LISA RAEBURN

W9-CNY-224

CULTURAL ANTHROPOLOGY

THIRD EDITION CULTURAL ANTHROPOLOGY

Daniel G. Bates
Hunter College
City University of New York

•

Fred Plog
New Mexico State University

McGraw-Hill Publishing Company

New York   St. Louis   San Francisco   Auckland   Bogotá   Caracas   Hamburg
Lisbon   London   Madrid   Mexico   Milan   Montreal   New Delhi
Oklahoma City   Paris   San Juan   São Paulo   Singapore   Sydney   Tokyo   Toronto

Cultural Anthropology

Copyright © 1990 by McGraw-Hill, Inc. All rights reserved.
Copyright © 1980, 1976 by Alfred A. Knopf, Inc. All rights
reserved.

Printed in the United States of America. Except as permitted
under the United States Copyright Act of 1976, no part of this
publication may be reproduced or distributed in any form or by
any means, or stored in a data base or retrieval system, without
the prior written permission of the publisher.

1 2 3 4 5 6 7 8 9 0   DOC DOC   9 5 4 3 2 1 0

ISBN   0-07-004066-4

This book was set in Zapf International Light by Waldman
Graphics, Inc.
The editors were Phillip A. Butcher and Mary Shuford;
the designer was Jack Ehn;
the production supervisor was Stacey B. Alexander.
R. R. Donnelley & Sons Company was printer and binder.

Part opener quotation sources:
p. 3   G. B. Harrison, ed., *Shakespeare: The Complete Works*
(New York: Harcourt, Brace & World), p. 901.

p. 95   A. Waley, *More Translations from the Chinese* (New
York, 1919), reprinted in J. Goody, *Cooking, Cuisine and Class*
(Cambridge, Eng.: Cambridge University Press, 1982),
pp. 13–14.

p. 233   W. Soyinka, *Mandela's Earth and Other Poems*
(New York: Random House, 1988), pp. 15–16.

Library of Congress Cataloging-in-Publication Data

Bates, Daniel G.
   Cultural anthropology / Daniel G. Bates, Fred Plog.—3rd ed.
      p.   cm.
   Plog's name appears first on the earlier edition.
   Includes bibliographical references.
   ISBN 0-07-004066-4 (text).—ISBN 0-07-004067-2 (instructor's
manual).
   1. Ethnology.   I. Plog, Fred.   II. Title.
GN316.B385   1990   89-13956
306—dc20

To the memory of
George and Lenore Bates

And to
Fred and Phyllis Plog

Contents in Brief

Contents

Anthropologist Napoleon A. Chagnon records Yanomamö creation myths on a solar-powered computer. (NAPOLEON A. CHAGNON/ANTHRO-PHOTO)

A Kwakiutl Indian village on the coast of British Columbia in a photograph taken in the 1880s. (COURTESY OF THE AMERICAN MUSEUM OF NATURAL HISTORY)

Chapter 3   Methods of Cultural Anthropology   50

Photography is important in ethnographic research and often serves to stimulate informant interest as well as to record data. (M. A. MACKENZIE/ROBERT HARDING PICTURE LIBRARY)

Chapter 4   Decisions, Adaptation, and Evolution   72

Virtually all native peoples of North America now have incorporated advanced technology into their way of life. This Inuit hunter is shooting caribou on Baffin Island, Canada, with a high-powered gun. (BRYAN AND CHERRY ALEXANDER)

Chapter 7   Pastoralism   150

In Navajo society, women usually own the flocks, tend them, shear the sheep, card the wool, spin it, and weave it into rugs. (JOHN RUNNING/BLACK STAR)

Chapter 8   Intensive Agriculture   176

Animal traction and plows such as this man is using to prepare his field near Lake Titicaca in Peru are characteristic of intensive agriculture, in which farmers use animal energy to produce more food for human consumption. (TONY MORRISON/SOUTH AMERICAN PICTURES)

PART III   THE DIVERSITY OF ADAPTIVE PATTERNS   232

Chapter 11 The Anthropology of Language 256

People use various stylized gestures and movements to communicate. With non-verbal eloquence, these Buddhist monks perform a stylized greeting. (RENE BURRI/ MAGNUM)

Chapter 12 Kinship, Marriage, and Household Organization 284

Kinship status in the United States is defined by a system of bilateral descent called a *kindred*. Except for siblings, each individual at this family reunion has a unique kindred, creating a network of interlocking relationships. (MICHAEL HAYMAN/STOCK, BOSTON)

Chapter 13   Social Groups and Stratification   316

These informal groups of men and women in Plains, Georgia, demonstrate the phenomenon of sexual segregation. In most societies, single-sex groups have traditionally played a central role at both informal and formal levels of social interaction. (OWEN FRANKEN/STOCK, BOSTON)

Chapter 14   Economics: Resources, Production, and Exchange   348

The percentage of workers in a population is determined in part by the society's concept of a productive life span. In this Niger community, young girls are part of the labor force. (MARK RIBOUD/MAGNUM)

Chapter 15   Politics, Social Control, and Political Organization   374

The accession to power of Pakistan's Prime Minister Benazir Bhutto marked the culmination of a long struggle. Among the odds working against her were the facts that her father, a former prime minister, had been executed following a miliary coup and that she was a female candidate in a society in which men dominate all areas of public life. (DOMINIQUE AUBERT/SYGMA)

Chapter 16   Religious Belief and Ritual   402

Important transitions in individual life cycles are marked by religious ritual and ceremony. These young Roman Catholic girls in Colombia have reached the age when they join with the adults in taking holy communion. (ULRIKE WELSCH)

Chapter 17   Cultural Change and Development: Anthropology at Work   430

People everywhere adapt to new technology when it becomes available, thereby changing their lifestyles and incorporating the new into already existing patterns of behavior. This !Kung hunter in Namibia sets off on his new bicycle in search of game. (ANTHONY BANNISTER/ABPL)

Preface

Our objective in all editions of this book has been to introduce cultural anthropology to readers with little background in the subject and to present the material in a unified rather than an encyclopedic manner. Traditionally, cultural anthropology texts have treated the many topics that constitute the field as a series of loosely interrelated subjects unified by the concept of culture. The concept of culture, which encompasses the myriad facets of human life that are rooted in learning and communication, is the hallmark of American anthropology. Our book, like all introductory texts, makes much use of this important tool for understanding unity and diversity in human social life. But the concept of culture itself does not offer a model for viewing change, and it is *change* that most accurately captures what is distinctive about humans. Our brief history on earth has been one of unparalleled dynamics, as the early representatives of our species spilled out of Africa to inhabit virtually every region of the globe. The concept of culture, as developed in many texts, seems to describe the relationship between culture and human behavior as virtually a one-way street. Culture and the rules of conduct it prescribes are often presented as the only factors molding our personalities and dictating how we act in many circumstances. In this view, culture is the script and people a rather unimaginative cast of actors mechanically performing their assigned roles.

We do not believe that this one-sided view of culture is adequate. A central theme of this book is that individuals are active decision makers, continually involved both in creating and using their culture, however misguided their creations may sometimes be. Faced with new problems and new situations in their environment, people will often attempt to find solutions that go beyond traditional customs and cultural prescriptions. In other words, behavioral variation constantly exists within as well as between societies. Those variations that prove adaptive are passed on to new generations; they become part of culture. Processes of innovation, adoption of new ideas and their transmission to others, lie at the heart of cultural variation and are part of broader ecological and evolutionary processes.

Decisions arrived at by individuals, the adaptive strategies of people and societies, and the evolutionary processes of which these are a part are central themes of this book. Our approach, then, is essentially an ecological and evolutionary one. However, while we stress the concept of adaptation, we do not slight what might be called the ideational or symbolic aspects of culture, ways of behaving and believing that validate our behavior, form our social identities, and satisfy our aesthetic needs. The ecological and evolutionary perspective includes much more than simply the material aspects of life. Religious and political beliefs and practices, even kinship systems, are as much a part of human adaptation as are subsistence strategies and economic practices. We will attempt to show this throughout the text and, in so doing, to show how the many topics customarily treated as basic to cultural anthropology are more than simply separate aspects of culture—politics, economics, religion are closely linked together in the adaptive process. We hope that we convey some of the excitement and controversy that are part of the ongoing, developing science of anthropology.

The Revision

In this revision of *Cultural Anthropology* we have made substantial improvements in the text. In general, we have attempted to streamline the material and make it more accessible to students.

■ In Chapters 2 and 3 we have extended and updated the presentations of the development of anthropological theory and methods and of research design. These topics, which frequently are presented chronologically or as abstract dos and don'ts of fieldwork and tend to be uninteresting for the student, are presented in a manner that makes them accessible, interesting, and relevant. Moreover, the methods and theory of anthropology are illustrated in the case studies and throughout the book in many of the boxes.

■ A new Chapter 4, "Decisions, Adaptation, and Evolution," which outlines the ecological-evolutionary perspective, is now in Part I, where it is better integrated with the discussion of theory and method. The chapter offers a concise and pertinent presentation of ecological concepts and decision making, and their relevance to understanding large-scale social phenomena are now presented in a more accessible manner. In addition to orienting students to the perspective which unifies the material that follows, Chapter 4 now also introduces Part II, "Adaptive Patterns."

■ In Part II, "Adaptive Patterns," the five chapters are organized according to commonly recognized strategies of food procurement; namely, hunting and gathering, horticulture, pastoralism, intensive agriculture, and industrialism. While this organization reflects a general evolutionary or historical scheme, it is not offered as a rigid typology or simple sequence of stages of development. It provides a closer look at the anthropological perspective in action; we use a number of case studies to illustrate how anthropologists view cultural evolution, analyze cultural adaptation, and attempt to understand diverse aspects of social behavior. Populations whose ways of life and livelihood are as diverse as the San People of Southern Africa and the farmers of Central California are viewed similarly as people responding to and, usually, coping successfully

with the problems facing them. What is emphasized are the costs and rewards of different ways of providing for necessities and the relationship of settlement systems, mobility, and economic and political organization to other aspects of adaptation. A distinctive feature of all these chapters is that they describe not only different societies but also a wide range of methods and techniques of studying them. This organization is intended to draw the student into interesting ethnographic material, give an insight into methodological concerns, and provide a foundation for understanding the more difficult topical chapters that follow in Part III, "The Diversity of Adaptive Patterns."

■ We have updated all of our case studies with new material and wherever possible attempted to place the populations in today's world. In Chapter 7 new ethnographic material on the Pokot of Kenya replaces the case study of the Karamojong, a neighboring East African population. The discussion of peasantry and intensive agriculture devotes more attention to change, including developments in China. Chapter 9 has new material on agriculture in the United States. All of the case studies, and the boxes, in Part II illustrate the variability and change that occur in every subsistence system: hunters and gatherers who incorporate farming and marketing; horticulturalists who irrigate; pastoralists who also farm, for instance.

■ Part III, "The Diversity of Adaptive Patterns," focuses on key topical areas of study in anthropology, ranging from exploring the relationship of the individual to culture to the anthropology of planned change. There are frequent references to the specific procurement strategies described in Part II. The chapters in this part have been extensively revised and updated. Chapter 10, "Biology, Culture, and the Individual," has an expanded discussion of sex and gender. Chapter 11, "The Anthropology of Language," now includes new material on sign, creole, and pidgin languages; the process of language formation; and a new discussion of sociolinguistics. The material in Chapter 12, "Kinship, Marriage and Household Organization," formerly covered in two chapters, has been updated and combined into one chapter offering a more concise discussion. Chapter 13, "Social Groups and Stratification," builds directly on the discussion of marriage and kinship to describe the dynamics of social groups and networks; the emergence of important, larger social constructs such as descent groups, tribes, and ethnic groups; and what are often the negative aspects of group-level social organization—structures that create and perpetuate inequality and stratification. The chapter amplifies the discussion of the organization of larger social entities, a topic often neglected by traditional anthropology, which tends to focus on small segments of larger populations. Chapter 14, "Economics: Resources, Production, and Exchange," moves the discussion of economic behavior beyond the academic debates that dominate much of the coverage of this important subject matter; Chapter 15, "Politics, Social Control, and Political Organization," draws on both the discussion of group-level organization and on economics to outline the dynamics of decision making, leadership, and the processes that determine who gets what in society. Chapter 16, "Religious Belief and Ritual," devotes more attention to the importance of ideology in terms of religion and politics, social change, and social control. The last chapter, "Cultural Change and Development," much more than in the previous edition, examines processes of planned and unplanned change, including the events that are so rapidly transforming the world today. It also looks at the ever-increasing role played by anthropologists in development work. It concludes with a timely discussion of current ethical concerns in the profession—focusing equally on traditional academic practice and on applied efforts.

■ The boxes throughout this edition have been extensively revised; in some cases more recent research has been added to make them current, but most are completely new and are based on reports on new developments. While most of the boxes draw on the research of anthropologists, several cover research outside the discipline, which unobtrusively demonstrates the links that join anthropology to other fields. For example, there is a box in Chapter 13 that describes the history of Afro-Americans in the coal industry and there is one in Chapter 17 that describes the sociology of risk assessment. The anthropological research presented in the boxes goes beyond what might be easily conveyed in a general discussion. For example, we use boxes to see complementary and competing interests and alignments in a Mexican village, processes of religious conversion in Guatamala, and how anthropologists use their training in the battle against AIDS in the United States.

Acknowledgments

Under pressure of other long-standing academic commitments, Fred Plog was not able to devote the time to this edition that he had hoped; this revision, therefore, fell primarily to Daniel Bates, who benefitted greatly from regular consultation with Fred Plog as well as from his helpful criticisms, suggestions, and insertions. Nevertheless, final responsibility for the content of the third edition rests with Daniel Bates. Both authors wish to acknowledge the contributions of Francis P. Conant, who was initially planning to co-author this edition with Daniel Bates and Fred Plog. But he, too, was unable to do so due to pressures of fieldwork. Nevertheless, he was involved in the early stages of the revision in developing new materials for Chapters 7 and 8 and he took an active interest in the project throughout. Furthermore, he graciously made available his report on the Pokot, much of which has not been published elsewhere. Judith Tucker worked on the project from the earliest stages to completion and made numerous recommendations, almost always gratefully accepted, as to reorganization, style, and presentation. She also made a substantial contribution to the boxes in this edition, most particularly to those in chapters 1, 5, 6, 11, 15, and 16. Two other colleagues, Gregory Johnson and Susan Lees of Hunter College, contributed much throughout the long project; both commented extensively on the organization and content of this edition—their often acerbic or irreverent observations frequently resulted in substantial extra work for the authors, always to the ultimate benefit of the book.

This edition benefited greatly from the authors' participation in the American Anthropological Association's Gender in the Anthropological Curriculum Project directed by Mary Moran and Sandra Morgan. This project paired authors and consultants with expertise in the study of gender in an effort to broaden the coverage of gender in textbooks. We were extremely fortunate to have been able to work with Rayna Rapp and Ida Susser, and we feel that this edition is richer by far for their advice. Needless to say, any errors or infelicities in this area remain the responsibility of the authors alone.

We also wish to acknowledge the invaluable contributions made by our other academic critics and consultants: William Davis, Joshua DeWind, Nancy Flowers, Brian Foster, David Gilmore, Robert Graber, Daniel Gross, Howard Higgins, William Irons, Carol Laderman, Murray Leaf, Louise Lennihan, Michael Little, Thomas McGovern, Warren Morrill, Robert Netting, Thomas Painter, William Parry, Burton Pasternak, Dennis Reno, David Smith, Ida Susser, and Pamela Wright. We greatly appreciate their generous help.

During what turned out to be a much longer task than originally envisioned, we were assisted in numerous ways by many other people. Perhaps at the head of the list are our editors: Barry Fetterolf, Phillip Butcher, Sylvia Shepard, and Mary Shuford. The latter two guided this undertaking safely among the numerous shoals of editorial development and production. Barbara Salazar did an outstanding job of styling and copyediting this manuscript. John Schultz was extremely helpful in researching the photographs that contribute so much to the visual impact of the text. John Willis assisted with library research toward the end of the project. Finally, both authors wish to acknowledge the support of each of their families and friends during the long period of time when this project occasionally interjected itself into our personal lives when least opportune!

Daniel G. Bates
Fred Plog

30° 60° 90° 120° 150° 180°

LAPPS

CHUKCHEE

A S I A

EUROPE

YÖRÜK   TURKMEN

KURDS   HAZARA

HAWAASHLEH
BEDOUIN   PATHANS

CYRENAICA
BEDOUIN   KOHISTANIS   NEPALESE   KACHIN   CHUNGSHE

SIKH   LEPCHA   SHAN   TATIEH
GUJARS   GARO

FUR   MURIA   CHIN   LAHU   IFUGAO

AFRICA   KOYA   MONS   HANUNÓO   PACIFIC OCEAN

NUER   CHENCHU   ANDAMAN
MANDARI   SHILLUK   NAYAR   ISLANDERS   IFALUK   TRUKESE

GALLA   TODA   MUNDUGUMOR
POKOT   TURKANA   SEMANG   DUSUN   KAPAUKU   ARAPESH
LUGBARA   GUSII   PAPUANS   CHIMBU
BUGANDA   JIE   JALE   MANUS
SUKU   KIPSIGIS   IBAN   TSEMBAGA   LESU
BUTI PYGMIES   MASAI   EQUATOR   TCHAMBULI   KURTACHI
MARING   SIVAI
BUSHONG   NDENDEULI   ALORESE   MAE ENGA   SIANE   KWAIO
LELE   NYAKUSA   JAVANESE   KWOMA
NDEMBU   GWEMBE TONGA   TROBRIAND
LOZI   TONGA   ISLANDERS   TIKOPIA
SHONA   THONGA   TIWI
INDIAN OCEAN   MURNGIN   MOALA
KALAHARI BUSHMEN   YAKINANKARATE   FIJI
(INCLUDING !KUNG)   ISLANDERS
SWAZI   WALBIRI
KARIERA   ARANDA
XHOSA   AUSTRALIA

MAORI

30° 60° 90° 120° 150° 180°

PART I

The Anthropological Perspective

The four chapters in Part I introduce the main subfields of anthropology and emphasize concepts basic to cultural anthropology and to understanding the place of human society in evolutionary perspective. Anthropology is an exceptionally rich and varied discipline, both in terms of theoretical orientations and in terms of the ever-growing availability of data from around the world. The chapters in this section stress the underlying unity of the anthropological perspective and at the same time describe a broad range of ideas and foci. Chapter 2 covers the rise of anthropological theory and stresses important lines of continuity as the field has developed. Chapter 3 brings together a detailed overview of anthropological methods and a sense of what it is like to work in the field. The last chapter once more addresses the theme of human biological and social evolution and establishes the framework that will organize the subsequent sections. While we are not concerned with labels, the approach used can be called *evolutionary ecology*. However diverse the field may be, most anthropologists share a commitment to viewing humans holistically and, thus, to understanding human cultural unity and diversity in terms of regular processes—biological, behavioral, and cultural. By building on a clearly recognizable framework, our perspective emphasizes both the behavioral and cultural variability within societies and the crucial role of individual choice and decision making in understanding cultural change and evolution.

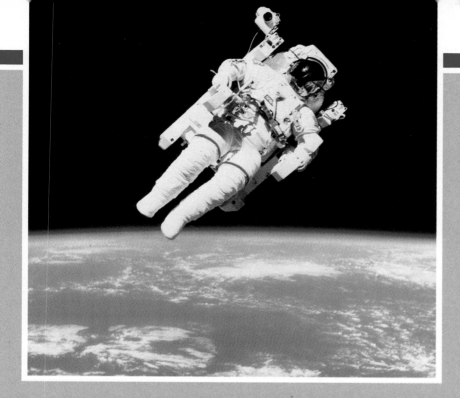

An astronaut in space is part of our relentless efforts to probe the outer limits of the universe. (COURTESY OF NASA)

A glimpse of an ancestor. Dr. Mary Leakey studies a 3.6-million-year-old human footprint in Northern Tanzania. (BOB CAMPBELL/ NATIONAL GEOGRAPHIC SOCIETY)

A teacher in Zaire. Human knowledge is cumulative because of our ability to pass on to the future what we have learned in the past. (PHOTOGRAPH BY ELIOT ELISOFON. NATIONAL MUSEUM OF AFRICAN ART, ELIOT ELISOFON ARCHIVES, SMITHSONIAN INSTITUTION.)

Episcopalian monks at vespers. Religion and philosophy help us to give meaning to our world. (JAMES H. KARALES/PETER ARNOLD)

Namibian mother and child. (ROBERT HARDING PICTURE LIBRARY)

Alaskan mother and child.
(STEVE MCCUTCHEON/ALASKA PICTORIAL
SERVICE)

Children in a refugee camp. (WILLIAM CAMPBELL/SYGMA)

Relics of the genocidal war in Cambodia. (STEVE PATTEN/BLACK STAR)

Reflections

What a piece of work is a man! How noble in reason! How infinite in faculty! In form and moving how express and admirable! In action how like an angel! In apprehension how like a god! The beauty of the world! The paragon of animals!

FROM WILLIAM SHAKESPEARE, HAMLET, ACT II, SCENE II, LINES 315–319

What we call anthropology is simply one facet of a universal urge to understand ourselves. We express our curiosity and our visions of ourselves in all manner of artistic, philosophical, and religious formulations. If there is a human intellectual universal, surely it is this restless seeking to define oneself.

We probe the outer reaches of our universe because we see ourselves as part of it. Our quest for knowledge is not without risk; we do not always like what we discover. Galileo was almost executed by the Catholic Church for his views about the universe. Sigmund Freud suggested that history is a series of blows to human narcissism. We know now that earth and all that is on it is a miniscule part of our solar system, let alone the universe. Charles Darwin has shown that we are one species among countless millions. In the last two years, evidence has emerged suggesting that all humans share a common ancestor alive as recently as 200,000 years ago, making us relative newcomers on earth. Freud has taught us that our most intimate behavior may be shaped by unconscious drives; recent research has shown strong continuities between the social life of humans and other species—kinship, sharing and cooperation seem to go together among all social animals.

Even if what we discover may humble us, there is a universal need to measure and somehow order the natural world; every person is to some degree a natural scientist. Some of what we wish to know lies beyond empirical explanation. We ask questions and formulate answers on the basis of ideas and emotions that do not depend on measurement and observation. For instance, emotionally charged debates rage in many countries: "When does human life begin?" "Is a fertilized cell 'alive'?" "Is a frozen embryo a 'person'?" Natural science cannot answer such questions and, when answered by law, the answers simply express the weight of particular ideas at that point in time.

We seek, too, to understand our social environment; what is a family, a marriage, a community? We are born into, live, and die in an ever-changing swirl of humanity out of which we try to make sense. We seek to define and understand special relationships. We come to recognize the meaning of family, neighborhood, and community. We probe and push in countless ways as we try, never fully succeeding, to find some pattern or order in the ways of those around us.

Every human being is also a social scientist. We know intuitively that much of what we think of as our culture comes to us simply because of our being in a particular setting at a particular time. Nevertheless, however much our beliefs are shaped by our associations, we see great variability in every society—not every Moslem is born into the faith; not every Catholic shares the same views on birth control. However forceful received ideas may be, people continually choose among ideas and different ways of solving problems, and thus adapt to ever-changing circumstances. What we seek to explain is forever transitory.

Intellectual curiosity is not divorced from the world as we observe and experience it. The words and concepts we use to describe the world are already loaded with meaning derived from our own experiences before we can ever bring them into use to describe others. We are products of what we would explain. What we express in poetry, in our myths, in our sciences, and in our arts is as much reflection as illumination. This is the human dilemma: We cannot go backstage to study the drama in which we are the actors.

Even so limited, our quest for understanding can and does build on what has been learned before us; our knowledge of the world, however imperfect, is a cumulative endeavor. In some areas our quests for explanation seem daily to reveal new understanding—more progress has been made in medicine, chemistry, and physics in the last fifty years than in the preceding millennia of recorded history. In others, always those which strive to probe the essence of our humanity, understanding is slow and hard-won. Nevertheless, there is progress. The fields we collectively label the social sciences, anthropology among them, have all contributed. We now know more than ever before about human origins; the nature of social, economic, and political organization; varieties of religious expression; and the diversity of means of livelihood. Simultaneously, we confront the fact that no explanation is final. We may never fully comprehend how individuals who, in some part of their lives, are loving, gentle, and self-sacrificing can also participate in torture and genocide. Love of family, kin, and community transforms all too easily into fear and murderous intent directed at outsiders; ideals of cultural or ethnic identity, political visions, religious sentiments all too often transmute into instruments of war, enslavement, and oppression. This should not cause us to halt in despair; it underscores the urgency of our quest.

Chapter **1** Anthropology and the Study of Culture

Human beings are relative newcomers on earth, but by most criteria we are an extremely successful species—certainly the most widespread and numerous of the large animals. We are distributed throughout the world and live under the most diverse and extreme conditions. Despite the enormous variety of local problems and hazards that humans must overcome to survive, all of the world's peoples are very similar in biological makeup and physique. In comparison with many other animals we are remarkably homogeneous and even a rather dull lot, lacking plumage and other specialized survival equipment. What accounts for the success of our species, and what can we surmise about our future? Why is it that humans vary considerably in social life and customs while differing only in small degree biologically? Such concerns underlie much anthropological research.

Anthropology, more than any other discipline, emphasizes the connections between human society and the larger web of life. Only by appreciating the fact that we are subject to the same forces that affect all other living organisms can we come to understand those many aspects of human behavior that distinguish us from other species. And if we more fully appreciate the extraordinary diversity evident in the ways of life of the world's peoples, we may come to a better understanding of our own society.

A perspective on humankind encompassing nonhuman life forms is relatively recent in European thought. For millennia Europeans were accustomed to thinking of the world, its peoples, and all other living things as eternally fixed and unchanging. Though similarities among species were widely noted, these similarities were not thought to represent the outcome of a shared and ongoing process of change—the process we call evolution. Instead each species, even each distinctive human society or culture, was seen as a unique entity with its own "essential" or unique characteristics. No such group was related to another or to anything else except in the seemingly obvious sense that the world existed for humans, in particular for those favored to be participants in European civilization.

In some respects early voyages of discovery reinforced the prevailing notion that nature in its diverse splendor was specially created for human enjoyment and exploitation. The great voyages of discovery in the fifteenth and sixteenth centuries introduced Europeans to forms of plant and animal life whose existence had never been suspected. The voyagers also encountered societies whose religions, marriage customs, and ways of life appeared quite alien to those of the West. Some accounts from North and South America in particular gave rise to debates as to whether these newly encountered people were actually human. It seemed implausible at first that all of the bewildering forms of newly encountered life could be interrelated.

Nevertheless, the tales of travelers, the scientific journals, and the newly discovered plants, animals, and people brought back to Europe all ultimately had a very valuable consequence: they stimulated further study, including the systematic recording of the customs and practices of non-European societies. Soon most religious thinkers, philosophers, and scientists were accustomed to thinking of the unity of humankind, and by the late eighteenth century it was widely acknowledged that Euro-

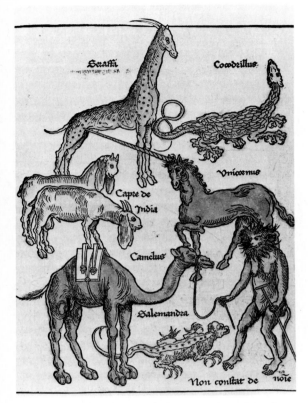

Depictions of non-European animals such as these from Bernhard von Breydenbach's *Journey* of 1486 aroused curiosity about the relationships between human beings and other species. This curiosity gradually led to scholarly interest in other human lifestyles. (SMITHSONIAN INSTITUTION PHOTO BY JOE GOULAIT)

pean civilization might in fact have developed from what they considered simpler societies, such as those encountered in the New World.

While the modern discipline of anthropology is a product of this long tradition of European exploration and inquiry, this fascination with humanity's diversity is not unique to the West. The Arabs and Chinese, for instance, have for thousands of years shown a systematic interest in their own and other societies. Ibn-Khaldun, an Arab scholar and historian of the fourteenth century who was familiar with African, European, and Middle Eastern societies, proposed a general theory of social change in which simpler societies, based on ties of family and tribe, were transformed into urban focused civilizations. So close is his thinking to that of recent students of society that some sociologists and anthropologists consider him to be the father of their disciplines. Still, it was only in European centers of scholarship that the systematic study of human diversity came to flourish.

Undoubtedly the major impetus for this development was the commercial and political ties being forged between Europe and the rest of the world. But this type of study also flourished because European scholars gradually came to recognize the explanatory value of systematically organized collections of data. As early as the mid-sixteenth century, a manual was published listing various physical and cultural attributes, some three hundred in all, that travelers should record when they visited foreign lands. Very diverse materials came to be organized in terms of similarities and differences, and the idea that change was a natural and ever-occurring process was increasingly accepted. Out of this habit of thought emerged the idea of **evolution**—the process by which small but cumulative changes in a species can, over time, lead to its transformation.

By the mid–nineteenth century the idea of evolutionary change was respectable in scholarly circles, in large part as a result of the tremendous impact of Charles Darwin's famous book, *On the Origin of Species by Means of Natural Selection*, published in 1859. The thesis of this book is that species are related to one another by descent, with modifications, from common ancestors. Darwin postulated that such modifications occur primarily through differential reproduction, or the ability of some members of a species to have more surviving offspring than others. These favored individuals pass on their traits to the next generation, whereas the less favored do not do so to the same degree. Darwin called this process **natural selection** and demonstrated that it can change the characteristics of an entire species over time, or even give rise to new species.

The idea that human society also may be a product of a long sequence of ongoing change received support of a rather startling variety: the discovery of human-like fossils in association with stone tools. **Fossils** are naturally mineralized remains of organic matter—earlier forms of plant and animal life turned to stone and thus preserved—very often lying underground for thousands of years until chance discovery brings them to light. During the seventeenth and eighteenth centuries many such fossil remains of extinct plants and animals were collected and classified, and the similarities and differences between them and living species were duly noted. These discoveries, along with Charles Darwin's theory of natural selection, established the idea that not only human societies but human beings themselves were the products of evolution—that is, development from earlier forms. Over millions of years the human body and human societies had emerged from earlier human and prehuman forms, through a combination of *physical evolution*—adaptive changes in biological make-up—and *cultural evolution*—adaptive changes in thought and behavior. The study of contemporary peoples and their social behavior is closely tied to this view of the world, the evolutionary view.

WHAT IS ANTHROPOLOGY?

All science is an effort to describe and explain natural phenomena. The aim of anthropology (the name of the discipline is derived from the Greek *anthropos*, "man," and *logos*, "account") is to describe and explain one particular natural phenomenon: **Homo sapiens,** the human species. Much of what anthropologists study in

their investigation of the human species concerns culture. Broadly defined, **culture** is a system of shared beliefs, values, customs, behaviors, and artifacts that the members of a society use to cope with their world and with one another, and that are transmitted from generation to generation through learning.[1] This definition includes not only patterns of behavior but also patterns of thought (shared meanings that the members of a society attach to various phenomena, natural and intellectual, including religion and ideologies), artifacts (tools, pottery, houses, machines, works of art), and the culturally transmitted skills and techniques used to make the artifacts. In short, culture includes almost any form of behavior that is learned rather than instinctive. We will leave until later the difficulties that may arise in attempts to apply this distinction.

Anthropological investigation involves comparisons of contemporary cultures and investigations of cultural and biological changes. In other words, anthropology takes as its object of study all human peoples, across the globe and across time, treating subjects as varied as their teeth, their diseases, their ways of getting food and shelter and rearing children, and their ideas about their place in the world. It is this breadth of inquiry that gives anthropology its vitality. Anthropologists continually probe the essence of human existence, asking philosophical as well as pragmatic questions.

The Subdisciplines of Anthropology

The field of anthropology is too vast to be mastered by any individual. For historical and prac-

---

[1]Because human culture is so elaborate, complex, and various, cultural anthropologists have as much difficulty agreeing on a definition of culture as aestheticians do on a definition of art. In 1952 Kroeber and Kluckhohn listed 164 definitions of culture used by various anthropologists, and many new ones have appeared since then.

tical reasons, the discipline is organized in North America in four subdisciplines: physical anthropology, archaeology, linguistic anthropology, and cultural anthropology. The differences between these areas of study, however, are less important than the dynamic way in which ideas and findings in one area influence ideas and research in the others.

Physical Anthropology

The study of the human species, past and present, as a biological phenomenon is known as **physical anthropology** (or, increasingly, *biological anthropology*). It is concerned with three central areas of study. The first is the reconstruction of the evolutionary history of our species[2]—the description and explanation of the changes that caused our lineage to diverge from its shared ancestry with other primates. The second area is concerned with describing and accounting for the biological variation among living human populations; such investigations extend to the relationship between human biological makeup on the one hand and culture and behavior on the other. The third area, an important specialization within physical anthropology, is primatology, or the study of our primate relatives—their ecology, evolution, and social behavior.

To reconstruct our evolutionary history, physical anthropologists sometimes engage in what many people consider the most glamorous task of anthropology—they search for fossils, especially fossils of our human and prehuman primate ancestors. Without doubt the

most widely publicized events in contemporary anthropology are the announcements of new evidence of early hominids (as our ancestral line is called), such as the spectacular discovery in northern Kenya of preserved human-like footprints over 4 million years old. Many of the fossils that physical anthropologists study have been retrieved by **paleontologists**—experts on the life forms of the distant past. But the actual discovery and excavation of fossils is simply a preliminary step. A fossil, once found, has to be interpreted. What creature did the bones belong to? When did it live? How did it live? How is it related to our species or to other species? One key to the answers to such questions is comparative anatomy—the comparison of the fossil's anatomical features with those of humans and other living primates.

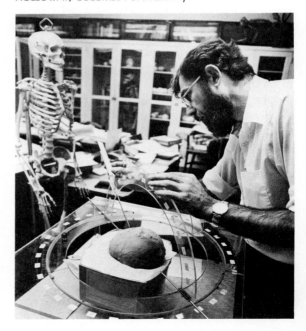

Physical anthropologist Ralph L. Holloway employs a craniometric stereoplotter to map the contours of a human brain. He has used this technique on fossilized hominid cranial casts to study brain evolution. (RALPH HOLLOWAY, COLUMBIA UNIVERSITY)

---

[2]A **biological species** is a group of interbreeding populations that is reproductively isolated from other such groups (Mayr 1963). Animals of one species, in other words, cannot mate successfully with animals of another species, and it is this fact that establishes them as members of a separate species. As all living human populations can interbreed, they constitute a single species.

Primates are a group of mammals that includes humans, apes, and the New and Old World monkeys. A human-like fossil skull, for example, will be studied to determine whether the teeth and cranial structure are of human proportions or whether its characteristics indicate it should be classified either as a "cousin" to our lineage or as a remote ancestor. To reconstruct the way fossil species lived—the foods they ate, their means of protecting themselves from predators, the kinds of social groups they formed—physical anthropologists study closely the total adaptive patterns of living primates: the ways in which their anatomy and behavior can be interpreted as adaptations to a particular environment and way of life. Then, using these patterns as guides, they infer from the evidence of anatomy and environment how a fossil species may have lived.

In the second area of study, biological variation among and within modern human populations, physical anthropologists ask such questions as: Why are some peoples dark-skinned and others light-skinned? Why is blood type B only half as common among white Americans as among African Americans, and why is it nonexistent among the Australian aborigines? Why can most northern European adults digest fresh milk, whereas most Chinese adults cannot? Though these sorts of biological differences are apparent, the sources of the variations are not.

To explain biological variations and to understand the processes that underlie them, some physical anthropologists apply the principles of **genetics,** the science of the biological transmission of traits from parents to offspring. The genetic differences within and between populations are linked to evolutionary processes, especially to the process of natural selection, whereby the genetic makeup of a population changes as a result of reproductive differentials among individuals. Anthropological geneticists, like other human geneticists, are concerned with all factors that affect the dis-

tribution of genetic materials in a population. What distinguishes the anthropological approach is its interest in accounting for the impact of social behavior on genetic transmission. Mating and marriage patterns, travel and trade relations, health status, and access to certain resources can all affect the genetic structure of the population.

The third major focus of research by physical anthropologists is **primatology,** or the study of living nonhuman primates. Primatologists come to their specialty from, in addition to anthropology, such fields as zoology, ethology (the study of animal behavior), and psychology. They look to our primate relatives to find clues to our ancestry and to probe the limits of the family tree of which we are a conspicuous part.

Until the pioneering work of an English scholar, Jane Goodall, most studies of primates took place in laboratories or by observation of their behavior in zoos. In the late 1950s, however, Jane Goodall undertook a field study of a free-ranging population of chimpanzees in Tanzania. She was surprised to find a far more complex and varied social life than anyone had expected. Since then there has been great interest in the study of primates in their natural habitats, and as a consequence we have a vastly broadened appreciation of their ability to learn, of their social organization, and of the commitment of the vast majority of such species to group life. Other studies have dealt with such varied problems as the communicative capabilities of nonhuman primates. To what extent can chimpanzees, for example, be taught a human language? How do free-ranging chimpanzees make and use tools? What is the significance of sexual differences in the social organization of a baboon troop?

Archaeology

Just as physical anthropologists try to reconstruct the successive stages of human physical evolution, the archaeologist tries to reconstruct

Archaeologists at work on a historic site in New York City that may have been the Almshouse of 1735. Excavation of the site is providing interesting clues about eighteenth-century attitudes toward the homeless and indigent. (JACK MANNING/NEW YORK TIMES PICTURES)

the processes of human cultural evolution and the effects of those processes in different parts of the world. **Archaeology** is the study of the relationship between material culture and behavior; archaeologists investigate the ways of life of earlier peoples and the processes by which their ways of life changed. While the study of early periods, usually referred to as "prehistory," is central to archaeology, recent history is also examined. *Historical archaeology* is concerned with patterns of everyday life in periods from which written documentation has survived, such as the colonial era in North America.

To reconstruct early societies, archaeologists, like physical anthropologists, must collect material remains, often by excavation, or systematic digging. Their interest, however, is less in

human or prehuman fossils than in cultural evidence—signs of ancient peoples' customs and beliefs, including anything they made: clay pots, fishhooks, hearths, beads, burial urns, tools. It also includes our ancestors' garbage— the stone flakes left behind by their toolmakers, the piles of animal bones left over from their meals. Even our ancestors' fossilized feces (known as coprolites) constitute useful evidence, for they can tell us what prehistoric people ate and how they prepared it, and even what diseases they had. Finally, the archaeologist must also collect environmental evidence—clues as to the climate, plants and animals, and water resources of the area.

Again, the collection of evidence is simply a preliminary step, and one that may be handled in collaboration with specialists in related fields. The archaeologist's central task is to interpret the evidence. By studying the cultural remains of a prehistoric group and piecing them together with the environmental evidence and, perhaps, the anatomical evidence provided by physical anthropology, archaeologists try to determine how large the group was, how its members procured their food, how they dealt with one another and with neighboring groups, whether they had class distinctions, how they buried their dead, and even, to the extent that the evidence yields clues, what they thought about the world they lived in. By gaining insights into individual groups, archaeologists gradually reconstruct prehistory, which spans the many thousands of years during which ancient peoples had no written language to record the concerns and events of their lives. And from the record of prehistory, archaeologists try to infer general processes of cultural evolution—how, for example, agriculture transforms societies or under what conditions cities tend to emerge.

Such interpretation often requires the careful analysis of immense amounts of data. Interpretation of these data, however, requires imagination. Archaeologists must try to determine which tools were used for which tasks. They must be able to draw conclusions about a wide range of human activities from the small preserved portion of the remains of those ancient activities. What are we to surmise, for example, about the social organization of a group that built lodges with rows of hearths rather than individual houses with individual hearths?

Ultimately, archaeologists must ask themselves *why*. If the evidence indicates that a people practiced a particular form of agriculture or trade, then how did they come to do so, and what advantages did this practice confer, if any? Just as the physical anthropologist often interprets fossils by analogy with living primates, archaeologists often interpret cultural remains by analogy with contemporary socie-

ties. If, for example, remains indicate that a group practiced a simple form of agriculture, the archaeologist may look to modern groups for possible clues as to the social correlates of this technology. Whatever guides archaeologists use, the key to accurate interpretation is recognition that cultural developments are responses to the physical environment, neighboring peoples, and a group's internal dynamics.

Linguistic Anthropology

Language is the primary medium through which culture is passed from generation to generation. To a large extent the ability to speak

Linguist Francesca Merlin studies a hitherto unknown language group north of Mount Hagen, Papua New Guinea. (IRVEN DEVORE/ANTHRO-PHOTO)

determined the direction our species took in its physical evolution. The major anatomical difference between modern humans and our ancestors of two and a half million years ago is that of brain size. And there is no doubt that the elaboration of language contributed to the growth of the human brain to its present proportions.

Early anthropologists used linguists, experts in the study of language, to help them understand the languages of nonliterate societies. Eventually some branches of the discipline of linguistics came to form a subdiscipline of modern North American anthropology as well. **Linguistic anthropology** is distinguished by its primary concern with unwritten languages (both prehistoric and modern), with variation within languages, and with the social uses of language. Linguistic anthropology is traditionally divided into three branches: descriptive linguistics, historical linguistics, and sociolinguistics.

Descriptive Linguistics. *Descriptive linguistics* is the systematic study of the way language is constructed and used: the way people combine sounds into words and words into meaningful statements. These systematic studies have produced grammars and dictionaries of many previously unwritten languages. Descriptive linguistics is concerned also with the intricate relationship between thought and language, the ways people use language to categorize their experiences, and the distinctive patterns of thought revealed by the structure of a language.

Historical Linguistics. *Historical linguistics* is the study of the origin of language in general and of the evolution of the languages people speak today. As spoken words leave no trace, linguists, unlike archaeologists and physical anthropologists, have little material evidence to aid them in the task of reconstructing the past. By comparing modern languages, however,

they have been able to identify families of languages, descendants of the same ancestral tongue. To some degree they have even succeeded in reconstructing those ancestral tongues, such as proto-Indo-European, the ancestor of such diverse modern languages as English, Greek, Russian, Farsi (Persian), and Hindi.

Sociolinguistics. A more recently developed branch of linguistic anthropology explores the connection between language and social relations. This field of study, called *sociolinguistics*, examines, for example, the effect of social class on the use of dialect; the ways in which people adjust language to fit the social demands of everyday life; and, in bilingual situations, why one language will be given preference. (The findings of linguistic anthropology will be examined in closer detail in Chapter 11.)

Cultural Anthropology

Cultural anthropology is the study both of specific contemporary human societies and of the underlying patterns of human culture. Often the terms "social anthropology" and "cultural anthropology" are used interchangeably; both combine the description of particular societies with the effort to understand the reasons for similarities and differences among them. These latter aspects of cultural anthropology are known as *ethnography* and *ethnology*, respectively.

Ethnography (literally, "writing about peoples") is the gathering of information on contemporary cultures through fieldwork, or firsthand study. Generally, ethnographers spend a year or more living with, observing, and interviewing the people whose culture they are trying to describe. In the course of their fieldwork they may gather data on economic processes (the way the population sustains itself materially); technology (the people's tools and their methods of using them); social organization (including the people's ways of reckoning kinship, contracting marriage, and organizing families); political behavior (the formation of action groups within the society, methods of settling disputes, means of dealing with outside groups, and ways of making decisions that affect the community); and finally, the group's religious, magical, and/or scientific strategies for explaining and attempting to control the world around them. The concerns of ethnographers are as varied as culture itself. In addition to acquiring a general picture of a society, an ethnographer concentrates on a particular problem. One ethnographer might go to the field to investigate the relationship between economic development and child rearing, for example, while another might study the influence of a group's environment on its family organization.

Ethnographers are increasingly turning from efforts to describe entire societies and are instead asking specific questions about social organization, family structure, land-use systems, or some other aspect of human societies that captures their interest. In attempting to get answers to their questions, ethnographers use a variety of techniques, from the study of official literary and legal documents to the statistical analysis of census data. (These and other techniques are discussed in Chapter 3.)

Some ethnographers concentrate on the process of societal change itself by reconstructing the recent histories of groups that have undergone rapid cultural change in recent years but have no written records of those changes. **Ethnohistory,** as such study is called, involves analysis of official documents; reading of explorers' and missionaries' journals; collection of oral histories, myths, and folktales; and interviews with people who remember the old days or their parents' and grandparents' stories of the old days. Much of what we know of American Indians' experience in the last two centuries has been compiled by ethnohistorians.

Ethnology. In their role as ethnographers, cultural anthropologists study and describe contemporary peoples. In their role as ethnologists, they go beyond description to interpret the data collected in the field and elsewhere. **Ethnology** is the uncovering of general patterns and "rules" that govern social behavior. To formulate these rules or to identify cultural patterns, ethnologists may use ethnographic data collected by several generations of fieldworkers all over the world. If the data from a number of societies seem to suggest a general pattern—a connection between small-scale agriculture and large, extended-family households, for example—then the ethnologist will review the data from other societies to see if this pattern holds true in general. If so, the observation may serve as the basis for generalizing about the relationship between family and household organization and technology in human society as a whole. In this way, our understanding of the way human groups organize their lives is gradually extended.

Contemporary Cultural Concerns. Although traditionally cultural anthropologists have concentrated on isolated nonindustrial societies, contemporary concerns lead them to work in a wide variety of societies, from the simple to the complex, from rural to urban, from isolated to cosmopolitan. Their studies range from the theoretical and abstract to practical efforts to bring about specific changes in societies. (Some efforts of this kind are discussed in Chapter 17.) Cultural anthropologists, like other social scientists, rely increasingly on computers to analyze their data, and often work in large research teams. Most, too, rely heavily on the work of other specialists in the social sciences and natural sciences. Contemporary anthropology is vital and far-ranging. Cultural anthropologists write books on the social history of sugar, on Balinese dance, on the nutritional consequences of rural migrant labor, and on a multitude of other topics that seemingly have little in com-

Careers for Anthropology Majors

In 1972, 75 percent of those people who held Ph.D.s in anthropology were employed in academic positions. By 1988, only 48 percent were so employed; the remaining 52 percent had entered fields as diverse as the law, personnel management, philanthropy, and civil service (data from American Anthropological Association). These increased opportunities are available to anthropologists with B.A. and M.A. degrees as well. In the private sector, environmental and engineering firms have hired anthropologists to deal with the human impact of their endeavors. Multinational firms, especially those operating in developing countries, need individuals with knowledge of local circumstances and customs to advise on employment practices and other conditions. Advertising, market research, public relations, sales, personnel management, whether domestic or international, are all fields that demand the ability to understand the workings and variation of culture. Many anthropologists now have their own consulting firms.

Hundreds of B.A. and M.A. anthropologists are now employed by federal, state, county, and city agencies to preserve our cultural heritage, whether it be the preservation of an archaeological site or the protection of a threatened community. Many state and city governments employ staff archaeologists to advise on building and development projects. And at least one federal judge has a background in anthropology.

The nonprofit sector also has many positions open to those with degrees in anthropology. For example, natural history museums offer opportunities to those trained in cultural anthropology, archaeology, and biological anthropology to work as educators running small classes and workshops; to prepare exhibits; and to research, catalogue, and curate their collections. Many institutions run internship programs that provide practical experience and training. Often anthropologists who participate in such programs can accumulate college credits while they work in stimulating jobs.

International human rights organizations, such as Amnesty International and Survival International, regularly employ people with anthropological training because their sensitivity to different cultural perceptions of individual rights, different notions of land tenure, and so forth are vitally important.

In the public sector, United Nations agencies, such as the UN Environmental Program (UNEP) and the UN Development Program (UNDP) need individuals with an understanding of cultural variation. In organizations such as Save the Children Fund, which maintains field offices throughout the developing world, almost the entire staff has some sort of a background in anthropology. The World Bank, following the recommendations of a 1985 report by Michael Cernea, has begun hiring more anthropologists on its permanent staff. One particular issue staff anthropologists have addressed is the resettlement of populations that have been displaced by major changes in land and water use such

mon. All, however, are concerned with aspects of human culture.

THE ANTHROPOLOGICAL PERSPECTIVE

All anthropologists tend to specialize, to reduce their subject matter to manageable proportions. But even when they apply themselves to specific questions, they try to retain a breadth of view. In short, what distinguishes anthropology among the social sciences is the comprehensiveness of its inquiry into the nature of humankind. This breadth of perspective, one of anthropology's distinctive features, is best demonstrated by two principles of anthropological research: holism and cultural relativism.

Holism

Holism is the philosophical view that no complex entity can be considered to be only the sum

as the construction of highways and dams. During 1986 and 1987, anthropologists also took part in eighty-four World Bank project missions to India, Nepal, Pakistan, Indonesia, China, Burma, Brazil, Argentina, Colombia, Guatemala, Ecuador, Turkey, Yugoslavia and other countries. The United States Agency for International Development (USAID) also employs anthropologists in positions ranging from senior management to country and regional specialists.

Academic anthropologists also are becoming increasingly involved in projects with direct practical applications. Norge Jerome, for example, a nutritional anthropologist, taught for twenty-one years at the University of Kansas Medical Center before being appointed director of the Office of Nutrition, Bureau for Science and Technology, for USAID. Jerome originally received her B.A. in nutrition and dietetics; only while doing graduate work did she discover anthropology. As a teacher she has done much important research in nutritional anthropology; in her new role she is expected to address important nutritional and food science problems in developing countries, a task she has described as her ''destiny'' (Fishman 1988).

H. T. E. Hertzberg (1989) applies his knowledge of physical anthropology to designing aircraft seats and crash dummies. Measurements of the body—anthropometry—can be used to determine the center of gravity of the human body. Such information is necessary, for instance, to design ejection seats for fighter planes that will not spin violently, killing their occupants.

Payson Sheets (1989) uses his knowledge of chipped stone tools to design better scalpels for eye surgery. Sheets has determined that flakes of obsidian (volcanic glass) are sharper than the best steel we know how to manufacture; this insight has resulted in surgical tools that produce less damage during and quicker healing after surgery.

In 1988, approximately 4,000 students received B.A. degrees in anthropology and 375 Ph.D. degrees in anthropology were awarded. Of the Ph.D.s, 12 percent were minority students, a large increase from 1971, when only 3 percent were minorities (data from American Anthropological Association). In a further effort to increase minority student exposure to anthropology, in 1988 the American Anthropological Association announced the formation of a Committee for Anthropology in Minority Institutions, chaired by Johnnetta B. Cole, president of Spelman College and a cultural anthropologist. The aim of this committee is to develop and administer a program to increase anthropology teaching in traditionally minority institutions. Many of these institutions offer little or no anthropology because limited funds have restricted their curricula. The work of this committee should result in more minority majors, and increase minority participation in both the academic and nonacademic aspects of the discipline.

Anthropology is a field that while growing apace, remains small enough to allow serious young scholars to make major contributions. The many new developments in the discipline mean that anthropologists today are no longer confined to the traditional pursuits of research and teaching, but are increasingly becoming involved in countless exciting and varied careers.

of its parts. As a principle of anthropology, it is the assumption that any given aspect of human life is to be studied with an eye to its relation to other aspects of human life. Anthropologists attempt to understand specific problems or questions of interest within a wider context. Carol Laderman, who has worked with rural Malaysian women in an effort to understand traditional medicine and childbearing and midwife practices, writes:

> The strength of anthropology lies within a paradox. The broad philosophical and theoretical concerns of anthropology must be approached through studies of a particular people, living in a particular place and time. But in order to understand the particular, we must approach it from a generalist viewpoint. The specific nature of our inquiries cannot be allowed to limit our field of investigation. Data must be collected even in those areas which at first glance seem to impinge only peripherally upon the problem. For example, understanding a people's dietary habits requires a knowledge of their economy and ecology, as well as their religious, social and aesthetic ideologies. An analysis of childbirth practices must include an investigation into sex roles, rules of

marriage and divorce, and the status and training of childbirth attendants, as well as the medical system of which these practices are a part. [Laderman 1983:1]

Thus an ethnographer studying child nutrition in Brazil will probably consider how the occupations of parents affect family diet, and then how differences in nutrition arose and what causes them to persist. The political implications of nutritional differences among ethnic groups may also be explored. The physical anthropologist studying the evolution of the human brain will take into consideration not only the shape and size of fossil skulls but also evidence in regard to the evolution of language,

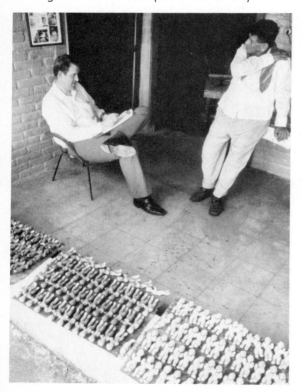

Archaeologist John Clark, director of the New World Archeological Foundation, Chiapas, Mexico, interviews a Zoque potter in an attempt to gain insight into ancient figurine manufacture. (D. DONNE BRYANT)

toolmaking, social organization, and of hunting and gathering techniques, all of which are related to the growth of the brain. Likewise, the archaeologist studying prehistoric stone tools and the linguist investigating the origins of language will take all these matters (and more) into account. Scientists in other disciplines are consulted as well. Geologists, paleontologists, botanists, zoologists, geneticists, physicists, geographers, and specialists in other fields all provide information relevant to the anthropologist's concerns.

By taking a holistic view, the anthropologist is able to surmount some of the academic obstacles that separate, for example, the study of human biology from the study of human social behavior, or those that divide the social sciences into such discrete disciplines as sociology, psychology, history, and economics. Such specialization is of course necessary if researchers are to obtain a thorough understanding of any one facet of human existence. But specialization has its dangers. Foremost among them is the tendency to ignore important causes or consequences of a given phenomenon that lie outside the confines of the researcher's discipline. It is this danger that anthropologists try to avoid by taking a holistic view.

Fifty years ago ethnographers went to the field with the intention of describing all that was important about the society they had chosen to visit. As anthropologists have become increasingly specialized, however, ethnographers have tended to concentrate on one or two aspects of a culture in order to be more systematic and thorough. In fact, as we shall see in Chapter 3, they go to the field with specific questions derived from theoretical models. The holistic view has not been abandoned, however. On the contrary, it is considered indispensable. Anthropologists have narrowed their subject matter but not their vision of it. Whether they focus on a fossil tooth, a prehistoric campsite, or a village wedding, they try to understand it in relation to larger questions about our species and its culture.

Cultural Relativism

The second important principle of the anthropological perspective is **cultural relativism**— the ability to view the beliefs and customs of other peoples within the context of their culture rather than one's own. This ability does not necessarily come naturally. Our perceptions are obviously adjusted to our own cultures. So, at first sight, an African man with ritual scars on his face or a Middle Eastern woman in purdah (that is with her face and body largely covered), is likely to appear strange to us. Unfamiliar food preferences (dogs, rats, grubs) may seem revolting. When the practice in question is one that we consider a matter of morality rather than simply one of taste—as, for example, the ritual homosexuality found in some New Guinea tribes, or the infanticide practiced by the Yąnomamö of Venezuela—our reactions can be far stronger.

Such cultural self-centeredness, the tendency to judge the customs of other societies by the standards of one's own, is called **ethnocentrism.** It is by no means a phenomenon exclusive to Western societies. People in every society tend to view outsiders and their customs with suspicion and often condemnation. If we consider infanticide cruel and unnatural, those peoples who practice it may consider equally appalling our own custom of shutting old people away in homes for the aged.

A perspective of cultural relativism aids understanding; it allows the anthropologist to see the customs of other societies as ways of solving problems, problems that all societies share to some extent. Throughout the world, for example, people have a desire for sexual activity that outstrips their desire for babies or their ability to support them. Americans tend to solve this problem by artificial birth-control mechanisms and, in some cases, abortion; other societies solve it by enforced sexual abstinence or late marriage; others by infanticide, which, when understood in its cultural context, is seen to be most often an extreme measure taken by parents who, in times of food shortage, sacrifice a newborn infant to secure the well-being of another child. Even so, the concept of cultural relativism does not imply that one condones or justifies any particular behavior just because it occurs; rather, it is a means for understanding why it does occur and its significance for the society in question.

When we can see cultural differences through the prism of cultural relativism, we approach other cultures with open minds and an appreciation for human diversity. We need not and we should not surrender our own ethical or moral standards; we simply adopt an approach that fosters scientific objectivity. At the same time, it encourages empathy with other peoples—an ability to see things, to some degree, as they see them. These products of cultural relativism—objectivity, empathy, and informed judgment—are indispensable to the anthropologist, as they are to anyone who tries to understand the customs of another society. Indeed, if anthropology has any "message" to offer the world, it is the need for cultural relativism in an era of global communication and trade, in which people of disparate cultures are coming increasingly to depend on one another.

CULTURE AS AN ANALYTIC TOOL

Earlier we broadly defined culture as a system of shared beliefs, values, customs, and behaviors that members of a society use to cope with their world and with one another, and that are transmitted from generation to generation through learning. While holism and relativism are important to the anthropological perspective, culture is a key concept and analytic tool. Although the term is susceptible to a wide range of interpretation, virtually all anthropologists agree on the importance of the concept of culture in the analysis of human social behavior.

Culture as Learned Behavior

Behavior may be instinctive—that is, genetically controlled—or it may be learned. Those behaviors that are learned constitute a very large percentage of human behavior, far outweighing instinctive behavior. We might visualize this situation by thinking of the difference between the behavior of a very young child and that of an adult in the same family. All animals have some capacity to learn, and learning is important to the survival of most species. But no other animal learns, can learn, or needs to learn as much as the human animal. In order to function as independent members of our societies, we require not only a long period of physical care but also a long period of "training" in how to think and behave; in other words, training in a society's system of behaviors—its culture.

A child born into Eskimo society, for instance, begins to learn behavior, language, and skills appropriate to Eskimo culture from the day of birth. The child's toilet training and feeding habits, the encouragement (or discouragement) given its first experiments in interacting socially with others, the rewards offered for correct deportment—all amount to an intensive training course in how to be a proper Eskimo. The child goes on to learn social roles specific to its biological sex, useful technical skills, his or her people's religion and moral codes. This training in one's own culture is sometimes called "socialization" or "enculturation." And what we become is greatly influ-

Humans tend to interact extensively with their peers, and a person's age affects how others behave toward him or her. (SHOSTAK/ANTHRO-PHOTO)

enced by the persons who carry out that en-culturation and the way they do it. In many societies a fairly narrow circle of people, primarily parents and kin and community elders, are responsible for the bulk of an individual's socialization. In other societies, as in our own, much of this training is provided by specialists outside the family or immediate community—we send our children to schools, churches, summer camps, and universities. To a considerable extent our behavior as men and women, our conduct as parents, our expectations, and our attitudes are shaped by this process.

This is not to say that these learned behaviors have no basis in biology. Our basic physiological requirements—the need for food, water, shelter, sleep, and sexual activity—underlie a good deal of our behavior. Rather than being a sharply distinct alternative to instinct, learned behavior is often guided by instinct or by information inherent in the genes (see Gould and Marler 1987:74). Speech learning is a good example. "Human infants innately recognize most or all of the consonant sounds characteristic of human speech, including consonants not present in the language they normally hear" (Gould and Marler 1987:82). Learned behavior, quite apart from instinct, serves biological purposes because of the practical advantages it confers, advantages that are attested to by our success in reproducing and surviving in virtually every climatic zone on earth. Even our universally shared taste for sweets, fats, and salts, and hence the underlying basis for our dietary systems, is the result of a long evolutionary process. It has been suggested that human systems of knowledge—religion, magic, science, philosophy—are based on a uniquely human, inborn need to impose order on experience. This is not surprising, as pattern recognition, for example, seeing a dangerous situation, is a key means for processing information critical to survival.

The biological basis of human behavior, then, is important. But *how* we go about sat-

isfying inborn needs and developing successful coping strategies is largely a matter of learning. Whether we feed ourselves by growing yams and hunting wild game or by herding camels and raising wheat, whether we explain a thunderstorm by attributing it to meteorological conditions or to a fight among the gods—such things are determined by what we learn as part of our enculturation. Enculturation prepares us to function as members of a given society—to speak its language, to use its symbols in abstract thought, and so forth. This ability depends in turn on genetically inherited physical traits, notably a brain of awesome complexity. But even though cultural behavior may be guided by genetically rooted limitations and propensities, it is obvious that we do not inherit genes for speaking English as opposed to Swahili, or for training as a doctor as opposed to a pilot. It is more difficult to assess the contribution of our biological heritage to the shaping of very basic aspects of social organization, sex roles, aggression, and family.

Knowledge and Language

Culture is transmitted via the symbolic communication system that we call language. Although humans are the only animals that use a fully developed language, we are not the only ones to use a communication system. All animals communicate with one another, using various kinds of cries, calls, gestures, and chemical emissions. Such means of communication are usually genetically determined, however, and therefore are more inflexible than human languages. A bird's danger call is the only call it can produce in a dangerous situation; the bird cannot add any refinements to the call to indicate, for example, the source of the danger or the direction it is coming from. Bees, however, are known to have very sophisticated systems of communication, and in some species "scouts" are sent out by the hive and return to inform the others of the way to proceed to reach a newly discovered food source. Even so, this pattern is far removed from human language, with its nearly infinite flexibility and capacity to generate new meanings.

Human language has an arbitrary quality: words can change their meanings; they can be combined and modified to create new meanings; perhaps most important of all, they can be used to represent things that are not actually present—events of the past and future, abstract qualities, and strictly mental phenomena. Language thus enables people to communicate what they *would* do if such-and-such happened, to organize their experiences into abstract categories ("a happy occasion," for instance, or "an evil omen"), and to express thoughts never spoken before. Morality, religion, philosophy, literature, science, economics, technology, and numerous other areas of human knowledge and belief—along with the ability to learn about and manipulate them—all depend on this type of higher-level communication. Cultural knowledge, then, is not only transmitted through language; it is to a large degree created out of language.

Rituals such as the Holy Eucharist are intelligible only if one is familiar with the cultural context, in this case with Catholic beliefs and ritual. (JEAN A. FORTIER/ROBERT HARDING PICTURE LIBRARY)

Culture Gives Meaning to Reality

Culture encompasses not only social behaviors but also ways of thinking. From our cultural training we learn what meanings to attach to the events of our world, and especially to the behavior of others, so that we can make some sense of those events and know how to respond to them. The meanings of specific actions can vary with the cultural context in which they are interpreted.

Because meaning is supplied by cultural context and because such contexts differ, people of various societies can view the world in quite different ways. For example, members of societies that speak different languages and follow different religious traditions may well make very different distinctions between the "natural" and the "supernatural." For the Australian aborigines, certain rocks, animals, and places have souls that are very much a part of them. The sacred sites of Christianity, Islam, and Judaism have meanings for their adherents that are not shared by outsiders. The beliefs and values of a society are a cultural reality. Whether marrying more than one spouse is treated as a crime or as a preferred form of marriage depends on culturally defined rules of behavior. Even so, we cannot regard our ability to define reality and to make rules for appropriate behavior as completely open or arbitrary. While different systems of marriage, mating, or cohabiting are practiced by societies around the world, we can easily think of variations that no society has adopted or condoned. There appear to be universal constraints on sex roles, as on other areas of human behavior, within which variation occurs. As David Gilmore points out, "All societies distinguish between male and female, providing institutionalized sex-appropriate roles for adult men and women. Most societies also hold consensual ideals—guiding or admonitory images—for adult masculinity and femininity by which individuals are judged as worthy members of their sex and are evaluated more generally as moral actors." While gender ideals differ from culture to culture, "underlying the surface differences there are intriguing similarities in sex stereotypes in cultures that otherwise display little in common" (Gilmore 1990:1–2).

Culture Is Integrated

The religious, political, and economic institutions of a society are shaped by common adaptive forces operating over long periods of time, and as a consequence they tend to "fit" with each other. The many ways in which cultural practices are interrelated gives stability and continuity to cultural evolution; changes are incremental and often occur very slowly. The political, economic, and legal functioning of society remains the same from day to day, as do items as mundane as the shape of stop signs and the colors of traffic lights. We do not wake up each morning with a burning need to reconfirm the existence of institutions on which we depend or the symbols through which we interpret our reality. It is probably just because stability and continuity are so important to our survival that change and innovation are usually so conservative. It is as though humans were generally guided by the maxim "If it ain't broke, don't fix it." Sometimes we see this tendency toward stability and continuity most dramatically when it is violated by the cataclysmic events of war or other disasters; people

who are suddenly cut off from their customary practices and familiar ways of doing things experience stress not unlike what is sometimes called "culture shock"—the feeling of disorientation one may experience when thrust into an unfamiliar cultural setting.

Culture Is Differentially Shared

The members of every society are differentiated by sex, age, health status, and occupation, and also very often by ethnicity, religious practice, and socioeconomic status. Indeed, a complex society may be seen as a cluster of ever-shifting groups unified by a system of economic exchange and political administration.

Each of these groups has a set of socially acceptable behaviors that to some extent differentiate it from the others—a subculture. The fact that the members of each group share certain special needs and interests and that they tend to interact with one another more often than with members of other groups encourages the development of distinctive attitudes and behaviors, even ways of dressing and talking, specific to that group. If, for example, a polling organization asked groups of Protestants, Catholics, and Jews to rate the desirability of legal restrictions on abortion on a scale of 1 to 10, the three groups would show different average scores. Likewise, Catholic men and Catholic women would probably reveal somewhat different attitudes on this topic, as would college-educated people and those without college degrees. Thus the values, behavior, and experiences of members of any society are differentially shared within the subgroups of the society.

Culture Is Adaptive

So far we have emphasized the effects of culture on the individual. Yet the behavior of individuals also affects the shared behavior of their society. By fitting cultural experience to new situations, individuals in every society experiment and arrive at innovative solutions. Sometimes these new solutions are taken up by others and become part of the larger cultural repertoire. Ways of doing things that are widely shared and passed on are usually ones that in some way facilitate the well-being of a large segment of the population, by emphasizing appropriate behavior or discouraging behavior that threatens the group in some way. Indeed, the customary patterns of behavior and thought that we inherit are nothing more than a complex of our ancestors' adaptive strategies, those that still seem to work. And by devising new solutions to fit our own circumstances, we modify those strategies before passing them on to the next generation (Boyd and Richerson 1985). To understand this dynamic interchange between people and their culture—that is, their systems of behavior—we must look more closely at the way individuals actually deal with behavioral practices and rules.

In any society, most people know what is appropriate to do in a given situation, but they do not always act according to a rigid formula or set rules. And when we look at the ways in which people break the rules they espouse, an interesting pattern emerges. For one thing, most of us "sin" in more or less the same way our neighbors sin; that is, we deviate in packs. A simple example of this phenomenon is seen in drivers' tendency to exceed the speed limit— just a little. When the legal limit is 55 miles per hour, most people can be found driving at 60 to 65. In fact, most of us look askance at people who obey all rules to the letter. The rigid bureaucrat who plods through every inch of red tape, refusing to cut corners, is generally considered a deviant—an "obsessive-compulsive personality." Likewise, though few Americans would openly condone lying, all would agree that in many social circumstances, telling the complete truth would be a mistake; we tell "white lies."

This curious situation holds in all societies. People everywhere establish rules for acceptable behavior and then proceed to break the rules in more or less regular ways. The reason for this behavior is the necessity of making received rules and values fit changing circumstances. Though most people feel a need to do what is "proper," and though their culture provides time-honored definitions of "proper" for them to fall back on, survival nevertheless depends on the ability to cope—to solve problems in the immediate environment and adapt to changing circumstances. And adaptation depends on smartness, not propriety—"ingenuity, not piety, . . . resourcefulness, not goodness" (Freilich 1971:286).

People spend much of their time, then, looking for solutions to their problems. Though usually they fall back on established ways of doing things, occasionally they strike out in new directions; such words as "invention," "discovery," and "innovation" refer to this aspect of adapting. Once people develop a new solution, they usually begin to argue not that it is new but that it is good—not expedient but proper.

Changing sex roles in our own society is a case in point. At one time it was not considered desirable for women to work outside the home, and usually only those who had no alternative did so. In time certain kinds of work in offices, hospitals, and schools came to be viewed as quite appropriate for women, and families began to invest in the training of their daughters as secretaries, nurses, and teachers. With the advent of World War I, industry and the civil service needed women to fill jobs left vacant by men who had gone off to war. Following the war, women not only continued to be employed in large numbers but the right of women to vote was secured. Slowly the employment of women in wider and wider sectors of the economy came to be viewed as legitimate and even desirable by a substantial percentage of the population. In recent years the right of women to be employed in every occupation became established in law, though not necessarily in practice. Still, almost no one, however conservative, questions the political rights of women or the appropriateness of their employment in most jobs. Once a new behavior, with its newly acquired moral value, gains enough adherents, it becomes a shared practice that is taught to the next generation as part of "the right way to do things."

In time some new solutions will be retired in favor of newer solutions. But the rule remains the same: individual ways of coping, if enough people find them useful, will become part of the system of shared behavior. Through such constant revision adaptive strategies evolve. It is on this process of adaptation and evolution that we will focus in the following chapters.

Summary

Exploration, observation, and curiosity about the diversity of the human species helped to engender the discipline of anthropology, and the scientific study and understanding of humankind have remained its dominant concerns. Anthropologists look at the human species from both cross-cultural and evolutionary points of view. For research purposes the discipline has been divided into four subdisciplines: physical anthropology, archaeology, linguistic anthropology, and cultural anthropology.

Physical anthropology, the biological branch of the discipline, is concerned with both reconstructing the physical evolution of our species and describing and accounting for the physical variations that are found among populations. *Archaeology* is the study of the relationship between material culture and behavior. Archaeologists explore both prehistoric and more recent societies. *Linguistic anthropology* is concerned primarily with unwritten languages. It is divided into three branches: *descriptive linguistics* is the study of the way language is constructed and used; *historical linguistics* is the study of the origin of language and of the evolution of the languages people speak today; *sociolinguistics* is the study of the connection between language and social relations. *Cultural anthropology* is the investigation of specific contemporary cultures (*ethnography*) and of the patterns that underlie human culture in its totality (*ethnology*). Some ethnographers study the process of societal change by reconstructing the histories of groups that have undergone rapid cultural change in recent years but have no written record of those changes; this approach is known as *ethnohistory*.

Though anthropologists tend to specialize in one of the four subdisciplines, they maintain a *holistic* approach: they assume that any given aspect of human life is to be studied with an eye to its relation to other aspects of human life. Of vital importance to the holistic perspective is *cultural relativism*, or the ability to view the beliefs and customs of other peoples within the context of their culture rather than one's own. Although everyone is somewhat *ethnocentric*, judging the customs of other societies by the standards of his or her own, anthropology underscores the need to view other cultures with objectivity and empathy.

Applying the concept of *culture*, anthropologists make certain assumptions about the behavior, beliefs, and experiences of individuals as members of society: that the human species learns rules of behavior and is dependent on learning for survival; that learned rules of behavior and thinking supply meaning to events and the behavior of others, although each society has its own interpretations; that knowledge is transmitted via language and is to a large degree created out of symbols; that experience is integrated, to varying degrees, within a society; that it is differentially shared within subgroups of a society; that behavior is adaptive, evolving from the constant revision of strategies to deal with changing circumstances. Anthropology deals with the adaptive strategies of both individuals and societies as wholes, as well as the evolutionary processes of which these adaptive strategies are a part.

Key Terms

archaeology	ethnocentrism	fossils	natural selection
biological species	ethnography	genetics	paleontologists
cultural anthropology	ethnohistory	holism	physical anthropology
cultural relativism	ethnology	*Homo sapiens*	primates
culture	evolution	linguistic anthropology	primatology

Suggested Readings

ANGELINO, E. (ED.). *Annual Editions: Anthropology 89/90.* Guilford, Conn.: Dushkin Publishing Group. A selection of articles by anthropologists focused on current topics in the study of anthropology. A good introduction to current research issues and approaches.

BOHANNAN, P., AND M. GLAZER. (EDS.). 1988. *High Points in Anthropology.* 2d ed., New York: Knopf. A book of readings that deal with what the field of cultural anthropology has been, what it currently is, and what the authors think it will be.

COLE, J. B. (ED.). 1988. *Anthropology for the Nineties: Introductory Readings.* Revised and updated. New York: Free Press. An anthology of introductory readings in cultural anthropology that explore human culture in both traditional and developed, Western and non-Western societies with an emphasis on race, gender, and social stratification.

JOLLY, C. J., AND F. PLOG. 1986. *Physical Anthropology and Archaeology.* 4th ed., New York: Knopf. A comprehensive introduction to the study of human biological, behavioral, and cultural evolution.

MAYBERRY-LEWIS, D. 1988. *The Savage and the Innocent.* 2d ed. Boston: Beacon Press. An anecdotal narrative of the experiences of an anthropologist and his family among the Sherente and Shavante Indians of Central Brazil. Updated to incorporate descriptions of the author's return visits to these peoples with his son and daughter-in-law.

PODOLEFSKY, A., AND P. J. BROWN. (EDS.). 1989. *Applying Anthropology.* Mountain View, Calif.: Mayberry Press. An introductory reader that emphasizes the practical application of research methods in biological anthropology, archaeology, anthropological linguistics, and cultural anthropology. The articles are timely and interesting; they offer a view of anthropology not available in any other reader. A number of these articles are cited throughout this text.

Chapter **2** ## The Development of Anthropological Theories

More straightforwardly than any other scientific discipline, anthropology asks questions that grapple with that elusive concept "human nature": why, for example, great imperial regimes arose in some places but not in others; why violence persists in a species that manifestly has the ability to see its horrible consequences. Such broad philosophical questions are apparent in the theories that guide anthropologists' research and writing.

The excitement that runs just beneath the surface of the formal discipline of anthropology arises from the dual tasks of collecting detailed data about often very remote and obscure societies and then fitting this array of facts into a broader philosophical framework. The ethnographer, in confronting the social practices of another society, often comes face to face with the question of where the outer limits of human social or cultural variability are to be located. When, for example, the anthropologist Bronislaw Malinowski found that the Trobriand Islanders assigned paternity not to men but to ocean spirits that impregnated women, he had to expand his notion of kinship and family ties.

For over forty years fieldworkers have been studying the San people of the Kalahari Desert in southern Africa. The San (referred to also as Bushmen) have maintained themselves in what others would consider a particularly harsh and unforgiving habitat: an extremely arid region known for seasonal shifts in the availability of food items and water holes that suddenly go dry. The researchers have addressed a wide variety of issues in their work, but most of those issues have to do with the life of hunting-and-gathering societies—the way of life that our ancestors pursued for many millennia before

they developed agriculture. The San are among the very few remaining groups that offer researchers a glimpse into our distant past. By the same token, as the San cope with the changes being thrust upon them by outsiders, we learn much about human resilience and ingenuity in contemporary life. The more we learn about the San, the better we understand the nature of human adaptability. The ethnographer goes out to the field not to "discover" facts that pertain to these overarching issues, however, but to ask very narrow questions or to address some very specific problem.

The kind of problem the researcher selects depends largely on the theoretical perspective in which the individual is trained. A researcher generally arrives in the field with a carefully formulated problem based on explicit and implicit assumptions that reflect a particular theory. In addition, the researcher inevitably brings some unwanted intellectual baggage in the form of biases and received wisdom of dubious utility. Clearly such biases may affect the objectivity of ethnographic reporting. No scholar in any scientific field begins research as a "blank slate"; the important issue is to be clear about one's own assumptions and biases. To attain such understanding, scientists, including anthropologists, rely on a variety of theoretical approaches, or "schools of thought." No field as complex as anthropology is monolithic; the variety of views among its practitioners is reflected in their research and contributes to the richness and diversity of the field. Regardless of theoretical focus, however, virtually all anthropologists share the belief that humans are part of a larger evolutionary process, that adaptation is the driving force of evolutionary change, and that, ultimately, individual motivations, strategies for coping, and decisions determine the nature of adaptation and larger evolutionary processes. In this chapter we will explore the meaning of theory and sketch the major theoretical perspectives that have guided anthropological research.

MAJOR THEORETICAL APPROACHES

Theories are the backbone of scientific research. A **scientific theory** is a statement that postulates ordered relationships among natural phenomena and explains some aspect of the world. There is some value in attempting seemingly open-ended description—that is, description of a phenomenon without strong preconceived expectations—particularly when the researcher is entering a totally unknown area. But all observations are ultimately affected by theory. Much early anthropology was highly descriptive, although, as we shall see, the researchers were guided by a general set of expectations. Increasingly, however, research is aimed at explanation or understanding of the regularities found in relationships among things or events. Theory is fundamental to this process, as the theoretical model chosen constrains the sorts of questions or interests that are investigated.

A theory serves as a framework for research by guiding researchers to ask certain kinds of questions and by helping them formulate specific hypotheses. A theory is never tested directly; one tests theoretical expectations by testing specific hypotheses. A **hypothesis** is a very special type of question or statement in research: it is a statement that stipulates a relationship between a phenomenon for which the researcher seeks to account and one or more other phenomena. Further, the statement is framed in a way that allows for its falsification.

Quite simply, a hypothesis is a statement about relationships which can possibly be shown to be untrue. The statement "Cigarette smoking is bad" is not a hypothesis because it does not define "bad" or specify the relationship between smoking and anything else. It seems like a valid or logical statement, but a skeptic might well argue that the economic, social, or psychological benefits of smoking outweigh the physical harm it causes. The similar statement "Cigarette smoking increases the risk of lung cancer" is a hypothesis because the risk of lung cancer can be measured among smokers and nonsmokers and a causal relationship between exposure to specific carcinogens in tobacco and smoking can be established. This distinction is important because unless a statement is logically falsifiable by appeal to relevant facts (or subjected to the appropriate test), it cannot enhance our knowledge of the world. If the actual results or observations are consistent with the hypothesis in a significant number of cases, the theory that generated the hypothesis is strengthened and perhaps expanded. But if the observed results of hypothesis testing repeatedly contradict theoretical expectations, the theory is eventually altered or abandoned. In short, theories survive as long as they continue to suggest useful approaches to the phenomena that scientists are trying to explain.

A theory may be the product of decades of diligent research. Or as in the case of Charles Darwin and Sir Isaac Newton, it may be the product of a young scientist capable of seeing through the preconceptions that block the insights of older and more experienced colleagues. Every theory has its blind spots: aspects of a subject that are underemphasized or disregarded in favor of other aspects. And new theories often displace the old by redirecting attention to those neglected areas. Through this dynamic process—the constant challenging and retesting of ideas—the discipline's theoretical framework is refined and developed over time.

A variety of theories have been developed over the hundred-year history of the discipline of cultural anthropology. These reflect both traditional issues that scientists have addressed and contemporary concerns. Most can be related in one way or another to the central issue of placing humans in some evolutionary context; all address the issue of cultural development and variation.

Humans in an Evolutionary Context

Humans are bound to the rest of nature by evolutionary history—that is, by descent from common ancestors. Our species is kin to every other living thing on earth—not just in a metaphorical or sentimental sense but in a strict biological sense, as two cousins are related by virtue of having the same grandparents. Of course, we are related more closely to some species than to others. Chimpanzees are much closer kin to us than are monkeys, not to mention nonprimates. Varying degrees of kinship are reflected in varying degrees of anatomical and behavioral similarity. Ultimately, however, all living things, ourselves included, are descended from the same forebears—minute organisms that lived billions of years ago in a world we would not recognize.

How, from such beginnings, did we and all the other species of the earth come to be what we are? The answer to this question did not become clear until the early twentieth century. In the eighteenth and early nineteenth centuries some scientists recognized that species could change over time, as organisms adapted to their environments. But they could not agree on how such changes occurred. Indeed, most of them did not believe that such changes could actually create new species. Natural processes of evolution might produce new "races" or strains *within* a species, but only God could create a new species. It was not until 1859, when Charles Darwin (1809–1882) published his treatise *On the Origin of Species by Means of Natural Selection*, that the major mechanism of evolution was finally described in a way that accounted both for change within species and for the emergence of new species without divine intervention.

Darwin: Evolution by Natural Selection

Darwin was convinced that new species arose not through acts of divine intervention but rather through a "blind" and mechanical process. He understood that all species of plants and animals tend to produce more offspring than the environment can support, and this results in intense competition for living space, resources, and mates. Only a favored few survive long enough to reproduce. Darwin noted also that individual members of a species differ from one another physically. In a given population of animals, for example, some may have thicker fur or longer limbs than others. These variations are *adaptive* if they enhance the animal's chances of survival and, more important, if they enhance its chances of producing offspring that survive to reproduce themselves. Needless to say, this process depends on the nature of the demands placed on the organism by its environment and by the changes that environment is undergoing. (Thick fur, for example, could mean a longer life in an increasingly cold environment, whereas it might be a handicap in an increasingly warm one.) Those individuals whose peculiarities give them a competitive edge in their particular environment produce more offspring, and those offspring inherit their parents' peculiarities, so they in turn survive longer and produce more offspring. Thus with each generation the better-adapted members of a population increase in number at the expense of less well-adapted individuals. In the process, the species as a whole changes.

This is the mechanism that Darwin called "natural selection." It served to explain not only gradual changes within a species but also the appearance of new species. For as different populations of a species adapted to different environments, they eventually diverged until the differences in their anatomy or behavior became so great that they could no longer interbreed. In other words, they became separate species. According to Darwin, this process—adaptation to environmental circumstances—accounted for the great variety of species observable in nature. *Speciation* is not in fact quite as simple a phenomenon as is described here. Many species are "ring species," which means that adjacent populations can interbreed, but nonadjacent ones cannot. Also, in studying populations of the past, it is not always possible to determine whether or not separate but fairly similar populations could have interbred. The concept of species, however, remains useful as a standard despite empirical problems in applying it.

Mendel: The Genetics of Natural Selection

A major weakness of Darwin's theory was that he could not explain how "favored" characteristics were inherited. And such a systematic explanation was needed, for the prevailing belief was that each individual inherited a *blend* of its parents' characteristics. If this belief were true, advantageous variations would be lost by dilution with less advantageous traits long before natural selection could act on them. It was an obscure Austrian monk named Gregor Mendel (1822–1884) who discovered the hereditary basis of natural selection.

In the garden of his monastery, located in what is now Czechoslovakia, Mendel spent years cross-breeding strains of peas and other plants in an effort to find out how traits were transmitted from one generation to the next. He discovered that biological inheritance was not an irreversible blending of parental traits. Rather individual units of hereditary information, later called "genes," were passed from

parent to offspring as discrete particles, according to certain regular patterns. In one individual a gene's *effect* might be blended with the effects of other genes, or even suppressed altogether. But the gene itself remained unchanged, ready to be passed on to the next generation, where it might express itself and thus be available for natural selection.

Mendel's work attracted no attention in the scientific community until both he and Darwin were dead. It was rediscovered in the early 1900s, but its relevance to evolution was not fully appreciated until the next generation. By that time other seeming discrepancies in Darwin's theory had been resolved, and it was finally accepted that the human species, along with every other species, was a product of evolution. Today evolutionary theory is at the very heart of all research in the biological and natural sciences. With the recent breakthroughs in modern genetics, population biology, and biochemistry, the utility of the "evolutionary synthesis"—as it is now called—is established beyond doubt.

The Early Cultural Evolutionists

As Darwin's evolutionary perspective became established in many areas of natural science, social scientists of his day also embraced at least some aspects of it. This development is not surprising, as Darwin himself was influenced by a social philosopher, Herbert Spencer. Spencer, like Darwin, promoted the idea of evolution, but Spencer's emphasis was on social evolution—the unfolding of human social life from simple to ever more complex forms. Spencer saw many analogies between Darwin's idea of evolution driven by natural selection and his own hypothesis that individual competition led to "civilization." In his view, a natural order in the world caused "advanced" forms of society and even races to displace less advanced ones. Though the explicitly racist aspects of Spencer's theory have been discredited, he did play a major role in directing systematic attention to worldwide cultural variation.

E. B. Tylor: Unilineal Evolution. One issue as important to explain today as it was earlier is why, although we are members of one species, we exhibit great cultural variation and our societies differ widely. Sir Edward Tylor, who defined the concept of culture in 1871, explicitly repudiated the idea that cultural evolution or "civilization" had anything to do with race or the superiority of any population or society. All peoples of the world, he said, shared a "psychic unity": all are equal in their innate capabilities, intelligence, motivations, and cultural potential. He invoked the concept of evolution to explain cultural diversity. Tylor and other **early cultural evolutionists,** as they are called, held to the basic premise that cultures progress through a sequence of evolutionary stages—a pattern that we now refer to as **unilineal evolution.** The reason that societies differ from one another, they reasoned, is that they began to travel this course at different points and are traveling it at different speeds. While some (notably European societies, in this view) had already arrived at an advanced form of social organization, others were still in earlier stages of development. They viewed society as being similar to a living organism, governed by its own laws of growth and thus passing inevitably from one developmental stage to another, each progressively more "mature" or advanced.

Contemporary tribal or "primitive" societies were regarded as akin to "living fossils," in which the characteristic features of early stages of cultural evolution were preserved. In the wedding rituals of the Balkans, for example, symbolic expressions of hostility between the families of the bride and groom were seen as vestiges of the days when men simply kidnapped or dragged off their mates. Societies in which inheritance or political office followed the female line were viewed as evidence of an early state of matriarchy, which eventually was replaced by a more "advanced" system—patriarchy. The ethnocentrism and sexism evident in the thinking of these early theorists makes it hard today to appreciate fully the positive contributions they made.

Lewis Henry Morgan: Technological Evolution. Lewis Henry Morgan, an American contemporary of Tylor, was a lawyer who became interested in anthropology as a young man when he helped his Iroquois neighbors in central New York with their legal fight for their land. In 1851 Morgan published his impressions of the Iroquois, the first full-length field report on an American Indian tribe. Soon he gave up the practice of law to pursue his new avocation full time. Like Tylor, Morgan believed that anthropology should be relevant to contemporary societal problems at the same time that it attempted to formulate general laws.

In his third major work, *Ancient Society* (1877), Morgan classified societies into three stages or levels of development: savagery, barbarism, and civilization. He divided each of the first two stages into lower, middle, and upper substages. Morgan defined his stages by the level of their technological sophistication. Upper Savagery, for example, was distinguished by the invention of the bow and arrow; Lower Barbarism, by the invention of pottery; Middle Barbarism, by the domestication of plants and animals. This formulation enjoyed wide acceptance at the time.

Each of these technological levels, Morgan claimed, was associated with specific cultural patterns or institutions—a particular kind of kinship structure, a particular type of legal system, and so forth. Morgan was particularly interested in the evolution of the family. In the earliest stages of human development, he postulated, there was no family structure at all; men and women mated indiscriminately. Gradually human society developed a form of communal marriage, in which groups of brothers married groups of sisters—in some cases their own sisters. In the next stage, sibling

Ethnography and Ethnology from Other Times, from Other Places

Anthropological theory is the product of a long tradition of scholarly inquiry in the West. Beyond this tradition, however, anthropology is, in its essentials, as old as human society itself. There is a universal nature to the spirit of inquiry and description that lies behind the discipline.

In *The Question of Hu*, historian Jonathan Spence describes the adventures and misadventures of a would-be ethnographer, one John Hu. In 1722 Father Jean François Foucquet, a member of the Jesuit mission in Canton and a noted scholar of Chinese literature, was granted permission to return to France with a collection for the king's library. Since he needed a Chinese calligrapher and secretary, he engaged Hu, the mission gatekeeper. Hu was semi-educated, a Christian convert, and eager to see the West. "Hu also believes," Foucquet noted, "he will be able to write up his travels in the form of a book that will make him famous among his countrymen when he returns" (Spence 1988:25).

After a lengthy and difficult voyage, in itself sufficient to cure the average person of any desire to see the world, Hu and his mentor reached Port Louis, France. Once on land, Hu set out to investigate the customs of the natives. But, making errors that modern ethnographers know all too well, he shocked then outraged his companions: he could not sleep in a proper bed and insisted on the floor, with an open window (unconcerned about the natives' beliefs in noxious nighttime vapors); he repeatedly wandered into kitchens, sampling the food uninvited; he borrowed a horse, left unattended for a moment by its owner, for a gallop of exploration through the city. Scolded, he was not contrite, asking "Why, if a horse is being left unused, may someone else not use it?" (Spence 1988:51).

When Hu, to Foucquet's consternation, decided he wanted to walk across France, which would have exposed him to great danger, he was packed unceremoniously into a coach to Paris. Nevertheless, his inquisitive spirit led to trouble: Hu stopped the coach to explore windmills, he jumped out to sample fruit in passing orchards, and one night at an inn he gave his best jacket to a beggar. His companions began to suspect that he was mad. Once in Paris, continuing his frantic explorations and still having learned very little French, he indeed gave local people every appearance of having lost his mind. Not content to observe and experience, he began to preach that men and women should be kept apart in church, as was the custom in China. Eventually his mentor and companions had him committed to a madhouse, where he remained in near-naked misery for over two years. Through the help of a priest, he was repatriated, and concluded his days answering such requests as, "Uncle Hu, Uncle Hu, tell us what it's like over there, in the West."

An early Chinese "ethnographer" who was more successful than Hu is Hiuen Tsiang who traveled in India in the seventh century A.D. Hiuen systematically described Indian society and culture in a manner that closely parallels the approach evident in many textbooks today. His descriptions include, among other topics, units of measure, the calendar, towns and buildings, dress, cleanliness, language and the arts, marriage, and education. His discussion of castes gives a sense of the detail he recorded:

With respect to the division of families, there are four classifications. The first is called the Brahman (*Po-lo-men*), men of pure conduct. They guard themselves in religion, live purely, and observe the most correct principles. The second is called Kshattriya (*T'sa-ti-li*), the royal caste. For ages they have been the governing class: they apply themselves to virtue (humanity) and kindness. The third is called Vaiśyas (*fei-she-li*), the merchant class: they engage in commercial exchange, and they follow profit at home and abroad. The fourth is called Sûdra (*Shu-t'o-lo*), the agricultural class: they labor in ploughing and tillage. In these four classes purity and impurity of caste assigns to every one his place.

An Arab missionary Ibn Fadlan was sent through Russia by his caliph in 922 A.D. He provides the only first-hand account we have of a Viking encampment on the Volga. Ibn Fadlan, like missionaries of many faiths, sometimes colored his observations with unfavorable judgments about "barbaric" customs. He, nevertheless, contributed a vivid portrait of the political hierarchy, costumes, trading ventures, and life of the Vikings in their great wooden houses. His inquisitive spirit led him to record their funeral rites:

Finally, the news was brought me that a prominent man among them had died. They laid him in a grave and covered it with a roof over it for ten days until they were through with the cutting out and sewing together of his garments. Thus it is: if the deceased is a poor man, they make for him a small bark, put him in it and burn the bark; if he is a rich man, they gather his possessions together and divide them in three parts: one third remains for his family; with the second third they cut garments out for him, and with the third part they brew nabid (beer) for themselves which they drink on the day when his slave girl kills herself and is cremated with her master. They drink the nabid to insensibility day and night. It often happens that one of them dies with his beaker in his hand. When a high chief dies, his family says to his slave girls and servants, "Which one of you wishes to die with him?" Then one of them answers, "I." When he has said this, he is bound. He can in no way be allowed to withdraw his word. If he wishes it, it is not permitted. For the most part, this self-sacrifice is made by the maidens.

While there are many more examples of early, non-Western ethnography, it is not only the ethnographic spirit that is universal. The need to systematize or generate theories about the cultural world also has a long tradition. Ibn Khaldun, born in Tunis in 1332, was an influential statesman and philosopher—one whose works still are read and valued today. While he trav-eled, as governor to Islamic provinces and as ambassador to Christian courts in Spain, he carefully recorded what he saw. But he was not content with observation. A highly educated individual, he wanted to understand the reasons why dynasties rise and fall, why great empires expand and die, and why people organize themselves in groups and live in tents, towns, and villages. He felt that "behind the external data is an internal, rational structure which, if understood, could explain the whys and wherefores, and render the external intelligible" (cited in Mahdi 1971:48).

Ibn Khaldun's theory of cultural evolution and what he saw as the laws of history are quite complex. However, it is not dissimilar to much contemporary theorizing. For example, he saw dynasties and empires as usually passing through five distinct stages: (1) the overthrow of an existing regime, (2) initial consolidation of the new regime in a period of recruiting and integration, (3) conquest and expansion, (4) a period of imperial glory and "contentment," and (5) corruption and decline. What makes this particularly interesting is that he postulates the mechanisms by which each phase leads to the next, something that any adequate theory of change must do:

The fifth stage is one of waste and squandering. In this stage, the ruler wastes on pleasures and amusements (the treasures) accumulated by his ancestors, through (excessive) generosity to his inner circle and at their parties. Also, he acquires bad, low-class followers to whom he entrusts the most important matters (of state), which they are not qualified to handle by themselves, not knowing which of them they should tackle and which they should leave alone. (In addition,) the ruler seeks to destroy the great clients of his people and followers of his predecessors. Thus, they come to hate him and conspire to refuse support to him. (Furthermore) he loses a number of soldiers by spending their allowances on his pleasures (instead of paying them) and by refusing them access to his person and not supervising them (properly). Thus, he ruins the foundations his ancestors had laid and tears down what they had built up.

unions were forbidden. People began to pair off but continued to live in large groups. Gradually, as society continued to evolve, men established the right to their own households, each with a wife, or more commonly with several wives. Only in the final stage of social evolution—civilization—did men and women become partners in monogamous marriage.

Though much of Morgan's language sounds old-fashioned and his bias toward Western society is obvious, his contribution to anthropological thought extends beyond the narrow confines of the discipline. Morgan has had a profound impact on modern intellectual and political history. Both Karl Marx and Friedrich Engels corresponded with Morgan and were greatly influenced by his findings, which they used in formulating their own theories regarding historical processes leading to communism. Engels' book *The Origin of the Family, Private Property, and the State* (1884/1972) has had a profound effect on the development of socialist thinking, and Morgan's *Ancient Society* was a major source of Engels' ideas. Thus Morgan's ideas became the basis for political ideology. Closer to our concerns here, Morgan's finding that there was a rough fit between social organization and technology is still valid.

The Place of Early Cultural Evolutionists in Anthropology. The early cultural evolutionists ultimately went far beyond the facts, and it was the facts that undid their form of evolutionary theory. They were unaware of or tended to ignore the vast amount of variability that exists within societies, historical evidence that some cultures become extinct, and evidence that there is no inevitable sequence of stages through which cultures pass. This is well illustrated in an anecdote involving an early evolutionist, Sir James Frazer, famous for his monumental study of primitive religions, *The Golden Bough* (1900). When asked if he

had ever seen any of the peoples whose religious practices he had described so eloquently, Frazer is said to have replied, "God forbid!" (Beattie, 1964:7).

Unilineal evolution proved to be a false lead. There is no neat or universal sequence to cultural change or development. Moreover, in their interest in broad features of cultural evolution, they lost sight of the role of individuals in society and of the great range of cultural behavior that occurs within some societies. Nevertheless, the early evolutionists made substantial contributions to anthropology. They reaffirmed the principle, fundamental to modern anthropology, that the variations we observe among contemporary societies are due to regular cultural processes. Moreover, in speculating about developmental sequences, they inspired many archaeologists to seek concrete data that would validate or refute their ideas.

Individual Actors: A Response to Cultural Evolution

One of the anthropologists who attacked the early cultural evolutionists was Franz Boas, who had begun his career as a physical geographer. In *The Limitations of the Comparative Method of Anthropology* (1896/1966), Boas argued that anthropologists knew far too little about preliterate peoples to construct valid theories about the origins of social life. He believed that anthropological research should focus on the relationship between individual action and custom. A great proponent of fieldwork, Boas spent years studying the Kwakiutl Indians of the American Northwest. He learned their language and dedicated much of his career to recording their beliefs and practices.

Boas was determined to refute speculative evolutionary theories about the origins of culture. His interest was not in discovering laws

Missionaries George Schwab and his wife also served as ethnographers in Africa in the early twentieth century. Although he had no formal training as an anthropologist, Schwab was affiliated with the Peabody Museum as a research associate for over thirty years. As with many early ethnographers who had dual roles, Schwab's ethnographic data must be viewed in light of his primary role as a missionary and agent of cultural change. (PEABODY MUSEUM, HARVARD UNIVERSITY)

of general evolutionary processes but in identifying laws that explained the relationship of individual actions to consensus and custom. Boas was one of the earliest anthropologists to recognize the importance of cultural relativism—the acceptance of society's behaviors, however alien to the researcher, within their cultural context, and the avoidance of negative value judgments. He instilled in his students an appreciation of the intricacy of nonliterate so-

cieties and of the need to understand them on their own terms, in meticulous detail, and in a temporal or historic perspective. The approach Boas adopted, now called **historical particularism,** is characterized by the collection of detailed ethnographic data.

It was largely through Boas's efforts that American ethnologists came to style themselves "cultural anthropologists" and to espouse the holistic view described in Chapter 1. Boas believed strongly that individuals are the products of their cultural systems and that the concept of culture is the keystone of anthropology. Further, it was largely due to Boas that cultural relativism became an established tenet of the field. Along with others, he effectively put an end to evolutionary studies of culture for the next thirty or forty years. American anthropologists concentrated instead on ethnography or

Pioneer ethnographer Frank Boas insisted upon detailed, firsthand ethnographic accounts of non-Western peoples. To this end, he immersed himself in the life and culture of the Kwakiutl Indians in British Columbia. Here Boas poses as a Kwakiutl hamatsa dancer in 1895. His meticulous attention to ethnographic detail set new standards for the field. (SMITHSONIAN INSTITUTION)

descriptive historical reporting on the rapidly disappearing tribes and traditions of the American Indians.

At the same time that Boas was making his contributions to the discipline in America, scholars in England and France were energetically exploring other aspects of anthropology.

Functional and Structural Approaches

The early British avocational and professional anthropologists collected vast amounts of data on a wide range of nonliterate societies, covering every conceivable topic from kinship, marriage, and sexual conduct to food, games, clothing, and houses. A picture of immense cultural diversity emerged in each area. How were these differences to be summarized? As ethnographic information became voluminous, a cross-cultural comparison of all known societies on all known traits became difficult. Anthropologists began to realize that approaches based on isolated cultural traits did not account for basic differences among societies. Patterns of behavior, they discovered, were organized—and the organization differed from group to group. Thus in order to focus on comparisons among societies, and ultimately to shed light on the reasons for cultural differences, some anthropologists began to investigate the variety of ways in which humans organize themselves. This focus, still the hallmark of British social anthropology, has had a profound impact on the field in general.

Functionalism

One major contributor to our understanding of social organization was Bronislaw Malinowski. Abandoning a career in physics and mathematics, he left Poland in 1910, studied anthropology in London, and then traveled to the Trobriand Islands in the western Pacific to do his fieldwork. Once he was there, however, World War I prevented him from returning home, and the year stretched to three years—a longer period than any other anthropologist had ever spent in the field. Malinowski became fluent in the language of the Trobrianders and immersed himself in their culture, noting in minute detail the routines of their daily life, their friendships, their fears, their ambitions, and the tones of voice they assumed in different situations. The result was one of the most thorough and vivid ethnographic studies ever done.

Malinowski's reflections on the material he collected in the Trobriand Islands led him to conclude that all the elements of a society are functional in that they serve to satisfy culturally defined needs of the people in that society. In this theory, called **functionalism,** Malinowski identified three basic types of human needs: biological needs (such as those for food and sexual activity), instrumental needs (such as those for education and the law), and integrative needs (such as the need for a common world view to facilitate communication).

To meet these needs, the society develops **institutions,** or recurrent patterns of activity, such as religion, art, a kinship system, law, and family life. Malinowski maintained that the institutions of a society dovetail not only with the needs they fulfill but also with each other. The function of religion, for example, is to establish and reinforce "valuable mental attitudes such as reverence for tradition, harmony with environment, courage and confidence in the struggle with difficulties and at the prospect of death" (1954:89). Though the Trobriand Islanders are highly skilled navigators and fishermen, for example, they perform magicoreligious rituals before embarking on long ocean voyages. They do not bother with such rituals for everyday fishing expeditions, but a long voyage on the open sea in a fragile canoe is far more dangerous, and the rituals help to allay some of their apprehensions. Reduced anxiety does not mean simply a more peaceful state of mind. A crew paralyzed by fear is less likely to complete a dangerous canoe voyage than one that is confident of the protection of providence. A culture, in Malinowski's view, is an integrated network of mutually supportive institutions ultimately related to human needs.

Structural Functionalism

Like Malinowski, Alfred Reginald Radcliffe-Brown argued that various aspects of a society should be analyzed in terms of institutions and their function. In his view, however, their central function was not to satisfy individual needs but to maintain the social structure—the society's pattern of social relations and institutions. To reflect this emphasis on social structure and to distinguish his ideas from Malinowski's, Radcliffe-Brown's theory has been called **structural functionalism.**

Radcliffe-Brown borrowed from the French sociologist Émile Durkheim the notion that a society is distinct from its individual members. A society has its own internal structure of beliefs and practices, governed by norms, which mold individual behavior. According to Radcliffe-Brown, the job of anthropology is not to concentrate on individual actions but to see through these particulars to the structure governing them. And the key to that structure is the society's norms.

Thus while Malinowski focused on institutions and individual behavior as the major organizing principle of society, Radcliffe-Brown concentrated on the norms that control behavior. In his view, all categories of social relationship in a society—the relationship between adult and child, man and woman, father-in-law and daughter-in-law, rich and poor—are regulated by such norms. Their purpose is to steer people through such relationships with a minimum of conflict. Radcliffe-Brown noted, for example, that many societies prescribe avoidance relationships between certain relatives by marriage, prohibiting them from entering the same room or speaking to one another. Other societies (including our own, to some extent) prescribe joking relationships between in-laws—superficial relationships dominated by teasing. According to Radcliffe-Brown, both norms serve the same function: to prevent conflict between potential antagonists, in the first case by keeping them apart and in the second by easing tension through laughter.

By reducing conflict in social relationships, norms perform the important function of stabilizing and perpetuating the social structure. A lawyer by training, Radcliffe-Brown appeared to think of norms as laws which people obeyed. He viewed societies as living organisms: highly ordered systems of differentiated parts, each of which contributes to the maintenance of the whole. By keeping the social "parts"—customs, practices, beliefs, relationships—working together in harmony, norms provide the structural stability that Radcliffe-Brown considered the necessary condition of existence in any society. Differences among societies depend on the way each society developed its own unique structure, its own characteristic arrangement of parts. Radcliffe-Brown believed that by uncovering the structures of a wide range of societies, anthropologists could ultimately construct a taxonomy, or comprehensive classification, of societies.

The Contributions of the Functionalist Approaches to Anthropology. Radcliffe-Brown's theories, like Malinowski's, stimulated interest in the internal dynamics of societies. And like Malinowski, Radcliffe-Brown traced the variations among societies to the means societies select to meet their basic needs—that is, to their behavioral norms and institutions. Yet neither theory explains why the cultural systems that developed out of the same basic needs vary so widely. Despite this serious shortcoming, these theories furthered anthropological study by supplying a theoretical framework for examining the internal workings of societies. Moreover, they encouraged anthropological inquiry rooted in **empiricism**—that is, reliance on observable and quantifiable data. Radcliffe-Brown's early view of anthropology as a scientific discipline that focuses on human society in the same way that biology focuses on other species is still held by a majority of modern practitioners (see Hughes 1988:18–20).

French Structuralism

To Claude Lévi-Strauss, a contemporary French anthropologist, and his followers, the key to cultural diversity lies in cognitive structures—the patterns that the human mind imposes on reality. This theoretical school is often termed **French structuralism.** But the interests of this group differ markedly from the "structural" concerns of Radcliffe-Brown. Radcliffe-Brown's followers in Britain and America concentrate on the structure of society and social relationships; the French structuralists try to identify the mental structures that they consider to underlie such social structures.

Lévi-Strauss's work draws inspiration from modern linguistics. After years of assuming that children learn language by imitating adults, prominent linguists in the 1950s and 1960s hypothesized that the fundamental rules of grammar are inherent in the human mind—that in a sense we come into the world preprogrammed for language. Similarly, Lévi-Strauss believes that certain codes essential to social organization are inherited, not learned. Cultural systems, he argues, are shaped by these inner structures. Lévi-Strauss has devoted much of his research to identifying the basic and universal mental structures.

One of these mental structures, he postulates, leads all humans to think in terms of logical "opposites." People everywhere recognize the distinctions between "us" and "them," animals and humans, adults and children, day and night, family and nonfamily, and—above all—self and others. This cognitive ability, Lévi-Strauss suggests, is one of the major differences between humans and other animals, between the world of culture and the natural order. Such distinctions establish reciprocal relations and obligations among groups and are reflected in the kinship system, myth, ritual, art, village layout, and overall organization of societies everywhere, regardless of the particular forms they take. Disparate subjects of myths in the Americas, for example—jealousy, potters, birds, sloths, comets, excrement—are actually interrelated. "Potter's clay," he writes, "undergoes extraction from the earth, and then firing to become a container designed to receive a content: food. Food itself undergoes the same treatment, but in reverse: it is first placed in a clay container, then cooked, then processed in the body through the operation of digestion, and finally is ejected in the shape of excrement." Myths, in his view, can be deciphered in terms of various systems of codes—sexual, zoological, cosmological, and so on.

Most anthropologists have rejected Lévi-Strauss's research and theories because his conclusions cannot be verified scientifically. Nevertheless, he has helped to direct attention to the relationship between cultural systems and the cognitive processes of individual members of those systems. And in the process of picking through cultural traits to find common underlying principles, he has revealed some interesting connections between the more imaginative side of culture—art and myth—and its more pragmatic aspects, such as technology and kinship systems.

Psychological Anthropology: The Individual and Culture

The structuralism of Lévi-Strauss comes closer than any of the other theories we have so far discussed to examining the dynamics of the interaction between individuals and broader cultural patterns. And yet it is individuals and the products of their behavior that anthropologists observe and from which they make inferences about culture and society. This important concern was initially addressed by anthropologists who had read and become interested in psychological approaches. They were strongly influenced by Boas as well; indeed, many were his students. In the 1930s psychological anthropologists who were influenced by Freudian theory began to examine the effects of society's child-rearing practices on personality, which has been defined as a set of distinctive styles of thought, behavior, and emotional responses which characterize a person's adaptations to surrounding circumstances. During World War II a number of anthropologists tried to identify basic personality structures in such complex societies as Japan, Russia, and the United States. Some of these studies formed part of the war effort. These national-character studies were based on the premise that similar childhood experiences produce a characteristic personality type. Because the war made field research difficult, anthropologists turned to secondhand

Psychological anthropologists investigating the interrelationships between culture, child rearing, and personality found that patterns of child rearing perpetuate a culture and its dominant personality type. (Top) A Tasaday man in the Philippines explains fire to his son. (Bottom) A kindergarten teacher discusses fire with her students. (TOP: JOHN NANCE/PANAMIN/MAGNUM; BOTTOM: BURK UZZLE/MAGNUM)

evidence, conducting interviews with immigrants to obtain their life histories and analyzing films, literature, propaganda, newspapers, and letters.

This interest in the psychological makeup of

people in various societies gave rise to a new branch of anthropological research called **psychological anthropology,** which focuses on the relationship between culture and individual personality. Most of the early psychological anthropologists agreed that they had to investigate the effect of culture on child rearing and personality. Child-rearing practices, they reasoned, mold the relatively uniform personalities of infants into the dominant personality type of the society, which in turn influences and perpetuates a particular cultural pattern.

Ruth Benedict: Group Personality

One of the earliest anthropologists to suggest that each society produces its own characteristic personality was Ruth Benedict. In her widely read book *Patterns of Culture* (1934/1959), Benedict claimed that from the grand arc of human potentialities each society unconsciously chooses a limited segment of traits to be cultural ideals, and that individuals gradually internalize these ideals. The result is a general similarity in ways of thinking and behaving—in other words, a group personality pattern.

To illustrate this process, Benedict analyzed the basic personality traits of two societies: the Kwakiutl Indians of the Pacific Northwest (the people Boas had studied) and the Zuñi Indians of the American Southwest. The Kwakiutl she depicted as an aggressive people prone to excess, constantly competing with one another for bigger and better supernatural visions, which they induced through self-torture. The Zuñi, in contrast, were portrayed as peaceful and restrained; distrustful of excesses and disruptive experiences of any kind, they always kept to the middle of the road.

Benedict's ideas have been sharply criticized as unjustified stereotyping. There is little evidence that any society is characterized by a single group personality. Later investigators have observed much more variety of temperament in the Zuñi and Kwakiutl societies than emerges from Benedict's portraits of them. Her work, in short, is regarded as an extreme oversimplification. But her basic approach, the effort to characterize a group by its cultural style rather than by its structural form, continues to be of interest to psychological anthropologists.

Margaret Mead: The Plasticity of Personality

Margaret Mead was one of the earliest and most prolific contributors to research on child rearing. Upon completing her graduate work as a student of Franz Boas and Ruth Benedict at Columbia University in 1925, Mead set out on her first major field trip: to study adolescents on the Polynesian island of Samoa. (Mead's research in Samoa is discussed more fully in Chapter 10.) Because puberty was presumably rooted in the biological nature of things, the social transition from childhood to adulthood was thought to be universally stressful. But Mead believed that adolescence might not be so universally stressful after all. If behavior and values differed from culture to culture, so might the experience of adolescence.

She found, in fact, that the Samoans followed a relatively short course from childhood to adulthood. In her famous book *Coming of Age in Samoa* (1928/1971), Mead reported these findings and stated her conclusions: "that adolescence is not necessarily a time of stress and strain, but that cultural conditions make it so" (1971:234). In later ethnographic studies she went on to argue that sex roles and personality traits—indeed, personality in general—are not biological givens but rather extremely plastic qualities, which are molded in the image of cultural ideals through child rearing. Thus men in one New Guinea society are found to be less aggressive and more nurturing of children than women, while in another, not so distant population, boys are reared to emphasize their fierceness.

Mead's work, like Benedict's, has been criticized on the grounds of stereotyping and for her overlooking of much of the variability in the societies she studied (see Freeman 1983). But by showing that a "fact of life" such as adolescence or masculinity can take very different forms, Mead pressed home the important point that often what the Western world regards as "human nature" is largely a cultural artifact.

Cross-Cultural Psychological Research

Psychological anthropologists have turned their attention to similarities and differences that cut across cultural boundaries. John Whiting and Irving Child (1953), for example, conducted a systematic cross-cultural study to determine possible correlations between child-training practices and adult attitudes toward illness. After comparing ethnographic data on seventy-five cultures, they did indeed find some significant correlations. They concluded, for example, that children who are nursed on a rigid schedule and weaned abruptly at an early age develop a preoccupation with and a negative attitude toward oral gratification. As adults they tend to attribute illness to events associated with the oral system—drinking, eating, and so on. Such cross-cultural studies are valuable in that they attempt to test the universal applicability of psychological theories through objective analysis of ethnographic data. Indeed, the contribution goes beyond psychological theories; it is an important impetus for rigorous hypothesis testing in all areas of anthropology.

The Culture Area Approach

Another approach or "school" of cultural anthropology that became prominent in the United States and had a lasting effect on the discipline is often referred to as the "culture area" approach. Clark Wissler, a curator responsible for laying out museum collections, set out to classify American Indian populations according to their most distinctive cultural traits and geographical locations. He noted a complex of traits common to all of the many tribes in the Great Plains region. Wissler thought it unlikely that this complex of traits had been invented independently by each of the groups. And since the complex appeared among peoples who lived in relative proximity, he explained the similarity as the result of **diffusion**—the spread of an aspect of culture from the society in which it originated by migration or imitation. Altogether, Wissler isolated a number of distinct **culture areas**—regions in which several groups have similar culture complexes—ten in North America, four in South America, and one in the Caribbean. He proposed that each of these areas had a "culture center," a place where all the typical traits could be found. This center, he maintained, must be where the complex originated, since the farther one moved from the location, the fewer of the component traits appeared.

While Alfred Kroeber contributed to almost every area of theory discussed in this chapter, his early research was carried on within the framework of the culture area approach. Kroeber added an important dimension to Wissler's work by showing the relation of the major culture areas of North America to such environmental variables as temperature and rainfall. In doing so, he introduced an important new line of investigation: the systematic study of cultural systems as forms of adaptation to the environment.

RECENT THEORETICAL PERSPECTIVES OF EVOLUTION

In the 1950s, anthropologists became interested once again in tracing broad patterns of cultural development. Reviving evolutionary theories, they enlarged and refined the classical evolu-

tionist approach on the basis of new information and ideas developed in the intervening years. Like the early evolutionists, they proposed that the key to cultural diversity was evolution, but they saw cultural evolution from a new perspective—as the product of human beings' interactions with their environment.

They also incorporated evidence offered by both archaeologists and ethnologists for broad regularities in the development of human culture. Moreover, the new wave of scholarship was able to analyze these broad developmental regularities without recourse to the antiquated notions of European superiority that underlay the concept of progress in earlier schemes. It had become clearer that the organizational and technological principles that nonindustrial people used in extracting resources from their environments were not simply "primitive" relics but often were practical, ingenious, and successful solutions. It was obvious, too, that sometimes these technologies were environmentally sounder than "advanced" Western practices.

The Return to Cultural Evolution

Trained in the Boasian tradition, Leslie White also greatly admired the work of the nineteenth-century evolutionists and regretted that their positive contributions had been ignored in the general rush to criticize their ethnocentricism. Like them, he believed that societies tended to develop progressively more complex forms of organization. Combining Herbert Spencer's idea that social evolution proceeded by decreasing entropy (randomness) with the theory that culture is an energy-capturing system, White (1949) sought to pinpoint the cause of cultural progress and to explain how it operated.

White reasoned that in order to provide themselves with the basic necessities of life, human beings have to expend energy. During the early stages of human history, they used their own bodies as the major source of energy, but gradually they began to harness fire, water, wind, and other resources to do some of their work for them. Energy capture increased as people learned to fashion more and more efficient tools, to domesticate animals, to construct power-driven machines, and so on. And at each step of the way, other aspects of culture evolved in response to the newly achieved level of usable energy. In other words, improvements in technology (that is, methods of energy capture) propelled the rest of culture forward. White's basic premise was that cultural development was rooted in technology, and that individual motivation and decision making were of little importance in the grand sweep of evolution. Here we see a return to the view of culture as an organism and of individuals as simply passive participants.

Cultural Ecology

Like White, Julian Steward was concerned with cultural evolution, but unlike White, he focused on the evolution of cultural systems through environmental adaptation. His work gave rise to an approach called **cultural ecology.** Steward's approach to cultural diversity required the simultaneous investigation of technology, culture, and the physical environment (including neighboring populations as well as climate, terrain, and natural resources). White had maintained that evolutionists should focus on human culture as a whole, and identify general laws. Steward believed that this approach to discovering such laws failed precisely because it dealt with culture in the abstract rather than with the actual development of particular cultural systems. Steward (1972) called for the replacement of universal or unilineal evolutionism by another approach, **multilineal evolutionism,** which would focus on the development of individual cultures or populations without insisting that all follow the same evolutionary pattern.

Like White, Steward regarded technology as

a crucial aspect of culture. He pointed out, however, that technology cannot be considered apart from environment. Cultures in different environments, for example, may have the same kind of technology, but that technology may not be equally productive and may entail diverse patterns of labor, economic management, and social organization. Hunters and gatherers who live in desert or arctic environments, where conditions are harsh and resources relatively scarce, tend to live in small, migratory bands with a relatively simple form of social organization and a meager material culture. Hunter-gatherers who live in more bountiful environments may develop a much more settled residence pattern and a more elaborate socioeconomic system.

Steward maintained that when one compared sequences of change in different societies, certain cross-cultural regularities could be seen. He noted, for example, that whenever complex state societies developed in the ancient world—in the Middle East, Mesoamerica, Peru, Egypt, and China—they seemed to develop under similar conditions. In each case, the people involved lived in arid or semiarid regions where they had learned to grow crops without iron tools but not without a rudimentary irrigation system. Steward concluded that people living under roughly the same environmental conditions with similar technologies will develop similar cultural systems, and that these systems will develop along similar lines. This approach, which Steward called **cultural ecology,** has had a major impact on current anthropological research and is the historical antecedent for the approach we use in this book.

Marxist Anthropology: An Alternative to Cultural Evolution

Both White and Steward were greatly influenced by Lewis Henry Morgan's work and by Engels' *Origin of the Family, Private Property, and the State,* which had itself been based in large part on Morgan's ideas. By the 1960s a large number of American scholars were interested in the internal sources of social change or disruption. By then the world had been shaken by two major wars and numerous less extensive ones; by dramatic revolutions in Russia, China, Egypt, Iraq, Indonesia, Algeria, and Cuba; and by a multitude of independence movements in Africa and elsewhere. Karl Marx's notion of "dialectical materialism," which postulates that historically societies move through distinctive stages, or "modes of production," seemed to have explanatory value in efforts to understand the broad sweep of historic change.

Each mode of production, Marx held, is characterized by distinctive social, economic, and political relations among members of the society. Thus any generalization about society is meaningful only in the context of a particular mode of production. Statements about capitalist society have little applicability to noncapitalist modes of production. Moreover, historically modes of production are transformed in a predetermined direction.

The causes of this transformation lie in the internal contradictions within any given mode of production, which ultimately are resolved by "progressive" change. In the capitalist mode of production, the contradiction is between the interests of those who control the society's means of production (capital and technology) and the interests of those whose labor produces economic goods. The owners or controllers of production are interested in increasing their wealth by exploiting the workers. The workers are interested in improving their position, and the only way they can do so is by rebelling against those who control the means of production. In the course of history societies have passed through feudalism, Oriental despotism, capitalism, and other modes of production, each with its own combination of distinctive elements and contradictions. The idea of universal progress through a limited number of stages is very similar to Morgan's early formulation. It differs, though, in stressing internal conflict as a primary source of change.

Marxist anthropology, then, is the study of internal sources of social change, with a focus on a society's distinctive set of elements and contradictions. The main contribution of this perspective to contemporary investigations, in our opinion, is the serious attention it directs to two critical questions: Who gets what and how in society? and what role does inequality play in the generation of social conflict? Considerable research on these issues has been carried out in recent years, particularly in efforts to understand the relationship between underdevelopment and the activities of industrial nations. By looking for general processes that go beyond national boundaries and narrowly defined social entities (tribes, communities, ethnic groups) and examining long-term interrelationships among people who may seem to have no connection with one another, we see the truth of the commonplace observation that we occupy one world (Wolf 1982:3).

Cultural Materialism

A further elaboration of the ideas of Marx, Engels, White, and Steward constitutes a perspective sometimes called **cultural materialism.** Marvin Harris, its leading exponent (see Harris 1988), emphasizes the material constraints on cultural adaptation. He views ideas, values, and religious beliefs as the means or products of adaptation to environmental conditions ("material constraints"): available food resources, climate, water, predators, disease, and so on. For Harris, the ideas people hold about food taboos, child rearing, and religion are best understood as having developed to further the survival of their culture in its habitat, though the people themselves are usually unaware of this function.

In some respects this approach is similar to that of the English functionalists who also stress the notion of society as a functioning system, each social institution playing its role in the maintenance of the structure of the whole. Harris's contribution is the notion of adaptation guided by a variety of cost-benefit calculations. Successful adaptations are those that promote a favorable balance of costs and benefits, usually from the standpoint of the society as a whole. Food taboos are a case in point. Both Islam and Judaism have dietary prohibitions on the consumption of pork (among other items). Harris has argued that this dietary law is an adaptive outcome of the fact that the raising of pigs in the arid Middle East would be an inefficient and environmentally poor use of resources (Harris 1987). This approach has been criticized for being, among other things, unclear as to how costs and benefits are actually weighed at a societal level and even as to how anything might be shown to be "maladaptive"—if it exists, it serves (or served) some societal purpose. Warfare, cannibalism, even female infanticide are explained in terms of large-scale utilitarian functions, such as population control or protein conservation. In short, the main criticism is that it explains too little because it explains too much. Anything can be asserted to be adaptive or cost-effective in the absence of a consistent system of measurement (Vayda 1987).

Sociobiology

While agreeing with the premise that humans have to be understood as products of a long evolutionary heritage, cultural anthropologists have generally emphasized the importance of learning and cultural plasticity relatively unconstrained by biological factors apart from obvious physiological requirements. In the 1980s, however, this position has been challenged by new theoretical perspectives on evolution that have emerged from the natural and social sciences, in particular from the areas of neurobiology, population genetics, ethology, and psychology. The main contention is that genetically controlled biological processes are responsible for shaping a good deal more social behavior than is generally acknowledged. The arguments are often controversial. As they have focused much attention on the relationship of biology and culture, we will look at them in some detail.

In the last fifteen years, a new approach to the study of social behavior, called **sociobiology,** has been propounded by biologists and others following the lead of E. O. Wilson. This view applies Darwinian ideas of natural selection to human culture and social behavior. The sociobiologists' position rests on the model of behavioral evolution in other social animals. Researchers have found a significant percentage of social behavior in nonhuman animals to be under the direct or indirect influence of genes, and they argue that such behavior has adaptive significance (Dyson-Hudson and Little 1983, Chagnon and Irons 1979).

The animal whose mating, defensive, and food-procurement behaviors "work" best within its given environment is the animal most likely to survive, reproduce, and rear its offspring to maturity. The argument is not, as is sometimes asserted, that there are particular genes for particular behaviors, such as aggression and jealousy, but that organisms have a genetically based propensity to behave in ways that are appropriate—that is, in ways that promote or facilitate individual reproductive success. Some aspects of the sociobiological approach are well established and not subject to controversy. Certainly genetically conditioned aspects of animal social behavior are the result of and continually influenced by the forces of natural selection (discussed in Chapter 1). Much social behavior involves cooperation among close kin, as this approach would predict. The genes that control behaviors that contribute to reproductive success are preferentially transmitted through generations, whereas genes that facilitate less adaptive behavior gradually disappear. So well established is this basic premise that virtually all behavioral research with primates and other social species takes it as given.

Should this line of reasoning apply only to nonhuman animals? A variety of studies point to the value of the evolutionary model for an understanding of broad patterns of human behavior: the importance of kinship and family and male-female reproductive strategies. The usual argument for exempting the human species from this line of reasoning is that once humans developed culture—and the behavioral flexibility that accompanies it—they parted ways with the other animals (see Gould 1986). Our social behavior came to be based primarily on learning, and our ability to learn can produce behavioral changes much more rapidly than natural selection ever can. Our behavioral repertoire has been passed down to us through our culture rather than through our genes. The behaviors that have survived have been of value less to individuals than to groups, for culture is the property of groups. Even granting these points, those who employ the evolutionary model argue that while culture is transmitted by learning, what is inherited is a built-in propensity to learn and pass on some cultural rules and beliefs at the expense of others. In other words, we learn what we are conditioned "by instinct" to learn (see Gould and Marler 1988). There is no simple resolution to this disagreement. We cannot doubt that lines of continuity run through the behavior of all animals. Nor can we doubt that human capacity for culture adds a unique dimension to human social life. Moreover, much of what anthropologists are interested in explaining is not directly addressed by this model; for example, the nature and persistence of inequality, the role of value systems and ideology in social life, and the evolution of contemporary political systems.

SOME OBSERVATIONS ABOUT THEORETICAL APPROACHES

The theories and methods we have discussed have been built upon, refined, or abandoned over the course of a hundred years. The ones anthropologists espouse are tentative; they change as the discipline evolves. It is this constant need for revision and testing of theories and hypotheses that propels anthropologists into the field. This is not to say that a year or even twenty years of fieldwork can prove a theoretical proposition beyond all doubt, thus elevating it from the status of theory to that of truth. Most modern scientists, conscious that one decade's truth is the next decade's reject, no longer talk about discovering absolute truth.

Even that mainstay, evolution, is continually being modified. Scientists continually aim to improve their theories, applying them to new areas and probing for oversimplifications. This, precisely, is the goal of anthropology. As a theory is strengthened, refined, modified, or refuted by one anthropologist's fieldwork, the revised formulation can then serve as a stimulus to other anthropologists, who in turn can refine, modify, or refute it through study of other societies. The hoped-for result of this halting process is less the elucidation of final truths than the formulation of the most probable and best-supported generalizations about human society.

Field research generates not only new theories but also new methods. For as theories are refined, they highlight new aspects of culture, stimulating the development of new techniques with which to explore them. New methods inevitably influence theory by allowing fieldworkers to uncover facts that have previously been overlooked or ignored—facts that call for modifications in current theories or, in the extreme case, explode current theories altogether.

In short, anthropological theory and method are mutually dependent. New theories produce new methods, and new methods produce new theories. Through this spiraling process, as anthropologists seek increasingly reliable means of gathering information and distill from that information increasingly accurate generalizations about human culture, the work of theory building is carried on. And our understanding of the complexities of human culture is extended.

Summary

A *scientific theory* is a statement that postulates ordered relationships among natural phenomena. Theory provides a framework for research, directing researchers to certain kinds of questions and leading them to expect certain results, against which they can check the results actually obtained. The many theories that cultural anthropologists have put forth revolve around basic questions: Why do societies differ? How do societies differ? What is the relationship between the individual and society?

Evolutionism explains the development of all species as the outcome of adaptation to environmental circumstances through the process of natural selection. The *early cultural evolutionists* applied evolutionary theory to culture. E. B. Tylor held that cultures progress through a sequence of evolutionary stages—a pattern now called *unilineal evolution*. Lewis Henry Morgan classified societies into three stages, differentiated by the level of their technological development.

Impatient with such speculative theories, Franz Boas held that the proper focus of anthropologists was the relationship between individual action and custom. Boas's approach, called *historical relativism*, stresses the collection of detailed ethnographic data.

The *functionalist* school, developed by Bronislaw Malinowski, holds that all elements of a society are functional in that they serve to satisfy culturally defined needs of the individuals in that society. Every society, Malinowski held, develops *institutions*—religion, art, a kinship system, law, and family life—to meet its people's biological, instrumental, and integrative needs. A. R. Radcliffe-Brown agreed that institutions are central to an understanding of a culture, but in his view their function was to maintain the social structure rather than to meet individual needs. His focus was less on individual behavior than on the norms that control behavior. Because of his emphasis on structure, his theory is called *structural functionalism*. Though neither of these theories explains why cultural systems that developed out of the same basic needs vary so widely, they formed a valuable theoretical framework for further research and encouraged *empiricism*—reliance on observable and quantifiable data. The *French structuralists*, led by Claude Lévi-Strauss, hold that the key to cultural diversity lies in cognitive structures—the patterns the human mind imposes on reality.

Psychological anthropology focuses on the relationship between culture and individual personality. Cross-cultural psychological research tests the universal applicability of psychological theories through objective analysis of ethnographic data.

The *culture area* approach identifies regions in which several groups have similar complexes of cultural traits and seeks to identify the "culture center" where it is theorized that the traits originated. Theorists of this school explain the similarity of culture traits as the result of *dif-*

fusion, or spread of traits from the culture center by migration or imitation.

Cultural ecology calls for the simultaneous investigation of technology, culture, and the physical environment. Julian Steward, who developed this approach, believed that unilineal evolutionism should be replaced by *multilineal evolutionism,* or a focus on the development of individual cultures without insistence that all follow the same evolutionary pattern.

Karl Marx's theory that societies move through distinctive stages, or "modes of production," has captured the interest of many anthropologists who seek to identify the internal sources of social disruption. *Marxist anthropology* focuses on a society's distinctive set of elements and contradictions in an effort to explain social change.

The approach of *cultural materialism* considers ideas, values, and religious beliefs to be the means or products of adaptation to environmental conditions. To Marvin Harris, an exponent of this approach, successful adaptations are those that promote a favorable balance of costs and benefits from the standpoint of the society as a whole. The *sociobiologists* apply Darwinian ideas of natural selection to human culture and social behavior. They argue that organisms have a genetically based propensity to behave in ways that promote or facilitate individual reproductive success.

Each of these schools of thought emphasizes different aspects of individual, social, and cultural behavior. Together they form the theoretical arena in which anthropological debate takes place.

Key Terms

cultural ecology

cultural materialism

culture area

diffusion

early cultural
　evolutionists

empiricism

French structuralism

functionalism

historical particularism

hypothesis

institutions

Marxist anthropology

multilineal
　evolutionism

psychological
　anthropology

scientific theory

structural functionalism

sociobiology

unilineal evolution

Suggested Readings

APPLEBAUM, H. (ED.). 1987. *Perspectives in Cultural Anthropology.* Albany, N.Y.: State University of New York Press. A history of anthropological theory that presents the major theoretical orientations that have influenced anthropological research and understanding.

CHAGNON, N. A., AND W. IRONS. (EDS.). 1979. *Evolutionary Biology and Human Social Behavior: An Anthropological Perspective.* North Scituate, Mass.: Duxbury Press. A collection of papers that together detail the

implications of sociobiology for anthropological explanations of human social behavior.

GARBARINO, M. S. 1983. *Sociocultural Theory in Anthropology: A Short History.* Prospect Heights, Ill.: Waveland Press. A concise survey of the history of sociocultural theory in anthropology. A good resource with which to familiarize oneself with the major figures in the field.

HARRIS, M. 1968. *The Rise of Anthropological Theory.* New York: Crowell. A comprehensive treatment of the history of theory in anthropology from an evolutionist materialist perspective. The emphasis of the book is on the development of this theoretical tradition within the discipline.

KAPLAN, D., AND R. A. MANNERS. 1986. *Culture Theory.* Prospect Heights, Ill.: Waveland Press. A survey of current anthropological theories and their origins, written at an introductory level.

LESSER, A. 1985. *History, Evolution, and the Concept of Culture.* Cambridge, Eng.: Cambridge University Press. A collection of selected papers that begin with Boasian anthropology, cover the author's thinking on cultural and social evolution, and end with the part the author feels anthropology has to play in the solution of modern social problems.

RIGDON, S. M. 1988. *The Culture Façade: Art, Science and Politics in the Work of Oscar Lewis.* Urbana and Chicago, Ill.: University of Illinois Press. An examination of the evolution of Oscar Lewis's ideas and findings about the culture of poverty; offers insights into the ways in which theory develops in anthropology.

STEWARD, J. H. 1972. *Theory of Culture Change: The Methodology of Multilinear Evolution.* Urbana, Ill.: University of Illinois Press. A collection of Steward's theoretical and substantive essays. These works provided the initial impetus for the development of an ecological tradition within anthropology.

STOCKING, G. W., JR. 1987. *Victorian Anthropology.* New York: Free Press. A probing look at the Victorian origins of Western European anthropological theories of human social and cultural evolution.

WOLF, E. R. 1982. *Europe and the People Without History.* Berkeley, Calif.: University of California Press. An analytic history of European expansion; the effects of this expansion on the "native" peoples of Africa, Asia, and the Americas; and how these peoples in turn affected the history of Europe.

Chapter **3** Methods of Cultural Anthropology

A scientific paper presents an account of research in a highly formalized manner: problems are laid out in accordance with implicit or explicit theory, methods of investigation are described, and findings are reported, with possible wider implications carefully noted. The fact is that the structure of most scientific papers is misleading—not because their findings are wrong but because the steps leading up to the findings stray far from the ideal format advocated by scholars. Such reports say very little about the way the research was conducted or the source of the original insights. Scholars rarely mention the role of serendipity or pure luck in pointing them toward their conclusions. Nor do they usually mention the role of old-fashioned intuition based on observation of a multitude of facts. The preferred language of science is *deductive* logic, or reasoning that leads one from the general principle to the meaning of particular facts. Of course, all recognize that in practice the opposite can be the case—the scholar starts with data that have to be accounted for and then finds a grand plan in which to incorporate them. In order to understand the process that led up to the results, one has to go backstage—get to know how members of a discipline are trained, the sources of the questions they ask and the way they formulate them, and even some of the professional surprises or hazards to be encountered, which are rarely reported. Much of what is unique in anthropological theory is formed in the crucible of fieldwork rather than in university libraries.

RESEARCH IN THE FIELD

Regardless of theoretical orientation, cultural anthropology relies heavily on **fieldwork**—that is, the firsthand observation of human societies—as a means of gathering data and testing hypotheses generated by theories. Most of the theoretical approaches discussed in Chapter 2 were not developed in quiet corners of university libraries, nor were they modified through laboratory experiments. They evolved through continual testing among the peoples whose ways of life they sought to explain.

Anthropologists gather data in the field in part through firsthand observation and reporting, living among the members of a group in an effort to understand their customary ways of thinking and behaving. They ask people questions and carefully record their answers. They closely examine the things the people produce: their tools, baskets, sculptures, musical instruments, weapons, jewelry, clothing, houses. Above all, they spend many hours simply watching the people's daily routines and interactions. From these activities emerge the fine-grained ethnographic descriptions that together constitute an invaluable repository of information about the breadth and variety of human culture. There is more to fieldwork than simple observation, as we shall see, but it is firsthand observation that gives anthropological reports a distinctive and vibrant quality.

Fieldwork is hard work and requires intense preparation. Today almost all anthropologists are trained at universities. Graduate programs are designed to give students a thorough grounding in anthropological literature, to make them aware of theoretical disputes and of what is already known about the cultures of a particular area, to enable them to establish a valid sample, and to formulate realistic research questions and organize and interpret the ethnographic data they collect. Anthropology as we know it today is firmly rooted in empirical data and, ultimately, in field research. Just as the development of precision instruments in the natural sciences has allowed scientists to probe previously uncharted areas of nature (the surface of the moon, for example), so improved techniques of field research have enabled anthropologists to explore more systematically the many ways of human life and thus to broaden our understanding of human nature. Methodical observation and questioning, systematic interpretation, controlled comparison, and sampling are the primary research tools of the anthropologist today.

But the process of observation is not neat and tidy. From the day the ethnographer arrives in the field to the day he or she departs, the course of research is being shaped by myriad chance encounters—often of a less than benign sort. The would-be researcher may be held up for months getting permission from local officials to visit the area targeted for investigation; lack of all-weather roads may make it impossible to visit a site during a critical period; local conflicts or strife may curtail movement from one community to another. Moreover, the data being collected are constantly affected by the researcher's own social presence: most ethnographers gain access to a community by associating themselves with a particular family or local grouping. Such an alliance, however tenuous, invariably affects the ethnographer's relations with others in the community—sometimes favorably but sometimes negatively.

People who are on poor terms with one's hosts tend to be cool or suspicious of the guests.

Any number of unforeseen circumstances can change the direction of a project. Dan Bradburd and his wife, Ann, went to Iran in 1973 to carry out a project among nomadic pastoralists. Their objective was to model formally the process of decision making as it applied to decisions to migrate or to remain camped. They spoke with many scholars and officials familiar with various parts of the country and determined that a population called the Komanchi would be suitable, as they were sheep herders who migrated over a substantial distance during the course of the year.

Once among the Komanchi, the Bradburds soon found their initial objectives less and less interesting (and less manageable in practice) than other aspects of Komanchi economic and social life. Decisions to move the tents and herds turned out to be based on a few fairly obvious criteria, and on balance the project seemed not very likely to add much to theory regarding information processing. At the same time, unexpectedly, they found very marked differences in wealth and social position among members of a tribe they had supposed to be egalitarian. Accordingly, they shifted their focus and methods of data collection to address issues related to animal husbandry, wealth, and economic mobility—a topic on which Dan Bradburd has since published extensively. Both the original topic of research and the new one were grounded in extensive but rather different bodies of theory—their evaluation of the field situation ended up determining which was pursued.

It is reasonable to ask why so much emphasis is placed on theory, method, and planning for the field when, in the end, things are likely to turn out not at all as one expected. The answer is partially just for that reason: command of theory or theories enables researchers to be flexible and to ask significant questions no matter what conditions they encounter in the field.

Bahram Tavakolian went to Turkey in 1969 to study the relationship between way of life and certain psychological variables among nomadic pastoralists and other rural populations. Unfortunately (as is often the case), the authorities denied him permission to work where he had planned. Instead of giving up his project, he pursued the general thrust of it in an urban setting, collecting data from workers in the city's marketplaces. The researcher who has a firm theoretical focus can tailor work successfully to accommodate ever-changing circumstances in the field. Fieldwork usually must be preceded not only by theoretical grounding but by training in the language and history of the area chosen and in specialized techniques of sampling, computation, and analysis of data.

Choosing a Problem and Designing Research

In the early part of this century, the primary goal of fieldwork was to describe a given culture, often previously unknown to Westerners, as fully and completely as the researcher's energy and funds would allow. Today, for reasons we have noted, more and more field research is problem-oriented. That is, the anthropologist focuses on one or more important theoretical issues—the relationship between child rearing and adult personality structure, for example, or between food-getting techniques and residence patterns—and then studies the aspects of a given society which relate to that issue.

Behind this switch to a problem-oriented approach is a major change in the interests and techniques of cultural anthropology over the past few decades. Quite simply, the subject matter has expanded. Whereas earlier fieldworkers were concerned primarily with normative patterns—a society's *typical* approach to child rearing, marriage, the settlement of disputes, or whatever—today's anthropologists probe these areas more deeply and explore the

variety of behaviors within each of them. Most anthropologists, working alone, limit their projects to an exploration of one or two aspects of a society or local community. More ambitious studies in broader contexts are often undertaken by a team of specialists. One researcher may concentrate on food getting and technology, another on child rearing, a third on religion. Or if the community includes distinct social classes or racial, ethnic, or religious groups, each member of the research team may focus on a different group. By pooling their individual efforts, the team can put together a more complete picture of a whole society or a research problem than a single researcher could accomplish. In some cases this sharing of knowledge may be interdisciplinary—the anthropologist may work with demographers, nutrition experts, agronomists, and the like.

Since 1981 a project called the South Turkana Ecosystem Project has been under way in northwest Kenya (see Little 1988:697–700; R. Dyson-Hudson 1988:701–704; and the box in Chapter 7). The project is set in the vast, extremely arid heartland of the cattle-herding Turkana tribe, and by directing primary attention to one segment of the tribe the researchers hope to understand the structure and function of an ecological community involving humans. Participants include five Kenyan scientists, thirteen American anthropologists, and fifteen ecologists, including experts in rangeland management, demography, livestock breeding, nutrition, and bioenergetics. The anthropologists, working in concert with the other scientists, have published articles on livestock production and human subsistence in a desert environment, human nutrition, and factors that affect human fertility and mortality (see, for example, Leslie et al. 1988:705–712). Though such large-scale and expensive projects are not the norm, interdisciplinary research is frequently employed and is invariably very strongly problem-oriented. As one member of the Turkana team puts it, "Research of this nature can provide solutions to previously intractable problems that were approached [previously] by single-science methods" (Little 1988:697).

A second reason for the development of a more problem-oriented approach is the recognition that theories inevitably influence the sort of data collected. Theoretical assumptions govern the kinds of questions researchers will ask in the field and therefore the kinds of information they will get. For example, a structural-functionalist theory of politics that stresses social stability and integration will direct a researcher to one kind of data; the researcher may well be looking for data on institutions that adjudicate disputes, release tension, and promote group solidarity. A Marxist theory of politics that emphasizes conflict and competition among those who control the means of production and those who supply the labor will direct a researcher to study instances of conflict reflecting class or economic divisions.

This is not to say that researchers see only what they are looking for and block out everything else. Still, perception is always selective and tends to be shaped by one's assumptions—in this case by what one expects or hopes to find. To prevent this issue from becoming a problem, anthropologists are careful to spell out their theoretical assumptions when they write up the plans for their research and later when they report their findings. Thus their biases, if indeed they have influenced the research, are at least not hidden.

Some researchers go into the field with one set of theoretical assumptions and emerge from it with another set. Though fieldwork is a dynamic process, it is far more effective when it is guided by explicit theoretical questions. In fact, funded research (research that is supported by a grant or a fellowship, usually awarded on a competitive basis) almost always requires the investigator to formulate a clear set of hypotheses and a design for research that includes precise details of the way the hypotheses will be tested. Most universities assume that their faculty and graduate students will secure funds for research by applying to outside agencies.

Methods of Gathering Data

Because anthropologists investigate so wide a range of problems, they must command an equally wide range of information-gathering techniques. Three techniques that are basic to almost every piece of field research are participant observation, interviewing, and collection of demographic and material culture data.

Participant Observation

The method most widely used by anthropologists to collect information in the field is **participant observation,** or actual participation in a culture by an investigator, who seeks to gain social acceptance in the society as a means to acquire understanding of her or his observations. Participant observation begins the moment an anthropologist enters the field and continues during the entire time of residence. In practice, "participation" can range from commuting to the village or neighborhood from a home nearby to almost total immersion in community life. In general, participant observers involve themselves in the cultures they study. Malinowski explains why it is essential for anthropologists to participate in the activities of the societies they investigate:

> Soon after I had established myself in [Omarakana, Trobriand Islands], I began to take part, in a way, in the village life, to look forward to the important or festive events, to take personal interest in the gossip and the developments of the village occurrences; to wake up every morning to a day presenting itself to me more or less as it does to the native. . . . As I went on my morning walk through the village, I could see intimate details of family life, of toilet, cooking, taking of meals; I could see the arrangements for the day's work, people starting on their

Participant observation, one of the main means of collecting ethnographic data, involves many hours spent in conversation. (Top) Richard Lee interviews a group of San of the Kalahari Desert. (Bottom) Margaret Keiffer records her conversation with a Guatemalan woman doing embroidery. (TOP: IRVEN DEVORE/ANTHRO-PHOTO; BOTTOM: YORAM KAHANA/PETER ARNOLD)

errands, or groups of men and women busy at some manufacturing tasks. Quarrels, jokes, family scenes, events usually trivial, sometimes dramatic but always significant, formed the atmosphere of my daily life, as well as of theirs. . . .

Also, over and over again, I committed breaches of etiquette, which the natives, familiar with me, were not slow in pointing out. I had to learn how to behave, and to a certain extent, I acquired "the feeling" for native good and bad manners. With this, and with the capacity of enjoying their company and sharing some of their games and amusements, I began to feel that I was indeed in touch with the natives, and this is certainly the preliminary condition for being able to carry on successful field work. [Malinowski 1922/1961:7–8]

Participant observation, then, helps anthropologists to see cultures from the inside, to see people behaving informally and spontaneously. Furthermore, it forces fieldworkers to learn how to behave according to the natives' rules.

Of course, fieldworkers must be more than just casual observers. They must observe systematically, making detailed and accurate records of their observations. The anthropologists Beatrice and John Whiting (1973) describe one useful technique for making systematic observations: to make schedules indicating where events are happening, at what time of day, and on what day of the week. In this way, fieldworkers can be in the right place at the right time to observe whatever it is they are interested in.

In taking their notes, anthropologists often use **code sheets,** checklists of observed behaviors and inferred motivations for or attitudes toward them. Such observational techniques have been used to study, for example, the relationship between personality characteristics in children and various child-rearing practices (Whiting 1963). Instead of measuring personality by using a traditional psychological test, which may not be meaningful in a culture other than the one in which it was devised, the researchers decided to observe children's behavior systematically and to assess their personalities on the basis of the frequency with which various characteristics were expressed in specific behaviors. A fieldworker might observe a child during a five-minute period and then assign a score for nurturance on the basis of the number of times the child gave food to a younger child or provided help, emotional support, guidance, or information. Similarly, the fieldworker might rate a child on aggression on the basis of the number of times the child hit, pushed, bossed, or verbally attacked other children within a five-minute span. These ratings would then form the basis of well-documented profiles of the personality characteristics of the members of several cultures.

One very promising method of collecting behavioral data which is largely free of cultural or observation bias is that of time allocation. The anthropologist designs a schedule that records types of activities throughout the day (Gross 1984). It is a way of sampling what people are actually doing as opposed to what they say or think they are doing. If one's research interest is to determine father–child relationships, one can select random times during the day and at each point closely record the interactions of the people observed, thus acquiring some insight into the frequency of various sorts of interaction.

The value of this approach is seen in the work of a research team led by Daniel Gross in central Brazil. Comparing four culturally similar Amazonian populations in different habitats and with different food resources, they found that levels of nonwork activity—particularly leisure-time pursuits—were sharply curtailed where resources were least abundant (Rubin et al. 1986). All the groups worked approximately the same number of hours but individuals in the poorer habitats engaged in fewer leisure activities and encouraged their children to play games that were low in energy costs, thus conserving their strength. In other words, people were adapting to hardship by adjusting their behavior so as to husband their energy, and even that of their children.

The advantage of combining time-allocation studies with participant observation is that researchers are able to observe commonplace events that are taken for granted and would not be noteworthy to the individuals being observed, or behaviors that individuals might not want to discuss (such as alcohol or drug use). Informants often do not remember relevant details accurately; they may also report what they think *should* happen, or only what they want the researcher to know. The researcher who lives among the people can check these statements against the observable facts.

Yet following the flow of events as they present themselves is not enough. Fieldworkers can easily misinterpret what they see, reading into a behavior meanings that do not apply. A fieldworker who sees a man beating his wife, for example, may assume that he is abusing her. But perhaps the people of that society believe flogging is the best way to drive away disease (Williams 1967:24). Interviews, questionnaire surveys, psychological tests, and other formal research methods are necessary to support fieldworkers' final interpretations of people's motives and behaviors.

Interviewing

Interviewing is the flesh and blood of ethnographic research—it reveals what individuals think and feel, how they see events and the world around them. Interviews are used to pursue topics that arise in less structured ways, to check participant-observation data, to gather general information about a community, and to obtain specific information about beliefs and behavior.

Interviews may be formal or informal. The **formal interview** consists of questions designed to elicit specific facts, attitudes, and opinions; the fieldworker plans questions in advance, arranges a specific time for the interview, and adheres to a preconceived plan. The **informal interview** is an unstructured question-and-answer session in which the informant is encouraged to follow his or her own train of thought, wherever it may lead. This sort of interview is really just an extension of participant observation. The advantage of informal, open-ended interviews is that they tell a researcher what the local people themselves consider important. Russell Bernard, who has worked many years in Greece, advises: "Get an informant onto a topic of interest and get out of the way. Let the informant provide information that he or she thinks is important" (1988:207). Informal interviewing can also be a point of entry into the community. Bernard, like many other anthropologists working in the Mediterranean region, discovered that he learned a great deal about the people he was studying by simply drinking wine at the local *taverna* and listening to their conversations (1988:207). He not only learned much about the life histories of the local sponge fishermen but made close friends among them. When he

wanted to shift to more structured questions and increasingly formal interviews, he found he could do so easily, as the men had gained a good sense of what he was doing.

The disadvantage of this method, were one to use it alone, is that since the informants are not responding to standardized questions or situations, it is difficult to compare and evaluate their responses. Variations in the wording of a question can elicit quite different responses. The researcher attempts to avoid this problem by supplementing informal exchanges with formal interviews. Often questions are carefully tested and screened in advance. To make sure that they are getting the kind of data they want, researchers may first try out a formal questionnaire on a few people and review the results. They may then eliminate confusing questions or sharpen those that elicit ambiguous responses. A vague question such as "Do you believe in witchcraft?" will be changed to a more precise one, such as "How many times did you visit the shaman last year?" Researchers may also revise questions that seem to influence informants' answers. Social scientists have found, for example, that more people will answer no to a question that is worded negatively ("You don't hit your children, do you?") than to one that is phrased positively or neutrally ("Do you hit your children when they misbehave?"). Finally, the fieldworker may decide to ask questions about new issues brought to light by the preliminary questionnaire. Once the final format has been worked out, a broader survey can be conducted.

Because formal interview questions are highly specific and leave little room for personal discussion, the answers tend to be limited and clear-cut. For this reason, and because the questions are presented in the same way to all informants, the responses can be compared and analyzed statistically.

Thus the formal interview and the informal interview have complementary advantages. The formal interview elicits more comparable information, while the informal interview gives informants a chance to reveal their own personal visions of the world and thereby point to new research directions. Today most fieldworkers make use of both techniques, either by combining formal and informal questions in a single interview or by interviewing the same people formally and informally at different times.

Regardless of the technique used, the interview can be a problematic tool for gathering data. Often local people assume that a stranger who asks a great many questions is a tax collector or worse, and they refuse to cooperate. (Hiring other local people as assistant interviewers may increase the rate of cooperation, but the practice creates other problems, for native interviewers often try to coax responses out of informants and influence the responses in the process.) Even when the local people are willing to be interviewed, their statements cannot always be accepted at face value, because many extraneous matters can affect their responses. Women may be reluctant to discuss certain topics if men are present, and vice versa; children may say only what they think they are supposed to say when adults are nearby. The social distance between interviewer and informant is also a factor. An interview with an illiterate person who is in awe of the researcher and perhaps anxious to please him or her is quite different from an interview with a member of the elite who regards the anthropologist as an equal or an inferior. Finally, informants may forget, idealize, or simply lie.

How, then, are fieldworkers to get at the truth? Though they probably can never get the complete truth, they can come close to it by checking interview responses against information elicited from other people, against repeat interviews with the same person, and, above all, against their own observations—Do people behave as they say they do? T. R. Williams (1967) learned in this way that although the Dusun of Indonesia boast about their sexual exploits, they are actually rather conservative in sexual matters. Conversely, they shy away from talk about aggression but are highly aggressive in their behavior.

Thus, like formal and informal interviews, interviewing in general and participant observation are complementary techniques. Each is truly useful only in combination with the other. Together they form the core of fieldwork and are continuing aspects of every field experience.

Collection of Demographic and Material Culture Data

Much of fieldwork is devoted to investigations of behavioral patterns—who marries whom and why; how people raise their children, carry out their daily routines, and conduct their rituals and formal transactions; and how they interact with one another generally. Anthropologists are also concerned with the demographic status of the population, with the material aspects of culture, and with the attendant technology and physical environment.

Toward the beginning of a field study, most anthropologists conduct a **census**—a comprehensive survey of their research population designed to reveal its basic demographic characteristics; the census may be extended to the regional population of which the community is a part. A census often takes the form of a simple household survey. Basic demographic items—occupation and income; the number, age, educational level, and marital history of family members; and so on—are usually covered, along with a few fairly standard questions about how members are related to one another, places of birth, and the like. Usually the fieldworker also collects relevant data to calculate fertility and mortality rates, estimate marital stability (divorce and remarriage), and to discover what dietary and other factors may affect the health of the population.

Mapping—drawing a map showing the physical features of the community—is usually an early step in a field project, for it allows the researcher to learn the lay of the land: the locations of fields, forests, sources of water, homesteads, streets, paths, and so on. By including dwellings and other structures in the map, the ethnographer not only gets to know the spatial layout of the community but may find useful information about social relations. People usually reside in groupings that reflect social relations. The map may also help the researcher gain a *complete* list of the people who actually live in the community. Very often, certain individuals may be socially invisible in that they are ignored by the community's establishment. People whose neighbors consider them socially undesirable or insignificant are rarely pointed out to strangers, but any researcher would want to work with a complete picture of the community, not an idealized one.

Also important is the study of material items that people make and use. During the initial phases of fieldwork, when researchers may still be perfecting the language skills needed to conduct extensive interviews, they can learn a good deal simply by describing and making inventories of tools, weapons, household utensils, buildings, vehicles, and the like. In any case, the fieldworker must at some point make a detailed study of technology in order to understand the relationship between the society and its physical environment.

Even more central to an understanding of this relationship is the construction of some form of **inventory of resources**—ideally, a catalogue of the kinds of materials the people under investigation take from their environment in order to clothe, house, and feed themselves; the amount of time they spend procuring these materials; the quantity of food they collect or produce; and the distribution of the research population per unit of land. A complete inventory is impossible, but even a crude one is invaluable.

Anthropologists have conducted more and more studies of this kind in recent decades, and some have produced important new insights.

After carefully measuring time expenditures and food yields among the Dobe !Kung in southern Africa, for example, Richard Lee (1968) found that hunting and gathering often yield a more abundant food supply—and allow people to have a more leisurely style of life—than earlier, less systematic observations had suggested. Though subsequent restudies have shown a less favorable food supply, their findings do not invalidate the point that impressions cannot take the place of careful data measurements.

Consider the investigations of the ethnographers Teresa and John Hart (1986), who carefully determined the caloric and nutritional values of food resources in the Ituri rain forest of Zaire. Their findings indicated that the Mbuti Pygmies—hunters and gatherers in the forest—could not live independently of the farmers with whom they trade. Mark Flinn (1986), too, found some interesting facts about sexual reproduction and parent–offspring interaction when he analyzed genealogical, demographic, and economic data collected in a village in Trinidad. He discovered that men and women with the most land, the major resource, have the most offspring; that the more land a man has, the more women he is likely to have sexual relations with; and that young adults, particularly men, whose parents live in the village have more children than those who live apart from their parents. The study shows the effect of wealth and family ties on reproduction.

Official documents (statistical and historical records) can provide valuable information. As we shall see in Chapter 8, Burton Pasternak (1983), working with historical documents and government census materials, was able to document precisely the migration and settlement of Chinese farmers in Taiwan over a century ago. The statistical and historical data, together with genealogical data gathered in interviews with living residents in the villages studied, made it possible for him to reconstruct family histories and to calculate such demographic variables as family size and rates of mortality, fertility, and longevity. In fact, fieldworkers with very diverse interests often spend a good deal of time working out genealogical relationships. Such information enables the researcher to go back a few generations in time even if historical records are absent or incomplete. Family history can be a good basis for a reconstruction of community history. One can also use genealogies to gain understanding of major events of the past—by inquiring systematically, for example, how individuals of an earlier generation were involved in a specific conflict or battle. Genealogies yield clues to patterns of violence and hostility, just as their evidence of marriages reveals past alliances and friendships.

Cameras and video recorders have become increasingly important as research tools and as means of studying social situations and interactions. Ethnographic films have recorded a wide variety of subjects, from the interaction of siblings and the ways mothers hold, feed, and bathe their infants in different societies (childhood socialization) to warfare and hunting expeditions. By watching such films carefully, much as athletes study films of their own performances, fieldworkers are often able to detect significant details of behavior that might otherwise have eluded them. Aerial photographs and satellite imagery can reveal unsuspected patterns of land use. In fact, photographs serve many useful purposes, from counting people on the streets more accurately than one can do with the naked eye to eliciting stories from informants; they have even gotten an anthropologist-photographer invitations to ceremonies and other private functions (see Collier 1967).

The Experience of Fieldwork

Although anthropologists arrive in the field armed with an impressive array of research techniques, they usually find their new world full of surprises from the moment they set foot in it. One of the most basic difficulties is language. While a knowledge of the native language greatly enhances the quantity and quality of data that can be gathered, it is not always possible for an anthropologist to learn that language in advance. Or there may be important dialect differences between the language learned and that spoken in the community that is ultimately chosen as the research site.

The first month or so in the field is usually spent making practical arrangements. The fieldworker has to find a place to live and a way to obtain food and supplies. Generally, anthropologists either rent a house in the community they are studying or live with a family. Some live in a tent or trailer, in a house that local people build for them, or in a school. Others commute from a nearby town. If the researchers intend to live in a remote village, they will have to purchase in advance many of the supplies they will use. "My main trouble was that I had no idea of what I might need," Elenore Smith Bowen recalled:[1]

> My own imagination carried me no further than a typewriter, paper, textbooks, and a miscellany for reading. . . . I had myself introduced to ex-traders and retired administrators. They all recommended a meat grinder to make goat meat edible and curry powder to make it palatable. . . . I was grateful, but I wanted to know more. . . . The best advice, in the long run, came from the ripe experience of two professors of anthropology. One said, "Always walk in cheap tennis shoes; the water runs out more quickly." The other said, "You'll need more tables than you think."   (Bowen 1964:3–4)

Food can also be a problem for anthropologists who work in remote towns and villages.

---

[1]Elenore Smith Bowen is the pen name Laura Bohannan used when she published her anthropological novel *Return to Laughter* (1964), based on her experiences among the Tiv of northern Nigeria. She explains in a foreword that all the characters except herself are fictitious but that the ethnographic details are accurate.

Eating and drinking with local people may be an excellent way to establish rapport, but it can also present difficulties. Bowen liked the roast yams and corn that her African neighbors prepared but could not swallow their mashes, viscous concoctions of grains and fluid. To refuse a host's food was considered a serious insult. She solved the problem by taking a child along on her visits: people thought her extremely good-natured to give the food to a child. Napoleon Chagnon, who studied the Yąnomamö of the Brazilian-Venezuelan border, did most of his own cooking, but found it an ordeal:

> It is appalling how complicated it can be to make oatmeal in the jungle. First, I had to make two trips to the river to haul the water. Next, I had to prime my kerosene stove with alcohol and get it burning. . . . Or, I would turn the kerosene on, hoping that the element was still hot enough to vaporize the fuel, and start a small fire in my palm-thatched hut. . . . Then I had to boil the oatmeal and pick the bugs out of it. . . . Eating three meals a day was out of the question.   [Chagnon 1983:12–13]

Fieldwork is sometimes a lonely undertaking. Inability to communicate effectively and culture shock—the disorientation one feels in a totally foreign social landscape—compound the fieldworker's sense of isolation. At some point during the first few weeks, nearly every anthropologist wonders, "What on earth am I doing here, all alone and at the edge of the world?" (Powdermaker 1966:51). Chagnon considered turning back the moment he saw the Yąnomamö:

> I am not ashamed to admit . . . that had there been a diplomatic way out, I would have ended my fieldwork then and there. I did not look forward to the next day when I would be left alone with the Indians; I did not speak a word of their language, and they were decidedly different from what I had imagined them to be. The whole situation was depressing, and I wondered why I ever decided to switch from civil engineering to anthropology in the first place. [Chagnon 1983:5]

In his work with the Yąnomamö, Chagnon spent months learning names and collecting genealogies, only to discover that the Yąnomamö have strict taboos against speaking the names of the dead and refer to a living person by name only to show lack of respect. His informants had made a game of inventing preposterous and obscene names. All his work was wasted. Nor was this the end of the fun the Yąnomamö had with Chagnon. They considered him (along with all other non-Yąnomamö) subhuman and had no qualms about relieving him of food and equipment whenever they had a chance. Finally he retaliated. After some men chopped up Chagnon's wooden platform in order to make paddles, Chagnon waded across the river, delivered a stern lecture to the culprits, and calmly cut their canoes loose to drift downstream. Thereafter his status rose dramatically among "the fierce people."

Sometimes the sex of the anthropologist poses special problems in the field. As men and women often move in very different social circles, a male anthropologist may find it difficult to interview women, collect their personal life histories, or closely observe the portion of their social lives from which men are excluded. Conversely, women fieldworkers may have difficulty moving in male social circles or be constrained by the limits of propriety that the society imposes on female behavior. In the end such constraints can usually be overcome, though sometimes some ingenuity may be called for. In the summer of 1974, while the Kurdish uprising was at its height, the anthropologist Amal Rassam was doing fieldwork in and around the city of Mosul, in northern Iraq. As part of her research she wanted to carry out a survey of villages belonging to different ethnic groups. Having obtained her official research permit, she hired a taxi and its driver, a native of a nearby village. Her notes read:

> On Tuesday morning, 'Ali my driver came to the hotel to pick me up to go to the village to begin my

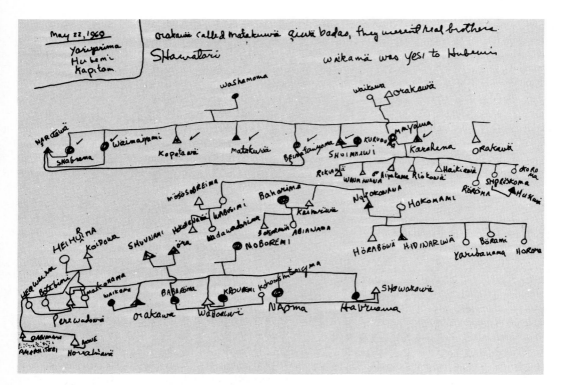

In order to remember complex kinship data given him by informants, ethnographer Napoleon Chagnon found it useful to make this detailed genealogy during his 1969 fieldwork among the Yąnomamö. (NAPOLEON CHAGNON)

survey. He was dressed in the traditional garb of his region, which marked him as a rural inhabitant, a qarawi, or villager. I sat at the back of the taxi and we drove off. A few miles outside the city we were stopped at a military checkpoint. The soldier ignored my driver and came around to my side of the car, put his head in the window and asked where I was going. I told him that I was on my way to the village down the road, upon which he asked to see my identification papers. Discarding my protestations and ignoring my work permit, he made us turn around and go back to the city, claiming that the road was mined and that he could not guarantee my safety.

On the way back, I expressed my frustration to 'Ali and my fears that I wouldn't be able to carry my survey through. Upon some reflection he suggested that we try again in a day or two, but this time he would put on his suit and I should wear the 'abaya (the black cloak worn by the more traditional women in Iraq). And so we did. When he came back two days later to pick me up, he was dressed like an effendi (an urban gentleman). As we reached the checkpoint, the soldier on duty came around this time to the window of the driver, asked to see his papers, and wanted to know where we were going. Without a direct glance my way, he waved us on, and we continued to the village. [Bates and Rassam 1983:219–220]

The first time Rassam set out, she was the one in the automobile who was socially visible: she was a woman traveling alone in Western dress and clearly a foreigner to the area. Her status was immediately recognized by the soldier, who ignored the driver and asked for her papers. Her dress identified her as a member of urban, educated society, and the fact that she had hired a car marked her as a person of potential significance. The soldier chose not to assume responsibility for the presence of such a person in his area.

On the second attempt, sitting next to the driver in her 'abaya, Rassam became publicly invisible; the soldier perceived her as belonging to the driver. Moreover, the driver, resplendent in his Western-style suit, had acquired both visibility and a certain amount of social standing. The confrontation now became one between the two men, the soldier at the bottom of the military hierarchy and the effendi representing the bourgeoisie. The woman in the car ceased to exist in any political sense. This, we might add, was one occasion when being a woman anthropologist in the Middle East was an advantage. A male anthropologist would have had to show his identification papers along with those of the driver, and on being found to be a stranger to the area would probably have been turned back.

Not all fieldwork is so chancy. Although the pioneer fieldworkers and many since them have ventured into extremely remote communities, hundreds of miles from the nearest bathtub, more and more work is now being done in urbanized areas. At the same time, more and more rural communities are acquiring electricity, modern plumbing, and transportation facilities. As a result, fieldwork has become less laborious and isolated—and perhaps less romantic as well.

DATA AND ANALYSIS

Romantic or not, difficult or easy, fieldwork is a means of furthering a scientific enterprise. It is one means of collecting a sample of a much larger phenomenon. When an ethnographer studies a village, that village is undoubtedly one community among many. No area of anthropological interest can be studied in its entirety; one can approach one's chosen subject only by looking at selected cases or instances of occurrence. When a researcher selects a village, that choice will determine just what aspect of a larger system he or she will experience. The utility of the study is vastly enhanced if the choice is made with some knowledge of where the sample falls in the **sampling universe**—the largest entity to be described, of which the sample is a part. The sampling universe may be a village, an ethnically defined population, a region, a town, or whatever. But however that universe is conceptualized, it is necessary to be clear as to its scope and to have a good feeling for the way one's data fit into it.

If one goes to a farming village, for example, one should know roughly how it compares with other such communities in the region, or in the country as a whole. In order to interpret the data correctly, the researcher must have a sense of just what kind of sample it does or does not constitute and the dimensions of the overall sampling universe. If a Nigerian anthropologist came to a rural Wisconsin community to study American farm family life, he or she could learn a great deal that was applicable to the society as a whole. But at the same time a **sampling bias**—the tendency of a sample to exclude some members of the sampling universe and overrepresent others—would preclude generalization about many American ethnic groups, about urban families, about non-English-speaking Americans, and about anything else that was excluded from the original sample (here the rural Wisconsin community). It is wise to be wary of generalizations that are based on very limited samples or that are purported to apply to a sampling universe that is not described.

Even when the community or population to be studied is relatively small, the researcher must take care that the persons who serve as informants, the times when questions are asked, the ages of the people interviewed, and the like are carefully chosen. It is never possible to get universal coverage of a topic. Knowing that the data they do collect are only a sample, most cautious researchers clearly stipulate the bounds of their samples. One cannot simply interview people on the basis of the fact that one knows them or that they are available at convenient times of day. The researcher considers the sorts of questions to be asked, draws up a complete list of possible informants, and then selects those who meet appropriate criteria. A very common unintentional sampling bias has to do with sex; some male researchers tend to treat sex as an unimportant variable when it is not, collect few data on women, or ignore them altogether (Eicher 1988:6–10, 66–70). Many researchers have underestimated the contributions of women to the economy of the populations they studied because they focused exclusively on male activities. In some societies women *are* socially invisible; but they should never be invisible to the researcher.

An ethnographer who wants household census data for a large area will have to make a compilation of all of the households in the population and then select those to be visited. In some cases a **random sample** may be appropriate—a sample in which each individual (in this case each household) in the population has the same chance of being selected as any other. Generally the universe being investigated is sufficiently large and complex (a community, a region, a tribe) that in order to ensure a realistic sample of it, the researcher has to divide it into categories representing distinctive characteristics and then select a random sample from each category. The result is a **stratified sample.** If a sample of households in a community characterized by differences in wealth is to be meaningful, all categories of wealth have to be represented in proportion to their numbers: if 35 percent of the population is landless, then 35 percent of the households to be visited should be landless, and so on. A re-

searcher who did not consider variability in wealth in stratifying the sample in this community might be seriously misled if he or she chanced to visit a disproportionate number of very rich or very poor households. Rich households in many farming communities tend to be larger than average (among other things). The researcher would similarly have to take care that female-headed households were proportionately represented, as they are likely to have distinct social or economic characteristics.

Statistical Analysis

Statistical analysis is the application of probability theory to quantified descriptive data. Statistical techniques provide an anthropologist with a standardized and clear method to describe the distribution of characteristics in a population and to determine correlations between these various characteristics. Consider an anthropologist investigating the number of people living together in households and the amount of work these people must do to make a living. One might hypothesize that farm families raising crops that require hand labor will tend to be larger than households in the same community whose land-use system and crops are less labor-intensive. In this hypothesis the variable defined as "need for labor" would be called an *independent variable* and "family size" would be called the *dependent variable.* In such causal models where one explains one phenomenon or factor as causing or influencing the behavior of another, the factor which is the causal agent is the independent variable.

The investigator will first find some way to quantify these variables. The dependent variable, household size, for example, could be measured in terms of the number of individuals living together, their sex, and their age; the independent variable, labor, could be measured by the number of hours per week spent at work in the fields. Then the anthropologist will collect these data for the households in the sample and see if there is a correlation between these two factors. Does household size in fact covary with hours of labor more than could be expected to do by chance?

Research Using Secondary Data

Fieldwork is distinctive to anthropology and, ultimately, most new data come from ethnographic reports. But a substantial amount of research also relies on secondary sources—materials already collected and available in archives and libraries. The basic types of questions that researchers address using secondary data can be included under two headings: diachronic, or historical, studies and synchronic, or nonhistorical, studies.

Diachronic studies, including ethnohistory, use descriptive data from one society or population that has been studied at many points in time. Historical studies are invaluable for determining long-term trends and for testing hypotheses about causal sequences. It has been suggested, for example, that human population growth is responsible for the development of intensive agriculture—an increasing pressure on food supplies resulted in a greater investment in farming. Archaeological and other diachronic studies indicate, however, that this is an overly simplistic formulation. While population change is one very important factor, in many instances intensive farming preceeds population growth; in many others, population growth occurs with no change in farming practices. Since all causal explanations rely on a sequence of events in which one phenomenon causes or acts upon another, such historical investigations are important. As we will see in the next chapter, our ability to see adaptation or evolutionary processes at work requires a historical perspective.

Synchronic studies rely on research that does not make use of or control for the effects of the passage of time. Ethnographic data collected in the field are usually published in reports, articles, or books. Often these reports represent a particular society or culture as frozen at a given point in time, which is called the **ethnographic present.** Any subsequent use of this ethnographic data is limited to this snapshot view. The western Pueblo Indians described in Chapter 6, for instance, bear little resemblance to present-day Pueblos, who, like other Native American groups, reflect both the traditional patterns and the sociocultural diversity of American society as a whole.

When we use secondary ethnographic data we generally use them *comparatively.* That is, we take data from two or more societies and compare them. Such comparative analyses usually are designed to test some hypothesis or proposition about how cultural phenomena are related.

There are many hypotheses that cannot be tested with synchronic data from only one society. For example, Yehudi Cohen predicted that incest prohibitions (that is, prohibitions on certain individuals as sexual partners) become less strictly applied and less inclusive as technological development progresses and as trade and exchange become more important (1974). We are not concerned here with why he formulated these hypotheses but only with how they might be tested. As a first step, data from numerous societies, at all levels of technological development, are required. Gregory Leavitt collated and analyzed data from a large sample of societies (1989:121) and found that, indeed, there is such a correlation: the incest prohibition emerged as significantly less inclusive and less strictly applied (specifically, the penalties are less severe) in technologically complex societies (1989:116–131). While we have simplified the results, the point is that Leavitt's research indicated an interesting relationship

Quantitative Methods in Anthropology

"The fundamental requirement of anthropology is that it begin with a personal experience and end with a personal experience, but . . . in between there is room for plenty of computers" (C. Levi-Strauss, as cited in Thomas 1986:vi).

Following World War II, all of the social sciences began gathering much more quantitative data. As the pool of anthropological research data burgeoned, paralleling the growth of the discipline, a need developed for ever-more efficient means of assessing the reliability of generalizations or conclusions based on behavioral data.

When sets of data are small, patterns and relationships are often apparent from a simple glance at the notebook or a column of figures. With larger arrays of data, however, it is not always possible to recognize patterns or interrelationships; while some very strong relationships may be clear, other more subtle but potentially useful ones may not. Statistical and mathematical techniques, greatly aided by computer technology, have developed to meet this need. Quantitative methods alone offer little, however. Far more important is the care with which questions are posed, data collected, and hypotheses tested.

David Thomas writes, "It has been said that anthropologists use statistics much as a drunk uses a street lamp—more for support than illumination." Shoddy research can be disguised with statistical jargon and masses of numbers. But it is for this very reason, Thomas argues, that one needs an elementary grasp of quantitative methods; at the very least, one must be able to assess the results of other anthropologists' analyses (1986:5).

One example of how systematic quantification and statistics can be used in ethnology is the work of Burton Pasternak (1978; 1983) who has used statistical methods to analyze data from two Taiwanese villages. His goal was to identify the factors influencing the timing of first births. He found that the reliability of food supply was the most likely factor to influence a seasonal distribution of first births. In other words, first births tended to be timed to coincide with a reliable food supply that became available during the six months or so following the fall harvest.

Let us take a look at Pasternak's methods. Fortunately, in addition to his firsthand observations in the field, Pasternak was able to use the household registry system introduced in Taiwan in 1905 by Japanese colonial authorities. This registry provided detailed demographic information on the village population levels for several generations. Since reporting of such information tended to be strictly enforced, it was not likely that many births went unrecorded. For the town of Meinung, Pasternak used data for 180 households drawn randomly from the approximately 4,300 households listed in the registry as of early 1947. For the village of Chungshe he was able to use the entire regis-

between certain cultural features and beliefs about incest that would not have been observable without using the comparative method.

There are a number of methods of comparative research used in anthropology. The two most common are controlled comparison and cross-cultural research. Each has advantages and disadvantages. In a **controlled comparison** of data, the researcher selects two or more societies that are similar if not identical in all

try, since in 1946 that community numbered only about 596 people.

After choosing his sample, Pasternak isolated the patterns of first births from those of subsequent children and charted the first birth frequencies by month. At each step in his study, Pasternak recorded his data in terms of variables that expressed fertility, seasonality, measures of wealth, and the like. He found seasonality, for the distribution of first births occurring when the food supply was greatest. To determine whether various associations were random, Pasternak then applied the chi-square test, a frequently used test for probability of randomness in associations. Chi-square tests showed an associated probability of less than .05 (1 chance in 20) for Meinung and less than .01 (1 chance in 100) for Chungshe. These results indicate that the likelihood of this relationship occurring randomly is very low.

Pasternak's task was not finished, however. A statistically significant relationship does not necessarily mean that there is a causal relationship. He, therefore, had to analyze the data to control for factors other than reliability of food supply as influences on birth seasonality—factors such as rainfall, work demand, timing of conception, timing of marriage, and temperature. Various statistical tests eliminated rainfall and periods of low labor demand as determining factors in the frequency of first births in both Meinung and Chungshe. Pasternak also considered, but was able to eliminate, the possibility that birth timing might be a consequence of conception timed to coincide with dry or cool months or when work was slack. He did find that Chungshe conception was more likely during cooler months or in the least busy time of the year, but no statistical significance showed up for Meinung.

An obvious possible factor that Pasternak had to consider was the influence of the timing of weddings on birth timing. Data for Meinung showed that most marriages did occur in the cooler and drier months of winter and spring and that there was considerable correspondence between peak birth and peak marriage months, with both occurring at times of peak food supply. But the data from Chungshe showed no comparable coincidence between seasons of birth and marriage, and only births were associated with food reliability. It would thus appear that this latter relationship was the more crucial one.

In both villages, frequency of first birth was found to be significantly related to temperature, with births generally occurring in the coolest months. But the coolest months were also the months of most reliable food supply. In order to determine which variable was the influential one, Pasternak had to hold the reliability of food supply constant and investigate the relationship between temperature and the frequency of first births. He found no significant linkage.

No scientific investigation is ever entirely conclusive. Data are always changing and refining earlier research. Since his original 1978 study, Pasternak has expanded his demographic sample in Taiwan and has launched new research in the People's Republic of China as well. Each new finding is likely to call into question some of the earlier ones. Today Pasternak, like many other anthropologists, makes extensive use of newly developed programs and powerful microcomputers to record, to store, and to analyze large sets of economic and demographic data that would be otherwise so time-consuming as to be impossible for the individual researcher to handle. But in the end computers, like the statistical routines they perform, are simply "tools of the trade"—by themselves they are meaningless until put to use in a responsible fashion.

areas other than those under investigation. The researcher then studies the comparable data from the areas of investigation in each of the selected societies to try to establish a causal mechanism that explains the variation among them. Burton Pasternak used this method to try to understand variations between Taiwanese villages (see Chapter 8). Noting that some villages in Taiwan had very cohesive forms of community organization while others were more focused on narrow family ties, he hypothesized that this variation was a consequence of economic differences.

To implement a controlled comparison, he selected two villages in which the inhabitants spoke the same dialect, had migrated together four generations earlier from China, and had in common numerous cultural beliefs, values, and practices. But the villages differed in their degree of community cohesiveness (the dependent variable), and in one major economic respect (the independent variable)—one practiced irrigation on rich land and the other, until recently, had relied on rainfall. This economic difference, he concluded, explained why the village using irrigation had a far more elaborate community organization. A relatively high level of community organization was necessary to facilitate both the defense of the fields and the cooperation required to use shared waterworks for farming.

The advantage of controlled comparison is that it allows one to try to emulate a laboratory experiment in which experimental conditions are carefully controlled. The disadvantages are that this control may be at least partially illusory, as the control can never be more than approximate and the researcher is usually aware of the results of the comparison before doing the research and thus the controlled comparison may become no more than an illustration.

Cross-cultural research (or *holocultural* research, as it is sometimes called) makes generalizations on the basis of global comparisons. While controlled comparative studies are usually designed to take into account internal variation within each of a limited number of societies (usually two) from one geographic region, cross-cultural studies treat each society as an entity that either has or does not have specific traits or has quantitative variation in the traits. Since internal variation is ignored, a society is seen as having a trait such as a "pref-

erence for polygamy" or a "weak, moderate, or strong preference."

Cross-cultural research usually tests a hypothesis by constructing a sample of reports from all over the world. These reports then become the source of raw data, which in turn are organized as variables and coded. In his study of incest, for example, Leavitt classified societies according to their general technological status and then established variables that measured the strictness and scope of the incest taboo. His data were drawn from the **Human Relations Area Files (HRAF),** an indexed collection of reports and documents on more than 330 societies.

Taking into account some very troublesome sampling problems, one can create a global picture of cultural variation: how people define incest, how many societies practice polygyny, allow for divorce, prefer marriage with a close relative, and the like. Moreover, using such a broad sample enables the researcher, as we saw with the incest study, to consider cultural evolution, as measured by cultural complexity, as a variable in the research (Levinson and Malone 1980:9). The shortcomings of the cross-cultural approach, however, are that the sample may be flawed by the fact that data collected at different points in time are treated as though they were synchronic, internal variation is typically obscured, and the researcher can easily be tempted to compare phenomena that are not strictly comparable.

It is impossible to detail all of the techniques and questions important to anthropological research. The main thing to note is that the field is constantly open to new ideas and new methods. The specific questions asked and the methods and approaches used are all affected in the final analysis by the material setting in which the study takes place.

Even if one is not interested in explaining cultural phenomena in economic or ecological terms, it is almost impossible to interpret any aspect of culture or social life without some appreciation of the people's means of coping with life's basic problems. This observation ap-plies as well to people who want to read or use anthropological studies—not just to the would-be fieldworker.

Summary

Cultural anthropologists depend heavily on *fieldwork*, the firsthand observation of people in other societies, as their primary means of gathering data and testing hypotheses gener-ated by theories. Most fieldwork today is prob-lem-oriented: the anthropologist studies a given society in order to test theoretical assumptions and then concentrates on those aspects of the society that are most relevant to that theory.

The two basic techniques of data gathering in the field are participant observation and in-terviewing. The researcher engaged in *partici-pant observation* seeks social acceptance in the culture to be observed as a means to acquire an understanding of it. This technique allows the researcher to view a culture from the inside and to observe aspects of it that interviews alone might not reveal. In order to be truly pro-ductive, the observation must be systematic; that is, the researcher should focus on a par-ticular category of information in any given situation. Notes can be taken systematically with the use of *code sheets*, or checklists of ob-served behaviors.

Observation alone is not enough. In order to go beyond surface impressions and find out how the people of a society actually think, field-workers conduct interviews, both formal and informal. Unstructured *informal interviews* en-courage informants to follow their own train of thought, so that they will reveal what is per-sonally important to them. But because the in-formants are not responding to standardized questions, it is difficult to compare their re-sponses. This problem does not arise in *formal interviews*, which consist of a standardized set of questions designed to elicit specific facts, at-titudes, and opinions. Because the two kinds of interview provide different kinds of informa-tion, most researchers use both approaches. They also check informants' responses against their own observations to make sure the infor-mation they are getting is accurate.

While the fieldworker's primary interest is usually the behavior of the people being stud-ied, demographic and material culture data are useful too. A *census*, usually in the form of a household survey, reveals the population's basic demographic characteristics. Fieldworkers also routinely *map* the area occupied by the com-munity, make inventories of its material goods—tools, weapons, vehicles, and so forth—and take notes on the use of natural resources. Fieldworkers gather additional data by con-ducting time-allocation studies, charting ge-nealogies, taking photographs, making films, studying official documents and folk tales, and administering psychological tests. The specific techniques that researchers rely on most heav-ily depend on the problem they are studying. But most fieldworkers use a variety of tech-niques, as this strategy allows them to gather a wide range of data and also to cross-check their information.

The day-to-day experience of fieldwork in-volves numerous difficulties, both practical and psychological. As they strive to become part of the community, fieldworkers find that the peo-ple's capacity to accept them is limited, and so is their own ability to participate in the society and still do the research properly.

The community chosen for investigation determines the aspect of the larger system—the *sampling universe*—that will be described. The researcher must take care not to overgeneralize from the data collected; otherwise the research will suffer from a *sampling bias*—the exclusion of some members of the sampling universe and the overrepresentation of others. Sometimes a *random sample* is appropriate—a sample in which each individual or household has the same chance of being selected as any other. If the universe being investigated is very large and complex, a realistic sample of it may require the researcher to divide it into categories and then select a random sample from each category. The result is a *stratified sample.*

Once gathered, data must be analyzed—a task that is largely postponed until the researcher returns from the field. Anthropologists have come to rely increasingly on statistical analysis as an objective means of isolating patterns in large collections of data. *Statistical analysis* is the application of probability theory to quantified descriptive data. Having quantified the data collected—determined the number of households, the number of persons per household, and so on—the researcher then draws conclusions on the basis of correlations between those data. This technique is essential for proving that suspected relationships between different social phenomena actually exist. Moreover, it can reveal unsuspected relationships. Above all, statistical analysis is indispensable for making cross-cultural comparisons. In statistical analyses the variable that is seen as the causal agent is called the independent variable and the variable acted upon is called the dependent variable.

Not all research involves fieldwork, even though most ethnographic data originates from fieldwork. Much research relies on secondary sources, available in archives and libraries. Such studies fall into two categories. *Diachronic studies,* including ethnohistory, use descriptive data from one society or population which has been studied at many points in time. Since causal explanations rely on a sequence of events in which one phenomenon causes or acts upon another, historical investigation is important. *Synchronic* studies rely on research that does not make use of or control for the effects of the passage of time. Ethnographic reports usually represent a particular society or culture as frozen at a given point in time, the *ethnographic present.*

There are many hypotheses that cannot be tested with synchronic data from only one society. Thus when anthropologists use secondary ethnographic data they generally use them comparatively and in the ethnographic present. Comparative analyses usually are designed to test some hypothesis or proposition about how cultural phenomena are related. There are a number of types of comparative research in anthropology. The two most commonly used are controlled comparison and cross-cultural research. In a *controlled comparison* of data, the researcher selects two or more societies which are similar if not identical in all areas apart from those which are the object of the investigation. The advantage of controlled comparison is that it allows the researcher to try to emulate a laboratory experiment in which experimental conditions are carefully controlled. The disadvantages are that this control may be illusory, as it can never be more than approximate and the researcher is usually aware of the results of the comparison before doing the research.

Cross-cultural research, or *holocultural* research, makes generalizations on the basis of global comparisons. Cross-cultural studies treat each society as an entity that either has or does not have specific traits or has quantitative variation in the traits. The advantage of this approach is that one can establish a global picture of cultural variation. The shortcomings of the cross-cultural approach are that the sample may be flawed by the fact that data collected at different points in time are treated synchronically, internal variation is obscured, and the researcher can easily be tempted to compare phenomena that are not strictly comparable.

Key Terms

census	diachronic studies	informal interview	sampling bias
code sheets	ethnographic present	inventory of resources	sampling universe
controlled comparison	fieldwork	mapping	statistical analysis
cross-cultural research (holocultural research)	formal interview	participant observation	stratified sample
	Human Relations Area Files (HRAF)	random sample	synchronic studies

Suggested Readings

BOWEN, E. S. 1964. *Return to Laughter: An Anthropological Novel.* New York: Doubleday/American Museum of Natural History. An extensive, amusing, and informative novelistic account of one anthropologist's experiences in the field.

BARLEY, N. 1986. *Ceremony: An Anthropologist's Misadventures in the African Bush.* New York: Henry Holt. A lively and amusing account of an anthropologist's attempt to witness an elaborate and fearsome circumcision ceremony in northern Cameroon.

BERNARD, H. R. 1988. *Research Methods in Cultural Anthropology.* Newbury Park, Calif.: Sage Publications. A practical guide to scientific enquiry in cultural anthropology that deals with the research process, the elements of research design, and data collection and analysis.

CRANE, J. G., AND M. V. ANGROSINO. 1984. *Field Projects in Anthropology: A Student Handbook.* 2d ed., Prospect Heights, Ill.: Waveland Press. In this compact volume, the authors present a series of projects that represent some of the most commonly used data-collection techniques.

LEVINSON, D., AND M. J. MALONE. 1980. *Toward Explaining Human Culture.* New Haven: HRAF Press. A systematic review of the theories of human culture and behavior that have been tested or developed through cross-cultural research.

ROSNOW, R. L., AND R. ROSENTHAL. 1984. *Understanding Behavioral Science: Research Methods for Research Consumers.* New York: McGraw-Hill. An easily read introduction to the application of research methods in the social sciences.

SPRADLEY, J. P. 1980. *Participant Observer.* New York: Holt, Rinehart and Winston. Step-by-step instructions are provided for doing fieldwork using participant observation methods.

WERNER, D. 1984. *Amazon Journey: An Anthropologist's Year among Brazil's Mekranoti Indians.* New York: Simon and Schuster. An informal and sympathetic portrayal of modern anthropological field data collection and analysis.

Chapter **4** Decisions, Adaptation, and Evolution

The Dobe !Kung, a subgroup of the San people of the Republic of Botswana in southwest Africa, live in a dry, sandy plain at the edge of the Kalahari Desert, where dependable agriculture is impossible and where food and water resources are constantly fluctuating. However, the Dobe !Kung have until recently lived by hunting game and gathering wild plant foods, the most ancient of all human subsistence strategies, and one that has allowed them to exist rather comfortably in the environment. This fact in itself merits investigation.

Study of the Dobe !Kung people began some two decades ago as a two-man project at Harvard University, with Richard Lee and Irven DeVore investigating subsistence patterns and social organization. The project has since grown into a collaboration of twenty-four specialists, including ethnographers, demographers, child-development experts, archaeologists, medical teams, students of folklore and cosmology, and numerous other experts. The studies being conducted are both long-term and short-term.

The Dobe !Kung project is of particular interest because of the goals and methods on which it is based. The goals of the project are highly ambitious—to put together a complete picture of a hunting-and-gathering way of life. To do this, many different facets of the !Kung's existence must be explored.

First, one must study the group's relationship to its environment and the effect of this relationship on population and social organization. How, precisely, do the !Kung respond to seasonal variability in the supply of game, wild plants, and drinking water? How do they spend their time and expend energy? How does the necessity to move regularly affect their birth and death rates? How does their commitment to hunting and gathering affect the way they organize their domestic groups?

Second, the health and nutrition of the !Kung must be examined. How hard do they have to work to keep themselves alive and healthy? What is the incidence of nutritional deficiency and of stress-related disorders?

Third, one must look at child development among the !Kung. How is the experience of growing up in a hunting-and-gathering society different from that of growing up in an agricultural or industrial society? Do these children reach the development milestones—walking, talking, and so forth—more quickly or more slowly than children in other cultures? What impact does the hunting-and-gathering way of life have on sex-role development?

Finally, the cognitive world of the Dobe !Kung requires exploration. How do they perceive themselves in relation to other peoples? What forces do they see behind nature? How do they perceive their resources? How, in sum, do they see the world and their place in it?

The thread that unites these diverse questions is the assumption that they can be best answered by viewing the !Kung people as part of a larger environmental system. What the !Kung do for a living, their beliefs, and family organization can all be seen as closely interrelated and can be understood in terms of their adaptation to their environment. The theoretical orientation that emphasizes the adaptive significance of culture and behavior, from procurement systems to kinship systems to political and religious life, is called **evolutionary ecology.** In this chapter we will explore the rationale for this perspective in greater detail, building on our discussion of evolution in the first chapters. We will discuss what is meant by adaptation, the role of variation and decision-making in adaptation, and finally we will place evolutionary processes affecting humans in an ecological context.

EVOLUTIONARY ECOLOGY

As the term suggests, there are two aspects of evolutionary ecology: evolutionary theory and the science of ecology. **Ecology** is "the study of the relations between organisms and the totality of the physical and biological factors affecting them or influenced by them" (Pianka 1974:3). In other words, ecology is the study of the interplay between organisms (or the populations to which they belong) and their environment. Implicit in this definition is the connection between ecology and evolutionary theory. As we saw in Chapter 1, evolution operates primarily through the mechanism of natural selection. That is, certain characteristics become more and more common within a population because within the context of that population's environment these characteristics give individuals an edge in the competition for survival and reproduction. So a crucial factor in the evolutionary process is an ecological factor—the fit between organisms and their environment.

While evolutionary research is diachronic by definition, ecological research tends to be synchronic (that is, primarily concerned with the present). However, both focus on essentially the same phenomenon: **adaptation,** the process whereby within a given environment organisms or populations of organisms make adjustments, whether biological or behavioral, that increase their chances for survival and reproduction. An evolutionary study may trace adaptation backward through time in an attempt to under-

stand major causes of change within a given species as an outcome of natural selection and other evolutionary forces. Ecological studies, in contrast, tend to focus on the present and to look at the outcome of the adaptational process by analyzing the totality of relationships among organisms in a given environment. Evolutionary-ecological research unites these two approaches by studying living organisms within the context of their total environment to discover how their evolved characteristics and strategies for survival contribute to their success within that environment; in other words, how they have adapted.

Still culture, or aspects of it, has an identity quite distinct from behaviors that are *directly* acted upon by such evolutionary forces as natural selection. In fact traits adopted and favored by groups or cultures may, for a while at least, work at cross-purposes with individual strategies for adaptive success. People enthusiastically embrace beliefs and adopt behavioral traits that apparently have little immediate relevance, either to their own well-being or to that of a larger collectivity such as a group or a community.

Sometimes extreme examples are more useful illustrations than are ones commonplace where costs and benefits are obvious. Consider societies that have stressful initiation rites, including in some instances severe genital mutilation. It is hard to understand just how such practices, with the attendant risk of death or injury, can benefit the individual (or his or her parents) except in the context of social relations. Traditional practices of female circumcision and female infibulation (sewing closed of the vagina), found in the Sudan and East Africa, and male subincision (cutting open of the penis and the urethra) found among the Australian aborigines, hardly promote the well-being or reproductive success of the individuals who suffer through them, except as they contribute to the initiates' social acceptability. Such practices appear to be related to the na-

Rituals such as circumcision must be understood in terms of the particular cultural environment of which they are a part. For the young Masai male, the year of circumcision, the most important in his life, marks his emergence into manhood. (GEORGE RODGER/MAGNUM)

ture of the society itself—the way it forms its cultural identity, defines concepts of sexuality and social maturity, and effects social control.

Many of our beliefs and ideas about the world are passed on through social learning even when they do not appear to have immediate utility for the individual. Many anthropologists argue for a "dual inheritance" perspective, from which cultural transmission and change are seen as working simultaneously with a parallel process of natural selection (Boyd and Richerson 1985). This means that we should not expect humans to operate within the narrow constraint of immediately perceived costs and benefits, but rather to respond to and solve problems using a wide range of cultural tools. Further, culturally transmitted ways of doing things need to be shown to be adaptive—not simply assumed to be so. Any realistic approach to understanding human cultural behavior has to allow for a great deal of indeterminancy even though ultimately all behavior has implications for the success of the individuals involved.

Adaptation

We have seen that evolution is a process of cumulative change, which is itself the outcome, in large measure, of the responses of organisms to their ever-changing environments, or adaptation. Adaptation can be an elusive concept because it involves processes that seem to operate on several different levels at once. Furthermore, since adaptation is the process by which organisms adjust in ways that facilitate their survival and hence their reproductive success, which determines their genetic contributions to future generations, it can only be observed over long periods.

We do know that the long-term processes of adaptation are dependent on the ability of organisms to appropriately resolve each of the problems faced on a daily basis. Thus the concept also encompasses all of the responses and behaviors of the organism that affect its life chances, even though these may have no immediate implications for natural selection. Like many other species, humans adapt by learning new ways of doing things; the swelling human population is testimony to just how rapidly we can adjust our systems of food production and other technologies. Our ability to learn rapidly and to communicate learning is, in large measure, due to our ability to use language. As

Our Human Evolutionary Legacy: Unity from Diversity

It is easy to overlook the fact that evolution is an ongoing process. Our species and all of its constituent populations are continually being shaped by evolutionary forces. While most often we speak of natural selection as the major force acting on the genetic compositions of populations, any force that causes the genetic composition of a population to change is an evolutionary force. Interbreeding, or gene flow, is a major source of both unity and change in human populations. Our species is a quite recent product; it is also highly mobile and local populations continually interbreed. As a result, we are relatively homogeneous in terms of genetic material. In fact, most anthropologists feel it is inappropriate, or at best difficult, to speak of different races (Rensberger 1989).

C. Loring Brace has studied skeletal remains from Japan. His results indicate that the present population of Japan is the product of the interbreeding of two genetically distinct groups—the Ainu, which he says are the original inhabitants of the islands, and the Yayoi, who migrated from Korea and China only slightly more than 2,000 years ago. He further claims his evidence shows that the famed Samurai warrior class descended from the northern people of Hokkaido, the Ainu, that Japanese royalty and nobility intermarried with them, and that other Japanese were primarily descended from the Yayoi (Brace 1989). This view almost completely reverses traditional Japanese thinking about their heritage, in which the Ainu are considered to have no role. Today they in fact suffer from social discrimination. Whether Brace's theories turn out to be true or not, the point is that we have to be wary about considering any population as a fixed entity.

In January 1988, the popular media ran a series of major stories on what was widely described as "The Search for Eve" (see Tierney et al. 1988). The report that focused national attention was by Rebecca Cann, a biological anthropologist. Her work was based on new techniques of studying the origins, unity, and diversity of our species that do not rely on the examination of fossils or bones, but rather on the cell tissues of infants. The results offered compelling evidence that all living members of our species shared a common ancestor—more accurately, ancestress—as recently as 200,000 years ago (Cann 1988: 127–143).

As is often the case, this startling discovery was simply the latest development in a long process of research and debate. Allan Wilson had long argued for the recent divergence of hominids (our immediate ancestral line) from chimpanzees. He and other researchers using techniques similar to Cann's also find evidence of a very recent origin for *Homo sapiens*. They disagree, however, as to the likely locale (Wilson et al. 1987).

The evidence that Cann and her co-workers have found is based on the existence of a form of DNA that occurs in the mitochondria of the cells of placentas. While DNA in the nucleus of cells is a mixture of both parents' genes, that in the mitochondria is inherited entirely from the mother. Any change in this DNA would have to occur by mutation—unique but regularly occurring errors in copying the DNA code. Since any mutation would be both distinctive and unlikely to occur twice in exactly the same way, similarities in DNA are an accurate measure of closeness of common ancestry. With time, the fact that mutations are likely to occur will decrease the amount of shared mitochondrial DNA. By collecting and analyzing mitochondrial DNA from placentas of babies born throughout Asia, Africa, Europe and the Americas, Cann and her co-workers have been able to establish that about 200,000 years ago all present-day *Homo sapiens* shared a female ancestress who lived in Africa. The date is established by assuming that mutations occur at a constant rate and measuring similarities and differences among the samples from different regions of the world. Those taken from African populations showed more divergence, indicating a longer period of time in which to diversify. Variability among all the others was less, indicating that at some subsequent point a subpopulation had emigrated out of Africa and later spread around the world.

Cann's work is clearly exciting. Its significance lies not just in the possibility of our African origins—an aspect of her work that may be challenged by future research. She and, increasingly, others trained in molecular biology point to some very basic findings about ourselves: All humans are very closely related with very little genetic variation, much less than is the case with other widespread vertebrates; our closest primate relative is the chimpanzee and our mutual divergence is as recent as 5 million years ago; for substantial periods of evolutionary history there were co-existing hominid species. This last point is strikingly confirmed by the discovery in 1988 of both Neanderthal and modern human skeletons from the same time period in what is today Israel.

It must be noted that several aspects of Cann's findings are controversial. The notion of a recent origin for our immediate ancestral line has long been the subject of controversy. A recent origin would imply that some earlier hominids found in different parts of the Old World were not directly in our family line. Although the idea of our African origins is now well established, it is unclear whether our species evolved only there and subsequently spread or whether our species diverged earlier and evolved more or less separately in different parts of the Old World, coexisting with our linear ancestors before dying out. A common recent origin in Africa would have occurred in a population whose appearance would most likely have closely resembled modern Africans. It is interesting to note that those features which we often use to describe different peoples of the world—skin color, eye color and shape, stature, and hair—are all the products of very recent and minor adaptations.

Stephen Jay Gould, speaking of these recent research developments, says, ''It makes us realize that all humans, despite differences in external appearance, are really members of a single entity that's had a very recent origin in one place. There is a kind of biological brotherhood that's much more profound than we had ever realized'' (Gould, quoted in Tierney et al. 1988).

The major differences we see between human beings are the products of behavioral or cultural adaptation. As Lewis Binford writes,

''Our species had arrived—not as a result of gradual, progressive processes but explosively in a relatively short period of time. Many of us currently speculate that this was the result of the invention of language, our peculiar mode of symbolic communication that makes possible our mode of reasoning and in turn our behavioral flexibility'' (Binford 1989).

Microbiologist Rebecca Cann is studying patterns of mutation in the mitochondrial DNA of 147 women from four continents. (JAMES D. WILSON/WOODFIN CAMP & ASSOCIATES)

Stephen Jay Gould points out, our capacity for language is undoubtedly an accidental by-product of our having earlier developed a large brain (1989). Once our brain developed beyond a certain threshold, our evolutionary course was altered; some consequences are clearly positive, in the sense that we have developed technologies enabling us to occupy most areas of the earth—something no other large animal can do. But other consequences may result in our becoming a species with a relatively brief history: our technology may prove the source of our demise.

Adaptation involves changes of all sorts that continually affect the relationship of the organism to its environment. It results in changes that can never be ideal, as the environment is itself constantly changing. No adaptation or response is a perfect or final solution; each carries with it certain costs and hazards. Adaptation is always opportunistic because organisms, ourselves included, use whatever resources are available to them at a particular time, including available genetic and cultural materials.

The opportunistic nature of adaptation is amply illustrated by solutions to problems in our own society. For example industrialized societies began to use oil as a fuel at the beginning of the twentieth century. This adaptation solved the problem of furnishing an effective, cheap fuel to power modern machinery. Its use was opportunistic in the sense that the oil was there to be tapped and our technology happened to have developed to the point that allowed us to make use of it. In adapting to oil fuel, we made numerous commitments that have altered the structure of our society: we rely on food produced by heavy equipment; we grow crops dependent on fertilizers and pesticides derived from the petrochemical industry; we use rapid transport, cheap electricity, and productive systems too numerous to mention, all fueled by oil. In recent years, the environment has been changing in unexpected ways. We are faced with declining reserves of oil, with

the toxic consequences of a highly developed industrial society, and, perhaps, with long-term changes in the atmosphere, all consequences of heavy oil use. It is also certain that whatever other energy sources we turn to next will be imperfect solutions and will generate a host of new and unforeseen difficulties as well. Adaptation is at once the solution to particular problems and the source of unanticipated changes and new problems.

Variation

Variation, whether biological or behavioral, is the key to the process of adaptation. One of the main contributions of recent studies of animal behavior is the recognition that among animals of all sorts, systems of mating, male-female differences, feeding habits, food sharing, social interaction, and the like can be understood as the outcome of behaviors that start as individual strategies. Groups are never homogeneous; all contain individuals who respond somewhat differently to the problems at hand. Patterns of behavior, seen in this light, become increasingly interesting. As human culture is elaborated, new solutions that seem to work can be rapidly added to the repertoire of knowledge that is passed on. The recognition of variability draws attention to the process of selection among choices—the process of decision making. It encourages researchers to try to predict how individuals would behave under specific circumstances. Under what circumstances, for instance, would food be shared or territory defended? Who is most likely to share with whom, and how much? The nature of the decision-making process itself comes into focus when humans are viewed in an ecological context.

Decisions

To understand the nature of human decision-making or problem solving, we have to consider the environment in which it takes place. We are all too prone to treat the environment as a fixed landscape or static fact, and so fail to consider the nature of variation in all environments. Environments are complex. The environment of any individual or population consists of *all* external factors that effect it in any way—not only the obvious features of the habitat (the place where the population lives) but the presence of organisms that transmit disease, competitors, shelter, and climate. It includes the cultural setting in which the individual must operate. In a society in which male initiation rites are important, for example, this social fact is part of the individual's environment. The environment also includes the demographic structure of the population; often the most important feature of an individual's environment is the presence of other members of the same population.

Finally, environments are dynamic. One ecologist, Lawrence S. Slobodkin (1968), has argued that four patterns of change underlie the dynamics of all environments: changes in the novelty (how new), frequency (how often), magnitude (how much), and duration (how long) of environmental events of all sorts. The organism with the best chance of success is not necessarily the one most perfectly adapted to its environment at any particular point, but rather the one that maintains its ability to respond to the environment in a flexible variety of ways. Given that organisms have only limited means of responding to environmental challenges and that they have no way of predicting how their responses to these challenges will turn out, what is the best strategy? Generally speaking, it will be the cheapest possible response—the strategy that involves the least possible loss of future adaptive ability, the minimum sacrifice of flexibility. In other words, choices among alternatives should be made to minimize risk, not simply to look to large possible gains. As we noted in Chapter 1, this seems to be the case with humans, in that people are generally conservative in their behavior and hesitant to change ways of doing things that appear to work.

A multitude of strategies for coping with different environmental problems occur in any human population. Change can be in behavior or culture, in physiology or genes (Slobodkin, 1968). We will be concerned primarily with behavioral and cultural changes.

In general, behavior is fairly predictable and conventional; people tend to arrive at similar decisions under similar circumstances. Were it not so, group life would be impossible. People regularly make major decisions regarding such basic issues of subsistence as whether to plant one crop or another or whether to migrate to new pastures or not; they also make day-to-day decisions such as with whom to socialize or to whom one might send a greeting card. The structure of human societies provides the context for and information concerning choices among alternatives. At the same time, human society is itself the outcome of this process. As Frederik Barth has put it

> Social life [is] generated by actors who go about their activity by pursuing their interests fitfully, often thoughtlessly, and generally conventionally. Yet they are concerned about the outcomes of their efforts in so far as these affect themselves. In this concern their judgments are based on values which serve to organize choice and action by providing standards to compare different alternatives and outcomes, both prospectively and retrospectively. When doing so, people tend to maximize the amounts of value they obtain by pursuing benefits and avoiding losses and drawbacks inasmuch as they see a way to do so (Barth 1981:102).

Still, no one can imagine that he or she is capable of comprehending the ultimate outcome of any particular decision or choice among alternatives. No one can avoid making mistaken choices, or even failing to recognize alternatives that may be available. But we must and do continually make decisions or choices that differ in their potential costs and benefits.

Ultimately all complex social patterns rest on individual decisions, choices, and behavior. (Top) The myriad of such individual choices and decisions made in this open-air market in Suffolk, England, result in one pattern of group phenomena. (Bottom) Another pattern emerges when decisions are the result of a consensus. The women here are gathered for discussion in a Western Sahara refugee camp. (BOTH: ROBERT HARDING PICTURE LIBRARY)

Very often we do have in mind objectives that most people would recognize as rational—maintaining good health, acquiring shelter, avoiding danger, preparing our offspring for life as adults. However, sometimes we have objectives that are less clearly beneficial—making great sacrifices to achieve power or prestige, throwing ourselves into unrewarded public service, displaying self-consuming religious or political zeal. Finally, we encounter people whose decisions seem to be irrational by any standard.

Given the complex and ever-changing nature of decision making, why not simply study the outcomes of individual strategies, the broad patterns of social organization? We often do just that. But if we are interested in predicting the course of future behavior or the way a population may respond to some novel event, we have to make certain assumptions about human decisions or choices. This is, of course, just what we do every day in our dealings with others—we assume that people behave in ways generally congruent with their self-interest. Larger patterns or processes do not exist in and of themselves; they are simply the expressions of myriad individual acts and beliefs. Assumptions of rationality and individual self-interest are obviously too simple and too narrow to account for the entire range of cultural behavior. Despite their limitations, however, such assumptions are useful in that they allow us to form expectations of behavior with which actual behavior can be compared (Rapoport 1981:137–150).

Human social organization is a product of the decisions made by individuals; most of these decisions concern the trivia of everyday life, but cumulatively they direct the course of adaptation. Thus decisions, adaptation, and evolution go hand in hand.

The Ecological Context

Unless one can envision the setting in which adaptive processes are unfolding, one cannot fully appreciate them. Humans, along with every other form of life, are a part of a single **ecosystem**—the cycle of matter and energy that includes all organic things and links them to the inorganic. All organisms depend on energy and on matter. Most of the energy and matter that animals use are not taken directly from the sun and the earth. Rather, these are produced by other organisms and cycled among the species through feeding—eat and be eaten is the rule for all. Humans breathe the oxygen emitted by plants, and plants take in carbon dioxide emitted by humans and millions of other species of animals. Such relationships, taken together, constitute a vast network of individuals exchanging the energy, nutrients, and chemicals necessary to life; humans and bacteria are involved in the same process.

The usefulness of the ecosystem concept is, first, that it can be applied to any environment. Second, and more important, the ecosystem concept allows us to describe humans in dynamic interaction with one another, with other species, and with the physical environment. We can chart and quantify the flow of energy and nutrients and specify the interactions critical for the maintenance of any local population. Thus the ecosystem concept gives us a way of describing how human populations influence and are influenced by their surroundings.

There is usually considerable order and continuity in natural ecosystems. This is not surprising since, over time, the millions of component species of any ecosystem have come to mutually limit one another as they feed, reproduce, and die. The fact that ecosystems appear to persist through time does not mean, however, that they are static. While most ecosystems are viewed as being in **equilibrium** or near-equilibrium, in fact relations among the component populations are changing continually. One ecologist, C. S. Holling (1973), employs two concepts to describe continuity and change in ecosystems: resilience and stability.

Resilience is a measure of the degree of change a system can undergo while still maintaining its basic elements or relationships. **Stability** is a measure of the speed with which a system returns to equilibrium after absorbing

As demonstrated on this polluted beach in North Yemen, the handling of human waste products is a global concern and one that will affect our ability to sustain ourselves in the future. (MICHAEL JENNES/ROBERT HARDING PICTURE LIBRARY)

disturbances. Systems with high resilience but low stability may undergo continual and profound changes but still continue to exist as a system; that is, their constituent parts persist together, even though they take a very long time to return to their initial states. Systems with high stability but low resilience, on the other hand, may show little change when suffering some disturbances, but simply collapse suddenly.

These concepts have considerable relevance for our study of ecosystems. We often assume that if an ecosystem appears to be in equilibrium or is very stable that it is likely to persist unchanged. As pointed out, this is often not the case. A highly stable system such as the Arctic terrestrial ecosystems may in fact be very close to the threshold at which it could collapse as a system. And even the most resilient ecosystems are resilient only to a point beyond which they collapse. We should bear this in mind when we feel that we are having no serious impact on our ecosystems simply because we see little evidence of immediate changes. For example, the seas around us may appear little changed despite the dumping into them of oil and other wastes. Thus they would seem to be quite stable. Yet each new addition of oil or wastes requires the organisms and microorganisms of the sea to respond in some way, and there are limits to their capacities to continue to do so. The resilience of marine ecosystems is limited even if the threshold for change is obscured by the appearance of stability.

The Nature of Ecological Systems

The structure of ecological systems—the flow of energy and nutrients—puts fundamental constraints on the way of life of any human population. Applying the ecosystem model to specific human populations, we can address two major questions: First, what is the population's place in its particular ecological system—that is, what are its relationships with the rest of the living world? Second, how are particular behaviors characteristic of this population related to its place in the ecosystem?

Humans hold a rather unusual position in their ecosystems. First, they occupy a remarkable diversity of such systems. This fact becomes strikingly evident when we look at the habitats and the niches that our species occupies. The **habitat** of a species is the area where it lives, its surroundings. Its **niche** is its "way of making a living," as defined by what it eats, what eats it, how it reproduces and rears its young. Most animals are limited to a few habitats and a relatively narrow niche. By contrast, we occupy an exceptionally broad niche. (Think of the great variety of foods eaten by human beings and the many ways in which they are produced.) And we live in an extremely wide range of habitats. Indeed, there are very few habitats, from deserts to Arctic ice sheets to tropical rain forests, where human beings have not found a way to thrive.

Second, once humans enter an ecosystem, they tend to become its dominant species. We strongly affect the life chances and reproductive rates of the other populations. We are continually affected by other species, especially by those that threaten our well-being, such as malaria-bearing mosquitoes; but the influence we wield is far greater than theirs, for we usually alter relations dramatically among the species with which we come in contact. Our dominance is due to the sophistication of our tools. (We will see the effects of our toolmaking ability throughout Part II, where we will examine the various strategies human societies use to provide food for their members.)

Some other species use tools, but no other species has elaborated them to the extent we have, and no other species depends on tools for its survival, as we do. Our technological expertise has allowed us to transform a vast variety of materials—including some rather unlikely ones, such as fossil oils—into sources of usable energy. It has also enabled us to be creative in our use of the resources that we share with other animals. To use the energy stored in a tree, for example, other animals must drink its sap or eat its leaves and branches. Humans not only eat the tree's products but cut it down and use the wood to build houses and furniture; we use its energy in the form of fire to warm those houses and cook our food. Likewise, we can use the energy stored in animals' muscles, not only by eating them, as other animals do, but also by harnessing them to plows and by putting bits in their mouths and riding them. When a plant or animal is not suited to our needs, we can alter it through selective breeding to make it more useful to us. The use of tools has enabled us to create artificial environments, such as farms and cities, in which we maintain very high human population densities by greatly increasing the inflow and outflow of energy, materials, and information.

Human-dominated ecosystems are considerably less resilient than other ecosystems be-

Almost everywhere humans are the dominant species; they directly or indirectly affect most other species in their ecosystem. This whale has fallen prey to native hunters in Point Home, Alaska. The fact that they share its meat and do not hunt for the marketplace makes them less apt to overkill the species on which they depend. (STEVE MCCUTCHEON/ALASKA PICTORIAL SERVICE)

cause they can be maintained only by constant expenditure of human energy and ingenuity. Cities depend on surrounding ecosystems for their food, water, and other necessities. In fact, inhabitants of cities tend to organize the countryside around them, since they control the capital, markets, and transportation systems on which the rural farming sector depends. Cities also produce large quantities of waste products that the surrounding ecosystem must absorb.

When urban ecosystems become large or numerous, the balance between the cities and the food-producing areas that sustain them may break down. In any event, these ecological arrangements depend on massive and costly inputs of energy, and with the recent dependence on fossil fuel for energy, the stability of today's urban systems may be severely limited by future fuel shortages.

Technology has *not* made us master of our ecosystems, let alone independent of them. We are still as deeply enmeshed in them as any other group of organisms. Indeed, anthropologists interpret human customs in part as accommodations to the physical environment. What distinguishes humans from other species in their relation to environmental problems is the rapidity with which we respond through learning. Different human societies may develop wholly different ways of life as they adjust to their environment. Moreover, they can change rapidly as circumstances require. Thus human adaptation has a unique flexibility. We can most usefully study the nature of this adaptive process by combining ideas from evolution and ecology.

PROCUREMENT SYSTEMS AND ADAPTATION TO LOCAL AREAS

Of all the problems people face, securing adequate food is the most fundamental. When ecologists note that "you are what you eat," they mean that the source and variety of foods used by any population, human or otherwise, is critical to its maintenance. While a vast array of adaptive patterns can be found throughout the world, if we concentrate on the central issue of the way a population procures and distributes its food, we will note common strategies.

The behavioral strategies that a particular group uses or has available to secure foodstuffs can be termed its food-procurement system. The available strategies are so numerous that no two systems are exactly alike. In fact, it is rare to find two individuals within a society practicing precisely the same strategy. To understand some of the important generalizations that can be made about food-procurement behavior, we will first consider the nature of adaptation in this context and then identify major patterns of food procurement.

The assumption that a given food-procurement system is an adaptation to a certain *type* of environment still does not explain very much. It is certainly true that the characteristics of environmental zones of different sorts—grasslands, deserts, tropical forests, temperate forests, the Arctic, and the subarctic—place limits on the kind of life that can be sustained in them. One does not farm in the Arctic, nor does one herd animals in a tropical rain forest. Yet these broad environmental factors account for only a small portion of the variation we see in procurement systems. They do not tell us

why inhabitants of similar regions—indeed, of the same region—often practice widely different procurement strategies, or why inhabitants of different regions sometimes practice remarkably similar strategies.

In order to understand how and why specific procurement systems develop, we must consider them as responses less to broad environmental characteristics than to specific environmental problems in local areas. Some common problems faced by local populations are fluctuations over time and space in quantity, quality, and availability of resources and the activities of other human groups in competition for the same resources.

Adapting to Available Resources

Every local environment or habitat has a limited potential for supporting any of the forms of life within it. This demographic potential is called the environment's **carrying capacity**—the point at or below which a population tends to stabilize. The most obvious limiting factors may be the availability of food or water. Others include disease, temperature, and even the regularity and predictability of critical resources. It really doesn't matter so much that a food source is available during the year, for example, if the people who rely on it cannot predict with accuracy *when* it is going to be available. Of course, this leveling-off point can shift at any time as circumstances change. The best way to determine carrying capacity is to observe the demographic characteristics of the population—its rates of birth, death, and migration. Anthropologists may also estimate an environment's potential carrying capacity for a particular population by computing the minimum amount of water and of vegetable and animal matter available on a regular basis for human consumption.

It has been estimated that the ecosystem of the Kalahari Desert, for example, can indefinitely support about 40 humans per 100 square miles, if they live as the indigenous inhabitants did and if the technology and requirements of the population remain constant (Lee 1968). Here a major limiting factor—that is, a key factor in short supply—is water. Water holes in the Kalahari may be as much as 100 miles apart, and the average water hole can support only about 30 people in years when the rainfall is normal, fewer during periods of drought. Thus Kalahari residents of necessity live in small groups broadly scattered over a large territory. Regions in which food is scarce or supply fluctuates greatly show a similar population pattern. In areas where food and water supplies are more abundant, larger populations may be sustained in permanent sedentary communities.

The carrying capacity of an area is affected not only by the total amount of food available but also by the availability of essential dietary items such as protein, vitamins, and minerals. In other words, the nutritional *quality* of resources is as critical as their *quantity.* To avoid chronic malnutrition, humans must somehow adjust to the variations in nutritional value among available foods. While some physiological adjustment is evident among human populations in areas of diverse resources, generally people solve the problem through restrictive dietary practices and in the way they prepare their foods.

This adaptation process can be seen in the ways corn (maize) is prepared in many societies. Unless corn is processed with alkali (obtained from lime, wood ash, or lye) before it is eaten, it is deficient in several essential amino acids and in niacin, a member of the B vitamin complex. Individuals in any population that relied primarily on corn without alkali processing would suffer malnutrition, as did residents of the United States who suffered from "pellagra" before this relationship was understood. Researchers predicted that where corn was a dietary staple, people would tend to make the necessary cooking adjustment. A survey of fifty-one North

A low water supply may limit the number of people an environment can support. In Ethiopia's arid Omo Valley, residents search for water by digging under a dry riverbed. (GEORG GERSTER/RAPHO/PHOTO RESEARCHERS)

and South American societies confirmed this hypothesis (Katz et al. 1974). In Mesoamerica, shelled corn is boiled in a lime-water solution before it is ground. In some areas of North America where lime is not available, the necessary alkali is obtained from wood ashes or lye. Without this behavioral adaptation, people could not depend on corn as a dietary staple.

A final factor affecting carrying capacity is the human ability to recognize resources. Even the determination of what plants and animals are edible varies considerably among cultures. Goosefoot and lambsquarter, two plants that we consider weeds that now grow in fields and vacant lots, were important sources of both seeds and greens among many Native American groups. These and many other plants and animals that we do not now consider edible are staples and even delicacies in other societies. Many resources identified as usable by individuals in one culture are ignored by others.

As these examples illustrate, an environment's human carrying capacity is not a simple product of local resources. We cannot simply say that a given environment can support x number of human beings per square mile. The number varies with the nature of the procurement system practiced in the area. Also, as we will see in later chapters, carrying capacity depends on the organization of the society and on the exchange of food and tools among populations.

Adapting to Fluctuations in Resources

Populations must adjust not only to the quantity and quality of available resources but also to fluctuations in their availability. Over a five-year period, say, an area may produce an average of 100 kilograms (about 221 pounds) of corn per year, but if production drops to 50 kilograms (about 110 pounds) one year, the people must adjust or starve.

The Shoshone Indians of North America's Great Basin before the coming of the Europeans provide a good example of adjustment to fluc-

tuations in resources. Because of extreme variation in rainfall in this region, the Shoshone were never able to predict with any certainty where or how much plant and animal food would be available from one year to the next. A spot that was highly productive one year might offer little food the following season. The Shoshone adapted to these environmental uncertainties by relying on a wide variety of resources and pursuing a highly mobile way of life, changing their location and residence patterns according to the kind and quantity of resources available. During most of the year a Shoshone family traveled alone or with one or two related families, gathering roots and seeds and hunting small animals. Periodically, however, when rabbits or antelope became unusually plentiful, several families might band together temporarily for a collective hunt. And when isolated families heard reports that a resource such as pine nuts seemed promising in a particular locality, they would plan to arrive together in time for the harvest and would separate again after the resources had been collected (Steward 1953).

People who live by cultivating crops or raising animals generally have a more stable food supply than those who depend on wild resources alone. But these groups are also affected by seasonal and yearly fluctuations and must adjust to them. Since population is more concentrated in these groups than among hunter-gatherers, the effects of food shortages may be even more devastating to them. The Pokot of western Kenya depend on agricultural produce for the bulk of their caloric intake. However, droughts and fluctuations in rainfall can result in crop failure, in which case the Pokot can fall back on their cattle and goat herds for their food supply. Thus their cattle may be seen as a means of storing energy rather than simply as a means of producing energy.

Consumers in our society rarely experience sudden short-term fluctuations in resources, since we depend on the resources of a huge area serviced by an efficient transportation system.

A wide variety of fruits, vegetables, grains, meats, and dairy products are available to us throughout the year. This steadiness of supply is due to our technology—producers have means of storing and transporting food in such a way as to cover shortages, and our technology enables us to minimize some fluctuations in resources, although often at considerable cost.

When a rancher's pasturelands go dry, the rancher feeds his cattle by hauling forage and water to them with tractors and trucks rather than by moving the animals. Similarly, a farmer can bring water to his crops through irrigation, control insects with chemical sprays, and spread fertilizer to add nutrients to the soil of a depleted field. The farmer can even grow crops in the dead of winter by constructing hothouses. But these techniques have costs, which are passed on to the consumer. Modern agriculture depends on machine technology and is thus subsidized by the large-scale use of "cheap" fossil fuel in the form of gasoline and diesel oil.

Our techniques are of course much more complex than the Pokot's reliance on their cattle as famine insurance, but both address a basic problem that faces all societies—the need to minimize uncertainty in food production. We should not make the mistake of assuming that industrialized societies are somehow better at this adjustment process than technologically simpler ones. Perhaps the greatest paradox of recent human adaptation is that responses aimed at stabilizing and increasing food production are in many cases having the opposite effect. That is, they are creating a new and more serious threat to the stability of the procurement system. In order to diminish the threat of drought or irregular rainfall, for example, a community may increase its dependence on irrigation agriculture, only to discover that the increased irrigation has elevated the salt content of the soil to the point where it can no longer support crops.

Thus while people in technologically advanced societies may accomplish impressive feats of environmental engineering, they must still remain sensitive to the environment in which they live. Ultimately the success of a group's adaptation to its resources depends not only on its ingenuity in manipulating its ecological system but also on its care in maintaining that system. As a consequence, the internal distribution of resources among people through social interaction is as important as are the resources on which they depend.

Adapting to Other Groups

The type and distribution of basic resources are only one aspect of an environment—the natural setting. Human populations make up another and no less basic aspect. Every society must adjust to the presence and activities of neighboring peoples, just as surely as it must adjust to variations in local resources.

Humans engage in a great deal of exchange with people outside their own group. They also engage in competition with one another for access to resources. If we step back from the study of societies as individual entities, we see a vast, ever-changing social mosaic, with each local population occupying its place in the larger picture. Of all large animals, we have the widest range of local patterns of behavior, each an adaptation to the challenge of making a living in local environmental circumstances.

When different groups occupy different niches in the same habitat, or when they occupy different habitats in the same region, they may come to rely heavily on one another for trade, each group benefiting from the products of the other groups' economies. The Tewa Indians of the American Southwest, for instance, established a variety of trade contacts with fellow Pueblo peoples and with nomadic hunter-gatherers. Itinerant traders went from village to village, exchanging the specialties of their own community for local craft products. The Tewa also exchanged many resources with neighboring Plains Indian groups, who inhabited an environment very different from their own. With the nomadic Comanche, for example, the Tewa traded their own corn meal, wheat flour, bread, melons, and other agricultural goods for such things as antelope hides, horses, and buffalo meat (Ford 1972). But trade is not inevitable between neighboring groups.

Nor is it by any means inevitable that groups occupying the same environment will learn to coexist peacefully through niche specialization. Aggressive competition is just as common, if not more so. Such is the situation in highland New Guinea, where neighboring tribes regularly war with one another to increase their agricultural land (Rappaport 1967). In other places one group may be driven out or absorbed by a larger or technologically more advanced group. This is what happened when European settlers moved into regions occupied by Native American groups.

The niche occupied by a human group that has developed a distinctive adaptive pattern is very different from the niches of other animals in the same environment. An animal species commitment to its niche is much more binding than a human group's commitment to an adaptive strategy. Humans can decide to change their diet and food-procurement strategies in a very short time, and will do so if they have to. Thus if pastoralists' grazing lands dry up, they may quite suddenly begin to compete with neighboring agriculturalists for arable lands, and what was once peaceful coexistence will become open hostility. Adaptation to other human groups, then, is a shifting, dynamic process, as is adaptation to any environmental condition.

The procurement systems that result from these adaptive processes are diverse. Each case is unique to some degree, and there is substantial individual variability within them. But five major procurement patterns can be identified.

The Major Procurement Patterns

1. **Hunting and gathering:** the collection of wild vegetable foods, hunting of game, and fishing.

2. **Horticulture:** a simple form of agriculture (sometimes called extensive agriculture) based on the working of small plots of land without draft animals, plows, or irrigation. In contrast to hunters and gatherers, horticulturists *produce* food by managing domesticated plants and animals.

3. **Pastoralism:** an economy based on herding. Pastoralists maintain herds of animals and use their products and by-products (milk, curds, whey, butterfat, meat, blood, hides, bones) both to maintain themselves directly and to utilize in exchange with other populations.

4. **Intensive agriculture:** a form of agriculture that involves the use of draft animals or tractors, plows, and often some form of irrigation. Intensive agriculture produces far greater yields per acre of land with less human labor than can be obtained by horticulture.

5. **Industrialism:** food production and manufacturing through the use of machines powered largely by fossil fuels.

Because procurement systems are so varied, most societies do not fall tidily into one or another food-procurement pattern. When we refer to hunter-gatherers, horticulturists, pastoralists, agriculturalists, and industrial societies, we are merely pointing out a cultural *emphasis* on the use of particular subsistence methods to obtain food. The specific procurement systems that people use involve varying strategies and varied degrees of reliance on the same strategy. People typically combine several methods. In most societies, for example, horticulture is supplemented by hunting and the collection of wild foods. In others, horticulture is practiced alongside plow farming, the former in steep and rocky areas, the latter in flatter areas where plowing is possible (Lewis 1960). Pastoralism is generally found in conjunction with other procurement strategies—in some cases with hunting and gathering, in other cases with small-scale horticulture. And, needless to say, many agriculturalists raise animals not only for transportation but also as sources of protein, wool, and hides. In Part II we will explore each of the patterns in greater detail.

Summary

Evolutionary ecology is a theoretical orientation that emphasizes the adaptive significance of culture and behavior, from procurement systems to kinship systems to political and religious life. There are two aspects to this orientation: evolutionary theory and *ecology*, the study of the interplay between organisms and their environment.

Anthropologists are concerned with the ways in which individuals and groups adapt to their ecological environments. In its simplest sense, *adaptation* refers to the ways organisms make adjustments that facilitate their survival and hence reproductive success, which determines their genetic contributions to future generations. The success or failure of adaptive responses can only be measured over the long term, and the evolutionary consequences of any observed behavior are unpredictable. We, like many other species, adapt by learning new ways of doing things. No adaptation or response can be seen as a perfect solution; each carries with it certain costs and hazards. Also, any adaptation is opportunistic in that it makes use of whatever is already at hand.

Variation, whether biological or behavioral, is the key to the process of adaptation. The recognition of variability draws attention to the process of selection among choices, the process of decision making. To understand the nature of human decision-making or problem solving, we have to consider the environment in which it takes place. Environments are dynamic. One ecologist, Lawrence Slobodkin (1968), has argued that four patterns of change underlie the dynamics of all environments: changes in the novelty, frequency, magnitude, and duration of environmental events of all sorts. The organism with the best chance of success is not necessarily the one most perfectly adapted to its environment, but rather the one that maintains its ability to respond to the environment in a wide variety of ways, to be flexible.

A multitude of strategies for coping with different environmental problems are practiced in any human population. Nevertheless, behavior is usually fairly predictable and conventional. People guide their decisions according to expectations about consequences. To predict the course of future behavior or the way a population may respond to some novel event, anthropologists have to work with certain assumptions about human decisions or choices. Larger patterns or processes are simply the expressions of myriad individual acts and beliefs. Assumptions of rationality and individual self-interest are obviously too simple and too narrow to account for the entire range of cultural behavior. Despite their limitations, however, such assumptions are useful in that they allow us to form expectations of behavior with which actual behavior can be compared.

Anthropologists may use the concept of an *ecosystem*—the flow of energy and nutrients among the numerous species of plants and animals in a particular setting—to describe how human populations influence and are influenced by their surroundings. The matter (or nutrients) that flows through these elements is cyclical—that is, the same matter is constantly reused—while the energy is constantly resupplied by the sun. The area where a species lives is called its *habitat*. While an animal species' commitment to its *niche*—its adaptive strategy in the larger scheme—is relatively binding, the human species is distinctive in its capacity to alter its adaptive strategy and accommodate itself to many niches. However, humans are still subject to the rules established by the flow of matter and energy. We depend, as do all living things, on other species, and must adjust our numbers and activities to our environment and available resources.

An ecosystem may be in *equilibrium*—all of its components in balance—or it may not be, and thus be changing. The properties that allow an ecosystem to adjust to change are *resilience* (its ability to undergo change while still maintaining its basic elements or relationships) and *stability* (its ability to return to equilibrium after disturbances). All ecosystems are limited in their capacity for change; it is often human activities that place the greatest strain on natural ecosystems. Each local environment also has a limited potential for supporting any of the life forms in it. The point at or below which a population tends to stabilize is called its *carrying capacity*.

Specific human food-procurement systems develop in response to both general environmental characteristics and environmental variables in the local area. These variables include the quantity and quality of available resources, fluctuations in the availability of resources, and the number of other groups competing for the same resources. A population's long-term success in adjusting to its resources may depend on its ability to maintain its ecological system; in this respect, simple societies can be as successful as technologically advanced societies.

A vast array of adaptive strategies are employed throughout the world, but within that wide range are certain common patterns. Among food-procurement strategies, for example, there are five basic patterns: *hunting and gathering, horticulture, pastoralism, intensive agriculture*, and *industrialism*.

Key Terms

adaptation	**equilibrium**	**hunting and gathering**	**pastoralism**
carrying capacity	**evolutionary ecology**	**industrialism**	**resilience**
ecology	**habitat**	**intensive agriculture**	**stability**
ecosystem	**horticulture**	**niche**	

Suggested Readings

BARTH, F. 1981. *Process and Form in Social Life: Selected Essays of Fredrik Barth*, vol. 1. London: Routledge & Kegan Paul. A collection of essays that illustrates the application of decision theory, choice models, and utility to anthropology, as well as Barth's own influential approach to this topic.

BOYD, R., AND P. J. RICHERSON. 1985. *Culture and the Evolutionary Process.* Chicago: University of Chicago Press. Discusses the ways psychological, sociological, and cultural factors combine to change societies. The authors also develop models to analyze how biology and culture interact under the influence of evolutionary processes to produce the diversity we see in human cultures.

CAMPBELL, B. 1985. *Human Ecology: The Story of Our Place in Nature from Prehistory to the Present.* Hawthorne, N.Y.: Aldine. This book is intended as a supplementary text for social science courses dealing with our current ecological crisis. It uses the study of human prehistory as a means to understand our present evolutionary and ecological situation.

DYSON-HUDSON, R., AND M. A. LITTLE (EDS.). 1983. *Rethinking Human Adaption: Biological and Cultural Models.* Boulder, Colo.: Westview Press. A selection of papers by both cultural and biological anthropologists that analyzes biological and social adaptive systems by means of recent evolutionary, ecological, and anthropological theory.

MORAN, E. F. 1982. *Human Adaptability.* Boulder, Colo.: Westview Press. A review of principles of adaptation as well as an introduction to ecological concepts and methodology. The volume is particularly useful for its case-study approach to human adaptation in different environmental contexts.

MORAN, E. F. 1984. *The Ecosystem Concept in Anthropology.* Boulder, Colo.: Westview Press. A reassessment of the utility of the ecosystem concept and the current relevance of this ecological approach to anthropological explanation.

PART II Adaptive Patterns

The five chapters in Part II build directly on the ideas developed in Part I, drawing in particular on the ideas introduced in Chapter 4. Each chapter is concerned, at least in part, with adaptive strategies, how the members of a specific population cope with food procurement, the exigencies of their habitat, relations with other populations, and important aspects of domestic and community organization. Specifically, the chapters deal with hunting and gathering, horticulture, pastoralism, intensive agriculture, and industrial society. While the chapters are organized in what has come to be regarded as an evolutionary framework, each exemplifies a facet of the ongoing processes of adaptation that apply equally to every population.

Detailed ethnographic case studies in each chapter not only illustrate the various adaptive strategies, but also demonstrate how ethnographic data is used as well as how it is collected. While each case offers its own unique insight, several shared themes run through them all: internal variation and sources for change, environmental costs and consequences of different activities, and the larger environmental, social, and political implications of the activities described. The ethnographic materials highlight both the important lines of continuity that run through them and the differences between individual cases. Further, the discussions of the cases put them in a global context and emphasize how, through the actions and decisions of individuals, change is a continuous process—labels such as "pastoralist," "peasant," or "farmer" are no more than convenient glosses that encompass much variability.

A fresh-food market in San Cristobal de Las Casas, Mexico. (D. DONNE BRYANT)

Preparing and selling food in a market in Pisac, Peru. (MARTHA COOPER/PETER ARNOLD)

Drying salmon is a means to store food for the winter for the Inuit Eskimos in Alaska. (EVA MOMATIUK & JOHN EASTCOTT/WOODFIN CAMP & ASSOCIATES)

Women in India till a grain field by hand. (ROBERT HARDING PICTURE LIBRARY)

Harvesting rice by mechanical means in Louisiana. (D. DONNE BRYANT)

A Xavante man in Brazil divides morsels among the children. (NANCY FLOWERS)

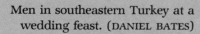
Men in southeastern Turkey at a wedding feast. (DANIEL BATES)

A mother and her sons share a quiet meal in Ghana. (CHRISTIANA DITTMANN/RAINBOW)

A family breakfast of dry bread and porridge in Mongolia. (NIGEL BLYTHE/ ROBERT HARDING PICTURE LIBRARY)

A Japanese family at mealtime. (NIGEL BLYTHE/ROBERT HARDING PICTURE LIBRARY)

Reflections

Where thirty cubits high at harvest-time
The corn is stacked;
Where pies are cooked of millet and bearded-maize
Guests watch the steaming bowls
And sniff the pungency of peppered herbs.
The cunning cook adds slices of bird-flesh,
Pigeon and yellow-heron and black-crane.
They taste the badger-stew.
O Soul come back to feed on foods you love!

Next are brought
Fresh turtle, and sweet chicken cooked in cheese
Pressed by the man of Ch'u.
And pickled sucking pig
And flesh of whelps floating in liver-sauce
With salad of minced radishes in brine;
All served with that hot spice of southernwood
The land of Wu supplies.
O Soul come back to choose the meats you love!

Roasted daw, steamed widgeon and grilled quail—
On every fowl they fare.
Boiled perch and sparrow broth—in each preserved
The separate flavour that is most its own.
O Soul come back to where such dainties wait!

FROM ANONYMOUS CHINESE POET, SECOND CENTURY B.C.

Early ethnographers were very concerned with unity and diversity in food habits in human culture. This topic has once more come to the fore. Life depends on the ingestion of the products and body parts of other species or, as one octogenarian put it, "So far, I've eaten every day and avoided being eaten in turn." On a daily basis we may not pay much heed to what we eat; what we choose from, what we avoid, even abhor, seem so obvious as to be a natural part of our makeup. But humans are omnivorous and can extract nutrition from a broad range of sources. Any given society seems to recognize only a small percentage of available possibilities. The Vedda of Sri Lanka eat rotten wood garnished with honey; while unlikely to be a popular item, there is no nutritional reason why this dish could not appear on a McDonald's menu or why a horse burger "as you like it" should not be a Burger King special (after all, the flesh of horses is eaten, even highly prized in many societies). Pork kebab is not to be found on the plates of Moslems, even though the pig is indigenous to the heartland of the Middle East; milk, cheese, cream sauces, and ice cream are rarities in China, even though the meat of cattle, sheep, and goats has been part of the Chinese diet for millennia.

So varied and seemingly arbitrary are food preferences and taboos, ways of preparing and categorizing them, that some anthropologists view a culture's cuisine as a form of symbolic expression, much like a language. Rules governing preparation, presentation, and sharing all constitute a complex system of communication and exchange. Others look to the politics of food usage; who eats what, shares with whom, sits where relative to special dishes, may depend on political power and social status. Foods may be introduced by new elites, for example in one-time European colonies, to replace traditional ones; control over food production and marketing may be a key to maintaining power. Still other anthropologists stress the biocultural or ecological aspects of food habits. Most of the world's adults, for example, are genetically lactase-deficient; that is, they cannot comfortably digest fresh milk products; those who can are mostly from Western and Northern Europe and hence our national penchant for milk and ice cream is a fairly local phenomenon.

While omnivorous, humans are biologically unable to cope with many items, for example the cellulose found in most grasses and trees, and this, too, structures our preferences. At a critical juncture in our immediate primate line, our ancestors undertook a major dietary shift from fruits available in treetops to roots and seeds, soon supplemented with meat. The need for meat or animal products is still strong; almost all vegetarians consume some animal products and no society culturally restricts them entirely. The allure of the sweet and the distaste for the bitter is also part of our heritage and guides our preferences. Societies vary primarily not in these needs, but in the most cost-effective manner by which to satisfy them given their ecological and political circumstances.

We think of regional cuisines, ethnic food preferences and taboos as fixed—part of seamless tradition. In fact, the foods we eat and how we grow, process, and otherwise prepare them change constantly. We all know how the American diet has been enhanced by the pizza, which became widespread only in the last thirty years, and the wet burrito, which is even more recent. In fact, the diets of all the world's peoples are in flux. The coming of the Europeans to the New World dramatically altered the production of food everywhere. Try to imagine Italian cuisine without tomatoes, Central European dishes without potatoes; corn is the staple of most of Africa today. Intensive trade and communication is creating what might be called a new global cuisine. Food in all its manifestations is what unites and differentiates us all.

Chapter **5** Hunting and Gathering

Humans and their hominid ancestors have lived on the earth for more than four million years, and for more than 99 percent of that time they grew no food of their own. They lived by hunting animals and gathering the plants that grew wild in their habitats. Today hunting and gathering is a subsistence strategy that is relatively rare and becoming rarer. A review of the approximately 860 historically known hunter-gatherer societies tabulated in the *Ethnographic Atlas* found that 179 survived into recent times (Ember 1978:440). Of those 179, far fewer remain today. Anthropologists, in describing any society in which they are not actually working at the time they are writing, employ the convention known as the "ethnographic present" (Chapter 3). The term indicates that the information being presented applies to the time when the data were collected; it doesn't necessarily describe the way the people in question may be living at the time the readers of the report make their acquaintance. All of the peoples we discuss should be understood with this fact in mind, for lifestyles and technologies can change radically from one year to the next.

In this chapter we will look at two hunting-and-gathering groups. The first are the people mentioned in Chapter 4: the Dobe !Kung, who live (or did live when the first studies were carried out) by gathering nuts, vegetables, fruits and by hunting wild animals on a semiarid plain in southwestern Africa. The second are the Eskimo of northeastern Canada, who support themselves primarily by hunting and fishing, but also increasingly by wage labor in the oil fields.

In certain respects, the lives of these modern hunter-gatherers, until quite recently at least, probably paralleled the lives of early or the earliest prehistoric humans. This is one of the reasons they are of such great interest to anthropologists. In time, the study of recent or contemporary hunter-gatherers may help us to understand why human culture developed as it did. This is not to say that the hunter-gatherers of today should be regarded as "throwbacks" or "living fossils." On the contrary, they are twentieth-century people with twentieth-century problems. They deal with governments that have jurisdiction over them and with neighbors whose cultures are quite different from their own. All hunter-gatherers have been drawn into exchanges with other groups, doing occasional wage labor for nearby agriculturalists and pastoralists, buying from and selling to industrialized societies, and even at times accepting welfare from their governments.

Hunters and gatherers are people for whom some version of this ancient subsistence strategy is still effective in their particular environments. We should bear in mind that most hunter-gatherers throughout history lived in areas far more hospitable than those they inhabit today. As we examine some of the methods of food procurement used by hunter-gatherers, their systems of kinship, residence patterns, and other cultural traits, we will see that these traits constitute solutions to the problems of making a living in their particular habitats.

THE DEVELOPMENT OF THE HUNTING-GATHERING ADAPTATION

The human pattern of hunting and gathering is unique in comparison with our primate

Marine resources are of vital importance worldwide and are exploited with a wide range of technologies. Present-day North American native peoples combine up-to-date technology with traditional and American social organization. These Alaskans are successful whaling captains with their crew members and wives. (STEVE MCCUTCHEON/ALASKA PICTORIAL SERVICE)

ancestors because it is based on extensive sharing. Other primates only occasionally share the products they have obtained, while sharing and the division of labor on which it is based is the very essence of the human system. Some animals—bees and ants, for example—characteristically share food with other members of their societies, but food sharing is not a common behavior among primates or other mammals, with the exception that parents provide for the very young. Two or three million years ago, some prehuman primates, for reasons that were essentially accidental, began to cooperate to secure food. Observations of the behavior of nonhuman primates suggest that kin systems are important to the manner in which behavior is structured, and this structure was the initial

basis for cooperation in the acquisition of food and in the sharing of products. Apparently this strategy was a successful one, and the groups that practiced it expanded in numbers and territory. In the process, the complexity of tool manufacture increased as communication developed from simple "call systems" (discussed in Chapter 11) into language as we know it. But it was cooperation among individuals, family groups, and eventually larger groups held together by shared ideologies and value systems that created the basis for the development of complex cultural systems. Sharing, the gift, is the fundamental element in the human adaptive pattern.

The Organization of Energy

Hunters and gatherers subsist primarily on wild plants and animals. Unlike agriculture, the hunting-and-gathering economy does not involve direct or intensive intervention to regulate the growth and reproduction of the life forms on which people depend. Thus the diet for hunter-gatherers is more strictly determined by habitat than that of other groups. In fact, abundant "wild" resources are available in any American city, but not in quantities sufficient to sustain a population of any great size. As local environments vary, so do the dietary staples of their hunting-and-gathering inhabitants. Peoples who live in areas where plant life is more abundant or reliable than game depend primarily on vegetable foods—nuts, fruits, and the like. Such is the case, for example, with the Dobe !Kung. The Eskimo, by contrast, rely much more heavily on meat and fish, for plant life is scarce in the Arctic. Whatever its emphasis, however, the diet of hunter-gatherers tends to be highly diversified. Since their diet is especially responsive to seasonal and annual fluctuations in resources, they must rely on a wide variety of foods.

This is not to say that hunting-and-gathering peoples do not manage their resource bases. In both North and South America, indigenous populations use fire to burn forest cover on a regular basis in order to promote the growth of vegetation supporting favored game animals (Clark and Uhl 1987, Lewis and Ferguson 1988). Coincidentally, this periodic burning may be instrumental in promoting the long-term health of the forest as well since it prevents the buildup of undergrowth, which can cause dangerous fires or harbor disease.

Most hunting-and-gathering peoples engage in varying degrees of exchange with other societies. The Mbuti Pygmies of Zaire, although often described as self-sufficient hunters, sell antelope and other game to visiting traders and buy the agricultural products and manufactured foods of their Bantu and Sudani neighbors (Milton 1985). It is extremely doubtful that they could have survived otherwise (Hart and Hart 1986). The Dobe !Kung also trade with and work for the Bantu farmers. The Eskimo hunt not only for themselves but also for the industrial market, as they have come to depend on numerous products of industrial societies—snowmobiles, kerosene, rifles, canned goods, even televisions and motor vehicles.

One of the reasons anthropologists find hunter-gatherers especially fascinating is that these people show us how humans can live on a low energy budget. A **low energy budget** is an adaptive strategy by which a minimum of energy is used to extract sufficient resources from the environment for survival. We humans are distinctively adept at extracting energy from the environment, but we also expend great amounts of energy. A single sack of potatoes, for example, represents a considerable investment of energy—in manufacturing the fertilizers and pesticides that were used on the potatoes; on powering the machines that planted, fertilized, sprayed, and harvested the crop; in packing and transporting the harvest; and so on. In comparison with other animals, humans—especially in industrialized societies—live on a high energy budget. Hunter-gatherers are the exception to this rule.

In general, the primary source of energy that hunter-gatherers expend in food procurement is that contained in their own muscles. While they may invest energy in building shelters, their energy is not diverted into the construction of a complicated infrastructure of food procurement—cleared fields, irrigation systems, or fuel-burning machines. As a result, hunter-gatherers spend much less energy to support a single unit of population than do other peoples. And since they generally support themselves rather well—in terms of nutrition, leisure time, and general physical well-being—their system must be regarded as remarkably efficient.

They are efficient, too, in preserving their resource bases. Because of their low expenditure of energy and because they tend to exploit a wide variety of foods, they place relatively limited demands on any one of their resources. At the same time, their way of life seems to limit their population growth; their numbers tend to remain proportionate to those of the animal and plant species on which they depend. The combined result of this adaptive strategy—low energy needs, a wide resource base, controlled population—is that hunter-gatherers interfere relatively little with other components of their ecosystems. Of course, they still have an impact on the environment. Because they are the most versatile predators in their habitats, they affect the populations of the species on which they feed. Still, their impact is relatively limited. Accordingly, their ecosystems appear to be in relative equilibrium and their resource bases remain unthreatened, at least in comparison with those of other economic systems.

This "conservationist" approach is probably inadvertent (and easily altered by new technology) but wise in regard to long-term resource management. Human history and prehistory show a general increase in populations accompanied by intensification in the use of resources. But this trend is not uninterrupted. Long periods of stable population levels tend to be followed by shorter periods of rapid growth.

One such rapid expansion of population accompanied the development of agriculture in most parts of the world, as some hunting-and-gathering peoples came to rely on domesticated plants and animals. Later, new agricultural techniques such as irrigation and plowing with livestock led to further growth in human populations. Since then periods of population stability have become shorter and shorter. Each new technological development seems ultimately to be translated into more people. The resultant demand for ever more food encourages people to increase their efforts to produce reliable harvests.

Thus people come to reshape their environments—digging canals, planting crops, eliminating insects—and in the process they lock themselves into a struggle to maintain themselves, at the expense of the equilibrium of the ecosystem. Of course, hunter-gatherers are also quite capable of overexploiting their resources. The Miskito Indians of Nicaragua, a group seri-

ously threatened by the current government's policies, have themselves almost wiped out the local turtle population. Though turtles are their primary source of protein, they have been lured by cash payments from turtle-packing companies to hunt the sea animals to the verge of extinction. Likewise, when the native North Americans suddenly found themselves in contact with a European market for beaver skins in the eighteenth century, they hunted nearly

The Miskito Indians of Nicaragua are currently wiping out the local turtle population—their primary source of protein—because packing companies offer high profits. (BERNARD NIETSCHMANN)

to extinction an animal on which they had depended for centuries. In both cases we see essentially the same process: once people who have been exploiting a resource for a limited market (themselves) are tied in to an unlimited market, the attraction of short-term gains often leads to the depletion of the resource.

As these examples suggest, those hunting-and-gathering peoples who have preserved their resource bases have not necessarily done so because they embraced a conservationist ethic. Nor can it be safely claimed that they deliberately limit their population in order to adjust it to their resources. It appears rather that several interrelated factors—among them the limits of their technology for storage, lack of fossil fuels, and lack of wider markets for the food produced, in combination with environmental conditions that limit population growth—have operated to maintain these peoples in balance with their resources. As we examine the Dobe !Kung and the Eskimo, we will see how people in two societies make a living and how various cultural practices contribute to their adaptation to harsh environments.

Social Organization

No one type of social organization inevitably issues from the food-procurement strategy of hunting and gathering. The way hunter-gatherers organize themselves into groups depends in part on the environment in which they have to make a living. However, since the environments of most recent and contemporary hunter-gatherers have certain characteristics in common—they tend to be the less desirable habitats, with relatively sparse and highly variable resources—they also share certain patterns of social organization.

Hunter-gatherers typically live in small groups, camps of closely related families. The size of the camps and of the society as a whole is limited by the local supply of natural resources. Unlike agricultural societies, hunter-gatherers cannot easily increase food production to accommodate an increase in population. Their population levels reflect the availability of food during the *worst* season of the year, since for the most part they lack the technology for bulk food storage. When food (or even water) cannot be stored, the season in which the least food is available limits population, no matter how abundant food may be in other seasons. And since their lands today are marginal, their population densities are generally low.

A critical factor in the adaptation of modern hunter-gatherers is the rule of **reciprocity**—that is, the sharing of food and other goods in response to fluctuations in resources. Food procurement is generally viewed as a family or household enterprise. The tasks that it involves may be divided along sexual lines; usually studies have noted that men hunt and women gather. Recent research has seen considerable variation on this theme. Among the Ache of Paraguay, men do considerable gathering along with the women (Hill et al. 1984); among the Agta of the Philippines, women do a significant amount of hunting (Estioko-Griffin and Griffin 1981). But no matter who does the hunting and who the gathering, when the people return to the camp, they generally share with the entire local group some or all of what they have gleaned. Thus rarely does anyone go hungry if others have adequate food, and no one has to work all day every day. Likewise tools, ornaments, and other material possessions pass from hand to hand in an endless round of gift giving and gift taking, so that inequalities of wealth are minimal.

Some members of a hunting-gathering band will have more influence than others and men tend to have more influence than women, but it is rare for anyone to have institutionalized power—that is, an office authorizing one person to make decisions for others. Decision-making power is spread fairly broadly among families of the entire group. Those who disagree are likely to simply move away.

Likewise, their systems of social control tend to be informal. Order is maintained on a day-to-day, consensual basis rather than through adherence to codified laws enforced by an administrative hierarchy. Codes of conduct and their enforcement are integral parts of the group's traditions, myths, and religious ideology. Both the definition of crime and the appropriate punishment reflect the consensus within the group at any given time. The Eskimo, for example, have "dueling songs" to resolve all disputes except those involving murder (Hoebel 1954). The two disputants, with their families serving as choruses, perform songs to express their side of the story and to vent their anger, and the winner is chosen by the applause of those attending the song duel. No decision is made as to who is right or wrong in terms of a body of law existing apart from public opinion. The most important thing is that the parties feel that the complaint has been raised and laid to rest; they then can resume normal social relations.

In extreme cases, individuals who repeatedly violate rules and social expectations in hunting-and-gathering societies may be ostracized by the group. But most commonly the dispute is between two parties, and if it cannot be resolved, the disputants and their families simply move apart.

This type of social organization, characterized by great fluidity and flexibility, is by no means inherent in the hunting-and-gathering way of life. When food resources are regularly available in relative abundance, hunting and gathering can support a quite complex cultural system accompanied by high population density. We know from archaeological evidence in the Old and New Worlds that some hunting-and-gathering societies of the past (much like fishing communities today) had large year-round settlements, numbering several hundred members, with considerable inequality of status and wealth (Price 1981). Indeed, various groups of Native American hunter-gatherers lived in permanent villages, had chiefs and hierarchies of other officials, and observed rankings of wealth and power, all predicated on a complex division of labor that involved castes and slavery. They traded with other groups, conducted warfare, incorporated captives into their labor force, and so forth. In short, they very much resembled advanced agricultural societies. But this was at a time when hunter-gatherers still occupied territories with abundant and predictable food resources that were amenable to storage.

Settlement Patterns and Mobility

A major concern of anthropologists who compare diverse procurement patterns is the manner in which people distribute themselves over the landscape. What is the nature of the settlements they occupy? How frequently, if at all, do they move their settlements? How are such decisions affected by the variability of resources from place to place and from time to time? Hunter-gatherer groups today tend to be nomadic. Their seasonal migrations on their home ranges are adjusted to the availability of resources in different places at different times. Once again, the limits of storage and transport technology are important. Most hunter-gatherers deal with variability in resources by moving people to the food rather than by moving food to the people.

Often the camps of related families form larger groupings, called bands, within a territory. The members of a band may come together at one or another of these camps for ceremonies, or the band may simply be an aggregation of people who regularly intermarry. The bands are strikingly flexible in their composition, expanding and contracting in response to fluctuations in resources. When certain resources are scattered, the members of the bands also scatter. Later, when game converges in one area or when large permanent water holes offer the only available water, camping groups come together again to exploit these resources jointly. Social habits also play a part in the flexibility of the bands. Groups are continually reforming as families visit or entertain their kin, move away from bands with which they do not get along, or move into bands that are short on people or long on resources and fellowship.

Nevertheless, more sedentary patterns can be found. The Kwakiutl of the American Northwest coast, the Chumash of Southern California, the Ainu of Japan, and the Andaman Islanders of India are hunter-gatherer groups whose members lived in large, sedentary villages. In such cases the key factor seems to be the availability of large quantities of stable and storable resources. Especially important are environments with great quantities of fish and shellfish, which are often fairly concentrated, predictable, and abundant.

This variability has led anthropologists to suspect that two patterns are characteristic. Louis Binford (1983) has contrasted logistical and foraging patterns; Robert Bettinger (1987) characterizes the same polarities as travelers and processors. **Travelers** follow a regular yearly round, occupying a series of campsites for brief periods when a valued resource is available in the vicinity of each site. Year after year they return to that site or abandon it for an adjacent one. While **processors** also move over the landscape, they occupy one permanent settlement, from which they move to temporary camps to exploit seasonally available resources. It is important to recognize that these two patterns are at the extremes of a continuum and that many intermediate behaviors, depending on the length of time each village is occupied, are possible.

In fact, groups that follow a strategy based on traveling may occupy what is essentially a processing camp for some portion of the year. Alternatively, a group that relies heavily on processing may use a traveling strategy during the season when local resources are scarce. Neither of the two groups we will consider lie at the extremes of the continuum, although the !Kung, as we will see, use a strategy involving somewhat more traveling than the Eskimos.

RESILIENCE, STABILITY, AND CHANGE

Of all the adaptive patterns, that of hunter-gatherers interfered the least with the resilience of their ecosystems. While interaction and exchange occur, ties of dependency between families and especially between groups are minimal. These people adjust to the environment by making use of any local resource that is abundant. At the opposite extreme are societies such as our own, which use a vast array of chemical and mechanical strategies to "control" the environment irrespective of changing conditions.

The viability of the hunter-gatherer strategy is based on the limited degree to which environmental problems are transmitted from one group to another. Some groups succeed; some fail. Yet this is the food procurement strategy that humans employed as they became the dominant species on earth. It is interesting to note one circumstance in which this form of adaptation came into direct competition with a technologically more advanced system of procurement. The Vikings of Norway settled Greenland in the tenth century and maintained colonies whose economy was based on farming, seal hunting, and fishing. They did not, however, adopt the patterns of hunting used by the indigenous Eskimo, whom they feared and despised. They failed. Because the settlers were unable to secure food in sufficient abundance to support themselves, the colonies died out, leaving Greenland once again the exclusive domain of the Eskimo (McGovern 1980, McGovern et al. 1988).

Adapting to Others: The Batak Foragers of the Philippines

It has long been recognized that hunter-gatherers rarely existed in total isolation, and that since the advent of farming, most had at least indirect contact with agriculturalists. Nevertheless, the prevalent assumption has been that as hunting and gathering societies take up farming, they become more integrated with and often dependent upon the wider social system almost immediately and they make a sharp transition from mobility to sedentism.

Many researchers are now questioning this assumption (Hart and Hart 1986, Headland 1988, Schrire 1984, Bailey and Peacock 1990). Others have suggested that pure hunting and gathering in tropical forests is difficult if not impossible—that hunter-gatherers have lived only at the edges of such forests and have always interacted with other groups. James Eder, who has studied the Batak of the Philippines, a tropical forest foraging people, extends this line of reasoning. He suggests that the nature and direction of the changes a hunter-gatherer society undergoes as it becomes increasingly incorporated into the wider society are to some extent determined by its own cultural characteristics (Eder 1988). Using historical accounts, interviews with the oldest Batak, and comparative observations of other hunter-gatherer societies, he has examined how Batak hunting and gathering practices have changed over the past hundred years as they incorporated other practices into their subsistence system. He also has found that the Batak become more, not less, mobile as they become integrated into the wider society.

The Batak inhabit the mountains of central Palawan Island where they are distributed in eight groups, each associated with a particular river valley. The number of households in each group ranges from three to twenty-four, and the groups are located between three and ten kilometers upstream from coastal Filipino villages. Like other contemporary hunter-gatherer societies, the Batak no longer rely exclusively on hunting and gathering for subsistence. Trade, horticulture, and wage labor are also part of their current economy, although foraging still provides about half their basic needs.

Trade and horticulture are probably not at all new to the Batak; but wage labor emerged more recently, with the arrival of the first lowland settlers during the latter half of the nineteenth century. As the Batak became more involved with the settlers their desire for lowland foods and manufactured goods increased and patron-client relationships rapidly evolved, tying individual Batak to individual settlers. An even more recent development has come in the form of foreign tourists, who have "discovered" the Batak, and now provide them with a minor source of income as guides.

The arrival of settlers also caused a change in the Batak settlement pattern. When root crops were the mainstay of Batak horticulture, periodic visits to swidden fields (partially cleared areas in the forest; see Chapter 6) were part of a pattern of year-round residence in temporary forest camps. Today the Batak plant their swidden fields exclusively with upland rice. During the agricultural season they now make periodic foraging trips to the forest from their field houses.

A further change in settlement patterns dates from the early twentieth century when government officials encouraged the Batak to come down out of the mountains and settle permanently on the coast. In 1930, five coastal settlements were declared reservations exclusively for Batak use. The legal disposition of the land was never clear and, in any case, the settlements were too small to provide the Batak with adequate subsistence. Thus, although the Batak did build houses on the reservations, they never occupied them fulltime. In fact, by the 1950s the reservations were overrun with non-Batak settlers, and the Batak, in a pattern of movement that still continues, began relocating their settlement sites further up their respective river valleys, leaving themselves relatively isolated but conveniently situated for access both to the lowland areas and the forests (Eder 1988: 40).

Eder's findings (1988: 44–49) are based on seven criteria against which he measured changes in Batak hunting and gathering practices: seasonality, encampment duration (mobility), encampment size, resource utilization, division of labor, hunting technology, and length of workday.

- *Seasonality:* Eder's data showed that forest camps are used more frequently during the first six months of the year, when the weather is dry and not suitable for agricultural pursuits, than during the latter six months, which are mainly rainy and swidden-oriented. Since the Batak do most of their hunting and gathering from forest camps, his data suggest a marked seasonality in contemporary foraging. Although he concedes that this may always have been the case, his view is that it is a more recent development.

- *Encampment duration:* According to Eder's informants, in the past, forest camps would be occupied for periods of up to three to four weeks. Today, the occupation periods are considerably shorter, usually two to seven days, because individuals now must balance the demands of hunting and gathering against those of cultivation and participation in the market economy. Not only are occupation periods now shorter, but forest camps are left not for other camps but to return to swidden and settlement houses. Although encampment duration is short, the Batak spend 40 percent of their time in camps of one sort or another, suggesting that they now have a greater rate of residential mobility.

- *Encampment size:* Eder found that it was rare today for more than seven households to camp together, whereas in the past between thirty and forty households would commonly join forces. In part, this is due to the fact that there are fewer Batak today. However, more significantly, Eder traces the change to the same types of scheduling conflicts that affect encampment duration.

- *Resource utilization:* Eder offers two explanations as to why the Batak today utilize a much narrower range of plant and animal resources than they did in the past. First, wild resources are seasonally available and cannot be utilized if their availability coincides with the planting or harvesting season. Second, the Batak regularly obtain many lowland foods (sugar, coffee, etc.) that may have changed their preferences for traditional foods.

- *Division of labor:* Eder found that there have been subtle changes in the division of labor as a consequence of discontinuing certain foraging activities, the depletion of game, and the fact that from August to October the women harvest the rice fields while only the men occupy forest camps.

- *Hunting technology:* The Batak hunted traditionally with blowguns. However, the use of blowguns ceased after World War II and the chief weapons now are spears, used in conjunction with hunting dogs, bows and arrows, and homemade guns.

- *Length of workday:* Although he has no time allocation data from the past with which to compare his own observations, Eder concludes that contemporary Batak work longer hours. He bases his conclusions on the fact that at least some foraging is for trade now as well as subsistence, and that the women are now involved in making articles for use in agriculture, such as harvesting baskets and rice-drying mats.

Eder concludes that despite the fact that the overall yields of hunting and gathering for the Batak today ought to be higher than in the past (fewer Batak forage in the same location and they stay for shorter periods of time) they are in fact lower. Because the Batak are now engaging in a range of economic activities, no one activity will be as remunerative as if it had been pursued full time. However, the Batak successfully maintain themselves and have been quick to incorporate new technologies into their subsistence system. Clearly, such change is not a simple process whereby traditional hunter-gatherers are absorbed or quickly overwhelmed by contact with farming populations. Nor can one assume that increased participation in agriculture is inevitably associated with increased sedentism and decreased mobility. People in general are resourceful and innovative; hunters and gatherers are no less adaptive.

The superiority of the indigenous hunter-gatherer adaptations to the European technology introduced into Greenland is not an isolated instance. In 1846 Sir John Franklin and his entire expedition (two ships, 200 men) starved to death in the heart of Netsilik Eskimo territory, presumably because they could or would not use Eskimo food-procurement techniques (Cyriax 1939). The Burke and Wills expedition of 1861 attempted to cross Australia from south to north and return; all but one explorer starved to death as they refused to forage and refused assistance from the Aborigines until it was too late (Moorehead 1963).

Let us now examine two hunting-and-gathering groups that illustrate the points we have been stressing. Keep in mind, though, the warning regarding the rapid changes that such peoples everywhere are undergoing. The two societies are those of the Dobe !Kung of southwest Africa and the Eskimo (or, as they are now more commonly referred to, the Inuit) of northeast Canada.

THE DOBE !KUNG

The !Kung are one of five physically and culturally related groups of Africans who are known collectively as the San.[1] The San are something of a historical mystery. An educated guess is that they once occupied most of southern Africa but were eventually displaced by successive waves of Bantu and European invaders. Those who were not killed or absorbed into the invaders' populations were gradually forced back into the arid wastes of the Kalahari Desert and its surrounding areas in Botswana, Namibia, and Angola. Most of the estimated 45,000 San who still live in and around the Kalahari are slowly being absorbed by the surrounding agricultural, industrial, and pastoral communities.

The several hundred !Kung San who live in the Dobe area, on the northern edge of the Kalahari, are an exception.[2] Although the Dobe !Kung have been in contact with Bantu and Europeans since the 1920s, share water holes with Bantu pastoralists, and sometimes work for them, the majority (over 70 percent) remain almost self-sufficient hunters and gatherers. In the mid-1960s, when Richard B. Lee lived with them, they had no interest in agriculture, herd animals, or firearms. They neither paid taxes to nor received services (except for smallpox vaccinations) from the government of Botswana. They traded with neighboring Bantu pastoralists but worked for them only occasionally. Thus although the Dobe !Kung are not isolated, until recently they were largely independent, mainly because they occupy territory that no one else wants.

Today they are in the middle of an international power struggle among white-ruled South Africa, Angola, and now Namibia, a newly independent state. As a consequence, the !Kung's traditional freedom of movement is severely curtailed. Parts of their territory are divided by a massive chain-link fence. Many !Kung are employed by the South African army as scouts, and all, willingly or not, are involved in the processes that are transforming this once re-

---

[1] Until recently, they were known as Bushmen, a name given to them by the Dutch who settled in South Africa in the seventeenth century. Africanists, however, now prefer the term San, which means "original settlers" in the Cape Hottentot dialect. To confuse matters further, the preferred usage of the Botswana government is Basarwa.

[2] In the mid-1960s their population was 466—379 permanent residents and 87 seasonal visitors (Lee 1968:30). In this discussion we will rely heavily on the preliminary work of Richard B. Lee and Irven Devore, along with the more recent writings of the rest of their Harvard team, many of which are collected in *Kalahari Hunter-Gatherers* (1976), edited by Lee and Devore. We also use Lee's monograph *The !Kung San* (1979).

mote land. Their situation is changing rapidly, and in all likelihood the life we describe will soon be transformed beyond recognition.

The Dobe Environment: Climate and Resources

The Dobe area is an inhospitable environment for humans, a fact that has protected the !Kung from invasion and assimilation. Dobe is a transition zone between the Kalahari Desert to the south and the lusher regions, inhabited mainly by agriculturalists and pastoralists, to the north. It consists of semiarid savanna, with a scattering of trees and grasslands and very few permanent water holes. The temperature ranges from below freezing on winter nights to 37°C (100°F) in the shade during the summer. Even more variable than the temperature is the rainfall. For six months of the year the area is completely dry; during the other six months there are heavy rains. Furthermore, rainfall varies considerably from year to year. In 1967–1968, for example, rainfall in the area was 250 percent greater than it had been in 1963–1964 (Yellen and Lee 1976). Such variation in rainfall, along with the sandiness of the soil, makes agriculture impossible. Nor is the area an ideal hunting ground; because the vegetation is scattered, it cannot support large migratory herds.

Nevertheless, the !Kung manage a livelihood in this environment, in part because they exploit such a wide variety of resources. Despite the extremes of climate, Dobe supports about 500 species of plants and animals. Of these resources the Dobe !Kung use about 150 plants and about 100 animals, and they eat approximately 100 species of plants and 50 animals (Yellen and Lee 1976). They gather wild nuts (chiefly from mongongo trees), berries, melons, and other fruits; dig for roots and tubers; collect honey in season; and hunt everything from warthogs, kudu, and leopard tortoise (three fa-vorites) to springhare, guinea fowl, and rock pythons. The larger animals, such as the antelope and kudu, are shot down with poisoned arrows. The !Kung hunt the smaller animals with dogs or trap them in ingenious snares. Very young animals, inept at running, are sometimes simply chased and snatched up. Although the Dobe !Kung definitely prefer some of these foods to others, their versatility in using a wide range of resources ensures that they are seldom without something to eat.

Most of their other needs are also easily supplied by the resources of the area. Their huts are constructed of branches and grass found throughout the area. Ostrich eggshells, also readily available, make ideal water containers. A wooden digging stick, whittled in an hour, lasts several months. A bow, arrows, and a quiver, which take several days to make, last years. The people's few luxuries—ostrich eggshell necklaces, thumb pianos, intricately carved pipes, and children's toys—are likewise made from materials readily at hand. Indeed, there is only one important resource that the Dobe !Kung traditionally obtain through exchange with other groups: iron for making tools. But even in this case they exercise a certain independence: they collect scraps of metal from the Botswana Veterinary Station fences to make arrowheads.

Limited in their needs and resourceful in filling them, the Dobe !Kung have little difficulty obtaining food and raw materials. The scarcity of water is the major problem, and it is this factor that in large part makes the Dobe !Kung a nomadic people.

Settlement Patterns

As rainfall determines the availability of water in the Kalahari, it also determines the people's settlement patterns. During the dry season, from June through September, the !Kung congregate in relatively large camps of about twenty to forty people around the large permanent water holes, the only available sources of water (Yellen and Lee 1976). In this period the people rely primarily on roots and tubers found within a day's walk, or about a six-mile radius, of their camps. The cool, clear weather makes for good tracking and hunting, and small groups of women periodically hike to the mongongo forests to collect nuts. By August, however, many of the preferred local foods have been eaten up, and rising temperatures make hunting and long gathering treks hard and uncomfortable. At this time the !Kung turn to less desirable foods—gums and the larger, bitter-tasting roots and melons that they passed up a month or two earlier.

But this period of austerity does not last long. In October the rains begin, filling the hollow trees and the standing pools in the upcountry with fresh water and transforming the parched landscape into a lush green, thick with new plant and animal life. This is the season of plenty. The !Kung now separate into groups of perhaps two or four families and scatter over the land to take advantage of the new crop of fruits, melons, berries, and leafy greens and the new generations of birds and animals that follow the rains. For seven to eight months the small groups move from camp to camp, staying an average of about three days in each spot and returning periodically to the permanent water hole. This pattern continues through April, when the pools of water begin to dry up. In May the wandering upcountry groups return to the permanent water hole to set up new camps, and the cycle begins again (Yellen and Lee 1976).

The Dobe !Kung, then, are an extremely mobile people. Accordingly, their goods are the kind that can be moved easily or left behind. Even houses fall into this category. When a group sets up camp, in a matter of two or three hours each woman constructs a small hut (perhaps 1.5 meters [about 5 feet] in both height and diameter) for her own nuclear family. The

A !Kung woman displays the foods she has gathered— tamma melons, grewia berries, a starred tortoise, and various roots. (ANTHONY BANNISTER/ABPL)

huts are arranged in a circle around an open space where the camp activity takes place. Very little goes on in the huts. Indeed, it is unusual to find anyone inside a hut, except perhaps a person who is taking a nap or seeking shelter from a storm (Draper 1976). A hut serves simply as a storehouse and as a marker, a sign of a family's residence in the camp. When the camp is broken up, the huts, representing little investment of time, energy, or material, are abandoned. Each member of the !Kung tribe can pack all of his or her possessions into a pair of leather carrying sacks and be ready to move in a few minutes.

Social Practices and Group Composition

The Dobe !Kung are very gregarious people; they spend about a third of their time visiting other camps and another third entertaining guests. (The size of the camp Lee studied varied from twenty-three to forty persons in a single month.) This tradition of conviviality, along with fluctuations in the availability of resources, keeps the !Kung on the move. The two factors should not be thought of as independent. In fact, the habit of visiting is probably an adaptation to the necessity of adjusting the populations of camps to local resources. It also facilitates exchange of information about game and other matters of concern to the dispersed local groups. Both Lorna Marshall (1961, 1965) and Richard Lee (1968) describe the constant babble of voices at night in !Kung camps, when residents and visitors exchange notes on rainfall and water holes, ripening vegetables and fruits, and animal tracks, in what amounts to a debriefing.

!Kung social customs provide not only for short-term visits but also for much lengthier stays. When a couple marries, for example, the husband moves to the wife's camp for an indefinite period of bride service—payment for his bride in the form of labor—and he may well bring his parents or a sibling with him. Usually he stays with his wife's people until the birth of their third child (about ten years). At that point he may return to the group into which he was born (perhaps taking some of his wife's kin along), or stay where he is, or move to a

The !Kung are extremely mobile. They construct huts in two or three hours and can abandon them in minutes. (SHOSTAK/ANTHRO-PHOTO)

camp where one of his brothers is doing bride service or where his wife's siblings have settled.

Such shifts are not limited to bride-service graduates. Any !Kung family may leave their group and move into another group where they have kin. Kinship is interpreted very broadly. The !Kung recognize ties among all individuals who share the same name, and address all of that person's relatives by kinship terms. Because the number of names used among the !Kung is limited, a person is quite likely to find a name-mate in camps where he or she has no relatives and be welcomed there too. Thus the !Kung have considerable freedom of choice with regard to residence. Lee (1968) estimates that every year about a third of the population makes a shift in group affiliation.

These changes in group composition, like the rounds of brief visits, help the !Kung to tailor the populations of their camps to local resources. At the same time, the flexibility of the group helps to prevent quarrels from turning into serious fights, which are carefully avoided. The !Kung are keenly aware that they all possess poisoned arrows and that fights have been known to end in killing. To avoid such an outcome, families that cannot get along together simply separate, one or both of them moving to another group.

Reciprocity

The !Kung have a saying, "Only lions eat alone." One of the characteristics that distinguish human beings from other animals, they are saying, is sharing and exchange. Though all humans share periodically, the !Kung system of distributing goods is characterized by continuous giving and receiving of gifts. Reciprocity is the basis of their economy.

Each morning a number of adults strike out from the camp in various directions to search for food. By working individually or in pairs they are able to cover a wider range and have a better chance of acquiring desirable foods than they could if they worked as a group. Whatever they obtain is brought back to the camp, and all the camp residents share it, whether or not they participated in that day's hunting or gathering.

It is easy to overromanticize the altruism of this system. The appropriate distribution of food is a common cause of quarreling among the !Kung. The way the day's take is divided depends on a variety of factors. In some cases, as when someone has brought in a large animal, the distribution is rather formalized. The owner (the person who owns the fatal arrow, whether or not he actually killed the animal) divides the meat into portions according to the size of the hunting party. The recipients then cut up their shares and distribute them among their relatives and friends, who in turn give pieces to their relatives, and so forth until everyone has eaten.

The size and distribution of shares of meat are matters of individual discretion, but the !Kung take care to meet their families' needs and to repay past generosity. Smaller animals and vegetables are distributed more informally. A family may invite someone standing nearby to sit at their fire, send children to neighbors with gifts of raw or cooked vegetables, or take fatty bits of meat and nuts with them on a visit. Thus each family's dinner is a combination of the food its members collected and the food they are given. The exchange of food constitutes an effective system that permits each family to store up goodwill and obligation against times of need.

The various artifacts used or enjoyed in daily life circulate in a similar manner. When a person receives an arrow or a dance rattle as a gift, he keeps it for a few months, then passes it on to someone else with the expectation of receiving a gift of more or less equal value in the future. As with food, the giver expects no immediate return; nor is there any systematic way to calculate the relative worth of gifts or to guarantee that the other person will reciprocate in kind. The !Kung consider bargaining and direct exchange undignified, and although they trade with the Bantu, they never trade among themselves (Marshall 1961:242). Food sharing and gift giving are based on norms of reciprocity that are understood and accepted by all !Kung.

The Quality of Life

We have briefly described the Dobe !Kung's way of life. Before Lee and his colleagues began their study of these people, it was widely assumed that the Dobe !Kung (indeed, all the San) waged a constant struggle for survival, battling hunger and poor nutrition from day to day. After all, they live in an area where game is scarce, their weapons are unsophisticated, and they have no way of storing their food. On the surface, they seem to lead a precarious, hand-to-mouth existence. Yet as Lee established through his painstaking research in the 1960s, the appearance bears little relation to the reality. In comparison with some other groups, the Dobe !Kung lead secure and easy lives (Lee and Devore 1968; Lee 1969).

Diet and Nutrition

From July 6 through August 2, 1964, Lee kept a diary of subsistence activities at an average dry-season camp. (Remember that this is a period of relative scarcity.) Each day he recorded the number of people in camp, the number that went out to hunt or gather, and the hours each spent acquiring food. He weighed all the animals the hunters brought back to camp during this period and all the bags of nuts and other foods that the women acquired in the course of each day's foraging. He even counted the number of mongongo nuts the !Kung cracked and consumed in an hour. By dividing the population of the camp in a given week into the total amount of meat and vegetable foods

acquired and then into the total number of hours devoted to their preparation, Lee was able to calculate the !Kung workweek and daily consumption of food. The results were surprising.

Lee found that the vegetable foods the women gather account for the bulk of the !Kung diet by weight; the meat that the men bring in amounts to only 20 to 25 percent. Meat, then, is a delicacy for the !Kung, not a staple. The reason is obvious: a man who spends four hours hunting *may* kill one animal (this is the average), whereas a woman who goes out to gather vegetable foods *always* finds something for her family to eat, even if it is not an especially choice item. Lee estimates that gathering is 2.4 times as productive as hunting in the Dobe area. One man-hour of hunting brings in approximately 800 calories; one woman-hour of gathering, approximately 2,000 calories. Thus the success of the hunt is not the critical variable in survival, as it was once thought to be. It is vegetable foods, not meats, that form the basis of the !Kung diet—and it is the women, not the men, who are the chief breadwinners in !Kung society.

Drought-resistant mongongo nuts are the !Kung staple, making up 50 percent of the vegetable diet. The average daily consumption (about 300 nuts) provides an individual with 1,260 calories and 56 grams of protein—the equivalent of 2.5 pounds of rice or 9 ounces of lean meat. In addition, everyone in the camp Lee studied ate an average of about 9 ounces of meat per day. Together mongongo nuts and meat gave each person 2,140 calories and 92.1 grams of protein per day—well over the U.S. recommended daily allowance (1,975 calories and 60 grams of protein) for small, active people such as the !Kung.

Leisure Time

Not only do the !Kung eat well; they do so with little effort. By counting the numbers of hours each person devoted to acquiring food during the twenty-eight-day period, Lee discovered that by Western standards the !Kung invest relatively little energy in the quest for food. Typically a man will spend five or six days hunting, then take a week or two off to rest, visit, and arrange the all-night dances that the !Kung hold two or three times a week. Furthermore, it is not at all unusual for a man to decide his luck has run out temporarily and take a month's vacation. The women also have considerable leisure. In one day a woman collects enough food to feed her family for three days. Household chores take between one and three hours. Plenty of free time is left to rest, visit, and entertain. Lee calculated that the average Dobe !Kung adult spends only six hours a day acquiring food, two and a half days a week—a total of fifteen hours a week.

Demography

The workweek figures are all the more surprising when one considers !Kung demography. It was once thought that few people in such societies lived beyond what we consider middle age. This assumption, too, has proved to be unfounded—at least for the Dobe !Kung. Lee found that 10 percent of the Dobe residents were over sixty years old. These old people do not participate directly in food procurement. Neither do the young, who constitute another 30 percent of the population. (!Kung do not expect young people to work regularly until they marry, usually between ages fifteen and twenty for women, twenty and twenty-five for men.) Thus 40 percent of the population are dependents, who live on the food that the young and middle-aged adults bring in. Such a proportion of nonproducers is surprisingly high, resembling that in agricultural communities.

At first glance these figures may suggest that if the Dobe !Kung worked harder, they could support a much larger population. This is not

A !Kung boy with toy bow and arrow. !Kung children do very little work until their mid-teens, and they live a generally secure and carefree life. (LEE/ANTHRO-PHOTO)

the case, however, for while the people as a whole could certainly spend, say, twice as many hours collecting food, the Dobe environment could not produce twice as much food for them to collect, to say nothing of twice as much water for them to drink.

This observation brings us to a factor that is crucial to the Dobe !Kung's way of life: the control of population growth. The well-being of any group, human or otherwise, depends in large part on the ratio of population to resources. For hunter-gatherers this ratio is especially critical, since, unlike agriculturalists, they cannot increase their resources.

The Dobe !Kung are particularly interesting in this regard, for their fertility is unusually low. On the average, !Kung women do not become pregnant again until four years after the birth of the previous child. The !Kung do not have a long postpartum taboo (that is, prescribed abstinence from sexual intercourse after childbirth), nor do they use chemical or mechanical birth-control devices. The women of Dobe attribute their low fertility to "the stinginess of their god, who loves children and tries to keep them all to himself in heaven" (Howell 1976:147). Prolonged breast feeding is probably a factor. Because they have no soft foods on which to wean infants, !Kung mothers nurse their babies for at least three years, until the child is able to digest the tough foods of the !Kung diet (Draper 1976). Breast feeding is not a guaranteed birth-control technique, but it does inhibit ovulation to some degree. Nancy Howell has suggested that gonorrhea, probably introduced through contact with Bantu and Europeans, may have reduced the fertility of some !Kung women. Of course, infant mortality, including occasional infanticide, is also a factor in the wide spacing of !Kung siblings. Twenty percent of infants die in their first year (Howell 1976).

This factor of controlled population, along with other factors that we have discussed—high mobility, flexibility of group membership, reciprocity, and a low energy budget—allows the !Kung to strike a balance with their environment. As long as their population continues to grow slowly and steadily—at a rate of less than 0.5 percent a year, as it does now—the Dobe area can continue to support them for a long time. By keeping their numbers and their energy needs low and by operating on the principle of flow—flow of groups over the land, flow of people between groups, flow of resources among people—they are able to fit their needs to what their habitat has to offer from day to day.

As a result, they live a relatively easy life; they eat well, work only in their middle years, and have time to rest and play. They are also well prepared for hardship. In times of shortage, Bantu pastoralists fare worse than the !Kung, and Bantu women turn to foraging with the !Kung to feed their families. Though the Dobe !Kung may not qualify as "the original affluent society," as Marshall Sahlins has termed the early hunter-gatherers, their adaptive pattern is still remarkable in that it yields them such a stable and comfortable existence within such an austere habitat.

THE ESKIMO

Until quite recently the Eskimo peoples who lived on the vast, treeless plains (or tundra) and along the changing coastlines of the Arctic were isolated from the rest of the world by their formidable environment. Like the Dobe !Kung, they occupied land that no one else wanted. And so for centuries they remained self-sufficient hunters and gatherers, relatively uninfluenced by the agricultural and industrial societies that grew up to the south of them, in the more fertile regions of the North American continent.

Since the beginning of this century, however, the isolation of the Eskimo has slowly broken down. Money has become an important factor in their relationship with their environment. While most Eskimo groups are fully settled today, some are still hunter-gatherers, and in some ways resemble the Dobe !Kung. At the same time, because of cultural changes resulting from their buying and selling in the world market and because of their unique climate, they provide an interesting contrast to the !Kung. Our discussion will be based primarily on Asem Balikci's study (1970) of the Netsilik Eskimo of northeastern Canada, with reference also to William B. Kemp's study (1971) among the Baffin Island Eskimo and a recent summary and synthesis by William Sturtevant and David

Damas (1984). Keep in mind that the various groups we describe are widely separated and that among the Eskimo there are many variations in language, custom, and ways of making a living.

The Arctic Ecosystem

If Dobe seems an inhospitable environment, the Arctic seems to most people simply uninhabitable. From October through July the waters are locked in ice, while the land lies frozen and almost bare of plant and animal life. During this period (the Eskimo's fall, winter, and spring), the Arctic animals, with the exception of seals and walruses, either migrate south or go into hibernation. By midwinter the ice is six to seven feet thick. Temperatures during the eighteen-hour Arctic nights may drop from a mean of $-16°C$ ($-30°F$) to $-27°C$ ($-50°F$). Forty-mile-an-hour winds with gusts up to 70 miles an hour are common. In the Hudson Straight area, 45-foot tides build walls of broken ice along the coast, making navigation extremely hazardous.

Most years the freeze continues into late July. Then this land on top of the world enjoys a brief summer. Temperatures rise above freezing, and daylight lasts as long as twenty-two hours. Lichens, mosses, shrubs, and tufted grasses sprout on the tundra, attracting a variety of wildlife—herds of caribou, musk oxen, polar bears, foxes, rabbits, and migratory birds. Seals and walruses bask in the sun; whales may appear; large schools of salmon run downriver to the sea in July or thereabouts, returning to inland lakes in August. But this Arctic summer lasts a short six to twelve weeks. The sea begins to ice over in late September, and the long freeze begins once again.

Hunting and gathering in this environment are quite different from living off wild foods in the Dobe area. Except for the summer berries, there are no vegetables, edible roots, or fruits in the Arctic; the long, dark winters, incessant winds, poor soil, and short growing season discourage plant life. The Eskimo's subsistence strategy is centered on animal life—on hunting, fishing, and, to a lesser extent, trapping and gathering of duck eggs, clams, and the like. And whereas the availability of water largely determines the migrations of the Dobe !Kung, it is the availability of animals and fish that structures the Eskimo's patterns of movement.

The Seasonal Migrations

Like the Dobe !Kung, the Eskimo are nomadic people, changing the sizes and locations of their camps as their resources change with the seasons. The pattern of these migrations is essentially the same as with the !Kung: dispersal in small groups in the season of plenty, concentration in large groups in the time of scarcity.

In the summer, when food is abundant, the Eskimo traditionally form small groups of twenty to thirty people, consisting of one or more extended families, and move inland to take advantage of fish runs and caribou migrations. Each August, for example, the Netsilik carry their belongings up the waterways to the stone weirs (circular dams) they have built to trap schools of salmon. Some of the fish are eaten raw, on the spot; the rest are dried and stored for the winter.

Toward the end of the month the group packs up once again and moves farther inland to await the coming of the caribou. Depending on the terrain, the Netsilik may construct knife-lined pits in the caribou's paths, which are well known to the Eskimo, or stalk them with bows and arrows. Another common technique is to stampede the animals into a trap. Howling in imitation of wolves, a few men drive the herd into a narrow valley, where hunters lie concealed, or into a river, where the hunters wait in kayaks. Caribou provide not only meat but also another crucial resource, skins for clothing. Balikci estimated that a family of four needs about thirty skins to see them through each winter (1970:47). In October and November the Netsilik live primarily on food stored during the caribou hunts, supplemented by occasional fresh fish and musk ox. The most important activity in this period is making winter clothing—a job that is performed by the women.

In December the scattered Netsilik come together once again in their winter camps along the bays and straits, where fifty, sixty, or as many as one hundred people join forces to hunt the major cold-season resource: seal. Although some seals migrate south for the winter, others remain in the Arctic, digging breathing holes up through the sea ice. (Seals need air every fifteen to twenty minutes and dig several holes.) Hunting seals in midwinter involves hours of silent, motionless waiting at the breathing holes, harpoon in hand. For much of the winter, seals plus an occasional fox are the only sources of fresh food.

In May or June, when the ice begins to melt, the Netsilik move to tents on solid ground. Hunting seals is easier and more productive in these months, for the animals often come out of the water. But in July the ice starts to crack and seal hunting becomes dangerous. Soon the Netsilik camps divide once again into smaller groups for their annual inland treks (Balikci 1970:chap. 2).

The Eskimo's seasonal round is similar to that of the Dobe !Kung. But there are important differences between the patterns of the two groups. For one thing, the Eskimo, unlike the !Kung, can store food. When fish are running and game is abundant, they collect as much as they can and smoke or store the surplus in stone or ice caches. However, the cold also requires the Eskimo to work on a higher energy budget than the !Kung. In such a climate, simply to stay alive, to say nothing of hunting, requires a relatively high-calorie diet. Furthermore, the Eskimo have to invest a good deal of energy in the task of protecting their bodies from the cold—building shelters (traditionally igloos in the winter, skin tents in the summer), making clothing (multilayered garments, boots, and mittens), and heating their shelters (with seal-oil lamps or kerosene stoves). And they have to feed their sled dogs, a vital component of their traditional nomadic way of life.

These activities require not only considerable energy but an accumulation of material goods. While the !Kung travel light, the Eskimo, with their dogsleds and snowmobiles, motorboats, tools, rifles, clothing, lamps, and stockpiles of food, have a good deal to carry around. Furthermore, their tents and igloos, unlike the !Kung's disposable huts, take time to build and cannot be lightly abandoned. Hence, even during the summer season, the Eskimo change camps much less often than the !Kung.

Demography

From what we can gather from early explorers' and ethnographers' accounts, this way of life did not enable the Eskimo to support sizable numbers of dependents, or at least not in bad years. Old and sick individuals who could not keep up with the group were occasionally left behind to manage for themselves—in other words, to die (Balikci 1970). Furthermore, the unequal sex ratio in some Eskimo groups at the turn of the century suggests that they also limited the number of the dependent young through female infanticide (see Freeman 1971; Balikci 1970).

In some cases, the population controls were probably quite deliberate attempts at family planning. The threat of hunger is a recurring theme in Eskimo conversation, even in communities where the evidence indicates that hunting accidents have caused many more deaths over the years than hunger (Kemp 1971). And one way to stave off hunger is to limit the number of nonproducers to ensure that at least some children survive. The archaeological record does contain evidence of

In addition to hunting and fishing, most Eskimo families supplement their livelihoods with seasonal employment. This house was built one summer as a temporary home for his family by a carpenter in Bethel, Alaska. Although all members contribute in some way to the family's subsistence, most Eskimos are also eager to send their children to school and to share in the modern consumer economy. (STEVE MCCUTCHEON/ALASKA PICTORIAL SERVICE)

some large and formal villages that were exceptions to this pattern, but they appear to have been short-lived.

The ratio of population to food resources may become a more realistic worry in the near future, for Eskimo populations are rapidly increasing. With improved health care, supplied by the United States and Canadian governments, the Eskimo's mortality rate has declined steadily in recent years. At the same time their fertility rate has increased. In the Eskimo community of Wainwright, Alaska, for example, the average woman gives birth to nine or ten live children in the course of her reproductive years; the average Dobe !Kung woman has five. As a result, the population of this group is growing at a rate of 3 percent a year (Milan 1970), six times the 0.5 percent rate of the Dobe !Kung. Other groups are expanding at similar rates, putting a strain on their ecosystems.

Social Relationships

The Eskimo, like most other hunter-gatherers, have extensive networks of kin, but the most important social unit is the extended family. This is considered to be the "real family." Jean

Briggs notes in her study of the Uktu in Hudson Bay (neighbors of the Netsilik), "Whenever possible, it is with their 'real family' that the people live, work, travel, and share whatever they have. Moreover, it is only with their 'real family' that they appear to feel completely comfortable and safe" (1970:39). These extended families are organized into larger kin groups that generally camp and work together. Like the Dobe !Kung, however, Eskimo families have considerable latitude in choosing the people with whom they will camp. It is common for everyone in an Eskimo society to be considered kin to everyone else—if not by blood, then by marriage, adoption, or shared names (a practice that we have already seen among the !Kung). These extensive ties allow families to shift about on short-term and long-term visits and thus enable the Eskimo to adjust the makeup of their groups according to the availability of resources and personal preference, especially in the scattered inland camps of the summer and fall.

In their personal relationships, the Eskimo place great value on restraint. Demonstrations of emotion are frowned upon. Briggs (1970) noted that Uktu husbands and wives and their older children never kiss, embrace, or even touch one another in front of anyone else. Even more unwelcome is a show of negative feelings, especially anger. To the Eskimo, the ideal personality traits are shyness, patience, generosity, and an even temper.

It is no surprise that the Eskimo have no formal group leadership. Though a man with a reputation for wisdom or expertise in hunting may come to have some influence in decision making, anyone who tries unabashedly to impose his will on others is regarded with deep suspicion. Likewise, Eskimo have no formal code for dealing with people who violate social norms. Stingy or bad-tempered Eskimo are not directly criticized or punished; rather, the others will try to soothe or tease them out of their folly. If this strategy does not work, the offender is simply avoided. The worst punishment that Eskimo societies can inflict is ostracism, a very serious threat in harsh Arctic conditions.

Energy Use: The Baffin Island Eskimo

The Eskimo's relatively high energy budget has been documented by William Kemp's (1971) careful study of energy use in one of the last all-Eskimo communities on Baffin Island, to the north of Netsilik territory. The village Kemp studied consisted of four households, whose total population varied from twenty-six to twenty-nine over the period of the study. Three of the families lived in quagmags, wood-frame tents covered with skins and old mailbags that the people had sewn together and insulated with a layer of dry shrubs. These tents were heated by traditional seal-oil lamps. The fourth family lived in a prefabricated wood house supplied by the government and heated by a kerosene stove. This house was not the village's only sign of industrial technology.

Among them the villagers owned two snowmobiles, a large motorized whaling boat, and a 22-foot freight canoe with an outboard motor, along with several large sledges and thirty-four sled dogs. Hunting is still the most important subsistence activity of these Eskimo, but now they hunt with rifles as well as harpoons. The younger men spend only part of their time hunting; they also mine soapstone and carve it into statuettes for export, and some of the young men leave the village periodically to work for wages at government construction sites. In one year village members earned $3,500 from carvings, $1,360 from animal skins, $1,225 in wages, and $670 in government subsidies.

Kemp's analysis of energy flow in this small community was similar to Lee's study of the Dobe !Kung's subsistence practices and standard of living. But Kemp had to take into account the use of fuel as well as muscle power, the hours spent working for wages as well as hunting and gathering, and the acquisition of store-bought as well as wild foods. To calculate the energy flow, he reduced both the number of hours individuals spent at various activities and the various foods they acquired and consumed to the common denominator of kilocalories (thousands of calories). This procedure enabled him to analyze in considerable detail the sources of energy, the routes along which it flowed, and the uses to which it was put.

Kemp calculated that over the fifty-four weeks during which he kept records of village activities (February 14, 1967, through March 1, 1968) the Eskimo expended some 12.8 million kilocalories of human energy in hunting, mining and carving, working for wages, taking care of household chores, traveling, and visiting. In addition, they used 885 gallons of gasoline, 615 gallons of kerosene, and 10,900 rounds of ammunition. During the same period they acquired 12.8 million kilocalories in wild food for human consumption (plus 7.5 million kilocalories in food for the dogs) and 7.5 million kilocalories in store-bought food. Thus important sources of energy lie outside the local economy, and indeed the Eskimo are as dependent on industry and fossil fuels as is the rest of North America's population. They may spend more time and energy in hunting, but such activities as wage labor and soapstone carving force them to depend on critical inputs of imported energy.

So far the Baffin Island Eskimo eat well. Game—primarily seal but also whale, caribou, and other animals—remains their dietary staple, accounting for 85 percent of their food. The villagers rarely buy canned meat and vegetables, though they do purchase sugar, powdered milk, quantities of flour and lard for bannock (a pan-baked bread), and small amounts of such delicacies as peanut butter and honey. Kemp estimates that this combination of wild and store-bought food provides each adult with 3,000 calories a day. The Eskimo's calorie in-

take, then, is about 50 percent higher than that of the Dobe !Kung. Their protein intake, accounting for 44 percent of their calories, is also quite high—a reflection of their heavy dependence on game. Of their remaining foodstuffs, 33 percent are in the form of carbohydrates, 23 percent in fat. Such a diet fortifies them for the exertions of Arctic life. Kemp noted, however, that when the men of one household abandoned hunting for a month to work for wages and the family ate only store-bought food, 62 percent of their diet consisted of carbohydrates and only 9 percent of protein—an unhealthy balance. Such a diet resembles that of the poor in North American cities, who rely heavily on factory-prepared snack foods.

The Changing Relationship with the Environment

The products of industrialization—motorized vehicles, high-powered weapons, store-bought foods—have affected the relationship between the Eskimos and their environment. The most obvious change that Kemp observed on Baffin Island is that the people have become sedentary. Snowmobiles and boats enable hunters to travel to their hunting grounds in a relatively short time, so it is no longer necessary for the whole village to pack up and move. Store-bought food provides the insurance against hunger which was once provided by seasonal moves to exploit a wide variety of game. Today the whole village moves only in August, when the families camp near the trading post to await supply ships bringing gas, kerosene, food, and mail.

The villagers express some ambivalence about their new high-powered equipment. On the one hand, they value it highly. On the other hand, they complain that it has destroyed the mutual trust between humans and animals. Seals are wary of the rumbling motors and rifle reports; only young animals can be coaxed within shooting range. Moreover, the Eskimo point out that rifles are not necessarily better than their old weapons. In the spring, for example, seals fast, losing their winter layer of fat; when melting snow reduces the salinity of the water, the animals are less buoyant. Unless an animal that has been killed by a rifle is immediately secured with a harpoon, it will sink—a fact that renders long-range weapons useless. Kemp notes that in one thirty-hour session of continuous hunting, the Eskimo killed thirteen seals but retrieved only five.

The danger of overkill, and consequently of the destruction of the Eskimo's resource base, is quite serious now that the hunters have high-powered weapons. In the area west of Hudson Bay the Eskimo have already virtually exterminated the once-large herds of caribou with rifles. In other areas, however, they have restrained their game harvests. This was the case with the Baffin Islanders that Kemp studied. Because the fall hunt yielded enough food to last through the winter, the villagers were able to spend more time visiting than hunting in February, March, and April. Although they might have used this time to collect extra skins for trading (and perhaps dangerously reduce the seal population in the process), they chose to travel instead. Whether this choice was based on conservationist concerns is debatable. The people may have been conscious of the need to preserve the supply of wild game. They may, too, have decided that the returns on hunting were simply less than those gained from the time spent on soapstone carving, or even than the rewards of visiting friends and relatives. Practices that limit hunting—visiting days, the soapstone industry, even the new custom of observing Sundays as a day of leisure—help the Eskimo maintain a balance between their needs and their resources.

The Baffin Island Eskimo also maintain balance in the distribution of resources among themselves. The snowmobiles are individually owned, but all the hunters contribute money

An Eskimo hunter drags home a seal he has harpooned. Most Eskimos have turned to modern, high-powered rifles, but they complain that these weapons have destroyed the mutual trust between animals and humans. (NFB, 5/58)

to pay for gasoline to run them. Although the men hunt individually, for themselves and their families, they store food collectively. And when a hunter brings in a big kill, the community feasts. All the people eat until they are full, and the leftovers are distributed equally among the families.

Thus adaptation is not simply a matter of the direct interplay between technology and the environment. Rifles and snowmobiles do not inevitably spell ecological disaster, for social customs intervene between technology and the uses to which it is put. The Eskimo ethic of sharing reduces the incentive to slaughter large numbers of animals for cash. The need to earn money through carving takes young men away from the hunt. And the same snowmobiles that enable them to kill more sea mammals give them the option to forgo hunting and visit distant kin when they have enough to eat.

Nevertheless, these social controls may break down if the temptation of short-term profits is great enough. For example, the Miskito of Nicaragua, mentioned earlier in this chapter, had at one time a strict obligation to share food with their kin—a social practice that discouraged the overexploitation of the turtle population for cash profits. But once the packing companies moved in and offered ready cash for turtles, many of the Miskito simply ignored their kinship obligations and threw themselves full-time into turtle hunting. As a result, both the kinship structure and the turtle population are endangered.

An optimistic postscript to our discussion of the Eskimos: In September 1988 the Canadian government passed legislation giving the Eskimo and other native peoples of the Canadian northern territories formal title to their extensive and potentially resource-laden lands. The economic and social future of the Eskimo is thus far brighter than that of other contemporary hunters and gatherers.

Summary

The hunting-and-gathering adaptive pattern, which has been dominant for much of human existence, is illustrated in this chapter by the Dobe !Kung of the Kalahari Desert and the Eskimo of northeastern Canada.

Hunting-and-gathering peoples traditionally have been self-sufficient, but they are becoming less so as they become less isolated from the dominant societies around them. Unlike societies that cultivate their food resources, hunter-gatherers eat what nature provides and diversify their diet to accommodate fluctuations in resources. Survival necessitates an adaptive pattern that balances resources, the group's technology, and its social organization.

Hunter-gatherers typically live in small, flexible groups that can scatter when natural resources become scarce and converge when resources again become plentiful. Some hunter-gatherers (*travelers*) move regularly from campsite to campsite as resources become available in various locations; others (*processors*) occupy a permanent settlement, from which they move to temporary camps to exploit seasonally available resources. Their kinship system creates ties over large areas, so that people can move in and out of groups as resources fluctuate. *Reciprocity*—the sharing of food and other goods—also allows hunter-gatherers to adapt to fluctuations in resources. Their systems of decision making and social control tend to be informal.

One reason for the success of hunter-gatherers is their *low energy budget.* They invest relatively little energy in the quest for food resources and obtain substantial returns. Their traditional adaptive strategy of low energy needs, a wide resource base, and a controlled population results in minimum interference with their ecosystem. Hunter-gatherers risk wiping out their resources when they attempt to exploit them for an unlimited world market.

The !Kung San occupy the Dobe area on the northern edge of the Kalahari Desert. They are able to satisfy their needs and live comfortably in this inhospitable region by exploiting a wide variety of resources. Seasonal migrations are necessary because of fluctuations in the availability of water. The nomadic !Kung possess only goods that can be moved easily or left behind. Social practices contribute to the mobility of the !Kung and the flexibility of their groups. The !Kung enjoy visiting kin in other camps, and bride service can take families to other groups for indefinite periods. Flexibility in group composition helps tailor population size to local resources and also helps to reduce friction among group members.

Although meat, hunted by men, is a prized resource, vegetables and fruits, gathered chiefly by women, are the staples of the !Kung diet. The quality of the !Kung's life is apparently quite high; their diet is nutritionally sound and procured with relatively little expenditure of energy, and they enjoy a great deal of leisure time. A low birthrate is crucial to the !Kung adaptive pattern.

The Eskimo have traditionally depended on a seasonal quest for animals to provide food, clothing, tools, and fuel. Contact with the world market, however, has eroded the isolation and self-sufficiency of the Eskimo.

The Arctic environment dictates the adaptive patterns of the Netsilik of northeastern Canada and the Baffin Island Eskimo. These people change the sizes and locations of their camps as their resources change with the seasons. In the summer they disperse to take advantage of abundant food, and in the winter they come together to hunt seals. Unlike the !Kung, they are able to store food for the long winters, but their climate forces them to adopt a higher energy budget than that of the !Kung and to accumulate material goods (such as heavy clothing, snowmobiles, lamps, rifles) that reduce their mobility. In the past the Eskimo have kept their population level in harmony with their food resources, but now their population is rapidly increasing, with resultant strain on their ecosystem.

Extensive kinship ties allow the Eskimo, like the !Kung, to move easily in and out of groups, but the most important social unit is the extended family. The Eskimo frown on shows of emotion or of negative feelings. They have no formalized leadership or code of social control.

A study of the Baffin Island Eskimo revealed that their intake of energy is high and their output low. They hunt seal, caribou, and other animals, and catch fish in weirs (circular dams) they have built of stone. Their natural resources are supplemented by store-bought food, particularly the ingredients to make bannock (unleavened bread baked in a shallow pan) and such items as snowmobiles and kerosene stoves.

Industrialization is changing the life of the Baffin Islanders. Seasonal migrations are no longer necessary, as they can quickly travel to their hunting grounds by snowmobile, and store-bought food provides insurance against hunger. The introduction of high-powered weapons has raised the danger of overkill and consequently of the destruction of the Eskimo's resource base. However, the Baffin Islanders seem to be aware, even if unconsciously, of the dangers these new tools represent: they continue to place a high value on sharing, which may prevent overkill; they have used their spare time to visit more than to hunt; and they have chosen means other than animal exploitation to achieve additional cash income. The greatest danger to the social controls of the Eskimo is the temptation of short-term profits, which would decrease both their self-sufficiency and the stability of their ecosystem.

Key Terms

low energy budget
processors
reciprocity
travelers

Suggested Readings

BICCHEIRI, M. G. (ED.). 1988. *Hunters and Gatherers Today: A Socioeconomic Study of Eleven Such Cultures in the Twentieth Century.* Prospect Heights, Il.: Waveland Press. Historical reconstructions and ethnographies provide a general perspective on the adaptations of hunters and gatherers.

HOWELL, N. 1979. *Demography of the Dobe !Kung.* New York: Academic Press. A thorough analysis of two years of demographic fieldwork with the Dobe !Kung that uses stable population theory for its perspective on the functioning of this group.

LEE, R., AND I. DEVORE (EDS.). 1976. *Kalahari Hunter-Gatherers: Studies of the !Kung San and Their Neighbors.* Cambridge, Mass.: Harvard University Press. This volume describes the results of field research carried out by a team of scholars. Together the articles constitute the most comprehensive study yet undertaken of a hunter-gatherer population.

LEE, R., AND I. DEVORE (EDS.). 1968. *Man the Hunter.* Chicago: Aldine Press. This compendium of studies by many researchers into the hunter-gatherer way of life was influential in refocusing anthropological attention on the oldest human adaptation. The articles, describing hunter-gatherers from all over the world, explore such topics as social organization, ecology, population, and systems of kinship and marriage.

SCHRIRE, C. (ED.). 1984. *Past and Present in Hunter-Gatherer Studies.* Orlando, Fla.: Academic Press. This collection of papers attempts to understand both the past behavior and current ways of life of hunter-gatherers by focusing on the history of their interactions with other peoples.

SISKIND, J. 1973. *To Hunt in the Morning.* New York: Oxford University Press. An intimate account of fieldwork among the Sharanahua Indians of the Amazon jungle. It is especially interesting for its emphasis on the way modernization is affecting this population.

STURTEVANT, W. C. (ED.). 1984. *Handbook of North American Indians:* vol. 5, *Arctic.* Washington, D.C.: Smithsonian Institution. Part of an encyclopedic summary of the information available about the prehistory, history, and cultures of the aboriginal peoples of North America in archaeological and ethnographic accounts. The organization of these volumes is by geographical area. Volume 5 deals with the special problems of the regions and populations that together form the Arctic habitat zone.

TURNBULL, C. 1961. *The Forest People.* New York: Simon & Schuster. An intimate view of the Mbuti Pygmies of equatorial Africa that explores the relationships of the people to the forest and to their horticultural neighbors.

WILMSEN, E. N. (ED.). 1989. *We Are Here: Politics of Aboriginal Land Tenure.* Berkeley, Calif.: University of California Press. An anthropological investigation that explores the issues of aboriginal relations to land and territory.

WINTERHALDER, B. AND E. A. SMITH (EDS.). 1981. *Hunter-Gatherer Foraging Strategies.* Chicago: University of Chicago Press. A collection of ethnographic and archaeological analyses that apply optimal foraging theory.

Chapter 6 Horticulture

Hunting and gathering, as we have seen, involves the collection of naturally occurring food resources of a given habitat. Agriculture involves the domestication and management of some edible species. Such species characteristically cannot survive or reproduce without human assistance. We have no direct evidence that people who lived in prehistoric times consciously or unconsciously tried to influence the reproductive cycles of the species on which they depended. But since they were intelligent, experiments certainly occurred. Over the ages, however, as people and animals and plants interacted, selective pressures changed the reproductive success of animals and plants favored by humans.

These changes need not have resulted from a conscious manipulation of a species by the people who used them; they could have come about as inadvertent by-products of the way people were altering their environment—being selective in the killing of members of a particular population, for example, or harvesting grain in such a way as to change the genetic makeup of seeds (Rindos 1980:752). Such selective pressures eventually led to **domestication,** the process by which people began trying to control the reproductive rates of animals and plants by ordering the environment to favor their survival—protecting them from pests, predators, and competitors, for instance, and supplying them with water and nutrients. Ultimately these efforts led to agriculture, one of the most significant achievements of the human species.

The development of agriculture irrevocably affected the course of human cultural history. The full impact of these changes can be seen in the societies that practice intensive agriculture (discussed in Chapters 8 and 9), the most productive and technologically sophisticated form of food production. But the distance from the hunting-and-gathering adaptation can be seen clearly even in societies that practice a modest and comparatively simple form of agriculture: horticulture.

Horticulture is almost always accompanied by some reliance on hunting, fishing, and the collection of wild plants. Unlike hunter-gatherers, however, horticulturists depend primarily on domesticated foods, especially plants, and unlike intensive or industrialized agriculturalists, they raise these plants in small plots, using relatively simple methods and tools. ("Horticulture" means "garden cultivation.") Agricultural techniques, along with other forms of behavior, vary widely from group to group. Yet the shared procurement strategy—production of food crops primarily for personal consumption—creates certain broad similarities in settlement patterns, social organization, and interaction among groups. First, we will examine how the strategy developed and its general features. Then we will focus on two specific groups of horticulturists: the Yanomamö of Venezuela and Brazil and the Pueblo Indians of the American Southwest. We must still keep in mind that all of the peoples we discuss are undergoing change; they are presented here in the ethnographic present.

THE HORTICULTURAL ADAPTATION

Development

About 12,000 years ago, people began to plant and harvest crops and to domesticate various animal species. This shift in adaptive pattern to horticulture is of great interest to anthropologists and archaeologists because the increases in social and technological innovations were significantly greater than any that had developed over the preceding millions of years.

The earliest evidence of cultivation and herding appears in the Middle East, where wheat and barley were the first staple crops. Horticulture also appeared early in China and Southeast Asia. Millet was the primary crop in early Chinese cultivation. The origin of rice, one of the world's most important crops, is still poorly understood. While our knowledge of the domestication process in Africa is incomplete, there is evidence for the cultivation of sorghum, millet, and a variety of other plants. In Mesoamerica and South America, cultivation appeared thousands of years later than in the Old World. Corn, beans, and squash were the important crops cultivated in higher altitude areas; manioc was grown in coastal zones.

Some archaeologists have suggested that agricultural experiments began when humans noticed plants growing from seeds in their garbage dumps. There is evidence that hunter-gatherers were well aware of the relationship between plants and seeds, and it is possible that horticulture began with the tending of useful herbs. The interesting question is why hunter-gatherers would give up a stable existence for one that requires substantially more work. Addressing it, archaeologists have identified certain traits that distinguish wild from domesticated plant specimens. Domesticated seeds, and often entire plants, are generally larger than their wild counterparts and they frequently have different structures. A key characteristic of domesticated plants is the absence of a seed-dispersal mechanism. Wild plants must have such mechanisms to insure that seeds are dispersed to locations with sufficient light, water, and other conditions favorable for growth. Domesticated plants are largely dependent on humans for their seed dispersal, through the practice that we call "planting."

Examination of the increasing amounts of data available on the origins of domestication has yielded several prominent theories. To begin with, learning appears to be an important component. However one judges the record, it is clear that people came to exercise more control over their environments. Ultimately, they selected more productive resources, stored seeds, selected from among the seeds those most likely to generate productive plants, and altered the conditions under which the plants were growing by removing weeds and supplying additional water.

The question arises, however, as to why people chose to learn more about their resources. Movement is certainly an important factor. Although people moved to a new environment, they valued resources from the old one. Bringing a plant to a new place required knowledge as to how to cultivate it there. Furthermore, despite many regional differences, there is a common thread underlying the growth of horticultural strategies: population growth and the instability that accompanied it. The most common early strategy for solving problems was to move to a new location. But as population levels became high, this alternative became less possible and more settled patterns of existence resulted. Thus sedentary lifestyles are associated with marked population growth, which probably upset the balance between human groups and the resources on which they depended. When infanticide, postpartum taboos, or migration were not sufficient to keep a population within acceptable limits, some groups began to manipulate the natural availability of resources. This strategy led to their being able to expand without depleting their resources. As these groups grew and spread, other groups imitated their practices. Because they could increase the carrying capacity of their environment in ways in which hunter-gatherers could not, horticulturists became more predominant.

It is important to emphasize that the initial expansion of horticulture did not occur because it was a universally superior adaptation to hunting and gathering. People had to work harder. Analyses of skeletal material from the time periods suggest that overall health decreased and disease and malnutrition increased. But the increased productivity and reliability of the food supply provided the basis for further population growth, a cycle that has continued to the present. Both depend on the elaboration of methods of cultivation.

Cultivation Methods

Horticulture differs from intensive agriculture in several ways. First is the relatively simple technology associated with this type of farming. Only small and often scattered plots of land are cultivated at one time, and they are worked without the help of plows, or animal traction, to say nothing of machines. The only tools used are simple hand tools—knives, axes, digging sticks, and hoes. In other words, horticulturists, like hunter-gatherers, still rely mainly on the energy stored in their own muscles in order to procure their food.

Second, in comparison with intensive agriculture, horticulture provides a relatively low yield per acre of land. For this reason it is sometimes called "extensive agriculture"; for every unit of energy produced, horticultural methods require much more land than intensive agricultural techniques require. The amount of energy horticulturists extract from the land is enough to sustain them, but they generally do not produce food surpluses for the purpose of trade. While trade is often of concern to horticulturists, usually it is for the acquisition of items produced by another population. Exceptions occur when horticulturists are in close contact with hunter-gatherer groups, from whom they may acquire animal products. The Mbuti Pygmies of northeastern Zaire, for example, are a hunting population that supplies its Bantu-speaking horticultural neighbors with meat and honey from the forest (Peacock 1984:15).

Third, in general, horticulture allows for household self-sufficiency. Each group, and in most cases each household, is capable of producing most of the food it needs. Most important productive decisions are made at the household level. Horticulturists need not depend on other groups for food because they cultivate a wide variety of crops with an exceedingly modest technology. This orientation toward self-sufficiency is one of the reasons that the production of horticultural societies remains low.

Most contemporary horticulturists occupy marginal territories—either tropical regions, where soil is thin, or arid regions, where water supply is a constant problem. In this respect they resemble hunter-gatherers. They often have been excluded by competing groups from better-favored lands, where intensive agriculture is possible. In such circumstances they cope with the challenge of agriculture in several ways. They may concentrate on crops that make few demands on the soil. They may plant next to rivers or in areas that flood in the rainy season. They may plant in several locations, so that if one field fails them, another may still feed them. Or they may shift their fields regularly to avoid depleting the soil. Many horticulturists use several of these techniques. The last, however, which in its present form is called slash-and-burn agriculture, is the most common.

Slash-and-burn agriculture, also called *swidden agriculture,* is a method of farming by which fields are cleared, the trees and brush are burned so that the soil is fertilized by the ash, and the field is then planted. Each field is used for perhaps two or three years; then it is left to regenerate for about ten years while the farmer moves on to other fields. Swidden agriculture was practiced in Europe until the beginning of the Christian era and in North America until about the seventeenth century. (Indeed, it has been suggested that one reason for the success of the European colonists in North America was that they imitated the

A Yąnomamö man uses a hoe to cultivate his garden plot in a clearing in the Brazilian jungle. (ROBERT HARDING PICTURE LIBRARY)

slash-and-burn techniques of the Native Americans.) Today the practice is confined mainly to the tropical regions. The reasons are complex but have to do primarily with the fact that where intensive agriculture is feasible, it produces more food. Unfortunately, all too often traditional horticultural plots are being consolidated into open-field farms and ranches in environments unsuited to such enterprises. The Amazon rain forest is being burned and bulldozed at an ever-increasing rate to make way for ranches and open-field farms (Posey 1984: 95–96). Whereas horticulturists, such as the Yąnomamö (whom we will meet shortly), have managed to exploit the rain forests without harming the environment under these forms of land use, the thin soil rapidly erodes.

The slash-and-burn technique demands a fine sensitivity to the environment. Swidden farmers must know exactly when to move their fields and when to replant a fallow field. They must also make rather precise calculations as to when to burn—on a day when there is enough wind to fan the fire but not enough to spread it to the rest of the forest. Horticulturists in general—swidden and otherwise—know an enormous amount about their environment, including minute details about different kinds of soil, about the demands of different kinds of plants, and about the topography and microclimate of their habitats. This knowledge is the secret of their survival.

Energy Use and the Ecosystem

The object of horticulture, as of any form of agriculture, is to increase the amount of energy that a given unit of land can yield for human use. Although horticulturists extract far fewer resources per acre than intensive farmers, they also expend less labor than intensive agriculturalists. They use neither their land nor their labor to the fullest. Simply producing enough to feed the family takes much less work than the people are capable of doing, so that many of the able-bodied, such as adolescents, may not have to work at all, while those who do work may do so intermittently and spend more time in hunting or other activities. That is not to say that horticulturists are lazy. They may simply have more options as to how to use their time. A comparison of four populations in the Brazilian Amazon finds that while all hunt to acquire needed protein, those who live in the best horticultural areas hunt the most—meat is a desired luxury and the men can afford the time to seek it (Werner et al. 1979:303–315). Horticulturists have time left over after the minimum required subsistence tasks to devote to elaborate food preparation, ceremony, and luxury items beyond their basic needs.

In general, the lower the energy demands a human group makes on its environment, the less the group alters that environment. Clifford Geertz, in the most influential discussion of the subject, has argued that swidden farmers in the tropical lowlands do not so much alter their ecosystems as create "a canny imitation" of it (1969:6). Their ecosystem contains a remarkable diversity of living things packed in a small area—that is, the ecosystem is generalized rather than specialized. Although tropical soil is often thin, it can support this dense variety because the nutrients are rapidly recycled rather than being locked up in deep soil. The dense canopy of trees prevents this layer of rich organic soil from being washed away by rain or baked hard by the sun.

The plots of the swidden farmers copy these qualities of the tropical forest. Unlike the specialized fields of most intensive agriculturalists—all rice or all tomatoes—the swidden plot contains a jumble of crops, from roots and tubers to fruit trees and palms, flourishing primarily in a bed of ash. Like the trees of the uncultivated forest, the domesticated trees of the swidden plot form a cover that filters sun and rain, thus protecting the soil from erosion or parching and at the same time reducing the encroachment of undergrowth. And, of course, within a few years this plot reverts back to forest.

The mix of crops, or polyculture, can vary considerably among swidden cultivators even in the same general region, as studies in the Amazon have shown (Flowers et al. 1982:203–217). Earlier studies have emphasized the diversity of crops and the apparent helter-skelter aspect of horticulture—a complex mix of plants and trees that is as ecologically diversified as the forest itself. Recent work shows that very often the people rely on one or two main crops but intersperse them with useful trees; the planting is not done in a random or unplanned fashion but is carefully patterned so that as the garden ages, different crops become available in turn (see Flowers et al. 1982, Beckerman 1983, Boster 1983). Thus even the return to fallow is carefully regulated, each stage providing some product to the cultivators.

This does not mean that swidden agriculture cannot or does not result in environmental degradation; quite the contrary. Many countries where tropical horticulture is practiced regard this technique as a scourge and try to prohibit its practice. If a piece of land is used too long, crops will fail, the soil may bake hard or erode, and the only plants that may grow there are species of Imperata (also known as savanna, razor, or elephant grass). This hard weed can survive in depleted soils; once it appears, the plot is effectively unusable for a long time. In the Philippines, for example, much land is taken out of food production each year because of this sort of mismanagement. As long as swidden farmers use their land carefully, however—cultivate plots for only a short time, allow them sufficient fallow periods—the danger to the environment is minimal.

Diversity and Stability in Horticulture

Polyculture (the planting of more than one crop in a field) has traditionally been considered the key to ecological stability and reliable yields; monoculture has often been linked to major disasters, such as the Irish potato famine of the 1840s and even the recent famines in Africa. Unfortunately, monoculture is usually the easiest way to increase yields. Many researchers have argued for years that polyculture is more "natural" than monoculture because a mix of species in a field parallels the diversity of the forest, because the use of many varieties of plants minimizes the risk of loss to pests and disease, and because the nutrient-enriching tendencies of some plants balance the nutrient-robbing tendencies of others. Also, polyculture is assumed to have preceded monoculture historically. The issue is an important one, as a reliable local food supply is the only thing that can avert starvation for many millions of people in areas that have traditionally practiced some form of horticulture.

Some researchers are now suggesting that it is possible to intensify horticultural systems through a form of monoculture without sacrificing reliability. What is crucial, they say, is not the diversity of crops cultivated by traditional farmers in any given field or area but the diversity of the larger system of which they are a part. "The element of risk arising from the interaction between cropping pattern and the larger system and the flexibility of the farmer is particularly significant" (Morren and Hyndman 1987:305). You can practice monoculture and reap its productive rewards without sacrificing flexibility if you have access to other food sources at the same time; if you space your fields widely and retain forest borders to shield your crops from pests; and if you interplant many varieties of the same species, a practice that decreases the risk of disease.

George Morren and David Hyndman found that the Mountain Ok of central New Guinea have practiced a sustainable and low-risk *Colocasia* taro monoculture for as long as anyone can remember. Taro is a starchy edible root crop common in the Pacific. Morren and Hyndman argue that these taro monocultures exhibit many ecological and systemic properties commonly attributed to polycultures. They dispute the claim that monoculture is less common than polyculture among traditional agriculturalists, and indeed they argue that monocultures were once more widespread than they are today, particularly in moist forested areas.

The Mountain Ok, numbering 28,000 and speaking eight closely related languages, inhabit an extensive region (20,000 square kilometers) that can be divided roughly into highland, mid-altitude, and lowland zones. Although these people exhibit considerable sociocultural variability, the Mountain Ok of all regions appear to have access to the same range of agricultural technology. They practice forms of slash-and-burn agriculture, show a cultural preference for *Colocasia* taro, keep large numbers of swine, engage in minimal tillage, and have short croppings and long fallows. Local swidden gardens, however, are clearly differentiated according to crop composition. The sweet potato is the

Social Organization

Horticultural societies almost always share other characteristics as well. One is **sedentism,** the practice of establishing a permanent, year-round settlement. Whereas hunter-gatherers invest much energy in moving from place to place to find food, horticulturists invest their

staple of the high-altitude dwellers, and they keep their taro gardens separate from their sweet potato gardens. The mid-altitude peoples plant only taro gardens, but these monocultures are highly flexible and low in risk.

The Mountain Ok of the mid-altitude range are able to practice an optimal long-fallow form of swidden cultivation because generally their population densities are low and their land is extensive. Their use of flat or gently sloping land reduces the risk of erosion. They clear secondary forest land, which tends to be more fertile than that of the primary forest. They make small gardens separated by large forest margins, which shield the crops from pests and enhance fallow periods. Rather than totally clear a field, they stunt the trees by scorching or ringing, and often plant in undisturbed forest litter, which also improves fallows. By postponing complete clearing until the crop is established, they ensure that young plants are protected, moisture is retained, and erosion is avoided. They harvest only once a year, saving vital nutrients for trees. And by letting the gardens lie fallow a minimum of twelve years, they allow for the restoration of essential nutrients. Morren and Hyndman also note that the Mountain Ok plant a great many varieties of the staple taro crop—some groups recognize more than a hundred varieties—and new ones are constantly being introduced through diffusion or by discovery and trial. It is notable that the Mountain Ok of the mid-altitude range gain between 81 and 89 percent of their cultivated foods by weight from *Colocasia* taro; that is as heavy a dependence on a single crop as can be seen anywhere (1987:308–309).

Even so, the high-flexibility–low-risk monoculture practiced in the mid-altitude region is potentially vulnerable to disaster, whether from pests, blight, or climatic changes. This potential is buffered, however, by the farmers' options to exploit other crops and resources. The Mountain Ok of this area have available a wide variety of alternative wild and domesticated foods, and the large array of taro varieties also mitigates the potential for disaster. And as these people have not yet cultivated sweet potatoes in any significant numbers, the sweet potato is another option available to them if the taro crop should fail.

The persistence of taro monoculture in this region is threatened by modernization. In 1981 a mining project was begun in the land of Ok Tedi, and as people moved there in search of employment, they carried with them taro planting stock infected by leaf blight, which has now spread throughout the region. Similar problems in other regions have led to the expansion of sweet potato cultivation at the expense of taro. And as a result of the pressures of life in the new roadside mining communities, polyvarietal taro monoculture has given way to polyculture of new staple foods.

The taro monocultures that Morren and Hyndman describe exhibit all the advantages attributed to polyculture: they simplify the ecosystem, provide biological variability, and minimize the vulnerability of the food supply. Nonetheless, these researchers warn that monoculture should not be regarded as an exclusive category. Rather, specific cases must be placed in the broader context of the surrounding ecosystem.

energy in increasing the food production of one place, their fields.

Population density is generally also higher. In a group that is not on the move constantly, in-

fants, old people, and sick people have a better chance of surviving. The fertility rate may go up, for when men are no longer called away to the hunt, they spend more time with their wives (Binford 1968). Similarly, storage, which equalizes the distribution of resources through the year, is easier in a permanent settlement. Sedentary groups, then, tend to have higher population densities than nomadic or semi-nomadic groups.

All three of these conditions—agriculture, sedentism, and increasing population density— tend to result in a more complex society. Agriculture is a group effort, involving considerable cooperation in clearing of fields, planting, harvesting, and storage of crops. The crops and fields have to be protected from predators, including the threat of theft by others. At the same time, since agriculturalists invest time and energy in the land, organization is required to regulate access to the land and to resolve disputes that accompany life in a large residential grouping. Finally, a group that contains many people, interacting on a permanent basis, needs to order the relationships of the group members—to determine who owes loyalty to whom, who can marry whom, who must give in to whom in a quarrel, and so forth. Hunter-gatherers have fewer such problems. They can work individually; they own the land collectively; and when disputes arise, they can simply pack up their belongings and move. But the horticultural life presents more social challenges, which must be met through a more complex social structure. Horticulturists frequently consider land to be the property of the group, but individual households have exclusive access to the crops they produce on a given plot. Though horticulturists, too, may move when disputes break out, once they have invested in a plot, it is harder to do so.

Relations Within the Community

The basic unit of a society heavily dependent on horticulture is the household, a small group of people closely related by marriage and kinship who work together to produce food, share in its consumption, and cooperate on a day-to-day basis. Thus it is a unit of production and consumption analogous in many ways to a small family firm in our society. These family-based households, as we have mentioned, are relatively self-sufficient, since their gardens allow them to produce almost everything they need. Nevertheless, they cannot afford to be completely independent of one another, for horticulture creates vulnerability. Once a family has invested all its energy in a single plot of land, crop failure or a raid by another group can wipe out its livelihood in one stroke. Therefore, as insurance, households must make alliances and integrate themselves into a larger social unit: the community. They achieve integration primarily through kinship ties and participation in community-wide religious or political groupings. In some respects, collective landownership by kin groups or small, closely knit communities goes hand in hand with one of the distinguishing features of horticulture in the tropical lowlands: long fallow periods during which the forest is regenerated do not encourage individuals to assert exclusive control over any given plot. And in most circumstances the fact of collective ownership limits incentives for long-term investment in the agricultural infrastructure, such as the construction of terraces or of systems to control the flow of water.

Kinship is often (though not invariably) the basis for recognition of individual rights to the use of land. Kinship is almost always the basis of extensive gift exchanges, which establish reciprocal ties and obligations throughout the community. By regularly passing along to friends and kin their surplus produce, horticultural families ensure that they will not be stranded if they fall on hard times. Indeed, it might be said that gift exchange is the horticulturist's way of storing food, just as among hunter-gatherers.

The second integrating force is political organization. While differences in wealth are usually slight or nonexistent in most horticultural groups, there are differences in power. Horticulturists tend to have better-defined leadership roles than hunter-gatherers, although the authority of the leaders varies from group to group. As we shall see, the headman in a Yąnomamö village is simply a man with influence; he has no formal office and no right to coerce others. Eastern Pueblo leaders, on the other hand, do hold office and have considerable sway over others. Whatever the allotment of power, the headman serves to integrate the horticultural community by helping families to settle their quarrels, arrange their marriages, and so forth, and by leading them in feasts, religious rituals, and raids.

Relations Between Communities

As social organization within communities becomes more structured, so do relations between communities, whether friendly, as in the case of exchange, or hostile, as in the case of conflict.

Exchange. Both of the groups we will be describing engage in some trade. The Yąnomamö acquire metal tools from neighbors, government officials, and missionaries. Their involvement in trade is expanding each year as they are increasingly drawn into the national economies of Venezuela and Brazil. Historically, the Pueblo used to obtain buffalo meat and hides from their more nomadic neighbors. (Today, of course, they use the same store that everyone else does.) Yet self-sufficiency is still the rule among horticultural communities, and most of their intergroup exchange is a form of gift giving rather than impersonal commercial trade. A Yąnomamö man gives a man in another village a dog; some months later the second man gives the first a bow. Neither party necessarily depends on what the other gives: both can acquire dogs in their own villages and make their own bows. What they do need is each other's support, either in warfare or in obtaining a

wife. Thus just as gifts passed within groups serve to foster goodwill, so gifts passed between groups help to create and cement alliances; exchange is as much a social as an economic transaction. The exchange of women through intermarriage is the ultimate expression of solidarity among the Yąnomamö and many other tribal agriculturalists.

Conflict. Intergroup cooperation is only part of the story, for horticultural societies are not always peaceable. The Yąnomamö engage in endless rounds of threats, duels, kidnapping, and raids. The Pueblo Indians maintained war societies and organized raids to overthrow the Spaniards and fight the nomadic tribes with whom they also traded. For many reasons—competition for new territory, raids by nomadic groups, exploitation by intensive agricultural societies—conflict is a frequent state of affairs in horticultural society.

More often than not, war consists of what Andrew Vayda (1974) has called "nothing fights": chest-pounding duels; club fights with definite rules; prearranged encounters with bows, arrows, and shields across wide spaces so that no one is likely to be mortally wounded. Some of these exercises are closer to our contact sports than to our wars. However, intervillage conflict can and does escalate to the point where people are murdered and whole villages are driven off their lands. A single raid may leave only one or two people dead, but frequent repetition of such incidents can result in a high casualty rate. In some horticultural societies, religious beliefs limit or regulate the slaughter. Even so, the practice of premeditated, organized armed combat between horticultural groups contrasts sharply with the near absence of war parties, raids, and the like among contemporary hunter-gatherers. At the same time, it is important to note that hunting-gathering societies of the past that lived in richer habitats with higher population densities were more warlike than their modern counterparts. Fur-

Horticultural societies are not entirely peaceable. In fact, violence is a salient feature of Yąnomamö social life. These Yąnomamö are preparing to depart on a raid. (NAPOLEON CHAGNON)

thermore, contemporary hunter-gatherers have been pacified by neighboring groups and national governments, whereas many horticultural groups have remained more autonomous.

We should not assume that relationships among horticultural groups alternate between utopian harmony and full-scale warfare, still less that some tribes are always peaceful and others always at war. Like their adjustment to the physical environment, the response of horticultural groups to the social environment is sensitive and flexible. War and peace are two ends of a continuum, with many intermediate stages, and most intergroup dealings take place in those intermediate stages. Even the Yąnomamö, a particularly bellicose group, have fine gradations of escalation in their warfare, as well as a graded sequence of stages in forming and cementing alliances (Vayda 1974:186).

In sum, social organization among horticulturists is decidedly different from that of hunter-gatherers. Hunter-gatherers form small, relatively amorphous groups whose resources and members flow back and forth in such a way as to blur boundaries between subunits. The nuclear family remains intact, but it is not a distinct economic unit; the economic unit is the band as a whole. Horticultural society, by contrast, is a complex structure made up of well-defined and largely self-sufficient households within relatively stable and self-sufficient communities. These communities in turn are likely to have relatively formalized relationships with one another, often mediated (as we shall see in Chapter 13) by a system of kinship-based groups, each with its own territory and insignia.

THE YĄNOMAMÖ

Napoleon Chagnon, who has worked among the Yąnomamö on and off for twenty-five years, believes them to be one of the largest unacculturated tribes in South America, numbering about 10,000 members. When Chagnon arrived among the Yąnomamö people in 1964, missionaries had already established posts in two villages, but many of the Yąnomamö knew of the outside world only indirectly, from the metal axes and pots they obtained through trade. Today interaction with outsiders in missionary settlements and through work for ranchers and government agents has brought the Yąnomamö into far greater contact with the external world. There are now few Yąnomamö who have never seen a non-Yąnomamö. This case study, thus, is presented in the ethnographic present, or as the Yąnomamö appeared when anthropologists first began to work with them.

The Jungle Habitat

The Yąnomamö live in villages of 40 to 250 inhabitants (the average is 70 to 80) widely scattered through the dense tropical jungle in southern Venezuela and northern Brazil. For the most part, the land is low and flat, with occasional rolling hills and mountain ridges. It is crossed by sluggish, muddy rivers that become rushing torrents in the rainy season. Palms and hardwoods create a dense canopy over a tangle of vines and shrubs. The rain pours down two or three times a day, increasing in intensity between May and August. The humidity rarely drops below 80 percent, intensifying what to us would be the uncomfortable year-round temperatures of 26° to 32°C (80° to 96°F).

This habitat provides the Yąnomamö with a variety of wild foods. They collect palm fruits, nuts, and seed pods in season; devour honey when they can find it; snack on grubs, a variety of caterpillars, and roasted spiders. They fish by a rather ingenious method known among many nonindustrialized groups: they dam a stream, pour a drug in the water, wait for the stunned fish to float to the surface, and then scoop them into baskets. They hunt monkeys, wild turkeys, wild pigs, armadillos, anteaters, and other species with bows and poisoned arrows. A survey of their hunting practices and game brought into the villages indicates that their intake of protein is approximately 75 grams per person per day, well above the 30 to 50 grams necessary to support an adult (Chagnon and Hames 1979).

Wild foods alone are not abundant enough to support the Yąnomamö at their present population level. Fruits and tubers are seasonal. Animals are small, many are nocturnal, and most live singly, so that they are difficult to hunt. Chagnon notes that although on one occasion he and a group of Yąnomamö hunters killed enough game to feed an entire village for one day, on another occasion five days of searching did not yield enough meat to feed even the hunters (1983). Moreover, the Yąnomamö's technology does not allow them to exploit the rivers as they might. Their bark canoes are too awkward to navigate upstream, and so fragile that they are generally abandoned after one trip downstream.

Thus the Yąnomamö depend on their gardens, which provide 85 percent of their calorie intake. The most important crops are plantains and bananas (which together make up 52 percent of their diet by calories); manioc, a root crop used to make flour for cassava bread; sweet potatoes, taro and maguey; and peach palm trees. Less important crops are maize, avocados, squash, cashews, and papayas. The Yąnomamö also cultivate cane for arrow shafts; cotton for hammocks, belts, and cords; hallucinogenic drugs; and a variety of "magical" plants—one (cultivated by men) to make women sexually receptive, another (cultivated by women) to calm male tempers, and others to cause miscarriages and similar calamities in enemy villages. Finally, every Yąnomamö garden has a sizable crop of tobacco, which is highly prized and is chewed by men, women, and children.

Like other Indians of the South American jungles, the Yąnomamö practice slash-and-burn agriculture. To clear land for a garden, they first cut away the undergrowth and small trees with steel axes obtained from missionaries and through trade (or from anthropologists). They let the cut vegetation dry in the sun, then burn it off on a day when the wind is right. This task done, they set about felling the large trees, which they leave in the fields to mark boundaries between individual family plots and to chop for firewood when the need arises. The most difficult part of planting a new garden is carrying cuttings from plantain trees in the old garden to the new site—an arduous job, for a single cutting can weigh up to 10 pounds (4.5 kg). Planting other crops involves little more than making a hole with a digging stick and depositing seeds or small cuttings. Gardens are individually owned while they are being tended, and each man plants a variety of crops on his land.

Newly established gardens produce in spaced cycles. Thus at the beginning there are alternating periods of scarcity and plenty. Then, in about two or three years, the gardens mature, and overlapping plant cycles produce a constant supply of food (Chagnon 1983: 71, 74–79, Meggars 1971:19–20).

The Yąnomamö do most of the heavy work of clearing the land during the rainy season, when swamps and swollen rivers make it impossible to engage in visiting, feasting, or fighting with other villages. Once established, a garden takes only a few hours a day to maintain. Men, women, and children leave for their plots at dawn and return to the village around ten-thirty (if the men have decided not to hunt that day). The women also gather firewood and supervise the children playing nearby. No one works during the midday heat. Sometimes a man will return to the garden around four o'clock and work until sundown. Most men, however, spend the afternoon in the village, resting or taking drugs, while the women go out to collect more firewood and haul water.

Cleared land in a tropical forest will not support crops indefinitely. Once a garden has been cultivated continuously for two or three years, the farmer begins to shift it gradually. Every year he abandons more land at one end of the plot and clears more land at the other end, transplanting crops to the new addition. The garden "moves" in this way for about eight years, after which time the weeding problem becomes insuperable and the soil unproductive. The plot is then abandoned and an entirely new site is cleared. Left fallow, the old plot recovers its natural forest covering in about ten years. It should be noted that the Yąnomamö are somewhat unusual in their swiddening. Most horticulturists use their plots for longer periods and carefully supervise the long fallow period, going back regularly to harvest wild fruits and other resources as they appear (Denevan et al. 1984:346).

Village Life

The Yąnomamö live near their gardens in circular villages they call *shabono*. Each man builds a shelter of poles and vines for himself, his wife or wives, and their children. These homes are arranged around a central courtyard, and the spaces between them are thatched to form a continuous roof with an open space over the courtyard. The shabono, then, is roughly doughnut-shaped. For safety, most Yąnomamö groups also construct a high pole fence around the shabono, with a single opening that can be barricaded at night.

What authority there is in the village rests in

the person of the headman, an individual who has proved his superiority in combat, diplomacy, hunting, or some other skill. Headmen have no official right to order others around; they lead only to the extent that people respect or fear them. Kạobawä, the headman of the village in which Chagnon lived in 1964–1965, is probably typical. Having demonstrated his fierceness in numerous raids and quarrels and enjoying a large natural following—five adult brothers and several brothers-in-law, who were under obligation to him for the sisters he had given them in marriage—he felt no need to prove his power to anyone. He simply led by example, with an air of quiet authority, and people came to him of their own accord for advice.

Most members of a village are related to one another, either by blood or by marriage. Kinship among the Yạnomamö is reckoned by **patrilineal descent;** that is, it is traced through the male line. Both men and women belong to their father's lineage. Typically a village consists of two patrilineages, whose members have intermarried over several generations. Within a single lineage, all males of the same generation call one another "brother," and all females call one another "sister." For a man, however, the really important ties are not with his "brothers" but with the men of the lineage from which he can acquire a wife. Wives cannot be chosen according to fancy. Yạnomamö marriage rules specify that a man must choose a woman from a lineage other than his own. In practice, his choice is narrowed to a small group of women in the village's other lineage (or perhaps two other lineages). This rule is closely related to the chronic hostility and violence that characterize Yạnomamö social relations.

Neither the composition nor the location of a Yạnomamö village is permanent. Villages move every few years. Sometimes the group relocates for the purpose of acquiring fresh lands. But as a rule there is plenty of land to cultivate in the immediate vicinity, for villages are widely separated. As with many other horticulturists, a growing shortage of firewood is an important reason for movement. However, the Yạnomamö also move because hostilities make it impossible for them to stay where they are. Sometimes internal feuds divide a village into two factions, which then go their separate ways. More commonly, a village moves because warfare with other villages has escalated to such a degree that the only way to survive is to flee. Kạobawä's group, for example, had made sixteen major moves in seventy-five years. One move was motivated by the need for fresh land, one by a desire to acquire steel tools from a group of foreigners newly arrived downstream, and the remaining fourteen by either bloodshed within the group or warfare with neighboring villages (Chagnon 1983:174–177).

Violence, in fact, is the most salient feature of Yạnomamö social life; internal hostilities are exceeded only by external hostilities. Intervillage duels, raids, ambushes, and kidnappings are almost daily fare. Why is there so much conflict? The apparent reason—the reason that is given by the Yạnomamö—is women (Chagnon 1983:86–87, 176; Horgan 1988:17–18).

Warfare and Women

The only forms of family planning the Yạnomamö practice are a long postpartum taboo—a woman may not have sexual intercourse while she is pregnant or while she is nursing a child—and infanticide. If, despite the taboo, a woman does become pregnant while she is still nursing her last child—a practice that itself decreases the likelihood of pregnancy—she will kill the new baby rather than deprive the older child of milk. A woman is also likely to kill her first baby if it is a girl, for her husband of course wants a son, and displeased Yạnomamö husbands can be brutal, even murderous. The practice of selective female infanticide creates a sexual imbalance among the Yạnomamö. The boys of a given village invariably outnumber the girls, sometimes by as much as 30 percent (Chagnon 1967:139). The fact that older, more powerful men usually take second and third wives makes the shortage of women a particular problem for the younger men. Chagnon has reported that men who have been successful in raiding and who are known to have killed enemies are far more likely than other men to have two or more wives—further exacerbating the situation (Horgan 1988:17–18).

The unbalanced sex ratio increases conflicts within and between villages. Competition for the limited number of women eligible as brides under the marriage rules turns biological and classificatory brothers into potential enemies. Suppose there are ten young men in a lineage, only seven young women eligible for them to marry, and older men take two of these girls as brides. The men grow up knowing that only five of them will be able to marry within the village. Somehow they must outshine or disgrace the competition, and this necessity tends to undermine whatever solidarity might develop among them as brothers. (A young Yąnomamö may seek a bride in another village, but most are reluctant to do so because they would have to undertake years of bride service.) In addition, the shortage of women increases the temptation to commit adultery—a temptation to which married men succumb as readily as bachelors, especially during the four years or so when their wives are taboo. If a man succeeds in seducing another man's wife and is caught, the husband will retaliate with all the ferocity he can muster. Club fights over women are the major cause of the splitting of villages. After they split, hostility between the two groups tends to continue on its own momentum, each group taking turns avenging wrongs inflicted by the other group.

Warfare between totally separate villages follows the same pattern. Fights over women may precipitate the conflict, or one village may suspect that its crops are being pilfered by a neighboring village. If a child falls sick, the illness will be blamed on sorcery emanating from another village. (The Yąnomamö are constantly invoking evil demons to steal the souls of children in enemy villages.) Whatever the original causes, contests over women are usually part of the ensuing hostilities. Typically a raiding party will kill one or two men and abduct any women they can lay their hands on. This raid precipitates a counterraid, to avenge the murders and recapture the women. The retaliatory raid in turn triggers another, and so on.

Eventually the members of one village will be put to flight. Abandoning their gardens and homes, they take refuge in another village until they can plant new gardens. This arrangement, while necessary for the group's survival, further exacerbates the woman-shortage problem, for the hosts are almost certain to take advantage of their guests' weakened position to demand temporary or permanent access to their women.

Thus the Yąnomamö, according to Chagnon's accounts, are locked into a vicious cycle. The more the men fight over women, the more eager they are to have sons who will help in the fighting, the more female infants they kill, the fewer women there are, and the more they fight. Moreover, the men encourage their sons to be suspicious, hot-tempered, and quick to take violent action against the slightest offense. Teasing fathers often provoke small sons to hit them and then reward the boys with laughter and approving comments on how "fierce" they are becoming. By raising their sons in this way, the Yąnomamö perpetuate hostilities in the effort to defend against them.

Chagnon's explanation for Yąnomamö warfare is not without its critics. Most observers agree with his data indicating a high frequency of fighting and high mortality associated with it. And most agree that warfare of the sort reported is (or was) widespread among Amazonian groups. But Marvin Harris and others have argued that the importance of women has been overstressed and that environmental factors are directly or indirectly implicated. Harris (1974:276–79) and Daniel Gross (1975) state that underlying the frequency of warfare is a shortage of game and other sources of protein. Although the Yąnomamö grow more than enough produce to fill their stomachs and have miles of virgin forest to clear for new gardens, the foods they cultivate do not provide large amounts of protein. To meet these protein requirements, they must hunt and fish. Harris suggests that at some point the Yąnomamö began to intensify their agricultural activities, and that their population level rose accordingly. As the population grew, they killed increasingly larger numbers of wild animals, thus depleting their game resources. Today, Harris argues, there is not enough protein to go around, and what the Yąnomamö are fighting over, albeit unwittingly, is hunting territory.

Gross traces not only warfare but also several other aspects of Yąnomamö culture to scarcity of protein. Above all, the settlement pattern—the establishment of small, widely dispersed villages, separated from other villages by a no-man's-land and abandoned every few years—is, according to Gross, a strategy for preventing the overexploitation of game in any one area. Likewise, infanticide and a long postpartum taboo keep protein demand in check by keeping the population in check. The hypothesis that Yąnomamö warfare—the most striking aspect of this tribe's culture—may be an adaptation to protein limitations is intriguing, but so far it has not been substantiated by any reports of protein deficiency among the Yąnomamö. One study has found some signs of infant malnutrition but also evidence that children who survive childhood mature to be healthy adults (Holmes 1985). Although warfare may indeed serve to preserve hunting territories, it does not appear that this is the immediate or conscious objective of the combatants (Chagnon and Hames 1979, Chagnon 1983). Such differences, while difficult to resolve, stimulate new and innovative directions for research.

Political Alliances

In this hostile social environment, the Yąnomamö devote considerable time and resources to cultivating alliances with neighbors. Overtures begin cautiously, with parties of visitors bearing gifts. The gifts are not free, however; the takers are obliged to reciprocate at some point in the future with gifts of equal or greater value. If visiting goes well, specialization in craft production may begin: one village may rather suddenly abandon the making of pots, the other the manufacture of arrow points, so that they become dependent on each other. These contrived shortages express growing trust; all Yąnomamö have the resources and skills to make everything they require.

After a period of trading, one group takes the next step toward alliance by throwing a feast for the other group. They harvest and cook great quantities of food, amass goods for exchange, and prepare elaborate costumes and dances. Because giving and attending a feast implies a higher level of commitment, the occasion must be handled with caution and diplomacy. The dances and songs are essentially displays of strength. Each side tries to impress the other with the fact that it does not really need allies and probably never will.

Almost invariably disputes break out, and the toughest men of the two villages challenge one another to contests of physical strength: chest-pounding duels, in which two antagonists take turns socking each other squarely on the chest, and side-slapping duels, in which the contestants take turns hitting each other on the flanks. The object is to stay in the game until your opponent withdraws or is knocked unconscious. If tempers get hot, these "chicken" fights can escalate into club fights, full-scale brawls in which the men of each village beat one another over the head with eight-foot poles.

An occasional club fight leads to full-scale violence, destroying the alliance altogether. Usually, however, these carefully graded levels

The wrestling match of these Yạnomamö men rapidly escalated into both a side-slapping duel and beating contest. (NAPOLEON A. CHAGNON/ANTHRO-PHOTO)

of hostility allow the Yạnomamö to vent their ever-present aggression, display their fierceness, and still finish the feast on a friendly note. If all goes well, the fighting ends in a draw and gifts are exchanged. The guests depart peacefully, the hosts can expect to be invited to a return feast, and each group assumes it can count on the other for refuge and food in times of trouble.

The final step is an exchange of brides between the two groups. This step is not taken unless the villages are convinced of each other's good intentions, or unless one is so weak it has no choice. Villages that exchange women usually can expect support in their raids and skirmishes with other Yạnomamö. But even alliances based on marriage ties are tenuous. No village honors a commitment when it sees some advantage in breaking it.

In sum, the Yạnomamö are great fighters and poor allies. Consequently, their social world is one of chronic suspicion and hostility. Warfare accounts for at least 22 percent of all male deaths (Chagnon 1967:140). The figure seems startling but it is comparable to those of New Guinea tribes and of Native American societies that feud regularly (Livingstone 1968:8–9).

THE PUEBLO INDIANS

The Pueblo Indian tribes of the American Southwest differ considerably from the Yạnomamö in the environment they inhabit, the agricultural techniques they employ, and the way their societies are organized. Furthermore, whereas the Yąnomamö until recently lived in almost total isolation from the outside world, the Pueblo have been beset for several centuries by competing populations—Spaniards, other Indian tribes, and settlers from northern Europe. Indeed, *pueblo* is the Spanish word for "village."

The Pueblo Indians are the cultural and biological descendants of hunter-gatherers who migrated to the American Southwest more than 10,000 years ago. The ancestors of today's Pueblos were skilled basketmakers, weavers, potters, and, above all, architects. They are famed (and named) for their pueblos—dwellings of three and four stories honeycombed by interconnected rooms, some of which open onto a protected inner courtyard, where a kiva—a round ceremonial chamber—is sunk into the pavement. Such compact structures housed entire villages of as many as several thousand people.

The prehistoric Pueblo experimented with various subsistence strategies and forms of social organization. That is the reason for some of the diversity among Pueblo settlements. Their diversity was once greater than it is now, but environmental pressures over the course of time eliminated the less adaptive strategies. More important was the destruction of up to 80 percent of Puebloan peoples by diseases brought by the Spanish conquistadors—measles, smallpox, plague, influenza—to which Puebloan peoples had no resistance. Two basic patterns remain. One of these patterns, the eastern Pueblo adaptation, is based on complex irrigation works. This was the most common pattern of prehistoric times, but in the last few centuries it has survived in only a few areas, most of them on the Rio Grande in New Mexico. The western Pueblo adaptation, found in eastern Arizona and western New Mexico, is based on the simpler techniques of rainfall and floodwater farming.

Thus we see an unmistakably horticultural adaptation in the western Pueblo and the beginnings of intensive agriculture in the eastern Pueblo. This contrast was most marked immediately before and after colonization by Spain; this is the period we shall be describing. Since that time the industrial economy of the United States has grown up around the Pueblo, transforming many aspects of their world. Even so, the basic technological and social features of the eastern and western adaptations survive today.

San Esteban Del Rey Mission at the western Acoma Pueblo covers seventy acres and is one of the oldest inhabited sites in the United States. (KENT & DONNA DANNER)

Two Environments

The Western Pueblo

The western part of Pueblo territory, a landscape of semiarid mesas and canyons, seems an unlikely spot for farming. The growing season is short; the frosts begin as early as September and can persist through May. There are few permanent streams, and rainfall, sometimes in the form of sudden torrents, averages only about 25 centimeters (10 inches) a year. As in most arid environments, climatic variability is a more important factor than aridity itself. Records obtained from tree rings show that the predictability of rainfall has varied greatly from year to year and that rainfall is very patchy; one valley may be quite wet during a given growing season while another remains dry.

In some prehistoric epochs the environment of the area was wetter, the rain less patchy and more predictable. Archaeologists find scant evidence of Puebloan ancestors during such periods. The inhabitants then followed a more mobile hunting-gathering strategy. During periods of variability ancestors of the modern Puebloan peoples developed sedentary strategies intended to counter such fluctuations in the food supply.

The western Pueblo developed several techniques to cope with the variability in rainfall, the most important of which was floodwater farming. Essentially, **floodwater farming** is the practice of planting crops in areas that are flooded every year in the rainy season, the floodwaters thus providing natural irrigation. Despite erratic rainfall, the western Pueblo's crops stood a chance of surviving, for the flooded soil could hold enough water to see them through the growing season. They also stood a chance of being uprooted and carried away in the violent rainstorms typical of this area. Or the rain might be too late or too little to provide adequate flooding for the growing season.

To protect themselves against these contingencies, the western Pueblo supplemented floodwater farming with other strategies. They did some irrigation farming in areas where it was feasible. They planted their maize in deep holes dug into the dunes, where the soil was wetter during the early part of the growing season and where the young plants would be shielded from sandstorms. Some people planted their crops in clusters, thus reducing the water requirements of the field and ensuring that in the event of heavy winds, at least the plants at the center of the cluster would survive. They chose their soils carefully, favoring spots where water was likely to seep into the ground rather than run off the surface.

Above all, they avoided placing all their eggs in one basket. Each village planted its crops—maize, beans, squash, and cotton—in three or four locations, chosen so that whatever the pattern of their climate in a given year, it could not affect all locations equally. In a year when rains were especially torrential, crops planted at the bottoms of gullies might be washed away, but those in a flat sandy area would still come through. In a year of sparse rainfall the crops in the gullies survived; fields in the drier lowlands might be parched beyond help, but those at higher elevations would still receive adequate rainfall. In a wet year the productivity of high or low elevations was reversed. As further protection, many western Pueblo planted early and late crops within about a month. If a late-spring frost ruined the late crop, the early crop would survive (Plog 1978).

Nevertheless, to ensure the success of the strategy they had to plant three times the crops they needed during any one season. One had to expect that only one-third of the crops would be successful in any one year, that crops would generally be successful in only one of every three years, or that the two outcomes would be combined.

In sum, the western Pueblo responded to a high-risk environment by diversifying their planting methods as widely and as ingeniously as they could. They knew that even in a normal year some crops would fail, and they took this factor into account when they devised their strategy. Consequently, despite the vagaries of their climate and their extremely simple technology (digging sticks, wooden shovels, and stone axes), they proved to be quite successful at farming. In good years they stockpiled enough food to last through the next growing season and sometimes the next two—necessary insurance in case of drought. For variety, nutrition, and further drought insurance, they hunted, kept turkeys, gathered small amounts of wild food, and harvested some wild plants that they left to grow undisturbed in the fields.

The Eastern Pueblo

Because of differences in environment and technology, the eastern Pueblo were less subject than the western Pueblo to the vagaries of nature. Both frost and rainfall are more predictable in the eastern region. Soil is richer, retains moisture better, and drains more easily. Valleys are smaller and more enclosed, so that the effect of violent winds is lessened. In all these respects the territory of the eastern Pueblo was more suitable for farming. Most important of all, the eastern groups, unlike those of the west, had a permanent water source: the Rio Grande.

The Rio Grande permitted the eastern Pueblo to regulate the flow of water to their crops through irrigation works. Near the river they cleared their garden plots, sometimes grading them into terraces in order to control the flow

The Rio Grande provided a constant water supply for the eastern Pueblo, enabling them to build permanent and centralized communities. Two of the Pueblo's artistic achievements—architecture and pottery—are visible here. (BUREAU OF INDIAN AFFAIRS)

of water and prevent erosion. Then, at elevations somewhat higher than the fields, they tapped into the river with canals, through which the water flowed downward into the fields. Climatic variation, floods, and insect pests created their own problems for the eastern Pueblo. But, overall, climatic variation was less extreme.

Until the Spaniards arrived, the eastern Pueblo cultivated the same major crops as the western Pueblo. And like the western groups, the eastern groups raised turkeys and did some hunting and gathering. In addition, they traded for buffalo meat and skins with neighboring hunter-gatherers. In general, however, while the western Pueblo poured their energy and ingenuity into diversifying their livelihood, the eastern Pueblo focused their efforts on water control, ditches, terraces, and other such devices. Aside from planting and harvesting, there were dams to build, ditches to maintain, and fields to clear, level, and grade. These substantial chores required the cooperative effort of the entire village. The subsistence strategy of the eastern Pueblo, then, was as concentrated or specialized as that of the western Pueblo was diversified. And this difference is reflected in the social organization of the two groups.

Two Social Patterns

Archaeologists working in the Southwest have shown that the social organization of the Anasazi ancestors of the Pueblo was highly varied. At different times and places, groups were more or less mobile, smaller and larger, more or less stratified. Significant evidence now suggests that before contact with Europeans, larger villages and groups with greater differentials in individual and family wealth and power were more common. These more stratified organizational forms appear to have been destroyed by environmental change and, more important, by the dramatic decline in the population following the arrival of the Spaniards. Thus these people's organizational patterns are less complex than they were in the past. Two are most prominent.

The Western Pueblo

Floodwater farming is a family affair, requiring ingenuity and patience but a relatively small input of labor and no major cooperative effort. The typical western Pueblo village was divided into extended families whose membership was determined by **matrilineal descent**—that is, kinship is traced through the female line. Daughters usually stayed in their mothers' households for life. Sons moved to their brides' households, but they continued to regard their mothers' houses as home and returned to them regularly to participate in rituals. The women and girls of each extended family tended the group's vegetables, prepared the meals, hauled the water, made the baskets and pottery and clothing, and cared for the children. The men and boys farmed and hunted for the family, collected fuel for fires, spun and wove cotton, and tanned leather for clothes. Each family, then, was relatively autonomous with respect to domestic and agricultural responsibilities.

Yet families were far from independent of one another. On the contrary, they were bound together into higher-level social units of equal if not greater significance. These were the **clans,** groups that claimed descent from a common ancestor—in this case a female ancestor—even though they could not trace their descent from her precisely. The clan owned the houses, fields, seeds, and stored food used by its members. More important, religious societies were the property of the clan. The eldest woman of the clan was recognized as its ceremonial head and her household as its religious center. Among one western group, the Hopi, each clan owned the rituals and ritual paraphernalia associated with a particular kachina—an ancestral spirit symbolized by a dancer wearing a distinctive and quite beautiful costume. Membership in kachina societies, however, was drawn from the community at large, regardless of clan affiliation. Individuals chose to join one society or another because they felt a calling or were dedicated to it; for everyone except the clan head, participation was voluntary. This cross-cutting of clan boundaries within the societies had the important function of creating ties between members of different clans. In this way nearly all members of a pueblo were related—if not by clan membership, then by society membership (Thompson 1950:66–70). This arrangement helped to prevent villages from dividing along clan lines under normal conditions.

Religion was central to the lives of the western Pueblo—a fact that may be related to the quality of their environment. Constantly plagued by the uncertainty of the rains, and therefore of their livelihood, they turned to the supernatural to explain and influence nature. Efforts to bring the divine forces over to their side were largely the responsibility of the kachina societies (Dozier 1970). In the kachina ceremonies masked dancers assumed the roles of the supernatural beings, who were petitioned to favor the crops. The western Pueblo believed that if they made these ceremonies as elaborate as possible and if they participated in them in a state of harmony with nature, har-

The late summer harvest is a time for feasting and family reunions. These men and women are performing the corn grinding dance at the western Pueblo of Santa Clara. (JOHN RUNNING/BLACK STAR)

boring no ill feelings toward anyone or anything, the spirits would send them rain. But the job of appeasing the spirits was not left to the kachina society alone. Other societies also petitioned for good weather. Even the medicine societies concerned themselves more with rainmaking than with curing.

Religious societies helped the people adapt to a marginal environment in another way as well. During important rituals, stores of food were brought out and shared among all the participants. As a result, families that had a lean harvest did not go hungry if others had surpluses.

Although the western Pueblo invested considerable time and energy in their religion, leaders of the kachina societies did not exercise control over other aspects of people's lives. They were religious leaders, not chiefs. When they met periodically, they confined their deliberations to ceremonial matters. The western Pueblo had no formal political leaders and no formal means of social control—no laws, judges, or trials. Gossip and ridicule—institutionalized in the so-called clown cult, which mocked deviants—kept most people in line.

The weakness of large-scale political integration and the strength of the clans were probably responses to a highly variable and unpredictable resource base. If times grew hard, a clan could simply break off from the village to seek its fortune elsewhere. Since government, religion, property, and community affairs were already organized around this social unit, the clan provided the ready-made core of a new village.

The Eastern Pueblo

As we have just seen, many aspects of western Pueblo social organization can be interpreted as a response to the unpredictability of their livelihood. The eastern Pueblos life was not so unpredictable; their irrigation works ensured a relatively stable harvest from year to year. But the irrigation works posed other problems. Above all, they encouraged the development of centralized authority. In many areas large labor forces had to be mobilized. Furthermore, decisions had to be made that would affect the entire community and require its cooperation: how was the water to be allocated? who would build and maintain the canals? and so forth. This situation worked against a social organization based on strong, independent clans. If the clans tried to work separately, the efficiency of the irrigation system would be reduced. The social organization that arose among the eastern Pueblo, in fact, was the reverse of the western Pueblo's: relatively weak subvillage social units united under a strong, centralized political leadership. This tendency was augmented by closer contact with Spanish colonizers than was characteristic among the western Pueblo. The Spaniards imposed a system of village leaders.

The eastern Pueblo tended to concentrate domestic and agricultural responsibilities in the nuclear family. In some areas they shifted from a matrilineal to a patrilineal kinship system. Thus the bedrock of organization, the matrilineal extended family, gave way; the clans became less and less important in eastern Pueblo society.

As the clans dwindled in significance, the societies became more important. The function of the eastern Pueblo societies was as much secular as sacred. Because of the security that the eastern Pueblo derived from their irrigation works, they did not petition the spirits continually to water their crops. Their religious ceremonies were aimed more at persuading the spirits to send them health and well-being. But it was their nonreligious functions that made the cults significant. They took over the administrative powers that in the west belonged to the clans.

When society leaders of the eastern Pueblo met, it was not only to arrange religious activities but also to organize war ceremonies and to coordinate communal hunts, planting and harvesting, work on the irrigation system, and maintenance of the kivas. Hence power came to rest in the society leaders. Together they made the community decisions and provided its leadership.

A formal system that divided the community into moieties arose. **Moiety,** which originally meant one of two equal portions, is used by anthropologists to refer to one of the two subdivisions of a society with a dual organizational structure. Every individual in an eastern Pueblo community was a member of one of two groups, each of which ruled the settlement for half of the year. Membership in an eastern Pueblo society was optional, but obedience to the societies' leaders was not. Medicine men,

backed by war chiefs, exercised considerable influence—in some cases great power—over the eastern Pueblo. A family that could not discipline one of its members turned to these big men. Not infrequently a group that disagreed with the medicine men's views was simply expelled from the pueblo and their holdings confiscated.

Thus whereas power was diffused among clans and families in the western groups, in the eastern groups it was centralized in highly structured, quasi-religious associations, with authority over the entire village. In fact, the village was the basic unit of eastern Pueblo society; all other social units—the family, the kin group, the clan—were subordinated to the needs of the community as a whole.

Summary

Horticultural societies depend on *domesticated* foods, especially plants; that is, people try to control the reproduction rates of their food resources by ordering the environment in such a way as to favor their survival. Human labor and simple tools are the primary means of working the land, and horticulturists do not produce consistently large surpluses for others' consumption. Their subsistence economies make both the group and the individual household largely self-sufficient and independent. Yet trade with neighboring groups is an important feature of their survival strategy and is integrated with their agricultural activities, as are some hunting and gathering.

Since contemporary horticultural societies generally occupy marginal territories and do not use major technological aids, they have developed a variety of techniques to exploit their environment. The most common technique is *slash-and-burn* (or swidden) *agriculture.* Trees and undergrowth are cut and burned to form a layer of fertilizing ash. Several varieties of

plants are cultivated for several years, then the area is left to lie fallow and new land is cleared. The success of swidden agriculture, and of horticulture in general, depends on intimate knowledge of the environment.

Horticulturists can support more people per unit of land area than can hunters and gatherers, but in comparison with other agriculturalists, they operate on a low energy budget. They do not have to use their resources or labor to the fullest in order to subsist. Their impact on their environment is minimal.

Among the social conditions that normally accompany a dependence on agriculture are increased *sedentism*—the practice of establishing a permanent, year-round settlement—and increased population density. These conditions tend to increase social complexity and interdependence.

The household is the basic unit in horticultural societies; the integration of families into a community is achieved primarily through kinship ties and political organization. Kinship networks are often the basis for both recognition of individual rights to the use of land and extensive gift exchange throughout the community.

Relations with other communities may be peaceable or warlike, or somewhere in between. Trade, alliances, and intermarriage foster peaceful relations, while competition for resources, raids, and exploitation provide excuses for war.

The two horticultural societies discussed in this chapter are the Yąnomamö of Venezuela and Brazil and the Pueblo Indians of the American Southwest. As the two peoples inhabit different environments, their adaptations have taken different forms.

The Yąnomamö hunt and gather in addition to practicing swidden agriculture in their dense tropical jungle. Authority in their villages rests with the headman, who leads by example rather than by institutionalized power. Kinship is reckoned by *patrilineal descent*, or through the male line, and a typical village consists of two lineages that have intermarried. Strict marriage rules specify that a man choose a wife outside his lineage.

Villages normally move every few years, mostly because of internal feuds or warfare with other villages. The Yąnomamö social world is one of chronic suspicion and hostility. Political alliances are cautiously negotiated by the exchange of gifts, followed by trading, feasting, and exchange of brides. But even alliances based on marriage ties are tenuous.

Some anthropologists attribute the hostile social environment to a shortage of sources of protein. Marvin Harris believes that Yąnomamö warfare is concerned, unwittingly, with hunting territory, and Daniel Gross holds that the settlement pattern—widely dispersed mobile villages—is a strategy for preventing the over-exploitation of game in any one area. Yet Napoleon Chagnon, who has studied the Yąnomamö longer and more intensively than anyone else, finds no evidence of protein deficiency among them. Chagnon attributes their bellicosity to intense competition for women, caused by their practice of female infanticide and the custom of powerful men to take more than one wife.

The subsistence strategies of the Pueblo Indians fall into two basic patterns. The eastern Pueblo adaptation is based on irrigation works. Because of their relatively stable environment and permanent water source (the Rio Grande), the eastern Pueblo were able to concentrate their efforts on the use of irrigation and terracing. The western Pueblo adaptation is based on the simpler technique of *floodwater farming*, or the practice of planting in areas that are flooded in the rainy season, so that the floodwaters provide natural irrigation. To compensate for the vagaries of their climate, the western Pueblo diversified their planting methods as widely and as ingeniously as possible. The basic features of these adaptations survive today, despite the Spanish conquest and the encroaching industrial economy of the United States.

Different subsistence techniques led to different social organizations. The floodwater farming of the western Pueblo is associated with extended family work groups, *matrilineal descent* (kinship is traced through the female line) and *clans*, and kachina societies that are ceremonial in purpose and focused on rain-making. The strength of both the kachina societies and the clans may be attributed to the uncertain environment. The religious societies represent attempts to influence nature through supernatural means; the clans provide the nucleus of a new village if a move is necessitated by a lack of resources.

The irrigation works of the eastern Pueblo required large forces, central authority, and cooperation. In response to these needs, the eastern group developed strong political leadership, a shift toward *patrilineal* kinship, and societies that dealt with both religious and secular concerns and took on administrative responsibilities. Each community came to be formed into *moieties*, or two subdivisions, each of which ruled the settlement for half of the year.

The invasion of the Spaniards intensified the contrasts between the eastern and western Pueblo. The western Pueblo were protected by their harsh environment from the full onslaught of the invaders, but the eastern Pueblo were more thoroughly exposed to Spanish culture. They became more technologically sophisticated and their villages more centralized as a result of Spanish influence. The contrast between the eastern and western Pueblo, products of differing physical and social environments, continues today.

Key Terms

clan
domestication
floodwater farming

matrilineal descent
moiety

patrilineal descent
sedentism

slash-and-burn
(swidden)
agriculture

Suggested Readings

CHAGNON, N. 1983. *Yąnomamö: The Fierce People*. 3d ed. New York: Holt, Rinehart and Winston. An account of fieldwork among one of the largest unacculturated tribes left in South America.

KELLY, R. C. 1976. *Etoro Social Structure: A Study in Structural Contradiction*. Ann Arbor, Mich.: University of Michigan Press. A general ethnography of a horticultural people, with a strong emphasis on concepts of social structure, religion, and ideology.

SAHLINS, M. 1968. *Tribesmen*. Englewood Cliffs, N.J.: Prentice-Hall. A now-classic discussion of the economic arrangements, social structure, and ideologies of tribal societies, most of which are horticulturists.

VAYDA, A. P. (ED.). 1968. *Peoples and Cultures of the Pacific*. New York: Natural History Press. The societies of the Pacific islands number some four million people, and historically much of this population has engaged in horticulture. This collection of twenty-four articles is an excellent introduction to the many peoples of the Pacific.

WERNER, D. 1984. *Amazon Journey: An Anthropologist's Year among Brazil's Mekranoti Indians*. New York: Simon & Schuster. An informal and sympathetic portrayal of modern anthropological field data collection and analysis among horticulturists in the rapidly changing Amazon.

WHITELEY, P. M. 1988. *Deliberate Acts: Changing Hopi Culture Through the Oraibi Split*. Tucson, Ariz.: University of Arizona Press. A detailed portrait of the history and social organization of a Hopi village that focuses on social change over a hundred-year period.

Chapter 7 Pastoralism

Pastoralism is **animal husbandry**—the breeding, care, and use of herd animals, such as sheep, goats, camels, cattle, horses, llamas, reindeer, and yaks. This highly specialized strategy of land use resembles hunting and gathering and is complementary to horticulture. Like most hunter-gatherer groups, pastoralists use lands whose vegetation they only minimally manage: they graze their animals on wild grasses and shrubs. Like agricultural populations, pastoralists invest time and energy in the *management* of productive resources—their livestock.

Most pastoralists are nomadic, moving their herds from pasture to pasture on a seasonal schedule within a well-defined territory. The degree of mobility varies from group to group, and even from year to year within a group, depending on such environmental factors as rainfall, vegetation, and the availability of water holes. Economic and political constraints also affect the pattern of nomads' movements. Pastoralists must deal with the demands of other groups, even governments, in order to gain access to pastures and to the markets where they can exchange animals and animal products for clothing, tools, weapons, and food.

There are two basic systems of nomadic movement, despite much variation. One pattern, plains or **horizontal migration,** is characterized by regular movement over a large area in search of forage, a necessary strategy where no particular area is capable of sustaining a herd for a long period of time. The Bedouin of the Arabian Peninsula exemplify this form of nomadism; members of Bedouin tribal groups are dispersed over hundreds of square miles as they make use of the scant vegetation of an extremely arid region. Although they gather in larger encampments around seasonal water holes, the density of population is strikingly low. This pattern has been widespread throughout the cattle- and goat-keeping portions of Africa, the deserts and steppes of Central Asia and the Middle East, and in later times the plains of North and South America.

The second pattern is that of seasonal movement of livestock between upland and lowland pastures, or **transhumance.** This form of nomadism has been found throughout the mountainous zones of the Middle East, parts of Eastern Europe, Switzerland, Central Asia, and in later times North and South America. Transhumant nomads often camp together for extended periods of time in two major grazing areas: summer pastures in the mountains and winter pastures in the valleys. During the migrations between seasonal encampments the roads and trails are crowded with people and animals on the move.

The extent of **specialized pastoralism,** the adaptive strategy of exclusive reliance on animal husbandry, varies with environmental and market conditions. Few groups rely exclusively on their herds for day-to-day subsistence. To do so would entail heavy risks in two respects. In order to keep their animals alive, pastoralists have to adjust to the vagaries of the environment—cold, lack of water, lack of pasturage, and so forth. At the same time they must deal with the existence of other groups with whom they may be in competition. Given these complications, it is no surprise that when the environment permits, pastoralists tend to pursue a more generalized subsistence strategy, raising at least some crops along with their animals (Salzman 1971, Berleant-Schiller and Shanklin 1983).

Camels in Saudi Arabia are rapidly being replaced by trucks, which have become the primary means of desert transport. Raising camels is no longer profitable, so most are being slaughtered for meat and are not replaced. (WILLIAM STRODE/WOODFIN CAMP & ASSOCIATES)

In fact, most pastoralists, no matter how specialized, subsist more on grains than on animal products. The camel-herding Bedouin of Arabia greatly prize their independence but are now, and always have been, linked by numerous economic and social ties to the larger, sedentary society. Even before the coming of trucks, camps in Arabia were regularly visited by merchants laden with wares to trade for camels. The merchants would set up shop in distinctive white tents (in contrast to the black tents of the nomads) and it was a breach of the codes regulating warfare to rob or harm these visitors, so important were they to the well-being of the pastoral community. Today, of course, most, if not all, Bedouin households have trucks or jeeps and can drive to the nearest town to shop.

Before we take a close look at two pastoral societies, let us see how pastoralism developed and what its social consequences are for groups that pursue it.

THE DEVELOPMENT OF PASTORALISM

The archaeological record indicates that mixed farming based on a combination of domesticated plants and animals preceded specialized pastoralism (Redman 1978). Mixed farming was a multifaceted strategy that provided a hedge against droughts, crop failures, diseases, and other natural calamities. For farmers, livestock not only provided valuable material (skins for clothing and shelter) and food products, but the animals themselves were a means of storing food against future use, a freezer on the hoof. At the same time, if the animals died, the crops were there. Diversification provided both the alternatives and the reserves necessary to survive fluctuations of food supply. Such diversification is still common in many parts of Africa, Europe, and the Middle East, particularly in mountain villages.

Despite the many advantages of diversification, changes in agricultural practices, especially the development of canal irrigation, created the preconditions for specialized pastoralism. Increased productivity, based on canal irrigation, made possible population growth and the expansion of settlements, with a consequent increase in land devoted to intensive farming and a decrease in land available for animals. It also stimulated interregional trade. Grazing areas were pushed farther from the settlement region into territory where forage was not so lush. To get adequate food and water for their herds, animal owners had to expend more labor and travel greater and greater distances. Furthermore, the animals were more vulnerable to predators and especially to raiders. Thus care of the animals began to drain energies away from agriculture. At the same time, agriculture became more time-consuming, for farmers now had to clear, tend, and repair the canals in addition to working the fields. The increased demand of each of these strategies may well have led to a divergence, with certain households specializing in increasingly intensive agriculture and others concentrating on animal husbandry or pastoralism.

Another factor in the divergence of strategies may have been the failure of canal irrigation for some groups. The technique had its drawbacks and limitations. Extensive irrigation systems may no longer be effective after a time. The **water table** (that is, the level of water under the earth) may drop, so that wells and canals run dry. Or the water may so increase the salinity of the soil that crops begin to fail. Canals were also built in areas where stream flow proved marginal; some agriculturalists who occupied poorer lands had incentives to concentrate their attention on animal husbandry. Eventually the differences in strategies between the farming and herding groups led to spatial and cultural differentiation as well, creating distinct groups of pastoralists and agriculturalists.

The Organization of Energy

Like horticulture, pastoralism is more productive than hunting and gathering. Hunters do not try to increase the numbers of animals or use the products of animals still living. They may, as we have noted, hunt in a conservative fashion in an effort not to eliminate their prey altogether, but they do not invest in animal management. Pastoralists do invest labor in breeding and caring for their animals and so increase their reproduction and survival rates. Tim Ingold notes that apart from reindeer herders, pastoralists are usually concerned with the production of milk, hair, blood, or wool and with traction, using animals as vehicles or sources of work energy (1980:87). Meat production is almost incidental with one or two notable exceptions. By investing human labor in the production of milk rather than meat, the herder gains a greater net return. The animal need not be killed to be useful. In fact, successful herders can generally increase their holdings at a faster rate than farmers, for as the animals reproduce, the offspring can be incorporated into their herds. Of course, this advantage is partially offset by the precarious nature of herding in most areas: animals are susceptible to disease, drought, and theft, any

Interdisciplinary Research in Action: The South Turkana Ecosystem Project

The South Turkana Ecosystem Project is a collaborative effort of scientists from universities in Kenya and the United States, with research interests as diverse as human genetics, demography, rangeland management, plant ecology, nutrition, and ethnology. About half of the scientists are anthropologists, many affiliated with the State University of New York at Binghamton. During the nine years the project has been in operation, many of the scientists have been graduate students.

The lands of the Turkana are subject to extremes of temperature; daytime highs average 87 to 100°F (35–37°C) and highly erratic rainfall varies from 5.8 to 19.5 inches (150–500 millimeters) a year. This low and variable rainfall, combined with intense solar radiation flux, results in a short growing season, and farming is limited. Most of the Turkana people of northwestern Kenya, a population of 150,000 to 200,000 distributed among a series of tribes and subtribes, exploit this region by "nomadic movements of their polygynous family settlements and the five species of livestock that they herd—camels, zebu cattle, goats, sheep, and donkeys. Home settlements will move, on the average, one or more times each month" (Little 1988:697). The Turkana live almost entirely on the products of their animals, and starvation is a constant specter.

As part of the project one study conducted by rangeland ecology specialists and ethnographers (Coughenour et al. 1985) addresses a key issue in the study of pastoral adaptations to extremely arid lands: how do these people maintain enough animals to sustain themselves without degrading their habitat? Using detailed measurements of energy expenditures, the researchers were able to map plant–animal–human food pathways. They not only studied animal requirements but also measured ground cover and the diets of a sample of nomadic households. They found that the Turkana derived 92 percent of their food energy from animal products—meat, milk, and blood—and from maize meal, sugar, and other foods that they acquired by bartering animal products. Though their animals produce less milk and meat than American and Australian breeds, they are more resistant to disease, heat, and drought-related stress. The Turkana can maintain an adequate diet and keep a critical reserve to face unexpected losses without degrading their rangelands because of two factors: (1) the number of animals they can keep is limited by the availability of water holes, and (2) they manage a mix of five species, each with its unique productive qualities. When milk from the cow fails, they turn to their camels; when meat is needed, they can kill small animals, such as sheep or goats. Cattle that do not produce milk provide blood, which is nutritionally rich. The livestock is often scrawny by European standards, but if the rains bring a bumper crop of vegetation, the animals put on weight rapidly and the fertility rate goes up.

Another study sheds light on the role of blood as human food in such a system (Dyson-Hudson and Dyson-Hudson 1982). Turkana cows yield only one-tenth the milk of well-fed American Holsteins, but their blood is a more efficient source of energy than meat (which involves much waste and of course requires the slaughter of the animals). Twenty-one pints (9.9 liters) of blood are taken from each thousand-pound steer every four to six months; lesser amounts are taken from breeding stock and smaller animals. The use of blood in the diet greatly enhances the herd's productivity, particularly because it can supplement the diet during

of which can reduce a rich household to poverty overnight.

Full-time pastoralism may be less efficient than farming in areas where cultivation is possible. People can produce approximately ten times as much food, measured in calories yielded per acre of land, by raising grains instead of livestock. But in areas where agricul-

the season when cows are not producing milk.

Among the people themselves, Paul Leslie and Peggy Fry (1989) found extreme seasonality in births, with more than half falling between March and June. The rate of conception, then, is highest during the early dry season (July through September), when the food supply has been at its peak for some time. The Turkana claim not to time their children's birth (as some African populations do) and attribute the seasonality of births to the separation of spouses during the pastoral cycle, high temperatures that inhibit coitus, and other factors. Whatever the reason, the human population closely tracks the environmental fluctuations.

In yet another study, three researchers (Little, Galvin, and Leslie 1988) examined the Turkana's health in an effort to determine the effects of a diet as high in fat as theirs, based as it is on milk, blood, and meat. Blood pressure is lower among all age groups than in a comparable American population, cardiovascular disease is rare, and general nutritional status is good, though the eye infections common to the area are prevalent. One of the researchers, Kathleen Galvin (1988), used project data to explore variation in the Turkana's nutritional status from season to season and according to food availability. She found that the nutritional status of a population at risk may be evaluated by means of dietary, ecological, and anthropometric measures of body fat and robustness: mid-arm circumference and skinfold thickness. She cautions against reliance on any one measure, particularly when little body fat is normally present in the population. Her findings, like those of the other participants in the project, have a significance far beyond the Turkana ecosystem.

These plus other completed and ongoing studies of the Turkana Ecosystem Project not only contribute to a much fuller understanding of the Turkana people and their ecosystems, but they also have a wider significance for pastoral, ecological, and medical research.

Masai pastoralists also use the blood of their cattle as a part of their diet, which allows them to utilize the animal's protein without having to kill it. (M.A. MAC-KENZIE/ROBERT HARDING ASSOCIATES)

ture is risky or impossible, pastoralism is a useful strategy for converting forage—sources of energy that humans cannot use directly—into milk, blood, and meat. These foods are stored in the form of animals until the people need them either to eat or to trade for agricultural foods, clothing, and other items they cannot otherwise obtain. Furthermore, the fact that animals can move themselves permits herders to move the production system to the resources. Pastoralism is a relatively efficient way of extracting energy from an environment not suited to agriculture. But since it produces much less food energy per acre of land than agriculture, specialized pastoralists necessarily have low population densities.

Pastoralism, then, may have developed hand in hand with intensive agriculture. Whatever the reasons for its development, pastoralism is a strategy predicated on agricultural surplus and on regular interaction between herders and farmers. Pastoralism may be an alternative to agriculture, but it is almost never independent of it.

Settlement Pattern and Mobility

In nonindustrial societies, **sedentary pastoralism,** or animal husbandry that does not involve mobility—ranching, say, or dairy farming—is relatively rare. The practice more generally followed is **nomadic pastoralism,** the adaptive strategy of moving the herds that are one's livelihood from pasture to pasture as the seasons and circumstances require. Land that is rich enough to support a herd indefinitely in one location will yield far more output if it is given over primarily to crops. By taking advantage of the mobility of herd animals and their own ability to group and regroup, however, pastoralists can adapt to marginal areas by moving as conditions dictate. Mobility is the key that unlocks widely dispersed resources and allows a population to gain a living from an environment that could not sustain a settled community.

While the main reason for pastoralist migrations is to secure adequate grazing on a year-round basis, this is not the only reason. William Irons (1975) has pointed out that the Turkoman pastoralists of northern Iran move more than is necessary if they were seeking nothing but grasslands. They also move to maintain their political and cultural independence. In the past, they also frequently raided non-Turkoman sedentary populations and caravans. If they were pursued by a more powerful force, they could simply disperse with their animals into inaccessible areas. Though they were "pacified" by the Iranian government in the early twentieth century, they have managed until recently to retain considerable control over their own affairs. They did so by using the one skill they had developed far beyond the abilities of other populations: moving.

Today, even within the boundaries of contemporary state bureaucratic systems, mobility often allows nomadic pastoralists to maintain greater political autonomy than settled communities enjoy. Today, in the context of political uncertainty in Iran, both nomadic and settled Turkomans are reasserting their claim to a separate identity, and the nomadic groups are apparently the more successful in their efforts. In other countries, nomads may be able to avoid onerous civic duties, such as military conscription and taxation.

Social Organization

There is no single form of social organization that is peculiar to nomadic pastoralists; such adaptations occur in varied environmental, political, and cultural contexts. The social life of Lapp reindeer herders may closely resemble that of neighboring Finnish communities. The Bedouin of Arabia may be culturally similar to tribal villagers in Iraq. Still, most researchers who have studied or worked with nomadic pastoral societies see certain aspects of social organization related either to the necessity (or capacity) for mobility or to the requirements of the animals they tend.

Virtually all nomadic pastoralists are organized in tribes, sociopolitical communities whose members are bound by ties of kinship, most commonly by presumed descent from one or more common ancestors. Such groupings can easily encompass many thousands of individuals through the expedient of recognizing subgroups defined by degree of kinship—clans, lineages, even large family clusters. Such groupings (which will be more precisely characterized in Chapter 13) do not depend on a definition of community that rests mainly on residence in a territory or locality; a member of one's tribe is a relative.

A member of the cattle-keeping Nuer tribe in Sudan, described by E. E. Evans-Pritchard (1940), is a Nuer wherever he or she may happen to be. Every Nuer is also a member by birthright of one of a series of "segments" or genealogical parts of the tribe, each having a distinctive name, not unlike a family name in our own society. Each segment of the Nuer tribal system is supposed to assist the others largely in accordance with the closeness of the presumed relationship between them. This "segmentary" lineage system, widespread in Africa and the Middle East, provides a highly flexible means of adapting group size to the resources at hand. Groups come together or split up along lines of kinship. Though not all or even most tribal societies are pastoralists, most nomadic pastoralists are organized in tribes of one sort or another.

Individuals and households in herding societies frequently change their patterns of movement and the groups with which they camp. They move in response to changing economic and political conditions and also to new social circumstances. Individual households camp with people with whom they enjoy good relations, and such people are most often kin. There appear to be strong constraints on the number of households that can readily coordinate their activities in an egalitarian society that lacks strong leadership roles. Two observers have noted considerable uniformity in the average size of nomadic camps or migratory groups—usually in the range of 100 to 300

persons (Tapper 1979:81, Johnson 1983:176).

When Gregory Johnson examined a large number of nomadic societies whose people lived together by choice rather than by coercion, he found that a camp group comprised on average six households or clusters of very closely related households, such as father-son groupings (1983:183). If conflict were to occur in the camp group, often the easiest solution was for the antagonists simply to move apart. In many respects the shifting composition of nomadic camping-and-herding groups resembles the camps of nomadic hunter-gatherers. People use mobility to minimize conflict and to associate with those they find congenial.

In most pastoral societies it is possible to speak of the co-resident household, a grouping whose members often dwell in tents as a basic economic unit and coordinate their herding and other productive activities. In a society in which groups move frequently and the composition of larger groupings changes regularly, the household takes on added social significance—particularly, Ingold contends (1980:188–189), when market relations engender competition. The household, like the camping group of which it is a part, must respond to changing economic circumstances—sometimes by an increase in size, sometimes by dispersal into smaller households.

While pastoralists' camp groups may resemble those of hunter-gatherers, most such societies have a more complex sociopolitical organization that unites the constituent households and camping groups in tribes. Some nomadic tribes, such as the Bedouin of Arabia and the Mongols of Central Asia, have strong leaders. Undoubtedly the existence of such roles reflects the fact that these peoples were in close contact, even regular conflict, with agricultural communities and lived within the boundaries of nation-states. The Qashqa'i of Iran, for example, have an elaborate hierarchy of leaders, each part of a fairly well-defined chain of command (Beck 1986).

A hierarchical tribal organization often has highly specified membership criteria (as by patrilineal or matrilineal descent) and is composed of well-defined subgroups. Such an organization allows for more than just communication across great distances. It is a means of coordinating large-scale migrations, gaining access to grazing land, holding and defending territory, and even on occasion gaining control over sedentary farming populations.

However we may think of nomadic pastoralists, we should not fall into the trap of perceiving them as inflexibly committed to a single way of life. As the anthropologist James Downs (1965) notes, "a pastoralist is no more anxious to move than is a farmer if he can maintain his herds while remaining in the same place." Nomadism is a strategy, a means of making specialized animal husbandry work. If it fails, nomads settle and pursue other livelihoods.

Consider a group of Navajo sheep herders called the Broken Foot outfit which consisted of an extended family made up of an elderly woman, her two middle-aged daughters, their husbands, and their children and grandchildren—about fifty people in all. Normally an outfit will fragment after its membership reaches about thirty, but the Broken Foot outfit stayed together because a dam on their land provided them with an abundant supply of water. The members of the outfit were constructing a relatively permanent homestead near the dam, and they lived there year-round except for brief migrations during the coldest part of the winter. The dam made their herding much easier than it had been when they had to search for water. Despite the outfit's size, tasks were handled cooperatively, and the members of the outfit themselves said that the dam was a major reason for their closeness.

The dam affected their relations with their neighbors as well. Because the outfit obtained all the water they needed from the dam, they never had to compete with others for this resource. Thus there was little tension between Broken Foot and other outfits. In fact, although the Broken Foot people considered themselves to be the owners of the water, they distributed it to anyone who wanted it.

Then came several years of serious drought. As the level of the water behind the dam began to fall, the Broken Foot outfit began to restrict its use, and some tense confrontations with neighbors ensued. Finally the members of the outfit forbade access to the dam altogether. Soon the water was not adequate even for their own needs, and they had to look elsewhere. Once a major distributor of this valuable commodity, they again had to compete with other groups. Their herding practices changed. To see that their animals were properly watered, members of the outfit had to be out all day with their herds. In the end this strategy did not work either, and they had to move their flocks temporarily to the land of a relative.

Meanwhile, tension within the outfit began to reach an intolerable level, and the family broke into two separate units. During the move to the relative's land they were still able to work constructively together from time to time and they never broke off all ties with each other, but essentially they had become two outfits. The homestead was dispersed and the people pursued different strategies.

The experience of the Broken Foot outfit illustrates several important points. It shows that a group can be more or less nomadic depending on conditions. It also demonstrates that people can organize themselves into sizable groups and stay together for extended periods when they gain advantages from that strategy. But they will work separately when that approach is more productive. Although we often speak of "group cohesiveness," "corporateness," and "economic stratification" as characteristics of a society, we should not lose sight of their ultimate origins in individual motivation. What we see as patterns of social organization are the outcomes of the strategies individuals adopt as they cope with their problems and evaluate their opportunities.

Livestock and Equality

The economic strategies of individual households within a given population of pastoralists often vary considerably. Such variations are sketched very clearly in the ever-changing composition of the camp group and in individual decisions on migration. Some individuals among the Navajo and the Pokot of Kenya, for example, may move frequently one year and be largely sedentary the next. Regular patterns often underlie this variability. In Turkey, Yörük households with many animals may move early in the spring to pastures in the mountains, braving cold weather to get to the first grasses. Others with smaller flocks may feel they cannot afford the risk of losing even a few animals to the cold, and so move later in the season.

In most instances, rights to animals are held by individual households. Some are better able to manage their productive capital than others, some may inherit more than others, and some may be reduced by disease, theft, or just bad luck. It is probably safe to say that distinctions of wealth are more evident among pastoral populations than among the horticulturists we discussed in Chapter 6. Among the Komanchi sheep herders of Iran, for example, Daniel Bradburd (1984) found not only great disparities of wealth among households but also systematic exploitation of poorer households by wealthy ones. Such disparities are reflected in marriage arrangements and in many other areas of social life; the poorer households have a limited opportunity to improve their lot (Bradburd 1984). This case may be extreme, but economic differentiation among households is common.

Nomadic Settlement

When we examine a pastoral population we often see families giving up herding altogether for other pursuits. This is what families in the Middle East tend to do when they have accumulated enough wealth to invest in a more secure form of capital, such as land or a shop, or when their herds have become so small that they can no longer support the household. In many regions settlement followed by a return to herding is a regular process (Salzman 1980). Agricultural households may shift to herding if they consider it advantageous to do so. Thus most of the people described as pastoralists have strong cultural ties in sedentary communities, and usually have relatives there as well.

We shall consider two groups of pastoralists, each with a distinctive adaptive pattern. The first group, the Pokot of East Africa, are farming pastoralists. The Pokot are among the African tribes for whom cattle are economically and culturally important. Yet they eat meat only occasionally. Milk, blood, and a porridge made of sorghum and other grains form the basis of a diet won from a harsh and unpredictable environment. The Pokot exchange very little with other groups, although they do take advantage of market or trade opportunities when they arise.

The second group, the Yörük of Turkey, raise their herds for the purpose of exchange with other groups. Traditionally the Yörük cultivated no crops, preferring to use the income from their stock to buy grain and other foodstuffs from the agriculturalists of their region. Nor did they have permanent settlements; they moved regularly and on a tight schedule in order to get adequate pasturage. Economic factors have caused them to change their pattern somewhat in recent years, however, and the majority now live in towns and villages.

THE POKOT OF KENYA

The Pokot of Kenya probably number some 200,000 persons if one includes the speakers of slightly different dialects of Pokot in western and northwestern Kenya. West Pokot District alone probably has about 100,000 persons, of whom about 75,000 are farmers and 25,000 are herders. Although farmers outnumber herders 3 to 1, a herding ethic predominates throughout the area (as in many other parts of East Africa), and cattle have a paramount and pervasive symbolic value. Melville Herskovits (1924) long ago identified this focus on cattle

This prize ox will have his horns cracked at their base and reshaped according to Pokot aesthetics. (KENNETH MALLORY/ANTHRO-PHOTO)

as the "East African **cattle complex**"—a socioeconomic system in which cattle represent social status as well as wealth. One feature of the cattle complex, Herskovits noted, was that cattle were raised in far greater numbers than anyone (apparently) could hope to use. Thus the role of cattle seemed to be less economic than symbolic. Early investigators were not aware of the rationale for the East Africans' subsistence strategy.

The essence of this strategy is the simultaneous exploitation of more than one environment. The great numbers of cattle involved allow the herds to be divided and dispersed over a wide area. This is a kind of insurance against loss of all one's cattle in one place to raiders from a neighboring group or to disease. Perhaps because of the symbolic importance of cattle (in ritual, dance, marriage, and other as-

pects of social relations), early observers also tended to overlook the fact that the herds of most East African pastoralists were *mixed*, and included not only zebu (oxen distinguished by a hump, much like a camel's, on the back) but also large numbers of goats, sometimes sheep, donkeys, and, in very dry areas, camels. The importance of the mixed herd lies in the fact that each species has its own feeding preferences; thus not one but several environments are exploited.

The Pokot Setting

The Pokot exploit a complex terrain with a wide variety of settings. Within West Pokot District alone, elevations range from over 11,000 feet to barely 2,000 feet above sea level. The escarpment that marks the eastern branch of the Great Rift Valley runs south to north through the center of the district. The top of the escarpment is cold and mountainous; at the bottom of the escarpment are plains with semi-desert to desert conditions. In the southern part of the district, high on the escarpment, rainfall can reach 40 to 60 inches a year; on the lowland plains, which occupy much of the northern part of the district, rainfall reaches at most 15 inches a year. The complexity of the terrain and the variety of potentials it offers provide the key to the subsistence strategy not only of the Pokot but of many other East African peoples. Wherever and whenever possible, more than one environment is exploited.

The Pokot's world is divided into high, cold areas, midslope elevations, and hot, lowland plains. Most Pokot live in the midslope areas, where, as farmers, they can strike uphill to take advantage of the rich soils in the forested areas of higher rainfall and downhill to exploit the areas of lighter soils and warmer temperatures. At midslope elevations the Pokot have combined a form of shifting cultivation (quite small

fields used for a short time only, then left to lie fallow) with much larger communal fields watered in part by rainfall and in part by irrigation ditches and bamboo pipes. The staple crops grown in these areas include a variety of grains, especially millet, sorghum, and maize.

Though some livestock are kept in the *masob* —the high, cold country—the cattle and wool-bearing sheep found at the higher elevations have been introduced relatively recently and are not plentiful. By far the greatest number of livestock are found on the lowland plains. Pokot herding families rely on mixed herds: camels, donkeys, and goats in the northern, very dry area; cattle, donkeys, and goats in the semiarid parts of the plains. The smaller stock (primarily goats but also some sheep) commonly outnumber the larger animals 5 to 1. The plains-dwelling Pokot do some cultivation as well, especially in lowland areas subject to periodic flooding. They obtain the greater part of their grain, however, by trading with kin in the farming areas.

The Pokot Community and Social Organization

The basic unit of Pokot social organization is the neighborhood, referred to as *korok* (Conant 1965). The physical aspect of the korok reflects the terrain in which it is found. In the upland regions, for example, the korok is generally a wedge-shaped part of an escarpment or mountainside, with the narrower part of the wedge at the higher elevation. Streams commonly mark the lateral borders of the korok. On the plains the korok is still partitioned by streams or rivers (which often flow only intermittently) but the slope is so gradual that to the unpracticed eye "uphill" may be barely distinguishable from "downhill." Some koroks are so placed as to include the forests at high elevations and grasslands at their lower limits.

The korok consists of a number of households (sometimes as many as 100 but more commonly about 50), spaced well apart. In a farming area each household is surrounded by fields under cultivation or lying fallow. In a herding area each household is surrounded by a corral (kraal) for the livestock and separated from its neighbors by stretches of land dotted by bushes and shrubs. The korok of either a farming or a herding area is regulated by a council made up of the heads of the resident households. Though the head of a household may be a woman, the representatives sent to the council are always men. The neighborhood council meets when anyone wants to call a meeting.

The council reaches its decisions by consensus. If someone persists in arguing a point after the others have said all they intend to say, they turn their backs to the speaker. Members of the council, who nominate one of their number as *kirwokiin*, or "big talker," have broad powers to recruit labor, levy fines, and mediate disputes.

In farming areas labor is generally recruited for construction and repair of fencing around communal fields and digging of new irrigation ditches. In herding areas there is less need for communal labor except in the dry season, when wells are dug sometimes fifty or sixty feet deep in sandy riverbeds to tap the underground water table. Neighboring koroks in herding areas often combine their forces to construct a common well.

Fines are levied for failure to comply with the council's decisions and for infractions of customary laws. Almost always the fines are levied in livestock, commonly goats. Only a few of the animals seized in this way are turned over to the aggrieved party; the greater number are slaughtered, roasted, and eaten by members of the council and their families. In effect the transgressors pay for their behavior by feasting the entire neighborhood.

Serious cases involving members of other koroks are discussed first separately and then at a meeting of combined councils. The complaints most commonly heard in both farming and herding areas involve marriage transactions. Accusations of adultery are common; so are cases of theft and wife abuse.

The koroks in farming and herding areas differ in several respects. Membership in a korok is a long-term affair for farmers, sometimes spanning many generations, whereas a herders' korok is a kaleidoscope of shifting membership. A korok in a herding area may dissolve after a single season; if it endures for a longer period, its membership is rarely completely duplicated from one season to the next.

Members of farming households are almost always close kin. Sons locate near their father, or if further land division is impossible, they open up new farming areas. Daughters marry out of the korok in which they are born. In effect a farming korok is inhabited by representatives of one or two localized clans. Households in herding koroks belong to many dispersed kin groups. Pokot kinship is reckoned by descent through the paternal line. Since members of farming families (especially younger men and women) often migrate to the plains and either found or join existing herding households, the kinship system also integrates farming and herding households. About 15 percent of the wives now in herding areas were born in farming households. Marriage among both farmers and herders is more a matter of a contract between households than a love match between individuals. The contract calls for the payment of **bridewealth;** that is, property given by the family of the groom to the family of the bride to compensate them for the loss of their daughter's services. Among Pokot herders, bridewealth takes the form of cattle; the number of animals to be given is determined by negotiation. Bridewealth is almost always delivered in three installments, one at the beginning of the marriage, one at the birth of the couple's first child, and the last at the birth of the second. Marriage is a process to the Pokot; it begins with betrothal and is considered complete only when the second surviving child is walking and talking. Since infant mortality among traditional Pokot can be as high as 30 or 40 percent and the mortality of women in their reproductive years may be as much as 5 percent, it is evident that the custom of paying bridewealth in installments is a safeguard against the possible failure of the new household unit to mature and grow. Although bridewealth is described in terms of cattle, the actual transaction among herders almost always involves a mix of cattle and goats, and among farmers it may involve no animals at all but equivalent amounts of grain, blankets, beer, and sometimes money. Marriage and the ties it creates are the primary means by which the Pokot exchange the surplus of their fields (grains, mainly) for the surplus of their herds (mainly milk and blood).

Seasonal Movements

Pokot herding households in their search for graze and browse disperse over a large area in the dry months of the year (October through February or March). In the driest months the household breaks up into two quite different units. In one, the base camp, the younger cattle and goats are maintained by older men, women, and children of both sexes. The second unit, stock camp, keeps the mature cattle, often far out on the plains. The stock camp is staffed by young unmarried men and older boys. The stock camp's personnel and their livestock may be drawn from as few as two or three households or as many as a dozen or so. The cattle in the dry-season stock camps are mature animals strong enough to withstand the rigors of being herded to distant grazing areas and to require watering only every three days or so.

The remote cattle camps place the Pokot herders at great risk from raids by neighboring groups, who, much like the Pokot themselves, are always searching for grazing and water resources in a region where both are diminishing.

The neighbors of the Pokot include Turkana, Samburu, Sebei, and Karamojong. The Turkana and Pokot are particular rivals for the use of water and grass. The two peoples may arrange dry-season herding partnerships, but such arrangements seem to break down regularly and lead to raids. It is when the dry season is prolonged that the Pokot (as well as other peoples in the area) construct their wells, best described as "step wells." Every eight feet or so they cut a step into the side of the well, where a person can stand to receive a calabash of water being handed up from below and pass it on to the person on the step above. At the top step the calabash is emptied into a log trough for the cattle. Pokot and Turkana disputes, sometimes resulting in raids on each other's stock camps, seem to arise principally over the use of the step wells.

Although the pattern is highly variable, the end of the dry season is heralded by storms brought about by shifts in the wind patterns over the Indian Ocean. Displays of lightning and local cyclones or dust devils are signs of the impending rains. In some areas the first "little rains" in March may be followed by a month or so of dry weather. Predicting when the little rains will begin is a major concern to the Pokot. The herders often set grass fires at this time, to burn off the dry overburden of the annual grasses, thereby encouraging the growth of new grass. The farmers sow sorghum and maize so that the seeds will sprout during the little rains and mature sufficiently to withstand the onslaught of the major rains.

Pokot herders begin to withdraw from the dry-season camps well before the arrival of the big rains, since from April through September the rains make stream and river beds, dry since October, severe obstacles to travel. The herding households relocate themselves in koroks close to the mountains and the farming areas. Twenty or thirty households may be found within a single korok, but they are not necessarily the same households that gathered there the year before. One of the best predictors of where a herding household will settle during the rains is the location of the farming area with which it has traded in the past. Ties of marriage are important links in these trading relationships. Other considerations, of course, also apply: herding households must locate themselves on higher ground to avoid flooding, and they must have access to nearby graze and browse.

Division of Labor

Household tasks are allocated according to age and gender among the Pokot, and the division of labor starts very early and lasts a lifetime. By age two or three girls and boys are encouraged to participate in symbolic activities that quickly become gender-specific tasks. Girls play at such chores as gathering sticks for fuel, carrying water, milking, and gathering food. Boys play at tending livestock, hunting, making spears and bows and arrows, and being warriors. By the time they reach age four or five, their play has become work. The small amount of water children can carry and the help they can give in managing livestock soon become measurable contributions to a household's energy budget. The children soon add the care of younger children to their tasks. While Pokot women are responsible for their own infants, almost all child care is in the hands of slightly older children and of some elderly men and women. In farm households men are responsible for the initial clearance of forested land, but at every step in this process women are at work also. Men are also primarily responsible for digging irrigation ditches and maintaining them, but here again women join in the work.

The women of Pokot herding households manage the goats, which browse on thornbush and shrubs, while men manage the cattle, which require more open, grassy areas. Because women tend goats, they not only widen the resource base to include shrubland but also keep the thornbush from spreading at the expense of grass. In many of the drier parts of East Africa, thorn shrubs and trees of the genus Acacia are dominant over the grasses; by keeping the acacias in check, the browsing activities of goats help make possible the grazing activities of cattle (Conant 1982).

Pokot women and girls commonly milk all the cattle, camels, and goats. Women and children gather most of the wild food—nuts, fruits, and several kinds of wild vegetables—which the women then process. Women supervise or carry out all the gathering of firewood, grass for thatching and the thornbush needed to build and repair fences. They haul water to the homestead and in the dry season help dig the step wells, and then they hand up the water to the cattle troughs. Women in herding households also plant sorghum in riverain areas subject to flooding at the outset of the rainy season. The gathering and foraging activities of women and girls are as crucial to the functioning of Pokot pastoral households as such activities are among the !Kung and other hunting-and-gathering peoples.

One of the women's crucial tasks is to transport surplus livestock products, especially milk and blood, to farming areas, where they exchange them for surplus grain and other crops. Donkeys are sometimes used to transport these loads on the plains, but because they are susceptible to diseases prevalent in the mountains, they cannot be used there. Pokot women are adept at backpacking loads of fifty to sixty pounds up and down steep mountain trails leading to and from the farming areas. Groups of twenty or so Pokot herdswomen may be away for weeks at a time to arrange exchanges of livestock for farm produce. When the women do return to the herding areas, they bring not only the much-needed grain and other farm produce but also a wealth of information on conditions throughout the region.

Among the Pokot as among many East African peoples, boys and men do most of the things that have caught the attention of observers. Men and older boys "blood" the cattle by shooting a blocked arrow into the jugular vein in the animal's neck; the blood is caught in a calabash and then mixed with milk. Only men butcher livestock. They kill cattle with spears, often in the context of a ritual; they kill goats by cutting their throats. Men and older boys also hunt—commonly buffalo, gazelle, warthog, and guinea fowl. Only men engage in raids on neighboring peoples. The herders often enlist the help of men from farming areas for major raids.

The main day-to-day activity of men and boys in Pokot herding households is managing the cattle. Although herding is sometimes punctuated by a burst of activity (as when a wandering ox must be driven back into line or predators are seen nearby, especially hyena and lion), it is not strenuous work. Not much more than an easy walking gait is required to drive cattle to a grazing area; and while the animals are grazing, the work can be so undemanding as to allow a herder to assume what is sometimes called the "Nilotic stance": he supports his weight on one leg and rests the other foot against it.

The light work that Pokot men do in herding areas leaves them a considerable amount of time to perfect their skills in making shields, spears, bows, and arrows. Much time is also spent in making personal items, such as wooden headrests, and, above all, either constructing or repairing the mud "helmet" every Pokot man is entitled to wear once certain ritual requirements are met. To make a helmet, a man packs clay into his hair. After the clay is sculpted into a highly stylized helmet, it is pierced so that quills and other ornaments may be stuck into it. When the clay has hardened in the sun, the helmet is painted in elaborate patterns announcing the individual's age grade, warrior status, and descent group. The helmet is a kind of identification card that can be interpreted from some distance away. It is also a

A Pokot male applies mud to another's hair to make a mud helmet. People everywhere often attempt to distinguish themselves from their neighbors by dress and other symbols. Headdresses are particularly effective badges of identity, as they can be identified from afar. (FRANCIS CONANT, HUNTER COLLEGE)

perfect excuse to forgo the use of the headband worn by women to balance heavy loads; nor can the wearer of a helmet stay out long in the rain lest it melt. Toward the end of its useful life (about ten weeks) the growing hair will have lifted the helmet several inches off the scalp. Men spend hours repairing one another's helmet and poking stiff straws through the quill holes to dislodge insects and the tangle of hair beneath it.

The Age Grade

Households in a pastoral korok belong to a dozen or more groups that trace their kinship through the paternal line. From one season to the next each household can drastically alter its herding strategy, change herding partners, or move out of the district entirely. Conventional administrative and international boundaries have little meaning to pastoralists. A large household, one with several wives and married sons, may split up into smaller units, which then scatter over thousands of square miles of rangeland. Ties of kinship are obviously more difficult to maintain and manipulate among pastoralists than they are in the more densely populated and far more stable farming areas. In such circumstances, people tend to establish ties of pseudo kinship through the device of age grades. An **age grade** consists of people of the same sex and approximately the same age who share a set of duties and privileges. The institution is widespread throughout East Africa and is particularly prominent among such pastoral groups as the Masai, Samburu, Turkana, and Pokot. Among the Pokot the age grades serve primarily to regulate marriage and to recruit groups of men for such activities as digging step wells, clearing land, digging irrigation ditches, and—rarely these days—organizing for a raid or a counterraid on a neighboring people.

Pokot men of the same age grade, who regard themselves as brothers, must not marry each other's daughters, and they are not supposed to marry the sisters of men in the next younger age grade. Wealthy older men who can offer large amounts of bridewealth sometimes do marry women of a younger generation. Such brides are sometimes women from farming areas, who thus assure the pastoral household of regular grain from farming in-laws. The Pokot age-grade system, like that of many other East African peoples, is a highly complex institution with multiple functions.

A common feature of East African age-grade systems is known as "cycling": there are only a limited number of names by which the grades are known, and the named grades appear in a regular order. The Pokot have five named age grades, but at any given time there are only three or at the most four age grades with living representatives. When the last members of the eldest age grade become too few and too weak to resist the young men clamoring to be formed into an age grade, a new age grade is formed. The threat that the new age grade represents to the authority of the elders is a continuing source of tension between older and younger Pokot men.

The Pokot cyclical age-grade system is complicated by the inclusion of "sets" within each grade, each set consisting of a group of men who were circumcised at the same time in conjunction with a coming-of-age ceremony known as *sapana.* From boyhood on, Pokot men are locked into a series of rituals, all of which involve the slaughter of livestock. Important events are celebrated by the slaughter of oxen, or if a household is poor in cattle, then a sheep or goat. Despite the high regard in which cattle are held (or perhaps because of it), meat frequently becomes available to Pokot households participating in rituals that call for livestock sacrifice.

Pokot pastoralism traditionally seems to have been conditioned largely by local factors, such as the range of environments that could be exploited by mixed herds of goats, cattle, and camels. Until Kenya attained independence in 1967, Pokot culture looked inward, and responses to external events were relatively rare. But since independence such external factors as government-provided health and education services and public-works projects—the construction of dams, irrigation systems, and roads—have forced basic changes in the Pokot way of life, especially among farmers and herders living near administrative centers. Pokot men now wear shirts and shorts, and their sandals are made from old automobile tires instead of buffalo hide. Pokot women in the villages cover their breasts and have given up the traditional skin shirts for clothing made of imported cotton. The old Pokot way of life survives in the hinterland, away from villages and towns, but for how long, no one can tell.

In fact, it appears that the Pokot's way of life is threatened by more than simple acculturation through their increasing involvement in the modern nation of Kenya. Ton Dietz, a Dutch geographer, has documented the pressures that threaten the very livelihood and existence of the Pokot today: drought and famine, competition from neighboring groups, and, most of all, such a breakdown in security that they must fear heavily armed robbers whenever they accompany their cattle to their pastures (Dietz 1987:299).

THE YÖRÜK OF TURKEY

The Yörük are transhumant sheep herders who move their flocks back and forth between two grazing zones in southeastern Turkey. In winter they camp on low plains on what is geographically an extension of the Syrian steppe. In spring, when the weather warms, they move the herds inland some 100 kilometers (62.14 miles) to craggy, mountainous summer pasturelands. The Yörük traditionally kept camels to transport their belongings during migrations, while their economy was organized around the herds of sheep (Bates 1973). Today the nomadic Yörük use trucks and tractor-drawn wagons to move their flocks and possessions. The Yörük's sheep, unlike the Pokot's cattle, serve almost exclusively as the capital basis for market production. Although the nomadic Yörük do eat some of their animal products—milk, butter, cheese, yogurt—for the most part these products, along with wool and male lambs, are sold. And with the money they receive the Yörük buy their necessities—above all the agricultural products that constitute most of their diet.

This, then, is not a subsistence economy. The Yörük are completely dependent on a market economy not only to sell their animal products and buy their food but also to rent the lands on which they graze their sheep. They actively use the market system to increase, if possible, their holdings in livestock, to accumulate cash to buy consumer goods, even to acquire land or urban houses. As a result, even relatively small fluctuations in market prices can bankrupt a household—or make it rich. As long as wealth and poverty are relatively temporary conditions, and as long as each household may reasonably expect to increase its herds in time, the society remains relatively egalitarian. By and large, no one family or elite group comes to hold substantial economic or political power over others. This is the situation among many herding peoples, since, as Harold Schneider (1970) notes in regard to Africa, the volatility of animal capital precludes the long-term perpetuation of rule by a special class within the society. Today the situation among the Yörük is changing with the emergence of a group of well-to-do merchant families who may well constitute a distinctly privileged group.

The Market Economy

The market economy is part of the Yörük way of life. All transactions are made on the basis of established market values, even when goods and services are bartered. If a Yörük family trades wool for tobacco, for example, the exchange is made according to the relative market value of each item. Supply and demand within a particular area can alter the values, of course, but such variations only restructure market prices to fit local conditions. The vast majority of transactions, however, involve cash or promissory notes. Often a herd owner will contract to supply animals or milk at a future date, accepting an advance payment in cash. Fluctuations in the market prices of animal products, of the foods the Yörük buy, and of the land they rent become significant problems to which they must continually respond.

A large cauldron used for washing clothes goes on top as a Yörük family loads its household possessions onto camels during fall migration. (DANIEL G. BATES)

As the Yörük are dependent on the market, they are dependent on other groups—the condition of the crops grown by those other groups, their needs, the value they place on their own and the Yörük's goods. For the Yörük the presence of other groups constitutes an all-important environmental variable that shapes their economic decisions at every turn.

Probably the most significant feature of such interactions is the Yörük's reliance on other groups for pastureland. The Yörük do not own or even have traditional claims to the pastures they use; they must rent them. In some cases they also have to pay for access to lands along the migration route. Thus, although the outer limit of their migration schedule is established largely by climate and topography, political and social factors help determine the actual schedule. When Yörük herd owners want to move their animals, they must take into account the wishes of the people who own the land that the animals must cross. This land is predominantly agricultural. The herders would almost certainly keep the animals longer in the lowland plains were it not that moving too late in the season would cause extensive crop damage. And they would return to the plains earlier in the fall if they did not have to wait for the harvest.

As one might expect, disputes often develop between pastoralists and agriculturalists over crop damages. In recent years the Turkish government has intervened to regulate the migrations and to see that all claims for crop damage are satisfied. Without governmental regulation, some agricultural lands would probably have to be abandoned, because damage would be too frequent and too costly. This was a common problem in the past. Each annual migration, then, is a complex strategy determined by the availability of grass, planting or harvest schedules, and the restrictions set by the government.

Social Organization

As with the Pokot, the composition of Yörük camp groups changes regularly. As many as twenty households or as few as two may camp together; larger clusters generally gather in the summer pasture areas. Although in some pastoral societies the labor of herding is pooled among members of a camp group, the Yörük household is in effect a self-contained producing unit: it relies almost exclusively on its own labor. The rental of pasturelands is an important function of the larger camp group. Though the families that make up the camp do not generally pool their labor, they do pool money to rent their grazing lands jointly.

The composition of a camp group depends on several factors. Kinship is one. The Yörük place great emphasis on patrilineage, and often families that camp together are patrilineally related. Some households, however, camp with people more closely related to the wife than to the husband. Sometimes this arrangement simply reflects the woman's wish to be with her sisters or brothers for a season or two. Or it may be a way for the family to secure better grazing than they could get by cooperating with the husband's patrilineal relatives. Or it may be the result of a family quarrel. Thus while kinship to some degree determines the camp membership, sentiment and economic strategy keep such communities highly flexible. They have to be. The amount of grazing available in any single location changes from season to season and from year to year, and the herders must be able to respond to these changes.

Changes in Strategies

In recent years the Yörük have had to face a variety of new situations. One major problem is inflation, especially in the rents charged for pastures, which initially rose much faster than the prices of animal products. This development has resulted in a significant transformation of Yörük society. At the same time, new developments in mechanized transport and in the opening of new markets in the oil-rich Arab world created new possibilities for some Yörük.

The Yörük today actually practice three adaptive strategies: nomadic pastoralism, sedentary agriculture, and trade or shopkeeping in town. The nomads, as we have seen, have developed a very specialized adaptation, engaging in animal husbandry and trading in animals and animal products. At the same time, entire villages of settled Yörük now engage in agriculture, shopkeeping, and commerce. Some families combine strategies. They may, for example, operate a mobile dairy and follow the herders, buying their milk and converting it to cheese for urban markets. Others own large trucks, which in the 1980s, they used to transport goods to war-torn Iran and Iraq. Some have become brokers, buying up large numbers of animals and shipping them to distant markets in Arab lands, where meat is in great demand. Very frequently entrepreneurs engage in several of these activities simultaneously, sometimes coordinating their ventures in town, sometimes camping in tents.

One point must be stressed. Yörük society, like most others, is changing rapidly, and the challenge to the ethnographer is to describe a way of life without implying that what is observed is a timeless pattern. Daniel Bates first went to southeastern Turkey in 1968, but few of his initial economic observations still hold today. Culturally, too, the Yörük are changing. In 1968 patterns of male–female interactions, recreation, and socializing were very different. Now even pastoral households have access to television sets, refrigerators, and other modern appliances. They usually keep them in village or town dwellings, where they spend part of each year and where children of school age live while attending school.

While the nomadic herders and the new class of businessmen and farmers are economically distinct, they differ little in cultural identity and there is no antipathy between them. Some of the strategies are actually complementary: the town-based businessmen often depend on the herders for their trade, while the herders depend on the small businessmen for the credit they need in order to go on herding in a volatile market economy. The different strategies are also interrelated in that families move from one to another as circumstances warrant. Many people who were settled in a town when Bates revisited the area in 1978 were once again living in tents in 1983. The reason was not dissatisfaction with town life: they could simply make more money raising livestock than selling shoes.

Wealth or access to capital determines whether a household herds or settles down to

In Yörük dairy tents such as this one, sheep's milk is processed into cheese, which is then canned and sold in urban markets. The dairies, which follow the herds at spring milking time, are important as a means for families to get the cash they need to rent pasture lands. (DANIEL G. BATES)

other endeavors. Wealth is no longer spread as evenly among the Yörük as it used to be. We can understand their new economic system better if we consider the circumstances of those at the lower end of the economic ladder.

The poorer herders, those with just enough animals to make herding viable, are often in debt and seldom have the ready cash they need to rent pastureland, pay for winter grains, or, more recently, hire truck transport. To pay debts accumulated during the winter, they are forced to shear their sheep at the beginning of spring. But early shearing leaves them at a disadvantage in the migration to high pastures: they must wait longer before leaving, as shorn sheep are vulnerable to disease in snow and extreme cold. When they finally do leave, they may travel over lands already grazed by sheep belonging to wealthier herd owners, who could afford to forgo an early shearing. The poor grazing leaves the last flocks tired and hungry by the time they reach summer pasture. The sheep of the poorer herd owners are more likely

to die during migration than those of the wealthier ones. Really affluent herders are likely to own a truck in which to carry animals and belongings to distant but choice grazing areas.

Even after selling their spring wool, many Yörük herders do not usually have the cash necessary to rent summer pasture. So they need an additional source of income or credit, and in recent years they have found one in selling milk to the mobile dairy tents that follow the flocks. Many of these dairies are owned by the wealthier herders. Just as there is a limit below which a flock is not economically viable, there is an upper limit as well. Huge numbers of animals require a large deployment of labor, so the wealthy have an incentive to diversify rather than to enlarge their herds. They have bought land or stores, or they have established dairy businesses.

The dairies are rather sizable enterprises with a ready supply of capital that enables them not only to buy the herders' milk but to buy it in advance. Such milk futures are purchased at a relatively low price, but they give the poorer herders the money they need for pasture rental. Once the dairymen have the milk, they process it into cheese and sell it for a substantial profit in urban markets. Thus the dairies allow the herders to fend off bankruptcy at the same time that they yield high profits to the dairymen.

It is easy to see that such a system encourages economic stratification, the creation of increasingly fixed classes of rich and poor. In the past the Yörük had no such permanent economic groups. As long as the people remained herders, they could expect to go from rags to riches and back again several times in the course of their lives, because animals are such a volatile form of capital. But once the temporarily wealthy began to invest their wealth in more fixed forms of capital, such as farms, shops, and dairies, their wealth ceased to be temporary, and indeed, it began to increase. The in-

crease in wealth enabled them to settle down. The traditional way of life—nomadic, egalitarian, sheep-centered—is slowly giving way to a more complex, stratified pattern, with a variety of strategies feeding into one another and reinforcing economic differences.

In 1978 and later in 1983 Bates found that the herders who were using trucks to transport their animals between pastures no longer migrated as a group. Herding has become a form of ranching, only the "ranch" is not a contiguous tract of grazing land. It is many pastures used sequentially as sheep are trucked among them. Often the household stays behind in a town or village, leaving herding to the menfolk or hired shepherds. In fact, by 1983 some herders were making so much money from animal export that they could afford to rent wheat fields and turn them into pastures, and thus could spend most of the year in one place.

Far fewer families were being supported by pastoralism in 1983, and those few were the better-off members of the society. The majority of households that had been nomadic in 1968–1970 had settled in villages and towns as laborers and tenant farmers, unable to continue making their living in the traditional way because of the rising costs of pasture and feed. Some were living precariously; those who had invested what they had in a shop or some other business had prospered.

The adaptation of the Yörük, then, is a matter not simply of accommodating to the physical environment but of finding a niche in a larger social system. To understand even their pastoral economy, we must take into account who owns what. Likewise, it is impossible to discuss the specialization of nomadic pastoralism among the Yörük without reference to other specializations within the larger society on which the Yörük depend for their buying and selling. Thus the effective environment of the Yörük has a political and social dimension as well as a physical and biological one.

Summary

Pastoralists engage in *animal husbandry:* the breeding, care, and use of herd animals, such as sheep, goats, camels, cattle, horses, reindeer, or yaks. Most pastoralists in nonindustrial societies are nomadic. But both the mobility of pastoralists and the degree to which they rely on animal husbandry varies with environmental, social, and economic conditions. Few pastoralist groups rely exclusively on their herds; they tend to pursue a more generalized subsistence strategy.

Nomads follow two basic patterns: *horizontal migration,* characterized by regular movement over a large area in search of grass, and *transhumance,* or seasonal movement between upland and lowland pastures.

Specialized pastoralism, or exclusive reliance on animal husbandry, may have developed from a farming/herding pattern. Changes in agricultural practices, such as the use of canal irrigation, may have pushed grazing lands farther from settlements. The consequent increased demands of both herding and agriculture may have led some families to specialize in agriculture and others to choose herding exclusively. The divergence of strategies may have been encouraged by the failure of irrigation for some groups. Extensive irrigation may cause the *water table* (the level of water under the earth) to fall, or it may increase the salinity of the soil until crops no longer thrive.

While pastoralism is a relatively efficient means of extracting energy from a harsh environment, it produces less energy per acre of land than agriculture, and population densities are correspondingly low. Pastoralism is an alternative to agriculture, but it is almost never independent of it. If pastoralists don't raise vegetable foods, they acquire them through trade.

In nonindustrial societies, *sedentary pastoralism,* or animal husbandry that does not involve mobility, is generally rare. The usual pattern is *nomadic pastoralism*—the practice of moving one's herds from pasture to pasture as the seasons and circumstances require. The main reason that pastoralists migrate is to secure adequate grazing land in a marginal environment. However, migration may also be a means to maintain political autonomy or even to control settled groups. The composition of local groupings in pastoral societies often shifts as nomadic camping units move, break apart, and come together with other units.

Virtually all pastoral populations are organized in tribes, communities of people who claim kinship, usually by descent from one or more common ancestors. Tribal organization provides for positions of leadership and allows for coordination of social and economic activities.

The basic economic unit is the household. Households may move frequently one year and be largely sedentary the next. One household may herd alone, while others may temporarily combine forces. Families may shift between agriculture and herding, or they may give up herding for other pursuits, such as shopkeeping.

The Pokot of Kenya maintain a subsistence economy through a balanced and diversified strategy of keeping cattle and growing crops. They exploit the arable land during the rainy season and use the more arid land for herding. The Pokot are part of the East African *cattle complex,* a socioeconomic system in which cattle represent social status as well as wealth. The cattle play a significant symbolic role in social ties, obligations, and rituals. They also provide most of the protein consumed by the Pokot and serve as a reserve food supply to be tapped in the event of crop failure.

The basic unit of Pokot social organization is the korok, or neighborhood. A farming korok consists of households belonging to one or two localized clans. Households in herding koroks belong to many dispersed kin groups, in which kinship is traced through the paternal line. Members of farming and herding koroks intermarry to a limited extent. The groom's family gives *bridewealth* to the bride's family to compensate them for the loss of their daughter's services. The labor of women and girls is crucial to the functioning of Pokot households. The men's activities are less arduous.

Pokot herdsmen are organized in *age grades*, each grade consisting of men of approximately the same age, who share a set of duties and privileges. The age grades serve to establish ties of pseudo kinship in areas where real kin tend to be scattered.

The Yörük of southeastern Turkey traditionally have been nomadic pastoralists, who move their sheep between summer and winter pastures. The Yörük are dependent on a market economy to sell their animal products, buy their food, and rent the lands on which they graze their sheep. The activities of the Yörük are shaped not only by climate and topography but also by political and social factors; the strategy of their migrations is determined by the availability of grass, village planting or harvest schedules, and the restrictions on migration set by the government.

Yörük social organization is flexible. The composition of a camp group may be determined by kinship, sentiment, or economic strategy. Each family within the camp group is a self-sufficient producing unit, although the camp group does rent pastureland jointly.

In recent years the nature of animal husbandry has changed. The rents charged for pastureland have risen but new opportunities have also opened up. Now many Yörük avail themselves of truck transport and sell animals in Arab countries. As a result, they now practice diverse and complementary strategies: sedentary agriculture, trade, brokerage, and shopkeeping, as well as pastoralism. Until recently, wealth determined whether a household herded or settled down. The rich herders tended to diversify into trading or farming, while the poor struggled to keep their herds. While some of the poorest herders of earlier years have become rich in today's market, this economic system has created increasingly fixed classes of rich and poor for the first time in Yörük society.

Key Terms

age grade	**cattle complex**	**sedentary pastoralism**	**transhumance**
animal husbandry	**horizontal migration**	**specialized pastoralism**	**water table**
bridewealth	**nomadic pastoralism**		

Suggested Readings

ABU-LUGHOD, L. 1988. *Veiled Sentiments: Honor and Poetry in a Bedouin Society*. Berkeley and Los Angeles: University of Los Angeles Press. A person-centered ethnography of a community of Bedouins in the Western Desert of Egypt that focuses on the oral lyric poetry

that is used by women and young men in this once nomadic but still pastoral society.

BECK, L. 1986. *The Qashqa'i of Iran*. New Haven, Conn.: Yale University Press. This political ethnography of elites is a historical and anthropological account of the

Turkic-speaking Qashqa'i. The Qashqa'i are a predominantly pastoral nomadic people but they have highly developed sociopolitical institutions, including a ruling elite that has participated in national and international politics.

BLACK-MICHAUD, J. 1986. *Sheep and Land: The Economics of Power in a Tribal Society*. Cambridge, Eng.: Cambridge University Press. An examination of the Luristan region of western Iran and the ways in which different populations relate to each other through exchanges between sedentary agricultural and nomadic pastoral populations.

EKVALL, R.B. 1968, *Fields on the Hoof: The Nexus of Tibetan Nomadic Pastoralism*. Prospect Heights, Ill.: Waveland Press. A clearly written case study of pastoralism in a region that is poorly understood ethnographically.

JANZEN, J. 1986. *Nomads in the Sultanate of Oman: Tradition and Development in Dhofar*. Boulder, Colo.: Westview Press. A comprehensive and insightful analysis of the traditional living conditions and economic circumstances of the nomadic-peasant population of Dhofar and the rapid changes to which they have been subjected.

KHAZANOV, A. M. 1984. *Nomads and the Outside World*. Cambridge, Eng.: Cambridge University Press. A good discussion of the many ways in which nomadic pastoralists are integrated into states and empires. The author is a specialist in Central Asia but deals with pastoralism in general.

PELTO, P. J. 1973. *The Snowmobile Revolution: Technology and Social Change in the Arctic*. Menlo Park, Calif.: Benjamin. A study of how the Skolt Lapps of Finland incorporated the snowmobile into their traditional economy, which was focused on reindeer herding.

TAPPER, R. 1979. *Pasture and Politics: Economics, Conflict and Ritual among Shahsevan Nomads of Northwestern Iran*. London: Academic Press. A socioanthropological study of the interrelations between distinctive grazing rights, community politics, and ritual behavior, and of the ways in which these dynamics contribute to the patterns of inequality and competition found within the primary nomadic communities of the Shahsevan.

Chapter 8 Intensive Agriculture

*I*f one were to observe the heartland of the Middle East from an earth-orbiting satellite, most striking would be the sharp contrast between the great expanses of desert and the lush green of cultivated areas. One can stand with one foot in a wheat field and the other in the desert. The Middle East, where agriculture began some 10,000 years ago, is the home of some 200 million people, most of them supported by the crops produced on less than 10 percent of the land by a land-use strategy referred to here as intensive agriculture. The impact of intensive land use is evident in Egypt. In 1984, 98 percent of Egypt's population was concentrated on less than 4 percent of its territory; an average of 1,200 to 1,400 people occupied every square kilometer of arable land (Kimball 1984:16–24). Today Egypt has to import large quantities of foodstuffs from other regions of the world. The irony is that both great productivity and accelerating social and economic hardship all too often march hand in hand. An ancient historian, Ibn Batuta, said that when famine strikes Egypt, whose lands have been irrigated longer than those of any other area, the world itself cannot feed her people.

Similar patterns of recurring famine and rural hardship are found in other regions where civilizations arose with the development of intensive farming. China, for example, where 1.1 billion people are supported by the produce of 11 percent of its land area, has a long history of chronic famine and mass starvation, particularly among the people who themselves produce the food that sustains the country. The present government apparently has reduced the possibility of a recurrence of famine in the near future. But even with increased production and improved food distribution, the threat of hunger is real. As China's population continues to grow, the country has not only more people to feed but less land with which to do it. As urban centers spread and the fertility of the soil diminishes, land is being lost at a faster rate than it can be reclaimed (Smil 1984).

India and Bangladesh experience even greater pressure on their land; Indonesia, once the most productive region of Southeast Asia, is seeing its people's well-being decline. To arrest such decline, governments often encourage even greater efforts in agriculture, including the destruction of tropical rain forests to support, however tenuously, people forced out of other areas. In Africa south of the Sahara, where newly instigated intensive land-use programs have often led to devastating environmental problems, the specter of mass starvation looms. Nevertheless, within each of these areas we find numerous striking instances of human resourcefulness in the face of environmental problems. This chapter deals with the rise of intensive agriculture and its social corollaries: urbanism, social stratification, and the emergence of a class of peasant farmers.

THE DEVELOPMENT OF INTENSIVE AGRICULTURE, CITIES, AND STATES

The interrelated processes of agricultural intensification and ever-rising requirements for food in combination with declining resources are seen throughout the world. Anthropologists and scientists in other fields have long been concerned with the origins of intensive farming and early civilization, with the social and economic structure of rural society, and with the strategies that have enabled diverse populations to adapt to environmental and other problems.

The most dramatic change to occur following the shift from hunting-gathering to agriculture was the appearance of a novel and distinctive settlement form, the city, and an equally distinctive form of political organization, the state. Archaeologists and anthropologists have argued for decades (as we shall see in Chapter 15) over the causal linkages among intensive farming, the development of urban centers, and the rise of states. But all agree that these developments are interrelated and mutually reinforcing.

A process as complex as the emergence of cities and states can be traced to no single cause. We know that even fairly complicated irrigation systems can be managed by local farmers themselves, although the record of conflict is substantial. Yet we see a widespread pattern of large-scale irrigation systems coming to be run by special managers, with a corresponding lessening of control by households, even by local communities. Centralized decision making facilitates the mobilization of large work forces, the allocation of water, the resolution of conflicts, and the storage of surpluses. In the emerging prehistoric states of Mesopotamia, this managerial role was first assumed by religious leaders; management by the temple was the precursor of management by secular rule. It is interesting to note that the earliest large-scale irrigation systems in the United States Southwest were managed by the Mormon Church.

The main impetus for irrigation, in most places, is simply the need to have water available in areas where rainfall is unpredictable— not a wish to increase the average yield of a unit of land. But with the advent of irrigation, slight differences in the productivity of different pieces of land became greatly magnified.

Those fields that lent themselves to irrigation— fields that were close to the water source or that drained well—produced far more than those less suited to irrigation. Where and when irrigation works, human societies tended to increase in numbers and in social and technological complexity. When farming produced more food than the farmers themselves could eat, segments of the population came to specialize in crafts—the making of tools, pots, and the like, which they then traded for food they had not produced themselves. The division of labor within society thus becomes more complex, with even spatially distant groups becoming mutually dependent.

Land fed not only the farming households and the craftworkers but other emerging classes of nonproducers: religious leaders, politicians, administrators. Increasingly the economic demands of urban populations and the political power of their elites came to exercise a profound influence on the life of rural peoples, although the country folk often sought means to avoid the power of the state. Town and country came to be part of an integrated system, though the results of increased productivity were not shared equally by all sectors of the economy (Redman 1978). As agrarian societies evolved into large-scale states, as in the ancient Middle East, some communities inevitably prospered and grew; those far from the major markets, religious institutions, and other products of the urban centers languished. Such regional differentiation may be the basis for significant social and cultural variability within a society.

One element common to all large territorial states with great urban centers is that they arose on the foundation of intensive agriculture. Thus while some horticultural societies, such as the Yąnomamö of Chapter 6, have remained politically autonomous until now, and can be studied as distinct societies with distinct cultures, intensive farming communities are closely interdependent. They are invariably part of a larger agrarian society, with much of their organization tied to distant cities and national administrative offices. They cannot be understood outside the context of the larger political and economic system of which they are a part. In fact, some social scientists argue that most important rural events reflect the influence of regional and metropolitan political and economic organizations.

The Organization of Energy

In the final analysis it is energy that distinguishes intensive agriculture—both energy invested in crop production and energy extracted from the land. The exact point at which horticulture becomes intensive farming is not always clear, but one can recognize the consequences of the shift, even without employing economic criteria. Rarely can large numbers of people maintain themselves in stable year-round communities without engaging in intensive food production, and nowhere do we see urban centers without a hinterland of highly productive farming. The vast energy surpluses that flow from the countryside to the city result from the investment of energy in agriculture. The increase in the energy invested can come from many sources: from animals yoked to plows, from human labor spent in terracing land or digging wells, or from farm machinery powered by fossil fuels.

Investment of energy in order to gain an even greater return in energy is characteristic of intensive agriculture, and is expressed in the management of fields and paddies. A crucial factor is fallow time—the time that must be allowed between crops for the soil to rest and regenerate its organic and chemical content. The fallow period, more than simply the yields of a particular year, is critical to a high level of food production over the long term. When other factors—availability of water, type of soil, and the like—are equal, sustained agricultural yields vary with the length of the fallow period.

The shifting agriculture practiced by the Yąnomamö is a long-fallow system, since they may have to wait as long as ten to twenty years before they can replant a field whose nutrients have been depleted. Intensive agriculture shortens the fallow period or even eliminates it altogether. The land permits nearly continuous cultivation, and in some areas can produce multiple crops each season. This approach requires developed technology, large inputs of human labor, and investment in other forms of energy. Fields have to be prepared, often specially laid out for irrigation; plow animals must be cared for, water controlled, fertilizers or other nutrients spread on the fields, and crops carefully tended throughout the growing period. But the result is a vastly increased amount of food per unit of land.

Both land and farmers work harder under intensive agriculture, and the result is a great increase in the production not only of food but of such crops as cotton and flax. It may sometimes appear that the possibilities of intensification seem almost limitless. Even with modern techniques, however, only 11 percent of the earth's land area is suited to intensive farming (Grigg 1974:6), and the potential for intensification is limited. A point is always reached at which increased investment of labor or capital is not matched by productive gains. We will return to this point later.

Environmental Resilience, Stability, and Change

Intensive agriculture is accompanied by a massive reshaping of the landscape—a process that is ever accelerating. In swidden horticulture, the forest is partially cut or burned, only to be allowed to grow back. Intensive agriculture entails the laborious clearing of fields, building of terraces, and excavation of drainage ditches, ponds, and canals. These tasks completed, the work has just begun. The new agricultural environment must be maintained through constant effort; its continuity is a life-or-death matter for the people who depend on it.

In one respect people are caught up in a vicious cycle. When intensive agriculture is not very closely regulated in keeping with natural constraints, it can be as much a problem as a solution. By creating elaborate waterworks or clearing hillsides for terraces, a farming population may indeed protect their yields or even increase food production. But as agriculture becomes more complex and specialized, it becomes more vulnerable to disruption. Irrigation canals may silt up, fields may become unproductive as natural salts become concentrated in the soil, topsoil may erode—the list is long. These calamities accompany intensification as surely as the increased yields. A farmer who plants the same crop year after year to obtain the maximum yield is increasing the risk of total crop failure from soil depletion or disease.

The problem is not simply a lack of planning or a tendency of individual farmers to take this year's yield more seriously than environmental consequences a decade or a generation from now. In response to market demands or government inducements to produce more food, entire regions may be threatened by depletion or erosion of the soil, or by its contamination by chemical residues. These problems arise in all major agricultural nations. Stability or continuity requires investment in the infrastructure which is not immediately reflected in crop yields: soils protected from erosion, drainage maintained, crops rotated, and soils allowed to regenerate. If such investments are not made, the stability of the productive system is threatened.

So even as intensive agriculture solves some problems, it creates new ones. Irrigation has left such concentrations of minerals in the soil of California's Imperial Valley that productivity is leveling off and threatens to decline, and there is virtually no way to divert the contaminated water from the fields and downstream communities. Irrigation is often associated

with environmental problems of this sort. Paradoxically, one response is to intensify production further, by expanding the area under irrigation, building larger dams, digging deeper wells, using expensive chemicals to remove the salt, using more water. Again, such efforts may solve the problem in the short run only to create more serious problems in the long run—such as causing the water table in the area to drop or further increasing the salinity of the soil. Consequently, cultivators have to work harder

A farmer planting rice seedlings in Bali. Rice cultivation is highly productive, but very labor intensive. (DAVID MOORE/BLACK STAR)

just to maintain the same level of productivity.

Intensive agriculturalists clearly do not free themselves from environmental constraints. On the contrary, they seem to labor under many more constraints than people whose technologies are less sophisticated. Intensive agriculturalists rearrange their ecosystems and must make tremendous efforts simply to support the artificial balance they have created. Intensification increases vulnerability. It opens up new possibilities for mishaps and magnifies the cost of mistakes. It widens the area and numbers of people who are affected, too, should a major problem occur. A crop failure in Canada or the United States today would leave millions hungry on the other side of the world. All this is not to say that intensive agricultural systems inevitably fail or result in severe environmental problems. We have evidence of continuous, environmentally stable agriculture practiced in many parts of the world for thousands of years. But intensive agriculture is always something of a mixed blessing, and human dependence on it—now virtually total—has important social implications.

THE SOCIAL CONSEQUENCES OF INTENSIVE AGRICULTURE

The social consequences of intensive agriculture have been at least as far-reaching as its ecological consequences. In nonindustrial nations the absorption of the intensive farming community into the larger society is most striking. In such societies farmers tend to have little voice in the national social and economic system. They may lack control over the means of their production—the land, the other resources, the capital they need to grow their crops, and the labor they contribute to the process. The state directly or indirectly shapes the structure of their lives. Such farmers are traditionally termed **peasants**. While they may

participate in national institutions, these institutions are controlled largely by the town-dwelling literate classes. Peasant farmers trade and market, but they are often exploited by merchants and middlemen. Peasants' fields may be owned by distant landlords, but even possession of land does not usually serve as a basis for self-sufficiency or community autonomy. Money and energy left over from their labors are regularly siphoned off in the form of land rents, taxes, and even labor **corvée**—unpaid labor in lieu of taxes, usually in road construction and maintenance.

Varieties of Peasant Society

Peasants have been described as farmers, usually intensive agriculturalists, who produce primarily for family subsistence rather than for profits to be reinvested (Wolf 1966). Much of their produce may be sold, but the profits accrue to middlemen and urban elites, not to the peasants. For them farming is a way of life and a means of sustaining a household within a community. It is, then, much more than simply a strategy for making money. Such farmers, often materially poor, closely identify with their villages and way of life. The term "peasant" subsumes great diversity in standards of living, even within one country. The common element is a farming household whose efforts are directed to maintenance and subsistence—not reinvestment of capital for profits. In most cases peasant families are dominated by holders of power outside the local community. In tsarist Russia before 1889, for instance, a peasant household was bound to a landed estate, and to leave without permission was to risk death or imprisonment. The peasants of Western Europe acquired full civil liberties by the nineteenth century, and often their standard of living, however simple in comparison with that of the well-to-do, set them apart from the poor people of the cities. Still, their form of farming permitted little accumulation of capital or material wealth.

In Latin America, India, and the Middle East, many peasants gain access to land through some form of **sharecropping**—that is, they work land owned by others in exchange for a share of the yield. In fact, the sharecroppers of the American South, traditionally but not exclusively black families, are a domestic example of peasant farming in all but name, as are many Chicano farmworkers of California today. Sharecropping is one means of getting land to farm; there are others. The way people control the lands they farm is a major determinant of the degree of political freedom they enjoy, and usually of their material well-being.

Horticulturists who control their own land and tools, such as the Yąnomamö and the Pokot farmers, decide for themselves how hard they will work and dispose of their produce as they choose. Peasants do not have this freedom. Their access to land, equipment, and capital—even the allocation of their own labor—is regulated by people more powerful than they. Even the local agriculturalists who own their own land, elect their own leaders, and control their own labor are heavily dependent on an administrative and commercial network. In one way or another, the middlemen who link the farm with distant markets, the rulers, governors, and tax collectors, even the merchants in faraway cities or on local estates determine how and what the peasants produce and what they get for it (Wolf 1966).

To gain an understanding of the economic and social position of these peasants and to see how their position differs from that of other kinds of agriculturalists, let us look at the way they use what they produce.

The Peasant Household Budget

Peasants must of course use part of their resources to feed themselves, but the rest is put aside for essentially three other purposes. Eric Wolf (1966) calls these allocations the ceremonial fund, the replacement fund, and the rent fund.

The Ceremonial Fund. Peasants, like other people, devote a portion of their food and labor to religious and ceremonial activities—primarily calendrical feasts and rituals, weddings, birth rites, and funerals. The portion of the peasant budget allocated to such religious and social activities is the **ceremonial fund**. One function of expensive celebrations, Wolf suggests (1966:7), is "to explain, to justify, and to regulate" social relationships. By exchanging gifts and organizing displays and feasts, villagers emphasize their ties to one another, their relative social standing, and their commitment to the community as a whole. The ceremonies also serve to redistribute resources among families in such a way that differentials in wealth are mitigated: the more prosperous are expected to give more lavish feasts and to contribute more to community celebrations.

This expectation does not imply any lack of interest in a quest for personal advantage in peasant communities. Peasants who have gained prestige through participation in religious or other public activities may attempt to use it to add to their land or wealth. The ceremonies require the purchase of urban-supplied luxury goods, such as ceremonial dress, fireworks, musical instruments, tea and coffee, alcoholic drinks, and gift items. These goods are considered necessities, as they are important to the social self-respect of the participants. The purchase of these goods through the sale of village produce further draws the peasant household into the larger economic system and ensures that the surplus produced by the peasants is siphoned to the outside economy without the use of such overt devices as taxation.

The Replacement Fund. Peasants also must have a **replacement fund**—that is, a portion of their budget must be allocated for the repair or replacement of materials depleted by normal wear and tear. Intensive agriculturalists, unlike horticulturists, use a complicated technology. Plows can break, irrigation ditches accumulate silt, wells must be dug, terraces must be kept in repair. Peasants must also set aside seed each season for the next planting. Where horses or oxen are used for traction, they must further invest in the care of young animals. The family has to be clothed; peasants are rarely self-sufficient in either items of apparel or all items of daily food consumption. To fulfill these needs, they must participate in a market economy, in which the value of what they produce and the costs of what they need are determined by forces far removed from them—the forces of national or world markets. Furthermore, if the peasant is faced with an extraordinary replacement expense—if, for example, an ox dies—the household may well have to borrow money from better-off neighbors or an urban merchant. Such debts, compounded by the extremely high interest rates frequently attached to them, constitute one of the major factors that prevent peasants from accumulating much more than the basic needs of the household.

The Rent Fund. Finally, as peasants do not control the basic means of their production, they must have a **rent fund**—that is, they must allocate a portion of their budget to payment for the use of land and equipment. Taxes levied on land or produce are part of the "rent" paid for continued use of a field. Peasants may pay in cash, or by turning over a percentage of the harvest, or by working for a time for the person or institution that controls the land. The government may require peasants to work on roads or bridges without pay—the corvée we mentioned earlier, another form of taxation. These rents are an important mechanism by which the rural economy's products are channeled into the urban centers. However it is lev-

ied, the rent is usually the peasant household's greatest expense and often is more instrumental than the replacement fund in keeping peasants from accumulating wealth.

The rent requirement, based as it is on political subordination, is the primary factor that distinguishes peasants from other kinds of agriculturalists. Modern farmers, of course, are also dependent on markets; they, too, pay taxes, interest, and sometimes rent. But they are far more free to deploy their capital and labor. They are not politically subordinate to urban elites—indeed, farmers in much of Western Europe and in the United States display a political strength disproportionate to their numbers. Peasants, by contrast, because of the oppressive rent structure, (1) are required to produce at a certain level each year; (2) are deprived of much of their surplus, so that they rarely improve their standard of living; and (3) are often oppressed by political superiors, whose continuation in power depends in large part on their ability to keep the peasants from rising from the inferior position they occupy in society. The rent arrangement, then, is the most important bond that connects the traditional peasant household to the larger society and determines the exploitive nature of the relationship.

Access to Land

One way to understand the factors common to the structures of peasant societies is to determine how the rent is paid. Very often the material circumstances of peasant households and the degree of exploitation depend on the way the land is controlled, which in turn depends on the political configuration of the larger society. Wolf (1966) describes four basic systems (he calls them "domains") of land control. Although his is only one way of looking at land tenure, these patterns are closely related to the general political structures of the countries in which peasants live.

Where the Dove Calls: Land and Politics in a Peasant Community

Little is of greater importance to farmers than access to land and water, the resources on which they depend. The ways in which land is held can be complex in even a small community. Cucurpe—the name, according to the Opata Indians, means Where the Dove Calls—is a farming community in northwestern Mexico. According to Thomas Sheridan, who has done research there,

> To those of us who have grown up in the modern cities of Mexico or the United States, a place like Cucurpe seems idyllic, offering us a vision of a distant agrarian past. But if we go beyond that vision, we see that life in Cucurpe is predicated on struggle, not pastoral harmony: struggle to raise crops when the rains won't come or when floods wash away the topsoil; struggle to keep cattle from turning into emaciated ghosts; struggle to prevent neighbors from diverting your irrigation water or fencing your pasture or stealing your land (1988:xv).

In fact Cucurpe is, as it has been since the arrival of the Spanish, caught up in conflict between corporate and private land tenure. It is one of the more than 22,000 "corporate" farming communities in Mexico where 70 percent of Mexico's farm population live. "Corporate" here means that some village resources—in this case, about half the land and most water rights—are legally owned by the community as a whole. The villagers must fend off the private ranchers who are ever ready to intrude on Cucurpe's grazing lands and at the same time manage conflict among themselves—among those who have land and communal rights, those who have some land and no communal rights, and those who have no land at all and hope to acquire some.

According to the 1980 census, 1,160 people lived in Cucurpe—less than one person per square kilometer. Most of these people lived either in the village center or in small hamlets along the three seasonal watercourses. They have only limited electricity (a generator runs several hours each evening). Only a few families have propane refrigerators, but propane stoves are increasingly replacing cast-iron wood-burners. Diet has changed little since colonial times, except that wheat has replaced corn. The staples are still pinto beans and tortillas (now made with wheat flour); fresh meat is consumed infrequently. Some patterns of production and consumption have changed, of course, and now that beef is being raised for market, many families purchase their food with the proceeds of animal sales. This practice, while economically sensible, does increase their dependence on market forces beyond their control. Some families have invested in pickup trucks and TVs (Sheridan 1988).

The fact that the community is described as "corporate" does not mean that there is economic equality or even that all have equal access to resources. Communal lands are interspersed with private holdings, whose owners also can claim rights to corporate lands. Distinctions of wealth are extreme. The villagers recognize three categories of people. *Los ricos,* "the rich," produce entirely for the market, not for domestic consumption; they employ labor, use pumps and tractors, and own considerable land and cattle. The wealthiest ten households own over half of all private land in the community and have little interest in preserving any communal rights; generally they would prefer to privatize all resources. *La gente ordenada,* "the orderly people" or middle class—about 60 percent of the

The Patrimonial System

In the **patrimonial system** that developed in northern and central Europe during the Middle Ages, land was controlled by feudal lords who held their domains by hereditary right. Land rights were passed down in a lineage—the patrimony of a lord. The feudal lord gave peasants

households—are generally self-sufficient peasant-farmers who farm some private land and run cattle on the commons, or corporate lands. They work their own fields and do not employ labor. Their interests in the corporate resources are very strong, as they rely on free grazing for their cattle and free water for their fields. *Los pobres*, or "the poor"—about 18 percent of the families—have no more than five or six cattle, own little or no land, and must work for others to make ends meet. The poor tend to feel that they should be given community-owned land; the others view these claims as threats to their own interests. However extreme these differences may appear, care is taken to minimize them socially. The wealthy do not flaunt their wealth, and all take pains to avoid conspicuous consumption within Cucurpe.

As the region is extremely arid, water is a critical resource. There are three major forms of land use, distinguished largely by the availability of water. *Milpas* are fields created laboriously by hand: the villagers clear them of stones and brush, level them, and then dig canals from one of the drainage systems to irrigate them. Milpas are usually privately owned or treated as though they were, even if technically the title is held by the community. *Temporales* are fields carved out of the margins of watercourses; they are not irrigated but absorb sufficient runoff water in good years to support squashes and other vegetables. These fields, too, are treated as though they were private. *Agostadero* or grazing land is communal and members can use it at will, unless the community decides otherwise. These three forms of land use allow people to pursue a diversity of strategies: they can raise cattle for market, cash crops, or subsistence crops, or pursue some mix of these strategies plus wage labor. For families that wish to specialize in ranching—and most would like to—a privately owned spread of less than about 2,500 acres (1,000 hectares) would be an unreliable economic base. Any

family without an outside source of income—some people have jobs on ranches or receive remittances from relatives in the United States—requires access to at least two of the three major forms of land use; no family can make a living by committing itself to only one. Here lies the root of both conflict and cooperation.

Surface water is held corporately. The rich can drill wells and run pumps, but most families must use surface water diverted to the fields by canals and dams. Families must cooperate if they are to have access to water. Here the middle class of peasants get little support from either the rich or the poor—both one way or another would like to get access to milpas and temporales. All small landowning families assist in the building and maintenance of these canals, and each has a right to a specific amount of water for the household's milpa. The milpa is the key to a middle-class family's survival: they may make more money from cattle, but they can rely on the milpa for food.

Thus the ranchers and the wealthy continually spar with those who defend the corporate rights of the community; those with fields contend with those without, while those without strive to get the community to grant them land on which to farm. The landless and the smallholders join in defending the grazing areas from the rich, but even in this enterprise there are bitter divisions: some of the farmers own many cattle while others own only a few. All know that the grazing land is being damaged by overstocking, but as it is held in common, there is little regulation. Thus families that own only a few cattle believe they are victimized by those who own many. Still, Thomas Sheridan finds, "Cucurpe is not a battle ground between collectivism and free enterprise. On the contrary, most Cucurpeños want to be as independent as possible—to run their own cattle, farm their own fields" (1988:146). Close examination would reveal that most peasant villages show similar sentiments and similar divisions.

the right to make a living on small plots of land. They paid for this right in labor, in produce, or in money. The raw economics of this arrangement were often surrounded by an aura of be-

nevolent reciprocity, and in fact the arrangement did often have a large personal element. Even the layout of the village, focusing on the lord's great house or castle, expressed this relationship. The peasants labored for their lord, and the lord in return protected the peasants (or at least the land they occupied), settled their disputes, and sponsored feasts on holy days.

The Prebendal System

State ownership, or a **prebendal system,** was common in the highly centralized bureaucratic states that arose in China, Mogul India, Peru, and the Ottoman Empire. There autocratic nonhereditary rulers retained ultimate control over most agricultural land. Instead of granting hereditary rights to feudal lords, as in Europe, they allowed prominent individuals to collect peasant tribute or taxes for specified periods of time. In return, the administrator provided services and revenue to the crown. Thus the administrator, or landholder, changed regularly. This system, like the patrimonial system, had its personal and ceremonial aspects, which helped to legitimize it in the eyes of the peasants. In China, for example, the local state official served as "magician of the people," interceding with the gods to stop floods, bring rains, and so forth. This system did not give rise to villages built up around a particular elite family, as in the patrimonial case.

The Mercantile System

The private property or **mercantile system,** the form of landholding most prevalent today, is associated with profound societal changes stemming from the rise of capitalism and industrialism in eighteenth-century Europe and the beginning of colonial empires. Land came to be viewed not as the hereditary privilege and responsibility of a local lord or ruler but as a commodity like any other—the private property of individual owners. Land became another form of capital, with rents or the sale of crops providing the return to the owner. Wherever European colonialism reached, this form

of land tenure was encouraged (Wolf 1982). When land became a commodity, it was relatively easy to encourage increased production and the settlement of Europeans in the new colonies, such as those in Africa and the Americas. Mercantile systems usually lacked the reciprocity that we saw in the patrimonial and even the state systems. But the mercantile system encouraged landowners to reinvest rents in their lands and to modernize their farm technology.

The transition from state control to mercantile or private ownership can be seen in the vast and varied lands of the former Ottoman Empire in the Middle East. In 1858 the Ottoman government transformed most state or crown lands into private holdings in order to stimulate agriculture. Urban investors and local leaders bought title to much of the best farmland. Agricultural production and investment did increase, but at the expense of the peasants who actually worked the land. The new owners were concerned with extracting maximum income, and the peasants no longer enjoyed their traditional right to farm. This experience—the disadvantaging of the peasantry by a move to private ownership (often in the guise of "land reform")—is not uncommon. When land becomes a commodity, those who supply only labor may be seen as expendable or at least replaceable.

The Administrative System

Finally, the twentieth century has produced the **administrative system,** in which land is owned and managed by the state. In most communist countries such as China (until 1980) and the Soviet Union collective and state farms are the basis of most agricultural production. Peasants on a state-owned farm work under the direction of government agricultural experts, who set production quotas and determine how labor will be allocated. Collective farmers may escape the extreme poverty and

The use of small tractors has transformed peasant agriculture in Southeast Asia. This early model tractor is being operated by a farmer in Huang-do, China. (BILL PIERCE/RAINBOW)

social degradation that often characterize peasant life under the other forms of land control, but as their labor and income are at the disposal of a bureaucratic ruling class, they are still peasants in the economic and political sense of the term. Variants of this arrangement are seen in the large state-run farm projects in some parts of Africa and Latin America.

Collectivization has seemed attractive to many governments for several reasons, not all of them laudatory. The main argument in favor of collectivization is that large agricultural enterprises gain from economies of scale; that is, expensive equipment can be shared, large fields tilled and irrigated efficiently, and labor pooled. In developing countries particularly it often seems easier to provide schools, clinics, and marketing facilities to large concentrations of people than to dispersed hamlets and villages. Another reason for collectivization is one

not often openly argued: it is one means of controlling rural people and ensuring a level of agricultural production adequate to meet the objectives of the ruling elite. Two examples illustrate some of the positive and negative aspects of modern collective farms.

A Sudanese Irrigation Project. The giant Rahad irrigation project in Sudan, established in 1973 to harness the waters of the Blue Nile for cotton production, regulates the lives of some 100,000 people in forty-six villages. Each farm family is regarded as a tenant and is given up to twenty-two acres to farm, according to an administrative plan governing all decisions in regard to crops, crop rotation, and animal production. Tenants receive housing, schools, and other community services. The project maintains strict authority in most areas of community life: it recruits and evicts tenants, provides all services and agricultural inputs, and markets and processes the cotton produced. It monitors each household's use of its lands, imposes sanctions it considers appropriate, and determines the profits the household is to receive (USAID 1982:4–6).

The Rahad Project has made some important positive contributions to the national economy of the Sudan and it has offered a substantial improvement in the quality of life of many tenants, in particular, by providing better access to schools and clinics. Still, most aspects of the economy are regulated, often to the detriment of the individual farmer who is called upon to produce cotton needed for Sudan's foreign markets rather than crops that would be more useful or profitable locally. Farmers see the most immediate return from their individual garden plots and from raising livestock, endeavors the authorities try to restrict. The immense scale of the project has caused some difficulties in management, and decisions are sometimes made that are almost impossible for farmers to implement if they are to survive. Most seem to cope by manipulating the rules, by raising more foodstuffs for private sale and adding to their herds of goats and cattle. However, they then run the risk of punishment or eviction.

Chinese Communes. China has radically transformed its land tenure and rural society in this century—not just once but several times. Following the success of the Communist Revolution in 1949, the traditional patrimonial estates were abolished and family private holdings were restricted in size, with much land being redistributed to the landless. Very rapidly this arrangement gave way to collectivization on the Soviet model, and by the early 1950s all farming was organized around collective farms or communes. At first these communes were relatively small and often consisted of closely related families. But soon the government ordered them consolidated into far larger entities, with all planning and administration carried out centrally. In 1956, for example, the government forced cooperatives to purchase over a million double-wheel, double-blade plows, even though they were virtually worthless in paddy cultivation. Authorities even dictated a specific planting density for rice, regardless of local conditions (Lardy 1985:38). By 1960 the government eliminated almost all aspects of rural entrepreneurship and private trading, closely controlled the prices of all produce, and set rigid quotas for grain production. The most consistent aspect of agricultural policy was the underpricing of rural products so as to support a large urban population.

Because central planning was unresponsive to local conditions and prices were low, production of critical food crops dropped drastically while the authorities continued to set high production quotas in an effort to feed the teeming cities. It has been estimated that between 1959 and 1961, food shortages and rural economic dislocations resulted in the deaths of 10 million Chinese (Lardy 1985:41). Most of these deaths occurred in the countryside, where 80 percent of China's people still live. Agriculture improved somewhat after 1961 but then stagnated until 1978, when the post-Mao government decided to return to decentralized, family-run farming. In the subsequent four years the proportion of people earning less than 100 yuan a year (the rural poverty line) fell from 30 to 3 percent—an achievement hailed around the world. Yet some Chinese communes had prospered during the years of collectivization, particularly those that were small, that enlisted members who trusted one another, and that offered greater rewards for shared labor than members could reap alone. When farming was returned to the private sector, many, but not all, profited (Parish 1985).

The Moral Economy Approach. In some respects the Chinese experience reflects an ongoing debate as to the kind of land tenure and farming system that is most appropriate in developing countries: family-run farms or collectives. There is no question that the Chinese government seriously mismanaged its collectivization policy, as it undoubtedly stifled food production and depressed living standards in the countryside. It is argued, however, that in some circumstances collective approaches to land use and tenure are indeed appropriate. James Scott (1976) suggests that most peasants are less concerned with individual profit than with the security of knowing they will be protected in adversity. This is sometimes called the **moral economy approach** to village life. Many traditional communities, its advocates hold, are built on this philosophy. People think less of their individual or family self-interest than of the moral value of membership in a society that culturally envelopes them and protects them through communal sharing in bad years. Traditional, "closed" villages in the Mexican state of Oaxaca, to be discussed shortly, are part of such a moral economy. The villagers place great emphasis on the village as a community in which all have a more or less secure place and in which culturally defined rules encourage sharing and tend to level distinctions of wealth. In such a community, investigators who stress the moral economy argue, a cooperative approach to rural development would be most appropriate.

The Political Economy Approach. According to the alternative approach, sometimes called the **political economy** (or *rational peasant*) **approach**, it is difficult if not impossible to build strong collectives except under special circumstances (Popkin 1979). Peasants, it is argued, rationally calculate the advantages their immediate families can expect to derive from a collective venture and decline to participate unless they see a benefit in doing so. They are motivated not by abstract notions of communal well-being but by self-interest. The only circumstances that would favor collectivization are those in which participation is voluntary, the work units are small, the labor contributions are honestly measured and proportionately rewarded, and the collective produces something that would be difficult for the farmer to handle alone. If farmers are to participate in such a venture voluntarily, it will have to appeal to their self-interest, not to their community spirit.

Louis Putterman (1981) found that this was the case in Tanzania: peasants joined a collective farm when it served their interests to do so. They joined collectives for the production of sugar cane and fruits, where the joint effort paid off to members directly; they did not join collectives organized to produce subsistence crops that a farm family could raise very well on their own. They responded to a collective when they had faith in the honesty of its leadership and felt that they could gain something they could not gain by their individual efforts. In short, they calculated their self-interest rather than the probabilities of strengthening community ties.

The lesson of these various experiences is probably that there is no best choice between collective and private farming: the appropriate choice depends on the circumstances and on the rewards for the farmers involved.

Peasant Responses to Oppression and Change

Although the lot of rural peoples varies widely, it is rarely enviable; "peasants of all times and all places are structured inferiors" (Dalton 1972:406). Wherever a peasantry exists, it represents a politically dependent and often oppressed segment of the society. Some observers say that peasants have been beaten down too long to be able to change their circumstances;

generations of oppression have turned them into passive drudges, resigned to the injustices of their position and indifferent to political events outside the confines of their villages. Others argue that peasants' "passivity" is a rational, conservative response: poor farmers or peasants simply cannot afford to take risks.

Still, we see that all over the world peasants have effected drastic changes in the way they live. In communities throughout southern Asia, for example, small tractors are used to till the paddies, entrepreneurs start up rice mills, and people almost everywhere are raising crops and animals they never raised before. Rural change is highly visible in China, where peasant farmers are now encouraged to reap the benefits of agricultural entrepreneurship. The Soviet Union is at last taking the same approach.

Anthropologists report that peasant farmers are far from passive and are quick to seize an opportunity. A study by an American anthropologist working with an Egyptian colleague documents a long history of entrepreneurial activity in a Nile Delta village, with effects that varied over time. In the early part of the century, rural entrepreneurs invested their profits in the accumulation of land and the community benefited little from their activities. With the enactment of strict laws limiting landownership in Egypt, entrepreneurs started to invest in other endeavors that stimulated the village economy. One entrepreneur began to raise chickens for sale in Cairo. He built incubators, sheds, and cages, and he purchased feed and equipment suited to a modest initial probe of the market. Soon his business was prospering and expanding. His success motivated others in the village to follow his example. Today raising chickens has become a major village industry (Saunders and Mehenna 1986:84–85).

Not all farming families can solve their immediate economic problems by adopting new agricultural techniques. Often the prosperity of one village household depletes the resources of a less fortunate one. One very common re-sponse is to pack up and move, just as thousands of Oklahoma farmers did during the great Dust Bowl era of the 1930s. Tens of thousands of Brazilian farm families are attempting to settle in the Amazon region, and even more turn to the cities in the hope of betterment. We may deplore the social and environmental consequences of pioneer settlements in the rain forest and of the proliferation of urban slums, but we must recognize the tenacity of people who are doing their best in a world that does not always serve them well.

Peasants do periodically mobilize themselves into armed opposition. Indeed, history has witnessed a series of exceedingly bloody peasant revolts, in which centuries of accumulated resentment, masked by seeming docility, burst forth in massive waves of violence. England in the fourteenth century and Germany in the fifteenth and sixteenth centuries were shaken by peasant uprisings. In more recent times, the Mexican, Russian, Chinese, and Cuban revolutionaries owed much of their success to peasant uprisings that furthered their aims.

As Eric Wolf (1966) points out, peasant uprisings are usually motivated by a drive not just for practical social change but for utopian justice and equality. Such hopes may serve to unite the peasants but not to organize them. The organization and leadership are usually provided by politically sophisticated outsiders.

When a government is strong, the usual outcome of a peasant revolt is the death of many peasants and the return of others to their fields. (An awareness of this likelihood has no doubt served to limit the number of peasant uprisings.) When, on the other hand, the government is already weakened, especially by war, then it may in fact fall if a strong leader manages to rally the peasants to his cause. This was the case in China, where Mao Zedong's revolution was furthered by the devastation of China's long war with Japan. Even when peasant revolts succeed, their success rarely brings complete equality, since urban elites often re-

In recent years, farmworkers in the United States have organized to seek better pay and working conditions. These Mexican-American farmworkers are members of the AFL-CIO. (AFL-CIO, GEORGE MEANY ARCHIVES)

place the earlier or traditional elite. In China, as we have just seen, even the newly installed Communist government continued policies that disadvantaged people in the countryside, particularly peasants. While the system of land control is usually changed and poverty may be alleviated, a sizable class of rural producers remains in a subordinate social and political position, so there is still a peasant class.

The remainder of this chapter is devoted to two peasant societies. First we shall see how peasant communities in Mexico's Valley of Oaxaca are coping with urban market demands for agricultural intensification. We will then investigate two externally similar but internally somewhat different Taiwanese villages.

THE VALLEY OF OAXACA

For more than two thousand years cultivators in the Valley of Oaxaca, in southern Mexico,

have been building brush-and-stone dams to control floodwaters from the mountains and diverting streams into irrigation canals to water their crops. On the valley floor, some peasants still irrigate by hand, drawing water in buckets from wells and carrying it to the fields. Recently some of the wells have gone dry after two to four hours' use. The pump of one farmer interferes with the well of another. Urbanization and the extension of irrigation farming are threatening the valley's water supply.

The city of Oaxaca is growing and the demand for water for domestic and industrial use is increasing, so water once available for farmers is now being diverted to the city. Agriculture is also being intensified. Demand is growing for fresh vegetables and for alfalfa. Farmers are tapping their water resources more extensively than ever before because the government of Mexico has subsidized the construction of concrete canals and dams and the installation of high-powered diesel pumps. This equipment enables Oaxacans to grow alfalfa, which is far more profitable than the former major cash crops of wheat and sugar cane or the traditional subsistence crops of corn, beans, and squash. Alfalfa is profitable because dairy farmers use it for feed, and dairy products are in demand in Mexican cities. But it requires a great deal of water and puts a serious strain on this critical resource.

The remains of the ancient canals, dams, and reservoirs indicate that this is not the first attempt to raise the level of productivity in the valley. Nor is the farmers' involvement in a centralized political state and a broad market economy a new development. Archaeological excavations in the ruins of the pre-Hispanic city of Monte Albán reveal that a complex, stratified urban civilization developed in the valley between 2,300 and 1,200 years ago, alongside other Mesoamerican states. When the Spaniards arrived in the sixteenth century, they found a large class of peasants and a small elite of professional governors and nobles, who regulated intercommunity relations and maintained order within the villages. The Spaniards eventually replaced the upper levels of the Indian nobility, but by and large they left local Oaxacan communities to their own devices, thus stimulating a gradual process of political and economic decentralization that is mirrored in the development of very inward-looking, self-contained villages—so-called **closed corporate communities.** Such a community strongly emphasizes its identity and discourages outsiders from settling thereby restricting land use to village members and prohibiting the sale or lease of property to outsiders.

Many such communities in the valley were incorporated in haciendas—self-sufficient landed estates ruled by wealthy landlords, who granted the peasants the right to farm the land in return for high rents. This is a form of the patrimonial system of landholding described earlier. The Mexican Revolution of 1910–1920 purported to bring the hacienda system to an end. Many farmers were granted titles to their fields. As before, the peasants' economic affairs remained subject to the forces of the larger society, but control of their villages and of their irrigation works was put into their hands.

Irrigation Management

In a survey of twenty-four Oaxacan villages conducted between 1967 and 1970, Susan H. Lees (1974a) focused on the management of irrigation systems. Were it not for irrigation, most of the land could not support crops reliably. Rainfall is highly variable, averaging between 51 and 76 centimeters (20 and 30 inches) a year, most falling in June and July. Except for those farmers who own land on the moist valley floor, Oaxacans depend on dams and canals. Lees reasoned that given the importance of water, she could learn a great deal about the political structure of Oaxacan villages and

about the relationship between irrigation and forms of social organization by determining who was in charge of water control in the villages, how the water was distributed, when and how often individuals irrigated their fields, and who was responsible for maintaining dams and canals.

Lees found that the mechanisms of water control varied from community to community. There was no single system. The *presidente* or mayor of one village had complete control over its irrigation system; he decided who received water, when, and for how long. The presidente of another village left the matter of water control to five lower-ranking officials, each of whom supervised one of the main canals. Residents of another village elected a full-time water commissioner. In two other communities, no one was in charge; each household made private arrangements with an upstream village that could shut off the water that flowed into their irrigation ditches. In nine of the villages that Lees visited, village household heads were required to pay water councils for water, the amount varying with the amount of land they were farming or the length of time they used the water. In others, payment was indirect; the greater a family's contributions in money or labor to the church or to the building and maintenance of the village school, the more water they were allotted.

Despite these variations, Lees found important relationships between irrigation practices and social and political structure. In general, the Oaxacans were intensifying their use of irrigation in order to increase their production of cash crops. And this stepped-up pressure on the water supply was related to a decrease in local control over resources and to a general centralization of the production system. In the process the Oaxacans were gradually abandoning some long-standing social practices that had served to discourage overexploitation of their environment.

Sharing and Production

All of the villages Lees studied were essentially egalitarian, democratic communities. In general, the standard of living in the valley was low, as most families produced just enough to get by. Inequalities existed; every village included poor and not-so-poor households. But no one owned what could be called a large farm or estate. And no matter how much land a family owned, there was always a chance that their crops might fail and that they would have to borrow money in order to get through the year. Oaxacan farming, then, is a risky endeavor. The villagers reduce individual risk by sharing their good and bad fortune through two closely related social customs: *guelaguetza* and fiestas.

Guelaguetza is the delayed exchange of equivalent goods and services. When it is time to plant or harvest, men form teams and move from the field of one to the field of the next until all of the work is done. When a child is born or a couple married, friends and relatives donate candles, bread, chocolates, coffee, a few pesos—whatever they can spare—with the expectation of receiving equivalent goods in the future. A man who has had a good year lends to one who has not (Lees 1973:13–14). Guelaguetza is a **leveling mechanism**—a social or economic practice that serves to lessen differentials in wealth—and so is the lavish fiesta that each village holds on the day of its patron saint.

Every couple is expected to sponsor at least one fiesta in their lifetime—perhaps more if they are relatively well off. The fiesta, the major social event in a Oaxacan village, is a source of great pride and prestige to the sponsor. Couples compete in the provision of extravagant amounts of food and liquor and spectacular fireworks and music. As a result, sponsorship of a fiesta requires large expenditures. A family may plan and save for years—and even then,

few can bear the total cost alone. The solution is guelaguetza. The sponsor borrows money and goods, mortgaging future surpluses for a day's celebration. Thus the fiesta siphons off surpluses, preventing anyone from accumulating substantial wealth, and at the same time perpetuates the guelaguetza system of exchange (Kirkby 1973).

Constant lending and borrowing distribute the risks of uncertain harvest across the community. Virtually everyone has made loans to some villagers and owes food or money to others. If a family's crops dry up or wash away, they can collect old debts and borrow from friends, relatives, and neighbors. There is no shame in borrowing. The household that has food to spare this year knows it may run short in the future. In this way small surpluses continually circulate in Oaxacan villages. Extra food and money find their way to the people who need assistance, to feed their families or to sponsor a fiesta.

At the same time, guelaguetza and fiestas encourage underproduction. If members of a household work harder than their neighbors and produce a surplus, they can expect to see their neighbors coming to collect old debts and to incur new ones. All their extra effort may profit them little in a material sense, although they enjoy the prestige of sponsoring a fiesta and sharing with their fellow villagers. Consequently, most household heads consciously aim to produce only a little more than they need. If the spring rains are light, boding a poor season, they plant a little more than usual; if the rains are heavy, they plant a little less.

Given low levels of production, an obligation to share what one has, and large expenditures for fiestas, such farmers have very little left over to invest in new equipment, fertilizers, or other improvements. But they have little incentive to intensify their efforts. On the one hand, Oaxacans have traditionally had a relatively low standard of living. On the other, they have until recently maintained a balance between their own needs and those of the environment: they have not overused critical resources, above all water. Thus guelaguetza and fiestas have served both social and ecological functions (Kirkby 1973). Recent urban growth and the consequent intensification of agriculture are testing their ability to continue to perform those functions.

Political Power

Lees (1973) found similar social limits to private ambition in village politics. In general, Oaxacans consider the holding of public office a necessary evil, not a route to self-aggrandizement. In most villages each household contributes to a communal fund used to build and maintain the church, school, roads, and so on, and every able-bodied man is required to devote a specified number of days a year to public works. In addition, all men are expected to fill increasingly responsible political offices, beginning as young men with the job of *topil*, a combination night watchman/messenger boy. Higher officials—presidente, school commissioner, judge, and so on—are elected or appointed; most officials are not paid.

Social pressure, public scrutiny, and limited terms of office prevent individuals from using public office for personal gain. Indeed, to be eligible for election to a higher office, a man first has to sponsor a fiesta out of his own pocket. Failure to accept an election or an appointment is considered a crime, punishable in some villages by a fine or a term in jail. Just as there is little advantage in accumulating a surplus, so there is little advantage in serving in office and accumulating political power. It is no surprise, then, that the villages Lees surveyed turned out to be relatively egalitarian and democratic.

The Pressure to Intensify Agriculture

The state of Oaxaca is undergoing a profound transformation. The Mexican government is encouraging Oaxacans to modernize and intensify their agriculture. Its subsidizing of the construction of new irrigation works and the purchase of new farm equipment created something of an economic boom in the valley, at least prior to the debt crisis of the 1980s.

A farmer in the Oaxaca Valley irrigates his flowers, which will be sold in Mexico City, by the time-consuming method of hand watering the rows. Today most irrigation is through larger-scale canal systems, often set up by the government. (UNITED NATIONS)

The social order of the peasant villages is already changing. The young welcome the new intensification program as an opportunity to improve their families' standard of living and status. They are eager to make more money and they consider the sponsoring of a fiesta old-fashioned and a waste of money. The social controls that served to inhibit the accumulation of wealth and limit exploitation are breaking down.

One consequence is that the ecological balance has been altered. The water table responds to mechanized pumping. As it fluctuates, the Oaxacans must dig deeper and deeper wells and invest more and more in equipment just to maintain current levels of production. And even as they do so, the water table continues to drop during critical seasons as many farmers pump water at the same time.

As a corollary to this process, the villages are gradually forfeiting their political autonomy. The Oaxacan peasants have neither the funds to purchase the elaborate equipment they now require nor the skills to maintain it. Of necessity, they are becoming increasingly dependent on the Mexican government and its experts.

The process of agricultural intensification, intertwined with political centralization, will continue until a critical element in the system is disrupted, crops fail, and a family can no longer maintain itself by farming. At that point, many cultivators will have to seek alternative ways to make a living. The "organizational response to short-term degradation of environmental resources is centralization while long-term degradation elicits responses of decentralization" (Lees 1974b:160). Perhaps this process helps to explain why states expand and contract in cycles.

Whether Oaxacan cultivators will turn to factory jobs, slash-and-burn agriculture, or some other alternative when they reach the point of diminishing returns is difficult to say. What is clear is that intensification of agricultural production does not solve the problem of supplying growing populations and states once and for all. Instead, it creates a situation that is both politically and ecologically unstable. Intensification inevitably draws the small farming community into an arena where powerful political systems and national and world markets are at play. And when these forces impinge on the community, traditional methods of maintaining social and environmental equilibrium may break down.

The next case study leaves some of these general issues to one side and treats the important question of the differential effects of two forms of irrigation agriculture on the social organization of the communities that practice them—even when those communities are parts of one cultural system. Burton Pasternak based his study on a carefully controlled comparison of two communities with very similar histories but with differing approaches to water use in agriculture.

TWO CHINESE VILLAGES

In many respects, Tatieh and Chungshe, two peasant communities in southern Taiwan, are twin villages. In 1967 each consisted of somewhat over a thousand people in households of about six members each. Both are situated near sizable cities, which are beginning to attract their young people. Both villages are almost entirely dependent on agriculture; the people make their living from their rice paddies and their fields of sugar cane, sweet potatoes, and other crops. With irrigation, these fields are able to feed the villagers and still produce a surplus that is marketed commercially. In both villages the average family income is quite high—between $7,000 and $8,000 in 1967 (Pasternak 1972:58).

Physically, however, the villages present somewhat different impressions. Tatieh is a tidy, well-kept village. Small shrines mark the entrances to the residential center, with its brightly lit, paved roads, neat brick houses, and small shops at the crossroads. Chungshe, thirty miles away, appears less prosperous: no shrines at the village center, no temple comparable to the one in Tatieh. The roads are unpaved, and the mud-brick and bamboo houses seem shabby. Even the fields seem less prosperous. Chungshe's soil is poorer than Tatieh's, and though both villages have erratic rainfall, Chungshe has less water to use in irrigation than Tatieh.

These surface details are not the only differences. Pasternak found that Chungshe and Tatieh differ considerably in political and social organization. Thus even though the circumstances of all peasants have much in common, two peasant communities—even communities only thirty miles apart—may vary widely in the way people order their relationships with one another.

Kinship and Power

The descendants of one of Chungshe's original settlers, Lai Yuan, have always dominated the village's political and economic affairs. In the old days, this lineage owned much of the land surrounding Chungshe, and because so many villagers were their tenants (and hence owed them loyalty), the lineage effectively controlled the local political offices as well. Today the nine sublineages (called *fangs*) that recognize Lai Yuan as their founding father still control a total of 20.3 hectares (50.1 acres)—far more than any other descent group in either Chungshe or Tatieh controls. Members of these sublineages are markedly better off than the other villagers and consider themselves socially superior. Entrenched in adjoining compounds at the head of the village, Lai Yuan's descendants spurn

those who live in the village "tail" as ignorant and lazy. Reforms instituted by the national government in recent decades have weakened the Lai Yuan lineage's hold on the town's political offices, but once their control of these offices slipped, so did the importance of the offices. Political power in Chungshe today is largely unofficial, and still in the hands of Lai Yuan's descendants. When disputes arise or villagers need loans, it is not the elected headman and neighborhood chiefs who settle the matters, but "big men" who are invariably members of the old and wealthy lineages and sublineages.

Powerful landholding lineages have not developed in Tatieh, the apparently more prosperous of the two villages. Residents do maintain ceremonial ties with branches of their lineages in other communities, but kin ties with the other villages are not emphasized. Households belonging to the largest descent groups—the Liu, Hsu, and Ch'en, which together account for 46 percent of all households—are scattered all over the village and are no better or worse off than their neighbors. The three lineages maintain corporate estates; that is, they hold land collectively, as a lineage, like the wealthy fangs of Chungshe. But together they control only about 1.5 hectares (less than 4 acres) so they wield no special power. Two other descent groups have set up modest trust funds for their members. Otherwise, kinship has virtually no effect on the villagers' access to Tatieh's land, water, or labor.

The people of Tatieh prefer to keep family and business matters separate, in order to avoid the embarrassment of having to accuse relatives of defaulting on contracts. Like many peasants, they require some means of convening large labor forces, for planting and harvesting require more hands than any one household can supply. The Chungshe farmers handle this problem (like most other problems) through kinship, calling on their relatives to assist them, but Tatieh farmers call on friends and neighbors, whom they pay in wages or in equivalent amounts of labor.

The fact that Tatieh residents can depend on people outside their families—that they have ties throughout the village—is due in part to the number of non-kin-based organizations to which they belong. Each household head in Tatieh is a member of the *hsiao-tsu* ("small group") in charge of the irrigation system that waters his land, and since most households own land in two or more areas, most villagers belong to several irrigation associations, with overlapping memberships. Many villagers invest in "grain associations" that function more or less as banks, making loans to members when they need money to pay for a new plow, a wedding, or some other extraordinary expense. Also common are "father-mother associations," whose members help one another with the cost and labor involved in funerals. Finally, most households in Tatieh own shares in the Make Prosperous Corporation, a public corporation that manages 17 hectares (42 acres) of public land.

Such organizations, cutting across kin lines, unite Tatieh villagers in overlapping networks of rights and obligations, and thus diffusion of loyalty and reciprocity throughout the community helps to prevent individual families from monopolizing power or resources. Tatieh has less wealth and poverty than Chungshe, and it is much more democratic. There are no "big men" operating outside the official political system. The people of Tatieh take elections seriously, vote without regard to kinship, appeal to their elected headman when disputes arise, and generally abide by his judgments. Important decisions in regard to the community are made in town council meetings, convened every two months or so and attended by a male representative of every household in the village. The village council of Chungshe, in contrast, is largely a formality; it rarely meets unless an outside government official calls household heads together for announcements. This

difference is understandable, for in Tatieh the basic social unit is the village, in Chungshe it is the kin group. The people of Chungshe have little notion of identity with their community. The village is simply the place where they live; they belong to and identify with their lineage.

Ceremonies

The contrast between the lineage-focused organization of Chungshe and the community-focused households of Tatieh shows up clearly in their approaches to marriage and other ceremonies. One way to preserve the integrity and exclusivity of a patrilineage is to acquire brides from other villages—the farther away, the better. Once the bride is removed from her kin, their influence over her becomes negligible; the new couple is unequivocally under the authority of the husband's kin. This is the preferred form of marriage in Chungshe. The villagers say that marrying someone from the same community is asking for trouble, and that in-laws get along much better if they see each other only infrequently. Less than 21 percent of all marriages contracted in Chungshe between 1959 and 1964 were intravillage arrangements. By contrast, 48 percent of the marriages contracted in Tatieh during this period took place between residents of the village.

The people of Tatieh consider marriage an opportunity to acquire new friends and allies within the village; they prefer that their children marry people they have watched grow up. In-laws in Tatieh are frequent visitors; they exchange gifts, labor, and financial aid, attend each other's celebrations, and often maintain ties over two or more generations.

Tatieh wedding ceremonies symbolize this reciprocity. The bride and groom honor each other's ancestors in turn, and many friends and relatives on both sides of the family are invited to help prepare and share in the wedding feast. In Chungshe, the marriage ceremony centers on the honor paid by the groom to his ancestors; the bride's ancestors are ignored. Only a few of the bride's kin are invited to the wedding feast. The trouble and expense are also kept within the groom's family. If the family needs help with these responsibilities, they hire outside assistance rather than call upon friends and neighbors.

Thus the people of Chungshe treat ceremonies as private family or lineage affairs, whereas Tatieh villagers celebrate not only with kin but also with friends and neighbors. The elegant temple in Tatieh, carefully maintained and improved by succeeding generations, is a source of pride to all villagers. Old people gather there each morning; the temple provides a nursery for village children and a dormitory for lay devotees. Bimonthly and annual festivals draw individuals from all over the village. The comparatively drab, square, concrete building that doubles as a temple and a meeting hall in Chungshe is locked most of the time.

On feast days in Tatieh, people honor their ancestors at home, then gather at the temple to honor the village gods. These celebrations involve unrelated households in cooperative labor, joint expenditures, and communal worship. On feast days in Chungshe, families borrow symbols of the gods and celebrate in their own homes—a custom that reinforces privacy and underlines class differences, since the members of different classes celebrate separately.

History, Ecology, and Kinship

Pasternak traces both the elaboration of patrilineages in Chungshe and the deemphasis of kinship in Tatieh to historical and ecological conditions. Land around Tatieh, long under irrigation, is highly productive and therefore highly desirable. Since the village was founded by immigrants from mainland China, its residents once had to defend themselves against attacks by native Taiwanese and by other immigrant groups. The need for collective defense encouraged the residents to band together in a fortified multilineage settlement and to establish ties with other villages as well. Moreover, the irrigation system—six main canals, each of which supplies water to a large number of fields—has been in existence for many generations, so the village has a long history of cooperation among unrelated neighbors.

By comparison with the territory around Tatieh, the land on which Chungshe was founded was nothing to fight over. The soil was relatively poor and the rainfall relatively sparse. Pioneer families—again, immigrants from the mainland—could claim large tracts of virgin land and live in relative isolation. Untroubled by fear of incursions, they had little incentive to form ties with other descent groups or neighboring villages. Nor did irrigation serve to unite them. Until a few decades ago, Chungshe had no irrigation works. Before then, residents depended entirely on rain, and rain requires no cooperation among neighbors. Furthermore, when irrigation works were built, they were on a scale too massive to be handled by the community. In the 1920s, the Japanese, who at the time ruled Taiwan, constructed a vast irrigation system to water the entire Chianan Plain, on which Chungshe sits. Since this system requires professional management, it is outside officials, not the town residents, who make and enforce decisions regarding the distribution of water and the maintenance of the canals. In short, neither the need for defense nor the need to administer the irrigation system ever forced the Chungshe lineages to establish ties with one another, and so they remained separate.

Rainfall, Family, and Demography

Dependence on rainfall rather than canal irrigation in Chungshe affects not only the choice of a marriage partner (usually an outsider) but

Two ways of celebrating a festival point up the contrast between two Taiwanese villages. (Top) The villagers take part in the celebration of the birth of village sons in Tatieh. Each household that produced a son during the year provides cakes, which are distributed from the temple throughout the village. (Bottom) A priest brought in from the outside officiates at a village festival in Chungshe, where ritual labor is more often hired than exchanged. (BURTON PASTERNAK)

also the demography of the village. In a more recent study, Pasternak notes that when field preparation depended on rainfall, all families in Chungshe raced to prepare their fields at the same time, as soon as the rains came (Pasternak 1983). Labor could not easily be exchanged between families. Since field preparation was assigned exclusively to men, the demand for male labor increased. Since labor could not easily be hired (given that all households had the same problem at essentially the same time), Chungshe (and other villages of the region) often deviated from the expected norms of residence after marriage. The norm in Chinese society was for the bride to join her husband in her husband's father's home; to do otherwise was felt to disgrace the husband and his family. (This norm of postmarital residence is usually called "patrilocal," as we shall see in more detail in Chapter 12.)

Many Chungshe men joined the families of their wives at marriage (matrilocal residence). Usually these men were from very poor families with no prospects of inheriting land to cultivate. A woman therefore did not have to leave her parents at marriage, move to a strange village to marry a man she had never seen (since matrilocal husbands usually come from the same community as their brides), or accommodate herself to the woman's network within a new community.

From the point of view of the women, therefore, these marriages were far less stressful. Moreover, it seemed that female children were treated better as infants, as their mortality was lower than elsewhere, probably because their parents realized that they might well remain at home after marriage and directly contribute to the long-term support of the household. We are not surprised to learn that women who married this way were more fertile than those who married patrilocally (Pasternak 1983). Nor is it unexpected that remarriage rates were

especially high here, even among older men and women. As a widow still required the labor her husband had provided, even a widower of advanced years could find a wife. Finally, Pasternak found that Chungshe households delayed the division of family lands among heirs longer than was customary elsewhere in order to keep adult brothers together. Once canals were introduced in the area of Chungshe, the frequency of matrilocal marriages declined, and families divided their lands earlier. In short, Pasternak's findings demonstrate the value of anthropology's holistic perspective. He has shown how the specific form of technology (irrigation) can influence social organization, here marriage and family structure, and how the latter can affect demographic behavior.

Thus while the people of Tatieh and Chungshe make their living in the same way—and, as measured by average income, with equal success—they have developed different forms of social organization. In one, the historical necessity of cooperative action has resulted in a breakdown of lineage barriers and a diffusion of reciprocity throughout the village—a process that has kept the community relatively unstratified. In the other, the lack of a need for cooperation has allowed residents to confine their loyalty and reciprocity to members of their own lineages. The strength and persistence of lineage ties have encouraged the development of economic stratification, and since the kinship system prevents any equalization of power and resources, the rich and poor have remained so.

Summary

Intensive agriculture is distinguished from horticulture by both increased investment in energy and increased productivity per unit of land. The additional energy may come from a variety of sources, including animals yoked to

plows, fossil fuels for farm machinery, fertilizers, and human muscles. Methods of intensification include irrigation canals, terracing, crop rotation, and selective breeding of crops and livestock. Through these techniques, the output of cultivated fields is increased, more fields can be cultivated, and fallow periods can be decreased or eliminated. While both the land and the farmer work harder under intensive agriculture, the result is a great deal more produce.

Intensive agriculture substantially reshapes the environment. By constructing irrigation systems to overcome the problem of insufficient rainfall, for instance, farmers may create new, complex problems that become increasingly difficult to solve. The more people alter their ecosystems, the more labor and organizational effort are required to maintain their bases of production.

The social consequences of intensification are far-reaching. The development of irrigation is associated with the emergence of cities and territorial states, with accompanying social changes: higher population densities, economic stratification, increased trade, the appearance of craft specialists, and the development of hierarchical civil and religious organizations. The need for centralized authority to make decisions, variations in the productivity of land in the region, and a surplus of food all contributed to the rise of cities and states. Farming communities that were at one time autonomous were absorbed by the states, and the farmers, or peasants, lost control over the social and economic system and the means of production. *Peasants* are agriculturalists, usually villagers, who do not control the land, capital, and labor on which they depend; further, they are often subject to *corvée*, unpaid labor to build and maintain roads and bridges. In some parts of the world peasants gain access to land by *sharecropping*, or working land owned by others in exchange for a share of the yield. In addition to supporting a household, peasants must allocate resources to *ceremonial, replacement,* and *rent funds*. All of these expenses, but especially the rent, tie the peasant to the larger society and determine the nature of that relationship.

There are four basic patterns of land tenure. Under the *patrimonial system,* which prevailed in northern and central Europe during the Middle Ages, land is controlled by decentralized feudal rulers who hold domain by hereditary right. The *prebendal system,* once common in China, Mogul India, and the Ottoman Empire, is similar to the patrimonial system except that land tenure is not hereditary. Under the *mercantile system,* land is regarded as the private property of the individual owner. And under the *administrative system,* found in some communist countries, the state owns the land and can control much of the peasant's labor and income.

The administrative form of land control has had a mixed record. Collective farming led to the near collapse of food production in China and was largely abandoned there as public policy. Some collective enterprises do prosper, particularly those that are small, that offer participants some advantage, and that produce items that farmers could not produce by their individual efforts.

Advocates of the *moral economy approach* to village life hold that peasants are less concerned with individual gain than with the security of knowing they will be protected in adversity. Advocates of the *political economy,* or *rational peasant, approach* argue that peasants will refuse to join a collective enterprise unless they see some advantage to their immediate family in doing so. Experiences in various parts of the world indicate that the appropriate choice between collective and private farming probably depends on the circumstances and on the rewards for the farmers involved.

Under exceptional circumstances, peasant farmers may find their situation intolerable and rise in revolt. In this century they have supported revolutions in Mexico, Russia, China, and Cuba. Even when such uprisings are successful, the farmers often remain disadvantaged in relation to the urban population.

This chapter focuses special attention on the

inward-looking, self-contained villages—*closed corporate communities*—of Mexico's Valley of Oaxaca and on the peasants of two Taiwanese villages.

Following the Mexican Revolution of 1910–1920, many peasants in the Valley of Oaxaca gained control of their villages and irrigation works. Studies of water control and social organization in the valley revealed nearly as many ways to organize access to irrigation as the number of villages. But two common social practices maintained a balance between the needs of the villagers and those of environmental stability—guelaguetza, an exchange of equivalent goods and services, and the annual fiesta. Both practices served as *leveling mechanisms*—a means of distributing goods and preventing the accumulation of wealth. Because there was not much advantage in having wealth, underproduction was encouraged. Because there was little advantage in accumulating political power, the villages were relatively egalitarian and democratic.

With pressure from the Mexican government to modernize and intensify production, however, the social controls that have inhibited overexploitation are falling into disuse and the environmental balance has been disturbed. The water supply is threatened. Because greater investments are needed to maintain current levels of production, the villages are increasingly dependent on the federal government.

The intensive agricultural villages of Tatieh and Chungshe in Taiwan resemble each other in size, physical layout, access to urban centers, and technology, yet they have evolved very different modes of political and social organization. In Chungshe, the descendants of one of the original settlers dominate village politics, economics, and access to resources; in Tatieh, kinship has virtually no effect on villagers' access to the critical resources of land, water, and labor.

The contrast between the lineages of Chungshe and the households of Tatieh is apparent in their different approaches to marriage and to ceremonies. The people of Chungshe preserve the exclusivity of the patrilineage by acquiring brides from other villages, while in Tatieh, marriage is regarded as an opportunity to acquire new friends and allies within the village. Similarly, ceremonies in Chungshe are family affairs, while Tatieh villagers celebrate with both neighbors and kin.

The elaboration of patrilineage in Chungshe and the lesser emphasis on kinship in Tatieh can be traced to historical and ecological conditions. Tatieh land is highly desirable and has long been irrigated. The historical necessity of cooperative action for defense and distribution of water in Tatieh resulted in a breakdown of lineage barriers, which kept the society relatively unstratified. Chungshe land is less desirable and until recently was without an irrigation system, so the lineages were not obliged to cooperate with one another.

Key Terms

administrative system	leveling mechanism	patrimonial system	prebendal system
ceremonial fund	mercantile system	peasants	rent fund
closed corporate	moral economy	political economy	replacement fund
community	approach	approach	sharecropping
corvée			

Suggested Readings

FREEMAN, J. M. 1977. *Scarcity and Opportunity in an Indian Village*. Menlo Park, Calif.: Cummings Publishing. A study of a small village in India that has experienced an ever-widening gap between the privileged high castes and the less privileged lower castes. The economic basis of this gap seems to be that the higher castes have benefited from the growth of a nearby city while members of the lower castes have little opportunity to improve their lot through urban contacts.

GAMST, F. C. 1974. *Peasants in Complex Society*. New York: Holt, Rinehart & Winston. A valuable introduction to the anthropological study of the peasant community and its relations with the larger society.

PASTERNAK, BURTON. 1983. *Guests in the Dragon: Social Demography of a Chinese District, 1895–1946*. New York: Columbia University Press. An analysis of the relationship between domestic institutions and demographic behavior in one Hakka district of Taiwan that details the different choices among the possible forms of marriage and the implications these choices have for rates of adoption, mortality, and fertility.

SMIL, VACLAV. 1984. *The Bad Earth*. Armonk, N.Y.: Sharpe. A detailed but readable description of the environmental consequences of China's postrevolutionary efforts to modernize.

SCOTT, JAMES C. 1976. *The Moral Economy of the Peasant*. New Haven, Conn.: Yale University Press. A study of peasant politics and rebellion that focuses on the critical problem of a secure subsistence as the explanation for the technical, social, and moral arrangements of these societies.

Chapter **9** Industrial Society

The products of industrial society are so much a part of our everyday lives that it is difficult to imagine living without them. Even those of us who have lived and worked in what have been called preindustrial societies have found that no population is untouched by the products of industrial nations. People as remote from us as the Pokot farmers and herders of Kenya learn of national events from their portable radios and television sets. Not only modern firearms and aluminum pots and pans are part of everyday life in the Amazon basin; so are items that only a few years ago would have been called high-tech: miniature cassette players and radios. Lapp reindeer herders go about their business on snowmobiles and the camel has been virtually replaced in the Middle East by Japanese made trucks.

Even without venturing beyond our own society we can see immediate costs and benefits of life in our postindustrial world. It has been designated "postindustrial" because its dominant technology has shifted from that of heavy industry (steel mills, locomotives, automobiles) to those of electronics and biochemistry, which make possible nearly instant global communications, space travel, and genetic engineering—not to mention the ever-present potential of nuclear catastrophe.

Among the benefits afforded by industrial and postindustrial society we count advances in the medical sciences. The CAT scan (computer-aided tomography, a way of enhancing X-ray images of the body) was an exotic diagnostic instrument in the 1970s, available only at a few hospitals and at great expense; CAT scans are now routinely available. Computers that twenty years ago existed only in research facilities are now home appliances. Another benefit of industrial and postindustrial society is the enormous growth in public and private educational facilities. More than ever before, knowledge is power. Access to training is an essential component of survival in the modern world. Money, power, social standing are all now coming to be linked as firmly to what you know as to whom you know: young persons looking for jobs in technological fields cannot rely solely on their family and friends, the conventional support networks of the past.

But industrial society imposes equally obvious costs. Pollution from industrial sites in the Midwest ends up as acid rain in the Northeast and Canada. The controversy over nuclear waste dumps rages wherever sites are proposed. The polluted waters off our coasts have disastrous effects on marine life. The much-discussed greenhouse effect and the lowering of the ozone level in the upper atmosphere are clear and present dangers—even though no one can say with confidence just what the consequences will be. One thing seems to be certain, however: industrial pollution, together with the effects of the massive loss of rain forests in the tropics, are causing global temperatures to rise.

Another and different kind of cost is the high level of stress and anxiety that seems to be built into the special socioeconomic system associated with industrial and postindustrial systems—irregular alternations between boom and bust can have devastating psychological consequences for large segments of our urban and suburban communities.

THE DEVELOPMENT OF INDUSTRIALISM

Understanding how we got where we are and the effects of industrial society on the rest of the world are relatively recent concerns of anthropologists. Urban anthropology and the study of complex societies emerged as areas of study only after World War II. Anthropologists quickly learned that no one discipline could hope to comprehend the very complex processes at work in modern societies. The disciplines of economics, history, political science, and sociology, as well as anthropology, are needed for adequate analysis of those processes.

The traditional subsistence systems we have discussed—hunting and gathering, horticulture, pastoralism, and intensive agriculture—are rural systems of food production. The first cities and until recently many African, European, and Asian cities were little more than administrative and trading centers, established to serve the surrounding countryside that provided them with food. The priests, military leaders, and artisans who were not serving the governing elite were serving the farmers. Only after about the fifteenth century (with a few exceptions) do we see a change—the rise of cities not as agricultural trade centers and administrative centers but as manufacturing centers. The production of goods in great volume went hand in hand with the spread of trade and invention. Improved armaments and navigational equipment on sailing ships gave European cities access to all the world's seas. European cities grew, fueled at first by the power of water, wind, and human and animal muscle. Finally, in the early nineteenth century, steam and internal combustion engines were harnessed to machines of both transport and manufacture. Soon industry acquired the means to provide energy and technology for agriculture, and thus the system of production based in the city spread throughout the world. Given their background of interest in earlier, simpler societies, anthropologists are particularly interested in two aspects of industrialization: the impact of industrial society on rural areas and the incorporation of rural values and organizations into the industrial system.

Industrialism and all its ramifications can be seen as a series of adaptive responses much like those we have already examined in other subsistence systems. It is a way of coping with challenges and resolving specific problems. As in all other instances of behavioral adaptation, the very act of coping creates the potential for negative as well as positive effects. The success or failure of industrial adaptations to human problems can be seen only in terms of long-range survival. What we call industrialism is a major societal commitment that has been under way for some 250 years. Not all the consequences are clearly understood even now. Further complicating the picture is the fact that industrialism is not an adaptation to a single local set of constraints or problems, and so the costs and benefits vary widely among people caught up in industrial society. Can we truly say that unemployed steelworkers of Ohio are benefiting from the system to the same degree as computer specialists in California's Silicon Valley? Are the unemployed young people in the ghettos of Chicago, Los Angeles, and New York as advantaged by supersonic transports as the commercial travelers who regularly commute to Europe?

The Organization of Energy

Howard Odum (1971) observed that the structure and function of animal, plant, and human social systems are understood at least to some extent by the way in which they acquire, channel, and expend the energy necessary for their maintenance as systems. Anthropologist Leslie

White was one of the first to recognize the importance of the role of energy in cultural evolution (as we saw in Chapter 2). What we have called the industrial age, White (1949) has called the fuel age.

The development of mechanized procedures for harnessing new forms of energy—first coal, then oil and gas—is closely related to the evolution of specialized production units. We know that many human populations had learned to extract the solar energy stored in plants more efficiently by domesticating them, harnessed animals to plows, used wind or water to power mills, traveled over the seas on boats powered by sail, and waged war with explosives. But the exploitation of energy sources outside the human body was relatively limited. It was only with the invention of the steam engine and later the diesel and internal combustion engines that populations were able to harness the concentrated solar energy stored in the fossil remains of organic matter (coal, oil, and gas). With these new sources of energy, industrialized populations have vastly increased the scale of mechanization, specialization, mass production, and so on. Modern industrial techniques harness more energy per capita than ever before in history.

Industrial societies may employ more energy than other groups, but they do not necessarily use it more efficiently. On the contrary, farmers in industrial societies often invest more energy in fertilizer and gasoline for their tractors than they harvest in calories of food energy, even with high-yield grains. Moreover, large quantities of energy are diverted to non-food-producing activities. Thus an industrial society is significantly less efficient than any other kind in the sense that it requires more energy to support a unit of population. Nevertheless, new sources of energy and the technology to harness them laid the groundwork for expansion of production on a scale never witnessed before—a dramatic, if costly, change.

Mechanization

Much of the energy involved in industrialism is channeled through machines rather than through animals and humans. **Mechanization**—the replacement of human and animal labor by mechanical devices—began long before the industrial age. Sails have been used to power ships for millennia. Mechanical devices of increasing size and complexity have been developed over the centuries for a variety of purposes—waging war, forging metals, constructing monumental buildings, grinding grain, making cloth. It is quite astonishing to note how far mechanization had proceeded even during what are sometimes called the Dark Ages. Outside of Paris in the sixteenth century an ingenious system of hydraulic pumps drew water from the Seine for manufacturing purposes. Despite the ingenuity of these machines, it was not until the relatively recent development of sophisticated metallurgical techniques and power-transmission systems that a breakthrough was achieved in the amount of power that could effectively be delivered to the job at hand. Such machinery has transformed our idea of work. Labor is increasingly devoted to the management and maintenance of machinery rather than to the products the machines make. The whole field of robotics is a case in point. Specialists in programming and maintaining industrial robots are now key personnel in heavy, light, and service industries.

Some key components of the industrial era are as important for their cognitive as for their technological effects. The development of precise instruments for measuring time was critical to most sophisticated technologies and processes. At the same time, the gears that drove elaborate mechanical clocks were pivotal elements in the directing of human attention to a mechanical view of the world, which in turn became a key to the physical knowledge on which industry is based. The view of the world as a machine provided a model for complex systems of power transmission and regulation; this is the view that underlies the concept of the assembly line. It also encouraged a mechanical view of human interaction.

Specialization

Specialization is a direct outcome of the linking of new energy sources to the working power of new machines. Regions, cities, even neighborhoods become associated with particular products. Agricultural districts come to depend on a limited array of crops—a far cry from the self-sufficiency that marked local adaptations in earlier eras. Even before the industrial period, cities were dependent for food on the lands within a one- or two-day walk from their walls. The city's workplaces or factories come to be highly specialized, each producing only a limited range of products, but often of exceptionally high volume and quality.

Quality, or more accurately precision, is a critical element. Specialization in high-volume production depends on the availability of interchangeable parts, a level of precision that did not develop in a significant way until the early nineteenth century (initially in the weapons industry). Even on the assembly line, tasks are broken down into simple components. This division of labor permits the employment of unskilled labor, the worker becoming one more component in the productive process.

Specialization is not limited to factories. When agriculture becomes specialized, farmers tend to view their work as a business, emphasizing cash flow and yield per unit of capital invested. Contemporary American farmers and their European and even many Third World counterparts concentrate on producing cash crops; they buy food for themselves in the marketplace. In Turkey nomadic herders now sell their milk and wool, and use the cash to buy margarine and polyester shirts. When a rural family makes the transition to market dependency, it has removed an important distinction between itself and urban households.

This homogenizing effect is particularly evident when market dependency is coupled with industrial forms of transport and communication. Widely separated households end up eating, dressing, entertaining, and in general living very much the same way. Farm families in this country share most of the expectations and values of urbanites of the same cultural backgrounds. Even their daily diets are very similar. While "living like city people" may be attractive to many country dwellers, it does bear a cost. Reliance on cash crops increases the risk of failure, as we saw in Chapter 8. Moreover, this risk increases as intensified agriculture moves toward industrialism. Now many of the world's most important cash crops are not only volatile in price but inedible. A farm family cannot eat the cotton it cannot sell. We will return to this matter shortly.

Social relations change as the organization of the workplace changes. When agribusiness supplants traditional farming, the farm family is increasingly removed from the family network on which it once relied not only for social interaction but for labor and loans. In places of urban employment, kin groups become removed from production or redistribution: people rely less on family members than on fellow employees or associates. Social class, professional affiliation, ethnicity, and union membership take on functions of mutual responsibility and support formerly restricted to relatives. This is not to say that kinship is unimportant (we will see the contrary in Chapters 12 and 13), but its functions change.

Charlie Chaplin's image of a worker caught up in the relentless cogs of a production line, powerless and somewhat disoriented, is in some ways accurate. Workers often come to see little of themselves in their product. Their labor is used impersonally and they respond in kind. Perhaps belatedly, industrial employers are realizing that this is not necessarily the most efficient way to organize production in a high-

An all-female production line in an electronics factory in Shanghai, China. Industrial technology and production is not limited by international boundaries; new factories are opened continually in new places in order to take advantage of local skills and to keep labor costs down. (DON KLUMPP)

technology society. General Motors recently built a new facility at which teams of workers have responsibility for producing entire cars. Increasing amounts of knitwear are being manufactured in New England homes in a return to cottage industry, which had almost died out by the end of the nineteenth century. Japanese workers are encouraged to use statistical and other evaluative techniques to improve the efficiency of their efforts. Even the spread of small but powerful computers is having an impact on the structure of the workplace: more and more business people are working at home and communicating by computer modem and fax machine.

Changes in Settlement and Population

The industrial age ushered in a whole host of social changes. First, and perhaps most obvious, population increased rapidly. Europe's population grew from 100 to 187 million between 1650 and 1800, then leaped to 400 million in the nineteenth-century coal age—an increase of 260 percent (White 1949:384). Today it is doubling every thirty-five years (Ehrlich and Ehrlich 1972:450). Birth rates are significantly higher in the Third World than in industrial nations today, while death rates are declining; the result is explosive population growth. The Central American nation of El Salvador, the most densely populated country in the Western Hemisphere, has more than 670 people per square mile, or 5.6 million people packed into an area smaller than New Hampshire. In the industrialized nations the rate of population growth has leveled off.

The changes that are occurring in human populations around the world are part of what demographers call the great **demographic transition** (Ehrlich and Ehrlich 1972:18–20)—a rapid increase in a society's population with the onset of industrialization, followed by a leveling off of the growth rate. Until approximately two hundred years ago the world's population stayed remarkably constant relative to today. Then, with urbanism and industrialization, it started to grow rapidly, and the point at which it will again stabilize is still distant. Every country appears to follow roughly the same trajectory as it develops: a spurt of rapid growth followed by a slowing of the increase rate. The economically advanced nations may have zero growth rates as the existing population simply maintains itself. The reasons for rapid explosion followed by a declining rate of population growth are exceedingly complex. The initial spurt of growth may be caused by a declining death rate, attributable to improved health care in combination with high fertility. One factor that encourages high fertility is the value of child labor. Peasants in largely rural El Salvador say that "every child is born with his bread under his arm"; not surprisingly, the birth rate in that country is over 45 per thousand of population—more than double that of the United States. More and more families come to depend on the sale of labor to meet their needs, and very often the income they derive in this way buys less food than they could produce directly. Mechanization and commercialization of agriculture precludes that option for most families. Rural people who have migrated to the cities simply do not earn enough to get by unless their children work as well. Children can help in the fields, work in the factories, peddle or produce crafts, scavenge, and otherwise bring in needed income. Given high rates of infant and childhood mortality, the more children a couple has, the more likely some will survive to take care of them when they are too old to support themselves. In countries that have no publicly supported health or welfare programs, these are vital considerations.

The reasons for a decline in the rate of growth following economic development are equally complex. It appears that the decline in the usefulness of child labor together with a rise in the costs of education are often important factors in the decision to limit the size of one's family. Changes in the work force are important, too, as women who work outside the home find it difficult to care for many children. Burton Pasternak and Wang Ching (1985) found that Chinese women who worked in factories tended to stop breast-feeding their infants in favor of buying prepared foods for them. This change is not necessarily a positive one in terms of the health of the child, but it does free the mother to work. It also has an impact on how women's employment may affect decisions to limit family size.

Unfortunately, many developing countries in which fertility remains very high for a considerable time after mortality has dropped find that their population levels are so high that the standard of living cannot be raised. All that can be said for certain is that present rates of growth cannot long continue: if they did, in 700 years there would be one person for every square foot of earth!

Population Movement

The process of devaluing agricultural products and labor in relation to other commodities, along with the mechanization of agriculture, serves to push people off the land and set up population movements both within and between nations. The migration of Europeans to North America, closely paralleling the spread of industrialization through Europe, reached a peak at the turn of the twentieth century. More than 52 million people, or a fifth of Europe's population, migrated overseas between 1840 and 1930. By and large, the immigrants were displaced from farming by mechanization, monoculture, and other changes. They came to America believing that U.S. factories offered opportunities for wage labor. Today rural people are pouring into cities all over the world for similar reasons. Others have adapted to changing patterns of food production by becoming migrant farm laborers. (Of course, migration is not limited to rural populations. The true nomads of industrial society are middle-class, white-collar workers who move from job to job or from city to city in the same job.)

Concentration of Wealth

The difference in productivity between richer and poorer lands was multiplied with the advent of intensive agriculture, which both created and amplified regional disparities. Similar processes of regional or national differentiation apply to industrial societies, with more extensive effects. Regions with access to cheap energy and sources of capital, labor, and appropriate raw materials may develop rapidly, while adjacent areas suddenly appear underdeveloped by comparison. Within countries, the people who control land and capital can reap far greater rewards than those who have only their labor to sell, so that great social and economic disparities develop.

Decreasing Cultural Diversity and Increasing Interdependence

Although concentration of wealth may increase the differentiation of economic classes, some cultural and ethnic distinctions have lessened, with resultant worldwide similarities within class lines. Robert Murphy sees "little doubt that by the year 2000 there will no longer be primitive societies" (1986:16). Eskimos use jeeps and snowmobiles, and watch the same TV shows as people in Florida and Brazil. Across continents, people are drawn into one global system, and styles of life reflect this convergence.

The increasing congruence of the world's cultures is a direct product of industrialization. Advanced transportation and communication systems, along with international migration, have brought peoples once isolated into contact with other societies. Above all, geographical barriers have been broken down by the economic forces of an international market system. Products are manufactured on one continent from the raw materials of another and sold on still another. The decisions made by Iowa wheat farmers affect the price of bread in India; the cost of oil in the Persian Gulf helps determine the cost of corn in the United States. In essence, the world's people are coming to live and produce under increasingly similar economic conditions.

When anthropologists study contemporary society, they must keep the wider context in view. Rather than study industrialism exclusively at the community or even the national level, anthropologists must view it as a global phenomenon, one in which all nations, industrial and nonindustrial, are to some extent interdependent. Thus when anthropologists try to determine the factors that shape social or economic relations in a local community, they have to consider the impact of the outside world.

As the manifestations of industrialism are too numerous and complex to be examined in the scope of a chapter, we will concentrate on just two of them. The first is the industrialization of agriculture and the adaptations that people have made to it. We will trace the urbanization of a rural farm community in Wasco, California, and later elsewhere in the San Joaquin Valley; the consequences of the introduction of sisal into a rural community in Brazil; and the influx of displaced agricultural people to the cities, with special attention to

Over the Mountains Are Mountains: Korean Peasant Adaptations to Industrialization

"Over the mountains are mountains" is a Korean proverb that suggests that as soon as one crisis is overcome, another one looms. Clark Sorensen took this proverb as the title for a book that examines Korean villagers' responses to the rapid industrialization of their country in recent years. He finds that traditional family structure can be instrumental in shaping a society's response to change. Family and household values and organization need not undergo massive shifts, as is often assumed. Even as families are drawn into the larger world and come to rely on such conveniences as electricity, television, and the telephone, social organization can remain much the same as before.

Sorensen went to the town of Sangongni for the first time in 1976. In his effort to analyze the social organization of this relatively stable, isolated, and undisturbed village in relation to ecological adaptation, he collected genealogical, demographic, and agricultural data. He noted that agricultural technology was rapidly changing: "Vinyl greenhouses were used to sprout rice seedlings. Composite fertilizer was used in the fields. There were even a few motor tillers and power sprayers that had been introduced into the village in 1975" (1983:37). Nevertheless, the overall impression was of tradition and stability. Patrilineages were well organized, and household organization appeared to adhere to traditional rules: the eldest son and his wife lived with his parents and gradually assumed the duties and rights of the household head and mistress. The household was still the mainstay of rural production and the means by which labor was organized.

By the end of his first year of fieldwork, however, Sorensen had begun to question his first impression of stability. When he looked at genealogies, he found that many families present in them were no longer represented in the community. Some lineages of the previous generation had broken apart and their descendants had become affiliated with other lineages. Some villagers had formerly lived in joint households (two or more brothers, for example, had lived together with their wives and children) but none were doing so in 1977. People were speaking of Japanese quotas on silk cocoons and world export patterns, inflation and labor shortages, the rising prices of land and agricultural inputs; some discussed migrating to the city; and all talked about the impending electrification of the village, which would enable them to watch television. He then realized how closely the village was integrated into the world economy and began to see the scale and importance of national politics, the market economy, and off-farm migration. It was not realistic, he concluded, to view the community as a small system narrowly adapted to its immediate environment.

Experiences in other countries have led to the assumption that the effects of industrialization on rural farming communities follow a fairly predictable course: peasant handicrafts are replaced by factory goods; peasants purchase in the marketplace much of what they used to produce at home and thus become dependent on money; farmers concentrate on cash crops

the new urban poor of San Juan, Puerto Rico. Second, we will broaden our focus by examining multinational corporations, which are emerging as vehicles for world trade and production, and are now taking on policy functions usually associated with governments. These two trends are interrelated. Multinational corporations are deeply involved in agri-industry, and the people displaced from the land by agri-industry have come to form an enormous low-wage labor force on which multinational corporations draw.

rather than on production for immediate consumption; and wage labor largely replaces reciprocity and family-organized farming. The social consequences of this process at the village level are usually assumed to be negative: poor farmers are unable to compete in a fully monetarized economy and lose their lands; small farms and plots are consolidated into larger units that are run as businesses with hired laborers, usually the people who have lost their own lands; and as the scale of agriculture increases, more and more labor is provided by migrant farmworkers—the poorest of the poor. This is the scenario that has been played out in many places, but it is not an inevitable one, as Sorensen shows.

Some of the expected developments did occur in Sangongni with rapid industrialization after the Korean war. Few handicrafts are to be found there now. People have acquired urban tastes, and all participate in the national market economy. There has been a massive migration to the cities, where many natives of Sangongni have become wage laborers, and average family size has decreased as sons and daughters have moved away to seek employment off the farm. Farm size has increased in response to market pressures. But even after twenty years of rapid development, landownership has not become seriously concentrated. Town and country have become so closely integrated that rural wages are almost as high as urban ones, with the result that farmers invest in modern technology and use new techniques on quite small holdings. The shortage of rural labor does not favor the large farm. By 1983 farm size had increased from less than 3 acres (1.14 hectares) to 3.28 acres (1.33 hectares); agricultural wages had more than doubled since 1977; more than a dozen motor tillers were in use, and they were needed because labor was scarce; household size had decreased slightly and at least thirteen families had left for the city. But contrary to the usual predictions, those who remained in the village had fared well. Though not all had done equally well, no impoverished class of rural worker had emerged. Virtually every household in the village was self-sufficient, despite its integration into the market economy. Sorensen found that even with mechanization, demographic shifts, and the new economy, the household was still the basic unit of production and consumption.

Industrialization had added a new dimension to decision making within households, however: now, in addition to deciding what crops to plant and how to use the land, they had to estimate the rates of return on capital and labor in market terms. Should all family members farm, or should some take up factory work? Would it be better to rent one's land out to others and seek urban employment, or would hiring farmworkers be more profitable? Should one sell one's land and open a business? "Industrialization provides rich and poor alike with choices," Sorensen observes (p. 206). Family labor thus remains central to successful agriculture, much as it has done in many parts of Europe and the United States. In many ways this situation has reinforced family ties rather than eroded them.

As for those who could not make a go of farming in a market-centered economy and moved to cities, many invested the proceeds from the sale of their land in small businesses or secured good jobs in the industrial sector. They have not, however, cut themselves off from their rural kin; they continue to visit, and some of them still keep their houses and fields in the village.

INDUSTRIAL AGRICULTURE

Industrialism has had a great impact on farming and farm society. One of the first areas in which factory production made itself felt was the farm. Steel plows, threshers, combines, reapers, and mowers, developed in the nineteenth century, were followed by the gasoline tractor early in the twentieth. Farming in industrialized countries soon came to depend on inputs that originated off the farm. The less

Even in areas as remote as this one in Bolivia, modern farmers use advanced technology. The use of expensive equipment means that capital has become as important as family labor on the farm; those who cannot secure it usually abandon farming, often to take up urban pursuits. (ULRIKE WELSCH)

industrialized world, often lagging behind in agricultural productivity, came to import the same technology.

The application of industrial technology to farming, while undoubtedly necessary to feed the world's burgeoning population, has wrought profound changes in almost every country. When tractors and other equipment are introduced, the richer farmer is usually the one to benefit. Poor farmers lack the capital to purchase equipment, and their fields are too small to make any such investment pay. New technology always entails a risk. Large farms offer their owners the security that enables them to assume the risks entailed by the adoption of innovations, such as new high-yield

seeds. As we saw in Chapter 8, rural people have responded in diverse ways, but rarely have avoided being drawn into new markets and a near total dependency on distant sources of energy.

Urbanized Rural Society: The Changing Face of California

American anthropologists were somewhat slow to recognize the importance of studying farming communities in their own society. In the early 1940s, however, Walter Goldschmidt (1947) undertook a study of Wasco, California, a town of 7,000 to 8,000 people, most of them involved in various aspects of industrialized commercial agriculture. By living in the town, participating in local organizations, conducting interviews, and examining official records and historical documents, Goldschmidt was able to trace the radical transformation that the town had undergone in the previous few decades. More recently the study of rural America has become a major focus of research, and not surprisingly, much of it has been directed to California (see Chibnik 1987).

The Development of Agribusiness in Wasco

Until the first decade of this century, the land on which Wasco's farms now sit was desert, and the main activity in the area was sheep herding. Wasco itself consisted of one store, one hotel, and a handful of saloons frequented by ranch hands and an occasional homesteader. Then in 1907 a developer persuaded the corporation that owned the entire Wasco area to sell part of its holdings and began to advertise for homesteaders, promising to provide the necessary irrigation. The sales pitch worked (the land was bought quickly) but the irrigation system did not. In all probability, the farmers would have abandoned Wasco to the sheep if a power company had not brought in a line, enabling the settlers to install electric pumps. This was the beginning of the industrialization of Wasco.

For small farmers, as most of the original settlers were, an electric pump is a major investment. In order to recoup that investment, the farmers turned to cash crops, specializing in potatoes, cotton, sugar beets, lemons, or grapes. Both profits and the settlement grew. In some years the payoff for commercial farming was spectacular. In 1936—a Depression year—one farmer was rumored to have made over $1 million from his potato crop.

Such booms encouraged Wasco's farmers to expand. Some of them rented land on which to grow profitable but soil-depleting crops for a year or two. (Once the soil was exhausted, the owner would revitalize it by planting alfalfa and then rent it again.) This strategy of expansion required the planter to hire large numbers of workers and to make substantial investments in tractors and other motorized equipment. Other Wasco farmers used their profits to expand in other areas. Having made a large investment, a farmer would look for ways to maintain a steady flow of produce and income. He might, for example, buy the fruits of another landowner's trees and hire his own laborers to pick them. Or better still, he might purchase more land. In this way, the average size of landholdings increased from about 20 acres when the homesteaders first moved in, to about 100 acres at the time of Goldschmidt's study—a 500 percent increase in about thirty years.

In no time Wasco was attracting outside corporations—first the utility companies, then a national bank, oil companies, and chain supermarkets. These developments changed the social landscape. The representatives of the state and national government agencies and of corporations, whose loyalties lay outside Wasco, tended to become leaders within the town. Even farmers with relatively small holdings began to see themselves as entrepreneurs rather than as tillers of the soil. One informant told Goldschmidt, "There is one thing I want you to put in your book. Farming in this country is a business, it's not a way of life" (1947:22).

Wasco began to attract large numbers of unskilled laborers who could find work in the town and dream of buying a place of their own one day. First Mexicans (Chicanos), then (after World War I) blacks, and in the 1930s refugees from Oklahoma, Arkansas, and other drought-stricken states poured into the town. They were markedly poorer than the Wasco farmers, who did not consider them their racial, cultural, or social equals. The social contact between the two groups was very limited. At the time of the study, the Mexicans, the blacks, and to a lesser extent the Oklahomans lived in their own separate communities with their own stores and churches. They were outsiders in every sense, and that was just what Wasco's commercial farmers needed—"a large number of laborers, unused to achieving the social values of the dominant group, and satisfied with few of the luxuries of modern society" (1947:62). In its urban orientation, its commercial production and consumption, and its economic gap between owners and laborers, Wasco might as well have been an industrial center. Above all, in its social structure—the impersonal, purely economic relationship between the landowners and the laborers—the town showed its urban-industrial face.

The Farmerless Farm in the San Joaquin Valley

Mark Kramer describes the subsequent phase in the transformation of California agriculture: the farmerless farm (1987:197–278). It is tomato harvest time in the San Joaquin Valley, 3:00 A.M., and 105,708,000 ripe tomatoes lie ready for picking—altogether some 766 absolutely flat acres of irrigated cropland. Out of the darkness rumble giant tractor-drawn machines resembling moon landers—two stories high, with ladders, catwalks, and conveyors fastened all over and carrying fourteen workers each. As they lumber down the long rows, they continually ingest whole tomato plants while spewing out the rear a steady stream of stems and rejects. Fourteen workers sit facing a conveyor belt in the harvester, sorting the marketable tomatoes from the discards.

It is a giant harvest carried out almost without people; only a few years ago more than 600 workers were needed to harvest a crop that 100 manage today. There are no farmers involved in this operation: only corporation executives, managers, foremen, and laborers. The word "farmer" has virtually disappeared; in this operation one refers to "growers" and "pickers." Managers take courses in psychology to help them determine appropriate incentives to offer tractor drivers for covering the most ground (if speed is too great, they may damage equipment; if they go too slowly, productivity falls). Managers similarly calculate pickers' produc-

tivity very precisely and regulate it by varying the speed of the conveyor belts and by minimizing the time spent turning the machines around at the ends of rows, when the workers are prone to get off for a smoke. Right now, Kramer reports one manager as saying, the industry is moving to a new-model harvester that will do the job of fourteen men with only two. The other twelve can move on to other employment if they can find it.

Tomato consumption closely reflects the changing eating habits of American society; these days each of us eats 50.5 pounds of tomatoes every year, whereas in 1920 consumption was 18.1 pounds. This change is accounted for by the fact that far more of our food is prepared somewhere other than in the home kitchen. This development has produced a demand for prepared sauces and flavorings, such as catsup and tomato paste. The increased productivity required to meet demand has resulted in dramatic genetic changes in the tomatoes we eat.

Processors of tomatoes demanded a product that is firmer; growers needed standardization of sizes and an oblong shape to counter tomatoes' tendency to roll off the conveyors; engineers required tomatoes with thick skins to withstand handling; and large corporate growers needed more tonnage per acre and better resistance to disease. The result is the modern American tomato: everything but flavor. "As geneticists selectively bred for these characteristics, they lost control of others. They bred for thick skins, less acidity, more uniform ripening, oblongness, leafiness, and high yield—and they could not also select for flavor" (1987:213). Even the chemists made their contribution: a substance called ethylene (which is also produced naturally by the plants) is sprayed on fields of almost ripe tomatoes in order to induce redness. Quite like the transformation of the tomato itself, the ownership of the farms that grow them has been altered. As one might expect in view of the massive inputs of capital needed to raise the new breed of tomatoes, most are raised on corporate spreads. The one Kramer describes consisted of more than 27,000 acres and was owned by several "general partners," including a major insurance corporation, an oil company, a newspaper, and thousands of "limited partners," most of them doctors and lawyers who invested in the operation for its tax benefits. There is little room under these conditions for the small farmer—or so it would seem.

Recent Developments on the Farm

Before we conclude that the farm future lies only in ever-increasing size, we must take a close look at a broader range of agricultural activities and developments. One activity, unfortunately, involves the production of illegal substances—opium, cocaine, marijuana. Many farmers, and not just those in the so-called Third World, have turned to such crops, for they respond well to labor inputs and have not yet attracted competition from corporations. A report in the *Economist* of April 1988 suggested that marijuana, grown largely on public lands, was California's largest cash crop. Even in food production there are limits to the efficiency of large farms: they require middle-level managers and get less out of individual workers than do smaller, family-managed operations. Large, corporately managed farms can make large-scale mistakes. Kramer reported that one worker in California sprayed a huge area with the wrong insecticide, and some managers' heavy investment in unsuitable crops resulted in big losses. In fact, the large farm Kramer describes subsequently sold off half its holdings as unprofitable. Under some conditions, a smaller farm can be more efficient than a huge one, but it will nevertheless bear little resemblance to the traditional family operation. It will be highly capitalized and employ modern equipment, up-to-date accounting methods, and trained management. Most successful

farmers in the United States are college graduates.

Some observers report a revival of the family farm in the southern states (Gladwin and Butler 1982). The family-run farm now often involves a new division of labor, with the wife assuming primary responsibility for farming operations, often of a specialized nature, while the husband holds down a salaried job and helps out when he can.

Another agricultural development is a new twist to what was traditionally a very exploitive farming arrangement: sharecropping (Wells 1987). Sharecropping reached its peak in the United States during the Great Depression of the 1930s, when more than 25 percent of American farms were operated on this basis. The arrangement had advantages and disadvantages. It did ensure the landless of access to farmland even when market conditions left them so poor that they were unable to rent land for cash. At the same time, it yielded far greater profit to landowners than they could realize from rents. Sharecroppers were invariably among the poorest of the poor. These days, however, with the price of land high and rising, many family and corporate farms engage in sharecropping of a sort: they invest in equipment rather than in more land, use it to farm land belonging to someone else, and pay the landowner in a share of the crop. These sharecroppers are among the more successful farmers in their communities.

In yet another development, Miriam Wells (1987) reports, some migrant workers are becoming sharecroppers. When crops require a great deal of skill and much labor to raise, it can make sense for the landowner to give the farmworkers a share in the proceeds. California is once more a case in point. Strawberry production has shifted to sharecropping in recent years, with much of the work being done by the same Chicanos who were formerly migrant laborers. By and large, the workers have benefited from this arrangement, as they are their own bosses and share in the profits produced by their labor. Though few have yet moved from sharecropper to farm owner, many are hopeful.

Rural Hope and Rural Poverty in Brazil

Farming people have always striven to increase their security by making their livelihood more dependable. Expectations are not always met, however, as in the case of farmers investigated by the anthropologist Daniel Gross and the nutritionist Barbara Underwood (1971) in the *sertão*, an arid region of northeastern Brazil.

The sertão has always been a place of hardship and uncertainty. Historically its people relied on cattle raising and subsistence farming. However, the years of self-sufficiency were regularly punctuated by disastrous droughts, with resultant starvation and mass exodus from the region. In the 1950s many subsistence farmers thought they could see an end to the cycle of uncertainty. A new drought-resistant crop, sisal, was beginning to be harvested as an export crop. Sisal takes four years to mature and produces a tough fiber used in the making of twine. The extraction of the fiber from the leaves, a process known as decorting, is a long and arduous task requiring heavy machinery.

The first sisal plantations were owned by wealthy landholders. Soon smallholders came to abandon subsistence crops in the hope of sharing in the ever-rising profits from sisal. While waiting for the sisal to mature, they worked as laborers on the plantations of others. Unfortunately, by the time their own sisal had matured, the market price had fallen, leaving them with little or nothing to show for their investments. At the same time, even the harvesting of the sisal was costly; the smallholders had to rent decorting machines. Once planted, sisal is extremely hard to eradicate, and many formerly self-sufficient farmers were forced to remain as day laborers on the large plantations.

Another aspect of this shift to wage labor concerns nutrition. Gross and Underwood measured the calories the laborers expended while they worked on the sisal plantations and the amount of food they could buy with their wages. They found that many workers could not afford to buy enough food to meet their own needs and those of their families. Forty-five percent of the children of sisal workers were significantly undernourished.

In contrast to the hopes raised by the shift to a cash crop, the result was a poverty more severe than the small farmers had originally experienced. Moreover, their poverty was compounded by their new dependence on the people who owned the large farms and controlled the machinery. This is the reason that rural people in many countries leave the countryside, even though the city offers them little but the squalor of an urban slum.

THE DISPLACED

One of the consequences of large-scale industrialized agriculture is the displacement of small agriculturalists from the land. Some settle in towns such as Wasco, where they work as unskilled farm laborers when there is work to be had. Some settle in large urban centers. Still others become migrant laborers. Northern Europe is dotted with temporary settlements of Turkish, Greek, Yugoslavian, and Spanish laborers who travel north every year for a few months of labor in the factories or fields and then return home. Many more migrants establish long-term residence in large cities. The organization of this mobile labor force varies considerably, as does the profitability of the arrangement for the laborers.

The Turks—nearly a million of them—who labor as "guest workers" in the factories of northern Europe generally receive the same wages as native workers and are able to return to Turkey with substantial savings. But at the same time, they are the first to be fired in times of recession and they suffer considerable social isolation and discrimination in their homes away from home. Migrant workers in the United States, most of them Mexicans or Central Americans, are seldom able to earn a living that is considered adequate by North American standards or to save enough to allow them to upgrade their salable skills. Throughout the year they move from harvest to harvest, staying in crowded and often squalid migrant camps. Most such camps are under the direction of crew leaders, who make the arrangements between the farmers and the laborers and provide the trucks to transport the laborers from place to place. Laborers are heavily dependent on their crew leader. When work is delayed, as it

often is, they must borrow from him to buy their food. And often it is the leader who sells them their food—at an inflated price.

The rural landless have options other than settling in industrial farming communities or joining the migrant labor force. The overwhelming majority have chosen to try their luck in the cities. Since the Industrial Revolution, population has moved in a steady stream from the countryside to the city. In many nations now becoming industrialized, the stream has become a flood as unskilled rural people pour into the cities. In most countries, one or two cities become the targets for the majority of the migrants, and these cities swell beyond their

A family of migrant workers in Denizli, Turkey. Rural poverty and landlessness are problems that farmers face in countries throughout the world. (WAUGH/PETER ARNOLD)

capacity to provide employment or social services. In the Arabic-speaking countries of the Middle East, only 30 percent of the population were urban in 1962 but today more than half are. The population of Cairo, for example, increased from 3 million in 1947 to over 12 million in 1988. Mexico City, now the world's largest city with more than 20 million inhabitants, is experiencing massive problems: the world's worst air pollution, frequent breakdowns in public transportation and other services, and high rates of infant mortality. Like similar cities around the world, much of Mexico City's growth is due to an influx of rural dwellers. As elsewhere, these recent migrants form an extremely disadvantaged and socially distinct segment of the population, with a high rate of unemployment, a high rate of crime, and substandard housing. In some respects these poor city dwellers are fortunate. A UN study indicates that more than 12 million people around the world live in refugee camps, often on the brink of starvation, displaced not just by a changing global economy but by the brutal facts of war, famine, and political oppression (*New York Times,* August 21, 1988).

Many anthropologists have now turned their attention to cities. The last few decades have produced a variety of ethnographic reports on the new urban society that industrialization has created and the life of the poor in that society. One such report is Helen Icken Safa's *Urban Poor of Puerto Rico* (1974).

Villagers in the City: Los Peloteros

In the early 1940s the government of Puerto Rico initiated a sweeping program of economic development. Called Operation Bootstrap, the program called for millions of dollars to be pumped into public services—housing, education, medical care—and industry. The goal was to launch the island economy into the modern industrial world, thereby creating new jobs and raising the standard of living for the average Puerto Rican.

Operation Bootstrap set off reverberations in the countryside. Puerto Rico's population at that time was mostly rural and mostly poor. The day of small, self-sufficient farms had already passed. In their place were large commercial farms and plantations, where families of unskilled workers labored for incomes of perhaps $500 a year, living as squatters on the land of the *patron* and surviving "dead season" layoffs four or five months of the year. As Operation Bootstrap got under way and urban industrialization took hold, the peasants began to hear reports of jobs in the city—jobs requiring less toil and paying higher wages than they could ever hope to get on a farm. The exodus from the countryside began. Family after family packed up, most of them headed directly for San Juan, Puerto Rico's major city. Between 1940 and 1960 the population of San Juan more than doubled.

No housing awaited them, of course, and they could not afford to rent apartments. They gravitated to underdeveloped public lands and constructed shacks from any materials they could find, creating their own squatter settlements. A favored spot was the strip of land along the Martín Peña Channel, which at the time was the main sewage dump of the city. Foul-smelling and swampy, this was nevertheless a spot on which the rural immigrants could settle, since the city considered it unfit for residential or commercial development.

By the early 1960s, the five-mile stretch of land was covered with shanties housing almost 86,000 people. By that time there was no longer any free space. Newcomers did not build houses; they bought them. The settlements were true neighborhoods, with former country folk and their children constituting a new social group: the urban poor.

Safa (1974), in her study of a channel-side settlement that she called Los Peloteros, sought to understand the impact this change had on

In the 1940s and 1950s, the rural poor of Puerto Rico flocked to San Juan in search of well-paying industrial jobs. No housing awaited them, so they constructed squatter settlements in swampy, channelside areas. By the 1960s, these communities had become true neighborhoods. (MARC AND EVELYNE BERNHEIM/WOODFIN CAMP & ASSOCIATES)

the social and cultural life of the immigrants: how they adjusted to city life, what changes this adjustment required in their customs and attitudes, to what extent they embraced urban ways and abandoned their traditional ways, how they fared economically, and how they organized themselves politically.

Life in a Squatter Settlement

At the time of Safa's study, 1959–1960, most of the residents of Los Peloteros had electricity and indoor water taps. But they had no sewage system, no garbage collection, no paved roads, no street lights. Indeed, they barely had streets. There were only a few dirt roads that in the dry season spread dust over the whole neighborhood and in the rainy season became mudholes that even pedestrians had difficulty navigating. Houses were crowded against one another, and most of them could be reached only by makeshift sidewalks consisting of planks and old doors laid over the mud. Joined to the stench of the channel was the stench emanating from the wooden latrines behind the houses. Garbage clogged the paths and floated at the edges of the channel. The neighborhood had no church, no medical facility, no shopping area, and no school. (The children attended schools outside the neighborhood.) The only businesses were bars, where the local men congregated, and a few tiny stores that sold a limited range of canned goods and other basic household items.

Despite its lack of physical amenities and its crowded conditions (about 200 people per acre), most of the residents of Los Peloteros were relatively content with their neighborhood. Above all, they were proud of their houses. Owning their own homes was extremely important to them, for it symbolized a degree of independence. They knew that no matter what happened—layoffs, illness, no money, no food—they would still have a place to live among people they knew. Those who could afford to do so took great care in improving their homes. Many families had two bedrooms; some had three. Linoleum covered the floors; gas stoves and other conveniences were fairly common. Great value and status were attached to shiny new furnishings and appliances. In this respect the squatter families adopted urban values very quickly. In the ideal home, the old-fashioned wicker furniture had been replaced by a less sturdy "living-room set," protected by plastic covers; the china closet, traditionally the focus of the house, had been pushed aside to make way for a television set; and a refrigerator was proudly displayed in the living room. Not all households, of course, could afford such luxuries, and many were minimally furnished.

As the variation in housing conditions suggests, Los Peloteros was itself a stratified society, with many degrees of status and material comfort. The residents were quite conscious of these disparities, and many of them strove, by economizing and saving, to improve their situations in relation to those of other families. Ultimately, however, their situation depended on their jobs.

Economics

Getting and keeping a job was a major problem for the families of Los Peloteros, even for those who had been in San Juan for years. There were almost no jobs available within the neighborhood itself; for employment the residents were completely dependent on the shifting economy of the outside community. Most of the men worked as unskilled laborers on the docks or in factories. Others were service employees—busboys, parking attendants—in San Juan's tourist industry. The fortunate ones, those who had a marketable skill, worked as artisans on construction projects. But all of these jobs were subject to frequent layoffs, and by the standards of the larger society, none of them paid well. Annual family incomes, like housing conditions, varied widely, from under $500 to over $5,000 in 1959, but most of the families that Safa interviewed were clustered in the $2,000–$3,000 range.

The poorer families supplemented their incomes by various stratagems—selling bootleg rum, taking numbers for the illegal lottery, selling ices, sending children out to shine shoes. Many women took part-time work as laundresses, maids, or (if they were lucky) factory workers; full-time employment of women was considered a threat to the husband's status in the home and in the community. The very poor—female-headed households—went on welfare, but these people considered welfare degrading and avoided it whenever they could.

The major factor barring the residents of Los Peloteros from stable employment was lack of education. Of the men in Safa's sample, only 40 percent had received any schooling beyond the fourth grade; in fact, in the countryside, where most of the residents were raised, schools often stopped at the fourth grade. Over 20 percent of the women in the sample had no formal education at all. With good reason, the more upwardly mobile families made great efforts to keep their children in school.

The families of Los Peloteros were as dependent on the outside community for their material needs as they were for employment. Once a week the father or the mother of the family would make a trip to the Barrio Obrero, a nearby commercial center, to buy food—rice and beans, which were the basis of their diet (almost the total diet of the very poor), along with perhaps some eggs, tomato sauce, milk for the children, and coffee. Meat was a luxury reserved for holidays. Clothes, too, were bought in the Barrio Obrero. The residents did little sewing, since store-bought clothing carried much more prestige than homemade goods. This desire for manufactured commercial items, encouraged by exposure to television and radio, extended to every area of their lives.

Community and Family

While fully urban in such matters as their buying habits, Los Peloteros families clung to rural traditions in other respects, especially in their social relationships within the community. These families bore no resemblance to the stereotypical isolated and autonomous urban household. On the contrary, each household was enmeshed in a tight network of reciprocal-aid relationships with kin, friends, and neighbors, perhaps even more so than they had been in their villages.

The majority of households were limited to nuclear families, averaging six members, but almost all families had kin in the neighborhood. And since people preferred to marry within the neighborhood and generally named their neighbors as *compadres* (godparents), the neighborhood kinship network was constantly growing by accretion. Neighbors who were not related by blood, marriage, or baptism nevertheless knew and helped one another. As in the Oaxacan villages described in Chapter 8, there was a constant informal exchange of goods and services in Los Peloteros. Any family that had a television set could expect a contingent of neighbors to arrive daily in time for the soap operas. When a house was being repaired or improved, as the houses often were, all the men in the neighborhood helped. When a woman had to take a part-time job, she left her children in the care of relatives or neighbors. Indeed, for the children the whole community functioned as a sort of extended family; a child could expect to be comforted, scolded, and sent on errands by any adult in the neighborhood. At any time of day the community buzzed with informal socializing—the men in the bars, the women on the stoops and in the small shops.

This cohesive and intimate community acted as a buffer between individual families and the large, complex, and perilous urban world into which they had migrated. In the world outside, jobs might vanish and prices soar, but in the shantytown people could expect to have their troubles listened to, their values reaffirmed, and, if necessary, their plates filled by people like themselves. As in Oaxaca, the sharing network had adaptive value as a leveling device, spreading good and bad fortune more evenly, so that even the severely disadvantaged had opportunities for survival. The intimacy of the neighborhood provided psychological protection against the stresses of adjustment to urban life.

Yet the stresses were still felt, and their impact could be measured within the nuclear family. In the world of the Hispanic family, the man's pride and authority emanated largely from his role as protector and provider, the woman's from her role as keeper of the house and the children. In the urban job market, however, many of the men were, of necessity, poor and erratic providers; consequently their authority was somewhat eroded. At the same time, the women's role of holding the house and family together became all the more important. Los Peloteros families, like many urban poor elsewhere, were decidedly **matrifocal** (centered on the mother): the woman and her relationships with her children and her female kin formed the core of family life. Indeed, men spent little time at home. When they were not working, they were generally at the local bar with their cronies. Home life was given over entirely to the function of child rearing. Thus husbands and wives occupied different spheres, and the emotional bond between them was weak in comparison with the mother-child bond. Their marriages tended to be more stable than those of the mainland urban poor. Of the men in Safa's sample, two-thirds were still living with their original wives.

Politics and Political Attitudes

The intimacy and reciprocity that marked relationships within the settlement contrasted sharply with the impersonal, utilitarian quality of the residents' dealings with people outside the community. Most important of all, the poor were excluded from any meaningful participation in extracommunity political processes. The squatter settlements had their own committees and local leaders, usually long-time residents of the community, but these committees and leaders had no power. All they could do was receive people's requests—a water pipe in need of repair work, a brother in need of bail—and petition the appropriate agency for action.

This is not to say that the needs of the poor were ignored. On the contrary, many of them were swiftly attended to. But the government rendered such services, and the people received them not as citizens' rights but as favors, just as a needy family might receive a bag of rice from the landowner for whom they worked. In return for these favors, the recipients were expected to vote for their benefactors, and they faithfully did so. In return for their votes, the poor were given small, personalized services to alleviate specific hardships, but they were never given the means to climb out of their poverty— good jobs, honest labor unions, a decision-making role in the political process. In time the people were marginalized, effectively isolated from the sources of community decision making and made to feel that they were outside the social mainstream.

The social and political alienation of the very poor has been noted by other anthropologists who have worked among groups of rural settlers in urban slums. Oscar Lewis (1959, 1961) has claimed that this alienation is responsible in large part for the social pathologies—drunkenness, violence, family disorganization—that he observed among the urban poor of Mexico City. These problems, Lewis claimed, were due less to material want per se than to the gulf that poverty opens up between the underemployed and the affluent middle class in an industrialized society—a society that seems to promise upward mobility. Believing that somehow they should be "making it" but denied the means of doing so, the urban poor fall into what Lewis calls the **culture of poverty**—a self-perpetuating complex of escapism, impulse gratification, despair, and resignation which Lewis sees as an adaptation and reaction of the poor to "their marginal position in a class-stratified highly individuated, capitalistic society" (1966:xliv). Hence their high rates of alcoholism, adultery, family instability, and debt, all of which operate in a vicious cycle to keep them poor. The way out of the culture of poverty, Lewis suggests, is through the development of social cohesion: perhaps joining a union, working for a political cause—in some way pressing for change.

Beyond the Squatter Settlement: Los Peloteros Ten Years Later

In the early 1960s, as part of the Model Cities program, Los Peloteros was knocked down and replaced by a highway and a new housing project. The families were paid for their homes and dispersed, the more affluent moving to private residential developments, the poorer to public housing. In the process, the unique society that Safa had described—an intermediate world, urban in its aspirations, rural in its social relations—was destroyed. The people in the projects came to look like full-fledged urban slum dwellers; those in the private residences, like full-fledged members of the middle class.

In 1969, ten years after her study of Los Peloteros, Safa returned to San Juan and was able to track down all the families she had interviewed in the settlement. Among those who had moved to the projects, she found a general dissatisfaction. Though the projects had physical advantages over Los Peloteros—more space, less dirt, gas stoves, flush toilets—they utterly lacked the social amenities that Los Peloteros had so richly provided. In comparison with the warm, intimate environment of the old neighborhood, the social world of the projects was cold and dangerous. Alcoholism, delinquency, crime, vandalism, and marital instability were common; there was a severe drug problem, particularly among the teenagers.

This outbreak of social pathologies was attributable in part to forces outside the projects; crime and drug addiction were also on the rise in the remaining shantytowns of the city. Another unquestionably related factor was that those who landed in the projects were the most disadvantaged of the former settlement residents—the very poor, the unemployed, the fatherless families. Still another important factor was that the informal social controls of the settlement—neighbors keeping an eye on each other's children, people needing the approval of their neighbors—were gone, along with the mutual-aid network of the old community. The people's former ties to kin and neighbors had been severed in the move from Los Peloteros, and they had formed no new ties, in part because the projects offered no facilities for informal socializing—no bars for the men, no front stoops for the women. Relationships between neighbors ranged from indifferent to hostile. As one man remarked, "One can die here and no one would do you a favor" (Safa 1974:82).

Safa's study shows the urban poor in two stages of progressive assimilation into an industrial society. In Los Peloteros, the urban village, people had to rely on the outside society for their jobs and their material needs, but the reciprocal-aid network within the community allowed them a degree of self-sufficiency. In the second stage, the move to public and private housing outside Los Peloteros, they came to depend entirely on the formal, impersonal institutions of the larger community to provide for their needs. They had entered fully into a politically centralized industrial society. In the process they lost the warmth and texture of a close-knit rural community, however materially poor it may have been.

BEYOND INDUSTRIALISM

The technological and social transformation we call industrialism started on a small scale and was restricted to certain forms of production in a few countries. But it did not remain limited for long. In a relatively short period peoples all over the world were affected by it. Today we have moved into yet another era in the organization of production and integration of peoples. This has been termed variously the communications era, the age of the computer, the high-tech age. The labels are not important. What is interesting from an anthropological perspective is that the processes of change appear to occur at an increasingly rapid rate.

The organization of commerce and industry is changing. The historian David Noble (1984) describes this transformation as the triumph of "numerical control" in industry. Following World War II there was a great advance in the development of servomechanical and electronic controls capable of running complex precision tools. This development, Noble suggests, opened up the possibility of moving the effective control of manufacturing from the shop floor to the main office. The outcome is a lessening of blue-collar power in industry and further centralization of control in productive organizations. This thesis is interesting, though in some instances the same technology has broken up large industries into smaller components—another outcome of high-speed communications. Certainly it is clear that job opportunities for production-line workers are rapidly decreasing while new ones open up for people who have skills appropriate to the new technologies.

The Organization of the Postindustrial World

Richard J. Barnet and Ronald E. Muller (1974) have written on a phenomenon closely related to the organization of production in the postindustrial era: the growth of multinational corporations. They suggest that the degree to which international corporations have taken over functions once performed by governments and succeeded where governments have failed in creating a "global organization for administering this planet" is difficult to comprehend. This is not to suggest that corporations have consciously evolved into multinationals in order to dominate the world. They simply make use of the communications and transport technology available to compete in the world marketplace. The sheer size and complexity of their operations, however, have made them a force unto themselves.

In 1974 the operating budgets of about five hundred giant multinational corporations exceeded those of most nation-states. In the 1980s the operating budgets of global corporations grew at over twice the rate of the GNP of the United States and other advanced industrial nations. This fiscal expansion is based on what has been called the corporations' "global reach"—today they know no boundaries. About 30 percent of corporate profits in the United States were derived from overseas operations in 1974. More than 25 percent of the employees

A Tokyo man and his son place an order at a local McDonald's. In the past three decades, multinational corporations have mushroomed, creating a privately run global economy. Note, too, the dress of the people outside this McDonald's franchise—around the world, people within similar social classes are beginning to dress in similar ways. (JAMES R. HOLLAND / STOCK, BOSTON)

of the largest international corporations based in the United States lived and worked outside this country.

Through expansion and diversification, global enterprises insulate themselves from many political and market pressures. High-speed communications permit a multinational corporation to control everything from raw materials to final distribution. It may, for example, buy raw materials from a subsidiary company at less than the actual market price in order to avoid taxes, or it may sell to another foreign division at inflated prices in order to transfer income out of a country. Price fixing cannot really be controlled under such circumstances. Further, and of greater social consequence, a giant corporation can easily shift operations to areas of low labor cost. Such a move can be catastrophic for the workers the corporation leaves behind. The very fact that a corporation operates on a global scale places it beyond the reach of national governments. Regulatory agencies lack the information and in many cases the jurisdiction to investigate global enterprises. "Corporations plan centrally and act globally, and nation-states do not" (Barnet and Muller 1974:109).

A more subtle problem, which underlies Barnet and Muller's analysis, is the instability that such global interdependence implies. India's ability to feed its people depends on modern farming, which in turn requires reliance on chemical pesticides, fertilizers, fuel, and machinery. All of these inputs are globally interconnected. Local disasters can now have immediate global repercussions, be it the Bhopal chemical factory disaster in India, the nuclear fires of Chernobyl in the Soviet Union, Arctic pollution, or acid rain in the United States and Canada. There is an obvious good side to interdependence: global trade and communications even out some disparities—the goods of the industrial states are widely available, people can move great distances to seek out a livelihood, the effects of famine and natural disasters can be mitigated. But is also puts all of us at the mercy of events in distant places. Interdependence and vulnerability are two sides of the same process.

Postindustrialism is a recent development and it remains to be seen how humans will adapt to its consequences. The problem is that change is coming so rapidly that it may outrun our ability to respond appropriately, especially with regard to natural resources. We must keep in mind that individual behavior is basic to adaptation; people generally alter their behavior to serve their self-interest as they see it. What is in the interest of elites and corporations may not be appropriate for long-range conservation of the world's resources and habitats. In earlier eras of human adaptation, people were severely constrained by their technology and by their limited access to sources of energy. By and large, people had to deal directly with the environmental consequences of their activities. Farmers who allowed their fields to erode

might face hunger. Now many decisions that affect the environment are made by people far removed from the consequences. The manager of the factory whose sulfuric wastes contaminate a distant water supply may receive a bonus for efficiency. Perhaps we shall have to devise ways to reward those who, in the words of the ecologist René Dubos, "act locally but think globally."

Energy, Resources, and Waste

Since World War II, per capita energy consumption throughout the world has risen at an ever-increasing rate. New technology makes low-cost fossil fuel, nuclear energy, and solar energy widely available. We already see the material effects: millions of people routinely move from country to country, homes are filled with appliances, foods from around the world are available in neighborhood grocery stores. In short, the material culture of the world is rapidly becoming homogeneous. The availability of cheap energy and high rates of consumption have stimulated the mass use of numerous items that only a few years ago would be considered luxuries, if they were imagined at all. Thirty-five years ago few homes or workplaces in the United States were air-conditioned; today most are. Even the poorest individual in almost any country has access to vehicular transportation, uses facilities that run on electricity, and consumes imported goods.

The energy that pulses through human society affects where and how people live, the material goods available to them, and their relations with their physical environment. Cheap energy allows huge cities to emerge because they are sustained by foods grown in distant fields and by water from distant reservoirs. Because energy is cheap, people are consuming the world's resources at a phenomenal rate; it has been estimated, for example, that tropical forests that once covered great portions of

A clean-up crew at work following the Exxon Valdez oil spill in Alaska. A major concern today is containing the toxic by-products of industrial society. (MICHAEL BAYTOFF / BLACK STAR)

South America and Southeast Asia will be gone by the year 2000. A giant new dam has been completed in the middle of the Brazilian rain forest. When it is in operation, it will flood more than 600 square miles of forest in order to produce electricity for the city of Manaus, on the banks of the Amazon. Manaus's population has recently swollen to over a million inhabitants—many of whom come to the Amazon to escape intolerable conditions elsewhere. Similar projects are under way throughout the Third World as governments respond to the need to feed ever-growing populations. Once such resources as the rain forest are gone, they cannot be reestablished; most of what we consume is nonrenewable.

Quite apart from the matter of how we will cope with the depletion of our resources is the ever more urgent problem of how we will dispose of the toxic by-products of what we have already consumed. All of the industrialized countries are faced with the unanswered question of what to do with nuclear and other radioactive wastes. There is still no easy and safe way to dispose of highly toxic chemicals such as PCBs.

Less apparent, but still very important to our future, the world's oceans are under siege: in the Pacific and Atlantic vast amounts of human waste, toxic and nontoxic, threaten marine life as never before. The same crisis threatens the Caribbean and Mediterranean: the fishing industries of these areas are experiencing severely declining catches. In 1987 the American National Academy of Sciences reported that each year the world's fishing fleets dump 350 million pounds of plastic debris in the world's oceans (*New York Times*, September 6, 1987, sec. 4, p. 16). It is thought that over 30 percent of the world's fish have ingested bits of plastic, which can interfere with their digestion. The 1989 Exxon Valdez disaster in which a supertanker released 240,000 barrels of oil (11 million gallons) into Alaskan waters is only a symptom of a global problem. The problem of pollution and waste disposal is not, of course, restricted to the oceans. Over half of the solid landfill areas available to American cities in 1980 are now full. Each year the United States produces more than 20 million tons of plastics, most of which require more than five hundred years to degrade fully. Every country has petrochemical plants churning out polyethylene and other plastics. Archaeologists of the future will find this accumulation a treasure-trove, but meanwhile the time is rapidly coming when our wastes will overwhelm us.

If our industrial and postindustrial adaptations are to be successful in the long term, solutions must be found to the problem of toxic-waste disposal. As history has shown, an increase in energy sources creates as many problems as it solves. The impending advent of superconductors—materials that can transmit electricity with no loss to resistance—will make available even more usable energy. If we merely use this energy to support more people and to speed up consumption, the results are quite likely to be disastrous for the environment.

As we shall see in Chapter 17, anthropologists have become increasingly concerned about the social and economic transformations taking place around the world and about their impact on the quality of life of local peoples. They are concerned for our own society as well as for those of the Third World. Individually we may deplore many aspects of modern society and view with alarm the emergence of an increasingly integrated global system, with all of its attendant inequities and loss of cultural texture. But we must understand that there is no turning back to a simpler age. It is a fact that, however vulnerable we are made by advanced technology, the level of the world's population today cannot be sustained without it. What anthropologists and other scientists can contribute is an understanding of the ways in which the impact of these changes can be made more equitable and local peoples given a greater role in their implementation.

Summary

Industrialism is characterized by a highly developed factory system of production based on the harnessing of vastly increased amounts of energy, on specialization, and on *mechanization*—the replacement of human and animal labor by mechanical devices. The rise of industrial society has provoked dramatic changes in our physical and social environments. The more energy industrial societies extract, the more they require for their survival.

Industrialism has numerous social consequences. Human populations are increasing more rapidly than ever before, with consequent pressure on natural resources. Industrialization brings a *demographic transition*: the population increases rapidly and persistently before the growth rate finally levels off. And massive migrations both between and within nations have occurred as people have left rural communities for the cities in the hope of industrial jobs. Increasing specialization of labor and concentration of wealth have resulted in new kinds of social relations and organizations. Differentiation between classes has increased, while differentiation based on cultural and ethnic distinctions within classes has declined. The economy brought about by industrialism has transcended geographical barriers. This chapter focuses on the industrialization of agriculture, the adaptations that people have made to this phenomenon, and the impact of technology and multinational corporations.

In the experience of Wasco, California, we see the urbanization of a rural community by mechanization—the transformation of farming as a livelihood to farming for profit, the change in social reference from the local community to that of the wider world, and the breakdown in social relations from close personal ties to relatively impersonal ones. In the San Joaquin Valley large corporations run giant farms without farmers, relying on managers and foremen to supervise crews of migrant laborers.

A group of small farmers in Brazil, hoping to share in the prosperity of the large landowners, abandoned their subsistence crops to plant sisal for export. By the time their crops matured, the price of sisal had dropped, and they were forced to work as laborers on the large plantations to survive.

Vast numbers of such displaced farmers all over the world finally seek a better life in the cities, where they slowly adapt to an urban and industrial society. Helen Safa's *Urban Poor of Puerto Rico* examines the plight of a new class

of urban poor who migrated from the countryside to Los Peloteros, a squatter settlement in San Juan.

The people of Los Peloteros relied on the outside society for their jobs and their material needs, but a reciprocal-aid network within the community and the fact that their houses were their own gave them a degree of self-sufficiency. The wives in these *matrifocal* households held their families together. The larger society depended on the shantytown dwellers for cheap labor but excluded them from any meaningful participation in their institutions or political processes. The poor, enmeshed in the *culture of poverty*, believed that their poverty was a personal rather than a political failing, and so had no sense of class solidarity and no idea of the possibility of political change. They wanted only to better themselves through their personal efforts.

The second stage of Safa's study explored the impact on these people of a forced move to public and private housing outside Los Peloteros. Isolated from one another and cut off from mutual aid, they came to depend entirely on the formal institutions of the larger community to provide their needs. Despite increased economic pressure and decreased social rewards, the people had no desire to return to the shantytown, since they felt it would be socioeconomic regression.

With the advent of the postindustrial era have come new problems. No longer can technology and cheap energy be seen as the solution to all of humankind's ills. The by-products of high rates of energy consumption increasingly threaten the quality of life.

Multinational corporations developed to provide centralized organization of a global flow of energy and materials; their operations have increased the interdependence of nations. Insulated by their sheer size and complexity from both market and governmental pressures, multinational corporations now function as major powers in the world economy. Their power rests on their access to vast amounts of capital, their control of advanced technology, and their grasp of communications and marketing-techniques.

As industrialization is a relatively recent development, it remains to be seen how societies will adapt to its consequences—assuming that they have the time and the ability to adapt.

Key Terms

culture of poverty   **demographic transition**   **matrifocal**   **mechanization**

Suggested Readings

CLARKE, L. 1989. *Acceptable Risk? Making Decisions in a Toxic Environment.* Berkeley: University of California Press. This book provides a concise analysis of what actually happens when industrial disaster strikes—in this case the filling of a New York State office building with deadly toxic soot.

LEWIS, R. L. 1987. *Black Coal Miners in America: Race, Class, and Community Conflict 1790–1980.* Lexington, Ky: The University Press of Kentucky. An account which vividly details both political oppression and the responses of those who suffered the effects of legal and social discrimination in pre-industrial and industrial America. As such it goes beyond simply documenting one ethnic group's experience; it describes the exploitation of a class of workers, coal miners.

MARTIN, P. L. 1988. *Harvest of Confusion: Migrant Workers in U.S. Agriculture.* Boulder, Colo.: Westview Press. A basic resource document providing the factual background necessary for an understanding of the misconceptions that surround the issues of the numbers and characteristics of migrant farmworkers and their role in the American system of industrialized agriculture.

MULLINGS, L. (ED.). 1987. *Cities of the United States: Studies in Urban Anthropology.* New York: Columbia University Press. Using traditional ethnographic approaches, this collection of original essays looks at urban inequality, crime, family structure, reproduction, welfare cheating, and the failure of some community organizations. It also includes a discussion of methodological techniques in urban anthropology.

WARD, B. E. 1985. *Through Other Eyes.* Hong Kong and Boulder, Colo.: Chinese University Press and Westview Press. A collection of essays devoted to understanding different aspects of Hong Kong society as it has been transformed over the past thirty years.

PART III — The Diversity of Adaptive Patterns

Part III explores in detail many of the ideas introduced in Part II. The topics are basic to understanding the anthropological perspective in action.

Although the chapters are designed to stand alone, each shares a number of common themes including a focus on individual behavior, variability within society, coping with problems arising from the environment and from within and outside one's own society. Although independent, the chapters are presented in a logical sequence. Chapter 10 examines the individual as a biological and cultural being. Chapter 11 follows with a discussion of language, which is at the heart of all human social behavior. Our treatment of various aspects of social life begins in Chapter 12 with a discussion of kinship, marriage, and family—key building blocks for social formations of a larger scale. Chapter 13 considers the nature of social groups and networks; special groups such as lineages, clans, and tribes; and the basis for hierarchical social divisions such as class and caste. The treatment of economic and political organization in Chapters 14 and 15 extends the discussion of the basic organization of social groups. The discussion of religion in Chapter 16 makes use of concepts introduced in our discussion of economics and political life. The last chapter focuses on the important issues of social change, planned or unplanned; the way in which anthropologists can contribute to understanding processes of change; and the ethics of anthropology.

At a funeral in Nepal, a body is ready for cremation. (BILL O'CONNOR/PETER ARNOLD)

A Berber man offers tea. Such gestures of hospitality are important rituals in many societies. (NIK WHEELER/ BLACK STAR)

Pilgrims bow in prayer before the sacred mosque in Mecca. (ARAMCO WORLD)

A young Jewish boy passes into manhood at his bar mitzvah. (CHRIS RIDLEY/ROBERT HARDING PICTURE LIBRARY)

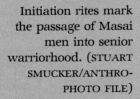

Initiation rites mark the passage of Masai men into senior warriorhood. (STUART SMUCKER/ANTHRO-PHOTO FILE)

A Thai couple marries in a Buddhist ceremony. (ULRIKE WELSCH)

An American wedding party.

Samburu tribesmen in Kenya perform a ritual dance. (KAL MULLER/WOODFIN CAMP & ASSOCIATES)

Indian folk dancers at a folklife festival in San Antonio, Texas. (BOB DAEMMRICH/THE IMAGE WORKS)

Reflections

We wish to bury our dead. Now, a funeral
Is a many-cultured thing. Some races would
Rope a heifer to the slaughter stone, or
Goat/ram/pig or humble cockerel,
Monochrome or striped, spotted, seamless—
The soothsayer rules the aesthetics or,
Rank and circumstance of the dear deceased.
Market rates may ruin devout intentions.
Times austere are known to sanction disrespect,
Spill thinner blood than wished. Still,
Flow it must. Rank tunnels or transition
Must be greased, the bolt of passage loosened,
Home-brewed beer or smuggler's brands, prestigious,
Froth and slosh with ostentation, belch
In discreet bubbles like embarrassed mourners
At the wake. The dead record no disavowal.

    FROM WOLE SOYINKA, "FUNERAL SERMON, SOWETO"

The human need to commemorate, to ceremonialize, is universal. Rituals range from the sacred to the mundane, they may be public or private, personal or political—as the funeral described by Soyinka. We all tend to organize the routines of our daily lives into private, personal, and sometimes idiosyncratic ceremonies. For example, do you eat your boiled egg from the shell or from a cup? Do you clean your teeth before or after breakfast? While these rituals are not issues of any particular significance in themselves, through them we gain a sense of security, of control over our lives.

How much more emphasis we put on the major events in our lives—the so-called rites of passage such as birth, puberty, marriage, and death—is amply illustrated by the fact that these events are universally celebrated as public rites. Yet the ways in which they are celebrated, the appropriate behaviors, the preferred colors, even the range of people permitted to participate, vary in ways that seem to be limited only by human imagination. Nevertheless, since Arnold Van Gennep's work in 1909 we recognize that most rites of passage have a clear structure: The individuals at the center of the situation are symbolically separated from society for a period, then given instructions or tests and ultimately reincorporated into society in a new status. The need for ritualization is social in nature: Changes in status occasion disruption in the lives of those around the individual—changes in expectations, rights, and obligations. Rituals by virtue of their predictability and fixed protocol facilitate the move to a new status, whether it is the investiture of a pope or the graduation of a child from high school.

Rituals and ceremonies are not compartmentalized activities. From a religious point of view, when one approaches the sacred, one takes steps to transform oneself into a sacred state appropriate to the ritual—perhaps by fasting, confessing one's sin, or performing special ablutions. Furthermore, participation may be an economic, social, or political statement. Many rituals are expensive and difficult to carry out; when one is successful, one's social standing is enhanced. One of the paramount rituals of Islam is making the once-in-a-lifetime pilgrimage to Mecca and the performance of a sequence of rites that symbolize events in the life of Muhammad. The would-be pilgrim prepares well in advance so as to be in a state of ritual readiness, dons special garments, and abstains from foods and activities that spiritually pollute. Having completed the rituals of the pilgrimage, the individual returns to his or her community with a distinctly altered social status. While piety and religious commitment are usually genuine, the pilgrimage often has beneficial economic and political consequences as well.

A funeral, such as that of a young man in Soweto, South Africa, described in Soyinka's poem may also be a political event. Not simply the funeral oration, but who attends, the positioning of the mourners, the numbers of people involved all constitute the structure of a readily interpreted political declaration. During the mounting rebellion against the Shah of Iran, each death of a protester brought renewed protests as the death was memorialized seven days and then again forty days later, as required by Islam. When certain opposition leaders started attending, when soldiers disobeyed their orders not to attend, when left- as well as right-wing student groups attended together, a powerful message was directed at the regime.

In another sort of ritual, the New Guinea *keiko* feasts, warriors and allies for other groups are honored; while the liturgy or content of the rituals is predetermined, what is not is also of great significance: the order in which the names are sung out; the number of pigs slaughtered; the blankets, coppers, pearlshells, and so on provided. Men whose names are not sung prominently are dishonored; men from other groups who attend and dance thereby announce their commitment to be allies in the next round of war.

Given its close association with myth, ritual serves as a means of expressing abstract but important relationships: king to subject, priest to layman, parent to child. Equally important is the way in which ritual can help relate people to the natural world. If the Mbuti pygmies of the Ituri Forest are plagued by sickness or poor hunting, the adult men gather nightly to hold a *molimio* ritual to awaken the forest to their plight and to restore balance and harmony to their world. No priests lead the ceremony and there are no specific invocations; people simply sing and chant.

Chapter **10** Biology, Culture, and the Individual

On August 31, 1925, a twenty-three-year-old anthropologist disembarked from an ocean liner in the sweltering Pacific heat of Pago Pago, American Samoa. Margaret Mead was about to undertake a field study that was to have a lasting impact on American anthropology—indeed, on the way many people view that elusive thing called "human nature." Many of us speak of human nature as if the entire human species were united by a single cluster of behavioral traits. Male assertiveness and female passivity, the trauma of adolescence, sexual jealousy, and the frequently competitive relationship of siblings are often assumed to be universal human characteristics, the behavioral hallmarks of our species.

Mead selected for research a topic of great interest to her mentors, Frank Boas and Ruth Benedict: she intended to investigate the adolescent behavior and maturation of young people, particularly young women. Her research was to test the hypothesis that human maturation is a passage through biologically fixed stages that are little affected by cultural conditioning. Part of her research would involve adolescent sexuality; she wanted to find out if the Samoan adolescent experienced the same stress that American young people seemed to suffer as they underwent puberty. Though it is popularly assumed that anthropologists have always had an interest in the sexual practices of people in other societies, this type of research had been quite rare. But it was not the pioneering aspect of her venture that made her topic of vital concern to so many people, or even the fact that she was a young woman pursuing her research in an exotic setting. Mead was putting herself squarely in the middle of an intellectual controversy that had long raged in Europe and America—one that touched on far more than the academic careers of the principal protagonists. It had political overtones as well.

The pressing problem, as Boas put it in 1924, was knowing "what is hereditary and what is not"; that is, what is the relative importance of biological and cultural factors in human behavior. This controversy, often called the nature–nurture debate, was usually expressed in terms of absolute contrasts—human personality and behavior were determined primarily either by people's biological makeup or, as the proponents of nurture would have it, by their cultural upbringing. The controversy was of immediate concern because legislators in Europe and the United States considered laws governing migration, interracial marriage, education, and social welfare in its light. In an extreme version, those who held that biology was destiny proclaimed doctrines of racial and gender superiority; others, somewhat less extreme at the time, argued against public education for the masses as a waste of resources. Boas, Kroeber, Benedict, and many of the other anthropologists introduced in Chapter 2 were strong proponents of the primacy of culture over biology as a determinant of individual behavior. Thus Margaret Mead placed herself in the thick of an important national and international debate.

Mead settled for her first study on the small island of Ta'u and began work with a sample of fifty young women in three villages. At the conclusion of her fieldwork, some seven months later, she returned to New York and began to write up her observations. Chief among them was the finding that adolescence in Samoa was almost wholly lacking in the trauma that characterized growing up in

American and European society. Young people there, she reported, were encouraged to engage in premarital sex, and were attached not exclusively to their individual parents but to a large, less authoritarian cluster of individuals that included kin and non-kin alike. Rape, sexual jealousy, and adolescent violence were virtually unheard of, as a result, in her view, of the permissive and relaxed Samoan approach to child rearing. Thus, she claimed, Samoan social relations proved that human nature does not of necessity involve a tension-ridden puberty.

Her book *Coming of Age in Samoa* (1928/ 1971) made her an almost instant celebrity. In her last chapter she attempted to apply the insights gained from the Samoan experience to American child rearing and family life in the hope of mitigating the stresses of growing up. As Nancy Scheper-Hughes writes (1979:444), the publication of her book began the sexual revolution in America: "It became a bible for reform-minded and progressive parents, educators, pediatricians, and guidance counselors throughout America, and it greatly influenced the man who, in later years, was to become the pediatrician of Mead's only child, Cathy: Dr. Benjamin Spock."

Margaret Mead (1935) pursued her interest in sex roles and related issues in her study of three New Guinean societies. In the 1930s, when Mead set out for New Guinea, many people believed (as some still do) that biological differences programmed women to be gentle, nurturing, and passive; men to be tough, independent, and aggressive. Among the Arapesh, the first society that Mead visited, she found that the women fitted the female stereotype quite well—but so did the men. As Mead saw it, "The whole adventure of living [among the Arapesh] was centered on making things grow—plants, pigs, and most of all children" (1975:214). Accordingly, men and women alike were nurturing types—gentle, kind, eager to help others. Violence and selfishness were equally frowned upon by both sexes.

Similarly, the second group that Mead studied, the Mundugumor, who had been (reputedly, at least) cannibals, had no conception of a double standard. But here, according to Mead, the uniform standard was one of "male" aggressiveness. Both men and women were expected to be fierce, selfish, and highly sexed. All adults were prone to violence. They slapped and ridiculed their children. They bit and scratched each other during lovemaking. They invoked evil magic to ruin one another's gardens.

Finally, in the third group, the Tchambuli, Mead at last found sex-role differentiation as pronounced as ours, but the roles, she asserted, were the reverse of our sex-role stereotypes. The women were the sexual aggressors and the household breadwinners of the society; they dressed simply, worked well with one another, and were generally brisk, hearty, businesslike creatures. The men tended to be vain, jealous, and moody. They adorned themselves with feathers and paint and spent most of the day in their ceremonial houses, gossiping, carving and painting, bickering with one another, adjusting their finery, and practicing their dance steps. Thus it appeared that sex roles were not biologically determined universals. As Mead was among the first to point out, such behavior is in large part a cultural construct.

Since then Mead's studies have been at the center of much debate, including allegations that her observations were, quite simply, wrong. Derek Freeman, an Australian anthropologist, has raised the question of the reliability of Mead's early studies. His challenge, published in 1983 (just after her death), has led to a vigorous round of charges and countercharges. He found that during the period of her fieldwork rape was at least as common in Samoa as in the industrialized nations, as was other adolescent male criminal behavior. He found, too, that contrary to Mead's observations, premarital sex was much frowned upon, that violence arising from sexual jealousy was common, and that children were, and still are, vigorously supervised and punished by their natural parents. Freeman concludes that human nature is the same everywhere and so are human passions. In short, his picture of Samoa is directly at odds with Mead's. As for the Tchambuli, what is often not noted is that after the men have perfected their dances, they go off on headhunting expeditions; and the fact that the Mundugumor women are the primary producers of food leaves "the men free to plot and fight" (Mead 1949).

Most scholars familiar with the issues agree that Mead overstated her case by ignoring both the considerable variability within the societies she studied and the contrasting evidence that others have seen in her case studies (Feinberg 1988). Most seem to agree that she underestimated the incidence of aggressive behavior among the Samoans but that she is generally correct in her reporting of Samoan sexuality (Scheper-Hughes 1979). One ethnographer, Allen Abramson (1987), who worked very close to Mead's original field site, suggests that both Mead and Freeman are at least partially correct but that they are looking at rather different aspects of Samoan culture. Abramson found that sexual contact was indeed common before marriage, but that the young people's parents disapproved. As Mead worked with adolescent girls, often spending hours in their company with no other adults present, she may have uncovered a reality that eluded Freeman, who concentrated his attention on senior men—who would have been unlikely to admit that such "deviant" behavior was widespread. The consensus is that Mead's general proposition is valid, that sex roles are variable and that individuals can be and often are socialized and enculturated to quite different gender-specific behaviors in different societies. At the same time, it is very likely that men and women do differ significantly; what socialization can do is either minimize or exaggerate such differences (Konner 1988).

Our understanding of the relationship between the biological and cultural dimensions of behavior is far greater now than it was in 1925. In fact, Margaret Mead often emphasized her belief that sex-role variability is constrained by physiology—a point often overlooked by her admirers and detractors alike. Today the nature–nurture argument sounds facile, as neither extreme position has been substantiated. We have, in short, no answer to the question that Mead herself posed: What would happen if a boy and a girl were raised with precisely the same role expectations and models?

THE IMPORTANCE OF LEARNED BEHAVIOR

Though all animals have the ability to learn, much animal behavior appears to be closely controlled by genes. Even learning itself can be directed by built-in propensities to learn certain things more easily than other things. The ability of songbirds to learn a call system appropriate to their species is a case in point. Birds learn the call system of their species, together with modifications that mark their particular population. They show no interest in learning the calls of even closely related species. Such "hardwired" or strongly constrained behavior has been well documented in regard to many species. In fact, many species of animals are distinguished more by their behavior than by their physical characteristics (for example, what they eat, how they attract mates, and how they defend their territories).

Konrad Lorenz (1965), an Austrian ethologist (student of animal behavior), discovered that for a short period after goslings are hatched, they will attach themselves to anyone or anything that produces the proper quacks—even Lorenz himself, who became "Mother Goose" to a small brood he was observing (Lorenz

1965). Lorenz and others have shown time and again that animals raised in isolation from their kind and thus prevented from learning through imitation will still perform complex behaviors typical of their species. They are genetically programmed to respond in a certain way when they are exposed to a particular environment or stimulus.

Without question human behavior is similarly constrained, though to a lesser degree. All human beings are born with certain fundamental biological needs and limitations. We cannot survive very long without food and water, rest and sleep, and our body chemistry pressures us to fill these needs. We get hunger pains when our blood sugar is low; there are times when no amount of effort will keep our eyes open. Many muscular acts are involuntary—sneezing, for example, and such complex facial expressions as those that indicate fear, pain, and pleasure.

In fact, our basic repertoire of senses and our mental system—that is, the brain itself—are products of biological evolution. This system sets the ultimate constraints within which behavior can develop. In some respects, we can say that the complex and changing phenomenon we call culture comes in a rather drab biological envelope, and even our ability to envision other ways to exist is far less than infinite.

Yet most behavior is not hard-wired and thus can rapidly change to accommodate new circumstances (though we all know of many instances when it does not). Learned behavior has another important attribute: we can transmit it to people who are not biologically related to us. Thus ways of doing things, ideas, values can be shared rapidly and widely. One's teachers or even schoolmates can be as instrumental in this regard as one's parents.

Going hand in hand with social learning, the need for social contact is as basic to humans as the need for food, rest, and sexual satisfaction. Children require attention from other human beings in order to develop normally. (The same is true of our nearest relatives in the animal kingdom, the apes and the monkeys.) When institutionalized infants who are ignored by busy nurses or other salaried caretakers are compared with children raised in families, they are found to be slower to learn to sit up, grasp objects, walk, and talk, and are often undersized even when they receive adequate food. Any infant usually becomes extremely attached to the person who cares for him or her. In our society, at least, infants go through a stage when separation from this caretaker makes them intensely anxious. The infant's joy in being handled and fussed over lays the foundation for a widening circle of attachments in the coming years (Bowlby 1969). The need for social contact remains strong in adults—so strong that most of us suffer acute psychological or even physiological distress when we are isolated from others for any length of time. As Aristotle said, humans are gregarious animals.

To these **biological imperatives**—the basic human drives for food, rest, and sexual satisfaction and the need for social contact—we might add another that Eugene d'Aquili (1972) claims is the "supreme adaptive specialization" of our species, the **cognitive imperative**—the human need to impose order on the world by mental processes. Our brains have evolved in such a way as to permit mental operations far beyond the reach of other species—abstract thought, complex problem solving, and subtle communication through the symbolic medium of language. These operations allow humans to impose order on their observations of reality. Yet, according to D'Aquili, the universal human habit of seeking order in reality is not simply a socially learned behavior. It is a product of highly evolved brains. It is also the product of a neurologically rooted "need to know," which evolved simultaneously with the biological capacity for knowing. Human beings tend to become quite anxious if they cannot impose order—at least in their minds—on the bewildering array of external stimuli. Thus we have invented magic, religion, science, philosophy, and other systems to explain the cosmos, to name and then to tame the unknown. In the process we have become cultural animals.

All people share certain biological traits that account in part for some of the broad similarities in human behavior. But biological makeup also accounts for behavioral differences. On the individual level, a person's build, health, and stamina affect ability to perform certain kinds of activities. Malnutrition during the first years of life, for example, prevents full development of the brain and in extreme cases may cause mental retardation. Even with an excellent diet, some people are simply not strong enough to work as stevedores or professional athletes, just as some lack the manual dexterity to assemble minute transistors or to perform intricate passages on the piano. Physiology sets upper limits on individual capabilities which training cannot always overcome.

We are beginning to learn more about the biological bases of certain kinds of behavior. As people have known for centuries, such drugs as alcohol and marijuana can significantly alter behavior by altering body chemistry. By the same token, many scientists now suspect that some behavioral states as well as behavioral disorders may have a biochemical basis. It has been discovered, for example, that when some people are severely depressed, their nerve cells do not fire as quickly as usual. The severe psychosis called schizophrenia has been shown to have a genetic basis. It has also been found that deficiencies of the B-complex vitamins can have significant effects on the nervous system, causing confused thought processes, severe anxiety, and exhaustion. Many scientists now believe that the emotional basis for male-female bonding may have a chemical component (Fisher 1987). Even the amount of sugar in the blood can affect behavior: blood-sugar level is an important factor in some manifestations of aggression.

Study after study has shown that men are more prone to physical violence than women, whether it is evidenced in warfare in a tribal society or in the crime rate in an industrial one. In a study of bullying behavior in the Norwegian school system, Dr. Dan Olweus, professor of psychology at the University of Bergen, found that of 568,000 schoolchildren, 41,000, or over 7 percent, bully others regularly. The majority of the bullies were boys, and the tendency increased with age in boys but declined in girls.

While socialization factors cannot be excluded, one hormonal cause seems to be implicated also: the blood level of testosterone, the male sex hormone, is linked to aggression in both sexes, and males are more likely to have elevated levels of the hormone. In a smaller study of teenage boys Dr. Olweus found a close link between testosterone levels and intolerance with frustration and response to provocation (cited in Konner 1988). When Dr. June Reinisch, director of the Kinsey Institute, studied twenty-five boys and girls who had been prenatally exposed to an artificial hormone similar to testosterone, she found that they were more aggressive than their same-sex siblings (ibid.). A parallel example in the case of females is the nurturing behavior that results from the enhanced levels of the hormone prolactin generated when women nurse (Trevathan 1987). In short, biological factors affect individual behavior in ways of which most of us are only superficially aware.

THE INFLUENCE OF SOCIAL LEARNING ON HUMAN BEHAVIOR

Studies of the biological foundations of human behavior tell us in general why we are all so fundamentally alike, whatever our culture. Yet anthropology must also explain how and why we differ in our behavior and our customs. As we know, behavior and perception vary considerably from society to society. For some reason, individuals within a given group will grow up acting and thinking differently from members of other groups. What is the basis for this cross-cultural variation?

As we saw in Chapter 2, some anthropologists have conceptualized this variation in terms of varying "group personalities." To use Ruth Benedict's metaphor, from the "great arc" of human personality potential each culture chose some traits to emphasize, and it fostered those traits in each new generation through its child-rearing practices. In this way the group personality lived on through time. Margaret Mead saw culture as the primary influence on personality traits.

Later theorists have criticized this "cookie-cutter" version of group-personality theories, which implies that all of an individual's qualities are imposed by her or his culture. Their more rationalistic approach recognizes that culture supplies individuals with alternatives for behavior in the form of "models," or general guidelines for behavior; "standards" (Goodenough 1970) or sets of "mazeways" (Wallace 1970) for coping with the problems of living; and values and beliefs as a basis for behavior.

Socialization

Socialization (often also termed *enculturation*) is the process by which a person acquires the technical skills of his or her society, the knowledge of the kinds of behavior that are understood and acceptable in that society, and the attitudes and values that make conformity with social rules personally meaningful, even gratifying. Socialization involves both explicit instruction and unconscious modeling by the family and by the society as a whole. As children absorb such lessons, they are gradually transformed into knowledgeable and more or less cooperative and productive members of their society. Socialization, then, is the process whereby a society reproduces itself in each new generation.

Socialization is by no means uniform for all members of a society. In our own society, for example, some parents raise their children quite strictly, setting clear rules and clear punishments for violations. Others take a more permissive approach, making large allowances for experimentation and failure on the child's part. Nor are the parents the only socializing influences. Each child has a unique constellation of friends, relatives, and neighbors, and hence each learns a somewhat distinctive version of the culture. Moreover, the exact content of the socialization process varies along gender, ethnic, socioeconomic, religious, and regional lines.

We have seen how Yąnomamö boys are encouraged by their parents to be aggressive and to display anger and rage. Their sisters are not encouraged to behave in this way, although we may assume that their capacity for anger and rage is as great as that of boys. Among the Yomut Turkmen of northeastern Iran, young men are brought up with a high regard for physical prowess and the necessity of defending one's kin and community, by force if necessary. One tribe or descent group among the Yomut, however, is considered holy, and the men do not fight. In fact, it is considered a serious religious offense to strike a member of this holy tribe or to steal their property. Boys in this group are socialized quite differently from those born into other Yomut groups, with little emphasis on fighting or self-defense.

Nevertheless, there are broad similarities in how and what the members of a single society are taught. The members of a given society tend to take such similarities for granted (often marking them up to "human nature") and to notice only the differences. But to the outsider, individual differences in thought and behavior within a society may be less striking than the similarities.

Every society teaches its own unique version of what life means and how it should be lived, but the lessons are conveyed through much the same channels in all societies. We will examine four of these channels, or media, of socialization—child rearing, education, role learning, and rites of passage—keeping in mind that they all overlap.

Child-Rearing Practices

The people responsible for raising children (usually the parents) teach and train them, molding the biological drives and instincts of infancy into socially acceptable behaviors. Children must be weaned; they must learn the general customs associated with elimination, sex, and the expression of love and aggression; and finally, they must learn a degree of independence from their parents and family.

The most obvious way in which this training varies from culture to culture is in its harshness or severity. Should children be permitted simply to outgrow their infant behaviors, or should they be compelled in one way or another to drop them? Each society has its own answer to this question. Among the Kwoma of New Guinea, for example, children are not toilet-trained until they are old enough simply to be told how to go about it, usually at age five or six. Among the Dahoemans of West Africa, on the other hand, children of four who soil their beds are disciplined by having ashes and water poured over their heads, or the parents may tie a live frog to the child's waist to frighten or humiliate him or her. Sometimes cross-cultural differences are truly startling. The Marquesan Islanders of Polynesia wean their children at six months, the American middle class at about eight months, the Chenchu tribe of India at six years. Among the Lepcha of India, it is not unknown for a mother to nurse a child until the age of puberty (Whiting and Child 1953). Even within a society, there is great variability, ranging in the United States from those who do not breastfeed at all to those who wean only after one year or more.

Some societies are generally more severe or indulgent in all aspects of childhood training, but most cultures indulge children in one area and discipline them strictly in another. The Marquesans, for example, whose culture is one of the most severe in its weaning practices, are indulgent in sexual training, encouraging early sex play and masturbating children to quiet them. The Kurtachi of New Guinea, in contrast, are severe in sexual training and indulgent in weaning.

A relationship between child-rearing practices and personality development has been widely recognized. As we have seen, the group-personality theorists based their studies on this relationship. Mead (1935), for example, noted that the differences in adult behavior between the gentle Arapesh and the fierce Mundugumor were closely associated with differences in child discipline. The Arapesh trained their children gradually and were highly solicitous of their needs. An Arapesh woman would offer a frightened child her breast even if the child was past weaning age. The Mundugumor, in contrast, were generally indifferent to children's needs and beat them soundly when they did not comply with an adult's demands.

Education

Education is "the transmission of the knowledge, understanding, attitudes, sentiments, and ways of doing things that characterize a particular society" (Goldschmidt 1971). Habit training in early childhood is part of education, but only a small part. As children grow, the scope of their education expands. From parents, neighbors, and friends and from religious and civic authorities they learn what they can expect in life and what is expected of them. They also learn the values and skills that will allow them to get along with others and make a living.

The Cultural Environment of a Deadly Virus: The Global AIDS Epidemic

C. Everett Koop, then surgeon general of the United States, reported in 1988 that since the count began in June 1981, more than 52,000 Americans had been reported as having AIDS, and that the projected cost in medical care alone would reach nearly $5 billion a year by 1992, when an estimated 142,000 people would be in various stages of the fatal illness. Despite massive outlays of resources, this is a disease that will not go away soon. The U.S. Public Health Service (1986) has estimated that 1.5 million people are infected with HIV (human immunodeficiency virus), which can be carried for up to ten years before the first overt signs of AIDS appear, and which kills by destroying the immunological system.

While most diseases have a cultural component that affects the rate of infection and largely determines the population at risk, probably no current life-threatening epidemic is more closely linked to patterns of behavior than AIDS. During the long period during which the infection is carried before the appearance of symptoms, it can be passed on through unprotected contact with semen and blood. Since 1981, most American adults infected with AIDS have been homosexual or bisexual males (65 percent) and homosexual or bisexual male intravenous drug users (8 percent). The bulk of the remaining victims (about 21 percent) are heterosexual drug abusers; only 6 percent of the cases occurred as a result of only heterosexual contact or blood transfusions (Curran et al. 1988:19).

The disease is commonly viewed as an outcome of a "gay lifestyle" (Schneider 1988:100–101). But as anthropologist E. Michael Gorman (1989) points out, homosexual culture simply reflects the larger heterosexual society, which had come to accept a "busy sexual lifestyle." Anthropology, he writes, can promote an understanding of AIDS by identifying high-risk behaviors, directing preventive educational measures to alter behavior, and developing greater understanding of

sexuality, particularly homosexuality (p. 200). A distinctive gay lifestyle has developed in urban areas; "gay people—men and women—have taken on characteristics of certain ethnic communities," with distinctive argot and symbols, distinctive social conventions, special churches, banks, and clubs (p. 199). These developments offer the anthropologist a window through which to see how diseases shape cultural development.

But AIDS is a global problem. In Africa, which has the highest incidence of AIDS after North America, AIDS is viewed as a disease of urban elite heterosexual men. Yet an interdisciplinary research team based in Kinshasa, the capital of Zaire, found more than half of the people infected by the virus were women (Schoepf et al. 1988). The disease had been transmitted almost exclusively through heterosexual vaginal contact.

AIDS emerged and spread in Central Africa as a result of specific social and economic conditions: recently many areas have experienced an economic crisis, with declining food production, soaring food prices, high unemployment, and massive migration from the country to the cities. Women, the major AIDS risk group in Central Africa, are most severely affected. Professional prostitutes are not the only women at risk; many other women have had multiple sexual partners, often because of the difficulty of feeding and caring for their children. Polygyny is widespread among all social classes, and spouses do not restrict their activities to socially recognized partners. A woman in a polygynous marriage usually resides with her children in a separate dwelling, and is likely to be abandoned or neglected by her husband. Women are virtually excluded from formal employment, and when economic crisis strikes, men provide less and less, particularly if they have multiple households to support. Many poor women report that "they need to find a 'spare tire,' men to whom they offer sexual services when they need cash to obtain health care for a sick child or meet social obligations." Since multiple sexual partnerships put people at risk, Schoepf and her colleagues note, "AIDS has transformed what appeared to be a survival strategy into a death strategy" (1988:176–177).

As recently as 1985, many educated Africans referred to AIDS as an "imaginary syndrome invented by Europeans to discourage African lovers," but by 1987 most people were fully aware of the fatal nature of the disease and felt powerless to prevent it. Anthropologist Christine Obbo (1988) points out that foreign examples and approaches are not useful in the Ugandan situation. The association of AIDS with blood invoked strong personal and symbolic images that worked against possible campaigns to educate Ugandans to alter risky behavior. People became fearful of the Red Cross, which they associated with blood. Obbo identifies a number of myths that have to be dispelled before an effective AIDS program can be mounted in Uganda. One is that Africans not only are promiscuous but engage freely in sex-related discussions. Wrong. While some dances and

rituals refer to sex, people usually use euphemisms, are prudish about sex, and take great care to avoid "rude" language. Attempts to educate must be presented in a manner that will not give offense. Another myth is that body scarification and female circumcision are widespread and that they cause AIDS. Not so. Female circumcision is not widely practiced in Uganda, and the notion that it causes the disease merely distracts people from the real causes. Ugandans have their myths, too. Urban elites say that villagers should not be encouraged to use condoms because they will reuse them. On the contrary, Obbo writes, villagers are fastidious about sexual body fluids and are familiar with condoms but often reject them because they believe that penicillin cures sexually transmitted diseases. Ugandans in general tend to believe that prostitutes—and all single women in towns are assumed to be prostitutes—are responsible for passing on the disease. Quite apart from stigmatizing women, this notion ignores the long period when the HIV carrier, male or female, has no symptoms and can communicate it to others. In short, any message about AIDS will have to be translated into a cultural medium accessible to the people. One imported video on AIDS depicted it as a disease of homosexuals, and in the discussions that followed people focused more on "the funny and strange ways of Europeans" than on the grave matter at hand.

Brooke Schoepf and her colleagues write:

"Zero Grazing," the motto of Uganda's AIDS Control Program, conveys the message encouraging sexual fidelity in a way that is appropriate to the culture. (INTERNATIONAL DEVELOPMENT RESEARCH CENTER-GARY TOOMEY)

> Breaking the chains of AIDS transmission will require rapid and widespread behavioral change. . . . AIDS prevention is both personal and political. What appear to be personal or individual behaviors (and problems) are actually embedded in culturally conditioned gender roles arising out of psychological expectations and material conditions [Schoepf et al. 1988:179].

Effective local programs to limit the spread of AIDS will have to be closely tailored to the specific cultural environment in which the disease occurs.

Education is more than just the teaching of the technical skills necessary for survival—it is part of the socialization process itself. This process may be informal or formal. (Top) Socialization by observation and imitation is an informal and often unconscious method common to all societies. The Congolese girl learns to weave straw matting by watching her grandmother. (Middle) In a slightly more formal way, the Tuareg nomad boy learns to read the Koran in Arabic from his father and the village elders. (Bottom) In most societies today, much social learning takes place in the formal framework of a classroom. (TOP: LEON V. KOFOD; MIDDLE: MARC AND EVELYNE BERNHEIM/WOODFIN CAMP & ASSOCIATES; BOTTOM: DAVID STRICKLER/MONKMEYER PRESS PHOTOS)

Role Learning

Much of education takes place in the course of role learning. Every society classifies its members in a system of social positions, according to age, sex, family background, wealth, occupation, achievements, and the like. Each of these positions carries with it a **role**, a set of behavioral expectations appropriate to that position. The position of mother in a traditional American household, for example, carries with it the expectation that mother will bear children, cook dinner, remember birthdays, and listen sympathetically to her family's troubles. Likewise, the position of shaman (a curer or doctor) in an Eskimo community requires that the individual in that position act in a dignified manner, have conferences with spirits, and solve problems for the community. Roles determine not only behavior but also ideas (such as the belief that spirits speak to shamans). This is not to say that the individual's thought and behavior are rigidly dictated by his or her role; each person will interpret a given role in a somewhat distinctive way. Nevertheless, roles do channel our actions and mental processes in certain prescribed directions.

Gender Socialization. There is no society that does not recognize, encourage, and even demand differences between the physiologically distinct sexes. What varies is the form and intensity of the set of distinguishable characteristics associated with each sex. Each set of characteristics is a cultural construct that is usually referred to as **gender**.

Parents in all societies begin to train their children at an early age in the social behavior, or gender roles, considered appropriate to their biological sex. Gender identity is one's feeling of being male or female. Gender identity and gender roles usually develop in tandem (Frayser 1985). Gender roles tend to be defined by the society and establish the kind of behavior that is appropriate and inappropriate for a male

and a female. Children are socialized also to respond favorably to what are perceived as the social tasks or jobs appropriate to their gender. The Hopi, for example, traditionally gave a little girl a doll to reward good behavior; when she is especially well behaved, they say glowingly that she will grow up to be a fine cook. Boys were rewarded with arrows and praised with hints that they are destined to become swift runners (Thompson and Joseph 1947). Similarly, boys in Los Peloteros, the Puerto Rican shantytown described in Chapter 9, were allowed to run free after school; much like their fathers, they generally turned up at home only for meals. Girls, in contrast, were expected to stay at home and help their mothers with the cooking, cleaning, and care of younger children (Safa 1974).

Not all gender roles are neatly defined as simply male and female. Several North American Indian societies recognized and respected at least one clearly defined alternative: the *berdache*, or biological male who does not conform to a society's normative expectations for masculine behavior. It had been thought that the status of berdache had died out among Indian groups, but Walter Williams (1986) demonstrated otherwise when he reported his extensive research among contemporary berdaches in the United States and Mexico. Europeans who encountered the berdache tradition in earlier centuries ridiculed it and tried to suppress the custom. Berdaches were men who opted out of masculine gender identity; they declined the roles of warrior, husband, and hunter and assumed a distinct identity. They were regarded as a special group, and sometimes were honored as healers, shamans, and seers. Some were asexual; some married and lived as the wives of other men. Most tribes did not regard it as proper for two berdaches to have sex with each other (Williams 1986:93); to do so was seen as incest. The identity "masculine" as opposed to "feminine" was viewed as a "character" that one assumed independent of biologi-

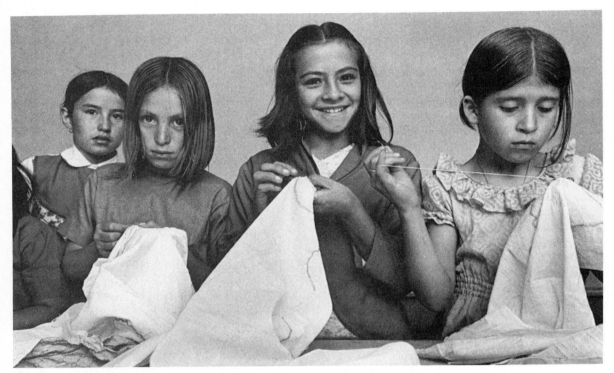

Gender socialization begins early to train the individual in the roles and behaviors the society sees as appropriate to the biological sex. Here girls in Colombia are learning to sew; it is unlikely that their brothers would join them in this activity. (ULRIKE WELSCH)

cal sex. Thus a man who lived with a berdache retained his masculine identity through his general deportment in society: he asserted his masculinity, performed appropriate tasks, and undertook the role of husband and provider.

In some Native American societies biological females could take on masculine gender identity; they have been referred to as "cross-gender females" (Blackwood 1984) and as "Amazons" (Williams 1986:234), after the legendary Greek female warriors. The Spanish explorer Pedro de Magalhães de Gandávo gave this name to the great river in Brazil after he encountered the Tupinamba in 1576.

There are some Indian women who determine to remain chaste; these have no commerce with men in any manner, nor would they consent to it even if refusal meant death. They give up all the duties of women and imitate men, and follow men's pursuits as if they were not women. They wear their hair cut in the same way as the men, and go to war with bows and arrows and pursue game, always in company with men; each has a woman to serve her, to whom she says she is married, and they treat each other and speak with each other as man and wife. [Quoted in Williams 1986:233]

Evelyn Blackwood (1984) writes that some thirty-four North American Indian societies recognized cross-gender females as a distinct and respected gender classification. The roles and status of cross-gender females, like those of berdaches, vary from society to society, but they were respected as a special instance of gender identity. Clearly the notion of gender has to be taken as culturally malleable, not something that is everywhere the same and unchanging. It is less clear whether our various cultures represent only a symbolic veneer masking a common bedrock of sexual thinking (Gilmore 1990:2).

Thomas Gregor, who has conducted cross-cultural studies of sexuality, believes that while gender ideals vary from culture to culture, underlying the variations are intriguing similarities in sexual stereotyping (Gregor 1985:200). Cultures may be more alike than different in this regard. David Gilmore (1990), in investigating what lies behind the notion of masculinity, found that widely separated and otherwise unrelated people had very similar notions as to what masculinity should be and how a man achieved it. In fact, "achieve" was the word Gilmore found best suited to express a man's attainment of masculine gender identity: men almost everywhere have to demonstrate masculinity by passing tests, performing certain tasks, and undergoing various forms of initiation. Gilmore shows impressive regularities in what seems to define masculinity in a wide variety of cultures: arduous tests of strength, risk taking, and demonstrations of bravery and resistance to pain.

We have to avoid thinking that biology is destiny. While gender distributions and by extension gender roles are grounded in biological distinctions, there is nothing biological in the gender-based allocation of economic, social, and political rights and responsibilities. As we see in the United States today, our view of gender, including that of people who do not conform to the societal ideal, such as homosexuals, is continually subject to change. Human society has few roles that cannot be filled by both males and females. The most important exceptions are those related directly or indirectly to childbearing and child rearing.

Age Roles. Societies also teach us age roles, and as we are constantly getting older, at each stage

of our lives we have to learn the types of behavior—the privileges and obligations—appropriate to our years. Our own culture makes rather vague distinctions among infants, children, and adolescents and among young, middle-aged, and elderly adults. Different degrees of responsibility and self-reliance are expected of people in the various categories, but we are not greatly shocked when people act older or younger than their years. In most of the cultures that anthropologists have studied, such relative indifference to age roles would be un-

There are very few jobs that cannot be performed equally well by individuals of either sex. This man and woman are supervisors in an iron refinery in Brazil. Whether or not such jobs are open to both sexes is determined by many factors; individual choice, cultural values, access to appropriate education, and even laws may result in some job categories being largely limited to one sex or the other. (ULRIKE WELSCH)

thinkable. Many societies treat aging as a passage through very distinctive states, not as movement along a chronological continuum.

Many African societies in particular have developed elaborate systems of age roles. We have already seen the age grades among the Pokot of Kenya (Chapter 7). Every Pokot male, along with the other males of his generation, belongs to an age class (or age set) whose membership remains fixed throughout his life. We recognize a similar grouping in our own society when we identify ourselves as members of "the class of '92," for instance. Among the Pokot from infancy to old age, each class of males moves through a series of five clearly defined and named age grades. The class occupies that grade—and the well-defined set of social roles that goes with it—for a period of years and then is initiated into the next higher grade. Just how long members of a junior grade must wait before moving on is a matter of some contention. With each advancement comes increased status and responsibility, which may threaten the status of older men. The group occupying the final age grade, for example, is expected to exercise major military and governmental responsibilities. Thus at each stage of the cycle, the society instructs its members on the roles appropriate to their grade, and in some measure the members become what the role dictates.

The matter of age roles illustrates an important point about socialization: it does not end with childhood. We learn more new material in childhood than in adulthood. Nevertheless, even as adults we are constantly stepping out of old roles and into new ones—from housewife to worker, from married to single and perhaps to married again, from parent of dependent children to parent of independent adults, from middle-aged person to old person, from employee to retiree, from spouse to widow or widower. With each role change comes a shift in behavioral expectation, and to some degree in values as well. Thus the individual is affected by and reacting to the processes of socialization from birth to death.

Rites of Passage

One of the most effective means of formally inducting an individual into a new role is participation in a rite of passage. Among the Pokot each move from grade to grade is celebrated with feasting and the sacrifice of animals. Such rites as the Jewish bar and bat mitzvah and the Catholic confirmation give the person a sense of identification with his or her new role, a notion that its privileges and obligations are not mere abstractions but are to be translated into action. Rites of passage are important signals to the larger community that an individual has changed roles. (We will discuss rites of passage further in Chapter 16.)

The Limits of Socialization

Anthropologists generally accept socialization as a useful concept, but with some reservations. One of its limitations is that it does not tell us very much about some widespread or very commonly shared patterns of behavior. Why, for example, is polygyny (one man married to more than one wife) so common while polyandry (one woman married to more than one husband) is rare? The concept of socialization is limited also in its ability to account for behavior that violates the "rules," behavior that deviates from the society's norms of propriety.

Deviance. We have stressed the vast amount of variation that exists within any society. Every society perceives some variant patterns of behavior as wrong. Often such behavior is seen as chosen simply to be different. The problem is complex because it is so difficult to define "deviance" precisely. Is alcoholism deviant behavior or is it a disease? Is homosexuality a psychological disorder (as it was long thought to be) or is it merely behavior not condoned by the majority?

Alfred Kinsey found that about 4 percent of American adult males were exclusively homosexual. A more recent study (using data from

1970 released in 1988) suggests that 20.3 percent of adult men had had sexual contact to orgasm at least once with another man; 6.9 percent had had such contact after age nineteen; and 3.3 percent had had regular homosexual contact (Fay et al. 1989:338–348). These results highlight the difficulty of defining proper and deviant behavior, even in an area as surrounded by cultural codes and norms as is sexuality.

Cookie Stephan and Walter Stephan (1985) have summarized two basically different schools of thought on the issue of deviance. From the perspective of the first, deviant behavior is behavior that is not proper, is not in accord with established norms. From the perspective of the second, deviant behavior is simply behavior that is labeled as such by individuals or groups powerful enough to impose their views.

The first approach presumes the existence of strong and well-defined norms within a society and individuals who choose, more or less consciously, to behave in a manner contrary to those norms. Several reasons for such a choice have been suggested: the deviants may be members of a group from which they have learned norms that are different from those characteristic of the majority; they may be unable to achieve goals to which they aspire by approved means; or they may have a negative attitude toward themselves, expressed by defying the established norms. In each case, the theory presumes an action that is deviant. A poor boy in a shantytown, for example, chooses to steal because all the other boys do it, because thievery is the only means he perceives of getting something to eat, or because it boosts his morale to outwit the shopkeeper and the police.

From the second perspective, that which is labeled deviant has little to do with the actions of the individuals who are said to be deviant. Instead, the actors are individuals or groups who isolate another individual or group by labeling their behavior as deviant. Deviance in this sense is viewed as a social construct and not as a fact. The dominant groups may label

The growing acceptability of homosexual relationships not only challenges perceived notions of what constitutes deviant behavior but also what constitutes marriage and family. (DONITA SIMPSON)

social practices, customs, even the religious beliefs, music, and art of a minority group as deviant. When a minority is thus stigmatized, it becomes further marginalized and effectively excluded from important areas of public life.

However we approach the issue, it is important to recognize the very important role that variation in behavior plays in societal change, even when that behavior is termed deviant. Behavior that is said to be strange or in any case outside of the established range of variation can become the very essence of change, the basis for the survival of the group. A member of an agricultural society may be termed deviant or abnormal because he spends too much time hunting. In the year when crops fail, however, this person becomes a hero. If crop failure continues, he is the founder of a new way of life.

In this respect, it is important to understand the powerful effect that circumstances have on the behavior of individuals and the equally powerful role that individuals can play in shaping situations and culture.

Culture versus Circumstances. Quite apart from socialization, individual development is not a play with only two actors—the individual and an outside agent, the culture. Many other factors bear heavily on what we become. An important one is the concrete circumstances in which we find ourselves. Consider, for example, the problem of alcoholism. One might think that society creates the conditions and the personality traits that lead people to drink excessively. Stereotyped views of drinking problems among some Native American groups follow this line of reasoning. It is sometimes said that Native Americans drink because something in their culture discourages abstinence and drives people to excess.

Theodore D. Graves (1970), however, drew the opposite conclusion from a study of drinking problems among Navajo migrants in Denver. In comparison with other urban groups (including other minorities), Native Americans do have a high rate of arrests for drunkenness and alcohol-related offenses—twenty times the rate for Anglo-Americans and eight times the rate for Hispanic Americans in Denver. But in interviews with more than 250 Denver Navajos, Graves found a high correlation between problem drinking and circumstantial factors: lack of parental models for wage labor, inadequate training for successful urban employment, the absence of family ties in the city, and unrealistically high expectations in regard to their new urban way of life. Another significant variable was marital status. Navajos who were single were arrested more often than Navajos who were not, and more Navajo immigrants to Denver were single than either Hispanics or Anglos in a comparable economic bracket.

Graves concluded that the high rate of alcoholism among the Denver Navajos was due not to their culture but rather to the situation in which these people found themselves in urban centers. He maintained that, "generally speaking, recourse to a group's 'culture' for explaining their behavior simply serves to conceal our ignorance of the underlying processes in operation" (1970:50). Admittedly, it is convenient for dominant groups in a society to explain the problems of minorities as the result of deviant subcultural values rather than as a result of social disadvantages. But the truth probably lies somewhere in between. As Graves rightly points out, the socialization model tends to obscure the role of circumstances.

INDIVIDUALS AS MANIPULATORS OF CULTURE

Those who hold that a given culture largely structures people's behavior view human beings in a passive role—blank slates that are gradually filled in with the wisdom of the past. This sort of determinism marks the theory that situations are the dominant influence on our lives, that people are reactors rather than actors. This position, when rigidly applied, ignores the fact that both cultures and circumstances are themselves creations of humans, and that people are always shaping and modifying them in various ways. The relationship between culture and the individual can be better understood, therefore, if we view culture as a set of guidelines that exists in order to be used by human beings (Leaf 1972).

Culture, some people hold, is only a set of codes and general rules, which individuals use to interpret their environment; they adjust the rules to fit the situations in which they find themselves. Furthermore, as we pointed out in Chapter 1, people look not just for proper solutions but for smart solutions—solutions that may be somewhat less than strictly proper but that enable them to overcome difficulties and achieve their ends. Morris Freilich (1971) has suggested that we are all scientists of a sort, constantly gathering data to apply to decisions. We make decisions on the basis of expert authority, use experience to predict the consequences of an act, and sometimes base decisions purely on theory. Many of the data we use are part of the content of our culture, but some are acquired through experience, group interaction, or our own powers of reasoning. In this view we are all individual actors in the culture, not stamped out by a cultural mold. Our relationship with our culture is one of dynamic interaction.

COGNITION AND CULTURE

Few anthropologists would dispute that at some level culture underlies individual behavior. Yet there is another factor that much more immediately underlies behavior—that is, thought. In the effort to avoid simplistic equations between culture and the individual, some researchers have turned their attention to **cognitive processes**—ways of perceiving and ordering the world. It is in the course of cognitive operations, after all, that the individual's knowledge of culture has whatever effect it is going to have on behavior. Therefore, it is not unreasonable to assume that cognitive patterns are a key to cross-cultural differences and similarities in behavior.

How, then, is cognition affected by culture? If societies differ in their social organization, economic strategies, religious beliefs, and so forth, do they also differ in their thought processes?

Cross-Cultural Differences in Cognition

A. C. Mundy-Castle (1966) showed four simple line drawings (like the ones in figure 10-1) to

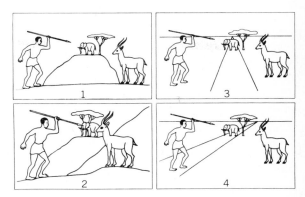

FIGURE 10-1.   (MUNDY-CASTLE 1966)

a group of Ghanaian youngsters. A Western child of seven or eight who looked at these pictures would perceive that the elephant is some distance beyond the man and the deer in all four drawings. But the Ghanaian children saw nothing of the sort. To them it was obvious that the man in card 1 could not see the deer because the hill blocked his line of vision. The fact that the elephant was small in proportion to the other figures did not evoke the impression of distance in their minds. Mundy-Castle associates their two-dimensional perception with lack of experience with picture books, drawing materials, and the like. Perception of depth in a drawing on a flat surface is an acquired skill. What the Ghanaian children lacked was familiarity with a certain symbolic technique, a culturally learned way of constructing reality. Although this technique may be common to Europeans, it is by no means a cultural universal (D'Andrade 1973). Thus Mundy-Castle's study shows that visual recognition of patterns, a process that most people consider strictly physiological, does in fact vary from society to society.

Other cognitive differences have appeared on cross-cultural tests. For example, experiments in Europe and America have shown that as children grow they go through a fairly well-defined sequence of developmental stages in cognition. From birth to age two, they master certain specific mental operations; from two to seven, others; and so on. Jean Piaget (1954), the Swiss psychologist who originated this theory, claimed that the developmental sequence was universal, and his claim has generally been substantiated by cross-cultural research. Piaget's theory likewise holds that children show a developmental increase in causal thinking: as they mature, they become more interested in and more accurate in determining what causes what.

Cognition, Personality, and Adaptation

Even though the differences that show up on cross-cultural tests reflect disparities merely in knowledge and experience rather than in ability, they may still give us insight into the interaction between culture and the individual. Such insight is offered by recent studies of perception.

Perceptual tests of pattern recognition have shown that people vary in what is called field independence versus field dependence. **Field independence** is the tendency to see the objects in one's field of vision as discrete units, distinct from the field as a whole. **Field dependence** is the reverse—the tendency to see the field as a single unit, with separate objects existing only as parts of the whole. J. W. Barry (1965) hypothesized that these different styles of perceiving might be related to different subsistence patterns. Specifically, field independence would seem to be necessary to hunting peoples, since they must be able to pick out an animal against a background and focus all their attention on that one object, distinct from its surroundings. Furthermore, in order to track the animal and get back to camp with the carcass, hunters must be able to see themselves in extremely precise relation to their surroundings. This hypothesis was confirmed in a study of eight communities (Barry et al. 1959). The greater the community's reliance on hunting as opposed to agriculture, the greater the tendency toward field independence on perceptual tests.

Interestingly, these perceptual styles have also been related to styles of child rearing. J. L. M. Dawson (1967) found field dependence is most common in societies that raise their children most strictly and field independence most common in societies where children are allowed more self-direction. These two correlations—perceptual style with procurement strategy and with child-rearing practices—may well constitute a single three-part relationship. Societies that rely on agriculture or herding—in other words, cooperative enterprises—are likely to raise their children to be submissive and obedient, to see themselves as subordinate to the group, an attitude that tends to foster field dependence. By contrast, hunting societies, in which survival depends on the resourcefulness of the individual hunter, are likely to encourage independence and individualism in their children, which in turn tends to encourage field independence.

Though speculative, this theory offers a good example of the type of relationship sought by cognitive researchers: a relationship in which the cognitive processes characteristic of a given society reflect and reinforce that society's subsistence practices, child-rearing practices, and other cultural attributes—all parts of a single adaptive pattern.

We may relate these findings to our earlier discussion of personality. According to one group of investigators, subsistence strategy may be the greatest single cultural influence on the individual personality. In 1961 Walter Goldschmidt, Robert Edgerton, and their colleagues launched the Culture and Ecology Research Project, to assess the impact of environmental factors and economic strategies on attitudes and behavior. The investigators located four East African tribes whose members were divided into farming and pastoral communities.

If culture is the dominant factor in personality development, they reasoned, there should be little or no difference between farmers and pastoralists of the same tribe. However, if personality is an integral part of adaptation to the environment, as the researchers believed, farmers and pastoralists of the same tribe should exhibit different personality traits (Edgerton 1971).

The researchers' hypotheses as to what those different traits might be were based on the requirements imposed by the two subsistence patterns. Farmers are committed to their land; they live in relatively stable, fixed communities. As a result, their social survival depends on maintaining good relations with people who will be their neighbors for life. Edgerton hypothesized that for this reason farmers would generally refrain from overt expressions of anger but would harbor secret hostilities and engage in indirect, covert forms of aggression—invoking demons to harm one another, for example. Pastoralists, in contrast, are highly mobile. If hostilities between individuals or groups build to the point where they can no longer live together, they can simply move. Because of this escape valve, Edgerton predicted, pastoralists would be much more open about expressing their feelings, good and bad. Farmers are at the mercy of the weather; when droughts come, there is little they can do except wait for rain. Pastoralists, again because they are mobile, are somewhat less vulnerable. They can move on to greener pastures and can fight the animal predators and raiders that threaten their stock. Furthermore, the pastoralist's livelihood depends on the ability to make quick decisions.

The farming life, in contrast, depends on hard, repetitive work; it is demanding but rarely dangerous. Edgerton predicted, accordingly, that farmers would be somewhat passive and fatalistic, whereas pastoralists would take the initiative more readily and would in general be more action-oriented and independent-minded.

The observations of four ethnographers, along with batteries of psychological tests, largely confirmed these expectations. Of course, not all pastoralists were open, resourceful, and independent, and not all farmers were furtive and passive. But in all the tribes the tests revealed statistically significant personality differences between farmers and pastoralists.

After examining both the biological and the cultural influences in human behavior, we must concede that in general it is very difficult to separate the threads of heredity and environment. Consider the unfortunate children who have grown up in total or near-total isolation from human contact. When such children are found, they are invariably mute. Must we conclude that language is the product of learning alone? Hardly; it has long been established that the capacity for language is dependent on certain biological, inherited structures in the brain.

Most human behavior, for that matter, is probably the result of interaction of biological and social influences. As F. T. Cloak (1975, 1976) put it, we all carry within us a set of biological instructions and a set of cultural instructions. At this point it is extremely difficult to determine the precise effect of each.

Summary

The focus of this chapter is the relationship between an individual and culture—the extent to which an individual is genetically programmed or shaped by social learning.

Margaret Mead's research in Samoa and New Guinea lent support to the nurture side of the nature–nurture controversy, for her findings indicated that sex-role behavior can be traced largely to child-rearing practices. Yet Mead herself viewed sex-role variability as constrained by physiology.

All people are born with certain biological traits that account in part for broad similarities in human behavior. In addition to two kinds of *biological imperatives*—the basic drives for food, rest, and sexual satisfaction and the need for social contact—Eugene d'Aquili has posited a third: the *cognitive imperative*—the need to impose order on the world. The creation of the explanatory systems of religion, magic, science, and philosophy result from this need. Biology also affects us on an individual level by setting limits—through our health, stamina, and body build, for instance—that cannot be overcome. In addition, biological factors affect certain kinds of individual behavior.

Through social learning, members of a society develop their own ways of behaving or perceiving, which differ from the ways of other societies. Social learning occurs primarily through *socialization*, the process by which the social group and the family, through formal training and unconscious modeling, pass on skills, knowledge, values, attitudes, and behavior to the next generation. Channels of socialization include child rearing, education, gender- and age-role learning, and rites of passage.

The goal of child-rearing practices is to mold the basic drives and instincts of infancy into socially acceptable behaviors; the relationship between child-rearing practices and personality development is widely accepted.

Education consists of both formal and informal instruction in the values, skills, and expectations that a person must have in order to get along in the society.

Role learning—adapting to a set of behavioral expectations appropriate to one's position—is an important part of education. While roles channel a person in certain prescribed directions, each individual interprets a given role in a somewhat distinctive way. Both gender roles and age roles are affected by socialization.

The form and intensity of the set of distinguishable characteristics associated with each sex—a social construct referred to as *gender*—vary from society to society. Many societies treat aging as a passage through distinctive states rather than as movement along a continuum.

One of the most effective means of socialization is the rite of passage, which marks the induction of a person into a newer, more responsible role. School graduations, weddings, confirmations, and bar and bat mitzvahs are all rites of passage.

The socialization model is limited in that it does little to explain behavior that deviates from established norms. It also fails to account for factors beyond the individual and the culture. In fact, both the individual's specific circumstances and his or her ability to manipulate the culture are vital elements in the determination of human behavior. The relationship between the individual and her or his culture is one of dynamic interaction.

Cognitive patterns may be the key to cross-cultural differences and similarities in behavior; if societies differ culturally, it is possible that they foster different *cognitive processes*—different ways of perceiving and ordering the world. Research has indicated that perception may vary (to a minor degree) from society to society. Certain perceptual skills, such as the capacity to perceive depth in a drawing on a flat surface, must be acquired. And research tends to substantiate the universality of Piaget's theory that children pass through a series of developmental stages in cognition.

People of different cultures have been shown to vary in *field dependence*—the tendency to see the objects in one's field of vision as discrete units, distinct from the field as a whole—and *field independence*—the tendency to see the field as a single unit, with separate objects existing only as parts of the whole. Such variations have been traced to styles of child rearing.

Differences in perceptual style have been identified and related to the society's procurement strategy as well. Such a correlation exemplifies the cognitive perspective, in which a society's cognitive processes reflect and reinforce its cultural attributes as a single adaptive pattern. And there is evidence that other aspects of the individual may be products of the same adaptive process. Personality, for example, was linked to subsistence patterns by ethnographers who studied four East African tribes of farmers and pastoralists.

It appears that most human behavior is the result of the interaction of biological and social influences. The precise effect of each is extremely difficult to determine.

Key Terms

biological imperatives	**cognitive processes**	**field independence**	**role**
cognitive imperative	**field dependence**	**gender**	**socialization**

Suggested Readings

CHAGNON, N. A., AND W. IRONS, (EDS.). 1979. *Evolutionary Biology and Human Social Behavior: An Anthropological Perspective*. North Scituate, Mass.: Duxbury Press. A collection of papers that investigate the implications of sociobiology for anthropological explanations of human social behavior.

GILMORE, D. 1990. *Manhood in the Making: The Cultural Construction of Masculinity*. New Haven, Conn.: Yale University Press. The author attempts to understand why so many societies, including our own, encourage boys and youths to adopt a pose of manliness. His conclusions are based on both anthropological and psychological theories.

GRUTER, M., AND R. D. MASTERS, (EDS.). 1986. *Ostracism: A Social and Biological Phenomenon*. New York: Elsevier. The essays in this volume explore the coercive exclusion of selected individuals by examining this behavior in groups of primates, in preliterate human societies, and in complex legal cultures.

KONNER, M. 1982. *The Tangled Wing: Biological Constraints on the Human Spirit*. New York: Harper. The author synthesizes data from both the biological and social sciences to determine to what degree human behavior is influenced by heredity. He contends that no theory of human nature is complete without an understanding of biology.

LADERMAN, C. 1983. *Wives and Midwives: Childbirth in Rural Malaysia*. Berkeley, Calif.: University of California Press. A vivid description that combines ethnographic data with medical data to demonstrate how a traditional medical system in Malaysia operates at the cultural, psychological, and physiological levels.

LEIBOWITZ, L. 1978. *Females, Males, Families: A Biosocial Approach*. North Scituate, Mass.: Duxbury Press. A wide-ranging look, from an evolutionary and cross-cultural perspective, at the prehistory, development, and diversity of the human family.

TURNBULL, C. M. 1983. *The Human Cycle*. New York: Simon & Schuster. A humanistic anthropological description of the human life cycle as experienced in a variety of cultures.

WHITING, B. B., AND J. W. WHITING. 1974. *Children of Six Cultures: A Psychocultural Analysis*. Cambridge, Mass.: Harvard University Press. A summary of the results of comparative studies of socialization that the Whitings have directed over several decades.

Chapter **11** The Anthropology of Language

The most distinctive single attribute of our species is language. Without it what we call culture would be impossible. Language allows us to make extraordinary use of intelligence, emotional capabilities, and even our more modest physiological endowments. Without language, our species could not simultaneously adapt to the rigors of space travel, conduct Arctic exploration, exploit the oil fields of the Arabian desert, and chart the depths of the Pacific Ocean. The ability to communicate through language underlies all aspects of culture: kinship, politics, religion, and family life, as well as science and technology. Language is the key to our ability to cope rapidly and effectively with new circumstances. It enables us to coordinate the activities of many people to achieve desired ends and allows us to codify and systematize our accumulated knowledge. Language enables us to transmit culture from generation to generation, as we teach our children.

HUMAN AND NONHUMAN COMMUNICATION

One way to appreciate the uniqueness of human language is to contrast it with nonhuman systems of communication. All animals seem to have means of transmitting messages to one another. Seagulls cry when predators appear. Honeybees, by means of intricate dances, tell one another where food is to be found. By releasing scents, dogs indicate their readiness to mate. Even amoebae appear to transmit rudimentary messages to one another, by emitting small amounts of carbon dioxide. Though we associate human language with speech, sounds are not a necessary aspect of language; people who cannot hear or speak can acquire and use language. Conversely, when a parrot imitates human utterances, it is not using language the way a human does. Language uses sounds, but what distinguishes it from other communication systems is not simply vocalization.

The primates, as we would expect from members of our own taxonomic family, have elaborate communications systems. Baboons threaten one another by baring their teeth and appease one another by smacking their lips. Chimpanzees, our closest evolutionary relatives, are even more communicative; they gesture, touch, hug, beg, smile, frown, glare, and so forth. Along with other animals, chimps also communicate vocally, through a **call system**—a repertoire of sounds (in the case of the chimps, about ten to fifteen different sounds), each of which is produced in response to a particular situation.

Language Versus Call and Gesture Systems

Presumably human language began as a call or gesture system. But language as we recognize it differs from such systems in several ways. Animal calls, probably because they are in large part genetically determined, are rigidly stereotyped; the call is always the same in form and meaning. Even so, the calls and songs of birds, for example, have important communicative functions and even resemble human language in that members of the same species occupying different territories may use slightly different songs, or what in humans would be called dialects. The same appears to be true of whales and porpoises. When chimpanzees find a plentiful source of food, they hoot. When attacked, they scream. In danger, they utter a resounding *"Waaa!"* To let others know that they are in the vicinity, they produce their distinctive "pant-hoot," roughly translatable as "Here I am!" (Goodall 1971). It is unclear whether chimpanzees, too, have territorial dialects, but signaling is clearly important. Neither the call nor its meaning appears to be consciously changed by the speaker. Moreover, animal call systems are closed. That is, elements of one call cannot be combined with elements of another to produce a new message. The calls are unique, limited in number, and mutually exclusive.

Human language is open—the number of messages that can be conveyed is infinite. Indeed, with language people can, and continually do, create entirely new messages—sentences that have never before been spoken—whereas call systems can generally convey only a very few simple meanings: danger, hostility, sexual excitement, the availability of food, and so on. As Bertrand Russell put it, "No matter how eloquently a dog may bark, he cannot tell you that his parents were poor but honest" (cited in Fromkin and Rodman 1988:346). Human language can be used to communicate a vast range of meanings, from subtle philosophical abstractions to complex technical information to delicate shades of feeling. This flexibility is made possible by the arbitrariness of human language. Unlike animal calls, the sounds of a language have no fixed meaning. Instead, meaning emerges from the way sounds are combined into words and words arranged to make sentences, in accordance with a complex set of rules (grammar).

Another distinctive feature of human language is that it is stimulus-free. That is, a linguistic utterance need not be evoked by an immediate situation. We do not have to turn a corner and come upon a tiger in order to say the word "tiger" or talk about "danger." We can discuss things that are not present—things experienced in the past, things that may happen in the future, even things that are not true or not real, such as unicorns and utopias. Little of this sort of communication appears to be possible in call systems, which lack the dimensions of time and possibility. While animals have been observed to send false signals, generally the use of call systems for deception is limited. It has been said, with some justice, that hominids became truly human when they became capable of telling a lie.

"Language" in Apes

Because language is fundamentally different from the communications of animals, and because children seem to learn language almost automatically, many anthropologists believe that linguistic ability must somehow be built into the human brain. In the words of the linguist Noam Chomsky, one of the major proponents of this view, language is based on "distinctive qualities of mind that are, so far as we know, unique to man" (1972:100). In recent years, however, other scientists have challenged this position, claiming that nonhuman species—especially the apes—have an undeveloped capacity for language. One way to test this question is to put an ape through language training, and that is what several researchers have done.

The earliest experiments in this area sought to teach chimpanzees to use spoken language, but since the chimpanzee vocal tract is not equipped for speech, these experiments were not very successful. This disappointment did not necessarily mean, however, that chimpanzees lacked the intellectual capacity for language. To get around the vocal-tract problem and test that intellectual capacity, two psychologists, Alan and Beatrice Gardner (1969), decided to teach their test chimp American Sign Language (ASL).

In four years this chimp, named Washoe, made astounding progress. She learned to use 130 signs. More important, she showed that she could manipulate them creatively. Having learned the signal "more" to persuade the Gardners to resume a pillow fight, she spontaneously used the same signal when she wanted a second helping at dinner. Furthermore, whereas chimpanzee calls, as we have seen, are never combined, Washoe spontaneously combined hand signals to make new words. Not knowing the signal for duck, for instance, she dubbed it "water bird." She learned to combine words in grammatical order, and she seemed to have an understanding of abstract concepts. One day when a new assistant was having some difficulty understanding Washoe's signs, Washoe, apparently sensing the problem, slowed her signing to make it easier for the woman to interpret. (The woman later commented that there are few experiences so humiliating as having a chimpanzee deliberately slow its language for your benefit.) Washoe seemed to understand the power of language and the way it could be manipulated.

Since the experiment with Washoe, another chimpanzee has been taught to communicate with colored plastic blocks; another, with a set of picture symbols on a computer keyboard. One of the most successful of the later experiments involved a gorilla named Koko. At age four she was able to use 251 different signs in a single hour. After five years of training in ASL, she scored between 80 and 90 (the equivalent of a five-year-old child) on an IQ test for nonreading children. Like Washoe, Koko could combine words creatively to name new objects.

Nonhuman primates are impressive in their communicative abilities and social skills. Here Koko signs the word for "smoke," the name of her pet cat, to her trainer Penny Patterson. (THE GORILLA FOUNDATION. © DR. RONALD H. COHEN)

She was also particularly adept at expressing her feelings. Whenever Penny Patterson, her trainer, arrived late at Koko's trailer, the gorilla would sign "sad." On other mornings, when asked how she felt, she would report herself "happy" or sign "I feel good." This was the first clear instance of emotional self-awareness on the part of a nonhuman primate. Koko also showed herself to be rather subtle in her emotions and in the way she expressed them. Once, when asked by a reporter whether she liked Patterson or Patterson's assistant better, Koko looked first at Patterson, then at the assistant, then back at Patterson, then back at the assistant, and replied, "Bad question." Whether she was being tactful or ambivalent, the response seems to indicate a rather intricate reasoning process, as did Washoe's handling of her new teacher's language problem. Such glimmers of human-like intelligence have led the ape trainers to argue that these animals have at least some of the advanced powers of reasoning that we associate with language; some observers assert that their linguistic ability differs from ours only in degree.

It would be incorrect, however, to conclude that these animals use language in the human sense. First, the languages that the test apes learned were in part iconic—the symbols imitated the things they stood for. There is a geometrical relationship between some of the signs and the things they represent. The ASL sign for book, for example, is two palms pressed together, then opened, much like the geometrics of opening a book. Thus, we still do not know whether apes have the intellectual capacity to handle a totally arbitrary language such as our own. Second, there is still some doubt as to whether the test apes put together sentences spontaneously or simply by rote. Third, even if ape language differs from human language only in degree, the distance separating them is vast. The suggestions of subtle reasoning in the apes' verbalizations are quite intriguing, but they are also quite rare. Finally, teaching language to an ape requires immense effort under highly artificial conditions, whereas human children learn it naturally, without training. Apes may share with us certain faculties necessary for language, but it is clear that these faculties have remained relatively undeveloped in their line.

THE EVOLUTION OF LANGUAGE

Because sounds leave no trace, researchers investigating the origins of language have to depend on indirect evidence: studies of the way children acquire language, comparisons of human and nonhuman vocalizations, guesses as to what kinds of brains and vocal tracts might have accompanied fossil skulls, and of course cultural evidence of the way our early ancestors lived.

The cultural evidence seems to indicate that language began to evolve as early as four million years ago. It was probably around that period, as we learned in Chapter 2, that our early ancestors made a crucial change in their way of procuring food—from individual foraging for vegetable foods to regular eating of meat and vegetables on a communal basis. The new pattern required cooperation and the coordination of hunting and gathering activities, for which at least an advanced call or gesturing system seems to have been required. The cultural evidence, then, suggests a very early date for the first rudimentary language skills. The physical evidence suggests a later date for the full development of language.

The Physiology of Language

To speak, the early humans had to have more than just the need to communicate. Speech requires physical mechanisms as well, such as certain structures in the brain. These structures allow us to associate incoming auditory messages with remembered messages from other sensory pathways—especially with the memory of the words that we will need to voice our thoughts. They also enable us to signal the muscles of the vocal apparatus to make the movements necessary to produce the appropriate sounds. Current research indicates that these operations are carried out mainly by three specific parts of the brain, all located in the cerebral cortex, the thick rind of gray matter that constitutes the outer layer of the brain.

Language and the Brain

Studies over the last thirty years have indicated that language abilities are located in a specific area of the brain. Early experiments indicated that in most humans it is the left cerebral hemisphere. The right hemisphere of the brain is thought to control such nonlinguistic activities as recognition of spatial relationships, mathematics, and art. This idea is based on observations of patients with **aphasia**, or, a language disorder resulting from brain damage. In 1969, John Bogen began to study patients in whom the *corpus callosum*, the major neurological bridge between the two hemispheres of the brain, had been cut in an effort to control severe epileptic seizures. Blindfolded, these patients were unable to name objects held in the left hand. Since the right hemisphere was known to control the left side of the body, the inability to name objects held in the left hand was attributed to the location of language in the left hemisphere of the brain. When the same object was held in the right hand, the subject could easily name it; the right hand was connected to the left hemisphere of the brain, where language was stored.

More recent studies, however, have indicated that the lateralization of language in the left hemisphere of the brain may be more appli-

cable to males than to females. Studies of patients with stroke- or tumor-caused brain damage indicate that damage to the left hemisphere caused aphasia three times more frequently in males than in females. Males with brain damage displayed strong laterality, the types of abilities affected depending on the location of the damage. Females tended not to show this difference, and researchers have concluded that language ability is more bilateral in females than in males. What this finding implies in regard to sexual differences in language capabilities and use is unclear. In any event, human linguistic capabilities are intimately tied to the structure and organization of the brain.

The cerebral cortex of the modern human brain is a recent development; it expanded rapidly and quite late in hominid history. Around the time of the transition to food sharing and meat eating, the early human brain was less than half the size of ours and its cerebral cortex was smaller still, so it seems unlikely that the language-producing structures of the cortex were developed at this time. It is a fair assumption, however, that the conversion from call system to language began about four million years ago.

By about 100,000 years ago, when the Neanderthals lived in Europe and the Middle East, the cerebral cortex had reached approximately its present size. Presumably these people had the mental equipment necessary for a complex language. Without doubt the cultural evidence, sophisticated tool manufacturing and deliberate burial of their dead, suggests abstract reasoning and well-developed modes of communication. Still, until recently it was thought that they may have lacked the physiological equipment necessary for fully human speech.

In addition to the cerebral cortex, a second physical structure is crucial to the production of speech—the pharynx, a tunnel of muscle connecting the back of the mouth to the larynx (windpipe). In human adults the pharynx expands and contracts to give different tones to the sounds made by the vocal cords and thereby produces the sounds that constitute intelligible speech. We are the only primates who make such extensive use of the pharynx. In other primates the pharynx is considerably smaller in relation to body size. It is also shaped differently. Whereas the human pharynx rises vertically to meet the back of the mouth at a right angle, in other primates it slopes upward in a broad curve. These differences in shape and size appear to affect its functioning, for the nonhuman primates do not move the pharynx when they vocalize. The pharynx serves only as a tunnel for air; the few differentiated sounds that nonhuman primates make are produced by movements of the mouth. (Hence the apes' physical incapacity for spoken language and the substitution of ASL and other systems in the ape language experiments.) The same is true of human infants until the age of about three months. Until very recently, it was thought to have been true of the Neanderthals.

This theory is the result of work by Philip Lieberman, a linguist, and Edmund S. Crelin, an anatomist (1971). On the basis of similarities among the skulls of human infants, the skulls of modern apes, and a reconstructed Neanderthal skull, Lieberman and Crelin concluded that the Neanderthals, like babies and apes, were equipped with a small sloping pharynx. After constructing a model of the Neanderthal vocal tract and measuring it, they fed their figures into a computer with information as to the resonances that can be produced by vocal tracts of various shapes and sizes. The results indicated that Neanderthals would have had difficulty in clearly differentiating the vowel sounds *ah*, *ee*, and *oo*, which are basic to almost every known human language. Furthermore, they could not have shifted very quickly from one sound to another. Indeed, if Lieberman and Crelin are right, the Neanderthals may have talked at about one-tenth the speed of modern humans. Some anthropologists and linguists question these conclusions, as they are

based on the hypothetical reconstruction of soft tissues (for which we have little direct evidence), and since only a single Neanderthal skull was studied. A Neanderthal skeleton excavated in Israel in 1989 with the small bones of the larynx intact appears to have had the physiological capability for human speech. Still, it is possible that truly fluent language is only a very recent achievement in the history of our species.

The Transition from Closed to Open Communication

Charles Hockett and Robert Ascher (1964) point out that the only plausible way the transition from a closed call system to an open symbolic language could have been made was through the blending of calls to produce new calls with more complex meanings. Presumably the ability to make combined calls had a definite adaptive value and therefore was favored by natural selection, gradually becoming part of the normal human genetic endowment. Then, as people came to regard the sounds made by their own voices as something they could combine and manipulate, the sounds eventually lost their association with specific situations and became instead arbitrary building blocks—the raw materials of an open and completely flexible language.

However the transition occurred, its consequences were incalculable. The use of language is undoubtedly responsible for the development of human culture. Groups whose members talked to one another hunted more successfully, gathered more efficiently, made more sophisticated tools, built stronger shelters, found more suitable locations for hearths, and argued and resolved their differences without necessarily coming to blows. The concomitant growth of language and culture in turn created strong selective pressures for more complex brains, which made possible the development of yet more elaborate language and culture. There arose, in other words, a feedback cycle: language, culture, and the brain evolved together, each stimulating and reinforcing the development of the others.

The study of language enables anthropologists to learn more about a people's culture, ways of thinking, and world view. It is a fundamental means of understanding human behavior—of examining how people view, describe, and analyze the events of the world in which they live. But such a study requires some knowledge of the language structure and of the way that structure varies from one language to another. Let us now look at the components of a language—the sounds, the way sounds are grouped into words, and the way words are combined to form sentences or utterances. In combination, these elements make up the formal structure of a language—what linguists call a **grammar**.

VARIATIONS IN LINGUISTIC STRUCTURE

Any person who has tried to communicate in a foreign country with the help of only a bilingual pocket dictionary can tell you that languages vary in subtle and complex ways. The differences are more than just a matter of vocabulary; every language has its unique repertoire of sounds. Further, every language has words for which other languages have no exact equivalents. Finally, every language has its peculiar structure. One cannot take an English sentence, translate all the words into Turkish, and expect the result to make sense to a Turkish speaker. The rules for proper word order, among other things, differ significantly in the two languages.

Thus, in order to understand a language, we must first understand its rules: the sounds that

it recognizes and the way it organizes sounds into words and words into meaningful statements. To discover these rules for English or French, we might begin by looking at a grammar book, where we could read how to form verb tenses and so forth. Yet some languages have no verb tenses comparable to ours; instead, they make linguistic distinctions (such as "manifested" versus "becoming manifest") that English speakers usually do not make. Therefore, in order to speak a particular language and to compare languages, linguists have had to develop a special set of descriptive categories, applicable to all known languages, as well as a special alphabet for transcribing the full range of sounds used in human languages.

Linguists describe the structure of any particular language by studying three central areas: (1) its **phonology,** or sound system; (2) its **morphology,** or the system by which its speech units are combined to form meaningful words; and (3) its **syntax,** or the arrangement of words into meaningful utterances. Language is thus describable in accordance with rules, most of them followed unconsciously by the speaker, which bring these three elements together. Linguists usually use "grammar" to describe the combinations of these three divisions.

Phonology

The human voice is able to produce thousands of different sounds. Yet out of this full range, every language community selects only a limited number of sounds from which to build its language. Languages vary considerably in the number of sounds they use, and no two languages seem to use exactly the same set of sounds. For example, the Spanish trilled *r*, as in *burro* and *cigarro*, does not exist in English.

The first job of the linguist in studying a new language is to record its unique repertoire of sounds. The linguist starts by acquiring a minimum vocabulary and then asking questions. "What is your name for that?" asks the linguist, pointing to a house, or to all the implements, one by one, in a family's kitchen. "And how do you say two of them?" As the people produce their replies, the linguist transcribes the sounds they make.

The linguist cannot depend on the people's writing system to transcribe a language. In the first place, most of the world's languages have no writing system. Second, even if there is a writing system, the linguist cannot be sure that it represents the sounds in any consistent way. Written English, for example, is notoriously inconsistent. If a linguist assumed that the "ough" sequence was pronounced the same way in "rough," "through," "though," "bough," and "trough," he or she would achieve a very poor grasp of English pronunciation. Finally, linguists need a universal writing system, one that can be used for any language and that can be understood by linguists of any nationality.

To fill these needs, linguists have developed the International Phonetic Alphabet (IPA), a notational system that can be adapted to provide a symbol for every sound that occurs in every known language.

Phonemes

Once linguists have identified the sounds of a language, they must determine how the people group these sounds into phonemes. A **phoneme** is a class of sounds that differ slightly from one another but that may be substituted for one another without any change of meaning. The sounds that belong to the same phoneme are called **allophones**; although the allophones may vary in accordance with the surrounding sound context, phonemes may not. Indeed, the sole function of phonemes in a language is to serve as differentiated sound elements, so that by using one phoneme rather than another a speaker can create recognizably different words.

Just as the total number of sounds varies from one language to another, so does the total number of phonemes, ranging from about 13 to almost 100. English has approximately 45 phonemes, Italian 27, and Hawaiian 13. Moreover, every language has its own unique way of classifying sounds into phonemes. In English, for example, the sounds [v] and [b],[1] though similar, constitute two different phonemes, and the contrast between them is crucial for differentiating numerous pairs of similar words, such as "vest" and "best," "vat" and "bat," "very" and "berry." The sentence "I want the vest" means something entirely different from "I want the best." In Spanish, on the other hand, [v] and [b] are allophones. When a Spaniard pronounces the word *beber* ("drink"), an English speaker may be unable to tell whether the word begins with a [v], a [b], or some blend of the two. Likewise, a Spanish speaker would understand the meaning of *beber* if an English speaker pronounced the consonants either as [v] or as [b].

To most native speakers, the phonetic distribution between one allophone and another is imperceptible unless a special effort is made to hear it. Most English speakers, for example, probably assume that the first sound in the word "pit" is the same as the second sound in the word "spit," even though they regularly pronounce the two sounds differently. If you hold your palm in front of your mouth while repeating both words, you will feel a slight puff of air in the case of "pit" but not in the case of "spit." In phonetic terms, the first is aspirated (written phonetically as [ph]), while the second is not (written [p]). But because the two sounds are allophones, we do not hear the differences between them. In Hindi, by contrast, the distinction between [ph] and [p] is crucial and

---

[1] We will follow the linguistic convention of using brackets [ ] for IPA phonetic symbols and slashes // for the phonetic symbols of individual languages.

distinguishes meaning. To substitute one for the other would be like substituting [p] for [b] in English.

Most of the phonemes in a language are vowels and consonants, such as we have just discussed. However, there are other kinds of phonemes as well: stress, juncture (that is, the linking and separation of syllables), and tone. Depending on the language, these phonemes may be as crucial as vowels and consonants in distinguishing one word from another.

Stress

Stress is a phoneme that exists in all languages, and in some cases it alone serves to differentiate words that are otherwise identical. Consider, for example, "desert," "address," "record," and "present." These words may be either nouns or verbs, depending on which syllables are pronounced longer and louder. *Ad*-dress, *de*sert, *rec*ord, and *pres*ent are nouns; ad*dress*, de*sert*, re*cord*, and pre*sent* are verbs. The vowels and consonants remain the same, but the difference in stress changes the meaning of the word.

Juncture

Stress alone is often insufficient for distinguishing words. Differences in meaning may also depend on **juncture,** the linkage or separation of syllables by pauses. Without a pause, we could not distinguish between such statements as "We're waiting for Jack's son" and "We're waiting for Jackson." "Jack's son" is differentiated from "Jackson" by a juncture plus a difference in stress.

Tone

Many languages use changes of tone, or pitch, to distinguish otherwise identical words. As one linguist found, low-tone and high-tone syllable distinctions must be observed very carefully:

"He who says *aSOoLAMBAboIli* instead of *aSOolaMBAboili* has stated that he is boiling his mother-in-law rather than watching the riverbank" (Carrington 1971:90).

The use of tones as phonemes makes it possible for people to communicate long-distance by using various instruments in imitation of the human voice. Drums are probably the most commonly used medium; in parts of traditional Africa one frequently heard messages drummed across the hills, announcing births and deaths or calling village leaders to assemblies. Other peoples used gongs and wind instruments for the same purpose. The Chin of northern Burma communicated with xylophones. Fiji Islanders drummed on canoes. Among the Mazateco Indians of Oaxaca, Mexico, anything that can be said with words can also be said with whistles.

Of course, whistled or drummed messages can be ambiguous, for tonal languages have many words with identical tonal patterns. This problem is sometimes solved by limiting conversations to topics that are clear by the situational context. Another solution is to substitute phrases for words. In their drummed messages, the Lokele of Africa replace the words "moon" and "fowl," which have the same tonal pattern, with the easily differentiated phrases "the moon looks down at the earth" and "the fowl, the little one which says 'kiokio' " (Carrington, 1949:33). People developed drum and whistle languages primarily to communicate over long distances or in other situations where the speakers are not face-to-face. But in some societies, whistle and drum languages have become routine means of daily communication, supplementing speech. The Mazateco sometimes switch back and forth between whistled and spoken language in a single conversation.

In each of these examples—unlike the Morse code, digital computer codes, or Native American smoke signals—the tonal messages are actual extensions of the spoken language. They

Re-creating the tonal inflections of his language on the drum, this man calls families scattered across the hills of Burundi to a tribal assembly. (LEON V. KOFOD)

adapt and pattern the tonal elements of the spoken language for long-distance transmission.

Morphemes

Sounds and phonemes are the raw materials of a spoken language. In order to create meaning, they must be combined. By themselves, the phonemes /g/, /o/, and /d/ have no meaning. But when combined, they produce a meaningful unit of speech—the word "god."

The smallest units of speech that convey meaning are called **morphemes.** Morphemes should not be confused with words, although in some cases a word does consist of a single morpheme. This is true of "god" and "dog"; neither of them can be broken into smaller units of meaning. The word "gods," on the other hand, can be broken into two morphemes: the root word "god" and the suffix -s (meaning "more than one"). Likewise, the word "ungentlemanly" can be divided into three morphemes: (1) un-, a prefix meaning "not"; (2) "gentleman"; and (3) -ly, a suffix meaning "in the manner of." Historically, of course, "gentleman" was itself formed from two morphemes. Most words in most languages consist of two or more morphemes.

As the breakdown of "ungentlemanly" suggests, there are two kinds of morphemes, those that can stand alone, as complete words, and those that cannot. Morphemes that are complete words when standing alone, such as "god," "gentle," and "man," are called **free morphemes.** Morphemes that must be attached to other morphemes (such as -s, un-, and -ly) to convey meaning are called **bound morphemes.**

Just as phonemes may include several allophones, so morphemes may include several **allomorphs,** forms that differ in sound but not in meaning. The morphemes meaning "more than one," for example, include three allomorphs: -s as in "hats," -s as in "cars" (pronounced like "z"), and -es as in "courses." Similarly, the morpheme meaning "happened in the past" has two allomorphs: -ed as in "cooked" and -t as in "built."

Morphology

Any English speaker will immediately recognize that the statement "George boil pot water" is not grammatical. The word order, or syntax, is essentially correct; it is the morphology that needs revision. Specifically, the sentence lacks the morphemes needed to express the tense of "boil," the number of "pot," and the relationship between "pot" and "water." To correct it, we need to add -s or -ed to the verb; "a" or "some" plus -s to specify how many pots; and "of" to indicate the relationship between "pot" and "water." This done, we have a grammatically well-formed English sentence: "George boiled a pot of water."

In other languages, however, this statement might require additional morphemes before it could be considered complete. In Spanish or French, for instance, the gender of the noun "pot" has to be specified. German requires that special bound morphemes, called case endings, be added to the nouns to indicate their grammatical role in the sentence—subject, direct object, indirect object, or whatever. A language such as Navajo may ignore number, gender, and case but require that certain bound morphemes be added to the verb stem to specify the pot's shape and size and whether the object of "boil" is animate or inanimate. Every language, then, has its own peculiar morphology.

In actual language use, words or morpheme constructions are related to a larger system of meaning; that is, to real situations, things, and behavioral consequences. If a man in a bar says "Make mine a light," he will be understood to have asked for a particular kind of beer. But the ambiguity of this communication has become the subject of a major advertising campaign. The study of the larger system of meaning created by words is termed **semantics**.

As children we learn the semantic system of our first language by observing the regular correspondence between acts of speech and behavioral consequences—the cry "Mommy!" attracts one individual's attention in particular. Linguists (and anyone who already knows one language) can also study the semantic system of a language by asking—one can ask a Turk what the word *arkadash* means and be told "friend." In many respects the child's system of semantic analysis through trial and error over a long period of time is superior; the context in which one uses a word or utterance determines its meaning. The fact that "arkadash" means "friend," for example, does not say very much about the social circumstances in which a

Turkish speaker would use the word. Depending on the social context and the way the word is stressed, the semantic value of "arkadash" can range from "old buddy" to "false friend." Semantic systems in every language are complex even though the morphology may be relatively simple. If one thinks about it, "friend" can be used in similar ways in English as well.

In comparison with other languages, English is quite modest in its morphological demands. Our words never become very complex; a word such as "ungentlemanliness," with four morphemes, is about the limit. By contrast, Fox, a language spoken by a Dakota Indian tribe, averages six morphemes per word. English is also modest in what it achieves morphologically. In Aranda, a language spoken by Australian aborigines, only one word, *erarijarijaka*, consisting of several morphemes, is required to say "full of longing for something that has been lost." Indeed, Aranda, Fox, Turkish, Latin, and many other languages convey meaning largely through morphology. English, on the other hand, relies more heavily on word order. What other languages express through morphology we express through syntax.

Syntax

In English—and to a somewhat lesser degree in the Romance languages—it is largely syntax, rather than morphological prefixes and suffixes, that indicates the relationships of the parts of a sentence; therefore English syntax is fairly intricate and rigid. Unconsciously, all English speakers know the grammatical rules governing the order of subject, verb, adjectives, and adverbs. When we say "Mary had three big red apples," we know there is no other proper way to arrange these words. The same is true in many other languages. The rules may be different, but they are equally strict. Spanish speakers, for example, would say "María tenía tres manzanas grandes y rojas" (literally, "Mary had three apples big and red"), but they too would have only one choice of word order. All native speakers follow these syntactical rules intuitively and meticulously, whether or not they are capable of stating them explicitly.

Because our language communicates so much through syntax, we can sometimes recognize a nonsense sentence as familiar through syntax alone. Consider the following excerpt from the poem "Jabberwocky," which appears in Lewis Carroll's *Alice Through the Looking-Glass:*

> 'Twas brillig, and the slithy toves
> Did gyre and gimble in the wabe:
> All mimsy were the borogoves,
> And the mome raths outgrabe.

Almost all the nouns, adjectives, and verbs are nonsense words. Yet by following the rules of English syntax and by using standard grammatical cues (such as "did" and "the"), Carroll makes us feel that somehow we understand the meaning of these lines. "Brillig," for example, must be a predicate adjective because it follows the verb "to be" ("'Twas"); we surmise that it refers to something like the condition of the weather. "Slithy," because it falls between "the" and "toves," must be an adjective modifying "toves." Likewise, "gyre and gimble," coming after "did," must indicate what the toves are doing, and "wabe," coming after "in the," must indicate where they are doing it. Of course, morphology helps too. The suffix -y (meaning "characterized by") at the end of "slithy" is a further sign that it is an adjective, just as the suffix -s on "toves" is a further sign that this word is a noun, and that we are dealing with more than one tove.

Our ability to learn through language and to use language creatively depends on this intuitive understanding of grammar. If, instead of learning grammatical rules, people learned only a vast collection of specific sentences, they would be unable to understand any statement unless they had already heard it and been told what it meant and remembered it. But by applying grammatical rules, people can readily understand statements they have never heard before, and they can continually make statements that no one has ever made before.

Transformational Grammar

Part of a speaker's capacity to generate new sentences is based on the ability to say the same thing in various ways. We can say, "Harry painted this lovely picture last spring." Or, by rearranging a few basic elements, we can say, "This lovely picture was painted by Harry last spring." This fact—that a single meaning may be expressed in different forms—is the basis of a major theory of linguistics, called **transformational grammar,** proposed by Noam Chomsky in the 1950s.

Chomsky claims that every sentence has two levels of structure: a surface structure and a deep structure. The particular arrangement of words that we hear or read is the **surface structure.** Beneath this surface lies the **deep structure,** a more abstract two-part mental model consisting of a noun phrase (say, "Harry") and a verb phrase ("painted this lovely picture"), with the optional addition of an adverb or adverbial phrase ("last spring"). This two-part deep structure can be translated into a variety of surface structures, according to the transformational rules of the language. Many different utterances, then, are reducible to the same essential meaning, and all the utterances of a language are reducible to the same essential pattern of meaning.

Going one step further, Chomsky speculates that differences among languages may be due simply to differences in **transformational rules**—the techniques by which deep structure is translated into surface structure—and that the same deep structure, presumably biologically determined, may underlie all human language. Thus the thousands of languages spoken on earth are merely surface variations of a deeper, universal grammar, rooted in the human mind. If this theory could be confirmed, it would help to explain the fact that children learn language with such amazing facility, and that they can learn any language with equal ease, depending solely on the linguistic environment in which they are living when they are very young.

CAUSES OF
LINGUISTIC CHANGE

We have seen how languages vary from society to society. But anthropologists are concerned also with the way the various elements of grammar change within a language, and with the causes of these changes. Some of them, as we will see, are merely the results of the accumulation of very slight and random variations that occur in every language. Others are adaptive—the result of accommodation to new social and environmental situations and needs.

Internal Processes of Change

During the Middle English period, between 1400 and 1600, speakers of English began to alter the sounds of their vowels. This change, known as the **great English vowel shift**, was by no means deliberate. Nevertheless, it eventually transformed every sound in our language. "Bot" and "stan" (rhyming with "cot" and "con") became today's "boat" and "stone." "Mus" and "cu" (sounding like "moose" and "coo") became "mouse" and "cow." "Win" and "min" (pronounced like "wean" and "mean") became "wine" and "mine." A similar regular and consistent change occurred in every Middle English vowel sound.

Grammatical structure, word order, and the semantic content of words have also changed somewhat over the centuries, in English as well as in other languages. Linguists are not entirely sure why these changes occur. They only know that dynamics peculiar to the structure of language promote change.

The tendency toward linguistic variation appears to be the key to the development of distinct languages. It is clear that languages in different geographical areas vary considerably. The French do not understand Chinese, and the Chinese do not understand Navajo. But even within geographical regions one can find linguistic differences, although they tend to be slight and gradual. Just how slight and gradual they may be was illustrated by Gillian Sankoff's study of language differences in a string of New Guinean villages. Sankoff (1972) proceeded from village to village, telling the people of each village a story in the dialect of the preceding village. In every case the story was easily understood. Indeed, the people often understood the story in dialects three and four villages removed. The villages at opposite ends of the line did not understand each other's language, but at no point along the line could one draw a boundary between two separate languages.

Within speech communities, the picture is also one of gradual and fluid variation. Within a single town there are differences in language based on the sex, social class, and educational level of the speakers.

As long as people speaking different dialects remain in contact with one another, reciprocal influence and the need to communicate will prevent the two dialects from drifting very far apart, as is the case with American English and British English. If groups speaking different dialects become isolated from one another, however, the dialects will diverge over time, eventually evolving into completely distinct languages.

This is what happened when geographical groups speaking different dialects of Latin be-

Signs and Survival: The Range of Natural Languages

When I was a small child I used to play with the girl next door. She didn't understand anything I tried to tell her, but it didn't matter. We played together all the time, using simple gestures to communicate. I thought something was wrong with her, but I adapted easily to her limitation.

One day when I was about four, I went inside her house. As I stood there, her mother came downstairs. Nothing happened between her and the girl that I could see. Then I saw her mother point at the doll house in the hallway. The girl ran and moved the doll house back into her room, as if she had just been told to do so. I was astounded. I knew it was different, something different. I knew that they had communicated, in a form I couldn't see. But how? I asked my mother about what I had seen.

"They are called 'hearing,'" she explained. "They don't sign. They are hearing. They are different. We are deaf. We sign."

I asked if the family next door are the only ones, the only hearing people.

My mother shook her head. "No," she signed, "it is us that are alone."

I was very surprised. I naturally assumed everyone was like me.   [Sam Supalla, quoted in Perlmutter 1986:515]

Linguists and laymen alike have been slow to recognize that human languages are of two kinds—signed and oral—and sign languages are still generally omitted from surveys of the world's languages. It is not even clear how many sign languages there are, since their boundaries do not coincide with those of oral languages. Oral American English and British English are mutually intelligible languages, but American Sign Language (ASL) and British Sign Language are not.

In Germany a number of distinct sign languages are in use, so that a deaf theater company, for example, performs in mime because its sign language is not understood in other German cities. In the United States, by contrast, the National Theatre of the Deaf, performing in ASL, is understood throughout the country, and is winning national acclaim for its performances (Perlmutter 1986).

It is reasonable to assume that sign languages, like oral languages, have existed throughout human history. And while little is known about the genetic affiliations of sign languages, it is clear that none of them is the same as the oral languages spoken in the place where it is used. Though ASL is not related to British Sign Language, it is related to French Sign Language, which in turn is related to several other European sign languages, including Irish, Swedish, Latvian, Dutch, Swiss, Austrian, and Russian (Perlmutter 1986).

Research has demonstrated that sign languages are natural and complete languages, with an expressive range that is indistinguishable from that of any oral language. ASL is *not* a form of English; it has a distinct grammatical structure, which must be mastered by nonnative speakers in the same way as that of any oral language, and its acquisition as a first language follows essentially the same pattern as that of oral languages. There is also evidence that the system of manual gestures used in ASL has a structure similar to that of the phonological system of an oral language (Wilcox and Wilbers 1987).

In some instances, however, sign languages fail to mature to full and complete languages, just as in the case of some oral pidgin languages. William Washabaugh's study of Providence Island, a tiny island off the coast of Nicaragua, provides an interesting illustration. Isolation and inbreeding have produced a very high percentage of congenital profound (and of course pre-lingual) deafness among the population of 3,000—a rate of 6.7 per thousand (compared to a rate of 0.4 per thousand in the United States). With a rate this high, the numbers of deaf are so large that they always have other deaf people to communicate with. Further, the hearing islanders on Providence, unlike those in North America, accept deafness and do not hesitate to communicate with the deaf by signing, although their signing is clearly distinct from vernacular deaf signing. Nor have deaf islanders undergone schooling and the concomitant linguistic pressures it brings: they are not literate; they do not fingerspell, nor do they have access by any other means to nonsigned linguistic models or inputs (Washabaugh 1986:9–10). It has been supposed that in situations in which the deaf can interact with each other, are encouraged to sign, and are given some signed input, they will construct a mature sign language. Washabaugh found, however, that deaf Providence Islanders in fact have not developed a complete language.

Providence Island Sign Language (PSL) is an efficient communication system, but it is entirely context-dependent. PSL has no metalanguage, that is, no expressions for signing about signs. Washabaugh found that deaf signers do not play in sign, do not play with signs, and do not teach in sign. Lexical expressions are highly variable; different signers produce different expressions for the same phenomenon, and quite often signers will change their signs from one occasion to the next. Signs made with parts of the body other than the hands are very common, but are ill defined and difficult to understand. Compound signs, which in ASL are highly conventionalized and unified, in PSL are extremely variable, and components can be moved about, added, or subtracted at the whim of the signer. Finally, it is difficult to discern any principle of syntax directing PSL utterances. Even close kin of deaf signers have difficulty in interpreting their signs when the context of the utterance is removed. And neither the hearing nor the deaf correct or revise each other's signing. Thus Washabaugh concludes that "PSL seems not to be what we would consider a mature language. It lacks . . . 'syntacticization.' It lacks the conventionality and rule governedness which we have come to expect of complete, mature human languages" (p. 74).

Given the apparently optimal circumstances for the development of a mature sign language on Providence Island, why should this be the case? Washabaugh sees the answer as lying in the social circumstances of the deaf. While fully accepting of deafness, the hearing do regard the deaf as handicapped and "smother [them] with a paternalistic care which prevents them from ever carrying their own weight in communicative interaction" (p. 145). In general, interactions between the deaf and the hearing are unbalanced; behaviors on both sides indicate the superiority of the hearing and the inferiority of the deaf. The hearing care for the deaf and are willing to sign with the deaf, but they do not sign among themselves. And the deaf do not appear to be interested in defining themselves as a distinct community with a distinct language. Their interactions with the hearing almost always take precedence over interactions with other deaf persons.

Historical and demographic conditions on Providence Island may to some extent explain the deaf's devotion to the hearing world. The mountainous and rugged fifteen-square-mile island is inhabited only around the perimeter, and the road connecting the villages that have sprouted in the bays and inlets was cut only in 1961. The resulting isolation has been a barrier to interaction among the scattered deaf islanders, who have perforce to interact with the hearing. "Deaf islanders do not want to be culturally deaf, and so they avoid the very real opportunities for language acquisition which they could create for themselves. Deaf islanders want to be hearing islanders, but the hearing will not lead them in that direction. Hence they remain stalled, arrested with an immature sign language" (p. 142).

came culturally isolated from one another during the early stages of the Christian era; eventually these dialects became separate languages—French, Spanish, Italian, and Rumanian. English and German evolved in the same way. Both are descended from an ancestral Proto-Germanic tongue spoken 1,500 years ago.

There are several ways to trace the development of various languages from their common ancestral language. First, we can look for regular correspondences between the sounds of two languages. We find, for example, that many words that begin with /t/ in English correspond to words beginning with /z/ in German—"to" and *zu*, "ten" and *zehn*, "tame" and *zahm*. Likewise, an initial /d/ in English often corresponds to an initial /t/ in German, as in "daughter" and *tochter*, "day" and *tag*. Their vocabularies include many **cognates,** words so similar from one language to the next as to suggest that they are both variants of a single ancestral prototype. All the German-English pairs that we just enumerated are cognates. Numerous other correspondences suggest that German and English are modern variants of an older Proto-Germanic tongue. Similar comparisons indicate that this same ancestral language also gave rise to modern Swedish, Dutch, Icelandic, Flemish, and other northern European languages.

We have no written records to prove that Proto-Germanic existed or to show how the modern languages of northern Europe developed from Proto-Germanic dialects. But we can reconstruct the process by tracing certain regular patterns of sound change backward through time. Indeed, by going back still further we can reconstruct the development of Proto-Germanic from an even earlier language.

During the early nineteenth century, Jakob Grimm—who later, with his brother Wilhelm, developed his linguistic interest while compiling fairy tales from various parts of the world—noted that regular phonemic changes took place from one language to another over the centuries. He found, for example, that the Sanskrit word *brata* ("brother") became *phrater*

in Greek, *frater* in Latin, *broder* in Old English, and *bratu* in Slavonic. Similarly, Sanskrit *admi* ("eat") became Greek *edomai*, Latin *edo*, Old English *etan*, and Slavonic *jadetu*. Numerous regularities of this type suggest that all these languages are related. Linguists now classify them as members of the same language family, Indo-European. All are descended from a single original Proto-Indo-European tongue, a language probably much like Sanskrit (see Figure 11-1).

By analyzing the vocabulary of various Indo-European languages, anthropologists have tried to reconstruct a picture of this early speech community's culture. This is done largely through the study of cognates. For example, cognates for "snow" appear in so many modern Indo-European languages that it was undoubtedly part of the original proto-vocabulary. It is probably safe to assume, then, that the Proto-Indo-European community did not originate in a snowless southern area such as India (Bloomfield 1965). Likewise, since cognates for "milk," "yoke," and "wheel" are fairly widespread, it is assumed that this speech community had domesticated cattle and used wagons.

By similar comparative studies, anthropologists have discovered a good deal about the movements and historical relationships of various cultural communities. We know, for example, that the Semitic languages—of which Hebrew is one—originated in the Arabian Peninsula. At some point, probably as early as 2500 B.C., the Semitic speakers began to extend their influence over wider areas of the Middle East. Subsequently, there developed local dialects and eventually distinct languages. Today, more than 200 million people speak Arabic, a Semitic language.

Linguistic Borrowings and Cultural Contact

Much linguistic change occurs when speech communities learn to adapt to one another. People use language to communicate, after all,

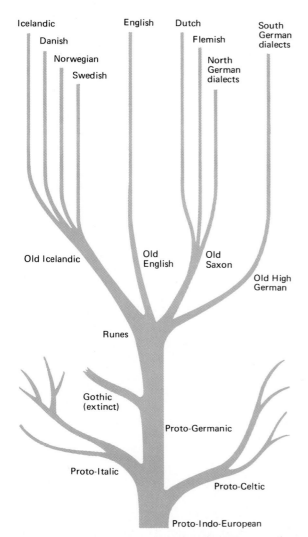

Icelandic

Danish

Norwegian

Swedish

English

Dutch

Flemish

North German dialects

South German dialects

Old Icelandic

Old English

Old Saxon

Old High German

Runes

Gothic (extinct)

Proto-Germanic

Proto-Italic

Proto-Celtic

Proto-Indo-European

FIGURE 11-1 All germanic languages descended from a single original Proto-Indo-European tongue—a language probably similar to Sanskrit.

and when their communication is hindered by their current usages or by the lack of important vocabulary elements, they may adapt their language by borrowing terms from another group. Such borrowing rarely affects grammar, the most conservative aspect of language. But vo-

cabulary rapidly crosses language frontiers. Consider the menu for an American breakfast: A typical meal might begin with juice or fruit—perhaps grapefruit (a compound of two French words first joined on American soil), melon (of Greek origin via French), or cantaloupe (named after a town in Italy). Or the meal might begin with an orange, derived from the Arabic *naranj*. After juice or fruit, the American breakfast usually consists of cereal (derived from Ceres, the Roman goddess of agriculture) or bacon (French) and eggs (Old Norse), with toast (French), butter (Latin), and marmalade (Portuguese). The beverage may be coffee (Arabic), tea (Chinese via Malayan Dutch), or cocoa (Nahauatl via Mexican Spanish) (Farb 1974: 296–297). All of these words reflect a history of trade and transport of food products across national and linguistic boundaries.

Borrowed words are seldom adopted wholesale. Pronunciation is usually changed in accordance with the native sound system and patterns of stress, tone, and nasalization. For example, our pronunciation of "petits fours" and "chaise longue" bears little resemblance to their pronunciation in the original French.

Lingua Franca, Pidgin, and Creole Languages

Two further dimensions of language change have to do with contacts between speakers of different languages. In many areas of the world where more than one language is spoken, one comes to the fore. In medieval times a trade language evolved in the Mediterranean region consisting of Italian grammatical structure mixed with Arabic, French, and Spanish vocabulary, and was called **lingua franca,** or "the language of the Franks." The term is now generalized to mean any language used as a common tongue by people who do not speak one another's native tongue. A contemporary lingua franca is English as it is spoken in India and Pakistan. Here individuals who may speak

Vocabulary, along with other cultural phenomena, rapidly crosses language frontiers. In Taiwan, Mickey Mouse asks people not to litter. (JAMES R. HOLLAND/ STOCK, BOSTON)

Pidgin languages sprang up along the coasts of Africa, China, and the New World during European colonization. In some places pidgin languages have become the native language, a process called "creolization." A **creole** language is a pidgin that has evolved into a fully developed language, with a complete array of grammatical distinctions and a large vocabulary. Some linguists suggest that Proto-Germanic developed about 1000 B.C. out of a pidgin used by the Germanic tribes of the Baltic region. If this supposition is correct, then English, Dutch, and German all originated in a former pidgin language (Fromkin and Rodman 1988:263).

A sign in New Guinea explains in pidgin that the bridge is broken and the road closed. (ROBERT HARDING PICTURE LIBRARY)

one of several hundred languages as their first tongue use English to communicate. Yiddish, derived from German, has served a similar role among Jews of Eastern Europe. What distinguishes a lingua franca is that it is used by a substantial population for whom it is a first language, and then spreads out as a second or trade language, picking up new vocabulary and forms.

A contrasting form of language that facilitates cultural contact is **pidgin,** a language based on a simplified grammar and lexicon taken from one or more fully developed languages. For example, Melanesian Pidgin English, or Tok Pisin, has about 1,500 words, 80 percent of which are taken from English. It is used widely in Papua New Guinea. Though simplified, Pidgin English is governed by rules for verbs and word order. In Tok Pisin, verbs that take the direct object must have the suffix -m (Fromkin and Rodman 1983:262):

Mi driman long kilim wanpela snek.
I dreamed that I killed a snake.

Bandarap em i kukim.
Bandarap cooked [it].

THE INFLUENCE OF CULTURE ON LANGUAGE

There is little question that language reflects social processes. As psychologists have pointed out, people tend unconsciously to focus on and respond to stimuli that they perceive to be important to them, to the exclusion of other stimuli. This same principle, called **selective attention,** seems to underlie language as well. Something that is of no adaptive importance to members of a given society may have no distinctive name in that society's language, or it may be included in a general name that covers a range of related phenomena. But what is of great adaptive importance to a society may have not only one name but several, to specify subtle variations that the language speakers perceive and feel the need to distinguish.

As we saw in Chapter 1, this matter of linguistic classification is a major focus of linguistic anthropologists. Linguistic anthropologists call groups of related categories—for example, all the color terms of a language, or all its kinship terms—**semantic domains.** By studying semantic domains, we can uncover a society's system of meaning—not only major concerns of the society but also the way those concerns have come to structure thought processes within that society.

The Koya of southern India, for example, distinguish seven kinds of bamboo, yet they do not have separate words to distinguish dew, fog, and snow. This is not terribly surprising, as they live in a tropical environment. English speakers have a separate term for snow, but only one. (That is, unless they happen to be avid skiers, in which case they may apply a more extensive classification system, distinguishing corn snow, powder, and deep powder, for example.) The Eskimo carry snow classification further, with separate words for snow on the ground, falling snow, drifting snow, and snowdrift, among other related phenomena

(Boas 1940). Interestingly, however, Eskimo have no general term meaning simply snow. Similarly, the Garo of northeast India have at least a dozen words for different types of ants, but no generic name for the whole class that corresponds to the English word "ant." In general, those domains characterized by large vocabularies are ones that are important to the survival of these groups. The Eskimo have many words for snow not simply because of its abundance but because the condition of the snow figures prominently in their reckoning of the safety of a particular sled trip or the success of a hunt.

Analyses of language as a mirror of culture have concentrated mainly on vocabulary, especially sets of adjectives and nouns that constitute semantic domains. However, some anthropologists have also studied **grammatical structure**—the rules for organizing elements of a language into meaningful utterances—as a key to a society's world view. Harry Hoijer (1954), for example, has suggested a relationship between the grammar of the Navajo language and Navajo religious beliefs. The Navajo religion attaches great value to preserving a harmonious balance between humans and nature. The Navajo have a lively sense of nature's power over humans. Consequently, in their religious ceremonies they never try to alter nature—to bring rain, for instance; they merely try to realign themselves with the dynamic scheme of events. Likewise, when they do something, they do not see themselves as actually performing actions; rather, they are simply participating in ongoing universal processes. These attitudes are also expressed in the structure of their language, in which every action—running, baking, weaving, whatever—is expressed in terms of a few universal processes. When the Navajo say, *"Ninti"* ("You have lain down"), they are literally saying, "One animate being [you] has moved to a position of rest [have lain down]." The position or process is already there; one has simply moved into it. This is quite the opposite of the Western view, in which human beings are generally seen as powerful and responsible actors, creators of processes—an image that is reflected in our very different use of verbs.

THE INFLUENCE OF LANGUAGE ON CULTURE

It is possible that cultural processes are not so much reflected by language as they are molded by it. Edward Sapir was one of the first linguists to argue that humans are in some respect prisoners of language. He believed that our view of reality is an abridged version of the world that has been edited by our language.

The real world is to a large extent unconsciously built up on the language habits of the group. No two languages are ever sufficiently similar to be considered to represent the same social reality. The worlds in which different societies live are distinct worlds, not merely the same world with different labels attached (Sapir 1929:214). In other words, people in different societies see a different reality because they speak different languages and because each language forces reality into a distinct mold.

Drawing upon Sapir's ideas, Benjamin Lee Whorf made an intensive study of the language of the Hopi Indians to determine whether radically different linguistic structures do in fact result in contrasting views of the world. Concentrating on grammar rather than vocabulary, he found that Hopi does not categorize the world in the same way as English. For one thing, Hopi has no verb tenses comparable to our own. English forces us to specify when an event occurs and encourages us to think of time as divided into three distinct units: past, present, and future. Hopi, on the other hand, classifies events in terms of objective versus subjective, or "manifested" versus "becoming manifested." The objective, or manifested, em-

braces all that is or has ever been physically accessible to the senses, with no distinction made between past and present. The subjective, or becoming manifested, comprises all that is not physically accessible, including not only what we call the future but also whatever we label as mental events, such as wishes, thoughts, and intentions (Whorf 1956).

While Sapir and Whorf emphasize the interconnections of belief and language, it is equally if not more likely that the linguistic structure grows out of the beliefs and then serves simply to reinforce them. One way to approach this question is through cross-cultural comparison. If language shapes a people's thought world,

Despite differences in language, worldwide communications systems have transformed social behavior in virtually all cultures. For example, during the June 1989 student uprising in Beijing, China, the conduct of demonstrators was in part determined by their ability to communicate with sympathizers throughout the world via television, telephone, and telefax. (ULRIKE WELSCH)

then two groups that speak closely related languages should also share similar cultural beliefs and practices. This is not the case. The highly ritualized culture of the southwestern Navajo has little in common with the cultures of tribes that speak closely related languages, such as the Hupa of northwestern California, a loosely organized hunting-and-gathering society; or the Apache of the Western plains; or the simple fishing-and-hunting tribes of western Canada and Alaska (Sapir 1921). At the same time, the Navajo do share many cultural similarities with tribes that speak languages utterly different from their own. The same is true of societies in general. Two societies may speak completely unrelated languages and still arrive at very similar social and economic arrangements.

Thus the evidence for the structuring of social processes by linguistic characteristics is not very strong. It is no doubt true, as Sapir and Whorf claim, that language, social behavior, and thought are closely interrelated. It also seems likely that language and thought are more readily changed by social and economic realities than vice versa. However, since language and other aspects of culture evolve together, it is almost impossible to point to simple lines of causality among them.

SOCIOLINGUISTICS

We have seen that speech communities adapt their languages to new situations and new needs. In much the same way, individuals adapt their language to different social situations. The study of this phenomenon, the interrelationship of social variables and language, is called **sociolinguistics**. As sociolinguists have discovered, it is not only geographical separation that causes the same language to be spoken in a variety of ways. The formality of the speakers' relationship and their situation, status, sex roles, and even age are expressed in distinctive linguistic behavior. On hearing language, individuals continually seek out clues to the status and intentions of the speaker, and in speaking, deliberately or not, send out information regarding themselves to the listener. All of these messages are exchanged in addition to the nominal content of the utterances spoken. Within any society, the choice of expressions, vocabulary, dialect, or even language reflects social status, education, geography, and the way the speaker wishes to be viewed by others.

Language and Ethnicity

One striking phenomenon within such complex societies as nation-states is seen in the distinctive ways in which ethnic and other socially distinct groups use the national language. Communities emphasize their uniqueness by developing a **speech community** or dialect. This variety of language diverges from the national language in vocabulary, pronunciation, and even grammar. One language form—the dialect of the dominant social or political group—is usually considered standard. In contemporary society, the mass media—radio, television, and newspapers—promote the standard language. Network newscasters do not use ethnic dialects unless they are attempting to be humorous.

Regionally or ethnically localized dialects often have social and political significance. Black English, a dialect of some African Americans, is perpetuated because it promotes a sense of shared communal identity. Most speakers can move between the use of Black English at home or in the neighborhood and a variant of standard English at work. Often such dialects are regarded by people who do not speak them as "substandard," but this is an ethnocentric (better, linguacentric) perspective. After all, everyone speaks some dialect or other; the denigration of some dialects simply reflects the social ascendency of the group whose dialect is considered standard. Sometimes the use of a dialect may have negative repercussions, particularly when the dialect is not prestigious or is politically charged. Americans who speak a southern dialect in the Northeast may find themselves stereotyped as rural unsophisticates, or worse. The same social stigma may be experienced by a Yankee in a small southern town. Still, dialects persist because of their association with a wider set of cultural values and community identity.

Quite apart from dialects, several languages may be spoken in one country; indeed, this is the case in the majority of countries. In the United States, Spanish is the most widely used language apart from English. In New York City, more than 100,000 students were enrolled in bilingual high school programs in the mid-1980s—75 percent in Spanish programs, followed by Chinese, Creole, Korean, and Hindi (*New York Times*, August 25, 1985, p. B-3).

Whether bilingualism should be encouraged is a controversial political issue. In November 1986 three-quarters of the voters of California said that it should not be, although the final word still lies with the courts, which may rule otherwise. Here we see the political importance of language. Nationalists in many countries, notably France and Germany, have often equated the use of foreign vocabulary with unwanted "foreign influence," even though historically no language evolved in isolation.

In modern Turkey, not only is standard Turkish regularly reviewed for foreign loan words (which are replaced by newly minted Turkish ones) but the use of any language other than standard Turkish in the media or in public institutions is forbidden (with a few exceptions, such as the use of English in some schools). Kurdish, spoken by at least 2 million people, is suppressed because the government fears a Kurdish political movement. Yet the Kurdish population retains its language as a badge of cultural identity.

Sociolinguists have noted another, more subtle variable behind linguistic differences: a sense of **community identity**—that is, an effort by speakers to identify themselves with a specific locality and to distinguish themselves from outsiders. William Labov (1964), for example, found that pronunciation of the phonemes /ai/ and /au/ varied considerably on Martha's Vineyard, an island off the coast of Massachusetts populated largely by vacationers and somewhat poorer locals. Those locals who resented the intrusion of "summer people" pronounced these phonemes differently from other, less culturally defensive locals. In other words, the "island-tradition" speakers used pronunciation to identify themselves with the island and to separate themselves from mainlanders.

In the case of groups that are struggling for or have recently achieved political independence, such efforts to differentiate one's language from that of outsiders may be far more extreme, taking the form of what has been called linguistic nationalism. Consider the case of Hebrew. For centuries this language was barely used by the Jews outside their religious ceremonies. Today it is spoken daily by most of the citizens of Israel. As many Jews had some knowledge of Hebrew and it had great symbolic significance, it was the logical choice for the national language of Israel, with its population of immigrants from all over the world. However, the return to this ancient language was also a powerful symbol of the Jews' return to their ancient homeland. Likewise, in Ireland and Wales efforts are being made to revive Gaelic and Welsh, which all but died out under English influence. In India and Burma special commissions have been set up to create "native" substitutes for the English terms that crept into the languages during the period of colonial rule.

To many observers these efforts to breathe new life into languages that have been threatened or replaced for political reasons seem historically naive. Yet the theory behind them is sound. As we saw earlier in this chapter, language mirrors, reinforces, and arguably even molds a culture. If a people's language is replaced by that of another people, their culture is replaced as well. Language, then, is a great deal more than a symbol of a group's culture. To a large extent, it reinforces the group's identity, its particular ways of thinking and behaving.

Formality and Informality

Another domain of sociolinguistics is that of the context in which speech occurs. Depending on who is addressing her, a woman may be either Professor Johnson, Mrs. Johnson, Ms. Johnson, Elizabeth, Beth, mommy, ma'am, or darling. These terms are by no means interchangeable, for each carries a distinctive social connotation. Professor Johnson's husband would be unlikely to greet her as Professor Johnson, and a student would not address her as "Hey, Beth." By the same token, her husband and her friends will feel freer than her students in their choice of words and tone of conversation when they speak to her.

Situations too may be formal or informal, the degree of formality affecting word choice and terms of address and in some cases choice of language. While Professor Johnson's husband may call her darling and speak very colloquially to her at home, he will probably call her Beth and use more refined language when her students are present. In much the same way language is used to structure or establish the tone of a situation. Should Johnson's husband greet her at the door with a term more formal than Beth or darling, he is indicating something of his attitude toward her arrival.

Even young children's speech varies in accordance with the formality of the situation. While studying child rearing in a small New England town, J. L. Fischer (1958) found that the children he interviewed, all under the age of eleven, dropped the -g from the -ing suffix much more frequently in informal interviews than in formal interviews. One other curious finding was that the pronunciation of the suffix was affected by the formal or informal connotations of the verb to which it was attached. The children would say "correcting," "criticizing," and "visiting," but "hittin'," "chewin'," "swimmin'," and "punchin'."

Social Status

Closely related to formality is social status. Indeed, it is quite common for a language to use the same signals both for status differences and for formality of relationship, even though the two are not always congruent. In America, for example, there are two main forms of address: title plus last name (Professor Johnson, Mr. Jones) and first name alone. This system tries to do two things at once: to signal the degree of intimacy and to signal the relative status between the speaker and the person being addressed. The system can create problems. For example, if a younger colleague joins the faculty at Professor Johnson's college, he may have trouble appropriately addressing her at first. If, in view of the fact that she is older and that they barely know each other, he calls her Professor Johnson, he is incorrectly suggesting that her social status is higher than his. But if he uses Elizabeth, he is suggesting that they are friends, which they are not.

Of course, social status also has a profound effect on a person's language in general, regardless of whom he or she is addressing. In complex societies, where status differences are marked and where formal education increases these differences, the rich and the poor, the educated and the uneducated speak what amount to separate dialects, with considerable variation in vocabulary, grammar, and pronunciation. Until recently, most New Yorkers, like other residents of other major Eastern cities, did not pronounce /r/ following a vowel when it preceded a consonant or fell at the end of a word. The word "bartender," for example, was (and still often is) pronounced something like "batenda." Since World War II, however, it has become more prestigious to pronounce the /r/, a mark of upper-middle-class speech.

It is possible that historical changes in language often evolve through people's efforts to climb this linguistic social ladder. A number of sociolinguists have noted that people tend to imitate the speech of social groups that they admire or aspire to join. Tribal peoples in eastern Burma are quite likely to learn Shan, a dialect of Thai spoken by members of a higher social class. But Shans rarely bother to learn any tribal languages. Sometimes both tribal peoples and Shans learn Burmese, the language spoken by the most politically influential group. Few Burmese, however, learn Shan, and fewer still learn the tribal languages (Leach 1954).

Similarly, William Labov (1964) found that although the dropping of /r/ by New Yorkers generally increased as social status decreased, the people most likely to use the /r/ in formal situations—when they were especially conscious of their speech—were those of the lower middle class, the group most concerned with improving its social status. One sociolinguist speculates that as aspiring lower-status groups attempt to imitate upper-class speech, the upper class may unconsciously attempt to resist this encroachment by changing their habits of pronunciation, thus keeping their linguistic distance from the commoners (Burling 1970).

Gender Roles

Gender distinctions, as culturally defined, also structure the use of language. For example,

Fischer (1958), in his study of the -ing suffix, noted that the girls he interviewed pronounced the -g twice as often as the boys. In the United States, females may try to speak more "properly" than males. A variety of polite expletives, such as "my goodness" and "dear me," along with the intensifiers "so" and "such" ("It was such a delightful party!"), are often characteristic of female speech, though this usage seems to be disappearing. One reason is that gender roles are rapidly changing and such usages are associated with patterns of submissiveness. It is interesting that not only does vocabulary vary by sex but so do patterns of conversing. It has been found that American men interrupt women in conversation far more frequently than women interrupt men and that most topics of conversation are introduced by male speakers. Some homosexual males adopt female speech patterns in intonation, vocabulary, and conversational habits.

Male–female linguistic differences are even more marked in many non-European languages, although "propriety" may fall on either side of the sexual barrier. Among the Yakinankarate of Madagascar, for example, men strive for diplomacy in speech. They are discreet, hide their feelings, and avoid open confrontations. This is the avowed ideal form of speech behavior. This ideal, however, applies only to men. Women have to express their emotions directly and bluntly. Whenever direct confrontations are unavoidable, the men incite the women to handle the unpleasantness on their behalf; women are also expected to do the haggling in the marketplace and to reprimand children (Farb 1974).

Summary

While all animals apparently communicate through *call systems*—repertoires of sounds, each of which is produced in response to a specific situation—humans are the only animals that use language. Human language presumably began as a call system. Language differs from animal call systems in that it is open—the number of messages that can be conveyed is infinite. This flexibility is made possible by the arbitrariness of human language—sounds have no fixed meaning—and the fact that it is stimulus-free: an utterance need not be evoked by an immediate situation. The training of apes to use limited sign language has convinced some researchers that their linguistic ability differs from ours only in degree; however, while apes may share with us certain faculties that are necessary for language, it is clear that these faculties have remained relatively undeveloped in their line.

Observations of patients with language difficulties resulting from brain damage, or *aphasia*, seem to indicate that language ability is located in the left hemisphere of the brain. More recent research, however, indicates that such lateralization applies more to men than to women. The significance of this finding is unclear, but it is certain that linguistic capability is tied to the structure and organization of the brain.

Researchers can only speculate on the origins of language. Cultural evidence suggests a very early date for the first language skills; the physical evidence suggests a later date for the full development of language. It seems likely that the change to language from call systems began about four million years ago and proceeded only gradually. Studies indicate that Neanderthals, who lived 100,000 years ago, lacked the physiological equipment for fluent speech. It is believed that human language developed through the blending of calls to produce new calls with more complex meanings. This transition is largely responsible for the development of human culture. Language, culture, and the brain evolved together, each stimulating and reinforcing the others.

Languages vary in subtle and complex ways.

Grammar—the formal structure of a language—consists of *phonology, morphology*, and *syntax*. To study and compare languages, linguists have developed an alphabet and a special set of descriptive characteristics applicable to all known languages. The International Phonetic Alphabet provides a symbol for every sound that occurs in every known language. Once the sounds of a language have been identified, the linguist must determine how the people group these sounds into phonemes. A *phoneme* is a class of sounds, or *allophones*, that differ slightly from one another but may be used interchangeably. The total number of phonemes varies from one language to another. Most phonemes are vowels and consonants; other kinds of phonemes are stress, tone, and *juncture*—the linking and separation of syllables.

Phonemes, when combined, produce meaningful units of speech. *Morphemes* are the smallest units of speech that convey meaning. Most words in most languages consist of two or more morphemes. Morphemes that stand alone as complete words are called *free morphemes*; *bound morphemes* must be linked to other morphemes. *Allomorphs* are those morphemes that differ in sound but not in meaning. Semantic analysis is the study of the larger system of meaning. *Syntax*, or the arrangement of meaningful words into utterances, is the means by which semantic complexity is achieved.

Chomsky's theory of *transformational grammar* postulates that many different utterances (*surface structure*) are reducible to one essential meaning (*deep structure*), and that all the utterances of a language are reducible to the same essential pattern of meaning. Chomsky further speculates that the same deep structure, presumably biologically determined, may underlie all human language, and that differences among languages may be due simply to differences in *transformational rules*.

Linguistic diversity may evolve as the result of certain internal processes in a language—changes in sounds, grammatical structures, word order, and meaning. During the period from 1400 to 1600, for instance, the *great English vowel shift* gradually transformed every sound in our language. The tendency toward linguistic variation may be a key to the development of distinct languages. Within geographical regions, linguistic differences tend to be gradual; distinct languages apparently evolved when groups speaking different dialects became isolated from one another. Through comparative studies, linguists have determined regularities among those languages they classify as the Indo-European family. Many words in those languages are *cognates*—so similar as to suggest that these languages are descended from a single Proto-Indo-European tongue. Similar comparative studies of language have revealed information about the movements and historical relationships of various early cultural communities.

The accumulation of random variations in a language accounts for linguistic change. So do the accommodations a people must make to their social and physical environment. In this way language and culture are interrelated.

People who do not speak one another's language but are in regular contact with one another often adopt a *lingua franca*, another language that all understand although it is the native tongue of none of them. Another form of language that facilitates cultural contact is *pidgin*, based on a simplified grammar and vocabulary taken from one or more fully developed languages. If a pidgin language becomes a fully developed language in its own right, it is called a *creole* language.

Social processes influence language through the mechanism of *selective attention*: people unconsciously focus on things that have adaptive importance for them and ignore things that do not. Thus a phenomenon of great adaptive importance to a society may have several names, so that speakers may distinguish among subtle variations in it, whereas other phenomena of little or no adaptive importance may have only one name or none.

The influence of culture on language has been studied by linguistic anthropologists, who analyze *semantic domains* (groups of related categories) to uncover a society's system of meaning, and examine a language's *grammatical structure* (its rules for organizing its elements into meaningful utterances) as a key to the society's world view.

Language also reflects culture, in that people choose to respond to stimuli that are important to them. But according to some observers, culture is molded by language; different ways of speaking create different ways of thinking. This statement is not definitive because of the simultaneous evolution of language and culture, and evidence for the structuring of social processes by linguistic characteristics is weak. Linguistic change is also brought about by elements borrowed from other speech communities.

Sociolinguistics is the study of interrelationships of social variables and language. Ethnic and other socially distinct groups emphasize their uniqueness by developing a *speech community* or dialect, which diverges from the national language in vocabulary, pronunciation, and grammar. Other groups may develop a *community identity*, making an effort to distinguish themselves from outsiders by their speech. The context of a situation—its formality or informality and the relationship between the speakers—is a factor in the choice of terms of address and of words or even languages. Social status influences a person's use of language; it is possible that historical changes in pronunciation may occur because of attempts to climb the linguistic social ladder. Gender roles also affect linguistic variables.

Key Terms

allomorphs	deep structure	morphemes	sociolinguistics
allophones	free morphemes	morphology	speech community
aphasia	grammar	phoneme	surface structure
bound morphemes	grammatical structure	phonology	syntax
call system	great English vowel	pidgin	transformational
cognates	shift	selective attention	grammar
community identity	juncture	semantic domains	transformational rules
creole	lingua franca	semantics	

Suggested Readings

FROMKIN, V., AND R. RODMAN. 1988. *An Introduction to Language.* 4th ed. New York: Holt Rinehart and Winston. An introduction to the study of linguistics. This latest edition reflects the newest developments in linguistic theory and related fields.

GIGLIOLI, P. P. (ED.). 1986. *Language and Social Context.* Harmondsworth, Eng.: Penguin Books. A selection of readings that discuss varied aspects of the social organization of speech. Particular emphasis is given to face-to-face interactions, the relationship between social and cultural structures, and the study of social change and social conflict through language.

GUMPERZ, J., AND D. HYMES (EDS.). 1965. The Ethnography of Communication. *American Anthropologist* 67, no. 6, pt. 2 (special issue). The essays in this volume describe language behavior in specific communicative contexts.

LABOV, W. 1972. *Sociolinguistic Patterns.* Philadelphia: University of Pennsylvania Press. A stimulating and important book on sociolinguistics that covers the author's work on contemporary language usages in the United States, especially black English.

PARKER, F. 1986. *Linguistics for Non-Linguists.* Boston: College-hill Press. This is a good book for the nonspecialist who wants to be familiar with the fundamentals of linguistic theory.

TRUDGILL, P. 1983. *Sociolinguistics: An Introduction to Language and Society.* Harmondsworth, Eng.: Penguin Books. A synthesis of contemporary sociolinguistic research with a special emphasis on the varieties of spoken English, as well as several related pidgins and creoles.

WARDHAUGH, R. 1986. *An Introduction to Sociolinguistics.* New York: Basil Blackwell. A sound, basic coverage of most of the topics concerning the relationship between language and society that draws on a wide variety of sources.

12 Kinship, Marriage, and Household Organization

The single most important aspect of human adaptation, as we have stressed earlier, is the ability to respond to problems in a flexible, creative fashion. Our ability to work in cooperation with others in large social groupings and coordinate the activities of many people to achieve particular purposes—to live, work, even to fight and compete as members of a social group—is a vital part of human adaptation. One important aspect of human adaptation consists of people's perceptions of their relatives, their ways of organizing themselves in kin groups, marrying, establishing households, and using ties of kinship and other relationships to accomplish their ends. Social organization can be difficult to unravel, given the multiplicity of ties that can serve to relate individuals to one another. This difficulty is compounded by the fact that to understand social organization we have to go beyond the social categories or expectations that people recognize and examine actual patterns of behavior. What people do may be quite different from what they say they do, of course, as people frequently idealize their own behavior and stereotype that of others.

Kinship is a basis for social organization we share with all social species, including other primates. This chapter deals with the very basic ideologies, or models, of kin-based social organization. Chapter 13 deals with some of the larger societal consequences of these ideologies. "Ideologies" here refers simply to the fact that our ideas of family, ancestry, descent, and relatedness or kinship are cultural constructs, mentally carried images, much like our religions and other beliefs. It is best to think in terms of ideologies because ideas of family and kinship, although they exhibit some regularity across cultural boundaries, also vary greatly. So we will begin with a general discussion of kinship and proceed to the ways in which ties of kinship are created and used socially. While we describe some simplified analytic models, human behavior is so varied that no single model can encompass all practices, even within one society.

KINSHIP AND SOCIAL ORGANIZATION

To say that society has organization is to say that people behave toward one another in predictable or at least patterned ways. Social behavior fits rough patterns, and we often have reasonable expectations that we can use to predict with some degree of accuracy how one person will deal with another in a given situation. Social scientists use the concepts of status and role to describe this phenomenon. A **status** is a position in a pattern of reciprocal behavior. In terms of kinship, for example, there are the statuses of father and daughter, nephew and uncle, to name only a few of the many possible in American society. Each of these statuses carries with it a *role*, which, as we saw in Chapter 10, is a set of behavioral expectations—the rights and duties appropriate to a given status. In any given pattern, those roles interlock with one another. With regard to kin statuses, for instance, the American father traditionally has the responsibility to provide material support, education, and social guidance for minor children. Sons and daughters, for their part, are expected to be respectful of parental authority, to be affectionate, and to respond to "fatherly" advice in choosing their friends.

These behavioral expectations or roles may of course vary greatly even within one culture and very often may not be followed in everyday practice. The traditional role of mother in American society is close to but still distinct from that of father. A mother is usually viewed as less authoritarian and emotionally more supportive—sometimes we say more "nurturing." Needless to say, these and other kin roles are changing. As increasing numbers of households come to be headed by women, sometimes very young women, the kin status of mother takes on new implications: breadwinner, disciplinarian, primary source of guidance and support, and so on.

It is the interlocking or complementarity of statuses and roles that gives coherence to social relationships. We see the roles associated with different statuses as overlapping but reinforcing one another, again as with mother and father in American society. In the United States we also see great variability in these roles when we compare people of different ethnic and economic backgrounds, families in which one parent is employed, those in which both parents have jobs, and households in which partners are simply living together, with or without children.

One way to look at a system of kinship is to see it as a model of statuses and reciprocal roles. The model used by one society may differ from the model used by another, so that the first may give prominence to statuses that the second does not emphasize or even ignores. As we shall see, many cultures recognize one's mother's brother as a very special uncle and use a special word to specify him. This status does not exist for most English speakers, who use the word "uncle" to describe all the brothers of both parents. In most small societies, kinship is the basis for social relations that link people across generations, and hence provide major channels for the transmission of knowledge through time—not just technical knowledge

but the more basic social knowledge of such things as what a person is, what a role is, what a status is, what a relation is, and what an obligation is. By the same token, it is usually the first system of social roles a person is introduced to; the major, sometimes the only system of roles applied to an individual from birth and unchanging throughout life. As Napoleon Chagnon (1983) puts it, "kinship is the heart of social structure."

Studies of kinship—the way people classify their kin and the way these classifications relate to social behavior and social organization—are a fundamental part of anthropology. Anthropologists have come to realize in the course of their research that kinship is important even in extremely complex industrial societies: most of us live with and carry on our most intense and enduring relationships with people related to us either by blood or by marriage. The new familial arrangements that are coming into being in the United States today because of the high incidence of divorce and remarriage are very interesting. Children of one or more previous marriages may live together with children of their common parent's current marriage. They may end up with large numbers of half-siblings or step-siblings, and even a substantial number of people who behave toward them as grandparents. Even so, kinship roles are universal organizers of behavior and hence are universal keys to the structure of society.

Kinship Terms and Social Behavior

Anthropologists are interested in the way people of different cultures classify their kin because people tend to structure their behavior in accordance with the way they perceive themselves in relation to others. Kinship terminology, after all, is part of a language system. A person whose kin terminology automatically separates father's kin from mother's kin is not likely to regard (and treat) his or her relatives the same way as one whose kin terminology lacks such distinctions. The Hopi of Arizona, who employ kinship terminology that anthropologists label "Crow," distinguish father's sister from mother's sister. A Hopi man has especially close and intimate relations with his *kya'a* (father's sister), and the relationship lasts throughout her life (Whiteley 1985:360). In fact, this relationship may be more meaningful than relations among members of the same matrilineage (the Hopi have matrilineal clans and lineages).

Classification systems tell us how people organize their perceptions of those relatives whom they view as belonging to the same category and toward whom they are expected to behave in a certain manner, and how they assign separate terms to relatives whom they perceive as excluded from that category and toward whom they are expected to behave somewhat differently. The terminology, then, both assigns and reflects important social roles. The following brief example illustrates this principle. In looking at it, we should keep in mind that it is presented from the perspective of a man in that society; women view some of the same kin relationships in quite a different fashion.

Yąnomamö Kinship

As we have seen, the Yąnomamö are a group of South American Indians who live in an environment marked by violence. Regular warfare between villages creates a need to establish allies; at the same time, men have difficulties in obtaining wives, because, Chagnon maintains, of the practice of female infanticide, which creates a shortage of women and thus encourages warfare. So to the Yąnomamö two things are especially important—finding a wife and finding allies. Underlying these two preoccupations, and reinforced by them, is a network of well-defined kin relationships. Membership in Yąnomamö named kin groups is inherited through

the male line; both males and females belong to the kin group, or lineage, of their father. The kin group to which a person belongs is particularly important in regard to marriage, for men and women are required to marry specific types of cousins in a kin group other than their own. This prescription often leads young men of different kin groups to exchange sisters. When the same two kin groups continue to exchange women for generations, strong bonds are created between them. Such alliances are extremely important in time of war.

The terms by which the Yąnomamö refer to many of their relatives reflect these marriage rules and the alliances they create. Within a particular generation, all the members of a kin group refer to one another as "brother" and "sister," a reflection of the prohibition of marriage between them. At the same time, a man refers to all his marriageable female relatives in other named kin groups (relatives that we would call cousins) as "wife"—whether or not he in fact marries them. Similarly, the same man refers to the brothers of all of his "wives" as "brothers-in-law," indicating their close potential ties through marriage. Among "brothers," as we saw in Chapter 6, relationships are often tense, for they are competing for the same "wives." Relationships among "brothers-in-law," on the other hand, are often quite friendly, since these men have much to gain—wives and wartime alliances—from one another. Among the Yąnomamö, kinship categories are critical to the establishment of patterns of social interaction. A person's status in most social situations can be described, in large part, by a single kin term. Chagnon describes the case of an orphaned adolescent boy who came to live in the village where Chagnon was conducting his fieldwork. The boy had no "real" relatives in the village, but he attempted to define his own place in society by calling the headman of one of the kin groups "father." This tactic established a basis for developing and manipulating his ties to others in the village.

Kinship classification systems, however, reveal only the structure of social relationships; they do not reveal people's actual behavior. If a Yąnomamö calls one man "brother" and another "brother-in-law," the terms tell us that he regards himself as playing two different roles vis-à-vis these two men. But it does not tell us what those roles actually are. To find out, the ethnographer must examine the society through observation and interviews. Once the ethnographer learns what the reciprocal roles of brothers and brothers-in-law involve, he or she can predict and interpret with some accuracy any male Yąnomamö's behavior toward any man to whom he refers by one of these terms.

Of course, kinship terms cannot predict behavior with absolute accuracy. For one thing, no two people interpret kinship roles, or any other roles, in precisely the same way; as long as certain guidelines are observed, the rules can be adjusted to suit the people involved. Thus, though we may try to remember both of our grandmothers' birthdays, we may visit one twice as often as the other simply because we enjoy her company more. Also, though kin terms may group people whom other societies would put in separate categories, they do not blind us to such distinctions. A Yąnomamö man may call eight women "wife," but he still knows which one of them cooks his dinner and hangs her hammock next to his. Likewise, we may lump together mother's brother and mother's sister's husband under the single term "uncle," but most of us, if we needed a loan, would probably turn to the uncle who was a "blood relative" before we approached the one who was related to us only by marriage unless we know the latter to be far more wealthy.

The Manipulation of Kinship

In adapting the general rules of kinship to the specific requirements of daily life, people manipulate not only kinship roles; they may also manipulate kinship terms. The terms we have discussed so far are **terms of reference,** the terms by which people refer to their kin when they speak about them in the third person. Most kinship studies are concerned primarily with terms of reference, for such terms reflect most consistently the society's system for classifying kin. However, the language of kinship also includes **terms of address,** the terms people use when they address their kin directly. Terms of address are particularly interesting because they are the ones that people are likely to manipulate to suit their needs in various situations. These are the terms used in direct, face-to-face speech and may be deliberately at variance with terms of reference.

A commonly observed social strategy is to use a kinship term with absolutely no genealogical justification in order to invoke a desired role relationship. During the Black Power movement of the 1960s, for example, many blacks adopted the practice of calling one another "brother" and "sister" in order to stress their group solidarity. For precisely the same reason, feminists sometimes refer to unrelated women as their "sisters." This ad hoc manufacturing of kin relationships for political reasons has been observed in nonindustrial societies as well, despite the fact that they sometimes seem to interpret kinship more strictly than we. Claude Lévi-Strauss (1943) has reported on a population of Brazilian Indians that included members of two tribes that did not speak the same language. The men of the two merged groups called each other "brother-in-law," a term they had previously applied only to the brothers of all eligible brides in their own separate groups. This manipulation of kinship terminology helped to promote peaceful relations in a situation of potential conflict.

The Classification of Kin

When we study kinship it is crucial to keep in mind how the people of a society classify kin, rather than how kin might be categorized on a biological basis. The manner in which biologically based relationships are sorted and grouped has more to do with values, beliefs, and economic practices than with biology. The classification of kin or the system of words used to describe relationships is a cultural and linguistic phenomenon as well as a social fact central to the operation of any society.

A Yąnomamö man, for example, uses the same word for his brother and for his father's brother's son; and a man has almost the same expectations of his father's brother's sons as of his biological brothers; they fight the same battles, marry into the same group of women, and interact in reciprocal ways. In much the same way English speakers call quite diverse relatives "cousin," and while we have few specific expectations in regard to our cousins, the term makes it clear that we do not distinguish much between those on our father's side and those on our mother's side. So when we study a community or population it is not enough to determine how people are related to one another biologically; one must also determine how the people themselves define these relationships. The key to such definitions is the society's linguistic system for classifying kin.

Criteria for Classifying Kin

People in every society have a diverse cast of relatives. First and often of primary importance are those who are related to us by birth—our **consanguineal kin**. One's brothers and sisters, one's mother and father, her and his brothers and sisters and their children, one's grandparents and *their* brothers and sisters are some, but by no means all, of one's consanguineal kin. One's **affinal kin** are the people related to one through marriage—one's spouse and all of his or her relatives, as well as the spouses of one's own consanguineal kin.

Consanguineal and affinal relatives are usually our most important kin, but the list does not stop there. In many societies, including our own, families may adopt otherwise unrelated individuals, who acquire the rights and obligations of kinship and are socially recognized as members of the family. In addition, people use consanguinity as a model to create relations, such as godparents, *compadres*, "blood brothers," and old family friends whom children call "aunt" and "uncle." These people are sometimes called **fictive kin**, although the relationship may be as intense as that between consanguineal kin.

In the Middle East, people recognize "milk" brothers and sisters: children who have been nursed, however briefly, by the same woman. Some women who are close friends briefly nurse each other's child just to forge such a bond between their children. In the United States, children who are biologically unrelated may be reared together as siblings, most often when people with children remarry after divorce or widowhood. In some ways the notion of fictive kin is interesting because in the broadest sense, most kinship terms are fictive in that they are cultural rather than purely biological categories. The main distinction between fictive and other kin types is that the terms of fictive kinship are imposed arbitrarily.

Every language distinguishes categories of relatives in a systematic manner. Anthropologists refer to the terms that systematically designate these distinctions as **kin terminology**. In no society do people refer to each and every one of their many relatives by a separate term. Instead, they group some relatives in a single category and refer to them all by one kin term: brother, sister, aunt, uncle, grandmother, grandfather, and so on. All systems of kinship terminology are to some extent classificatory.

All societies use a limited number of criteria for classifying kin, though not necessarily the same criteria. Most distinguish among relatives on the basis of sex, using different terms for male and female kin. We refer to our female parents as "mother," our male parents as "father"; we also distinguish brothers and sisters, aunts and uncles.

Many societies also distinguish the mother's side of the family from the father's side. Such a basis of classification, called **bifurcation**, is extremely important among peoples (such as the Yąnomamö) who inherit their membership in a named kin group exclusively through either the mother or the father. In such societies some distinction must be made between, for example, mother's brother and father's brother (both of whom English speakers call "uncle"): one belongs to ego's kin group—and therefore has certain rights and obligations in relation to ego—while the other does not. ("Ego" is the term conventionally used to indicate the individual who is the point of reference in a kinship relationship; that is, the speaker, who with no justification but convenience is always assumed to be male). Such distinctions are made by bifurcate terminology; that is, one divides one's kin into two groups.

Most systems of kinship also use different kin terms to distinguish between generations. English speakers have separate terms for grandmother, mother, daughter, and granddaughter. In addition, the majority of societies (including our own) make some distinction between **lineal relatives** (direct ascendants and descendants) and **collateral relatives** (people to whom one is related through a connecting person). An uncle who is related to ego through one of ego's parents is a collateral relative. Some societies, however (not including our own), go one step further and use separate terms for collateral relatives connected to ego through a female and those connected through a male. A distinction between mother's brother and father's brother is frequently found. So is the use of separate terms for **cross-cousins** (mother's brothers' children and father's sisters' children) and **parallel cousins** (mother's sisters' children and father's brothers' children).

Six Basic Classification Systems

Despite the many thousands of languages spoken, not to mention the nearly infinite ways in which people could potentially reckon kin relationships, only a limited number of basic patterns are to be found among the world's peoples. Although a society may have variations of its own, kin classification systems are of six very general types—Sudanese, Eskimo, Hawaiian, Iroquois, Omaha, and Crow, which derive their names from peoples that exemplify the types or from the areas in which such terminologies are widespread.

It is important to understand that these six general categories are idealized types. Although most societies have kinship systems that are more or less like one of these models, only a few conform to the model exactly. For example, in a study of forty-one societies identified as having Iroquois kinship terminology systems (to be described shortly), Ira Buchler and Henry Selby (1968) show that very few of the groups actually have *all* the traits associated with this system of classification.

Sudanese Kin Terminology. The kin terminology system known as Sudanese is used by Arabic, Persian, and Turkish populations throughout the Middle East and also by the Chinese. Its most striking feature is its descriptiveness. There are separate terms for father's brothers, father's sisters, mother's brothers, and mother's sisters—relatives whom we lump together under two terms, "aunt" and "uncle." Similarly, the male and female children of each of these relatives in ego's parents' generation are called by a separate term. This arrangement yields eight "cousin" classifications in ego's own generation. Thus in the Sudanese system, each of ego's sixteen possible consanguineal relationships in his own and his parents' generation has its own separate term. In the order in which they appear in Figure 12-1, they are:

1. father
2. mother
3. father's brothers

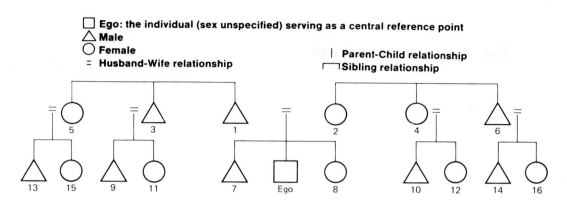

FIGURE 12-1   Sudanese kin terminology.

4. mother's sisters

5. father's sisters

6. mother's brothers

7. brothers

8. sisters

9. father's brothers' sons

10. mother's sisters' sons

11. father's brothers' daughters

12. mother's sisters' daughters

13. father's sisters' sons

14. mother's brothers' sons

15. father's sisters' daughters

16. mother's brothers' daughters

Sudanese systems of terminology are associated with descent groups defined in the male line (discussed later in the chapter). The Yörük pastoralists discussed in Chapter 7, like most Turkish speakers, use this system of terminology. The Sudanese system is also found in societies that have a high degree of class stratification and occupational differentiation, such as those in China and throughout the Near East, although the causal relationship is unclear. The emphasis on distinctions of relationship among even close kin may well reflect socioeconomic diversity within the group.

Eskimo Kin Terminology. People in our own society, as in many others, use what is known as Eskimo kin terminology (see Figure 12-2). In some respects, this system, too, is quite descriptive. For mother, father, sisters, and brothers the Eskimo system, like the Sudanese, provides separate terms that do not apply to other kin. Outside the nuclear family, however, the Eskimo terms are quite inclusive. No distinction is made between relatives on the paternal and maternal sides of ego's family. For example, the same terms—"aunt" and "uncle"—are used to refer to the brothers and sisters of both ego's mother and ego's father (and to their spouses as well, so that consanguineal and affinal relations are lumped together). Moreover, the Eskimo term "cousin" covers all the children of ego's aunts and uncles, making no distinction between male and female cousins, parallel and cross-cousins, cousins related through ego's father and cousins related through ego's mother. This term is also used to refer to the children of ego's parents' cousins and to still more distant relatives. Indeed, the word "cousin" in English once meant any relative or even a friend whom ego treated as a relative. To summarize, Eskimo kin terminology includes a mix of one-relation and catchall categories:

1. father

2. mother

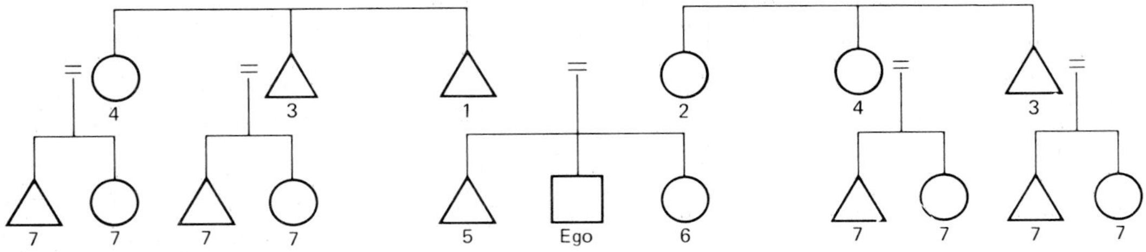

FIGURE 12-2   Eskimo kin terminology.

3. uncle (all of ego's parents' brothers and parents' sisters' husbands)

4. aunts (all of ego's parents' sisters and parents' brothers' wives)

5. brother

6. sister

7. cousin (the children of all of ego's parents' siblings, plus more distant relatives)

The most distinctive feature of Eskimo terminology is its emphasis on the nuclear family. In singling out ego's parents and siblings with exclusive terms, it provides the immediate family with a small, rather private niche in the kinship system which is not provided by other terminologies. Another notable feature of Eskimo terminology is the absence of bifurcation. Again not surprisingly, peoples who use the Eskimo system tend to inherit their kin-group affiliations from both sides of the family and therefore do not have to make fine distinctions between mother's kin and father's kin (Pasternak 1976:143–146).

Hawaiian Kin Terminology. Hawaiian kin terminology (see Figure 12-3) is almost as inclusive as the Sudanese is exclusive: it makes only two kinds of distinctions, that of generation and that of sex. Thus in ego's and ego's parents' generations there are only four kin terms:

1. all males of the parents' generation

2. all females of the parents' generation

3. all males of ego's generation

4. all females of ego's generation.

The Hawaiian system resembles the Eskimo in its lack of bifurcation, and like the Eskimo, it is frequently found in societies in which the individual is affiliated with kin groups on both the mother's and the father's sides of the family. At the same time, the Hawaiian terminology differs radically from the Eskimo in

FIGURE 12-3   Hawaiian kin terminology.

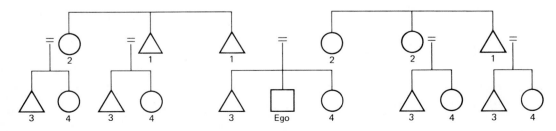

merging the nuclear family with other consanguineal kin—mother with aunt, brother with male cousin, and so forth. This approach to classifying kin is generally associated with societies in which the nuclear family is submerged in a larger kin group, so that in fact the nuclear family and other kin may have approximately equal importance in the individual's life (Pasternak 1976).

Iroquois Kin Terminology. The Iroquois system, named for the North American Indian confederation, is found in every part of the world (Pasternak 1976; see Figure 12-4). An important feature of this system is that it distinguishes between parallel cousins and cross-cousins. As we saw earlier, parallel cousins are the children of ego's parents' same-sex siblings, while cross-cousins are the children of ego's parents' opposite-sex siblings. Thus ego's parallel cousins are his father's brothers' children and his mother's sisters' children. In Iroquois terminology these cousins are called by the same terms as ego's own brothers and sisters. By contrast, ego's cross-cousins (the children of his father's sisters and his mother's brothers) are given their own separate terms. Cross-cousins, in other words, are thought of as being at a greater relational distance from ego than are parallel cousins.

Since parallel cousins are classified with ego's brothers and sisters, it seems logical that the parents of parallel cousins are classified with ego's parents. In the Iroquois system, ego uses a single term for father and father's brothers and a single term for mother and mother's sisters. Father's sister and mother's brother are

assigned separate terms. Thus in the Iroquois system, as in the Hawaiian, members of the nuclear family are classified with collateral relatives of both generations on the basis of sex in the parents' generation. The Iroquois kinship classification system can be summarized as follows:

1. father and father's brothers

2. mother and mother's sisters

3. father's sisters

4. mother's brothers

5. brothers and male parallel cousins (father's brothers' sons and mother's sisters' sons)

6. sisters and female parallel cousins (father's brothers' daughters and mother's sisters' daughters)

7. male cross-cousins (father's sisters' sons and mother's brothers' sons)

8. female cross-cousins (father's sisters' daughters and mother's brothers' daughters)

Yąnomamö kinship terminology follows the Iroquois pattern; hence the Yąnomamö's inclusive use of the terms "brother" and "sister." Ideally, a Yąnomamö man will marry one of his female cross-cousins. It is this group of relatives that he calls "wife," and it is their brothers (his male cross-cousins) that he calls "brother-in-law." The emphasis here is on defining two

FIGURE 12-4 Iroquois kin terminology.

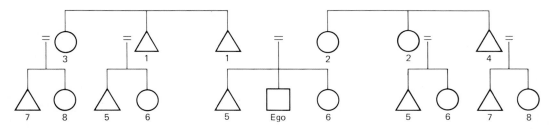

categories or groups of relatives and establishing a relationship between them. The members of each group are in-laws of the other group.

Omaha Kin Terminology. Omaha kin terminology takes its name from the Omaha Indians of North America, who lived west of the Missouri River. Most societies that employ Omaha terminology are divided into patrilineal kin-based groups—groups in which membership is inherited through the father. On ego's father's side of the family—the side that constitutes his kin group—we find father and father's brothers referred to by a single term. The merging of these two kin types serves two purposes. First, it indicates the great importance of the paternal uncles, who are senior male members of ego's own kin group and can claim the same respect, loyalty, and rights as ego's biological father. Second, it distinguishes them from ego's mother's brothers, who are not members of ego's kin group and do not share the same rights and responsibilities. In short, Omaha terminology is found almost exclusively among societies in which the patrilineal descent group has important functions, be they military or territorial.

In Omaha terminology, kin-group affiliation so far dominates classification on the mother's side that generational distinctions are erased. From the point of view of English speakers, their use of the term "mother" to refer not only to one's biological mother but to her sisters as well seems strange, as does the use of the term "mother" to refer to tiny female infants. Yet this is a feature of the Omaha kin terminology system (see Figure 12-5): mother, mother's sister, and mother's brothers' daughters are all lumped under the same term. Similarly, mother's brothers and mother's brothers' sons are referred to by a single term. This lumping together reflects the fact that careful distinctions need not be made in mother's kin group, for this is not ego's kin group and therefore his or her relationships with them have fewer socially prescribed obligations. But this does not mean that ego has no ties to mother's kin. On the contrary, precisely because they are not of his kin group—and are therefore removed from the kinds of political considerations that might discourage emotional attachments—ego may have strong affectionate ties with at least some of mother's kin group. Such ties are all the more likely to develop in that ego may well marry into his mother's kin group and thus form important alliances with them. Like the Iroquois, the Omaha kinship terminology system lumps brothers and male parallel cousins (father's brothers' sons and mother's sisters' sons) under one term, and sisters and female parallel cousins (father's brothers' daughters and mother's sisters' daughters) under another term. The rationale for this arrangement is the same as in the Iroquois system: the children of men and women whom ego calls "father" and "mother" should, logically, be called "brother" and "sister."

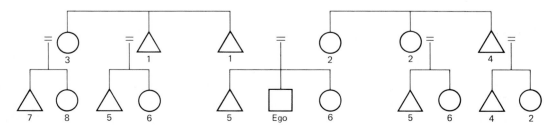

FIGURE 12-5   Omaha kin terminology.

Crow Kin Terminology. Crow kin terminology is associated with societies that establish membership in kin-based groups through the maternal line, and takes its name from another North American Indian society. It is as strongly dominated by concerns of matrilineal kinship as the Omaha is by those of patrilineal kinship. Indeed, as one can see by comparing Figures 12-5 and 12-6, the Crow system is the mirror image of the Omaha. Male and female parallel cousins on both sides of the family are grouped with brothers and sisters. All male members of father's kin group are lumped under one term, and all female members under another term, regardless of generation. On mother's side of the family, the side that constitutes ego's kin group, mother and mother's sisters are given a single term, and mother's brothers another term. Crow terminology, like Iroquois and Omaha terminologies, is associated primarily with less complex sociopolitical systems and with tribes in which lineality is critical in many areas of political life.

The Crow system of kin terminology, like any other, should not be seen as simply an extension of primary or close kin terms to include more distant relatives. The Trobriand Islanders, for example, whose Crow terminology was first described by Malinowski (1922/1961), use the term "taboo" to include all grandparents, anyone of the grandparent's generation, all ancestors, and any women of the father's clan or mother's father's clan. The fact that one term covers such an array of individuals does not mean that the root meaning of "taboo" is grandparent; rather it constitutes a category of people in some special relationship to the speaker. And remember that the use of the same classificatory terms does not imply that the speaker cannot actually differentiate among the various relatives thus lumped together.

To summarize, one has to understand the kinship system if one is to understand the behavior of individuals in a particular society. As we shall see shortly, kinship serves the important function of structuring at least one vital area of human behavior: whom one may and may not marry. Still, it is not possible to assume a close fit between a particular terminology and a particular way of life or cultural adaptation. Sudanese terminology, for example, is used by Bedouin pastoralists as well as by Chinese urbanites. The Inuit of Alaska use Eskimo terminology, and so do Londoners. Usually the most one can say is that each of the six systems is congruent with the patterns of political and economic organization that prevail in the societies where the system is found. One would not expect a terminology that emphasizes matrilateral distinctions to be employed by people who emphasize the political or economic roles of relatives on the father's side.

MARRIAGE, REMARRIAGE, AND MARITAL RESIDENCE

Of course the terminology and beliefs associated with kinship are only one dimension of the

FIGURE 12-6   Crow kin terminology.

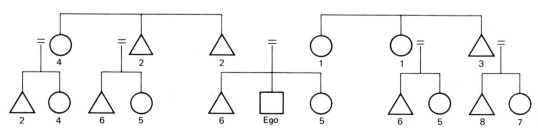

way people conceptualize their relationships with others. Another dimension is seen in the various ways people choose spouses and establish families and households. Such choices are influenced by socially prescribed rules, but not to the exclusion of other factors. In almost every society marriage is the institutionalized means by which new families are created and existing ones expanded, and family organization forms a basis for most domestic groups, or households.

Marriage is everywhere the occasion for ceremony and ritual, marking the change in the individual's status. (Left) A Maasi bride and groom walk unspeaking to the groom's house. (Right) In France, a couple is married before the town magistrate. (LEFT: ANNE RIPPY; RIGHT: ULRIKE WELSCH)

Marriage

Marriage is not easy to define. Anthropologists try to define marriage so as to cover all known variations, but the effort is inconclusive. In the United States, people debate whether homosexual couples should be permitted to marry and have legal standing comparable to that of heterosexual couples. The financial rights and responsibilities of men and women in legal marriages are rapidly being redefined. In Europe and the United States many couples are choosing, too, to ignore church or state-endorsed marriages and simply live together, but in every other respect to behave as a married couple. The colloquial term "significant

other" is sometimes used socially to refer to a co-resident sexual partner to whom one is not married. It avoids any implication as to the gender of the partner or legal status of the relationship. But almost all societies have some form of marriage in that special recognition is given to a sexual and economic union between two or more people which legitimizes their offspring and establishes reciprocal rights and obligations among husbands, wives, and their children.

Marriage is usually a legal contractual basis for the sharing of property, economic responsibility, sex, and obligations toward children born as a result of the union. Marriage almost everywhere involves some form of reciprocal economic obligations. Traditionally in American society wives were expected to provide domestic services; husbands, financial support. This arrangement is of course changing, but the notion that husbands and wives have different spheres of responsibility in marriage is still prevalent. Unless they arrange otherwise, a couple's private wealth and future earnings become joint property upon marriage. In addition, a husband and wife are jointly responsible for supporting and raising the children they have together, whether or not they remain married.

Marriage as legally and socially defined varies around the world, though everywhere it is bound up in notions of mutual rights to sex and responsibilities toward and rights over children. Simply in the matter of intended permanence, marriage customs vary. In Iran, members of the Shi'a faith can enter into a special form of marriage in which they stipulate how long their marriage contracts are to remain in force. What is considered appropriate sexual conduct is also culturally variable. We tend to view sexual relations as appropriately restricted to a monogamous couple. In many societies a man is permitted more than one wife at a time, and in a few others a woman is permitted more than one husband at a time.

The people of Lesu in the South Pacific consider extramarital sexual relations acceptable — provided the wife's lover presents her with gifts to be turned over to her husband.

Among the Nayar of Kerala, in India, until the practice was forbidden by British authorities, marriage did not prohibit a woman from having a sexual relationship with any suitor of an appropriate caste status; her ritual husband had no more claim to her sexual favors than any other qualified man. In fact, the term "group marriage" has been used, rightly or wrongly, to describe the practice whereby Nayar women took multiple "visiting husbands" and men similarly "visited" multiple women. While the Nayar no longer follow this custom, it is possible that the traditional emphasis on women's prerogatives underlies the higher status that women enjoy in Kerala than in the rest of India. Women here marry later, have fewer children, have high rates of literacy, and enjoy superior health (Weisman 1988).

The economic rights and obligations that accompany marriage also vary. A Trobriand husband is expected to help support his sisters but is only partially responsible for the support of his wife and children. A Nayar husband is not expected to provide any financial support for his ritual wife and her children at all. In fact, he may never even see his wife again after their wedding; the marriage is significant primarily as a political statement indicating relations among groups (Gough 1959, Schneider and Gough 1961:319–320). Hopi women find it relatively easy to divorce their husbands and, traditionally at least, have done so quite frequently; their children, like corn, their main crop, were seen as their property (Whiteley 1985). Of course, the converse is also found; under Islamic law, women inherit only one-half of the property that would fall to a comparable male heir, and in rural areas often do not inherit land at all. And upon divorce, women have no claim to their children or to any property that came to the couple from the husband's family (Bates and Rassam 1983).

Marriage is not a prerequisite for the legitimacy of children in all societies. A Nuer man in southern Sudan can legitimize the child of an unwed mother by making a specified payment. Nor are parents everywhere responsible for the care and teaching of their children. In Israeli kibbutzim, children may live apart from their parents in nurseries and dormitories. Although parents have a special relationship with their own children, the entire community assumes substantial responsibility for their upbringing.

Divorce and Remarriage

Helen Fisher (1987:22) quotes Samuel Johnson as saying that "remarriage is the triumph of hope over experience." However marriage is defined, divorce or dissolution of marriage by formal or informal means is an old phenomenon. While the norm may be marital monogamy, many individuals marry more than once.

In traditional Navajo society most people marry and divorce four or five times, and did not marry with the expectation of remaining together for life. And among the Kipsigis of Africa, when a wealthy man has enough children, particularly sons, to manage his farm, he may marry again, move to his new bride's home, and begin the family cycle again, maintaining what amounts to visiting relationships with his other wives. The Pokot, described earlier, do likewise, but few men wish to go through the formality of divorce, perhaps because of the ramifications of attempts to retrieve the bridewealth they paid the first wife, which they would need for a formal union with a second. The !Kung or San, hunters and gatherers of the Kalahari, have a divorce rate at least as high as any found in an industrialized country; Nancy Howell reports that of 331 !Kung marriages she recorded, 134 ended in divorce (Howell 1979).

Can any pattern be found in the data on marriage stability in various cultures? Fisher thinks so; she finds some basic regularities in both marriage and divorce. In a sample of fifty-eight societies at all levels of technology, she identifies three "divorce peaks," or life stages in which couples are most likely to divorce. The couples most susceptible to divorce are those who have been married for four years; next most susceptible are couples between the ages of twenty-five and twenty-nine; and finally, couples with no children or one dependent child who have been married more than four years.

These times of peak divorce are interrelated and arise, she asserts, from both the reproductive process and psychochemical processes. Fours years of strong bonding between the sexes is, she claims, the product of our evolutionary history. It is the period of time needed to have an infant and to bring it to a point where the combined forces of both parents are not critical to its survival. The main impetus for divorce or separation comes after four years of marriage, when the couple feels less strongly attached to each other. She terms it the "four-year itch," and she attributes it (as do others) to brain physiology: chemical processes in the brain foster an intense attachment or infatuation that can last no longer than two years, after which different brain chemicals, the endorphins, set the basis for strong attachment but without the sexual excitement and intensity of infatuation. A United Nations sample of fifty-eight countries indicates that 48 percent of divorces occur within seven years of marriages, most clustering around the four-year peak.

This is not to say that no significant economic or social factors are involved. Even if the peaks for divorce seem to be regular, the rates of divorce vary widely. Again Fisher suggests that rates of divorce are lower where men and women are economically dependent on each other, as in intensive agricultural societies. Thus with industrialization and the increasing economic autonomy of men and women, divorce rates rise. Even so, about half of American marriages last for life.

Despite its variations from one society to another and the possibility of divorce, the institution of marriage is nearly universal. United Nations records for countries that conduct censuses show that an average of 93 percent of women and 92 percent of men will marry (cited in Fisher 1987:26). One explanation is that marriage functions as a useful social and economic contract—bonding not just a man and a woman, but social groups as well. It is a means of binding family to family and kin group to kin group. Another reason for the prevalence of marriage is that it serves as a means of organizing economic sharing and cooperation.

Marriage as Exchange

When a man or woman marries, he or she acquires not only a spouse but also a new set of parents, brothers- and sisters-in-law, and other affinal relatives. Exchange is the most basic way of establishing a bond between individuals and groups. Quite apart from what is exchanged, the act of exchange itself creates a precondition for further social interaction. In many societies, marriage is the most important form of exchange. It is usually women who are the key figures in exchange marriages, in part because of the high value placed on a woman's labor and reproductive capacity. Very often women are seen to symbolize the wholeness of a group, be it family, clan, or tribe. Marriage represents either a union of the bride's group with the groom's or occasionally the submission of one to the other. The latter situation is seen when men of a dominant group take wives from people whom they would not permit their own women to marry. The Yörük of southeastern Turkey will arrange marriages with non-Yörük women, but even though they live in multi-ethnic communities, they will not give their own women to outsiders. Among Bedouin tribes, the giving of a daughter in marriage may resolve a blood feud: the family that gives its woman placates the other.

In some societies families create alliances by exchanging daughters directly. Among the Tiv of Nigeria a man may exchange one of his sisters for the sister of another man, binding their families together. But such direct exchange of women is relatively rare. More commonly, a man pays the family from which he takes a daughter in marriage (bridewealth or **bride price**) or works for them **(bride service)**; the payment helps the family replace the daughter with a wife for one of their sons. This indirect exchange of women is found throughout the world (recall the discussion of bridewealth among the Pokot of Kenya in Chapter 7.)

The reverse custom, paying the groom's family a **dowry** to take a daughter off one's hands, was common in medieval Europe, and exists today in parts of Eastern Europe and particularly in India. In India the practice has occasioned a great outcry as police have reported many incidents in which poor men have murdered their wives in order to remarry and collect a second dowry.

Marriage payments, because of their wider social or political significance, may involve a complicated form of social calculation, as can be seen among the Kwaio of the Solomon Islands. The Kwaio are obligated to contribute to a close kinsman's bride price. They consider many factors in determining whether they are closely enough related to the groom to be expected to make a contribution, and if so, the size of the payment the relationship warrants. The degree of closeness, and thus the size of a bride-price contribution, is calculated as follows: (1) Comembers of a descent group are more closely related than are nonmembers at similar genealogical distance. (2) Persons who lived together in childhood are more closely related than persons at similar genealogical distance who did not. (3) Persons who habitually

Elopement and Bride Theft Among the Yörük: A Problem Reconsidered

People do not always want to do what is expected of them. Departures from social norms often occur in the relatively minor decisions we make in the course of our everyday routines, but they may also affect major life decisions, such as marriage. People often marry in ways that not only displease their families but flaunt established norms and conventions. When Daniel Bates went to study the Yörük of Turkey in 1968, he knew from Turkish newspaper accounts that marriage conventions, not to mention the law, were sometimes violated. The topic offered, it seemed, a clear example of a discrepancy between real and ideal behavior: newspapers frequently contained lurid stories about women who had been abducted, raped, and forced to marry against their will (Bates 1974).

He decided to inquire about such "kidnappings," as the locals termed them. Yörük informants at first claimed no personal knowledge of such disgraceful behavior; that sort of thing occurred only in other families. As it turned out, a few nights later a young woman was abducted from the family with whom Bates was living; after the initial excitement died down, he learned that such "disgraces" were quite common—a source of local amusement but unfortunately also some violence.

In this patrilineal society, marriage to one's first cousin is strongly encouraged, especially to the father's brother's daughter or son. As a result of this preference, most members of any patrilineal group are closely related by numerous ties. Marriage is a serious matter,

and the heads of Yörük households take great care to arrange suitable matches for their children. Given this emphasis on arranged marriages, Bates was surprised to discover the number of marriages that were the result of elopement and "bride theft"—*kacirma*. A bride who is "stolen" is kidnapped and raped by her prospective husband. In a society that places a premium on virginity, this attack greatly diminishes her prospects for marriage and increases the chances that she will agree to stay with her abductor. Elopement, also called kacirma, is a couple's joint decision to run away together, in defiance of their parents' wishes. The Yörük frown intensely on both of these practices; when they occur, the result is extreme shame and outrage, particularly on the part of the girl's family. Yet Bates found that 23 percent of all Yörük marriages were contracted in these ways. What accounted for this high proportion?

Bates concluded that kacirma provided a means for the expression of individual choice in an otherwise highly structured system. That a boy and girl may love each other, for instance, traditionally played little or no role in the arrangement of a marriage. Furthermore, because it is through marriage that adult status is attained, kacirma allowed young men to hasten their entry into mature society by bypassing the normal procedure of marrying in order of birth and only after a substantial bride price has been raised (a project that could take several years).

---

live in the same settlement or in proximate settlements in adulthood are more closely related than persons at similar genealogical distance who are living apart. (4) Agnates (patrilineal kinsmen) are more closely related than are nonagnates at similar genealogical distance

(Keesing 1975, Buchler and Selby 1968:95–96). In addition, the potential donor's age, his reciprocal obligation based on the groom's contribution to his own bride price, his acceptance or opposition to the marriage, past quarrels he may have had with the groom, a closer rela-

As a group, kacirma marriages involved bride-price payments higher than average. But even though some were very high indeed, some husbands paid little or nothing. It appeared that wealthy families whose sons committed kacirma were obliged to pay very large sums in order to avoid legal action or prolonged hostility. Poor families, however, often paid very little or nothing at all. Once the act had been committed, there was little the girl's family could do to collect if the boy's family had little money. In this way, kacirma could also be seen as equalizing the burden of high bride prices for people of differing wealth.

Bates concluded that kacirma, although vigorously disavowed and discouraged as deviant behavior, played a significant—and in some cases even predictable—role in Yörük social interactions. Because couples who eloped more often tended to be from different social circles, Bates believed that elopement served to broaden and diversify kinship networks. He also assumed that this aspect of the Yörük marriage system had existed for a long time and was likely to continue.

On subsequent visits, however, Bates found that the prevalence of kacirma was declining, and by 1984 no kidnapping or elopement had occurred in a year. Moreover, he noted that the time-honored custom of bride price which had so preoccupied the people in 1968 had dwindled to a mere symbolic payment, and by 1984 had been almost completely reversed. Instead of large sums of cash paid by the groom's family to the father of the bride, gold was given directly to the bride, and her father was expected to contribute as well. In short, the arrangements had come to focus more on the couple and the establishment of their household (still patrilocal, or near the husband's kin, however) than on kin and lineage.

Why had kidnapping and elopement once been so common? Some of the original answers still held. When Bates considered the phenomena as features of the society, he ignored not only the possibility that they could suddenly cease but also their origins. When he looked over some old data, he noticed that the women who had been kidnapped fell within a fairly narrow age range, and that this group had reached its maximum numbers about ten years before his study. Kidnapping began to be frequent around the end of World War II, increased during the 1950s and 1960s, and by the early 1970s started to decline. Many, if not most, social preferences and practices—even deviant ones—are like that. In the Yörük case one might speculate that kidnapping and elopement roughly tracked the rapidly changing economic and political environment. Following World War II, many traditional grazing areas, sources of prestige, and sources of income were declining at the same time that the Yörük were being drawn into an all-cash market economy. Many people found new opportunities, and some flourished as meat and wool prices rose. Others did not do so well and fell into debt. All of these phenomena could have worked to disrupt normal marriage arrangements; but an additional factor was at work: bride price, which formerly had been expressed in terms of a few animals, became fully monetarized and then subject to rapid inflation.

Though any decision may have social consequences that one has not anticipated—such as a broadening of one's kinship network after elopement—such consequences do not explain one's decision. The discovery that kacirma is not, after all, a permanent feature of the Yörük marriage system suggests that it might be best to be wary of tidy explanations of social phenomena.

tionship with the bride than with the groom, and, finally, his financial circumstances are all weighed and evaluated. In this case bride-price payment is more of a social than an economic transaction.

Bride-price payment and bride service are most common in societies where a woman leaves her family to live with her husband's kin and the children she bears become members of his patrilineal kin group. In effect, the husband is compensating his wife's family for the loss of her economic services and reproductive

Marriage among the Fore people of Okapa, a subdistrict in the eastern highlands of New Guinea, is preceded by the payment of a bride price—goods presented by the groom's family to that of his intended. Here we see a formal presentation of the price, which includes pigs, bananas, and sugar cane; the bride's male relatives are examining the goods to ascertain their worth. (ROBERT GLASSE)

capacity. (When the couple remain in the vicinity of both kin groups and the husband's and wife's families have equal rights to the assistance of the couple and their children, reciprocal gift exchange is more common.) Bride payments and gift exchange help to ensure that neither the couple nor their families will take the marriage lightly. Perhaps more important is the fact that when potentially hostile groups intermarry over several generations, they establish a lasting bond. As each group has vested interests in the other, in terms of past, present, and future offspring, they have established a basis in kinship for cooperation and communication.

Two social customs, the levirate and the sororate, exemplify the widely held conception of marriage as an exchange between kin groups. These social customs extend the marriage contract beyond the death of a spouse. Under the **levirate,** a man has both the right to marry his dead brother's widow (or to demand bride payment from another husband she chooses) and the obligation to provide for her. The woman is seen as having an obligation to produce or rear heirs for her husband's family even if he is dead. Under the **sororate,** a widower has the right to marry one of his deceased wife's sisters, and her kin are obliged to provide him with a new wife. In American society, where one is not expected to marry one's deceased spouse's brother or sister, individuals often assume at least some continuing responsibility toward the family into which they marry.

Marriage and the Division of Labor

Many anthropologists have suggested that one reason marriage is so widespread lies in its economic advantages, quite apart from child rearing. Marriage unites two economically complementary people, a man and a woman. Among the !Kung (San) people, as we have seen, women spend many hours gathering vegetable products for the family and camp, while men range far afield in the hunt. Though the women may produce more calories of food energy than the men, their roles are basically complementary. Men can perform some physical tasks more easily than women, and more important, they usually have greater freedom of movement, as they are not burdened by a nursing infant on their backs. Because women bear children and usually assume primary responsibility for their care, women supervise more aspects of housekeeping and other work that does not interfere with child care. Such responsibilities and the attendant division of labor are not static, and have changed through history.

Carol Ember, surveying the data from a large number of horticultural and intensive agricultural societies, finds that as agriculture intensifies, women not only continue to work hard in food production, but take on added duties, mainly associated with the preparation of foods that require more labor (Ember 1983:290).

Particular divisions of labor within the household are of course by no means inevitable, and today traditional systems are rapidly changing. Even if a couple does not allocate tasks along customary lines, they can still share the burden of work in some way, thus reaping the benefits of collaborative labor. Marriage serves as a convenient way to institutionalize such economic cooperation.

Actually, the economic alliance in a marriage is more complex than a balancing of strengths and talents between wife and husband. In many societies, labor is scarce; a greater number of family members means more potential sources of labor. The economic strategies of husband and wife frequently shift as children are born, grow up, and then either leave the family unit or bring spouses into it.

Given the importance of marriage in the creation of bonds between kin groups, promotion of economic cooperation, and provision for the care and education of children, the arrangement is not taken lightly in any society. In fact, all societies have both explicit rules and implicit norms defining who is an appropriate spouse, how many people one should marry, and where a newly married couple should settle.

Marital Rules

Marriage rules are generally not inflexible, but they are often backed by strong social pressure. The rules establish regularities in the way people marry, and the resultant organization of marriages and marital ties can be viewed as a coherent system. The rules also serve to strengthen the potential for alliances and other bonds between groups. Perhaps the most significant marriage rules, at least in regard to the possible range of choices open to an individual, are those prescribing whom a person should and should not marry.

Whom Should One Not Marry? The Incest Taboo

In virtually every society, sexual relations (and, by extension, marriage) between parents and children and brothers and sisters are forbidden or "taboo." The exceptions are few. For religious and political reasons, the ancient Egyptians, the Incas, and the aboriginal Hawaiians required brothers and sisters of royal families to marry, a practice forbidden to other members of society. While the incest taboo is universal, the inclusion of first cousins among prohibited mates is not. Some societies ban cousin marriage, some tolerate it, and some even favor this form as a cultural ideal. And while incestuous relationships are disapproved of, they can be fairly common in practice. Many explanations have been proposed for this universal taboo on incest.

One explanation, popular at the turn of the century, is that people have no desire to mate with members of their own family (Westermarck 1889/1922). Familiarity leads to sexual disinterest: long-term close associations simply discourage eroticism. This view is supported by both observation and by psychological and biological theory. Marriages between people born and raised together at an Israeli kibbutz are extremely rare. In fact, one study of 2,769 second-generation kibbutz marriages found not one intrakibbutz marriage (Shepher 1983).

An explanation of the incest taboo favored by another early anthropologist, E. B. Tylor (1871), focuses on its sociocultural functions. In brief, the taboo prevents social isolation by ensuring that individuals participate in social units beyond the family in which they were raised. More recent alliance theories are related to Tylor's. They stress the positive consequences of "marrying out" to create interfamily alliances that enhance social cohesion.

Freud was also much interested in the taboo, and he speculated that it reflects the need to control a subconscious desire for incestuous sex. Certainly an instinctive recoil from sex with close relatives could be the mechanism by which this form of mating is avoided. However logical this position may seem, it is difficult to see why an instinctive taboo is needed to achieve such utilitarian social ends.

Still another theory, similar to Tylor's, centers on the social consequences of role disruption caused by incest (Malinowski 1927). The complex relationships that would ensue when men, for example, in addition to being husbands, were acting as both parents and lovers to their children within the same household at the same time would probably have proven disastrous among early hunting-and-gathering groups, in which cooperation was necessary for survival. On a large scale, the role confusion would have disrupted the transmission of culture through socialization.

Seymour Parker (1976) concludes that incest avoidance is "wired in" to humans and other vertebrates as a result of two factors. First, it evolved as an instinctive behavior through selective advantages that derived from outbreeding as opposed to the ill effects of inbreeding: individuals who avoided mating with close kin had more surviving offspring. Second, it developed as an adaptive behavior as groups learned the survival advantages of exploration and connection with a large social network. From Parker's point of view, the incest taboo is an example of "the complementary relationship of culture and biology." This perspective seems confirmed by growing evidence from behavioral studies with animals as well as with humans. Even a slight risk of genetic damage would be very deleterious to a species that reproduces slowly and whose adult members have a large investment in their offspring (Shepher 1983:150–200).

Whom Should One Marry?

Rules of Exogamy. Beyond the incest taboo, societies have a variety of rules that specify who is considered acceptable as a mate. Individuals in most societies are expected to marry outside a particular group with which they are identified. Where rules of **exogamy** apply to members of a village, men must seek their wives, and women their husbands, in other communities. More commonly, however, these rules apply to some or all of a person's kin. Because cultures classify kin in a variety of ways, rules of exogamy take many forms. In societies that do not have a concept of unilineal descent, such as our own, rules of exogamy generally apply to most of a person's consanguineal relatives. Americans frown on marriage between first cousins; the frowns are replaced by lifted eyebrows when second cousins marry. Such unions are not illegal (in most states; the laws regarding incest vary somewhat from state to state) and do not inspire the same negative feelings that incestuous mating does, but neither are they applauded. Traditionally the Chinese carried exogamy to the extreme, forbidding marriage between individuals who had the same last name on the theory that they might be related, however distantly.

In some societies with a concept of unilineal descent, rules of exogamy may apply to all members of a lineage. Thus in some patrilineal societies, individuals may be permitted to marry first cousins on their mother's side of the family but not on their father's. The prohibition usually forbids unions with all the people one calls "brother" or "sister." Many exogamous societies forbid marriages between members of a clan or even **phratry**—a group that typically consists of several clans that extend the rights and obligations of kinship to one another but retain distinct identities. But lineage exogamy, while prevalent, is not universal.

Rules of Endogamy. The choice of a mate may alternatively be regulated by rules of **endogamy,** which prescribe marriage within the particular group with which one is identified. Many Middle Eastern and North African peoples practice endogamy within a very narrowly defined kin group. First-cousin marriages of all sorts are common. In such a marriage, of course, both the husband and wife belong to the same descent group and usually knew each other as children. Indeed, in some Middle Eastern groups a man has a recognized right to marry his father's brother's daughter (his parallel cousin) and must be consulted and compensated amply if she marries another man (Bates and Rassam 1983).

Although we may not always think of it as such, endogamy is practiced in our own society. In fact, most Americans marry a person who grew up within a few miles of their own family's residence. Marriages across socioeconomic, religious, national origin, and racial lines are in a distinct minority, in part because our society is structured in such a way that we have more frequent social contacts with people whose backgrounds are similar to our own, and in part because parents and others pressure young adults to marry "their own kind." In complex societies such as our own, ethnicity often sets the outer limits to an acceptable marriage.

The Yörük of Turkey are an endogamous group; cousin marriages are common. These three Yörük brides are all from the same lineage as their husbands and are themselves closely related. Two are brides in the same household, married to two brothers. Thus the lines of kinship are complex—the brides are cousins and their husbands are their cousins as well. (DANIEL G. BATES)

Of course, such norms as exogamy and endogamy are not always consistently followed within a society. Many mitigating factors may cause individuals to depart from recognized marriage norms. One of the most powerful factors is proximity—the nearness of potential mates. Even on the tiny island of Tikopia in the South Pacific (two miles by three miles), people are far more likely to find marriage partners in the same or neighboring villages than farther afield. One study (Adams and Kasakoff, 1976) found that propinquity ranked as high as clan considerations or any other factor in determining the choice of a mate.

Cousin Marriages. Although many societies do not sanction first-cousin marriages, people in approximately one-third of the world's societies allow or prefer marriage of certain selected cousins. Let us suppose a young man belongs to an exogamous partrilineage. Marriage with any cousin on his father's side of the family would be considered incest if the kinship terminology labels members of ego's descent group in his own generation "brother" and "sister," as it does in the Omaha and Iroquois systems. Nor could he marry any of his parallel cousins on his mother's side of the family; he probably refers to those women as "sister" as well. But he could marry a cross-cousin on his mother's side of the family. Moreover, marriage with his mother's brother's daughter might have certain advantages. It would allow him to formalize affectionate ties he has developed with his mother's family and strengthen his ties to a family he knows and trusts. Also it would reinforce interfamily ties established in the preceding generation by his mother and father.

In matrilineal societies, marriage with one's father's sister's daughter serves the same purposes. Thus anthropologists generally believe that exchange and alliance are among the important functions served by cousin marriages and the cultural preferences that structure them.

How Many Should One Marry?

Just as societies have rules regulating who an individual may or may not marry, so they also have rules regulating how many spouses an individual may have. Historically, most societies have not followed the rule of **monogamy,** which restricts marriage to only one man and one woman at a time. Instead, they allow, or even prefer, some form of **polygamy,** or plural marriage. Many groups that prescribe monogamy consider it acceptable for a man to maintain one or more mistresses and their children in separate households—if he is reasonably discreet. In our own society, **serial monogamy** (divorcing and then remarrying, perhaps many times) is becoming an acceptable alternative to lifelong marriage to one partner.

It is difficult for those of us accustomed to thinking of marriage as an exclusive relationship to imagine a husband or wife accepting a "rival" into the home. How does polygamy work? There are actually two basic forms it can take—**polygyny,** marriage between one man and two or more women at the same time, and **polyandry,** marriage between one woman and two or more men at the same time.

Polygyny. Polygyny was the preferred form of marriage among the ancient Hebrews, in premodern China, and traditional India. It remains the preferred form in much of Africa, the Middle East (the Koran permits a man four wives), and Asia. In most polygynous societies, only a few wealthy and powerful older men actually have more than one wife. After all, since there are usually approximately the same number of males and females in a population, widespread polygyny within a society would require some men to remain single, at least during part of their adult lives. It is no accident that polygyny is closely associated with male competition and is a prerogative of the senior men. From a male perspective, women are an economic asset. Women not only perform a significant amount of work themselves; they also bear sons to support a man in his political struggles and daughters who can someday be exchanged for bride payments. The Siwai of Melanesia are quite explicit about the matter: the more wives a man has to tend his gardens, the more pigs they can raise; the more pigs he has, the more feasts he can give; the more feasts he gives, the more people will become obligated to him (Oliver 1955). Thus multiple wives are a source of wealth, power, and social status. Patricia Johnson found that the number of women in a household was a major factor in determining its wealth: the women were vital to agricultural success, particularly in growing cash crops (Johnson 1988).

Polygyny has its drawbacks, however. Unless the husband is an accomplished diplomat, the household may dissolve into bitter competition for his attention, sexual favors, and economic considerations. Gusii wives in Africa, for example, nearly always blame a miscarriage or a child's death on a co-wife's witchcraft and seek to retaliate (LeVine and LeVine 1963). To minimize friction, polygynous husbands usually provide a separate dwelling for each wife and her offspring. The one exception is with *sororal polygyny* (the marriage of one man and two or more sisters). Perhaps because they have learned to resolve jealousy over their parents' attention, sisters seem to have fewer problems about sharing a dwelling as well as a husband (Murdock 1949).

Conflict among co-wives, a potential problem when the wives reside together or not far apart, is usually mitigated by an established domestic hierarchy. The senior wife nearly always enjoys superior status and authority over younger wives. She, not the husband, assigns the other women's work. Sometimes wives encourage and even help their husband to obtain new wives, but as Lila Abu Lughod shows graphically in her study of the Bedouin of Egypt (1988), the taking of a second wife is usually a sad occasion for the first. However brave a face a woman may put on, when her husband decides to take a second and usually younger wife, she often feels personally wounded and embittered. Polygyny, it seems, is closely associated with sociopolitical systems that enforce male authority and gender inequality.

Polyandry. Polyandry is much rarer than polygyny, and is found in only four societies. The Toda of India and the Tibetans, for example, traditionally allowed a woman to marry a set of brothers **(fraternal polyandry)**, who shared her bed on an agreed-upon schedule and who jointly undertook responsibility for support of her children. Marquesan men thought it advantageous to marry a woman who had several unrelated lovers and make them subsidiary husbands, because co-husbands would then act as allies. Under certain conditions, polyandry may be advantageous for all concerned. If the ratio of males to females is seriously unbalanced, polyandry equalizes a man's chance to find a mate. If resources are scarce, it can also be a means by which limited land is shared by brothers, who otherwise would have to divide it up. On the other hand, it may not be favored by men under most circumstances because it reduces the number of offspring an individual man can produce (Hiatt 1980). This practice can still be adaptive when resources are scarce, as in Tibet, where much of the arable land traditionally was controlled by a multitude of monasteries. If brothers marry one woman and have only one set of children, and the sons continue to practice polyandry, their land (not large enough to support several families) passes intact from generation to generation. Interestingly enough, polyandry in Tibet was practiced mostly by the poor.

Nancy Levine, who worked for many years among ethnic Tibetans in northwest Nepal, has written the most detailed account of life in a polyandrous community. The Nyinba villages she studied were unusual in that fraternal polyandry was the norm. "Every man who has brothers—with the rarest exceptions—marries polyandrously, and virtually all the brothers remain in intact, fraternally polyandrous marriages throughout their lives" (Levine 1988:3).

As Levine had expected, the presence of more males than females in polyandrous marriages has important consequences for household organization and the domestic economy. The Nyinba are a tightly bounded and closed society in their marital and social arrangements. Land in their mountainous region is limited and villagers have little possibility of acquiring any by means other than inheritance. Households resist the partition or splitting up of domicile and land whenever possible. Against this backdrop, the members of the society see polyandry as a logical means of preserving resources intact. Sexual jealousy among men who share a wife is not prominent although difficulties are most likely to break out when the brothers are not full brothers.

Polygyny is far less common but is permitted in the same communities. Such a union usually comes about when a man marries the sister of his present wife. In many respects this is a male-focused domestic arrangement, as the household and its resources are passed on in the male line. Marriage in general is highly endogamous by category of wealth as well as by the narrow limits of the community. Even in regard to child care and consequently child mortality, boys are favored (Levine 1988:75). Men in a fraternal household frequently engage in trade or craft activities, leaving the farming and domestic work to the women.

Marital Residence Rules

All societies have norms governing where newly married couples will live. Our own norm is called **neolocal residence** ("neo" meaning "new"): a married couple establishes their own household apart from both the husband's and the wife's kin. This residence rule is comparatively rare. In many other societies, married couples move in with the kin of one spouse or the other, joining an established household.

Patrilocal residence—residence of a married couple with or near the husband's kin—is the preferred arrangement in most patrilineal societies. The couple may build their own dwelling in the compound or village of the husband's father or of another senior male of his kin group, or the bride may just move into her husband's father's house. But in all cases, they are residentially in the husband's kin group and are subject to its authority. Even so, there is always room for maneuver and deviation from the rules.

Matrilocal residence—residence of a married couple with or near the wife's kin—is also quite common. Matrilocal residence is usually found in matrilineal societies that favor marriage to someone in the same village (village endogamy), so most male members of the matrilineage remain in their natal neighborhood. In some matrilineal societies, however, sons move to their mother's brother's community and set up households there. This pattern—residence of a married couple with or near a brother of the husband's mother who is a senior member of his matrilineage—is known as **avunculocal residence**.

The Suku of Zaire (Kopytoff 1977) combine matrilineal descent with patrilocal residence—a situation that anthropologists once assumed was unstable. Members of a lineage are dispersed within an area that extends as far as thirty kilometers (twenty miles) and both men and women live with or near the man's father or brothers. But each kin group also has a ceremonial "anchor village," the matrilineage center, to which kin-group members return frequently for ceremonies and rituals. Because members of a matrilineage are in regular communication with one another, the combination of matrilineality and patrilocality has been stable.

In a fifth pattern, **bilocal residence**, a married couple regularly alternate their residence between the household or vicinity of the wife's kin and that of the husband's kin. Rather similar is **ambilocality,** a pattern in which the couple reside with or near the kin of either husband or wife, as they choose.

The preference for patrilocal over matrilocal residence (or vice versa) is a subject of much debate. For some time anthropologists have associated patrilocal residence with hunting, the herding of large animals, and complex agriculture, all of which require cooperative male labor. Matrilocal residence was thought to be adaptive for horticultural societies, where subsistence depends largely on female labor. But cross-cultural data do not support this view (Ember and Ember 1971). Although most matrilocal societies practice horticulture, more than half of all patrilocal societies are also horticultural. The data, they suggest, show that where warfare among subgroups or neighboring communities of a single society is common, residence is patrilocal. If the family has to be on the lookout for attack, it makes sense to keep sons close to home. Patrilocality ensures that men are closely associated with the communities they are called upon to defend.

FAMILY HOUSEHOLDS

Ties of kinship and marriage are basic to human social organization, and the most fundamental group in most, if not all, societies is the **household**—the domestic residential group, whose members live together in intimate contact, rear children, share the proceeds of labor and other resources held in common, and in general cooperate on a day-to-day basis. While households as residential and cooperative

groups need not be formed on the basis of kinship and marriage, most of them are. We will therefore refer here to the **family household**. The household is a residential unit that functions as a small corporation, regulating consumption and production. Households commonly own property or hold defined rights in society as a recognized entity.

We already have seen how marriage customs can vary. Since it is through marriage that family-focused households are formed, it is not surprising that variations in these customs can affect people's ideas about acceptable or preferred forms of domestic groupings. In essence, definitions of the family household vary from society to society in accordance with the way people conceptualize two relationships. First, there is the **conjugal relationship**, that between spouses. In most but not all societies, the conjugal bond is basic to the structure of the family household.

The conjugal relationship may, as we have seen, be monogamous, polygynous, or polyandrous. The second relationship, the maternal and paternal ties, are those of **descent** between mother and child and between father and child. The maternal relationship, no matter how it is conceptualized, is universally recognized; the paternal relationship may not be, although such cases are relatively rare. The Nayar of India, mentioned earlier, are one of the few societies in which the definition of the household excludes both the conjugal bond and the father–child relationship. The Nayar family is (or was traditionally) based solely on the bond between a mother and her children; it is therefore called a **matrifocal family household**. This term is sometimes employed in our society to describe a household that comprises a single mother and her children. Thus numerous variants of the household are possible, each depending on the relationships included in the definition and on the way those relationships are conceptualized or stressed.

Independent versus Extended Family Households

One axis of variation based on the conjugal and descent relationships is the number of generations of married adults who live together in a household. The **independent family household** is a single-family unit (be the marriage relationship monogamous, polygynous, or polyandrous) that resides by itself, apart from relatives or adults of other generations. The independent family household formed by a monogamous union, the most common type in the United States, is often referred to as the **nuclear family household**. Far more common in other parts of the world, as an ideal at least, is some variant of the **extended family household**, a multiple-family unit incorporating adults of two or more generations.

The composition of a household in every society, regardless of the type that is culturally prized, changes regularly with the processes of birth, marriage, aging, and death. Thus any family household may best be described in terms of a **domestic cycle**; that is, according to the series of demographic events that its members undergo over time. An elderly couple whose children have left home form a rather different household from that of a newly married couple who have not yet had children. Individuals are likely to reside in a variety of household arrangements in the course of their lives, each depending on their age, the number of spouses they or their siblings have (whether serially or simultaneously), the health of their parents, and other factors. Thus it is difficult to assign one household type to an entire society or even to a local community, even if one form or another is clearly the cultural preference. Because of the normal workings of the domestic cycle the household in which one lives changes in a regular fashion with time. Thus even in a society that stresses the importance of the extended household, the majority of people may actually be residing in independent or nuclear households.

Each domestic arrangement has its advantages and disadvantages, and the advantages and disadvantages will vary in accordance with one's position and gender. For example, the extended household in a patrilocal society may be less advantageous to a young bride than to her mother-in-law. The chief benefits of the single-family household unit are mobility, privacy, and independence. But the costs of independence may be high. The independent family household is relatively vulnerable to labor problems arising from illness, care of children, and other potential demands for more time and energy than its few adults can muster. Moreover, in times of crisis or conflict, smaller households may find it hard to compete for economic resources against larger and thus politically stronger households. It is not accidental that nuclear households are both favored and very common where the larger political system assumes much of the burden of security, health care, and education.

The extended family household provides economic benefits (through the sharing of expenses and labor), defense, social security (illness or death do not leave individuals stranded), and companionship. And extended families are flexible: the members of the family can divide into teams to perform different kinds of work simultaneously and share what they produce. But there are disadvantages, too: friction between parent and adult child and among adult siblings; domination by elders, who achieve positions of leadership on the basis of age rather than ability; and lack of privacy (Nimkoff and Middleton 1960).

Extended family households usually center on either the paternal or maternal descent relationship as expressed in rules of marital residence. A patrilineal extended household consists of a man and his wife or wives, his unmarried daughters, his sons, and their wives and children. In the small towns and villages of Turkey, a bride commonly moves into her husband's father's household. The couple may have their own room but the bride shares cooking chores with the other women of the household and the family members eat together and share resources. Even if adults work for wages outside the household, they are expected to pool their money for household use, largely as the head of the household determines. The groom's father is the recognized head of the household and his wife exercises authority over the younger women and gives them daily work assignments. This arrangement is quite common throughout Eastern Europe, the Middle East, and the Mediterranean area, though for demographic reasons it is unlikely ever to be the predominant mode of household organization.

Despite the Yörük stated preference for extended family households, for example, only 30 percent of the households are so constituted. One outcome of this preference is that closely related men tend to remain in close proximity to one another while women, if they are not close relatives, come to the neighborhood from elsewhere. Even if a man does not actually co-

In 1969, this Yörük family lives together in one household, consisting of a man and his wife, their married son with his wife and child, and their unmarried children. Along with several other families, this group comprised an important political unit in this society—the lineage, whose membership is determined by patrilineal descent. Even after marriage, the sons remain close to their father, and together with the father's brothers and their sons, form a closely interacting group. In 1988, this living arrangement remained the practice. (DANIEL G. BATES)

reside with his married brother or with his parents, he usually tries to settle as close to them as possible. Thus the household can be seen as a mirror of the larger community, a fact that has been noted in many cultures.

A matrilineally extended household consists of a woman and her husband or husbands, their unmarried sons, their daughters, and their daughters' husbands. The Pueblo matrilineal extended family, for example, placed great emphasis on the mother-daughter bond. The oldest woman headed the household, while husbands, as well as sons to some extent, occupied peripheral positions. Even the children were viewed as belonging to the women (Whiteley 1985:370).

In China, where strong emphasis is still placed on patrilineally extended households, some households find themselves without marriageable sons, only daughters. Such a household may take a son-in-law into the house, make him an heir, but exact a commitment from him to honor the woman's family line, care for her parents until death, and regard his children as descendants of her (not his) parents (Pasternak 1985:311, 1972:85). This practice has a long tradition but is both rare and held in low regard by most people. Only a poor man will accept the humiliation of living with his wife's parents. Pasternak found, however, that it is more common in households that face a serious labor shortage. Thus in Chungshe village (Chapter 8) where irrigation farming requires substantial labor, Pasternak found a correspondingly high rate of uxorilocal (matrilocal) marriage. Such an option not only helps supply the needed male labor but helps families short of sons to maintain their family lines.

A complex household, formed through polygyny or polyandry or through the decision of married siblings to live together in the absence of their parents, is often termed a **joint family household**. It is common for a husband of multiple wives to establish a separate dwelling for each wife, or at least to provide separate domiciles within a family compound or building. In the most common form of joint family household, married brothers live together, with the senior brother assuming a position of leadership. One advantage of this arrangement is that resources need not be divided. The disadvantage, much commented upon, is that interpersonal conflict frequently leads to the dissolution of the household, especially when the wives of the younger brothers, determined to protect the interests of their children, come to resent the leadership of the senior brother and his family.

Anthropologists have looked at a variety of social and economic relationships in an attempt to explain why the extended or joint family household is so commonly idealized and why in some societies (such as ours) the independent family arrangement is preferred. They have found that extended families are prevalent in agricultural societies, while independent families are more frequently associated with industrial or hunting-and-gathering modes of subsistence (over 80 percent of the world's hunters and gatherers spend most of the year in independent family groups). This statistical association has been basic to the traditional explanation for the dominance of one or the other type of family structure in a particular society.

Some observers hold that societies may have a high frequency of independent family groups because they have to: in hunting-and-gathering societies, resources are too variable to feed a large group throughout the year, while workers in industrial societies need mobility to pursue jobs and cannot take large families with them (Nimkoff and Middleton 1960). Extended families, on the other hand, can exist in societies that offer an abundant food supply, landownership, and a settled lifestyle. These observations do nothing to negate the possibility of great variability within communities, or even during the life cycle of an individual.

Summary

The three foci of this chapter are kinship—the most crucial factor in social organization—marriage, and the family household. Social behavior in the framework of kinship and marriage is determined largely by *status* (a position in a pattern of reciprocal behavior) and *role* (a set of behavioral expectations appropriate to a given status). Social organization may be seen as a network of reciprocal roles, each organizing in a predictable way the behavior of the individual who occupies it. In all societies, but especially in small-scale societies, important roles are defined by kinship—relatedness by marriage or by descent from common ancestors. Since kinship roles are universal organizers of behavior, they are universal keys to social structure.

In most small-scale societies kinship is the major system of social relations that links people across generations and hence provides major channels for the transmission of social and technical knowledge through time. Kinship must be understood in the terms the people themselves use to categorize kin both when they speak about them (*terms of reference*) and when they speak to them directly (*terms of address*). Although kinship terms use a biological idiom—"father," "mother," "sister"—they are cultural and linguistic creations. Hence they vary in accordance with the society's values, beliefs, and ways of making a living.

In studying a culture, one must determine both how people are related to one another and the kin terminology by which they define these relationships. There are various criteria for classifying kin, including the distinctions among *consanguineal kin* (relatives by birth), *affinal kin* (relatives by marriage) and *fictive kin* (persons such as godparents and "blood brothers"), between male and female, between the maternal and paternal sides of the family (*bifurcation*), between generations, between *lineal relatives* (direct *descent relationships*) and *collateral relatives* (relationships traced through a connecting person), between *cross-cousins* (mother's brothers' children and father's sisters' children) and *parallel cousins* (mother's sisters' children and father's brothers' children). Kin classification systems are of six general types—Sudanese, Eskimo, Hawaiian, Iroquois, Omaha, and Crow. The study of kinship classification is important because of the relationship between the way people classify others and the way they behave toward them. But kinship classification systems reveal only the structure, not the content, of social relationships. People adapt the rules of kinship to daily life by manipulating both kinship roles and kinship terms. The kinship language of some societies includes optional modes of address to be used in alternative situations.

Social rules are only one among many important factors a person will consider in a given situation. The family is a social construct based for the most part on ties of kinship. The term may refer to the co-residing domestic group or household, or to a broad network of relatives by birth and marriage; thus its form varies considerably from society to society. It is also necessary to distinguish between social norms of family organization, other family units, and the actual living arrangements people make. A household is a minimal residential unit but it is not necessarily a family, just as not all families are households.

Marriage is a contractual basis for the sharing of property, economic responsibility, sexual access, and the responsibilities of parenthood. But marriage is culturally variable in terms of permanence, sexual privileges, and economic rights and obligations. Moreover, legitimacy of children is not dependent on marriage in all societies. Marriage binds families and kin groups together. The act of exchange inherent in marriage creates a precondition for further social interaction. In some societies, interfamily alliances are created by the direct exchange of daughters. *Dowery* may be paid by the girl's family to the groom's. Usually, however, marriage entails a *bride price* or *bride service*, which is paid or rendered by the prospective husband to the kin of his wife. This custom is most common in patrilineal societies, where women leave their families to live with their husband's kin. A lasting bond is thus formed between the groups, which tends to alleviate any potential conflict. Some societies extend the marriage contract beyond the death of a spouse. Under the *levirate*, a man has the right to marry his brother's widow and the obligation to provide for her. Under the *sororate*, a widower has the right to marry a sister of his dead wife, and her kin are obliged to provide him with a new wife.

All societies have explicit rules and implicit norms concerning marriage and residence. Virtually every society maintains the incest taboo, which prohibits sexual relations—and therefore marriage—between brothers and sisters or between parents and children. Most also enforce rules of *exogamy*, which require people to marry outside a particular group. These rules take various forms, depending on the kin classification within the society. Many exogamous societies forbid marriage between members of a clan or even of a *phratry*—a group that typically consists of several clans that share the rights of kinship but retain distinct identities. In other societies, rules of *endogamy* apply, requiring a person to marry within a defined group. This form of marriage guarantees that one will marry and live within a circle of fairly close relatives. Cousin marriages are sometimes preferred or even prescribed. Such marriages enhance exchange and alliance with kin groups. Societies also enforce rules governing the number of people one may marry. Our society prohibits marriage with more than one person at a time *(monogamy)* but permits divorce and remarriage *(serial monogamy)*. Most societies practice (at least ideally) some form of *polygamy*. The two basic forms of plural marriage are *polygyny*, marriage between one man and two or more women, and *polyandry*, marriage between one woman and two or more men. Tibetans traditionally practiced *fraternal polyandry*, under which a woman married a set of brothers.

Rules dictate where a married couple must establish residence. Norms in our society call for a newly married couple to establish *neolocal residence*, apart from both the husband's and the wife's kin. Other societies prefer *patrilocal residence*, in which case the married couple lives with or near the husband's kin. Other alternatives are *matrilocal, avunculocal, bilocal,* and *ambilocal residence*. It has been suggested that residence rules reflect military rather than economic considerations: where warfare is common, it is advantageous for those who fight together also to live together.

Perhaps the most basic group is the co-residing domestic group, or *household*. Usually, but not always, the household is based on ties of kinship. Members of such *family households* share food, labor, and material resources. Inasmuch as marriage customs affect the composition of the family household, the *conjugal relationship* is basic to its structure. Male and female roles in the household are affected by the society's emphasis on *descent relationships*. The *matrifocal family household* is based solely or primarily on the bond between the mother and her children. A single-family unit that resides apart from relatives of an older generation is an *independent family household*. When the union is monogamous, it is usually called a *nuclear family household*. A polygamous or polyandrous household, or one formed through the decision of married siblings to live together with their spouses and children, is usually termed a *joint family household*. Far more common is the *extended family household*, which includes adults of two or more generations.

Because of the series of demographic events

that make up the *domestic cycle*, individuals are likely to reside in a variety of household arrangements in the course of their lives, whatever the cultural ideal. Each domestic arrangement has advantages and disadvantages.

Extended families tend to be prevalent in agricultural societies; independent families are more common in industrial and hunting-and-gathering societies.

Key Terms

affinal kin	**domestic cycle**	**joint family household**	**parallel cousins**
ambilocality	**dowery**	**kin terminology**	**patrilocal residence**
avunculocal residence	**endogamy**	**levirate**	**phratry**
bifurcation	**exogamy**	**lineal relatives**	**polyandry**
bilocal residence	**extended family**	**matrifocal family**	**polygamy**
bride price	**household**	**household**	**polygyny**
bride service	**family household**	**matrilocal residence**	**serial monogamy**
collateral relatives	**fictive kin**	**monogamy**	**sororate**
conjugal relationship	**fraternal polyandry**	**neolocal residence**	**status**
consanguineal kin	**household**	**nuclear family**	**terms of address**
cross-cousins	**independent family**	**household**	**terms of reference**
descent relationship	**household**		

Suggested Readings

BOURGUE, S. C., AND K. B. WARREN. 1981. *Women of the Andes: Patriarchy and Social Change in Two Peruvian Towns.* Ann Arbor, Mich.: University of Michigan Press. A feminist perspective on women, family, and kinship within a rapidly changing world. The authors' research focuses on the position of women in an agrarian society with a patriarchal power structure.

DRAGADZE, T. (ED.). 1984. *Kinship and Marriage in the Soviet Union.* London, Eng.: Routledge & Kegan Paul. A volume of articles by established Soviet anthropologists that demonstrate the variety of family and marriage customs maintained in spite of the influence of an ostensibly uniform economic and political system.

EMBER, M., AND C. R. EMBER. 1983. *Marriage, Family, and Kinship.* New Haven, Conn.: HRAF Press. A collection of previously published essays by the authors that examine in cross-cultural perspective variation in family and household, the incest taboo, postmarital residence, and related topics.

LEVINE, N. E. 1988. *The Dynamics of Polyandry: Kinship, Domesticity, and Population on the Tibetan Border.* Chicago: University of Chicago Press. A rare ethnographic account of life in polyandrous households. The author has carried out intensive fieldwork in Nepal among villagers of Tibetan ancestry who practice fraternal polyandry.

NETTING, R. MCC., R. R. WILK, AND E. J. ARNOULD (EDS.). 1984. *Households: Comparative and Historical Studies of the Domestic Group.* Berkeley: University of California Press. The editors introduce issues of methodology and theory in the study of household organization; the individual essays describe a wide range of current research.

SCHNEIDER, D. M. 1980. *American Kinship.* Chicago: University of Chicago Press. 2nd ed. An account of kinship as a system of symbols and meanings rather than just as a network of functionally interrelated roles. A clear and concise introduction to kinship in American society.

Chapter **13** Social Groups
and Stratification

Any human society is complex, given the many ways in which its members actually or potentially interact. Humans, as we have stressed, tend to solve their problems through cooperative efforts, and in general thrive best when they are interacting with others. While human societies vary widely in complexity, their structures have much in common. Here we shall look at the ways in which people categorize or differentiate themselves within larger social groupings and examine the importance of networks for individuals. We shall also explore more complex social arrangements, such as descent ideology, ethnicity, gender, caste, and social class.

Descent is of course an aspect of kinship, and ethnicity, gender, social class, and economic inequality are germane to politics and economics. Yet all of these domains of social organization ultimately rest on individual perceptions and behavior. In Chapter 12 we looked at notions of kinship or relatedness and at ideas about marriage and family; now we will see how these concepts are extended or applied to constitute the basis for social groups and larger social constructs, such as ethnic groups, gender groups, social classes, and castes. Very frequently these constructs do more than simply serve as a frame of reference for individuals—they often structure access to resources and political participation and thereby underlie social stratification.

Members of any society have some sense of distinctive identity. They may express it in religion or language or symbolize it in art. Within societies, people constitute themselves in an array of groups, each having a distinctive identity and claim on its members. From household to nation, these identities and claims are reflected in a pervasive "we–they" dichotomy. Societies at all levels of technology place a heavy emphasis on their uniqueness vis-à-vis outsiders; xenophobia (the fear of foreigners) is a global phenomenon. Band and tribal societies may have special insignia for clans or lineages, and the integrity of the whole is expressed in dress, dance, and ritual. The Yąnomamö, like many other tribal peoples, have elaborate myths that place them at the center of humanity, not unlike the creation myths of the Old Testament.

State-organized polities have formally demarcated frontiers, emblems of citizenship, and myriad signs of common membership in a social and political system. The overarching social and political structure of the state encompasses any number of smaller social and political groups, each announcing its own uniqueness, whether of religious affiliation, ethnicity, social club, or even family. Within any society the nature and activities of constituent groups is basic to the organization of the larger population. Ethnicity in state societies, for example, can become a major means of distinguishing local populations or segments, even though all may participate in the same larger social order. Sometimes, as we shall see, notions of ethnicity become a rationale for oppression or exploitation. Racism, as we usually term the use of ethnic criteria to restrict social or economic activities, is a case in point. Apart from ethnicity, it is impossible to ignore the fact that people often do not participate equally in society.

GROUPS

In addition to our natal or marital household, all of us belong to social **groups** whose members interact on a regular basis and have a sense of collective identity. This sense of collective identity, usually a vital part of social organization, is based on criteria that can range from age, sex, family, and kinship through more abstract categories, such as shared religion, ethnicity, and political views. Even very small aggregates of people tend to arrange themselves in groups set apart from the rest for some purposes. The San, described in Chapter 5, share food extensively and almost impartially but still focus on kin-defined families or households, each bearing final responsibility for its own well-being. In more complex societies, such as the settlement of Los Peloteros in Puerto Rico (Chapter 9), people not only are members of distinctive households but participate in a wide variety of other groupings. Any resident of Los Peloteros who has a job is likely to be a member of a union; most belong to a church congregation; some are affiliated with a political party. Men and women socialize in separate spheres and have distinctive social networks. Moreover, viewed as a neighborhood population, the people of Los Peloteros constitute a distinctive segment or social class within Puerto Rican society.

The Organization of Groups

Obviously, groups differ in composition and function. They also differ in degree of **formal organization**—the extent to which they restrict membership and make use of officially designated positions and roles, formal rules and regulations, and bureaucratic structure. Groups may also differ in permanence. Some are created to perform a specific function and are dissolved when the task is completed. Other groups may far outlive their original members. Most important, groups may also vary in degree of **corporateness,** or the sharing of members in specific rights, such as common property or resources. The ultimate definition of "corpo-

rate" is that in which a group is treated as if it were an individual. A family household is corporate in many ways: its members share rights to food, property, protection under law or custom, defense, and inheritance. A village is often a group with a high degree of corporateness if membership automatically grants the right to share in land and other resources. Some villages, however, are little more than clusters of dwellings, with little economic or social activity uniting the residents. This is the case where residence confers no special economic rights or political responsibilities (as in most suburban communities in the United States). Of course, in actual practice a quality such as the economic corporateness of a community may be difficult to measure. In most cases the rights and privileges bestowed by group membership are achieved through individual negotiation and through social and political maneuvering.

All societies are formed by the integration of smaller groups or subsets of the whole, whether the smaller entities are households, lineages, political parties, labor unions, or whatever. The great nineteenth-century French sociologist Émile Durkheim (1964) referred to this process as the **social division of labor.** Social processes are compartmentalized or specialized, with each segment or grouping occupying its own position within the whole.

Durkheim identified two contrasting forms of division of labor, a distinction that still is useful. One form of society is built up of similar parts; for example, societies in which all of the social units are comparable—households, lineages, or other descent groups. Every member of the society (of the same sex and age category) belongs to the same sorts of social groups as does every other member. This form of organization, which exhibits **mechanical solidarity,** is exemplified by the egalitarian social organization of the !Kung San people of the Kalahari.

The second form of social organization is more complex: society is built up from dissimilar, specialized social groupings. No individual can participate in all of them but each participates in at least some. Durkheim characterized this sort of society as exhibiting **organic solidarity** because it resembles the structure of a living organism, constructed from numerous but specialized parts, each with a separate function. Complex societies, such as Los Peloteros, are almost always structured so that some of the social groupings have preferential access to resources, prestige, and political power. In short, they are stratified.

SOCIAL CATEGORIES

The way we classify people greatly influences the way we behave toward them and the way we expect them to behave. Thus we must focus on the way people in a given society categorize one another if we are to understand that society's organization and patterns of interaction. Such a focus can also help us to understand social cleavages and the differences in access to resources and power among members of the society.

A **social category** is composed of all people who share certain culturally identified characteristics. For example, people classify others on the basis of certain perceived social characteristics that serve to set apart segments of society, as we saw in our earlier discussion of kinship. We are also using a system of categories when we refer to people according to their age, sex (or, more accurately, gender), and family status, not to mention such categories as social class and ethnicity. In other words, social categories often establish boundaries to our personal networks. Social categories are not groups or even networks, but such distinctions can and do supply the *basis* for the formation of groups and influence the composition of networks.

Among the numerous criteria that may serve as bases for social classification, three are universally used in every society: age, gender, and kinship. Each of these criteria has been discussed in earlier chapters. Here we simply illustrate how such categories may structure larger patterns of social behavior and influence the composition of groups and networks.

Age

In any society, our behavior toward others and our expectations of others' behavior toward us are influenced to some extent by age classifications. A young adult will behave quite differently toward a child than toward an elderly person. A child will behave differently toward another child than toward an elderly adult. More important, age categories are extensively used to structure rights and responsibilities in society.

In the United States, juveniles, those who have not reached full social maturity, are not legally responsible for their actions. Even among those who are legally "adults" under law, some are denied the right to participate in national politics. You have to be eighteen years old to vote, thirty-two years old to run for president, and so on. Forced retirement (now illegal in some circumstances) automatically deprives some people of continued employment after they reach a particular age. In many societies, the elderly constitute a class of individuals with special rights and high social standing. Men called "graybeards" among the Turkmen of Iran supply the political leadership of their villages; they all are of an age when their maturity is demonstrated by their long gray beards. Among many of the peoples of East Africa, as we saw with the Pokot in Chapter 7, each person is a member of an age grade, or a formally recognized group of people of approximately the same age and enjoying certain responsibilities and rights. Members of the older grades are in charge of religious rites, and so on.

Gender

Like age, gender can be the basis for the organization of groups. In our own society, fraternities, sororities, men's clubs, and women's organizations all limit membership on the basis of sex. Groups restricted to members of a single gender have traditionally played a central role in our lives, notably organized religion, the armed forces (until World War II), the Supreme Court (until 1985), and many labor unions. Some of the organizations simply reflect the different employment opportunities available to men and women, while others, such as the Army, were until fairly recently restricted by law and custom to males. In industrialized societies, gender criteria are being used less and less often to limit participation in the economy. The reasons for this change are complex, but certainly the prominent role women have played in education and the increased importance of high technology have encouraged women to enter the public work force in large numbers. The shift to a preference for smaller families also facilitated women's new prominence in the labor market. But until quite recently, even in the advanced industrial nations, many jobs were legally restricted to men.

Recent psychological studies indicate that sex-role or gender differentiation remains a powerful feature of life in the United States, despite two decades of assaults on stereotypes

Despite advances in gender equality, many sex stereotypes persist. Here men and women participate in the same endeavor, but as part of sex segregated groups. (JOAN LIFTIN)

(Goleman 1988a). Laboratory research indicates that when men and women are provoked, they have equivalent physiological reactions (heartbeat, respiration, and so on), but when they are questioned, men and women give very different responses. Men say they are angry, but women say they are hurt or sad. Quite apart from male-female hormonal differences, the conclusion that men and women are socialized to express their emotions very differently, confirmed by numerous studies, seems to be related in large part to the way boys and girls are treated by their parents as infants. Boys are expected to show their anger, girls are not. Boys are trained to suppress their emotions, girls are encouraged to emphasize emotional closeness. While sex roles are changing in American society, emotional differences are likely to persist as long as we continue to expect different emotional reactions from men and women.

Single-gender groups play a significant role in structuring social interaction in most tribal societies. The men's associations in many Melanesian societies are well known for their strict sexual segregation. Among the Siuai, a group of pig herders and cultivators in the Solomon Islands, the men's clubhouses have resident demons who are said to kill any female who ventures too near (Oliver 1955). Among the Mae Enga of New Guinea, all males except the youngest boys live in men's houses and married men are permitted to visit their wives only under strictly regulated conditions. Rules of exogamy often force men to find their wives in alien groups, with resultant hostility between spouses: they don't trust each other. Unmarried Mae Enga men belong to their own organization, which conducts purification rituals called *sangai*, during which the bachelors go into complete seclusion and even the glimpse of a female footprint is contaminating. These bachelor retreats serve not only to reinforce masculine identification but also to display the fighting strength of a village by massing the men together. In short, the men seem to band together to reinforce a gender hierarchy; that is, their own dominant position (Meggitt 1964).

Not all such single-sex groupings are male, although male groupings tend to predominate in the public political and economic arenas. Among the Yoruba of Nigeria, women traders constitute an important economic group and maintain a virtual monopoly over certain commercial activities. How and to what extent gender is used to structure participation in social life and public affairs varies in accordance with the larger economic and political context. In societies where legal rights and ownership of productive resources are vested primarily in males, gender stratification is likely to be pervasive in social life.

Kinship

Kinship has been treated extensively in Chapter 12 but here we will briefly note how this principle can be used to form more inclusive groupings. The importance of kin ties to the dynamics of social relations is hard to overestimate. One Scottish folk rhyme expresses it nicely:

> Adam Smith
> Was disowned by all his kith
> But he was supported through thick and thin
> By all his kin   [Mair 1965:66].

"Kith" are neighbors and close friends, who in this rhyme were fickle in their loyalties. Steadfast, however, stood the kin. The same attitude toward kin is reflected in an old Arabic saying, which also shows how even relatives who are on bad terms with one another may close ranks against outsiders:

> I against my brother; my brother and I against my cousins; I, my brother, and my cousins against the outsider (Bates and Rassam 1983:260).

The family-based support system is the most important element in most individuals' lives.

Most people spend most of their lives in family units, sharing food, lodging, and income with others who are kin of one variety or another. Expectations of mutual aid and shared social and legal responsibility all are affected by the ties of kinship. Even far-flung relatives may constitute an important source of support for the individual.

In Turkey, for example, kin networks are based on the economic and social need for close rural-urban ties (Duben 1986). Despite the great increase in urban migration, most migrants to Istanbul are not economically or socially committed to city life. They go to the city in the hope of earning enough money to support their families back home. Almost all urban migrants maintain land and homes in their native villages if they can. Close ties to rural kin play a crucial role in these economic plans. Urban and rural family members share resources and visit one another frequently. When newcomers arrive in Istanbul, they generally stay with relatives. If the migrants are successful in finding work, they often send money to their kin in the country.

KINSHIP IDEOLOGY AND DESCENT GROUPS

Kinship systems do more than mold social behavior and establish a pattern of statuses and roles. They can also sort the members of a society into groups—collections of people who interact on a fairly regular basis and who have a sense of common identity. The most significant of such kin-based groups is the **descent group**, a group of consanguineal kin united by presumed lineal descent from a common ancestor. The primary importance of descent as a form of kinship reckoning is that it can be the basis for unambiguous membership in a group; it may further structure property rights and political obligations. This concept is usually de-

scribed as **descent ideology**, as the biological facts of ancestry are less important than social perceptions; and most descent ideologies emphasize only one of many means of calculating descent from a given ancestor. Genealogies and ideas of descent and ancestry are every bit as ideological as kinship terminologies. They are just two complementary kinds of kinship ideology that interact—just as do our ideas of public domain and private property.

In societies with a strong descent ideology, the descent group's sense of collective identity is based not solely on a presumption of common biological ancestry but on a whole set of beliefs, myths, and symbols that have considerable religious and social significance. Of course, much more than ideology holds any group together; as we shall see, members of descent groups provide one another with many essential services. Yet the descent ideology serves both to reinforce group solidarity and offer justification for what in other respects are highly pragmatic relationships.

Descent groups fall into two general categories: **unilineal descent groups**, in which descent is traced through one parental line only, and **nonunilineal descent groups**, in which descent may be traced through either parent or through both. The ideological basis of descent groups is perhaps most obvious in societies with unilineal descent.

Unilineal Descent Groups

Membership in a unilineal descent group is inherited through either the paternal or the maternal line, as the society dictates. Such groups are known as **patrilineal** and **matrilineal descent groups**, respectively, and are often divided into more specialized segments such as clan and lineage (of which we will speak shortly). The point to bear in mind is that descent ideology alone does not constitute a descent *group;* it defines a category of people who are qualified to become members.

Patrilineal Descent

Under patrilineal descent ideology, which is very widespread, all children are members of the descent group or groups of which their father is a member (Figure 13-1). If a man is a member of a particular group or has specific social rights attributable to descent, his children share this membership or set of rights. This does not mean they are less attached to their mothers than to their fathers. A mother simply does not pass on her descent-group membership or social rights to her children in such a society.

The female member of the society who marries out of her kin group (as generally she must) cannot provide new members for her lineage in the succeeding generation; her children are members of her husband's lineage, not her own. The significance of this arrangement for the role of women varies. The role of Yąnomamö women is extremely subordinate to that of men. Women's political roles are more im-

portant in many African patrilineal societies, such as the Tallensi of West Africa. Though one cannot predict a patrilineal descent ideology on the basis of the technology a society employs or of its level of political integration, patrilineal descent is the most common form found throughout the world. Still, one can say that it is more likely to be found in some contexts than in others; for example, most (but not all) nomadic pastoral societies are patrilineal (Pasternak 1976: 112–113).

Matrilineal Descent

Under a matrilineal concept of descent, all children are members (or at least eligible to be members) of their mother's group (see Figure 13-2). Again, this is not to say that children in societies with matrilineal descent ideology are less attached to their father than to their mother. A father is simply not a member of the same descent group as his children. Matrilineal descent ideology is far less common than pat-

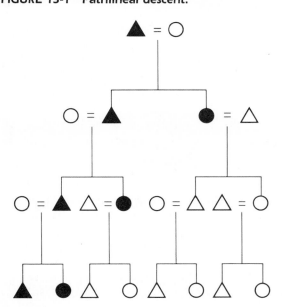

FIGURE 13-1   Patrilineal descent.

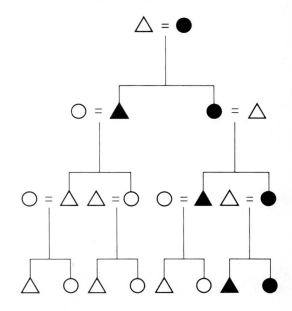

FIGURE 13.2   Matrilineal descent.

rilineal ideology, for reasons that are unclear.

Though one might suspect that women would have more political power than men in matrilineal descent groups, this is not necessarily—or even often—the case. The titular head of a western Pueblo matrilineal descent group was its oldest woman. As such she was accorded much respect and deference. But the person who took charge of the group's religious objects and directed its rituals was that woman's oldest brother. Indeed, women were barred from participating in certain rituals. Where, as with the Pueblo, matrilineality is combined with matrilocality (residence of a married couple in the wife's natal household), women may achieve higher status and more authority than they can in patrilineal and patrilocally constituted communities. A fairly similar pattern can be observed in most societies with matrilineal descent ideologies. In theory, while the descent group is defined by descent in the female line, in practice actual descent groups are headed by a woman's male siblings and/or her sons. Though the society, in keeping with the matrilineal descent ideology, may well prescribe that married couples establish residence in the wife's village and near the wife's natal home, men who marry within the village can also remain near the home where they were raised. This arrangement keeps a man near males of his kin group and facilitates strong male participation in public affairs.

Types of Unilineal Descent Groups

Unilineal descent groups follow certain basic patterns, whether the ideology involved happens to be matrilineal or patrilineal. Generally speaking, anthropologists categorize such groups according to their inclusiveness, from lineages through clans. Minimally, a descent group of any size or level of inclusiveness must have some recognized function in the larger society. It may be as important as owning resources the society needs or as simple as supplying individual identity.

A **lineage** is a unilineal descent group composed of people who trace their genealogies through specified links to a common ancestor. Depending on whether descent is traced through the maternal or paternal line, such groups are called **matrilineages** or **patrilineages**. Some societies have hierarchies of lineages, with individuals belonging to smaller minor lineages, as well as more inclusive larger lineages. The larger, more encompassing lineage is likely to be defined by descent from a more distant ancestor.

Kin groups may extend beyond the limits of known ancestry. Some societies have descent groups whose members believe themselves to be descended from a common ancestor and therefore have a sense of collective identity, even though they are unable to reconstruct exact genealogical connections. These are the groups known as *clans*, as we saw in Chapter 6—**matriclans** or **patriclans**, depending on which parent determines ego's affiliation. In many societies, a matriclan or patriclan will be named after a plant or animal, called a **totem** (from the Ojibwa Indian word *ototeman*, meaning "relative"). To clan members, the totem generally holds some special significance, usually related to the group's mythical ancestry. If little else, such symbols help to make a clan's sense of collective identity and unity more concrete.

Often clans appear to derive from lineages that became too large or too dispersed to keep track of their genealogies. Others may be formed when two or more lineages join forces, perhaps after a famine or invasion has reduced their populations, and invent a common ancestor to cement their union. The details of clan formation can only be guessed from the myths that commonly surround them. In some societies several clans band together and extend the rights of kinship to one another yet retain distinct identities for some purposes. Such a group, as we saw in Chapter 12, is called a *phratry*. An entire society, as we saw in Chapter 6, can be organized into two large descent groups, or *moieties*. Some moieties are not based on kinship. The Miwok Indians of California, for example, are divided into moieties, one called Land, the other Water. Alternatively, a society may be organized into several phratries, which are divided into a series of clans and subclans, which in turn are divided into lineages and sublineages. When groups of related phratries, lineages, and clans acquire a common name and identity, they become a tribe.

Tribes. The word "tribe" is used in several ways in anthropological literature. In its most general meaning, a tribe is a culturally distinct population that uses various principles of kinship and descent, a shared language, and a common history to distinguish its political limits. We are concerned here with a much more specific and restricted sense of the term. The **tribe** is a decentralized descent- and kinship-based grouping in which a number of subgroups are loosely linked to one another. Leadership is informal and constituent subgroups form cooperative alliances but these can easily shift or break up. There is no centralized system of authority, decision making, or social control, but the potential exists to unite a large number of local groups for common defense or warfare. The internal organization of the tribe is similar in principle to that of the lineage or clan. Just how the lineages are expressed and maintained varies from society to society. One system is for two or more groups, clans, or lineages to see themselves as related, even though each group generally will act autonomously in managing its affairs. However, the sense of common identity can be called into play for defense.

The Tiv of Nigeria, for example, are organized into **segmentary lineages**, descent groups in which minimal lineages are segments of minor lineages, minor lineages are segments of major lineages, and so on, with the result that all of the more than 800,000 Tiv are related in a single genealogical hierarchy (Bohannan 1965). Segmentary lineage systems may develop when tribes expand into territory already occupied by another group, as did the Nuer of Sudan in the nineteenth century (Sahlins 1961, Kelly 1985). It should be kept in mind that, however strongly a population expresses an ideology of patrilineal descent, ties of kinship among and through women are likely to be extremely important in practice: they will affect where one lives, whom one relies on, and many other aspects of domestic life (Gough 1971).

The segmentary system enables a particular lineage segment to enlist the aid of progressively larger and larger groups of related segments when its territory is threatened. Of course, the entire tribe rarely functions as a completely integrated whole. But the system does provide the basis for broad military alliances that endure as long as they are needed to ward off attack or defend newly acquired territory. The segmentary lineage system also serves to regulate the relations between the various segments. When conflicts erupt between minimal segments, for example, other minimal segments take the side of the party to whom they are most closely related. One segment joins another until minor and even higher-order segments are pitted against each other.

The Functions of Unilineal Descent Groups

No kin group in any society is formed simply because people perceive themselves to be related to one another through descent. For a group to exist at all, its members must have shared interests that give them a reason to join forces and view themselves as a collective entity. The anthropologist E. R. Leach has explained:

> Kin groups do not exist as things in themselves without regard to the rights and interests which center

in them. Membership of such a group is not established by genealogy alone. Properly speaking, two individuals can only be said to be of the same kinship *group* when they share some common interest — economic, legal, political, religious, as the case may be — and justify that sharing by reference to kinship ideology. The anthropological question that then arises is to discover these common interests   [Leach 1965:66, 1982].

Some anthropologists have argued that the common interests that usually underlie unilineal descent groups are economic: such groups develop when some permanent resource, such as land, requires allocation (Barth 1966). The Hopi of Arizona have a matrilineal descent system in which the clans and lineages hold rights to land and other property. They also are custodians of important rituals and ceremonies. Matrilines do not own land in an absolute sense; all productive land is seen as "owned" by an important deity, Maasaw, and men have the right of usufruct — that is, the right to use it. Once a man has planted a seed, however, it becomes the property of the clan of the woman for whom the man is planting, be it his wife, mother, or sister.

Hunting-and-gathering bands, whose ecological adaptation requires mobility and dispersal across large areas of varied landscape, seldom have lineages and clans. However, with the development of cultivation and the changes that accompany it — a sedentary way of life, increased population density, and exclusive ties to specific territories — we find unilineal descent groups proliferating, presumably to protect access to resources.

A related factor in the evolution of unilineal descent groups may have been warfare. After all, property does not have to be protected until someone else wants it. In a sample of a large number of societies, fighting between communities or between larger territorial groups was found to be common in 94 percent of those with a unilineal descent system (Ember et al. 1974). There appears to be a causal association between unilineality and warfare, although the precise linkages are complex.

Intergroup fighting may favor customs and institutions that provide affiliation with clearly defined groups of people who can be relied upon in time of need. In societies with a high level of political development, such affiliation may be provided by membership in a centralized political unit. But when political development is not so advanced, unilineal descent may constitute an especially fitting response to the challenge of competing groups (Pasternak 1976:107–108). Unilineal descent groups are not, however, incompatible with state forms of political organization. In some regions of the Middle East, where state-dominated societies have been in existence longer than anywhere else in the world, tribes or unilineal descent groups are important as a means of promoting local groups' autonomy in the face of powerful governments, with their tax collectors and administrators. The same may be true of China, where clan organization was important in some regions.

Whatever the common interests that prompt the development of unilineal descent groups, it is clear that such groups serve many important functions for their members. The regulation of marriage is one such function, as we saw in our discussion of the Yąnomamö. In societies with unilineal descent ideologies, lineages and clans (and very often phratries as well) are usually exogamous — that is, marriage within one's own descent group is strictly forbidden. By forcing its members to look to other groups for marital and sexual partners, the kin group presumably saves itself a good deal of internal discord. Perhaps more important, rules of exogamy create ties of alliance and cooperation between kin groups — ties that can be invaluable when resources are scarce and warfare is common.

Another extremely important function of unilineal descent groups is the regulation of land use. In patrilineal and matrilineal societies, it is often the descent group, rather than individuals or the village as a whole, that owns the land, allocating plots to its members for their use. By virtue of affiliation with a descent group, individuals have rights to the land on which they plant their crops or graze their animals. The descent group may also control other essential resources, such as water, and may have collective ownership of the tools that its members use to make their living. This arrangement is often called "corporate" ownership.

In addition to regulating marriage and allocating resources, unilineal descent groups provide mutual aid and support to their members. People who belong to the same descent group are bound together by a code of reciprocal rights and obligations. The strength of this bond varies with the closeness of the kinship ties. Mutual obligations between the members of the same lineage, for example, are usually quite strongly felt; those between members of the same clan somewhat less so; and the members of the same phratry or tribe are often so distantly related and so widely dispersed that they may feel virtually no obligation toward one another.

The mutual aid and support provided by unilineal descent groups cover both political and economic activities. In some unilineal societies, the entire lineage is held accountable for the actions of individual members if they infringe on the rights of members of other lineages. If a person murders a man from another lineage, for example, vengeance may justifiably be inflicted on any of the slayer's kin. By the same token, individuals can depend on their kin to help them exact justice for wrongs committed by members of other descent groups. In some societies people also have the right to expect food from members of their descent group when their own crops fail. In this case unilineal descent groups serve to redistribute wealth in the absence of such mechanisms as welfare systems and unemployment insurance.

Nonunilineal Descent Groups

Many of the societies that early anthropologists encountered had strongly unilineal descent ideologies, which led them to expect that most other societies in the world also had unilineal descent groups. The one large and obvious exception to unilineal rule—European and American society—was explained as the result of industrialism. In complex industrial societies, individuals could obtain help from many different sources: employers, friends, government agencies, clinics, and so on. Therefore, they did not have to align themselves with a strictly defined kin group.

This assumption proved to be false. Eventually anthropologists encountered many nonindustrial societies in which descent ideology was less strongly enforced, more ambiguous, or used less extensively as the basis of group formation than in unilineal societies. These peoples were not only nonindustrial; they were often hunter-gatherers, with exceedingly simple technologies. This discovery laid to rest the notion that nonunilineal descent was an idiosyncrasy of complex societies.

Anthropologists classify nonunilineal descent groups into two basic types, ambilineal and bilateral.

Ambilineal Descent

In societies with an **ambilineal descent** ideology, a person affiliates with kin groups on the basis of ties traced through either the paternal or the maternal line. In some ambilineal societies, a person is expected at some point to choose among the various kin groups to which he or she is in some way lineally related. In other ambilineal societies, a person is free to move from one descent group to another, as long as he or she affiliates with only one group at a time. And in still others, a person may affiliate, for whatever different purposes, with as many groups to which he or she claims ties.

Ambilineal descent systems, then, have more flexibility than do unilineal systems; they leave more room for individual choice concerning kin-group affiliation. On the Gilbert Islands in the Pacific, for example, membership in a land-holding ambilineal descent group, called *ooi*, is open to all individuals who can trace their descent to the person who originally owned the *ooi*'s land. If one *ooi* becomes overcrowded, people will affiliate themselves with another *ooi* that is short of heirs (Goodenough, 1955). As a result, the distribution of people in the various *ooi* is invariably guided by population pressure. Such flexibility may be quite useful, but it is achieved at the cost of clear-cut loyalties.

The same is true of ambilineal societies in general: as a rule, the looser the membership rules of the descent group, the less cohesive it is and the less impact it has on its members' day-to-day lives. In ambilineal societies in which the individual must choose a single descent group to affiliate with permanently, the functions served by descent groups are often similar to those in unilineal societies: collective ownership of land and other productive resources, regulation of marriage through rules of exogamy, provision of mutual aid and support. But when ambilineal descent permits people to have multiple or temporary descent-group affiliations, the functions of the descent groups tend to be fewer and less critical.

Bilateral Descent

With **bilateral descent,** the system that we use in our own society, individuals define themselves as being at the center of a group of kin composed more or less equally of their mothers' and fathers' relatives of all kinds—grandparents, aunts and uncles, great aunts and great uncles, cousins and second cousins, nieces and nephews, and of course the nuclear family.[1]

The resulting collection of bilateral kin,

called the **kindred,** is significantly different from the descent groups we have discussed so far. Indeed, a kindred is not a group at all in the true sense of the word, for most of its members do not perceive themselves as having a collective identity. Nor is there any reason why they should, since each member of a given kindred has a different kindred from everyone else (except siblings). Ego's kindred, for example, is not the same as his parents' kindreds, for his own combines relatives from both of theirs. And ego's kindred has only half its members in common with his cousin's kindred. A kindred, then, is not technically a group but a *network*, a set of interlocking social relations as seen by the ego to whom they are all related. This is why anthropologists refer to a kindred as being ego-oriented rather than ancestor-oriented. While descent groups consist of people who have a real or fictive ancestor (along with all the members of their group) in common, kindreds consist of people who have a relative (ego) in common.

A kindred, then, exists only in relation to one person. Furthermore, it changes through time. When we are children, our kindred consists of contemporaries and older kin; as we grow and bear children, and as our older kin die, the membership of our kindred shifts to contemporaries and younger kin. And when we die, our kindred ceases to have any meaning—unlike descent groups, which are self-renewing.

Because of its personal, changeable, and temporary character, the kindred is ordinarily less powerful than the unilineal descent group. While it may still regulate marriage through rules of exogamy, it generally provides fewer essential services for its members. In our own society, kindred may be called on for help, but

---

[1]The list could extend further, but the line is usually drawn at second cousins (ego's parents' first cousins). Otherwise, the kin group would become too large and too complicated.

they are usually assembled only for ceremonial occasions—when ego is christened, married, or buried. This type of loosely organized network is particularly well suited to a society that places a premium on personal independence and mobility, of which our own is a prime example.

In nonindustrial societies, however, the kindred may form ad hoc associations to perform important functions. For example, among the Iban of Borneo, a man who wishes to organize a headhunting or trading party calls on members of his kindred, who call on members of theirs. In this way, a large group is assembled in an astonishingly short time (Freeman 1961).

In some societies with bilateral concepts of descent, groups are more clearly structured and lend themselves to corporate enterprises. Among the nomadic reindeer-herding Lapps of northern Scandinavia, for example, residential kin groups are formed on the basis of bilateral descent, with sibling ties forming the core of such groupings (Pehrson 1957). Usually a group of brothers with their wives and children will band together, with other consanguineal kin attaching themselves to the sibling core. Although an individual may belong to several bands during his lifetime, each affiliation will be based on bilaterally reckoned genealogical links.

Descent, Ideology, and Behavior

It is a mistake to assume that all societies with the same descent ideology exhibit similar patterns of behavior with regard to kinship. Just as pastoralism takes different forms among the Yörük and the Pokot, and horticulture among the Yąnomamö and the western Pueblo, so a descent ideology may be reflected in different ways of behaving and thus we see different types of descent groups. As we suggested earlier, people everywhere always weigh the costs and benefits of various courses of action before they come to a final decision. Social rules alone, including rules of descent and kinship, can only partially predict how a person will act in a given situation; they are simply one among many important factors a person will consider. Systems of descent and kinship can never be rigid constructs.

ETHNICITY

Some criteria that define social categories are universal; others are not. In the case of more complex societies, ethnicity is a particularly important criterion. **Ethnicity** is a basis for categories that are rooted in socially perceived differences in national origin, language, and/or religion. In many respects, ethnicity resembles descent ideology: it stresses one's origins as part of one's social identity. Any society is the product of a long and varied historical process. People, whether literate or not, are conscious of this process, and often an awareness of the group's past serves to validate the present. Historical themes are used to inspire group loyalty, patriotism, loyalty to an organization such as an army or a religious body.

The Yörük of Turkey, whose pastoral way of life was described in Chapter 7, take pride in their Central Asian ancestry and the fact that they are among the first Turkish peoples to have settled in the region. While such an awareness of the past is a source of unity, it also emphasizes that which sets one segment of the population apart from others. What emerges is a "we–they" distinction. Within our society Native Americans, African Americans, Chicanos, Jews, Puerto Ricans, Chinese Americans, Japanese Americans, Irish Americans, Italian Americans, and Polish Americans are significant ethnic categories. Each group has a sense of a unique identity, derived from a sense of history, which other groups do not share. Ref-

In urban centers, members of different social classes and ethnic groups often find themselves in close proximity, as in this park in LaPaz, Bolivia. Proximity, however, does not always mean that people from different backgrounds will mix. (ULRIKE WELSCH)

erences to race, as in "racial equality" or "racial discrimination," are in fact usually references to ethnicity.

The ethnic categories in any state-organized society can be numerous and varied. Accra, the capital of Ghana, for example, encompasses more than eighty ethnic groups. A study of 423 residents in eleven apartment buildings on a single street in Accra revealed twenty-three distinct ethnic groups and fourteen first languages (Sanjek 1977). Roger Sanjek found a good deal of interaction among these ethnic groups, including intermarriage and widespread multilingualism. In one especially complex household he found representatives of three ethnic groups who regularly spoke seven languages. When asked to identify the "tribes" living in Accra, each of the local subjects who were sampled listed between one and fifty-five ethnic terms; the mean number was ten. Thus, Sanjek concluded, the residents of Accra are typically aware of the ethnic diversity, but no one person comprehends the total picture.

Because ethnic categories are culturally defined, they can be manipulated and changed.

The definition of an individual's ethnicity changes with his or her situation. In some circumstances, for example, each of us might identify ourselves by emphasizing the national origin of one of our many ancestors, and in other circumstances we might emphasize an ancestor of different national and religious origin.

A striking example of ethnic transformation associated with economic change can be seen in the case of the Fur of the Sudan. These are hoe-agriculture people, but some of them are abandoning their separate identity to become part of the Arabic-speaking, nomadic, cattle-herding society known as the Baggara. (Oddly enough, this process has come about not because people were being pushed off the land and into a nomadic group but because they had accumulated wealth to invest, and traditional Fur society provides no outlet for it.) But the Fur cannot simply leave the land and take up cattle herding without sacrificing an important part of their ethnic identity. As the Norwegian anthropologist Frederik Barth explains it, each subsistence strategy entails a whole style of life, which is subsumed under the ethnic label Fur or Baggara (Barth 1969:26). A Fur who herds cattle becomes a Baggara.

Many ethnic classifications largely define social roles. Members of some ethnic minorities, for example, are usually traders, sometimes to the exclusion of the native majority. The Chinese in Southeast Asia and the Asians in East Africa are two prominent examples. Brian Foster has examined the same phenomenon in Thailand, where the Mons are the traders. Originally from Burma, this group is similar to the Thai people in most ways except language. But the Mons who are traders are less likely to be assimilated into the larger society than Mons who are not traders. Foster hypothesizes that ethnic distinctions serve important functions. "Ethnic differences set off commercial people from the society around them in such a way as to (1) minimize the stress inherent in market transactions, and (2) free the merchants from the social constraints of an anticommercial peasant society that would otherwise strangle commercial enterprise" (Foster 1974:5). Traditional Thai society stressed generosity, lack of profit in dealings with others, and extreme civility to avoid conflict and competition. So long as villages were self-sufficient, these values proved viable. But as the possibilities for extensive outside trade developed, Thais faced the choice of either forgoing trade or flouting social expectations—a serious conflict. Only an outsider could violate the social rules without endangering the society.

When ethnic differences are expressed in economic deprivation or monopoly of a resource, they do not generally promote harmonious relations. Relations between members of different ethnic groupings within a nation-state are frequently characterized by conflict. Even societies that pride themselves on democratic access to political power, such as the United States and Great Britain, are not immune to such conflict. In 1985 Great Britain was rocked by violent confrontations between native Britons and ethnic Asian immigrants. In West Germany, 1.4 million Turkish "guest workers" are viewed with some misgivings by the German majority. Northern Ireland has been the scene of conflict between Protestants and Catholics for centuries. Southeast Asia seethes with constant hostility between the indigenous populations and communities of Chinese and Indian nationals involved in trade and commerce.

A common, if deplorable, feature of polyethnic societies is the use of ethnic categories to restrict access to resources or full participation in political decision making. This process can be seen most clearly when members of the dominant group in a society discriminate against other ethnic groups. In this country until quite recently, African Americans and members of other ethnic categories were routinely refused housing in "white" neighborhoods, enrollment in "white" schools, and access to many hotels, restaurants, and other public accommodations. Such restrictions expressed in terms of ethnic separateness often serve to maintain preferential access to resources for some members of society at the expense of others.

At the same time, ethnic distinctions, like social distinctions based on age and gender, may be the basis for the formation of special action groups. In the United States, members of ethnic minorities have joined in a large number of formal organizations to enhance their status and combat discrimination by the dominant society. The same process of ethnic-group formation can be seen in other societies as well. The Ibo of Nigeria who have migrated from the tribal territory to the cities, for example, have

formed tribal associations to assist newcomers, sponsor events that preserve Ibo culture, start businesses, educate children, and exert political pressure. In many respects, the very idea of ethnic identity is an important means by which people adapt to the realities of life in complex societies. By stressing a special identity and a separate heritage, thus emphasizing the "we–they" distinction, they create conditions that favor concerted and forceful action.

An experiment conducted by Charles Korte and Stanley Milgram (1970) revealed just how important ethnic boundaries can be. These researchers asked white volunteers in Los Angeles to send messages to eighteen "target" individuals in New York, nine white and nine black. The targets were not known personally to the senders, so the messages had to be passed through intermediaries, each of whom was requested either to pass the message to the target

Australian Aborigines are now organizing to secure their rights in a land that since colonization in the eighteenth century has largely ignored them. This "Aboriginal Embassy" is part of a political movement in Brisbane. (IRVEN DEVORE/ANTHRO-PHOTO)

or to relay it to someone else who might be able to do so. Five hundred and forty messages were sent from Los Angeles. Thirty-three percent of those aimed at white targets reached their destinations, while only 13 percent of those aimed at black targets were delivered. This study thus identified ethnic categories as important factors in the establishment of network boundaries. More recently the 1980 census revealed that less than 2 percent of those Americans who identified themselves as black had spouses who were not also black, and 85 percent of those who reported themselves as Jewish had Jewish spouses (*New York Times*, February 11, 1985).

NETWORKS

While social categories and groups are important, it is obvious that the business of society is also carried on through networks that connect people who may never join forces as a group. A **network** is a web of social ties of various kinds. From the customary vantage point, the individual is at the center of the network, connected with others by an intricate set of links, both direct and indirect. Although this person may perceive many of these links, certain indirect ties may become apparent only when an outside observer studies patterns of interaction.

It is clear that an individual's network of contacts serves many vital functions. It can help one accomplish a particular task or solve a given problem. It can provide intermediaries to be used as contacts to obtain information or to send messages. Furthermore, a person's network offers an important measure of psychological support. It "provides him with a surrounding field of friends and relatives who help give his life meaning, establish and maintain the norms by which he regulates his behavior, and protect him from the impersonal world beyond" (Bott 1957:200).

How Networks Vary

Like groups, networks vary in many ways. One way is simply the nature of the contacts a person has. Although one might assume that a person with many contacts could obtain help or communicate more quickly than one with fewer, this is not necessarily the case. The efficacy of a network also depends on who one's contacts are. The person whose contacts include a few very influential people often establishes a more effective network than the person whose contacts include more people but less powerful ones.

Networks vary also in the number of interests served by individual relationships. One may be both lawyer and cousin to another person. Generally speaking, the more interests served by a relationship, the stronger the tie. A lawyer is more likely to extend herself for the client who also happens to be her brother-in-law than she is for the client with whom she has no other ties.

Finally, a network varies in *density*—that is, it may be closely or loosely knit. If an individual's contacts are also linked to one another through other ties, the network is said to have a high density. This is the case in many homogeneous populations in which everyone is known to everyone else, and all interact on a regular basis. In complex societies such as our own, many of the contacts in a person's network are unknown to one another, being linked only indirectly through their individual relationships with that person.

Dyadic (Two-Person) Relationships

One prevalent feature of networks is the complex systems that may arise from the relationships between pairs of people. Such dyadic relationships take many forms, from the intense, often highly emotional ties of lovers to the more relaxed relations between old friends to the surface camaraderie of two people engaged in a business transaction. Any person's significant relationships are necessarily limited: there are practical limits to the number of close friends one can have and still maintain that the ties are in fact intimate. (We tend to discount the friendship of those who claim to be best friends with too many others!) When individuals have business to transact with strangers, particularly those of higher social or political rank or belonging to other ethnic groups, a common way of making contact is through intermediaries.

Intermediaries

In the Middle East, people who seek official favors, sometimes even routine administrative action, often approach administrators through intermediaries known to both parties. This tactic tends to personalize what would otherwise be an impersonal transaction. In the same part of the world, marriages are often arranged by families rather than by individual initiative. In such cases, the family of the boy makes its overtures to the prospective bride's family through an intermediary. They would never do so in person, as a negative answer would be a blow to family pride. In our own society we use lawyers in very similar ways; they may settle disputes between neighbors, settle damage claims out of court, or represent one in a court of law. The use of such go-betweens or brokers to mediate relationships or forge new ties helps a great deal to extend an individual's network.

The Patron–Client Relationship

One two-person relationship has attracted considerable attention: the **patron–client relationship,** a mutually obligatory arrangement between an individual who has authority, social status, wealth, or some other personal resource (the patron) and another individual who benefits from his or her support or influence (the client). Although their relationship is not symmetrical, in that one individual has a measure of control over the actions of the other, they have mutual obligations of loyalty. The patron is just as obligated as the client to fulfill the terms of the relationship. A person may be a patron in one situation and a client in another, depending on what he or she has to offer in the specific circumstances.

Her observation of patron–client networks in Bombay convinced Karen Michaelson (1976) of the pervasiveness and importance of patronage. As she points out, relationships between patrons and clients, and among patrons, are extremely useful to the social scientist because of what they reveal about the surrounding social, political, and economic climate, and about the historical processes that shaped them. Most societies have an official system, composed of formal institutions (codified laws, principles of government) at some variance from the way things actually work at the local level. When the official system fails to deliver, individuals tend to seek other solutions. Very often patronage plays an extremely important part in determining what happens at the local level. In effect, these patron–client networks serve to bridge the gap between various levels of social organization, be it family, caste, or government. The patron may be seen as a mediator between the different levels. In Bombay, Michaelson found, patron–client relationships aid in the dissemination of goods, the exchange of labor, and the distribution of power. For example, in the overcrowded city and environs of Bombay there are many housing developments and formal rules for getting into them, yet most people actually find their homes through friends of friends—that is, through patronage networks.

Overlapping Networks

While two-person relationships, such as those between patrons and clients, are important, there is more to social networks than merely a compounding of two-person transactions. Urban social structures are built up from subsets of networks that link quite diverse groups—ethnic groups, clubs, unions, trade associations, and the like (Foster and Seidman 1982). Membership in such groups and in informal cliques as well can be of great importance. Consider the activities of a business executive or politician who joins organizations of all sorts to "get ahead." The fluidity of larger, complex social structures rests ultimately on ever-changing interrelationships among overlapping groups and associations. The African American businessman who is at once a member of the chamber of commerce, the Rotary Club, his local church, a national fraternal organization, and the black caucus of his political party is participating in diverse but overlapping spheres of activity. Such multiple associations on the part of many individuals are an important element in the structure of the larger society. The businessman's network serves to link a number of subsets or social groups.

INEQUALITY AND SOCIAL STRATIFICATION

Despite the importance of networks and multiple associations, in complex societies entire groups may have very little or no access to processes of decision making and little access to the resources of the larger society. A society in which extensive subpopulations are accorded differential treatment is said to be **stratified.**

In no society do all people enjoy equal prestige or equal ability to participate in all social and economic activities. Even within the simple society of the San people, described in Chapter 5, some men acquire the title of "headman" and are accorded great respect. The agricultural Algonquin of the American northeast coast selected some women as leaders, or *sachems*, but most women could not aspire to this position. Many members of a society often have limited access to resources, little support to draw upon in conflict, and little likelihood of marrying and raising a family. Among the Tiwi of Northern Australia, for example, many men traditionally failed to marry or married only in middle age (Hart and Pilling 1960). Older men, through astute negotiation using their accumulated social credits and social status, acquired large numbers of wives, creating a shortage of mates for their peers.

While inequality of this sort may entail great hardship for some members of a society, it is not the same as socioeconomic stratification. Stratification is a process by which entire segments of a population are disadvantaged in comparison with other members of the same society. Moreover, this disadvantaged position is largely passed on to their children. They come to be not only disadvantaged but systematically constrained or exploited by other segments of the population over a substantial period of time. In this sense the groupings formed in stratified societies perpetuate inequality, and such inequality has little to do with the personal strengths or weaknesses of individuals. We can understand this phenomenon better if we concentrate on three concepts that describe stratification: class, caste, and slavery.

Class

Most modern state societies, including our own, can be viewed as stratified to some degree along lines of social and economic class. The term **social class** is used to describe people who have generally similar educational histories, job opportunities, and social standing. The term implies some consciousness of membership in a distinctive social group that is ranked in relation to others and is replicated over generations. Associated with each social class in a society is a differential degree of access to status and prestige, and the ability to pass both on to one's children.

Closely related to social class is **economic class,** a group that is defined by the economic position of its members in relation to the means of production in the society—the wealth and relative economic control they may exercise. Again there is the presumption that in societies marked by economic class distinctions, each class tends to replicate or perpetuate itself. Thus in a society that includes a class of landless farmers, one would expect most of the children of this group to remain in the same condition. People who form a distinctive economic grouping may or may not also form a social class. In general, social standing, political power, and economic position are closely interrelated.

Social classes are not cut-and-dried categories. It can be difficult to define the boundaries and differentiate among members of social classes. Indeed, the whole idea of class is controversial, and few social scientists now consider social or economic class as the only means for describing stratification or inequality in a society. Certainly stratification and inequality expressed along ethnic and gender lines are also of great importance (Smith 1984). Gender stratification is distinct from social class because it cuts across most if not all the criteria that define class. Sociologists have identified in American society a number of dimensions of social-class membership—power, job prestige, wealth, education, family position, and ethnic derivation, to name a few. Yet these variables do not correlate neatly.

In general, social class is closely related to political power and economic position. Native Americans in the United States, such as this Navajo family, have had very little access to influential, well-paying, or prestigious jobs, so they have tended to remain near the bottom of our social ladder. (SHOSTAK/ANTHRO-PHOTO)

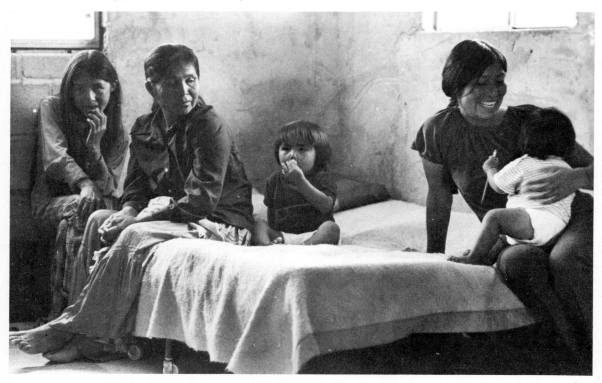

An Italian-American building contractor may have a great deal of money and considerable power in local politics but less prestige than a middle-income college professor with a similar background. The daughter of the same contractor may enter a low-paying clerical job while her brother goes into a prestigious law firm. The professor's children may find employment in a trade such as carpentry more to their liking than a profession. Thus such categories as "upper class," "middle class," and "working class" tell us only a little about American society. But at the same time, popular perceptions of such distinctions can be important: individuals spread along a very broad spectrum of occupation, income, and education regard themselves as middle-class. Social class is useful as a means of describing some dimensions of social identity and the relative position (real or perceived) of individuals in a stratified society.

Economic class is also an analytic construct, but it is perhaps somewhat easier to delineate with precision than the concept of social class. The concept of economic class is used by the anthropologist or sociologist to describe the way people fit into an economic system. The approach most commonly taken is to see how people relate to the organization of production: Do they sell their labor? Do they control primary resources? Do they control capital and the labor of others? Those who occupy a similar position in the productive system often share political interests—either in maintaining or in changing the economic system. But it may be difficult for members of such economic classes to organize themselves, particularly if they already lack political power. Moreover, it is often the case that people do not clearly perceive their own economic interests.

Perceptions of Class and Class Interest

It is doubtful that the various classes of a single society do in fact have truly separate value systems. Some Americans who oppose spending public money on improving education and job opportunities for the poor have argued that it is not inequality of opportunity that defeats the poor in the schools and in the job market but rather a lack of initiative and a work ethic. The evidence, however, is otherwise. Often what may appear to be "lack of initiative" is actually a realistic appraisal of the chances of success, given the opportunities available. Also, as we have seen in the case of Los Peloteros, economically deprived people may place a premium on sharing and reciprocity as a survival technique. As a consequence it becomes very difficult for any individual family or person to accumulate enough resources to make drastic changes in lifestyle.

Behind these vaguely differentiated stereotypes, some attitudes cut across class lines. In the United States, for example, materialism and an interest in job security are the preserve of no one class. Furthermore, any tendency for the so-called upper class to vote the same way or express similar interests is deeply rooted in economic self-interest rather than simply an expression of a value system. More significant than any value system is whether perceptions of social or economic class are translated into social action.

Some societies and some classes are probably more class-conscious than others. Not surprisingly, members of the American upper class find their networks and associations, derived in part from participation in select schools, clubs, and the like, useful in promoting their economic advantages. This advantage is certainly reflected in a self-conscious identification with others who have similar values, backgrounds, and economic interests. But class consciousness can vary with political currents. Political parties associated with working-class or minority interests draw heavily for support on people whose economic interests are at some remove from those of people who make their living by physical labor.

Also, rapid changes in the social or political structure of a society may cause disadvantaged segments of the society to realize that they have little to lose by organizing to resist exploitation that earlier they took for granted. Artisans who may have long accepted low pay in traditional workshops, for example, may decide to organize a union once they are brought together in large numbers in a modern factory. As Thomas Collins found in his study of the Memphis garbage strike of 1965 (1974), African American workers who had long accepted discrimination in pay and working conditions were suddenly galvanized into resistance. Far from passive, they organized unions and struck when circumstances were suitable.

Caste-Stratified Societies

Although social classes may perpetuate themselves, a family can change its class membership, sometimes in a relatively short time, sometimes over the course of generations. **Castes,** on the other hand, resemble a series of ranked ethnic groupings, each closed and each defined by its relative position. Membership in a caste is fixed at birth and usually is unchangeable. An Indian boy born into the Brahman (priestly) caste will always be a member of that caste, whether or not he ever performs a ritual. One must marry endogamously within the caste, and all of one's descendants will be members of the same caste despite changes in wealth, education, and class.

Caste in India

India is often cited as the classic example of a caste society. It should be noted, however, that caste observances are illegal in modern India, where all citizens are presumed to be equal under law. Nevertheless, de facto caste organization and social distinctions made on this basis are evident in many ways and are often the

The lives of many in class or caste stratified societies are largely spent "on the outside, looking in" in the sense that the resources, entertainment, and rewards of the elite are visible but unobtainable. (GEORGE BELLEROSE/STOCK, BOSTON)

subjects of bitter social commentary in Indian newspapers, novels, and films.

According to Hindu belief, humankind is divided into four basic categories: Brahmans (priests), Kshatriya (warriors and rulers), Vaishya (tradesmen), and Shudra (servants). The rest of the Hindu community, regarded as outside the overall religious hierarchy, was until recently called "Untouchable." These five macrogroups are further subdivided into about 3,000 subcastes: the goldsmiths, the blacksmiths, the potters, the water carriers, the barbers, the shoemakers, the oil pressers, the washermen, and so on. The term often used for these occupational subcastes is *jati*. The system of castes, or jatis, has to be understood as it functions in a particular locality, as the organization varies. In Gopalpur village, in southern India, for example, Alan Beals (1962) identified about 15 jatis comprising 113 households. The larger region of which Gopalpur is a part has about 50 jatis. Each jati is associated with definite economic, social, and ceremonial roles. While members of the castes of higher rank, such as the Brahmans, tend to be landowners, some are not. Many of the richest villagers are members of middle-ranked castes, and anyone of any caste can be poor.

Each caste, or jati, has its own occupational role and its own status, ranging from the Brahmans at the very top of the hierarchy to the Harijans—the so-called Untouchables, who were considered spiritually unclean and whose occupations traditionally reflected this belief. They served society in the most menial of jobs or engaged in such activities as leather working, which were thought to be "polluting." Often such a group is forced to live at the periphery of the community.

In keeping with Hindu belief, the various levels of status are perceived as degrees of ritual purity. Every general category must guard itself against pollution from intimate contact with members of lower categories (Mayer 1968). The degree of pollution depends on the caste distance between the people involved. Theoretically, anyone who eats with or has sexual intercourse with a member of a lower spiritual category has been polluted and must undergo purification. The code is not simple for the people who follow it closely, but many care little for strict adherence to it.

Discussions of the Indian caste system often focus on these religious rules. But underlying the religious rules is an extremely pragmatic economic system, based on the familiar principle of the "haves" benefiting from the labor of the "have-nots." In most Indian villages the resident jatis are joined in a complex network

of rights and obligations, whereby each individual has a predetermined task and a predetermined reward. Ultimately, of course, those who receive the most services are the landowners, often of high caste; in return they provide those who work the land with a plot on which to build a house and with a yearly allowance of grain. The grain the landowners do not distribute to the other castes is sold. Thus the lower castes may eat, but the higher castes profit. In sum, the religious code serves as a justification for an economic system that is extremely beneficial to the top castes.

Castelike Systems

Some theorists claim that India is not only the classic example of a caste society, it is the only example—that the caste system has been defined on the model of India and no other society has a comparably rigid system. According to other social scientists, however, caste systems, or at least castelike systems, exist in Polynesia, South Africa, Japan, Guatemala, and the Arabian Peninsula as well as in India. Indeed, it has been argued that African Americans in the southern United States formed a caste (Berreman 1972).

South Africa today is an extreme example: blacks are disadvantaged not only by a social position ascribed at birth by reason of their skin color but by the laws that prohibit sexual intercourse between races and forbid blacks to reside in white towns, or to use the same bathrooms, drinking fountains, and beaches as whites. One thing that characterizes caste distinction, in India and elsewhere, is that the boundaries separating stratified groups are reinforced by ideology: in India by the notion of spiritual cleanliness, in South Africa and even in North America by the notion of racial superiority. Certain minorities, not all by any means, are subordinated socially, politically, and economically in countries as diverse as Israel, the United States, the Soviet Union, New Zealand, Japan, and England—to name only a few.

Recently an educational controversy has again raised the issue of caste or castelike social categories in the United States. Educators have long been troubled by the fact that there is a gap of approximately 15 percentile points between the IQ scores of African Americans and whites in America. The width of the gap varies from decade to decade but it has been observed for the last seventy years (Goleman 1988b). Obviously the gap does not apply to all African Americans, and the scores of those who go on to attend university are virtually indistinguishable from those of whites. The gap is based on the averages of millions of test scores, and there are African Americans among the highest 1 percent and whites among the very lowest scores. Nevertheless, the gap is significant because IQ scores are good predictors of academic success. It has been attributed to everything from the home life of the individuals tested to their heredity. Anthropologists and many other scientists have long believed that the tests themselves are culturally biased and that they reflect the socioeconomic status of the people who devise them. New studies confirm this suspicion but also point to the castelike stratification that is reflected in the test scores.

The new theory is that African Americans and some other minorities—Mexican Americans, American Indians, native Hawaiians—are in a castelike position similar to that of minority castes elsewhere in the world, such as the Harijan of India and the Maoris of New Zealand. The IQ test scores of these children, too, are approximately 10 points lower than those of other children in their countries. John Ogbu, a Nigerian-born anthropologist, contends that this gap is found wherever castelike divisions exist in society (cited in Goleman 1988b:23). The divisions need not be based on race but may be based on religion, tribal identity, or ethnicity. Such gaps in IQ scores reflecting caste lines are found in many countries.

Among the social concomitants of belonging to a castelike minority are pervasive prejudice, lack of political and economic power, and the fact of being raised with a very limited set of expectations. Children reared in such an environment of discrimination and poverty have very little prospect of desirable employment and do not see education as making much of a difference.

When members of a subordinate caste move to a country where they do not face discrimination, their IQ scores rise dramatically. George DeVos, an anthropologist, has studied the IQ scores of a Japanese minority caste, the Burakumi, who were traditionally thought to be "unclean" because they worked as tanners. In Japan their test scores reflected their disadvantaged social and economic position; the gap between the scores of Burakumi and Japanese children was similar to the gap between the scores of African Americans and whites in the United States. But, Burakumi children whose families migrated to the United States achieved scores identical to those of other Japanese-American children (5 to 11 points higher than average white scores) (Goleman 1988b:24).

Slavery

An expression of extreme stratification is **slavery,** a practice that permits some people within a society to own other persons and to claim the right to their labor. Slavery is no longer practiced or at least recognized as such. Slavery does not constitute a type of society, as the conditions of slaves and the kinds of services they owed their masters varied among the societies in which slavery was practiced. In some cases slaves were bought and sold like animals; they had no rights whatsoever. At the other extreme, some societies allowed their slaves to own property, to take on responsible and respected work, and to earn their freedom. In the Middle East in medieval times, for example, slaves owned by the sultan became generals and governors, with all the powers and prestige that such offices imply.

Slavery in the antebellum American South is the most familiar instance of the system, but this was actually a brief and atypical episode in comparison with the widespread and long-standing slave systems that were prevalent in other parts of the world. Slavery was common in Africa long before Arabs and Europeans arrived on the scene. Four-fifths of the African societies included in G. P. Murdock's *Ethnographic Atlas* (1967) practiced slavery. Likewise, slavery existed in two-thirds of the societies bordering on the Mediterranean and more than half of those in Asia. And before the arrival of the European colonists, over one-fourth of the Native American societies of North and South America including some hunting-and-gathering bands had forms of slavery (Bourguignon and Greenbaum 1973).

Slavery is associated with certain subsistence patterns. It has been present but relatively rare in hunting-and-gathering societies. But it has existed in more than half the world's intensive agricultural societies, where landowners could benefit greatly from the increased labor supply. With the advent of industrialism, slavery has largely disappeared (Coult and Habenstein 1965). The reasons for its demise, unfortunately, have less to do with an improvement in human morality than with far-reaching changes in technology and production. There is little use today for human beasts of burden; the need now is for skilled and educated labor.

The Ideology of Inequality

Any stratified society usually has a set of beliefs that serve to justify and perpetuate inequalities, the beliefs varying with the nature of stratification. In Melanesia, where the "big man" is a self-made leader, qualities of leadership are thought to reside in the man himself. In Polynesia, where the office of high chief is inherited, the qualities of leadership are thought to reside in the office of high chief. The chief, simply because he is chief, is automatically endowed with wisdom, majesty, sanctity, and all the other traits necessary for command (Sahlins 1963).

As equality is a highly prized ideal in many modern industrial societies, the stratification within them is often a source of moral discomfort, or at least of political embarrassment. One result of this discomfort is a set of beliefs that seek to justify inequality of wealth and power as the result of individual moral worth, behavior, and gumption, rather than something that is built into the social structure. The rich deserve their wealth, according to this creed, and the poor have only themselves to blame. Another result is that public ideologies—or at least the claims of some important segments of society as to the way the society works—often contrast strikingly with social and economic realities. Indeed, there is no necessary connection between the true degree of stratification in a society and the prevailing ideology on the subject.

Invisible Ruling Classes

The variance between ideology and social reality is strikingly seen in the Soviet Union and the United States (and in most other industrial countries, for that matter). Soviet leaders and theorists claim that their country is an enlightened economic democracy. They claim to have no ruling class. Indeed, the stated aim of the 1917 revolution was to abolish the ruling class and to transfer the means of production from these oppressors into the hands of the people.

The result was quite otherwise. After the tsar was deposed, the Communist party took command of the government. Far from broadly sharing power with the people in whose name it ruled, the party abolished the Constituent Assembly elected by popular ballot in 1917 and did not permit another election until 1989. Most important government jobs are still filled from within the party and no other party is

Black Coal Miners in America:
Race, Class, and Conflict

When we think of black miners working under oppressive conditions, we usually have South Africa in mind. Ronald Lewis (1987) has written a comprehensive history of black coal miners in America. His account, vividly detailing political oppression and the responses of those who suffered the effects of legal and social discrimination, goes beyond the experience of one ethnic group; it describes the exploitation of a class of workers, coal miners. Lewis's study, which spans the 190 years from 1790 to 1980, shows the importance of a historical as well as a regional perspective when one considers a phenomenon as complex and varied as interethnic relations.

To some degree the history of Afro-American miners reflects the general experience of blacks in North America. From colonial days to World War II, blacks were an important part of the labor force in the coal industry. Their role, however, has been largely ignored. It would be satisfying to say that Lewis's analysis has a happy ending; it does not. Blacks today are virtually absent from the industry, victims of both discrimination and mechanization.

Lewis frames his analysis in terms of distinctive systems of race relations. In those systems we can see the various ways in which appeals to race and class can be used to subjugate or exploit people without political power. Until the end of the Civil War, most black miners were slaves, even those who held supervisory positions. Sometimes slaves, freedmen, and whites worked side by side. The work was dangerous and difficult. "Miners worked in very tight quarters, fre-quently pick and shoveling while lying on their sides. When small tram cars were filled, the miners positioned themselves on hands and knees and used their heads to push the cars to and from the outside coal bank. . . . Diggers worked on a task basis, being required to load four or five tons of coal before the end of each day" (Lewis 1987:8). Those who did were fed; those who did not were flogged. This system represents industrial slavery at its worst: depersonalized, relentless exploitation.

This system did not end with emancipation and the concluding shots of the Civil War. Soon after the war, Georgia, Alabama, and Tennessee instituted the convict leasing system, which remained in use well into the twentieth century. Mine owners could lease convicts from the state for a nominal sum. The convicts were mainly black, and the system bore a startling resemblance to slavery; as one mine owner put it, convicts were better than slaves because "we don't own them, one dies we get another" (p. 16). During Reconstruction many states took aggressive action to maintain white supremacy. Among popular mechanisms were vaguely worded codes proscribing "vagrancy" and other offenses which could serve as an excuse to arrest blacks for any behavior deemed inappropriate by white authorities. As a consequence, the convict population was approximately 80 percent black (p. 17). This practice remained in force in Alabama until 1928. On July 1 of that year, when black convict miners turned in their picks and lights, one remarked, "Boss, I'm no longer in slavery" (p. 35).

allowed to exist. Freedom of speech and assembly, though no longer subject to a total ban, is still not firmly established, and the press is cautious in exercising its new relative freedom of expression. The Soviet technocratic elite, though shaken by the popular rejection of some of its members in the election of March 1989, is still in control, still enjoying the privileges against which the maverick Boris Yeltsin inveighed in his successful election campaign in

Convicts were not the only source of labor, or even the predominant one. From the late 1890s through the 1920s the coal industry expanded in the south, in Appalachia, and in Pennsylvania and Ohio. West Virginia experienced a serious labor shortage, and blacks were generally welcomed there. They were paid the same wages as whites, were accorded the same rights, and faced the same tribulations as others who worked in the industry. Wages were low and danger was constant, but at least black miners were recognized as part of the local community, and when the work force became organized, blacks joined the union along with whites. The labor movement was born of armed conflict. The largest single armed conflict between labor and capital in America took place at Blair Mountain in September 1921, when more than a hundred men lost their lives. In this conflict, black and white workers fought side by side against company guards and local deputies for a common cause, establishing the basis for considerable interracial unity among West Virginian miners (pp. 162–164).

In the South, both black and white workers, the latter mostly European immigrants, struggled to organize and to improve conditions in the mines. Mine owners strenuously resisted unionization, often pitting one group against the other. When workers struck, owners deliberately recruited black strikebreakers, most of them impoverished farmers desperate for work, in the hope of dividing their workers' allegiances along racial lines. Blacks received lower wages than whites for the same work, and they were required to provide unpaid services in the mine camps as well. In short, southern "coal companies brutally suppressed all attempts to create a biracial unionism which promoted the economic, if not social, equality of blacks" (p. 48). It was

not until the 1940s that unionism took hold, and even then discriminatory practices persisted. As recently as June 1989 the coal industry of the United States was crippled by a seven-state strike marked by violence, charges of oppressive conditions, and strikebreaking.

The situation in the North was not much better; as in the South, mine owners resisted unionization and often encouraged racist attitudes in an effort to divide black and white workers. Violence between union and nonunion workers was common. Surprisingly, black union members usually remained loyal to their white colleagues even though they suffered from discrimination within the union movement. Many mines were operated with strikebreakers. In 1928, Bethlehem Steel's Ellsworth mine in Pennsylvania was surrounded by a chain fence, searchlights swept the compound, and machine guns were emplaced because, as its director testified, "you could not run without them" (p. 113). The mine was being worked by black nonunion workers. One result of this tactic is that blacks have borne the brunt of racial hatred in the coalfields of the region and the union movement has been slowed.

Today mechanization has virtually eliminated black labor in the mining industry. Mine operations were mechanized first in sectors where hand labor was the most intensive: loading, cutting, and lifting. Because of discriminatory practices, blacks were concentrated in such jobs. Workers were laid off by job category rather than by seniority in the mine. Further, blacks were denied access to segregated institutions that would have prepared them for the mechanical revolution. If the current trend continues in the mining industry, there will soon be virtually no blacks in the mines. "Machines, those mechanical slaves, will have taken their places" (p. 190).

Moscow; yet the Soviet leaders continue to claim that their country has no ruling class.

A somewhat similar though less extreme situation exists in the United States. Here, as in the Soviet Union, the existence of a ruling elite

is firmly denied in public policy. According to the national ideology, the government is chosen by the people and serves primarily to represent their interests. But many sociologists and political scientists have found the political system to be less open in fact. The sociologist C. Wright Mills (1959) has written of a "power elite," consisting of key figures in industry, finance, the military, and politics who have common interests and backgrounds and whose decisions effectively set public policy.

Ideology and practice vary to some degree in every society. People of high status may not have much more material wealth than their compatriots of low status. India is a case in point. Despite the great gulfs that separate the castes, wealth differentials within villages need not be extreme. In some villages the differences in wealth between Brahman and other castes may not even approach the wealth differences in a rural American town with an egalitarian ideology.

The same issues arise when one considers changing relationships among groups. Joseph Jorgenson (1971) points out that social scientists often use the term "acculturation" in a way that obscures reality. When Native American groups are described as semi- or partially acculturated—somewhere between their original organization and integration into the modern society and economy—continuing change is suggested. In fact, he argues, Native Americans are fully integrated into the economy, but in a subservient position.

Quite different ideologies can exist in reference to one's own group as opposed to others. André Gunder Frank (1969:390) has characterized the "world capitalist system" as structured inequality: developed countries keep other countries less developed to ensure their own continued growth. Yet many capitalist countries stress an egalitarian ethic internally. There is only a rough connection between sets of ideas and particular group interests; democracy and colonialism can go hand in hand (Wolf 1982).

Inequality is rooted in economic processes. No matter what social or political upheavals take place, social stratification is likely to continue in many instances. If a society is to have large-scale production and development of resources, whether agricultural or industrial, it must have ways of controlling and integrating them. When some person or persons must make decisions concerning the distribution of resources, they are often in a position to gain control of the resources and so have access to ever more power and wealth. Once they gain such access, they are not likely to surrender control, nor can they easily be forced to do so; they have the means to protect their positions and tend to endow their children with the ability to maintain themselves in a similar fashion.

Summary

Groups are associations of individuals who interact on a fairly regular basis and have a sense of collective identity. Groups vary in composition and function, in their degree of *formal organization* (the extent of their use of official roles, formal rules, and bureaucratic structure), in their relative permanence, and in their degree of *corporateness*, or the access of their members to group rights and privileges.

Numerous social groupings have some sense of collective identity. Such groups, be they religious congregations, clans, or political parties, vary widely in composition and function. Every society is formed by the integration of its smaller groups or subsets. Émile Durkheim called this process the *social division of labor*. Durkheim further identified two contrasting divisions of labor: *mechanical solidarity*, or the unity of a society formed of social units that are comparable, so that all members of the society have access to the same sorts of groups; and *organic solidarity*, or the unity of a society formed of dissimilar specialized groupings, each having a restricted function (as in an organic entity), so that membership in any group is limited.

The ways we classify or socially categorize others influence our behavior. A *social category* is composed of all people who share certain culturally identified characteristics. Three social categories found in every society are age, gender, and kinship. These categories tend to structure personal interaction, generally limit the network of social relationships, influence behavior toward others, and often supply the basis for the formation of groups.

Kinship is the basis for the formation of important social groups, the most important of which are *descent groups*. Underlying a descent group is not just common ancestry but a whole set of beliefs, myths, and symbols—a *descent ideology*—which reinforces group solidarity. A descent group is either unilineal or nonunilineal. *Unilineal descent groups* are those in which membership is traced through one line only, either the father's (*patrilineal descent group*) or the mother's (*matrilineal descent group*). In *nonunilineal descent groups*, descent may be traced through either parent or through both. Unilineal groups are generally categorized according to their inclusiveness. Members of a lineage trace their genealogies through specified links to a common ancestor—female links to a female ancestor in a *matrilineage*, male links to a male ancestor in a *patrilineage*. Members of clans, whether *matriclans* or *patriclans*, believe themselves to be descended from a common ancestor but are unable to trace the exact genealogical connections. Many clans are named for a *totem*, a plant or animal to which they claim a special relationship. Phratries and moieties are even more inclusive categories, comprising several clans or even a whole society. When related phratries, lineages, and clans acquire a common name and identity, they become a *tribe*. Tribes are formed of *segmentary lineages*, each lineage encompassed by a larger lineage, which is a segment of a still larger lineage, and so on until all members are related

in a single genealogical hierarchy. For a unilineal kin group to exist, its members must recognize some shared set of interests that give them reason to join forces; that reason may be economic or related to the need for protection. Whatever the common set of interests, it is clear that unilineal descent groups serve many important functions for their members, including the regulation of marriage and land use and the provision of mutual aid and support.

Anthropologists classify nonunilineal descent groups into two basic types—ambilineal and bilateral. In societies with an *ambilineal descent* ideology, a person affiliates with kin groups on the basis of ties traced through either the paternal or the maternal line. *Bilateral descent* ideologies define individuals as being at the center of a group of kin composed more or less equally of their mothers' and fathers' relatives of all kinds. It is a mistake to assume that all societies with the same descent ideology have identical systems of behavior with regard to kinship. Descent ideologies are regularly manipulated and may change with time.

A social category that is particularly important in more complex societies is *ethnicity*, a basis for categories that are rooted in socially perceived differences in national origin, language, and/or religion. Ethnic constructs can and do vary from society to society, and they can be manipulated and changed. Ethnic ascriptions can define social roles, impose boundaries on personal networks, and structure human interaction. References to "race" are in fact usually references to ethnicity. Ethnic distinctions commonly give rise to discriminatory practices and can be the basis for the formation of political action groups.

Networks are webs of social ties of various kinds. They serve many vital functions, such as helping one accomplish a task or solve a problem, providing intermediary contacts to send and receive information, and lending psychological support. Individual networks vary in quantity and quality of contacts, in the number of interests served by individual relationships, and in density, or the degree to which an individual's contacts are linked together by other ties. One prevalent two-person network is the *patron-client relationship*, a mutually obligatory arrangement in which an influential individual (the patron) extends support to another person (the client), who owes the patron loyalty.

Most modern state societies are *stratified* by class. Members of a *social class* have generally similar backgrounds, educations, job opportunities, and social standing, and share a perception of belonging to a distinctive social group. Each social class in a society is associated with a differential degree of access to status and prestige, and the ability to pass both on to their children. An *economic class* is defined by the economic position of its members. It is sometimes difficult to define and categorize classes, and there is some dispute about whether classes have distinct cultures. The various classes of a single society do not necessarily have truly separate value systems; moreover, class consciousness is highly variable.

Another form of stratification is the *caste* system. Castes resemble a series of ranked ethnic groupings, each closed and defined by its position in relation to the others. Caste membership is fixed at birth and is usually unchangeable. India had the classic caste system, based on Hindu religious beliefs. Each caste has not only its own level of status but its own occupational role. Strict religious rules serve as the justification for a very pragmatic economic system that benefits the top castes. Castelike groupings are found in many other countries, not always expressed in terms of religious ideology. Some people say the average gap of about 15 points between the IQ test scores of blacks and whites is consistent with the castelike positions occupied by African Americans and other minorities in American society, and a similar gap is seen in minority castes in other parts of the world.

Another extreme form of stratification is *slavery*, a practice that permits some people to own others and to claim the right to their labor. Historically, slavery was prevalent in most of the world. It is associated with certain subsistence patterns, primarily intensive agriculture.

In any stratified society, a set of beliefs serves to justify and perpetuate the stratification system. In modern industrial societies, stratification can be a source of moral discomfort. As a result, the public ideology in regard to inequality often conflicts with social realities. The differences in wealth between the upper and lower classes in America contradict an egalitarian ideology. Regardless of political and social upheavals, stratification is likely to continue because inequality is rooted in economic processes.

Key Terms

ambilineal descent	group	nonunilineal descent	segmentary lineage
bilateral descent	kindred	group	slavery
caste	lineage	organic solidarity	social category
corporateness	matriclan	patriclan	social class
descent group	matrilineage	patrilineage	social division of labor
descent ideology	matrilineal descent	patrilineal descent	stratified society
economic class	group	group	totem
ethnicity	mechanical solidarity	patron–client	tribe
formal organization	network	relationship	unilineal descent group

Suggested Readings

BEHAR, R. 1986. *Santa Maria del Monte: The Presence of the Past in a Spanish Village.* Princeton, N.J.: Princeton University Press. An examination of the social structure, customs, economy, and daily life of a small Spanish community. The author describes how these rural villagers have acted together to ensure the survival of their traditional forms of social organization.

COHEN, A. P. 1985. *The Symbolic Construction of Community.* New York: Tavistock Publications. Drawing on contemporary anthropological work on symbolism, meaning, and ritual, the author views the community as a cultural field with a complex of symbols whose meanings vary among its members.

GAILEY, C. W. 1987. *Kinship to Kingship: Gender Hierarchy and State Formation in the Tongan Islands.* Austin, Tex.: University of Texas Press. Explores how and why gender relations become skewed to subordinate women when classes and state organization emerge in a society. The author uses ethnographic research in Tonga, an area in the South Pacific, to look at wider issues of class and gender.

KELLY, R. 1985. *The Nuer Conquest.* Ann Arbor, Mich.: University of Michigan Press. A comprehensive examination of the causes and means of the most prominent and widely discussed instance of tribal imperialism. The author synthesizes nearly half a century of scholarly enquiry into the interrelationship between social and material causes in historical and developmental processes.

STAHL, P. H. (Trans. Linda Scales Alcott). 1986. *Household and Village Confederation in Southeastern Europe.* New York: Columbia University Press. A comparative presentation of the traditional social structures and property systems of the Romanians, Southern Slavs, Albanians, and Greeks that uses historical documents and direct observation.

Chapter **14** Economics:
Resources,
Production,
and Exchange

A daptation is the process by which people develop the means of coping with the problems they face. The ways in which people allocate their time among competing demands, use energy, and store and exchange resources of all sorts are central to successful adaptation. Economics is a means of studying some of the material aspects of adaptation. Economics, in its simplest definition, is the study of the way people use certain *means*, whether time, money, or even social skills, to obtain desired resources. In this broad sense, all societies have an economy and virtually every human activity has economic implications. The Pokot man in Kenya who gives a member of his age grade a cow, accepts no payment, but knows that he has gained future rights in his friend's herd, has engaged in an economic transaction with the expectation of a delayed return on his investment. He has also secured his perishable capital by moving it away from his main herd. The New York City stockbroker, buying and selling shares in unseen companies all over the world, is engaging in very similar economic transactions of a less personalized nature.

A society's **economic system** may be defined as the ideas and institutions that people draw upon and the behaviors in which they engage in order to secure resources to satisfy their needs and desires. An economic system, then, has the basic components of ideas, patterns of behavior, and special-purpose institutions.

Anthropology contributes to the study of economics by offering a perspective that looks beyond impersonalized, monetarized transactions to the culturally varied and often emotionally charged means by which people acquire critical resources. The anthropological approach stresses the cultural or social context in which people operate and the importance of social or kinship relationships in the shaping of economic behavior. To the Western economist, the fact that a man may sell his car to his brother-in-law for less money than a stranger would pay is of little consequence in terms of the millions of cars sold each year. But when one deals with a relatively small population, as anthropologists frequently do, transactions involving relatives or socially close individuals are the norm, not the exception. And, as we shall see, social relationships in every society affect what we might think of as straightforward material exchanges.

CONCEPTS OF ECONOMIC BEHAVIOR

The study of economic processes lies at the heart of social science research and has generated considerable controversy. At the end of the eighteenth century, Adam Smith, the founder of the discipline of economics, posed a question fundamental to the social sciences: How is it that the independent actions of people made without reference to one another result in orderly patterns or processes? Why does not chaos reign as people pursue their separate interests? The answer, Adam Smith suggests, is that if people have free will and if they act rationally, chaos will not erupt because people will be making similar decisions under similar circumstances; the result will be orderly patterns. In a free market it is expected that prices of goods will follow orderly patterns related to supply and demand as a consequence of many choices made by many people acting rationally to maximize gains and minimize costs. A central concept in this approach is that of **scarce resources:** people inevitably have many more wants than they have resources to satisfy them. Therefore they must make **rational economic decisions,** weighing the available alternatives and deciding which will benefit them the most at the least cost. In short, classical economic theory views individual rational behavior as the driving force behind all economic dealings.

This assumption of individual free will and rational, self-interested decision making is not universally accepted. Social scientists of the nineteenth century, including Karl Marx and Émile Durkheim, argued that society imposes its own rationality on people, and that social and economic institutions perpetuate themselves regardless of the needs of the individuals concerned. In the middle of the twentieth century this intellectual conflict about the nature of people and of culture and society began to influence anthropology. The economy is seen as the process by which a society is provisioned by its own institutions. This view does not assume individual rationality and choice; instead one looks to the way institutions, whether explicitly economic or not, serve the material needs of society. Different societies, it is argued, may have quite different economic structures, and individuals will behave in ways that the classical assumptions cannot predict.

Proponents of this view note that most economic theory is rooted in industrial capitalism, and its basic concepts—capital goods, surplus, the profit motive, the allocation of scarce resources—are abstractions developed in the effort to study that system. They suggest that these concepts are not very useful in efforts to study the economic systems of people who are not involved in market or capitalist economies. This school of economic anthropology is called **substantivism.** According to the substantivists, analyzing nonindustrial societies according to the concepts of Western economics is misleading: it would wrongly attribute motiva-

These two men in a Berber market are bargaining over the price of sheep. In almost every part of the world, market transactions are the primary means by which goods and services are exchanged. (NIK WHEELER/BLACK STAR)

tions, such as the profit motive, to these people. Substantivists propose to develop theories that will enable them to understand economic processes as the maintenance of an entire social or cultural order (see, for example, Durrenberger 1984). Individual decision making and choice, which are of primary concern in classical economic theory, are of secondary concern in substantivist studies.

Other anthropologists, drawing on mainstream economic theory in the tradition of Adam Smith, argue that if the concepts of formal economic theory are broadened, they can serve as analytic tools for the study of economic systems quite unlike those of market-structured societies. This approach is called **formalism.** The fact that individuals in a nonmarket society do not pursue profits in an immediate material sense, the formalists argue, does not mean that the concept of profit is irrelevant to their behavior. In the broadest sense, profit is the maximizing of something scarce or limited, which need not be money or even a material possession. If in their economic transactions people are looking for profit in terms of prestige or establishing a social network, they are seeking to maximize some perceived advantage. People everywhere, formalists argue, direct their behavior toward maximizing scarce ends; that is, toward making a profit, however it may be measured.

As Harold Schneider (1974) has noted, in many African societies cattle are capital goods, savings, and consumer goods all in one. They are capital goods in the sense that they produce calves, milk, and manure; savings in the sense that they are a means of keeping and accumulating wealth; and consumer goods in that ultimately they are eaten and their hides used. They are also, as we have seen with the Pokot, a primary social institution in many instances. These observations suggest to Schneider and others that there is a universality to human economic behavior. Studies in this vein stress individual variation and diversity in the making of choices, entrepreneurship, individual strategies, and their attendant costs and benefits.

This is not to say that people are assumed to operate on the basis of what is immediately gainful or gratifying. Herbert Simon, for example, suggests that rationality in economic decision making is not necessarily getting the most for the least, but simply the "selection of preferred behavior alternatives in terms of

some system of values whereby the consequences of behavior can be evaluated" (1966:75–76). Thus if the desire for prestige or the need for good relationships with kin is considered more important than immediate material gain, one might "rationally" ignore material profits and seek to obtain only what one needs, giving away the rest or perhaps even ostentatiously wasting it.

In addition, as the economist Kenneth Boulding (1961) has pointed out, even in market economies people do not reevaluate their economic practices in terms of profitability every day. Rather, they tend to keep doing what they have been doing in the past unless they have some reason for dissatisfaction. According to Boulding, this practice—and not the effort to maximize short-term advantage—is the essence of economic rationality.

Finally, the rationality of economic decisions must be considered in relation to the situation of the person making the decision. As Scott Cook has pointed out, "tribesmen and peasants do not always choose the best or least costly alternative [that] is possible under the circumstances" (1966:844). Such choices may seem irrational to outside observers, but only because they are unaware of the specific situation.

This position finds support in Jan Newton's (1977) study of the consumer behavior of the rural poor in the United States. Newton asked a woman who had just bought a $25 second-hand dryer how she would have shopped for the dryer if she had had the money for a new one. She responded that she would have checked the prices in the newspaper appliance ads and compared the guarantees offered by the various manufacturers; she added that in the end she would probably have bought a Maytag, because it had the best reputation for durability. But she bought a nameless machine for $25 because that was all the money she had. Newton also investigated the popular assumption that poor people do less comparison shopping than the middle class because they are less

capable of planning and of deferring the gratification of the purchase. One of Newton's informants did in fact do most of her buying
without comparison shopping, but her reasons
had more to do with circumstances than with
values:

> "Look," she said, "maybe it does save money if you
> go around to different stores to check out prices and
> such. But you've got to have money to pay for the
> gas to go to all of them and the heart to do it. I've
> ate my heart out once too often, looking at things I
> can't have. I'm tired of hunting, and I won't put
> myself through it anymore"   [Newton 1977:58].

Once circumstances are taken into account,
seemingly senseless economic decisions begin
to appear more logical. Economic anthropologists believe that people in nonliterate societies
are as rational in their economic behavior as
are people in complex industrial societies, and
that if they appear irrational, the fault lies
either in an ethnocentric definition of rationality or in the observer's ignorance of the circumstances.

DIVERSITY IN THE ORGANIZATION OF ECONOMIES

In the actual measures it employs, Western economic theory assumes the existence of specialized economic institutions that exist purely for
the sake of mobilizing resources. It assumes
further that these institutions will be "subspe-
cialized"—that is, each will control a separate
aspect of economic life. In our own society,
these assumptions are reasonably valid. We
have stores for buying and selling, banks for
lending and storing money, and so forth. And
these institutions are, for the most part, exclusively economic. But in nonindustrial or nonmarket societies, we often find not only that

many economic functions have been lumped
together in one institution but also that this
institution serves many purposes other than
economic ones. In many societies, for example,
the household is the unit of production and the
center of economic life as well as the focal point
of religious activities, politics, kin organization,
socialization, and numerous other functions,
all intermingled. The economic institutions of
people living in nonmarket societies are embedded in the social structure, so that it is almost
impossible to separate what is economic from
what is not.

Even when we consider market-structured
economies, the economic institutions may be
very different from our own specialized ones.
If we need money for a major expense, we borrow it from a bank and then pay it back gradually. In many other societies, this function may
be performed by rotating credit associations,
rather like our credit unions. These are groups
of perhaps ten individuals who meet regularly
and contribute a fixed amount of their earnings
to the group's "pot." At established intervals,
the pot is turned over to one of the members
for his or her exclusive use. A new pot is then
accumulated and it is turned over to another
member.

In Cameroon, West Africa, just such an informal credit system, the *tontine*, exists side by
side with banks. The classical tontine is a financial arrangement in which participants
contribute an equal amount and the entire sum
goes to the one who survives the others. In the
Cameroon variant, they contribute an agreed-
upon sum each month and then periodically
loan it to one of the members. A recent innovation in Cameroon is the interest-bearing tontine—members not only borrow but receive interest on their contributions (Brooke 1987).
Variants of tontines are found throughout the
world and are vital means by which people
pool resources so that members of the group
can buy consumer items, make home improve-

ments, or even get the capital to open a business. Tontines work because of social pressure; people who might default on a bank loan will rarely let their friends down. Should they do so, they not only would face social disgrace but could never join another tontine. As James Brooke notes (1987), tontines are built on trust, and their participants generally are people of the same neighborhood and ethnic background.

Even when the economic institutions of two societies superficially resemble each other, they may in fact be organized very differently. Every country has markets today, yet markets are by no means uniform everywhere. In some places people of neighboring villages who specialize in certain kinds of production regularly congregate in a central market town to exchange their surpluses for necessities produced by other villages—potters buy baskets, basketmakers buy rice, and so forth. In such markets the interlocking specializations keep the producers in a state of mutual interdependence; the potters, for example, must continue making pots in order to procure the baskets they need. In other markets, ties are looser. Producers may haggle with one another, and if they do not like the proposed deal, they can go elsewhere; there is no sense of inescapable dependence.

Markets may also vary in the degree to which noneconomic dealings are combined with economic ones. Buyers and sellers in the Grain Exchange in Chicago are there only to buy and sell. But in peasant societies, farmers come to market not only to exchange their goods but also to perform a variety of other functions— to see the doctor, to have their children baptized, to arrange marriages for their older children, to vote, to attend meetings, and of course to socialize with relatives and friends (Cook 1966). This social exchange, not to mention the acquisition of critical information and political news, is inseparable from the actual marketing processes.

THE THREE DOMAINS OF ECONOMIC STUDY

Though many theoretical differences separate the substantivist and formalist positions, anthropologists find common ground in the way they actually describe the workings of a given economic system and variations among such systems.

Regardless of theoretical orientation, it is useful to think of economic study as having three major domains of inquiry. A population's strategy for securing and using a resource is generally based on some assurance of continued access to the resource. Thus access to resources and the rights by which individuals and groups hold resources is the first domain. The second is the nature and organization of production. Resources are rarely used exactly as they are found naturally; they are transformed through processes of production. Finally, goods, services, or resources are, by necessity, exchanged or redistributed by various means among individuals. This movement of goods and services is the third area of study. Despite intersocietal variation, it is possible to make a comparative study of the economic processes that are found in all societies:

1. **Regulation of access to resources**—control over the use of land, water, and raw materials.

2. **Production**—the conversion of natural resources to usable forms.

3. **Exchange**—the distribution of goods and services among the members of the society.

Regulating Access to Resources

In order to secure resources, a group must have some assurance of continued access to an area where resources are located. They can do so by establishing a territory and restricting its use to members of the group. People define and regulate access to productive resources in a variety of ways; the way chosen depends on the nature of the resources and the means available to control and use them. In many respects this aspect of economic behavior overlaps what is usually thought of as political organization.

Property Rights

Most agricultural and industrial societies maintain clear-cut rules that define rights to productive land and other resources. Among most hunting-and-gathering societies an individual's rights to use resources are virtually unrestricted. Hunters and gatherers such as the Eskimo and the !Kung must be able to move according to the seasonal availability of resources; otherwise they might starve when normal fluctuations in climate depleted the local water supply or altered the distribution of wild animals or plants. The more uncertain or mobile the food supply, the greater the need for flexible boundaries and collective rights of access.

The extent to which people define and defend a territory also depends on the gains versus the costs of maintaining exclusive rights. A group that stakes out and defends its own territory retains the resource supply in that territory. But to guard a territory requires time and energy that might be spent in other activities. It also involves risk; one can be killed defending a boundary. Finally, reliance on a restricted area for resources may be disadvantageous, as it would be for hunter-gatherers. To the degree that costs outweigh the gains, territoriality will be relaxed. To the degree that the gains outweigh the costs, territoriality will be strictly observed. Thus while hunters and gatherers have territories to which groups lay primary claim and stake out possession of strategic resources

such as wells or rich stands of vegetable foods, they do not necessarily defend the boundaries as vigorously as farmers defend their fields (Dyson-Hudson and Smith 1978). Generally, permission is readily granted to outsiders to visit wells or traverse territories.

The gains–cost formula is well illustrated by the Pokot, whom we described in Chapter 7. The Pokot's sorghum fields are critical to their survival, and they are relatively easy to defend, for they are small and located near the people's houses. The fields are carefully guarded against both intruding animals and human thieves. The pastureland on which the Pokot graze their cattle is almost impossible to defend, and it would be unwise to try to defend it. It covers too large an area, and the water resources and the quality of grass vary seasonally in any one area. A well-defended patch of brown grass with dry water holes would benefit no one. The Pokot therefore exercise far less control over grazing land than over fields and farmland.

Maintaining control over a territory, whether loosely or strictly, is only the first step in regulating access to resources. Every society has principles that govern who may use which resources and under what circumstances. One important principle observed in our own society is that of private ownership of property, or **freehold.** Americans regard land, water, minerals, machinery, and all types of productive resources as things that someone can own. Owners, whether individuals or corporations, decide who has access to their resources and when. They may exploit them in any way they wish; they may also rent or sell them.

Of course, even capitalist economies recognize that the concept of private property has limits. Systems that provide essential resources, such as transportation and electricity, are often considered "public utilities" and are heavily regulated, sometimes even owned outright by the government. Zoning laws further define actual use of private property. And social constraints may restrict the way one disposes of it. Few urban neighborhoods in the United States allow one to keep chickens in the backyard, although not too long ago this practice was widespread. At the same time, effective ownership may depend on active use: in many European and American cities squatters have taken over buildings that the owners left unoccupied. In many less-developed countries, entire sections of major cities are given over to illegal shantytowns formed by rural settlers who simply erect rough dwellings on vacant land, without municipal approval or title to the land. In Turkey, for example, such settlements are called *gecekondu,* or "built in the night." Taking advantage of a customary law that prohibits the destruction of one's domicile, poor people rapidly put up a house and dare the authorities to evict them.

In many nonindustrial societies, groups rather than individuals control the land and other productive resources, along with the equipment necessary for production. The individual gains rights to these resources only by virtue of affiliation with a group. We can see this form of **corporate ownership** best by looking at the way such groups control land.

Landholding Systems: Ownership versus Use

In traditional societies that do not recognize individual ownership of land, the kin group or the community at large either is the landholder or at least has a great deal to say about who uses what resources. Individuals or households may have the right to use these resources for limited periods, but they do not own them—they can neither buy nor sell the land they farm. Such kin-group or community landholding rights are often termed "corporate" rights, as we noted in Chapter 13.

Thus while people in most industrial countries acquire land and the resources on it

through inheritance, purchase, or rental, people in most nonstate societies gain their right to land as a birthright or through marriage to a member of a landowning group. As a member of a band, for example, a !Kung man or woman automatically has the right to hunt and collect wild foods within the area used by that band. The !Kung say it does not matter who owns the land itself, since one cannot eat the ground. Rather, each band collectively holds the right to exploit specific water resources and patches of wild plant foods (Marshall 1965). With few exceptions, pastoral peoples follow the same rule. Grazing lands are generally treated as a communal asset, open to all members of the tribe, or at least to all members of the large and cooperating kin groups that typically migrate and settle together.

Horticulturists, on the other hand, are generally concerned with allocating rights to use specific plots, for they invest a great deal of time and labor in these plots. Like hunter-gatherers and pastoralists, they acquire rights to land by virtue of group membership, but in order to retain the right to a particular plot, one must actively use it. Among the Tiv of Nigeria, for example, the head of the household is allowed to cultivate any unused piece of land within a territory belonging to his lineage. He may lay claim to as much land as his household can handle. So long as the household actively works these fields and keeps them clear, the members are entitled to their exclusive use. When fields revert to fallow, however, rights lapse and the land becomes part of the public domain, to be claimed by other families in the lineage. Nevertheless, a Tiv man always retains the right to some land—if not to one particular field, then to another—simply because he is a member of a certain kin group (Bohannan 1960). In other horticultural societies, rights of use may be acquired simply through residence in the village or through the performance of some social obligation, but again the land must

This Pennsylvania farm is a symbol of the concept of private property—ownership is in the hands of an individual farmer who has exclusive rights to both the land and everything on it. Only the owner can make decisions regarding the renting or selling of the farm and determine how and to what extent its resources will be exploited. (GRANT HEILMAN)

be cultivated if those rights are to remain in force.

As with hunter-gatherers and pastoralists, collective as opposed to private ownership of land may be critical to a horticultural group's way of making a living. Consider the Western Pueblo, discussed in Chapter 6, who must plant their crops in a variety of settings in order to ensure that some will survive. Each clan owns some lands in several micro-environments—some on the gully floor, some at the base of the hill, and so forth. If these properties were owned by individuals rather than by the clan and were therefore subject to sale, the actions of one or two individuals could destroy the entire group's intricate pattern of land use.

Commercial Farming and Private Ownership

In areas that were ruled by European colonial powers, European systems of private ownership usually replaced traditional land-use systems. As a result, the economic system became more impersonal and less tied to a larger system of social relationships. Sometimes already existing discrepancies between the property rights of men and women were amplified. Very often even in horticultural and pastoral societies property rights differ by gender, and even the egalitarian !Kung recognize different rights to possession for men and women. When the colonial powers imposed the concept of private property as a means of controlling productive resources, they usually allocated ownership to men rather than to all individuals (Etienne and Leacock 1988). Among the Buganda of Central Africa, for example, chiefs traditionally allotted portions of their estates to tenant farmers.

State ownership of resources provides the foundation for enterprises such as this collective farm in the Krasnodar Territory in the USSR. Farms like these attempt to utilize economies of scale to increase agricultural production and eliminate income disparities in agriculture. In fact, the opposite usually has occurred. In the absence of rewards for initiative, risk-taking, and hard work, most collective farms have produced far less than private farms, and the managers earn far more than those who do the farm work. (TASS FROM SOVOTO)

These grants could be revoked at any time. Once the British took control of this region, they passed a law enabling tenants to do as they liked with their land grants, even pass them on to their heirs without the chief's permission. The aim was to protect tenant farmers from exploitation—and, in the process, to bring them more thoroughly under colonial control through land registration and systematic taxation. As a result, in Buganda land is now individually owned (Southwold 1965).

By different routes the same process has taken place in many other societies. Private ownership allows a certain freedom for individuals to make a living by using their land for their own exclusive benefit. This freedom, however, significantly alters an individual's ties to the group, along with the psychological and social advantages they once afforded. Under a system of corporate rights, since ownership is collective, the individual has a sense of place—a knowledge of belonging, in perpetuity, to this group and this piece of land. Under private ownership, land is transferable, and it may well belong to someone other than those who work on it, so that individuals who must sell their labor because they do not own the land they farm may come to be commodities themselves, with few economic rights in and limited benefit from what is being produced.

Of course private ownership is not the only European model to have been transferred or adopted elsewhere. Various forms of collective farming, essentially products of European socialist or utopian philosophy, are found throughout Eastern Europe, South America, Asia, and Africa. One common denominator of these systems is that they are usually imposed on peasant farmers by outsiders so that in some respect they contain the most oppressive aspects of absentee landlordism: the people who farm have a limited say in the actual management of their work and must sell their crops at prices set by impersonal agencies.

The Control of Capital Goods

In addition to a system for allocating land, all peoples must have some way of establishing and coordinating rights to tools, storage equipment, means of transportation, and other capital goods. In our own society, most capital goods, such as factories, machinery, tools, trucks, and warehouses, are privately owned. In socialist countries many capital goods are owned by the state and access is regulated bureaucratically. In peasant farming societies, whatever the form of landownership, major implements and other agricultural inputs are often owned by individuals—even by those who may only work the land as sharecroppers. Animals in pastoral societies are almost always owned by individuals or by households, but as we noted, individuals may have shares in animals herded by others or have expectations of being given livestock held by others.

Among hunters and gatherers, a person may be said to own a weapon or a tool, but ownership seldom implies an exclusive right to the thing. A hunter who makes a spear thrower or a bear trap owns the implement only in the sense that he has first right of use; when he is not using the tool, others may lay claim to it. Since hunters work together closely and survival depends on sharing, tools and weapons are often lent and exchanged freely. It may be that proprietary rights usually become more fixed and formalized where productive goods are more complex and difficult to make or acquire.

Production

Manufacturing is largely a specialized activity in most agricultural societies, and it becomes even more specialized as industrialization increases. In agricultural societies, the specialist who makes plows or pottery is the owner and operator of the production equipment—the forge, potter's wheel, kiln, or whatever materials and instruments he or she uses. The maker sees the product through from start to finish and owns it until it is sold. In industrial society, however, the relationship of workers to their tools and their products is far less intimate. The factory workers who make tractors and combines will probably never use any of the farm machinery they produce. They are involved only in a specific and limited portion of the production process, and they own neither the product (unless they choose to buy it from the company) nor the factory and manufacturing equipment. They are simply selling their labor to a business at a rate set by the workings of the market system. Labor becomes a salable commodity like any other. **Alienation**—the fragmentation of individuals' relations to their work, the things they produce, and the resources with which they produce them—is one possible consequence of industrial specialization and private enterprise.

When we consider cross-cultural variation in production, we need to consider two major aspects of production: how production is organized and what productive strategies are used.

The Organization of Production

In every society production is an organized process. That is, it is handled by specific productive units—groups of people organized to do certain jobs. The nature of those productive units varies widely from society to society. In our own society, the basic producing unit is the business firm, be it an individually owned gas station, a farm, or a giant oil corporation with thousands of shareholders. Households in our society, for example, are typically consuming rather than producing units. As a consequence, production is usually far removed from the domestic economy. People who live in vastly different domestic circumstances may be working side by side on the same assembly line or in the same office. Productive tasks are divided up in complex and specialized ways. Rarely does one worker see an item produced from start to finish, and rarely is production based on local resources alone. Even on the family-owned and -operated farm, fuel, equipment, hybrid seeds, fertilizers—not to mention electricity and water for irrigation—are "imported."

In most nonindustrial societies, the basic producing unit is the household or domestic group. When technology is relatively simple, all the skills and many of the resources needed for production can be found in a single household,

specialized along gender lines. In most horticultural societies, such as the Yąnomamö, the members of a household will have among them the knowledge and abilities required to plant and tend their gardens, to hunt, to fashion hoes, spades, digging sticks, and other cultivating tools, to make clothing, ornaments, pots, baskets, and other implements and utensils. If a task is too large to be handled efficiently by a single household, the additional effort will simply be supplied by kin or friends. For the Trobriand Islanders, for example, the construction of a canoe is a village event; dozens of friends and kin cooperate in this large-scale project, which is also marked by ritual and

People rarely use resources exactly as they come from nature. Animals are butchered and cooked, plants are ground or sliced, stone and wood are shaped into tools and buildings. Here villagers in Niger pound wheat. (MARC RIBOUD/MAGNUM)

feasting (Malinowski 1922/1961). Nevertheless, most aspects of production are located in the household, which is also the main unit for organizing consumption. The organization of economic production and consumption primarily in the household is often referred to as the **domestic mode of production.**

Sometimes the risk of loss or damage dictates that a task be handled jointly by more than one household. Among the Pokot of East Africa, every man herds some of his friends' and kinsmen's cattle along with his own to minimize the risk that any one household's entire stock will be destroyed if disease strikes their herd.

Productive Strategies

In technologically simple societies, as we have noted, the productive unit serves many purposes other than just production. When a Oaxacan farm family gather together their kin and friends to harvest their fields, the resulting productive unit is largely the same group with which they share their religious, political, social, and other activities. Production in nonindustrial societies affects and is affected by noneconomic matters, whereas production in our own society is performed by people pursuing strictly economic ends, largely to the exclusion of social considerations, as we saw in Chapter 9.

In addition to productive units, an economy must use productive strategies—methods for converting natural resources into usable products. Productive strategies involve at least three major elements—natural resources, labor, and capital. Any one of these three elements can be varied in accordance with the needs of the society. Intensity of labor can be increased or decreased; capital can be saved, borrowed, or invested; the use of natural resources can be adjusted by a switch from one available alternative to another, as from a tobacco crop to corn. In industrial societies, the critical variable in a productive strategy is usually capital.

In traditional agrarian societies, the most important variable is often labor. In industrializing countries today, however, a characteristic of agriculture is a rapid increase in the importance of capital in relation to labor. Louise Lennihan (1988), who worked with Hausa farmers in northern Nigeria, notes that agriculture may appear to be carried on as it has been for generations—one still sees farmers in the fields with their hoes—but the social facts have been transformed by the increased presence of capital in agricultural production. Now the field a farmer hoes may not be his own, and if it is his own, it may be neglected because he is forced by circumstances to work for wages. Agriculture has come to require commercial fertilizer, hybrid seeds, and insecticides. Many farms and fields are owned by people who have made money in nonagricultural pursuits and wish to reinvest it. Such a change is often accompanied by changes in the gender-based division of labor. If men go away to work for wages, women must assume male responsibilities at home. If women are drawn into the wage labor force, this change will similarly have domestic consequences for men. Usually substantial time elapses before men come to assume some share of domestic tasks. The overall configuration of society affects the gender division of labor, so it is inevitable that major economic transformations, such as a shift to industrialized production, brings changes in the lives of men and women.

Variation in Labor Use

Anthropologists have paid considerable attention to the role of labor in different productive systems. Marshall Sahlins, drawing on the formulation of an early Soviet economist named Chayanov, has stated the relationship of labor to productive strategy as follows: Intensity of labor in a system of domestic production for domestic use varies inversely with the relative working capacity of the producing unit (Sahlins 1972:91). In other words, since people in a household work for what they need in a domestic mode of production, the more mouths they have to feed in relation to the number of people capable of producing food, the harder they must work. If a household is composed primarily of very young and very old people, for example, the few adults in their prime productive years will have to work quite intensively to supply the group's needs. At the same time, what people need depends on what they think they need, and thus if the opportunity to acquire and accumulate things is very limited, rational people do not work very hard. Conversely, if a household has many productive members and few dependent ones, its producers will find themselves in the enviable position of having much time to devote to leisure, unless they have access to some means of saving or investment (Durrenberger 1984:20).

Central to this notion is the relationship between household demographic characteristics and the way labor is deployed. All things being equal, the more consumers each worker in a household has to support, the harder he or she has to work. Since the very young and the elderly consume more than they produce, households with a large proportion of such individuals must bear a heavy labor burden. Michael Dove (1984) found this idea borne out when he investigated the household economy of the Kantu of West Kalimantan, Indonesia. A large extended household is a cultural ideal among the Kantu horticulturists, but social reality falls short of the ideal. Of the thirty households Dove studied, thirteen were nuclear. The nuclear households were smaller than the others, and, most important, the ratio of workers to consumers was proportionately lower. Using various measures of productivity, Dove found that households with adverse worker–consumer ratios did in fact intensify their labor output proportionately; some of them had to hire labor to make up for their own deficiencies. In fact, the organization of labor was a major problem faced by all households: some had to sell their labor to make ends meet and others had to hire them. The demographic measures of workers available to support consumers is a good predictor of labor deployment and the amount of work people have to do.

Households in preindustrial societies vary the intensity of their labor by modifying one of several factors, all of which are governed to some extent by cultural norms. First there is the speed and efficiency with which a person works, the amount of work he or she accomplishes in a given period of time. This amount is often referred to as output per worker-hour or level of **productivity.** The members of every society have a general notion of what the average person's productivity should be in a particular task. Productivity is of course greatly influenced by the kinds of tools people have at their disposal. A person with a tractor can obviously furrow a field more quickly than a person with an ox and a wooden plow. But even when they use similar equipment, people in different societies define the acceptable level of productivity in different ways.

Another factor that influences intensity of labor is the **productive life span,** the period bounded by the culturally established ages at which a person ideally enters and retires from the work force. The Bushong of Africa, for instance, define the productive years as those between the ages of twenty and sixty; the neighboring Lele regard the twenty years between the ages of thirty and fifty as an appropriate working life (Douglas 1962).

There is also the concept of **workday** or workweek—the culturally established number of hours that a person ideally spends at work each day or each week. Members of many hunting-and-gathering bands consider it normal to work three to five hours a day; and in most other preindustrial societies, underproduction —that is, the practice of working fewer hours a day than are available for work—is also the

The Invisible Woman: Cash Crops and Women's Labor in New Guinea

Until recently, anthropologists have sometimes minimized and even ignored women's economic activities. Women have been portrayed primarily as wives and mothers—that is, as reproducers rather than producers (O'Brien 1984). Yet when Patricia Lyons Johnson (1988) investigated the commercial production of coffee among the Gainj of highland New Guinea, she found that a household's commercial success in coffee growing was directly related to women's labor.

The Gainj live in the rugged and forested Takwi Valley, on the northern edge of the central highlands of Papua New Guinea. Their settlements are widely dispersed and there are no large aggregations of people that could be described as villages. The Gainj remain to a large degree subsistence slash-and-burn horticulturists, growing mixed gardens of sweet potato, taro, yam, banana, sugar cane, a variety of leafy greens, and some introduced plants, such as corn and pumpkin. They raise a few pigs and chickens, more for their ceremonial value than for consumption. Hunting is so sporadic that it contributes little to a household's diet. The Gainj men are responsible for the initial clearing and fencing of garden plots. Women are responsible for secondary clearing, burning, and planting. They also cultivate, harvest, carry, process, and cook garden produce. Since 1963, a large percentage of the men have worked as wage laborers for coastal copra (coconut) plantations, usually on two-year contracts.

Coffee was first introduced as a cash crop in 1973, and the manner of its introduction followed a pattern identified by Esther Boserup (1970:53ff.) in other parts of the developing world: regardless of the traditional division of labor in subsistence activity, cash crops and the technology that accompanies them tend to be introduced to men by men. Despite the clear identification of women with gardening, the male agricultural extension officer provided coffee seedlings and information about their cultivation, processing, and sale only to Gainj men. The men then established a new division of labor for this new garden product: men plant the coffee trees and sell the final product; all the remaining labor—cultivation, harvesting, processing, and much of the local transportation—falls to the women. Since the Gainj accord ownership of trees and their fruit to the person who plants them, and since men plant the coffee seedlings, the profits from coffee sales go exclusively to the men. "These profits are spent on investment in all-male business cooperatives, education (almost exclusively male), air travel by men to the provincial capital, and consumer goods," despite the fact that women do most of the work (Johnson 1988:111).

Taking as the unit of study the conjugal family household (that is, a household that has a male head and at least one of his wives), Johnson compared data gathered in 1978 and again in 1983 to analyze the effects on success in coffee growing of five variables: (1) age of male household head, (2) migration experience of male household head, (3) number of resident wives per household, (4) number of other women between the ages of twenty and sixty per household, and (5) number of dependents per household.

She discovered that migration experience had no significant effect on coffee growing, as measured by the number of coffee gardens a household cultivated: clearly one did not have to go out of the community to learn how to grow coffee. Age was marginally significant in that the younger male household heads, no longer able to achieve status in the traditional manner—by exhibiting prowess as a leader in warfare—tended to follow the cash-cropping path to glory, and worked hard to increase their coffee crop. The number of wives per household had a significant positive effect on success in coffee production: the more wives a man had, the more gardens he could manage. But the greatest effect on coffee production was produced by women other than wives of the household head—his unmarried daughters and sisters, the wives of sons who shared the household, and widows who chose to attach themselves to the household. This finding is explained in part by the fact that few of these women have to deal with the demands of children.

Johnson analyzed the effects of the number of dependents per household in terms of "dependency ratio"; that is, the ratio of nonworking dependents to female producers (both wives and other adult women). She found that the more successful households (three or more coffee gardens) significantly decreased their dependency ratios between 1978 and 1983, while the less successful households (fewer than three coffee gardens) had increased them. The decrease in the dependency ratio is "entirely attributable to an increase in the number of producers" (p. 117). Johnson points out that in all cases the producers are women other than the household head's wives. Between 1978 and 1983, she found, the number of such women declined in the less successful households and increased in the successful ones.

Those households considered in 1983 to be successful in producing coffee as a cash crop were the same households that in 1978 had had more dependents and fewer adult women other than wives of the household head. Johnson postulates that it was the pressure of the high dependency ratios that had motivated their move into cash cropping. But by 1983 these households had drastically altered their structure by adding women to lower their dependency ratios. Where did these women come from?

Fifty-four percent were young women who had not yet married. A mere 14 percent were women of marriageable age who had been brought into the household. The remaining 32 percent were widows who had joined the household. Most of the widows were close friends of the women already in the household and were related to the male head in such a way (either genealogical or classificatory) as to preclude their ever becoming his wives.

Johnson notes that both the retention of marriageable women and the admission of widows carries a cost to the household. The family that delays in arranging a marriage for a daughter forgoes, at least temporarily, the bridewealth that her marriage would bring, as well as the marriage ties that it would create. Widows more often than not bring dependent children with them; in fact, because widows with children are the least likely to remarry, they are the most likely to be available for incorporation into another household.

Widows currently seem to be making their decisions on the basis of strong sentimental ties with women of a particular household. Women have not yet made serious demands on men for compensation for their labor, and any material benefits they may acquire (clothing, pots, purchased foods) do not seem to weigh heavily in widows' decisions to ally themselves with a particular household. If women do come to demand some material compensation for their labor, same-sex affective ties may then become less important and the costs of such demands will have to be included in consideration of a household's economic success.

Johnson assumes that the addition of productive women enabled a household to increase its coffee production. But even if she were wrong—if, that is, it was the success of households with multiple coffee gardens that led widows to join them—the conclusion that there is a dynamic relationship between the number of female hands at work and the number of coffee gardens would not be affected. Johnson warns that ethnographers should recognize not only that women's unpaid domestic work is productive, but also that in many areas of the developing world women are "crucially involved in commercial, nondomestic production, in labor that must by any standard be recognized as productive" (p. 120).

rule. People in such societies attach a good deal of value to leisure and to the fulfillment of social obligations, and little value to the accumulation of food they can neither eat nor store and goods they do not need.

The concepts of productivity, productive life span, and workday, although culturally defined, are often redefined by individuals and households as they adjust to their own particular circumstances. We know in our own society, for instance, that some people ignore cultural guidelines in regard to the normal length of a workday and take on two eight-hour jobs, one in the daytime and one at night. Their reason may be the need to make ends meet or the wish to accumulate a large savings account rapidly. The same is true in preindustrial societies. A Lele household that found itself particularly short of members in the culturally defined productive years might well assign tasks to members under thirty or over fifty. A survey of a sample of Lele households would doubtless find significant variation in the ages of the youngest and oldest working members of each domestic group. Such variation reflects adjustment to individual circumstances. Households adjust the intensity of labor, the sexual division of labor, the working age, and working hours to meet their particular requirements.

As we mentioned earlier, intensity of labor is also affected by factors other than material need. Sahlins found, for instance, that among the Kapauku of New Guinea some households produced more than would be expected on the basis of their numbers, while others produced far less than their sizes seemed to warrant. The Kapauku have a form of political organization with well-established leaders known as "big men." These leaders and their families tend to be overproducers, while their followers and their followers' families tend to be underproducers. The big men maintain their authority primarily through conspicuous and carefully calculated generosity toward their followers. In the end, all receive enough to fulfill their individual needs. Among the Kapauku, therefore, political and economic decisions are very closely related.

Strong parallels to these observations on domestic production in nonindustrialized economies can be seen in industrializing countries. Egypt is a case in point. Agriculture is dramatically changing with industrialization, but the household still remains the primary unit of rural production and consumption. In one village in Upper Egypt, Nicholas Hopkins (1983) found considerable variation in the way households deployed their labor, the pattern chosen being determined largely by both the family's size and the amount of land to which they had access. Richer farmers had tractors, and did not work the land directly themselves. Poorer families sent their male members elsewhere to work for wages or to work as laborers in the fields of neighboring farmers. Though here the intensity of work is based less on the ratio of household workers to consumers than on ownership of land, the household remains the main vehicle for organizing the work force. Cultural ideals as to the work that is appropriate for men and for women also condition the household's strategy. Only in a family that has no other choice do women work in the fields.

Choices and Constraints

In manipulating productive strategies, a household almost always has choices. Such specialized pastoralists as the Yörük of southeastern Turkey, for example, are dependent on trade with agricultural communities and therefore are extremely vulnerable to fluctuations in the relative prices of animal and agricultural products. If the price of wheat goes up or the price of milk goes down—or if both fluctuations occur simultaneously—even owners of large herds may find themselves in severe financial straits. They may consume less of their animal products in order to have more to trade; or they may increase the productivity of their herd by investing more labor or capital in it; or they may join with other families under a single leader, the more prosperous members of the group helping the needier. All of these strategies are relatively cheap responses, in that they can easily be abandoned without great loss. Another alternative, considerably more costly, is selling the herd and trying to make a living by some other means—perhaps buying a farm, hiring out as an agricultural worker, or taking up urban employment (Bates 1973; Bates and Lees 1977).

In general, it seems that a household will first experiment with a wide range of cheap responses and only if absolutely necessary proceed to the more costly response of abandoning herding. Furthermore, when families do abandon herding, the transition is made according to a logical pattern. The first to give up herding are the rich, because they can buy farms and therefore have the least to lose by settling. The poor are the next to do so; with depleted herds, they have the most to lose from further price fluctuations and stand a better chance of surviving as agricultural laborers (see Barth 1961). Later, if economic pressures continue, middle-income herders may also switch to agriculture. In general, however, they will try to cultivate new lands, for they are usually neither rich enough to buy established farms nor poor enough to have to hire themselves out as laborers.

The Exchange of Resources

Some resources are kept and consumed by the producers, while the rest enter the society's network of exchange. Exchange, a basic part of any economic system, allows people to dispose of their unneeded surpluses and to acquire necessities from other people's unneeded surpluses. At the same time exchange serves as social cement. Indeed, some anthropologists have argued that regardless of what is exchanged, the very act of exchange is the primary bond that holds societies together.

Mechanisms of Exchange

The three mechanisms that characterize the various systems of economic exchange in human society—reciprocity, redistribution, and markets—broadly reflect the evolution of economic exchange in the course of human cultural history. **Reciprocity,** or mutual giving and taking between people who are bound by social ties and obligations, is universal (and also important among nonhuman species); **redistribution,** or reallocation of a society's wealth by means of obligatory payments or services, is a more recent phenomenon associated with specialized political institutions; **market exchange,** or the trading of goods and services through a common medium of value—money—arrived only with the advent of state societies.

People in most societies use all three mechanisms, as we do, but vary considerably in the mechanism they rely on most and the kinds of transactions they enter into by means of each mechanism. In agrarian and industrial societies, the majority of economic exchanges are conducted in highly specialized marketplaces. But in other economies (now quite rare) the market serves only a peripheral function; reciprocity and redistribution predominate. Where the market mechanism is nonexistent or is used only for certain goods, exchange is conducted through reciprocity alone or through a combination of reciprocity and redistribution.

Reciprocity. Reciprocity may play a more important role in nonindustrial societies than in industrial societies. While systematic reciprocity is important everywhere, in nonindustrialized settings gifts are given more often, in greater quantity, and to more people. The obligation to reciprocate is stronger; and most important, reciprocity plays a fundamental part in the actual production process, as it is likely to involve strategic productive resources—such as the cattle of East Africa (Dalton 1962).

Because reciprocity is so crucial to the economies of these societies, it does not always take place in the atmosphere of casual benevolence associated with our familial and neighborly exchanges of favors. Anthropologists have identified three forms of reciprocity, each involving a distinctive degree of intimacy between giver and taker, and hence a distinctive measure of formality and goodwill: generalized, balanced, and negative reciprocity.

Household members, other relatives, and friends usually engage in **generalized reciprocity**—informal gift giving for which no accounts are kept and no immediate or specific returns are expected (Sahlins 1965). Household members routinely provide services for one another with no calculation of expected return; a mother does not record for future use the cost of the breakfast cereal she feeds her children. Wage earners in households usually pool all or most of their earnings and share in their expenditures without close regard to who may be getting the most out of each transaction. Even the most casual form of reciprocity, however, operates with the implicit understanding that goods and services exchanged are to be balanced in the long run. Household members assume that they can rely on long-term mutual support; neighbors who "help out" assume that when they need help, others will come to their assistance. So in one important respect reciprocity is a form of storage or warehousing: you give goods or services to someone else and ultimately, even without close calculation, receive something comparable. This is particularly useful when the goods are perishable and cannot otherwise be stored for future use.

Generalized reciprocity historically was the characteristic form of exchange among hunting-and-gathering peoples and was essential to their adaptation. The Dobe !Kung, as we have seen (Chapter 5), have no means of preserving meat. So they exchange access to meat by sharing. When a hunter kills a sizable animal, he keeps only a small share for his family. The rest he distributes among his hunting companions, who share their portions with their kinsmen, who in turn share with other kinsmen. Tomorrow or next week, the favor will be returned. The result is that despite constantly shifting and uncertain resources, everyone eats (Marshall 1965). Of course, this is not to say that individual self-interest is lost sight of in these transactions. Melvin Konner, who worked many years with the !Kung, recalled that one respected man in the group approached him with the leg of an antelope he had killed and asked that the anthropologist keep it for him so he could consume it later (1983:375). It was clear that one reason why members of this group shared widely was that they had limited means of storage, and that it was physically very difficult to keep one's relatives and neighbors from eating one's food or using one's other possessions.

Somewhat more formal than generalized reciprocity is **balanced reciprocity,** gift giving that clearly carries the obligation of an eventual and roughly equal return. This form of reciprocity normally takes place between more distantly related individuals, friends of roughly equal social or economic status, or formal trading partners. The expectation is explicit: what is given must be balanced by a return of something comparable. As with generalized reciprocity, what is returned may be quite different from what is received, and the return gift or favor may be given later.

Many horticultural, pastoral, and agricultural societies have labor-exchange systems based on balanced reciprocity. (Remember the Oaxacan custom of guelaguetza, described in Chapter 8). At planting and harvest time, when the work load is too great for one household, neighboring households or kin groups take turns working one another's fields. The partic-

!Kung men return from a hunt with game, all of which will be shared in camp according to rules that take into account who killed the game, sex, relationship to the hunter, and need. (ANTHONY BANNISTER/ABPL)

ipants in such systems keep fairly close mental accounts of their debits and credits. A person who does not reciprocate within an appropriate time and with the same measure of labor or an equivalent gift will meet with severe social disapproval and future lack of cooperation.

Exchanges between enemies or strangers are generally impersonal transactions, with each side trying to get the better end of the bargain. Such exchanges, classified as **negative reciprocity,** involve an effort to get something for nothing or for as little as possible. They can range from unfriendly haggling to outright theft. The Mbuti Pygmies, for example, find it expedient to exchange meat and their own labor for the produce and metal of their horticultural neighbors, but these exchanges are marked by a good deal of mutual antagonism.

The villagers use threats and bribes in an effort to get as much from the Mbuti Pygmies as they can, while the Pygmies do their best to work as little as possible (Turnbull 1965). If negative reciprocity is to be truly reciprocal, the two parties must outwit each other by turns.

Redistribution. A society redistributes its wealth when it requires its members to make payments of goods, currency, or services to some central agency (a king, a chief, a religious leader, the state), which subsequently reallocates some of these resources in the form of community services, emergency help, or special rewards. Alternatively, the payments may be used to support public institutions and infrastructures, whether political or religious. In our own society, the federal income tax is supposed to function as this sort of **redistribution** mechanism. In nonmonetary societies, tribal chiefs typically redistribute unused land, hunting sites, and food surpluses to members of their tribes. This system has several advantages. It may help to guarantee adequate subsistence to all members of a society in the face of variation in the local availability of resources. It is a means of collecting some resource and storing it against future needs.

William Abruzzi (1987) describes how the Mormons colonized the valleys of Utah in the nineteenth century: each household was required to tithe to the church and to contribute labor to the community; when the Mormons experienced devastating floods or poor harvests, the church used these resources to support them through the crisis—or if a community failed, to help people settle elsewhere. Redistribution may also support specialists who serve the interests of the community—warriors, priests, artisans, and so forth. One social consequence of redistributive exchange is that it enhances the prestige, power, and authority of the person or agency responsible for collecting and controlling it. Whereas reciprocity is usually found between social equals, redistribution is based on the power of leaders over

In markets such as this one in Chinceros, Peru, goods are exchanged by barter or direct trade. Even so, the underlying values are established by market processes, much as though money were used. (CHRISTIANA DITTMANN/RAINBOW)

their subjects and is common in societies with marked political and social hierarchies (Sahlins 1965).

Market Exchange. Unlike reciprocity and redistribution, market exchange is a commercial transaction largely removed from social considerations. Goods and services may be traded (bartered) directly, but they are usually bought and sold through a standard medium of exchange—money. Beyond the requirement to pay the agreed amount and to deliver the goods or services paid for, the parties usually are under no social obligation to each other—they have no ties based on kinship, friendship, or political affiliation. Relative values of goods and services reflect supply and demand, and participants in a market economy have means of learning prevailing values—they can compare offerings by shopping, walking around a marketplace, or reading a newspaper. The seller can sell the product or service to anyone who offers the best return; the buyer can shop around for the best bargain. Not all market exchanges need be impersonal. People often establish long-term relationships with those with whom they trade. Yörük nomads, for example, usually do all their town shopping with merchants with whom they have a long-standing tie of friendship and, not incidentally, good credit. In almost any market setting some individuals play the role of middleman or broker, expediting the flow of information among buyers and sellers and, in many instances, personalizing and thus facilitating transactions.

Just as market behavior can be quite diverse, so the importance of market exchange in a society can vary widely. A West African farmer, for example, may meet most of her family's subsistence needs through her own productive activities. If she happens to have a small surplus, she may sell some of the extra crops in the marketplace and use the profit to buy a manufactured item or to pay taxes. The range of consumer goods sold in these peripheral market systems is usually quite limited; land, labor, and capital resources change hands only through reciprocity and redistribution. The economies of most industrial nations, by contrast, are based largely on market exchange. A vast commercial network, linking millions of individuals and business firms, allocates not only an enormous array of consumer products but also land, labor, and capital resources.

The Organization of Exchange

All three forms of exchange—reciprocity, redistribution, and market exchange—operate together to some degree in all contemporary societies, but certain rules determine to which particular goods each mechanism of exchange applies, and in what situations. Anthropologists describe this differentiation as the operation of **spheres of exchange.** Among the Siane of New Guinea, for example, luxury goods—tobacco, salt, nuts, oil—circulate in a free-market setting, but subsistence items are distributed through reciprocity (Nash 1966). In the Trobriands, ceremonial objects are exchanged according to the principle of reciprocity; subsistence items, through purchase and sale. The islanders keep these two spheres of exchange entirely separate: one can never sell a ceremonial armband for yams or a canoe. In our society we keep many transactions of household members distinct from those with outsiders; a wife does not pay her husband to wash her car, nor does a husband pay his wife for her care when he is ill. But the distinction becomes blurred when one borrows money from a relative and pays interest or employs one's child to make repairs on the family dwelling. In many societies that do not consider sex to be a market commodity, prostitution is nevertheless common; people everywhere find opportunities and strategies for such **conversion**—the use of a sphere of exchange for a transaction with which it is not generally associated.

Just as some rules dictate which mechanisms of exchange are appropriate, other rules govern the terms on which a given exchange is transacted. Supply and demand, of course, influence price, but other factors are also involved. Among the Kapauka of New Guinea, for example, the kinship relationship between traders and their relative statuses can affect the terms of the deal (Pospisil 1963). And in our own society, although we are fond of saying that business is business and a person always sells to the highest bidder, we may know of relatives and friends who could sell us items at cost rather than at retail prices.

ECONOMIC EXPERIMENTATION AND ADAPTATION

Like all aspects of adaptation, strategies of production and exchange are never static. By experimenting with new approaches or by being forced to deviate from traditional ones, people inevitably discover new methods that may eventually alter their economic organization.

The human capacity to cope with new situations is seen to good advantage in the phenomenon of **entrepreneurship**—economic innovation and risk taking. In their efforts to solve some pressing economic problem, some people even in socialist states manage to gain a personal advantage and ultimately effect a change in the larger economic system. Patricia Vondal (1987) describes the efforts of some small farmers in Borneo to break out of their poverty and obtain consumer goods by investing in ducks. Ducks could be sold on the regional market to satisfy an increasing need for low-cost meat in the cities. But to take advantage of this possibility, innovating farmers had to risk their land and homes to make the initial investment in the novel enterprise. Cages and other structures had to be built, bran and poultry feed either produced in quantity or pur-

chased, market outlets secured—all of which required capital and risk. Some duck farmers failed; others reaped the rewards of the successful innovator.

Lucie Saunders and an Egyptian colleague, Sohair Mehenna (1986), who worked together in a village in the Nile Delta, had good data on the economy and social life of this community spanning several generations. They found that certain families were consistently involved in risk taking through entrepreneurial innovation. At the end of the nineteenth century, when the transport system was rapidly improving and cotton was the dominant cash crop, one individual used proceeds from successful village shops to consolidate a modest estate on irrigated land. In the postrevolutionary era, land reform and new laws governing farm labor limited the profits from farming. Members of the same family, who had been innovators a generation earlier, sought out new activities. Most recently the grandsons were experimenting with the introduction of chickens. They purchased foreign stock, acquired the necessary equipment, and built hatcheries. As their profits mounted from the sale of poultry to Cairo families, others emulated their operations, and a new industry was founded.

Whether or not the efforts of entrepreneurs reflect a conscious strategy, they inevitably have important consequences. First, entrepreneurs most commonly engage in activities that take them over the boundary between traditional and modern economic organization. They recognize the potential of market exchange, for example, and bring the products of new factories or imported goods into the countryside to compete with traditional handicrafts and to create new needs. Second, while an entrepreneurial effort may originate with an individual, it rarely succeeds unless others join and support the new enterprise (Barth 1963). And finally, these entrepreneurial actions typically lead to fundamental changes in the systems of production and distribution. Farmers may begin to produce more cash crops; they—or their children—may choose to work in the factory rather than the fields. These changes in turn will begin to transform gender relations, social and family structures, and eventually the whole society.

But no matter how they are introduced, innovations are not always successful. People may experiment a good deal before arriving at an idea, technique, or product that proves more effective or socially beneficial than the old method. Changes can be relatively easy to effect in one situation but not in another. Or they may quite simply be inappropriate for a particular society or at a particular time.

Today in India, for example, the rush toward large-scale heavy industry that characterized

efforts at development after independence in 1947 has largely stopped, because the consequences often have been the opposite of what was desired and expected. The country simply could not compete with already industrialized nations. Now the development emphasis appears to be on light, high-technology industry, but the results are as yet unclear. One thing is clear, however: instead of experiencing large-scale reorganization and better distribution of wealth, the country is seeing an accentuation of the traditional dichotomy between rich and poor. A populous nation such as India does not always benefit from labor-saving innovations and mass-production techniques.

Summary

A society's *economic system* consists of ideas, behaviors, and institutions. Basic to classical economic theory is the idea of *scarce resources.* As people inevitably have more wants than they have resources to satisfy them, they must make *rational economic decisions*, weighing alternatives and deciding which will benefit them most at the least cost. Many social scientists have argued that social and economic institutions perpetuate themselves regardless of the needs of individuals. The economic view of anthropology sees the economy as the process by which a society is provisioned by its own institutions. One school of thought, *substantivism*, seeks to explain economic processes as the maintenance of an entire cultural order rather than the workings of individual decision makers. Another, *formalism*, argues that formal economic theory can be broadened to be made applicable to any economic system. Recent investigators have found that the rationality of an economic decision cannot be judged without an awareness of the circumstances surrounding it, and that in some societies markets serve noneconomic as well as economic functions.

In order to explain and compare the economic systems of different societies, anthropologists investigate three economic domains: *regulation of access to resources;* the *production* process; and the *exchange* of goods and services.

Strategies for securing natural resources are devised to ensure access to resource-rich land. Agricultural and industrial societies generally maintain clear-cut territorial boundaries, which restrict the use of land to certain groups. Hunters and gatherers, however, require greater flexibility to account for seasonal variation in the availability of resources. Typically, the more uncertain or mobile the food supply, the greater the need for flexible boundaries. The extent to which a territory is defended depends on the gains versus the costs of maintaining exclusive rights to a parcel of land.

Industrial societies observe the concept of private ownership of property, or *freehold*, emphasizing individual control of resources for individual benefit. This concept is alien to the majority of horticultural, pastoral, and hunting-and-gathering societies, in which the individual gains rights to resources only by virtue of affiliation with a group that controls them (*corporate ownership*). In these societies, individuals have the right to use the community's resources but they do not own them. As more and more societies are affected by industrialization, however, the practice of private ownership is replacing traditional land-use systems; economic systems are becoming less tied to the general system of social relationships. One outcome is *alienation*, the fragmentation of individuals' relations to their work, the things they produce, and the resources with which they produce them.

Producing usable goods is as important a part of survival as acquiring resources. In studying cross-cultural variation in production, one must consider how production is organized and what the productive strategies are. In industrial societies, the production unit is the business firm, whose function is strictly economic. In nonindustrial societies, the basic production unit is often the household, or domestic group. Nearly all the skills needed for production can be found in a single household; additional effort is supplied by kin and friends. In these societies that employ the *domestic mode of production*, productive activities are linked to many noneconomic functions. Like collective ownership of resources, this type of domestic production has declined with the spread of industrialism.

Productive strategies combine three elements—natural resources, labor, and capital. In industrial societies, the critical variable in a productive strategy is usually capital; in nonindustrial societies, labor decisions are generally most important. The more mouths people have to feed in relation to the number of workers in the household, the harder they must work. Factors that influence the intensity of labor include people's concepts of *productivity* (the amount of work a person accomplishes in a given amount of time), *productive life span* (the period bounded by the culturally estab-

lished ages at which a person enters and leaves the labor force), and *workday* (the culturally established number of hours that a person ideally spends at work each day). These culturally defined concepts are often redefined by individuals and households as they adjust to their circumstances.

After goods are produced, those that are not kept or consumed by the producer enter the society's network of exchange. There are three major exchange mechanisms: reciprocity, redistribution, and market exchange. *Reciprocity*, which plays a much greater role in nonindustrial societies than in our own, involves giving and taking without the exchange of money, between people who are bound by certain social ties and obligations. Three forms of reciprocity involve different degrees of intimacy between giver and taker—*generalized reciprocity*, *balanced reciprocity*, and *negative reciprocity*. *Redistribution* involves obligatory payments of goods, currency, or services to a central agency, which then reallocates some portion of them. *Market exchange* is the trading of goods and services through a common medium of value, a transaction removed from social considerations. Most societies use all three forms of exchange, but each society has rules that determine the *spheres of exchange* that apply to particular goods and situations. But these distinctions are often blurred; people everywhere find opportunities for *conversion* of a sphere of exchange to a transaction of a sort not usually associated with it.

A degree of economic experimentation and variation is usually necessary for survival. When we study *entrepreneurship*, or economic innovation and risk taking, it is clear that in every society the economy is part of the overall system of social organization; one aspect cannot be changed without provoking changes in the others. The needs and values of a particular society at a particular time may determine the course of economic change.

Key Terms

alienation	entrepreneurship	production	regulation of access to
balanced reciprocity	exchange	productive life span	resources
conversion	formalism	productivity	scarce resources
corporate ownership	freehold	rational economic	spheres of exchange
domestic mode of	generalized reciprocity	decisions	substantivism
production	market exchange	reciprocity	workday
economic system	negative reciprocity	redistribution	

Suggested Readings

BENNETT, J. W., AND J. R. BOWEN (EDS.). 1988. *Production and Economy: Anthropological Studies and Critiques of Development.* Lantham, Md.: University Press of America. Monographs in Economic Anthropology, no. 5. Original essays that explore anthropology and development through numerous case studies from different regions.

DURRENBERGER, P. (ED.). 1984. *Chayanov, Peasants and Economic Anthropology.* Orlando, Fla.: Academic Press. A collection of original essays that explore the utility of the Chayanov or domestic mode of production approach to understanding peasant economics.

ETIENNE, M., AND E. LEACOCK (EDS.). 1988. *Women and Colonization: Anthropological Perspectives.* South Hadley, Mass.: Bergin & Garvey. A presentation of case studies from twelve societies that focus on colonization and women. The authors examine women's economic, social and political roles before and after colonization.

LEACOCK, E., AND H. I. SAFA (EDS.). 1988. *Women's Work: Development and the Division of Labor.* South Hadley, Mass.: Bergin & Garvey. (paperback edition). Examines development and modernization in terms of changing rewards and costs for women.

NASH, J. AND H. I. SAFA. 1985. *Women and Change in Latin America.* South Hadley, Mass.: Bergin & Garvey. A collection of accounts that document the effects on women of the economic crisis in Latin America and the survival strategies they are employing, such as migration, industrial occupations, and mobilization through various forms of collective action.

ORTIZ, S. (ED.). 1983. *Economic Anthropology: Topics and Theories.* Lantham, Md.: University Press of America. Monographs in Economic Anthropology, no. 1. Original essays exploring theory and topical research in economic anthropology today.

SCHNEIDER, H. K. 1989. *Economic Man: The Anthropology of Economics.* Salem, Wisc.: Sheffield Publishing. An investigation of how culture affects resource allocation and how scarcity and conflicting needs determine how people cope with uncertainty.

Chapter **15** Politics, Social Control, and Political Organization

From an anthropological perspective, politics closely resembles economics in that virtually every social activity can be seen as having political implications. In every society there are scarce or limited rewards for which people compete, rules that govern this competition, and procedures for mitigating conflicts that arise among individuals and groups. **Politics** is the process by which a community's decisions are made, rules for group behavior are established, competition for positions of leadership is regulated, and the disruptive effects of disputes are minimized. Political organization is the larger context in which political processes unfold.

Politics is a universal aspect of all human relations. Politics has been succinctly defined as the process of "who gets what, when, and how" (Laswell 1936). Although this definition was formulated to characterize the political process in our own and other state systems, it is broad enough to apply to societies throughout the world. Even such small groups as families and households can be considered arenas of political behavior. Political scientists tend to focus on state-level institutions, national parties, state policy, and international diplomacy. Anthropologists, by contrast, tend to focus on individual communities and relatively small-scale political systems.

THE NATURE OF POLITICAL BEHAVIOR

At the bottom of all political competition lies disagreement—conflicting ideas about individual interests and community life. The specific issues involved can be almost anything individuals or groups consider important, anything they deem worth competing for. In all these cases the decisions that are eventually reached will benefit some people or groups more than others, in spite of lofty rhetoric to the contrary. But societies vary widely in the kinds of decisions people attempt to influence and in the nature of the rewards they expect.

Among hunting-and-gathering peoples, for example, political competition may arise over disagreements about where to search for game, marriage arrangements, food sharing, when to move camp, where a new camp should be located, or any other matter in which the entire group has an interest. The ways in which these disagreements are resolved is politics, even though the process may not seem very competitive by our own standards. A decision affecting the community has to be made, and often one group's or one individual's desires or needs prevail over those of others.

The Politics of Sociability

If there is a common denominator to anthropological studies of local-level politics, it surely must be the complexity of factional alignments and, for the observer at least, the bewildering shifts in loci of power and decision making. At the heart of this complexity, so it would seem, lies a factor that is hard for the outsider to comprehend: the unique ability of certain individuals to mobilize supporters and allies and to translate personal qualities of charisma and sociability into political power.

The Siuai of the Solomon Islands in the South

Pacific have no hereditary leaders, but they do have "big men" (Burling 1974:15–17). These men are important leaders who achieve their positions by economic and social activities carried out over a long period of time. First a man builds up his economic resources by opening up more fields, and he tries to marry several wives. These women work his gardens and feed his herds of pigs—all essential to the great feasts he must sponsor if he is to gain and consolidate a reputation as a big man. Eventually he builds a clubhouse for his entourage and engages in competition with other big men for prestige. Even though this competition is carried out largely in the social arena, certain big men acquire great influence over the actions of others. A big man has the ability to give away food in time of need, to mobilize public opinion, and generally to shape public policy. Hundreds, even thousands of people can be brought into political cooperation in this manner. But the society has no formal structure by which the big man can pass his position to an heir. When he dies, his power dies with him.

Almost all of the societies we have described in our discussions of hunters and gatherers, horticulturists, and pastoralists find their leaders, make decisions, and organize the succession of leadership in similarly fluid, personal, and informal ways. Pokot men spend a good part of each day in small groups discussing current events and, in effect, making group decisions. The same is true of the San people and the Yanomamö. Even in societies that have more formally designated leaders and even hereditary lines of succession, as with the Bedouin of Arabia and the Hopi of the American Southwest, most day-to-day decisions are made in the context of informal discussion and debate. Women participate in this process. Although women's discussions are usually dismissed as "gossip" by men (Riegelhaupt 1967), women's networks are vital lines of political communication.

The Environment of Political Behavior

Environmental factors can render a highly personalized and flexible system of local-level politics advantageous at every level of political complexity. These highly personalized political activities in turn affect the development and stability of forms of political organization and institutions that transcend local groups. Local populations, even individuals, by necessity cultivate and maintain multiple political and social ties that help them to cope with prevailing uncertainties of all sorts. Often one's allegiance is less to a set of abstract ideals or to a political party or faction than to specific individuals or positions of authority. In the Middle East and Africa, for example, membership in particular parties or allegiance to political leaders overlaps with important sources of one's social identity: religion, ethnicity, even tribal affiliation. But, as any politician knows, people are fickle in their loyalties and commitments. Often they have to be as a matter of survival.

Until very recently in the West, and still in many parts of the world, local populations were dependent on local food resources. At the same time, as we noted in Chapters 7 and 8, the potential for agriculture or other forms of food procurement is highly variable, with sharp contrasts between highly productive and marginal areas. Even within regions, members of particular societies are often differentiated in regard to access to critical resources and to their place in the system of production. There is inevitably a great deal of exchange of food items, labor, and other services both within communities and among them—virtually no local population is completely self-sufficient. Pokot farming and herding households exchange things continually, the pastoral Yörük sell their animal products in markets, the Pygmies of the Ituri Forest in Zaire trade forest products for grain with their Bantu farming neighbors, and so forth.

The result of this variability and interdependence is that prosperity is unevenly distributed, with affluent communities frequently abutting smaller and poorer ones; households and groups are simultaneously faced with the need to compete and to cooperate. Peasants and pastoralists may fight for the same well; upstream villagers may fight with downstream neighbors over water rights. Communities, neighbors, and even relatives may find themselves in competition even as they rely on each other for help and the exchange of goods. Individuals try to maintain as wide a range of contacts as possible and are continually prepared to shift alliances as their interest dictates.

Environmental uncertainty is another factor that encourages individuals and groups to maintain a multiplicity of political associations. Most communities periodically face conditions of drought, disease, and the like which require them to seek help from others—even from people with whom relations may be strained or hostile. Observers of social life in the Middle East have been struck by the great amount of time and energy people spend in socializing and politicking. Whether in the ubiquitous teahouses of rural Turkey, Iraq, and Iran, in the village guesthouses of Syria, or in the urban coffee shops of Egypt, clusters of men and women meet (usually separately) almost daily to reaffirm existing ties, to forge new ones, and to keep an eye on each other's activities.

As the level of social complexity increases, so do the number and scope of objectives that unite and potentially divide people. In our society, overt political competition is focused on access to public office and such issues as the portion of income and personal property that should be taxed, where a new housing project or nuclear waste dump should be built (or not built), and the kind of arms or trade agreements that should be reached with a foreign nation. Parties to the competition typically mobilize impressive support to bolster their posi-

tions and apply all sorts of legal and occasionally illegal pressure in an effort to turn the decision in their favor.

In state-organized societies, the working of politics is most evident in the working of bureaucracy—the formal system of specialists whose tasks are to ensure that rules are obeyed, that penalties are imposed on those who deviate, and that taxes and revenues reach their approved destinations. This system may have such formal groupings as the judicial system, the civil service, the legislature, and the executive or ruling cadre. Such a formal political system may overshadow the way the political process operates at the local or informal level, but the fact remains that the political process is rooted in the daily decisions and actions of individuals. And in every society, local-level politics is intensely personalized and extremely fluid.

THE POLITICS OF SOCIAL CONTROL

Political competition, whether heated or muted, is rarely a free-for-all; it is always governed by conventions or norms. Rules of conduct allow some types of political activity and prohibit others. Clearly, rules of some kind are necessary; they allow us to predict with relative accuracy what other people will do in a given situation and the way they will respond to our behavior. Yet, as we well know, rules are not necessarily followed, nor are all of a society's rules in the interest of all its members. Thus the potential for conflict is fundamental to all political processes, and when conflict becomes intense enough, it may erupt into violence or rebellion. Some features present in all societies, however, serve to restrain violence and disruption while conflicting interests are being resolved and thus prevent the political process from dissolving into chaos.

One such factor is the multiplicity of competing social demands for an individual's or group's loyalty. This factor is inherent in any social order, for individuals and groups are socially interrelated in complex ways. Thus opponents in one area may well be allies in another. Such cross-cutting ties tend to discourage wholehearted enmity and to reduce the potential for violence.

But cross-cutting ties may also limit the possibility for unity when important matters require solidarity. Consequently, although such ties tend to deter violence, they may also be a source of instability. In the idealized tribal political structure, ties of descent override all others as a principle for mobilizing people for action. But such unity may be very difficult to achieve. In reality, the local descent group is composed of individuals who are related in numerous ways and are involved in continually shifting alliances. Even if unity, say for warfare, is achieved, it is frequently short-lived. The result is a very dynamic political system in which violence is limited but long-term stability is highly elusive.

Conventions designed to keep political competition within reasonable bounds are also built into the formal structures of most political systems. Of course, political prescriptions cannot spell out exact behaviors in every situation. There is almost always room for individual interpretation and choice. "Thou shall not kill," for example, may sound quite unambiguous. Yet some individuals subscribe to the interpretation "Thou shall not kill except during wars or when acting on behalf of the state." Others may find killing justifiable only in cases of self-defense. Social rules set broad guidelines for much of our behavior, but individual decision making is inevitable, and with it comes variation in the way the rules are actually followed—or not followed.

Rules and Deviance

Deviance from social rules and laws is part of the fabric of daily life. Individuals are bound to differ in the ways they think, feel, and act. So it is not surprising that people deviate from social expectations. When an infraction is not considered damaging to anyone else (as in the case of scanty or bizarre dress), it is often tolerated, and eventually it may be considered acceptable. More serious infractions may or may not be tolerated. In the United States prostitutes are breakers of social conventions and, almost always, of laws as well. In some communities they are rigorously prosecuted; in others their infractions are overlooked, except perhaps during periodic crackdowns. In some counties of Nevada prostitution is legal. Every society labels certain acts as deviant, such as theft, incest, and murder. When an infraction is considered serious enough, a society's response can be extremely severe.

In view of the variability of human behavior, we might well ask why people do not deviate more often than they do, and how they are induced to follow the rules, even when such obedience runs counter to their apparent (or at least immediate) self-interest. The answer lies in social control. **Social control** restructures individual self-interest by providing a framework of rewards and sanctions that channel behavior. Every society has its own means, formal and informal, of dealing with deviance.

Informal Means of Social Control

The most obvious means of social control are often the formal or institutionalized ones. In our society, police forces, courts, reformatories, and prisons serve to deal with people who step too far out of line, but the average citizen seldom feels the full force of these agencies of social control. For most people, a society's informal means of control are sufficient to ensure a reasonable amount of conformity to the rules.

When people venture over the boundaries of their society's rules, **social pressure** often brings them back into line. Such pressure can be very subtle or very blunt; but regardless of its form, it can be highly successful. Social pressure can channel even political and economic action. During the civil rights movement in the American South in the 1960s and 1970s, social pressure helped mobilize black and white activists, while social pressure in some white communities was a primary means of continuing segregation in the face of legal penalties and black opposition.

In many societies satire and gossip are powerful social pressures. People everywhere dislike being publicly ridiculed or having their misdeeds broadcast to others. In the Arab village of Kufr al Ma in Jordan, satire has been honed to a sharp edge in an elaborate system of nicknaming (Antoun 1968). The system is organized in such a way as to indicate the degree of dissatisfaction caused by the violation of social expectations.

The hierarchy of terms begins with neutral occupational names, proceeds to slightly ironic names based on personal habits, and culminates in distinctly pejorative names based on physical or social defects. The villagers most often criticize slander and backbiting, behaviors that are expressly condemned in Koranic verses and traditions. The satirical use of such epithets as Gossiper and Busybody thus serves to humiliate a person who has violated an important social rule. The Yörük of Turkey do almost exactly the same but take great care never to use the derogatory nickname in the presence of the offender or his or her relatives. They achieve the same result because everyone knows that with unacceptable behavior they will acquire an unfortunate label.

David Gilmore (1987) found much the same situation in a small town in Spain, and came to the conclusion that conformity was enforced not by the laws of the Spanish state but by a moral structure reinforced by gossip, name-calling, and backbiting. People in this small town were intensely interested in one another's activities, jealous of those who were able to better their economic lot, and quick to attack through gossip and slander those who violated the social status quo.

Social pressure can also take the form of informal shunning and ostracism, the ignoring and exclusion of offenders. Being ignored is generally a painful experience, and even the threat of it can often be an effective means of social control. Among traditional peoples living outside of state systems, such as the Inuit and !Kung, ostracism can be tantamount to a death sentence, as one cannot survive alone. In close-knit religious communities in the United States, ostracism is sometimes a very powerful means of punishing one who has violated a moral code.

A widespread means of social pressure is rooted in beliefs about the supernatural. Moral codes expressed in religious terms are familiar to all of us. Not so familiar today but quite common in the past is the condemnation of individuals viewed as threatening to a community's interest as heretics or witches. In medieval Europe and in colonial America, individuals thought to practice witchcraft were driven from their communities or executed. Their real crime often merely was to have aroused the fears and hostility of their neighbors by behaving differently from others of their sex (generally female) and age group (usually elderly).

Informal social pressure can also be brought to bear in the form of threatened vengeance. Vengeance is an extreme response to assault or similar crimes against one's person. In one sense it is like a formal mechanism of control in that the response is highly predictable among members of the society. But it differs

Among the Huli of Papua, New Guinea, the public reprimand is the punishment for adultery. Here a wife accused of adultery is forced to the ground while her husband's kinspeople scream insults and point at her. The reprimand lasts for several hours and may include beatings and other forms of physical punishment. *(ROBERT GLASSE)*

from formal legal sanctions in that it is embedded in the structure of kinship relations rather than administered by an impersonal authority outside the family.

Violence, as in the case of the blood feud, pits kin groups or families against each other, with revenge as the principal motive. A typical blood feud starts when a member of one family is murdered or assaulted. The victim's relatives then seek to avenge the crime, attempting to kill the murderer or one of his close relatives. Such feuds occur among the Yörük; when a person is killed, close patrilineal male relatives feel a strong obligation to seek revenge on the aggressor's patrilineal relatives (excluding the women and children). Even if the state arrests and punishes a murderer, the victim's relatives still try to avenge the killing. Only then is it possible to conclude peace between the families. But this peace is an uneasy one, and one murder may result in a series of killings. The sense of mutual obligation arising from kinship is so strong that a man killed in the course of aggression toward another is usually avenged by his relatives, even when they agree that he was in the wrong. At the same time, this strongly felt sense of mutual responsibility encourages people to control the behavior of their relatives and to avoid confrontations in the first place.

Formal Means of Social Control

No society functions with only informal means of social control. Sooner or later, conflicts erupt between individuals and acts are committed that are viewed as threatening to the entire community. Such events are inevitable when human beings live together. Of course, the extent of conflict varies. But in most societies, conflicts and disputes are a normal part of everyday life. And most societies have established some kind of formal action to resolve such disputes before they become too heated or to deter the offenders before they rip the fabric of social life.

Law and the Legal Process

Laws and legal processes to implement them are the most formal means of social control. A **law** is a rule of social conduct enforced by sanctions administered by a particular source of legitimate power (Fried 1967). Laws serve the important functions of eliminating some areas of potential conflict and minimizing the degree of actual conflict. Without some formal means of social control, disputes or retaliation for wrongs committed could become very costly, even for those not directly concerned. Still, laws and the legal process usually benefit or penalize

some individuals in a society more than others. Thus, while laws may help to structure behavior, resolve disagreement, and penalize wrongdoers, they also may engender further inequality and conflict.

In nonliterate societies the legal tradition is oral rather than codified. In many ways these noncodified systems of social control—or law—appear to resemble codified systems, but there are some very important differences. The law administered by a codified legal system may be much further removed from the desires and needs of particular segments of the society. In fact, the general public may be ignorant of most of the actual body of law. This gulf between individuals and the legal apparatus gives considerable power to those who interpret, administer, and enforce laws and adjudicate disputes.

Between the extremes of informal customary practices and codified bureaucratic legal systems lies a broad range of forms, procedures, or mechanisms for settling disputes and regulating conflicting interests. All societies have methods of mediation or adjudication and modes of settlement or redress.

Methods of Adjudication

In our own society, trial before a judge and jury is a method of adjudicating or deciding a case. Two parties who contest the interpretation and application of a law in a particular situation are handed a decision by a judge and possibly a jury. Some method of adjudication is found in every society. Such methods typically involve some sort of hearing conducted in accordance with accepted procedures. The final settlement can be reached in any one of several ways. Disputants may, for instance, seek a solution through negotiation, which may or may not be mediated by an impartial third party; or they may state their case in the presence of an adjudicator, whose job it is to "hand down" a decision. There are numerous variations on these basic themes both within and among societies, which in a very general sense again can be termed informal and formal.

The Kpelle of central Liberia follow both formal and informal procedures. Formal adjudication takes place in a court, where procedures are basically coercive and authoritarian. Because of its somewhat harsh tone, the court is not suited for disputes in which reconciliation is of primary importance. In such situations the informal meetings, or "moots," are more appropriate. These proceedings take place in a home, where the complainants sit among a group of their kin and interested neighbors and before a mediator. Unlike the rigid structure of the courtroom, the structure of the moot is relatively loose; people mix freely and both sides are able to state their cases fully and to question each other and anyone else present. After all the evidence has been given, the group as a whole determines who is in the right. The guilty party then makes a public apology and gives token gifts to the wronged party; the winner reciprocates with small gifts of acceptance (Gibbs 1963).

Among the Nuer cattle herders and farmers of Sudan, if disputes break out among members of the same lineage, the parties are expected to turn to their oldest living common ancestor for mediation. Among most Middle Eastern tribes, they turn to the formally recognized leader of their descent group; among the Yạnomamö, they are likely to seek out the headman or possibly the shaman. The Nuer also have special chiefs called Leopard-skin chiefs who use supernatural sanctions to arbitrate feuds and other conflicts within groups. Lebanese villagers often turn to mediators, who tend to be men who are recognized for their impartiality or honesty. In our own society, the existence of courts tends to force most cases to a settlement outside the court; but the very existence of a formal process for adjudication serves to structure informal remedies.

It is important to realize that neither informal nor formal means of social control are ever completely effective. They do serve to reduce deviance, but they do not eradicate it. The social rules underlying mechanisms of social control are not necessarily agreed upon by all members of a society. Finally, the mechanisms of social control do not affect all people equally. Particularly in highly stratified societies, laws and methods of adjudication may be used by the rich and powerful to maintain their position. This has been said about some of our own mechanisms of social control—as when our laws and legal procedures work to the disadvantage of the poor and often of women.

Law and Tribes in the Twentieth Century

Autonomous tribal societies, such as those in North America, Africa, Australia, South America, and parts of Asia, once determined their own customs and sanctions and managed their own legal affairs. They used their own local procedures to settle disputes, regulate access to resources, and so forth. But with the spread of colonialism in the late nineteenth and early twentieth centuries (earlier in the Americas), many local populations were integrated into complex, codified legal systems, generally based on European models. Throughout the far-flung British Empire, for example, British administrators encountered legal systems quite different from their own. In few areas did they attempt to impose English law in its entirety on local peoples. Rather, local law or custom was modified to suit the purposes of the new rulers. Often this change was rationalized as a progressive move, as when women were granted greater legal standing. More often the revisions imposed and the new laws enacted served the interests of the colonial power and its local allies.

These systems have usually remained even after the populations gained their independ-

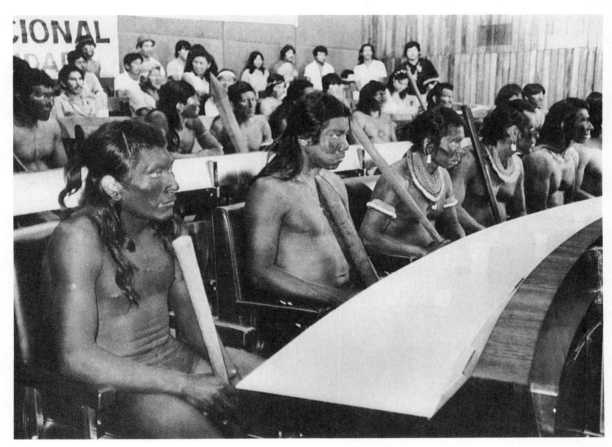

Kaiapo Indian leaders attend a 1988 meeting of the Constitutional Assembly in Belem, Brazil. The assembly was then voting on the rights the central government would grant to the Indians. (MARLISE SIMON/THE NEW YORK TIMES)

ence. In Africa today, for example, the legal systems of emerging or newly independent countries are based on various European codes. And except in very limited spheres, Native Americans are governed by the United States legal codes, which in turn evolved primarily from English common law.

Such integration of local systems into national—and, from the local community's point of view, alien—systems has created problems. In a bureaucratic, complex, and highly centralized legal system, access to the courts, to redress, and to protection of legal rights requires one to work through a series of intermediaries—lawyers, prosecutors, judges, and so forth. These legal intricacies tend to be in-

timidating, discouraging, and in many cases, costly.

In addition, these centralized systems of law were often introduced with the explicit purpose of transforming the political and economic basis of the colonized society. This transformation benefited the colonial power by making the local population more malleable and their elite dependent on the colonial regime (Wolf 1982).

A case in point is that of Bunyoro, a kingdom in western Uganda colonized by the British, who introduced a land-tenure act that registered all land as freehold. Bunyoro society had previously had a feudal structure: all land had nominally been owned by the king, who had allocated plots to the people who actually worked it. It might seem that giving title to that land to individuals would promote equal access to it. But, because the British gave title to a group of nobility who had formerly had the right to manage tracts on behalf of the Bunyoro king, the new system actually created a landed aristocracy. Whereas previously these notables did not own the land and had to maintain good relations with the people who worked it, they now became landowners, and their former tenants became workers, with no right to communal use of the fields. The new land-tenure system weakened the power of the Bunyoro king, but it also decreased the traditional access rights of many of the people who farmed the land (Middleton 1960).

ACCESS TO THE POLITICAL PROCESS

Every society not only has norms governing the way people may participate in political competition but also has both formal and informal rules that determine who may participate. While the results of political competition may affect every member of a society, it does not necessarily follow that everyone in the community is equally involved in the political process. All societies impose certain formal qualifications for participation in different areas of politics. Group membership is the most basic of these formal qualifications. Age and gender restrictions are also common; women are often excluded from political decision making.

But formal exclusion from the decision-making process does not necessarily imply lack of political influence. As anyone familiar with the American political system knows, formal offices and positions of authority do not tell the whole story about who actually holds power. Informal channels of access to decision making are frequently open to people who cannot or simply do not hold recognized positions of authority. In societies that formally restrict women's access to political office, they may exert informal influence on their husbands, brothers, and sons. Among the Iroquois, men held the dominant political positions, but women selected the officeholders. Thus we must not confuse the norms that govern formal participation in the political process with the actual exercise of influence and power. The two may be quite different.

The number of criteria restricting access to political roles increases with a society's complexity. In state societies, not only group membership, age, and gender but also ethnicity, religion, caste, wealth, and education may circumscribe political participation. These criteria can be embedded in formal rules as well as in informal practices. In our own society, neither gender, ethnicity, nor wealth is a basis for formal restrictions to participation in the political process; yet women, the poor, and members of some ethnic minorities are still not proportionately represented among officeholders and in positions of political influence. Access to the political process in societies such as our own is hierarchically organized. While the right to vote has given most minority groups access at one level of participation, the higher levels—the domain of the ruling elite—are still less accessible.

POLITICAL LEADERSHIP: AUTHORITY AND POWER

Naturally, restrictions on access to political influence affect the determination of leadership.

Some criteria for leadership may be highly idiosyncratic. Individuals may be able to influence others because they possess charisma or because they have persistently demonstrated wisdom or good fortune.

Leadership can also be established by success in mobilizing organizational support. The general rules because he has the support of the army; candidates are elected to office because they can mobilize the greatest numbers of voters. Often these two kinds of leadership criteria work together. In Melanesia, as we noted earlier, status and prestige are accorded to certain individuals known as "big men." A big man has typically demonstrated certain personal qualities, such as bravery or speechmaking ability, that make him worthy of admiration. But these qualities alone will never accord him the status of big man. He must also have a following, which he can acquire only through exceptional, habitual, and calculated generosity. Such generosity, in turn, is based largely on the skillful manipulation of food production or trade relations with others.

When we discuss political leadership, it is useful to distinguish between **power**, the ability to exert influence because one's directives are backed by sanctions of one sort or another (the ultimate negative sanction being the use of physical force), and **authority**, the ability to exert influence simply because of one's personal prestige or the status of one's office (Fried 1967). Among the !Kung, for example, some individuals may acquire authority but not power. They can affect the behavior of others because their opinions are respected for one reason or another, but they cannot effectively impose threats or sanctions of any kind. A Melanesian big man has a somewhat more clearly defined political position, but his authority rests ultimately on his ability to persuade. In state societies, however, officials exercise both power and authority. They can force citizens to behave in certain ways through the use of sanctions backed by armed force. Political authority may be either *ascribed* or *achieved;* that is, it may be based on ancestry or some other ascribed quality, such as divinity or holiness, or it may be achieved by military success, electoral success, demonstrated moral worth, or some other factor.

Power and authority need not always accompany each other, but we find that as population densities increase with the evolution of more effective food-production strategies, positions of authority become increasingly formalized and power is centralized in them. Many reasons for this development have been advanced, yet the lines of causality are not entirely clear. With the development of irrigation agriculture, for example, some communities and some regions emerge as especially favored, grow rapidly, and expand at the expense of others. Certainly the extension of political control, via warfare or otherwise, entails the development of mechanisms for enforcing orders over a large area.

Also, as population size increases within political entities, the volume of information that has to be processed, the number of decisions made, the number of possible communication problems generated are all so great that some political division of labor is essential—groups that develop an administrative hierarchy gain an advantage. After all, the chief or big man in a small community can talk to everyone face to face. But in a fairly large regional population such personal dealings are not practical. By delegating authority, leaders extend their control and in so doing create a form of bureaucratic hierarchy. This bureaucratic hierarchy can coordinate the activities of many workers, fighters, and food producers. In groups without administrative hierarchies, there are fairly narrow limits as to the number of people who can be coordinated without resort to division into subgroups, each with its own leader or spokesperson (Johnson 1983).

Responding to Oppression: Two Case Studies

There are occasions when apparently passive and powerless individuals galvanize themselves to rebel against authority. What combination of circumstances and motivations provokes active opposition to oppression, and what circumstances determine the success or failure of these small-scale revolutions? Let us look at two examples: the Memphis garbage strike of 1968 and the 1977 movement of *las madres de la Plaza de Mayo*—the mothers of the "disappeared" in Argentina.

Traditionally, Memphis had been the first stop for rural southern blacks on their way to Chicago and other cities of the North. Most of the migrants came from areas of high unemployment, had little money and minimal education, and consequently were willing to accept any job they could get in Memphis. Those who grew dissatisfied moved north rather than fight to improve conditions. The employment available consisted mainly of menial service jobs, since Memphis was a commercial rather than an industrial city. Garbage collection was one option for blacks, though the pay was only $1.30 an hour at the beginning of the 1960s and job security was nil.

By 1963 union organizing had begun, but Memphis had a long history of crushing municipal workers' unions, and it took the garbage workers' union five years to become powerful enough to sustain a strike. In those years, cutbacks in pay and in equipment maintenance created more reasons for dissatisfaction. At the same time, the black middle class had become frustrated by the slow pace of desegregation, and their frustration grew when a hard-line white mayor was elected in 1967. Thus, when the sanitation workers walked off the job over a blatant incident of racial discrimination in February 1968, they had a militant union

and a unified black community behind them. Despite intimidation, scab labor, and the use of outright force against them, the workers held out, and when the assassination of Martin Luther King, Jr., focused national attention on the strike, the city had no choice but to capitulate. The Memphis garbage strike marked a major turning point in the history of the civil rights movement.

The anthropologist Thomas Collins (1974) concludes that a combination of circumstances contributed to this success. The recent migrants were able to cushion their vulnerability as outsiders by maintaining close supportive ties within their own communities and by organizing groups to press their interests. Moreover, opportunities for blacks in the North were decreasing, and as more migrants stayed in Memphis, the motivation to press for change increased. Finally, the workers' success depended a great deal on the support of the black community, particularly of the black middle class.

Marysa Navarro (1989) describes a roughly similar situation in Argentina. A group of mothers in Buenos Aires, most of them housewives, transformed themselves into political activists and ultimately into symbols of resistance to military dictatorship.

In March 1976, President Isabel Perón of Argentina was deposed by a military coup that placed power in the hands of a junta composed of the commanders in chief of the army, the navy, and the air force. One of the junta's first acts was to declare war on "subversion." The war was waged on two levels: conventional confrontations with guerrilla forces both in the cities and in the countryside and, more ominously, a clandestine campaign of terror carried out by right-wing death squads under the control of the armed forces. The junta never officially acknowledged the existence

THE SOCIAL STRUCTURE
OF POLITICS

Political activity occurs within the context of a larger social framework. Procedures for making decisions and defining authority follow certain patterns, which can be seen as recurring in similarly constituted societal settings.

Essentially, political organization varies broadly along two dimensions. The first is the degree to which political roles and institutions

of these squads, much less responsibility for their activities. Tens of thousands of "subversives" (the term encompassed guerrillas, Marxists of varying persuasions, liberals, reform-minded Catholics and Jews, and anyone suspected of having a good word to say for any of them) were arrested—some formally, many others by summary abduction from their homes, on the street, even at school. All were held incommunicado in inhuman conditions and grotesquely tortured. As they were never charged, they were never brought to trial. Some were released after several years, but many others were never heard from again. These were the *desaparecidos,* the disappeared. Most of the disappeared were young people between the ages of twenty and thirty.

According to Navarro, "the existence of a parallel but hidden . . . structure of repression that carried out actions not acknowledged by the government and for which it did not take responsibility" meant that "all legal resources for redress available under normal circumstances" were "either shut or controlled by the armed forces." Even the Catholic church never clearly dissociated itself from the junta. Gradually this void was filled by human rights organizations, which persisted in their efforts although the junta did all it could to repress them.

In April 1977 a group of fourteen women who had met in various public offices while they were attempting to obtain information about their children decided to meet in the Plaza de Mayo (the main square in downtown Buenos Aires) to publicize their plight. By June 1977 the group had grown to one-hundred, and had established a weekly ritual: they marched silently around the square, each carrying a photograph of her lost son or daughter. Given the circumstances, this was "an extraordinary act of defiance that no human rights

group or political organization had dared to undertake." By 1982, the marching mothers numbered 2,500. The junta did not at first recognize the political nature of the women's actions, and the fact that it ignored them gave the women crucial time to strengthen and build their movement. At the end of 1978, however, the junta started a vicious campaign of harassment, which by 1980 forced the mothers to cease their marches in the plaza and meet in churches instead.

According to Navarro, what distinguished these women from other human rights groups was their militancy, which was rooted in the devastating impact of the disappearance of their children. Their socialization as wives and mothers forced them to act. Besides, they had more time than men to search for their missing children, and because they were older women, they could move about Buenos Aires without much fear for their safety. "In a society that glorified motherhood . . . they were implicitly excluded from the different groups defined as 'subversives.'" They were politically invisible. So many young people had disappeared that the mothers formed a critical mass of people who, though they varied widely in personal and social characteristics, had one all-important thing in common. And as most of them lacked any kind of political experience, they were not constrained by any previous ideologies, and were free to create new symbols and to take actions that no one had tried before. In the terrorist state created by the junta, motherhood protected them and allowed them freedom and power not accessible to traditional political actors. Ultimately, the actions of the mothers of the Plaza de Mayo contributed to the fall of the military junta and the transition to civilian rule in October 1983.

are specialized or differentiated from other roles and institutions. A society may have such political offices as king, chief, judge, or legislator, roles vested to varying degrees with power and authority. The more specialized or differentiated a society's political organization, the more formal its structure—that is, focused on institutions dedicated more or less exclusively to running the political system. The second dimension is the degree to which power and authority are centralized as opposed to divided among the members of a society. Where political power is highly centralized, one is likely to find a hierarchy of decision-making offices, and access to the political process may be restricted to members of certain classes or ranks.

These organizational attributes are not fixed and inflexible. A highly centralized state system, for example, can decompose into competing political, tribal, or ethnic factions, as we see in the unfortunate examples of Lebanon and Cambodia; and decentralized tribal systems can form more complex polities almost overnight when they are faced with particular problems or opportunities. Change in political organization is always possible.

THE EVOLUTION OF POLITICAL ORGANIZATION

It is generally believed that from the beginnings of human society until about ten thousand years ago, most groups were organized as relatively egalitarian societies. Over the last ten thousand years or so, human society has moved toward greater specialization of roles and institutions, including political institutions. Positions of influence and authority have become more centralized and increasingly restricted to a relatively small subset of the larger population, and centralized decision making and bureaucracies have become involved in more and more aspects of people's lives. These emerging bureaucracies are usually exclusively male, a fact that may further amplify the gender hierarchy.

The development of political centralization probably began not long after the Neolithic revolution in food production—the changeover from the hunting and gathering of wild food to the domestication of plants and animals. This is not to say that a shift from food collection to cultivation in itself required increased

political complexity, but the effects of this shift on the way people lived acted as selective pressures for greater political and social integration. With food production, human populations became larger and denser and sustained themselves through increasing economic specialization. Also, vital resources had to be protected from external threat and competition. In conflicts between groups, the one that is best organized and best consolidated will have an advantage (Carneiro 1981).

Though external threat or competition may have been a factor in the rise of centralized political systems, economic factors appear to be most important. Warfare does not generally need a permanent agency of coordination, but an increasingly specialized economy does. Once that agency exists in the economic realm, extension of its planning capabilities into other areas, such as warfare, is logical, and undoubtedly proves to be advantageous.

Egalitarian Political Systems

For most of human existence, people lived in fairly egalitarian political systems, or so it would seem. Nomadic hunter-gatherers are characteristically organized as egalitarian societies, although this is not a necessary outcome of a hunting-and-gathering procurement strategy. Groups of hunters and gatherers in areas of rich food supplies may well have a political organization similar to that of ranked or stratified sedentary agricultural communities. The relative abundance of the food supply affects the size and social complexity of local groups (Price 1981).

The most basic form of egalitarian political organization is sometimes referred to as the **band**—a loosely integrated population sharing a sense of common identity but few specialized institutions (Service 1971). The San or !Kung people and the Inuit or Eskimo are bands. In such a society, political life is simply one dimension of social life. There are no specialized political roles—that is, no political leaders with designated authority. Economic exchange is effected through reciprocity, with no individual having disproportionate control over resources or access to them. Some degree of competition for influence may arise over day-to-day problems, such as decisions to hunt or to move to a new camp, but it is resolved in give-and-take discussions involving all members of the group. A !Kung headman has no coercive power and only limited authority. He is essentially a symbol of the group, and as such is given certain ceremonial prerogatives, such as walking at the head of the line when the band moves. But the position carries no rewards of power and riches, and the headman hunts, works, and shares his food like all others in the band (Marshall 1960).

In egalitarian societies, an influential person, no matter how great his or her status, never has power beyond the charismatic power to persuade. Others are always at liberty to accept or ignore advice. For the most part, vital decisions affecting the entire group are made by consensus. A band is a society of equals who permit one of its members to lead them only because they think it is in their self-interest to do so.

Although we term such societies "egalitarian," the term has to be used cautiously. First, as we have noted, most positions of respect are reserved for men; in fact, many may be reserved for only a few successful, older men. John Speth, in a survey of the literature on hunting and gathering groups (1988), finds that women are frequently less well nourished than men, particularly hunters. And some societies do hold slaves, as noted earlier. Much of the egalitarianism of hunters and gatherers is probably a product of technological difficulties in the production and storage of food and in security. Unless you can safely store something of value, accumulation for personal ends is difficult, even futile. Since political power often

rests ultimately on economic clout, an inability to accumulate material resources prevents any individual from gaining great power. The archaeological evidence clearly indicates that societies are far more complex in areas of abundant, predictable resources than in marginal zones (Price 1981).

The band is not the only political expression of egalitarian society; many societies with a tribal organization provide comparatively open access to the political process. The term **tribe** is often used to describe an organization similar to that of the band but coordinating the activities of more people—perhaps even a large number of villages or small communities. A tribe, as we noted in Chapter 13, is a descent- and kinship-based grouping in which subgroups are clearly linked to one another, with the potential of uniting for common defense or warfare. The segmentary lineage system, also discussed in Chapter 13, typifies tribal organization. Tribal societies have limited or few specialized political roles, authoritative leaders, permanent centers of administration, or formal mechanisms of coercion. Like the band, the tribe is egalitarian inasmuch as everyone within certain age and sex categories has access to status and prestige.

Nonegalitarian Political Systems

Chiefdoms

Though the term "egalitarian" has to be used cautiously, it is possible to see organizational differences between what we have termed egalitarian societies and political systems in which power is concentrated in the hands of a few and specialized political institutions maintain social order. Such systems are sometimes referred to as "ranked." **Ranked societies** are those in which access to valued positions of status is limited in some way (Fried 1967:109). This is, of course, a far broader category than

Tribal leaders, all men, sit in council with the *mir,* a traditional paramount chief in western Pakistan. Chiefdoms are characterized by a simple decision-making hierarchy: the chief deals directly with the leaders of his constituency, without a bureaucratic chain of command. (JOHN LAUNOIS/BLACK STAR)

"egalitarian society," as it encompasses systems that range from very minimal differentiation to extreme forms of stratification.

An intermediate expression of ranking is exemplified by the chiefdom. A **chiefdom** is distinguished by the presence of a permanent central political agency to coordinate the activities of multicommunity political units. From an evolutionary perspective, chiefdoms mark a major stage in political development. As Robert Carneiro puts it, "they represent the first transcending of local autonomy in human history" (1981:37). With chiefdoms, we see political decisions occurring at two levels—that of the chief or senior leader and that of local subordinates who carry out commands.

Although the upper ranks may be composed of a large number of people, at the core is the office of chief. While chiefdoms vary widely, all are characterized by profound inequality (Service 1971:140). The paramount leader or chief occupies a hereditary position and typically has great powers over subordinates. Many chiefs had supernatural qualities, as in Polynesia, and were distinguished from other high-ranking individuals by elaborate dress, residences, and, upon death, special burial ceremonies. The archaeological record shows that often chiefs were buried with wives and retainers to serve them in the afterlife (Feinman and Neitzel 1984).

The office of chief is a specialized political position with well-defined areas of authority.

Hawaiian chiefs, for example, were considered the "owners" of the resources their people used and had the right to call on their labor and collect a portion of their crops. These chiefs filled great storehouses with goods of all sorts—food, hardware, clothing, and so on. Chiefs used the surplus to support lavish community feasts or to subsidize large-scale construction projects, such as irrigation works, all of which enhanced both their status and their potential for accumulating ever-larger funds. While most investigators see the redistributive activities of chiefs as important, it is not clear whether this function is the source or the outcome of their power (Carneiro 1981). In many respects, chiefs act like tribute takers, even though they may provide a service to the society at large by giving back some of what they collect.

Chiefs can deploy labor, give commands, and ask others to do things that they themselves might never do. Their authority is backed by sanctions of one kind or another. In most Polynesian chiefdoms religious status is probably the chief's most compelling tool of persuasion. Chiefs are believed to be richly infused with a supernatural force known as "mana," which sanctifies their right to office and otherwise protects their persons. Invested with this kind of strong spiritual power, chiefs are able to enforce their authority by threats of curses or other spiritual sanctions (Sahlins 1963).

A chief acquires his rank by heredity as the eldest son of a chief or of the chief's sister. Sometimes, however, kinship ties are so complex and overlapping that more than one person can lay claim to the position of chief. Kinship and ancestry are often the basis of many status positions other than that of chief. The chief's closest kin may form something of an aristocracy. In many cases a hierarchy develops in which those kin closest to the chief have a higher status than more distant relations. On Tahiti, for example, the population was basically divided into three grades of people (with levels of rank within each grade): the immediate family of the paramount chiefs; those of a lesser, intermediate lineage; and the commoners. The noble of a chiefdom may exercise various levels of authority and possess prestige and influence, but they are still more like a hierarchy among kin than a bureaucratic administration of the type that exists in state societies.

The fact that chiefs rule through bureaucracies largely composed of relatives may, according to Eric Wolf (1982:96), explain why chiefs are often quite eager to collaborate with outsiders, even to the detriment of their own people. Wherever European colonists went, they usually found local chiefs willing to collaborate in the exploitation of their own people. The reason, Wolf suggests, is that by acquiring European allies, money, and guns, the chiefs free themselves from the limits imposed by the need to rule through relatives who clearly expect to be part of the power structure. They gain what they hope is an independent source of power.

States

The most complex and centralized of political systems are states. A **state** is essentially a hierarchical set of institutions that transcend kinship in the organization of power. This is not to say that all power in such societies is preempted by the state. Kinship networks that possess limited authority not only usually coexist but may be fundamental to the political process. In the Nupe state of central Nigeria, for example, civil offenses came under the jurisdiction of the village and kinship groups, while criminal offenses were the exclusive province of the state (Nadel 1935). By definition, it is the state that holds ultimate power. Acts of coercion or violence not legitimized by the state are punishable by law. To maintain internal order and regulate relations with other populations, the state maintains mechanisms of coercive control: police force, militia, army, arsenals, and so on.

Perhaps the most useful way to describe the

state is in terms of the organization of lines of authority and decision making (Wright and Johnson 1975). States have at least three levels in their chain of command, as opposed to the two levels associated with chiefdoms. Thus decisions made by rulers or administrators are often implemented by a bureaucratic organization far removed from the upper level of government. As we saw in our discussion of the farmers of Oaxaca in Chapter 8, decisions regarding even very basic elements of production, here water rights, may be made by administrators who have little direct relation to the community.

State-level political organization is associated with large populations, substantial segments of which live in towns and cities. The complex of communities that make up a state is supported by intensive agriculture, relatively well-developed communications systems, markets, and extensive economic specialization, all of which in combination allow for the production of large surpluses, although the surpluses are not equally distributed among the population. In fact, the complex division of labor that sustains large populations and urban centers requires that much redistribution be centralized in bureaus of taxation, public works, social services, and the like. The people who direct or regulate the redistribution process achieve a great deal of de facto power. Also, state societies are usually stratified: access to factors of production—such as land and capital—is restricted in many cases to an elite group or economic class. Control of resources is a key to political power, and wealth and political power tend to be self-perpetuating.

The myriad social, economic, and political activities in a state require a centralized system of administration. At the hub of the system are the people with the greatest power. Members of this group create laws and formulate the overall political strategy of leadership. They often make use of a bureaucracy to carry out

their directives. Even where a single ruler has absolute power, a hierarchically organized bureaucracy is needed to implement policies at the local level. In fact, the leaders are dependent to a large extent on information given them by subordinates. The organization of states is closely tied to the need to assimilate and control the flow of information. Even ancient states, such as Egypt and Mesopotamia, maintained elaborate records and archives.

The Moral Basis of State Authority. Although coercive power is essential to state control, the state also exercises its authority and power through ideology. In any state system, some philosophical basis of legitimacy establishes the right of the state to govern. The legitimizing ideology of the state may be secular, as in most contemporary nation-states; religious, as in some of the Islamic states; or focused on a ruling dynasty, as in traditional monarchies. Whatever the source, the notion of **legitimacy**, or the right to rule on the basis of recognized principles, is a powerful force, and few regimes survive long if their people view them as lacking the moral authority to govern. Thus in state societies a great deal of attention is paid to maintaining the symbols of authority, be they the ceremonial stools of West African kings, great shrines and monuments, or national constitutions preserved in archives.

When new states or radically different national governments are brought into being, a great deal of attention is devoted to legitimizing the new establishment. Following the overthrow of the Shah of Iran in 1979, the moral basis of the new government was its claim to conform to the precepts of Islam and Islamic law. Accordingly, much attention was paid to passing new legislation to bring family codes into accordance with Islamic law, prohibiting alcoholic beverages, and enforcing female dress codes (Fisher 1980:232 ff.). One might think that a more pressing problem would have been

Mayoral candidate, David Dinkins, meets with leaders of New York's Jewish community. The fact that religious and ethnic identity are important determinants of voting patterns in many American cities reflects the overall importance of such factors in political organization. (JACK MANNING/THE NEW YORK TIMES)

the reorganizing of the bureaucracy; but first priority was given to establishing the moral basis to rule. We see it in our own history, clearly spelled out in a declaration and a constitution, and symbolized in the building of a brand-new capital city named after the hero of the revolution. Simon Schama (1987), a historian, interprets much of Dutch art of the sixteenth and seventeenth centuries as having political significance: it expresses the cultural unity and political legitimacy of the newly formed confederation of formerly Spanish-ruled principalities that had fought for their independence. Here art was used to help create a political culture and to validate a newly formed confederation—The Netherlands.

The Evolution of the State. No single factor was solely responsible for the emergence of state societies in various parts of the world, but a complex of interrelated factors probably contributed to their evolution. One might speculate that more efficient methods of food production (such as irrigation or greater specialization), coupled with social changes (such as village and town settlements, increased population density, the development of trade networks and centers of redistribution), stimulated the production of economic surpluses. These surpluses could be used to support large numbers of people not directly engaged in food production.

Dominant groups assumed control over much of that production and over the task of mobilizing surpluses. Of course, this chain of events did not proceed at the same rate in all communities. Those communities that controlled land highly suitable for intensified agriculture were able to produce more than others and monopolized access to strategic resources. Eventually they came to control food production over large areas, thus becoming important centers of redistribution that were able to wage war on weaker groups. As outlying groups fell under their control, these powerful communities gradually became the centers of economic, political, and religious life, as well as of technological, artistic, and scientific innovations. These developments in turn reinforced the advantages of the dominant societies over their neighbors. While this scenario is unverifiable in all its details, it does conform largely to what Robert Adams (1966) has described for the rise of the Mesopotamian state.

However difficult to unravel the fabric of state formation may be, it is clear that various economic and social pressures are central to political evolution. A complex interaction of population growth, intensification of production, nucleation of settlements, specialization of production, stratification, and the extension of exchange relationships, all of which require centralized authority, underlies the process of state formation. But these pressures will not always lead a society to a higher level of integration. Some groups may resolve resource and other problems they encounter by moving or limiting their own growth rather than by centralizing; other societies may revert to less integrated forms. A chiefdom threatened by another society's army, for instance, may at first unite, only to break apart and return to a tribal way of life should the external force be too strong to withstand. It is possible to envision conditions that would cause even our own state system to fragment, just as established states have so often done in the past.

POLITICAL RELATIONS BETWEEN SOCIETIES

Strategies and methods for dealing with outside groups are important aspects of every society's political system. Many of these strategies are peaceful: intergroup law, mediation, and diplomacy are common ways of regulating relations and resolving conflicts and disputes between societies. But inevitably some conflicts will be more difficult to settle peacefully than others, and many of them will ultimately reach the point of violence.

Mechanisms of Peace

Relations with other populations are often the most critical aspect of a group's environment—sometimes its most important resource—so it is not surprising that societies have evolved mechanisms to regulate intergroup exchange peacefully.

Some New Guinea tribes commonly hold ritual feasts to appease the ghosts of ancestors. These events are occasions to entertain neighboring groups and thereby to consolidate alliances. Often the relationships strengthened at these ritual feasts are further cemented through marriages (Rappaport 1968). In North Africa and the Middle East, where intergroup conflict has been common in some areas, religion also serves as a means of mediating disputes. Some lineages or lines of descent have come to be recognized as sacred or holy. Removed from the threat of attack because of their presumed sanctity (injuring such a person is a serious religious offense), these individuals have been free to play an important role in mediating disputes among warring groups. Among the Turkmen of northeast Iran, lineages comprised of such holy individuals, thought to be descended from early figures of Islam, actually occupy land between competing tribes (Irons 1975).

Among the Bedouin of the Arabian Peninsula, elaborate rules regulating hospitality to members of other groups and protection of travelers facilitate intergroup communication. Such communication is particularly important among nomadic pastoralists who live in a harsh and often unpredictable environment, where knowledge of rainfall and conditions of pasturage in different areas is critical to survival. Bedouin etiquette requires every head of a household to give three days of hospitality—a place to sleep, food, and entertainment—to anyone who enters their tent. If the visitor happens to be an enemy, the rule still holds; in addition, the guest must be given a head start out of camp when he leaves. The Bedouin also have rules protecting travelers from attack. As long as travelers are accompanied by the proper guides, it is considered wrong to harm them. Traveling merchants are also protected under tribal rules. If a raid occurs at a place where a merchant is camped, the raiders are required to make restitution. Despite conflict among groups, these rules ensure a constant flow of information.

Armed Conflict

Of course, not all political relations between societies are peaceful. Anthropologists have found that armed conflict occurs in all types of societies, regardless of their level of political organization. In less complex societies such conflicts are typically tied to specified perceived transgressions, while wars waged by the state are often justified by broad political and religious ideologies. Nevertheless, the frequency of warfare, when defined simply as combat between separate territorial groups, is apparently no greater among states than among bands (Otterbein 1970). This is not to say that all band societies make war against neighboring groups. But the majority of bands do engage in some form of armed conflict that can generally be classified as warfare. We can surmise, therefore, that warfare has existed for many thousands of years—probably since long before the development of tribes.

Evidence also indicates that the relative casualty rate for combatants in warfare is no higher among states than among less centralized political organizations, even though state societies clearly have more highly specialized and complex military establishments and more sophisticated weapons. In band societies people usually fight with spears, clubs, or bows and arrows, and often both sides of a conflict withdraw if they incur serious injuries. But since the total populations of bands are so small, only a few deaths can result in a significant overall casualty rate. Among the Murngin of Australia, 28 percent of all male deaths have been attributed to combat. The Yąnomamö have similarly high casualties. Among Western nations during this century, in contrast, less than 1 percent of all male deaths can be attributed to warfare (Livingstone 1968). These figures do not apply to any specific country considered individually, such as Germany or the Soviet Union, where war-related mortality has been much higher.

What does seem to distinguish modern warfare, and even warfare in the earlier state-level societies, is its impact on noncombatants. Today the effects of war are felt by every member of society, even if the actual fighting is distant. And, of course, modern technology, including elaborate systems of communication, draws more and more people into particular conflicts and increases the costs in lives and resources associated with warfare. For most societies warfare is a hazardous solution to a threatening problem. More than likely this problem will

have to do with something as fundamental as access to vital resources (Ferguson 1984:55–57).

Andrew Vayda (1976) has argued that warfare between horticultural societies is frequently precipitated by population pressures on scarce land resources. Vayda suggests that warfare can provide a mechanism for establishing a balance between available resources and human population, although this is only one possible solution among many.

Land is not the only resource over which armed conflict can arise. Among some Bedouin tribes of northern Arabia, camels were the objects of armed raids and counterraids. The camel was a strategic resource for the Bedouin, the foundation of their traditional economy: first, camels were a reasonably stable source of food, providing milk (a dietary mainstay) and occasionally meat; second, the camel was an effective means of transportation in a desert environment, allowing the Bedouin to reach areas inaccessible to sheep or goat herders, so that they could migrate long distances; finally, camels were valuable commodities for trade. Male camels and old or barren females could be exchanged in oasis town markets for such valuable items as grain, cloth, domestic utensils, and weapons. Because the camel was so central to the Bedouin way of life, tribal sections felt constant pressure to increase their herds. As a female camel yields only a small amount of milk each day, relatively large numbers of animals had to be kept merely to meet subsistence needs.

It is impossible to increase the size of a herd quickly through breeding, for camels reproduce

The rifles of these Korean soldiers (top) are far more sophisticated and destructive than the bows and arrows of the Pygmy tribe in Zaire (bottom). However, since less centralized groups have much smaller populations than organized states, their traditional weaponry can incur equally high casualty rates. (TOP: DAVID BURNETT/STOCK, BOSTON; BOTTOM: CHRISTA ARMSTRONG/ PHOTO RESEARCHERS)

and mature very slowly. Consequently, raiding proved an efficient way of replenishing a declining herd or just as a safeguard against future losses to drought, disease, accident, or theft. Elaborate rules governed raids between Bedouin tribes, all members of which were thought to be related to one another, however distantly. These rules ensured that no group that was the target of a raid would be completely routed; only camels (particularly adult females) were taken, and enough camels would always be left to permit the victims to reach their nearest kin for aid. In this way camel raiding served as a mechanism for distributing a valuable and scarce resource among groups spread over a large area (Sweet 1965). It was a costly but apparently effective way for each local group or tribal section to alleviate, at least temporarily, scarcity in a vital resource. And, as is often the case with warfare, each raid or act of armed aggression set the stage for a response in kind.

Two anthropologists have dramatically extended the idea of warfare as a means of adjusting population to resources. William Divale and Marvin Harris (1978, Harris 1984) propose that warfare is part of a distinctively human system of population control—or was until fairly recently. They argue that the impact of warfare on population was significant—and not solely through casualties lost on the battlefield. Warfare, they suggest, is often associated with a complex of "male supremacist" practices; most notable among these practices is the once-widespread killing of unwanted baby girls, or female infanticide. Chronic warfare creates an environment that favors males at the expense of females, and thereby limits future population growth. A society that rears more boys than girls often finds, paradoxically, that it is forced to wage war to secure marriage partners. This, you will recall, is the argument that Chagnon advances to explain the Yąnomamö's warlike tendencies. This view has been challenged by other investigators who find little evidence that population has ever been regulated in such a fashion or that warfare and male supremacy are causally linked.

Summary

The study of *politics* is concerned with who benefits in any competition for power and rewards. In a given society, particular rules govern political competition and leadership: who has access to the political process, how leadership is determined, and what mechanisms keep political competition within reasonable bounds.

At the bottom of all political competition lies disagreement about the way issues that affect individual interests and community life should be decided. Societies vary in the kinds of decisions that are regarded as important, in the intensity of political competition, and in the kinds of rewards that are distributed. Generally, as the level of social complexity increases, so do the number and scope of political objectives, as well as the use of force to achieve political ends.

All societies have mechanisms that act to restrain violence and disruption when political conflict becomes intense. One such mechanism is the multiplicity of competing demands for a person's or a group's loyalty. Other mechanisms may be built into the formal political structure, such as positions that endow their incumbents with authority to mediate issues.

Rules, or standards for proper political behavior, vary widely among societies, but every society has rules governing behavior and means of enforcing them. Rules give social relationships order and a certain amount of predictability, essential to the functioning of society. Social rules establish broad guidelines for behavior, but individual interpretation and decision making produce variation in the way the rules are actually followed or flouted.

Individual behavior can vary or deviate from social rules. Some deviations from prescribed behavior are tolerated more than others. Deviant behavior and the exclusive pursuit of self-interest are modified by a system of *social control* that channels behavior through rewards and sanctions. Every society has evolved mechanisms for dealing with deviance. These mechanisms of social control have been broadly classified as formal and informal.

Social pressure, in the form of satire, gossip, shunning, ostracism, and moral sanctions based on beliefs about the supernatural, is applied when infractions of the rules do occur. Vengeance or threatened vengeance is a form of social control embedded in the structure of kinship relations. Violence often erupts in blood feuds.

No society functions with only informal mechanisms of control. The conflicts that are an inevitable part of social life often need to be resolved through formal, institutionalized channels. Formal mechanisms help resolve disputes before they become violent, or they deter offenders before they can rip the fabric of social life.

Law is the most formal mechanism of control. Laws help structure behavior, resolve disagreements, and penalize wrongdoers, but they may also engender conflict, as they tend to benefit or penalize some individuals more than others. The elements of the legal process vary widely from one society to another. In our own and other industrialized societies, the legal process is highly developed. Laws are codified, or systematically recorded and preserved and interpreted by specialists, such as judges and lawyers. In technologically simpler societies, the legal tradition is largely oral and more directly related to the day-to-day concerns of the people.

Methods of adjudication are means of arriving at a decision in a dispute. Such methods typically involve some sort of hearing that is conducted according to accepted procedures. Settlement may be achieved through negotiation or through an adjudicator who makes a decision. Methods of adjudication may be formal or informal. An informal procedure involves mediation between parties and usually reaches compromise decisions. Formal procedures often take place in an established court, but formal and informal procedures may be used simultaneously.

Neither the formal nor the informal mechanisms of social control are entirely effective; they reduce but do not eradicate deviance. In highly stratified societies, these mechanisms are often used by the elite to maintain their position. Legal inequality is particularly pronounced in tribal societies that have had centralized and codified legal systems based on European models imposed upon them. The centralized legal system has had the effect of heightening the discrepancy in power between the rural class and the central bureaucracy.

In all societies, access to political power is limited by both formal and informal means; the numbers of such restrictions increase with the complexity of the society. Political leadership may be established either through a person's idiosyncratic qualities or through the ability to mobilize organizational support, or a combination of the two. In discussing political leadership, one should distinguish between *power* (the ability to exert influence because one's directives are backed by negative sanctions, such as the use of force) and *authority* (the ability to exert influence because of one's personal prestige or status).

Although individual political systems vary, four general organizational patterns have been identified: bands, tribes, chiefdoms, and states. The *band* is the least complex and probably the oldest form of political organization; it may be defined as a small group of individuals with a fluid membership. No overriding political institutions act to unite several bands into a larger polity, and no specialized political roles exist. In effect, political life is an integral part of all social relations.

The *tribe* is similar to the band in that it is egalitarian and provides comparatively open access to the political process. Bands and tribes are considered egalitarian in that most political positions are available on the basis of ability, although actual equality may be tempered by gender differences and extreme status differences based on age.

Nonegalitarian or *ranked societies* are those in which access to valued positions of status is limited in some way. Among such political systems, the *chiefdom* is distinguished by the existence of a central agency, headed by the chief, that coordinates economic, religious, and social activities. Another common feature of the chiefdom is greater specialization in the means of production, which allows for the production of surpluses and for support of a larger population. The office of chief is a specialized political position, with well-defined areas of authority backed by sanctions of one kind or another. In chiefdoms, positions of status and authority are not accessible to everyone, even though major resources may be commonly held.

The *state* is the most complex and centralized of political systems. It may be defined as a hierarchical complex of institutions that transcend kinship in the organization of power. The state also gains its authority through ideology, which serves as the basis of the state's *legitimacy*. State-level political organization is associated with densely populated, largely urban units, which are supported by intensive agriculture, sophisticated technology, markets, and a high degree of productive, administrative, and economic specialization. Control over the means of production, trade, and the surpluses created is not evenly distributed: state systems are socially and economically stratified. It is generally believed that most human groups were organized as bands until about ten thousand years ago. Since then political society has moved toward stratification, increasing role specialization, centralization of authority, and bureaucracy.

All societies must deal with outside groups. A variety of mechanisms have been developed to regulate intergroup exchange and to minimize conflict. The most obvious of such mechanisms are intergroup laws, mediation, and diplomacy, but other more subtle mechanisms are also operative. Among them are religion, as when certain people are designated as sacred and thus removed from the threat of attack. They then may act as mediators among warring groups. Etiquette and hospitality may protect some groups and provide for exchange of information despite conflict.

Despite these mechanisms, warfare is a universal phenomenon. For the most part people resort to warfare to deal with a threatening problem, often one related to a scarcity of resources and/or population pressures. In this case war acts as a mechanism for redistributing resources by establishing a balance between available resources and population.

Key Terms

authority	**law**	**power**	**social pressure**
band	**legitimacy**	**ranked societies**	**state**
chiefdom	**politics**	**social control**	**tribe**

Suggested Readings

BOEHM, C. 1984. *Blood Revenge: The Anthropology of Feuding in Montenegro and other Tribal Societies*. Lawrence, Kansas: University Press of Kansas. An account using ethnographic materials from Yugoslavia and Albania that detail the functioning of blood feuds as a mechanism of social control.

BURLING, R. 1974. *The Passage of Power: Studies in Political Succession*. New York: Academic Press. A cross-cultural study of power that, by using historic and ethnographic examples, encompasses a wide segment of known political processes.

FERGUSON, B. R. (ED.). 1984. *Warfare, Culture, and Environment*. Orlando, Fla.: Academic Press. A collection of eleven original essays on the anthropology of war. All focus on the need to understand the material circumstances involved in order to understand the nature of war itself.

GILMORE, D. D. 1987. *Aggression and Community: Paradoxes of Andalusian Culture*. New Haven, Conn.: Yale University Press. Traditionally aggression has been viewed as maladaptive and disruptive in small-group dynamics. Based on field research in rural Andalusia, the author argues for the usefulness of limited aggression in promoting social cohesion.

SEATON, S. L., AND H. CLAESSEN (EDS.). 1979. *Political Anthropology: The State of the Art*. The Hague: Mouton Publishers. A general reader that outlines the field of political anthropology and provides a sampling of the ideas and research used to explore such topics as power, ideology, reciprocity in political relations, clientelism, and political economy.

Chapter **16** Religious Belief and Ritual

Humans weave intricate intellectual webs of faith and imagination that relate them to the universe and to each other, that express basic premises linking event to event, past to present. Religious beliefs, cosmologies, myths, and rituals are basic to our perceptions of time and space, our views of our own behavior and that of others, and our conceptions of the world, as it is and as it should be. Religion is a human universal—perhaps one of the key distinguishing features of our species and undoubtedly as ancient as human language. We may never fully know just how and why the human brain evolved, but surely one consequence of its evolution is the universal need to explain the world and to position ourselves in it. Religions and cosmologies—world views—vary so greatly that any definition must remain extremely general. But be that as it may, there is no society in which religion does not play an important role. Religion and cosmology encode not only a model of the world but also a model for the world—a plan of what it should be like. Thus religion can, and often does, guide behavior, from family relationships to the ideology of ruling parties.

DEFINING RELIGION

Anthropologists are concerned with understanding how religious ideology or ritual behavior relates to a larger cultural pattern and to social, political, and economic processes in a society. Some anthropologists broadly define religion as any system of beliefs in supernatural forces, symbols, and rituals that serve to make life meaningful and intelligible.

If the Mbuti Pygmies of the Ituri forest in Central Africa are plagued by sickness or poor hunting and if every practical remedy has failed, a festival known as *molimo* is held to awaken the forest to their plight and to restore balance and harmony to their world. For about a month, all the adult men gather nightly to sing and "rejoice" the forest. No specific invocations are made for better hunting or an end to sickness. The purpose of the festival is simply to express through song the Mbuti's trust in the forest as the benevolent provider of all good things. Having done so, the Mbuti say that whatever happens must be the will of the forest and therefore it is good. This feeling is clearly expressed in the Mbuti creed: "The Forest is Mother and Father, because it gives us all the things we need . . . food, clothing, shelter, warmth . . . and affection. We are the children of the forest. When it dies, we die" (Turnbull 1965:312). The Pygmies' belief in the forest, the molimo ceremony, and the creed of the forest constitute the elements of a religion, a model of the world for its participants. No church or temple has been erected; the molimo is not led by a priest or other intercessor with the supernatural. In fact, the supernatural itself does not exist for the Mbuti as it does in Western tradition. Not only is there no intangible, other worldly power known as a god, but the object of the worship is exactly that which is most natural and tangible in the Pygmies' life: the forest environment.

Thus religion cannot be defined in terms of what is worshipped. In general terms, all religions have two common characteristics: they include a recognition of the supernatural or sacred, and they express (whether or not in specific terms) an ideology that orders the world.

Religion as a Belief in the Supernatural

The sociologist Émile Durkheim (1961) argued that the essence of religion is not a specific set of beliefs, attitudes, or practices, but a broader, more universal phenomenon: the expression of a community's moral values and collective beliefs, whatever they may be. He maintained that each society distinguishes between the **sacred**—the sphere of extraordinary phenomena associated with awesome supernatural forces—and the **profane**—the sphere of the ordinary and routine, the natural, everyday world. Religious beliefs express what a society considers sacred. These values may be represented symbolically by a cross, a star, a statue, a rock, an animal, a tree, or any object that a society selects; and this symbol becomes the focus of collective ceremonies—communion, dances, feasts, and so on—that serve to unite believers into a single moral community. In this sense, the annual ceremonies of the Australian aborigines which center on a sacred totem are religious in exactly the same way as are the celebrations of Easter and Ramadan—the latter being the Muslim Feast of Abraham.

It has been pointed out, however, that few societies make a clear distinction between the sacred and the profane or the natural and the supernatural. For the Mbuti, the forest is not an awesome, mysterious entity that exists on a different level of reality. It is an ever-present factor that shapes every aspect of their lives and must be related to in concrete, practical terms. Thus, while a supernatural dimension is common to all religions, the categories "sacred" and "profane" or "natural" and "supernatural" are analytic constructs and do not always reflect distinctions that people actually make.

In fact, upon examination, we find that the distinction between the natural and the supernatural is not very clear at all. On the one hand, the natural world is the center of many religions (like that of the Mbuti Pygmies), while on the other, the supernatural often plays a routine role in secular affairs. A case in point is the practice of **divination**, in which an element of nature—the configuration of tea leaves, the movement of a water witching stick, or the side on which a flipped coin lands—acts as a sign to provide supernatural information to the diviner. The Sisala of northern Ghana consult diviners at least once a month; they rely on diviners to diagnose some ills and prescribe treatments. **Witchcraft** is another practice that is as likely to involve the profane as it is the sacred. It has been defined as an "individual's use of religious ritual to control, exploit, or injure unsuspecting, or at least uncooperating, other persons" (Wallace 1966:144). While we associate the practice with bizarre tales of evil spells, witchcraft is not necessarily either furtive or even socially unacceptable, as we shall see in our discussion of the Vodoun church of Haiti. Many cultures regularly attribute illness, including psychological ailments, to **spirit possession**, the supposed control of a person's behavior by a supernatural spirit that has entered the body. Is a line drawn between the natural and the supernatural? For some religions, the answer is clearly not at all. For others, a sharp boundary is the essence of belief, and the dialogue concerning the boundary may be the essence of the faith in question.

Religion as Ideology

Clifford Geertz (1966) maintains that religion is essentially an ideology, or a system of very potent symbols that has a powerful emotional appeal and can provide a rationale for human existence.

Religious ideology can be understood on two levels. First, it provides a symbolic framework that allows an individual to understand his or her place in the universe. Here religion expresses itself in myths. The myths of the book of Genesis, for instance, describe in symbolic terms the creation of the world and people's place within it. Myths about dying, too, use a variety of images—such as passing between jaws, or entering a mountain that has no visible entranceway, or crossing over a bridge that has been filed to a razor-sharp point—to describe a journey that the body cannot make, but the spirit can (Eliade 1975:349–350). Such myths put complex ideas into a framework that people can relate to from their own experience. Typically the myths that are of greatest importance to a culture are ones people call sacred. These are myths that occur in "holy books" or "scripture" or tales told by a shaman, for example, and are, as Geartz (1966) has noted, "highly charged symbols."

Claude Lévi-Strauss and other anthropologists have argued that the symbolic expressions embodied in myths are arranged in a common pattern. The typical structure of myths and legends juxtaposes three sets of symbolic elements: those that define a value, a desirable object, or a course of action; those that define its antithesis; and a mediating set of values that resolve the conflict between the two. Thus myths may be symbolic formulas for the resolution of conflicts of values and moral quandaries within a society. According to Lévi-Strauss (1955), myths have an internal logic of their own, unrelated to the real world; since they are highly abstract models that are open to a variety of interpretations, they permit people considerable leeway in defining their positions in the real world.

A myth, writes Lévi-Strauss (1988), has an authority that cannot be denied—"it arises from the depth of time, setting before us a magnifying mirror that reflects, in the massive form of concrete images, certain mechanisms by which the exercise of thought is ruled." Apparently disparate subjects of myths in the Americas, such as jealousy, potters, birds, sloths, comets, and excrement, are actually interrelated. "Potter's clay," for example, "undergoes extraction from the earth, and then firing to become a container designed to receive a content: food. Food itself undergoes the same treatment, but in reverse: it is first placed in a clay container, then cooked, then processed in the body through the operation of digestion, and finally is ejected as excrement" (Lévi-Strauss 1988). Myths, in this view, can be deciphered as various systems of codes, including sexual, zoological, and cosmological ones.

Beyond providing a framework for understanding the cosmos and people's place in it, religious symbols can be understood on another level. They take on a potent significance in their own right—places, buildings, tombs and monuments, relics, books and writings, words, abstract representations such as the cross and the crescent all become sacred. They have meaning for their adherents and come to signify basic values and beliefs of the community. Such religious symbols, be they places (Mecca, Jerusalem) or sacred writings (the Koran, the Bible), often serve as rallying points for social and political activities. As previously noted, the 1979 revolution that overthrew the Shah of Iran made extensive use of both religious ideology and the symbolism of sacred places and writings.

BELIEF SYSTEMS

The nineteenth-century anthropologist E. B. Tylor (1871) was one of the first to try to understand and explain systematically the phenomenon of religion. Tylor asserted that the foundation of all religion is the idea of a soul, a spiritual essence that differs from the tangible, physical body. Tylor speculated that the concept of a soul developed from primitive people's curiosity and concern about the difference between living and dying, waking and dreaming. He called this belief in a personal supernatural force **animism**, arguing that primitive peoples applied the idea of a soul not only to humans but also to animals and plants.

R. R. Marett, a contemporary of Tylor, maintained that the concept of a soul was too sophisticated to have supplied the foundation of religion. He argued instead that animism was preceded historically by **animatism**, a belief in an impersonal supernatural force (Marett 1909). Animatism can be seen among the people of Melanesia, who attribute extraordinary events, unusual prowess, and both good luck and misfortune to *mana*, an invisible force, transmitted by touch, which may be harnessed for good or evil. Mana may reside in people, places, or things, and it affects anyone who comes in contact with it. An unusually shaped stone found in an especially productive garden, an exceptionally swift boat, a particularly skillful leader may all be said to possess mana. Similarly, the Fox Indians believed the *manitu* came to warriors in visions, endowing them with temporary supernatural power. Many people in the Near East believe a person may acquire *baraka*, or holiness, by touching the clothes a holy man has worn or the ground on which he has walked, or by visiting Mecca. Roman Catholics in many parts of the world attribute healing powers to saints' relics, holy water, and places where miracles are said to have occurred, such as Lourdes. The belief that supernatural forces may reside in both people and inanimate objects is widespread.

A belief in supernatural beings is also common, although these beings are conceived in a wide variety of ways. Some have human origins. The Tonga of Zambia, for example, believe that the souls of all who have died live on as *zelo*, or ghosts; the souls of people who have attained some prominence become *mizimu* (something more than ghosts). Mizimu maintain a lively interest in the kin they leave behind, in part because they cease to exist if no one calls their name or brings them beer and other offerings. The Tonga see mizimu as their protectors, since they punish evildoers. When one of the living violates tradition, mi-

zimu may inflict an illness on the person, on their own initiative or because they hear the elders grumbling. But in general, mizimu act in their kin groups' best interests (Colson 1954). The Ifaluk of Micronesia, in contrast, believe that malevolent people become malevolent spirits (*alusengua*), who delight in stirring up immoral behavior and making the living sick and unlucky. The Ifaluk spend much of their time worrying and complaining about alusengua. These spirits give the living a common enemy and help to defuse quarrels among them (Spiro 1952).

In many parts of the world, religion centers on one or more gods of extrahuman origin. Such a pattern of belief is called **theism**. Dahomeans in Africa, for example, worshiped a pantheon of Great Gods, each involved in Creation, each responsible for some part of nature, each endowed with a human or animal form and a strong personality. Like humans, Dahomean Great Gods occupied themselves with sex, war, economic endeavors, and mischief. Their intervention in life on earth was largely unpredictable (Wallace 1966:93–94). Similar forms of **polytheism** (belief in many gods) flourished in the Inca, Maya, and Aztec cultures of Latin America and in east Asian kingdoms, as well as in central African kingdoms, Greece, and Rome.

Judaism, Christianity, and Islam, all of which arose in the Middle East, recognize only one supreme God, who created the universe and all that is in it, watches over human affairs, occasionally sends messengers to earth, and works in mysterious ways. But **monotheism** (belief in one god) is relative. All three of these belief systems deify their saints and prophets to some extent, and all have made room at various points in their histories for other supernatural beings—angels, demons, and witches, not to mention the devil.

Some anthropologists have suggested that these patterns of religious belief are related to the way society is organized. Guy Swanson (1960) has conducted the most extensive such study to date. The highlights of his findings can be summarized as follows:

1. Animism is associated with a variety of social conditions found in less complex societies, among them the nuclear family as sovereign kin group, only one or two politically important groups, and organization in small hamlets or hunting-and-gathering bands.

2. Belief in ancestral spirits is related to a system of social organization in which the extended family is politically important.

3. Polytheism is associated with the existence of social classes and occupational specialization. Societies with a polytheistic belief system, however, are intermediate rather than extreme in social complexity.

4. Monotheism is strongly associated with a high degree of social complexity and is very common among societies with three or more politically important groups.

5. Supernatural sanctions for immorality are significantly related to economic and social complexity, measured by such factors as the private ownership of important resources, the prevalence of debt relationships, the cultivation of grain crops, and, most important, the existence of social classes widely separated by differentials in wealth. The elites in such societies invoke the authority of high gods to preserve their privileges and to prevent or at least to control rebellion in the lower classes.

Thus religious belief systems seem to reflect basic characteristics of the social order in which they appear. As social organization became more centralized and stratified, so did the conception of the supernatural.

RITUAL

It is difficult to distinguish religious beliefs and symbols from religious behavior. In all societies basic beliefs are embodied in rituals of religious observance. In simple terms, **ritual** can be defined as behavior (religious or not) that has become highly formalized and stereotyped; in the process its original function often changes. Viewed dispassionately, the behavior of the practitioner appears to have no direct stimulus; it is a response only to the rite itself. Religious ritual often involves the manipulation of symbols, including the combining of symbols of very different origins. In the modern Catholic-Mayan community of Chamula, for instance, the ritual display of religious symbols reinforces fundamental beliefs and values. The sun symbolizes all that is good and desirable to the people of Chamula. The ritual procession of saints' images in the church runs from the eastern side (where the sun rises) to the western side of the church, and candles are arranged so that the largest and most expensive are nearest the east, and the inferior ones are placed in the west (Gossen 1972). Beliefs, symbols, and ritual are closely interconnected.

Ritualistic behaviors may appear to produce little benefit for the people who engage in them. But in fact ritual can perform the basic function of reinforcing group solidarity. Genuflecting upon entering and leaving a Roman Catholic church, for example, helps integrate individual behaviors into a group structure, thereby reducing anxiety: one's sense of belonging is reinforced when one acts with the group (although the stated purpose is to acknowledge God's presence). Anthony Wallace (1966) has suggested certain broad categories of ritualistic behavior associated with religions in various parts of the world which provide a sense of solidarity. These categories include prayer, music, physical exertion, pleading, recitation of

Religious rituals often involve the display of symbols. Every year in the Sierra Madre mountains of Mexico, the Tateineira ceremony is held to thank the gods for sufficient rainfall to ensure a mature corn harvest. The children of the community, symbolized by the young ears of corn, are introduced to the gods on an imaginary pilgrimage to the god Peyote. Here the shaman is lifting a young ear of corn and singing of the pilgrimage in a rite similar to the Christian sacred communion. (KAL MULLER/WOODFIN CAMP & ASSOCIATES)

codes, taboos, feasts, sacrifice, congregation, inspiration, and the manufacture and use of symbolic objects. A given rite may include one or more of these ritual behaviors.

Another function of ritual is to promote change—although the actual change that occurs may be quite different from the one overtly desired by the group. For instance, there is no evidence that rain or war dances bring rain or victory, or that a healing rite cures a sick child.

But the ritual does have the effect of bringing about a measure of physiological change in the individuals who participate as tensions and excitement rise, peak, and then subside in the course of the ritual. This group experience also has the effect of reinforcing group solidarity.

Anthropologists identify two major categories of rituals, according to the kind of change they are designed to effect: rites of passage and rites of intensification. Because these two categories encompass much of ritual behavior, we will briefly explore each of them.

Rites of Passage

Rituals that mark a person's transition from one set of socially identified circumstances to another are known as **rites of passage.** Birth, puberty, marriage, parenthood, and death are all occasions for such ceremonies. According to Arnold Van Gennep (1960), rites of passage normally include three separate phases: rites of separation, rites of segregation, and rites of integration. In many societies the transition from childhood to adult status, for instance, is marked by an extended ritual that involves first a symbolic end to childhood status; then a period of physical separation from normal community life; and finally, ceremonial reintegration into society as an adult.

Among the Nbemdu of Africa, the ritual marking the transition from boyhood to manhood, known as *mukanda*, lasts four months. After a night of feasting, singing, and sexual license, the initiates receive a last meal from their mothers (rites of separation). Then they are marched to another camp known as the "place of dying," where they remain in seclusion under the supervision of a group of male guardians. Here they are circumcised, hazed, harangued, and lectured on the rules of manhood (rites of segregation). Finally, daubed with white clay that signifies rebirth, the initiates are taken back to their families. At first their mothers greet them with songs of mourning, but as each realizes that her son is safe, the laments turn into songs of jubilation. After the novices are washed and given new clothes, each performs the dance of war to signify his new status as an adult (rites of integration). The function of these rites is not merely to celebrate the changes in the life of an individual but to give public recognition to a new set of roles and relationships in the community (Turner 1967).

The transition from childhood to adulthood is marked by an extended ritual in many societies. These boys of Palembei, New Guinea, are undergoing part of an initiation rite in the "spirit house." (MALCOLM KIRK/PETER ARNOLD)

Rites of Intensification

Rites of passage are related to individual transitions, but **rites of intensification** are usually directed toward either nature or the society as a whole. Their avowed intent is to reinforce or bolster some natural process essential to survival or to reaffirm the society's commitment to a particular set of values and beliefs.

Many agricultural societies, for example, perform rites of intensification at the coming of spring and the renewal of fertility. Among the Iroquois Indians, ritual celebration was tied to important events in the agricultural cycle of the seasons: the rising of the sap in the maple trees, the ripening of the strawberries, the maturing of the corn, the harvest.

Weekly Christian church services are rites of intensification that are intended to reinforce the commitment of the believers. Similarly, the molimo festival of the Pygmies, described at the beginning of this chapter, is a social rite of intensification, its purpose being to strengthen the trust of the community in the will of the forest.

While these categories are useful for analysis, they do not always precisely reflect the actual ritual performance. A rite of passage—baptism, for example—can be performed as a part of a rite of intensification, a weekly church service. Similarly, the nature of a given ritual can change over time. Circumcision in the Judeo-Christian-Muslim tradition, for example, almost certainly began as a rite of passage marking the transition from boyhood to manhood. Among Muslims it is still practiced in this manner. A boy between the ages of eight and twelve undergoes circumcision in the context of a ceremony that explicitly emphasizes the fact that he is no longer an infant but rather a young adult ready to assume certain responsibilities. Among Jews, circumcision is performed when the boy is eight days old and marks his arrival into the community; no subsequent adult responsibilities are implied. This later transition is marked by a separate ceremony (the bar mitzvah) at puberty. When Christian boys are circumcised, the procedure usually is carried out in a hospital shortly after birth and is associated with no religious symbolism. It is done for putative health reasons, although no medical evidence supports the practice. Other familiar examples of the changing contexts or meanings of ritual can be seen in the incorporation of many pre-Christian rituals into the Christian liturgical calendar: Christmas and Easter are two notable examples, not to mention local practices accommodated by the local church in different countries.

The Organization of Ritual

In any society, ritual behavior does not occur at random: it is organized and closely structured. Not surprisingly, it is organized in different ways in different societies. It may be individualistic or communal or operate via intermediaries.

In individualistic rites, the individual worshiper draws on the powers of the supernatural. A Crow Indian man who wanted to excel in hunting or war, to find a cure, or perhaps to avenge the death of a relative goes off alone for four days (four was the Crow's mystic number) to fast, pray, and seek visions. This individualistic seeking usually produced revelations that fitted neatly into Crow traditions. Spirits nearly always appeared on the fourth day, bringing the supplicant a sacred song, describing special ways to dress and medicines to use, and imposing certain taboos (Lowie 1954: 157–161).

Religious rituals may also be organized communally, with everyone in a particular group or society participating. One person may be assigned a special role—dancer, speechmaker, prayer leader—just for the occasion. People who adopt these temporary roles are not imbued with unusual powers or vested with full-time religious duties.

Ritual Specialists: Shamans and Clergy

In most societies, however, people seek help from intermediaries who are specialists in the art of reaching the spirits and gods, men and women who are trained in or have inherited a special vocation that distinguishes them from others. They are seen to be more knowledgeable about the belief system and, more to the point, know how to use this knowledge. One such religious specialist is the **shaman,** a medium of the supernatural who acts as a person in possession of unique curing, divining, or witchcraft capabilities. In addition, chiefdoms and societies organized as states usually, if not inevitably, have a religious-ritual system that is organized in some form of ecclesiastical bureaucracy: specialized mediators with the supernatural who constitute a clergy or a priesthood. With such ecclesiastical organizations, religious practice takes a distinctive form: on the one hand is a religious specialist or priest who performs or directs ritual, on the other a more or less passive audience or congregation.

Shamans assume their religious status through birth (sometimes all the men or women of a particular family become shamans), through visions, through contact with some form of supernatural force, or through what amounts to simple vocational training. The word "shaman" can be traced to the Tungus reindeer herders of eastern Siberia, where part-time religious specialists are consulted for curing and communicating with the spirit world. They are able to transport themselves to the world of the supernatural (however it is conceived) and to act as mouthpieces for spirits, and often have privileged access to knowledge of the future.

In Greenland an Eskimo shaman yearly undertakes a dangerous spiritual voyage to the bottom of the sea to seek out the goddess Sedna, stroke her hair, and listen to her complaints against humans. When the shaman returns, he or she exhorts the living to confess their sins, so that Sedna will release the game

Shamans often assume their religious status through visions or contact with a supernatural force. Here a San healer has fallen into a trance. (MARJORIE SHOSTAK/ ANTHRO-PHOTO)

for another year and allow success in the hunt (Rasmussen 1929). On other occasions, shamans may be called on to reveal a witch or thief, to cure illness, or to help people make decisions. In all cases, the rituals involved are organized around the role of the shaman, who performs his or her services for a fee.

Many shamans have a substantial knowledge of pharmacologically active plants and herbs, which they employ along with healing or other rituals. Thus they may be offering more than what we would term psychological support—they may in fact be effecting medical cures. They also perform magic, perhaps chewing various plant and natural substances that congeal to form "stones" that are extracted from the patient. On the negative side, as we shall see, shamans can sometimes use their knowledge of plants and herbs to make effective poisons that add considerable authority to their reputations for supernatural power.

The mainstays of religion in many Eskimo, Native American, and other hunting-and-gathering societies, shamans of one sort or another are found throughout the world. In our society astrologers, mediums, and fortune-tellers are essentially shamans, and anthropological studies have suggested that the shaman's techniques do not differ greatly from those of the psychiatrist. Shamanism can exist very comfortably alongside organized churches, as we see in our own society. For example, astrology has no scientific basis and thus must be considered a form of supernatural belief and ritual, and the people who practice it shamans or diviners. It is big business in the industrialized world, where the rich and famous as well as the poor and disenfranchised spend a great deal of money to peer into the future. Even Nancy Reagan, wife of the former president, is said to have consulted an astrologer to determine auspicious days for the president's appointments and to have used her influence to persuade him to avoid certain activities on inauspicious ones. Human beings seem to have a compelling urge to seek out the future; the obviously vague and ambiguous advice found in newspaper horoscopes is sought by avid readers in even the most advanced industrialized societies.

In our own and many other stratified societies, religion is administered by a full-time professional clergy. Priests, like shamans, are religious specialists who act as intermediaries between the community and the supernatural. Also like shamans, priests are considered qualified to perform sacred rituals that lay people cannot perform, such as penance and communion in the Roman Catholic church. But priests differ from shamans in many important respects. Whereas shamans seek to resolve crises as they occur and usually work in the context of the family group, priests and other qualified members of the clergy more often perform rites for the community as a whole, in a public forum, on a regular, calendrical basis. Whereas shamans are individual entrepreneurs whose influence in a group depends on their ability to perform cures and the like, priests are part of a self-perpetuating organization. The training, sanctioned activities, dress, deportment, and responsibilities of the clergy tend to be much more highly regulated by rules or conventions; these people are members of a church—an ecclesiastical bureaucracy. In many societies, religious and political authority overlap: the head of the church is also the head of the state. In other societies, political and religious organizations are entirely separate. One thing that distinguishes any member of a clergy is that the individual practitioner is part of a larger, fairly closely organized system involving others who practice the same profession.

Established churches and priesthoods tend to be found in highly complex, stratified societies. Of course, as we have emphasized, people in complex societies may also practice individualistic or communal rituals, but the importance of the established, bureaucratic religion in maintaining social and economic stratification cannot be ignored.

RELIGION IN ACTION

Generally, as we have seen, anthropologists are more concerned with what religions do than with what religions are. Ethnographers go to the field to ask why a given culture or society has created a world of unseen entities and forces that lie behind the observable world. The consensus is that religions, first of all, *explain*. They answer existential questions about the origin of the world, the human species, and the meaning of life and death. Second, religions *validate* the established social and moral order—existing forms of governance, social hierarchies, codes of law, customs, and morals. As such they may well contain codes or models for action which have ecological or environmental implications. Third, religions assist people to *cope* psychologically and otherwise with the pains and disappointments that inevitably attend every life. In short, religion is part and parcel of a larger adaptive process as it is played out at both individual and societal levels. On the personal level, religious practices frequently answer a need for certainty which people's concrete experiences cannot fulfill. On a larger scale, too, religious beliefs and expressions are related to the economic, political, and social organization of society.

Religious Beliefs and Resource Management

Religion, in validating a prescribed course of action, may affect the relationship between people and their environment. Many religious beliefs include important environmental information, and ritual observances frequently mark or even trigger events critical to the success of economic production and distribution. For the Waswanipi Cree, a tribe of Canadian Indians, hunting success depends on acting in a responsible manner toward the animals that nourish them. An animal, they say, will not give itself to a hunter unless the hunter fulfills certain moral obligations: not to kill too many animals, to use all of what he takes, and to show respect for the bodies and souls of the animals by following established procedures for hunting, butchering, and consuming the game. Failure to live up to these responsibilities will anger the animals and bring a hunter bad luck.

According to Harvey Feit (1973), these beliefs and practices are a critical factor in the way the Waswanipi use their environmental resources. Because they live in a subarctic ecosystem in which productivity is low, they have to manage their resources carefully. Waswanipi hunters regulate the harvests of moose and beaver and control the distribution and population levels of these species by using alternative resources, such as fish, during some years and by occupying a different hunting territory each season. These practices allow the animal populations to expand for several years after each periodic harvest. In effect, Waswanipi religious beliefs and practices actually incorporate a basic ecological principle: people and animals will survive as long as they remain in balance.

The ecological significance of religious beliefs and practices may be unintentional. Among the Naskapi of Labrador, hunting strategies are sometimes regulated by divination. When food supplies are low and Naskapi hunters are uncertain where to find game, they usually consult an oracle, who tells them what direction the hunt should take. He decides the question by holding the scraped shoulderblade of a caribou over hot coals and "reading" the cracks and burned spots that appear in the bone. Thus the hunters select their routes on a random basis—wherever the spots and cracks indicate. As a result, the game supply is not depleted in particularly successful hunting places and the hunters follow no habitual routes that the animals can learn to avoid (Moore 1957).

Some religious beliefs and customs may seem maladaptive on first consideration. For instance, the Hindu prohibition against the killing or eating of cattle appears illogical in a land where hunger is prevalent. But the cattle produce three essential products: fuel and fertilizer in the form of dung, and traction with which to plow the fields (Harris 1966). To eat the cattle in times of famine would be rather like an unemployed worker selling the car needed to look for work. In the short run, the car money (or the beef) would come in handy, but in the long run the means of making a living would have been eliminated. Hence the taboo against killing cattle, Marvin Harris argues, is cost-effective, even in an area where hunger and starvation are chronic.

The attitudes toward cattle held by many East African peoples which are collectively referred to as the "cattle complex" serve a similar function, as we have discussed in Chapter 7. This is to say not that such religious prohibitions or taboos are a necessary component of resource management, only that religious belief and ritual usually encode information and encourage ways of behaving that have environmental impacts (Rappaport 1979). And as Michael Dove writes in regard to Indonesia (1988:17), "when traditional uses of the environment by peasants are investigated, they are usually found to embody sound principles of utilization and conservation—which are often expressed through the idiom of ritual."

Ritual and Resource Management

Like religious beliefs, ritual cycles serve important functions in the regulation of the relationship between people and their resources. The Pueblo Indian groups of the American Southwest, for instance, celebrate most major occasions in the life of an individual and all major religious festivals with an exchange of food throughout the community. Given the unpredictable climate, the variable land quality, and the social setting, in which one family may be living in abundance while another faces lean times, these practices ensure that all individuals receive ample food from time to time during the year.

The most important mechanism of redistribution, however, is not randomly occurring rituals but the time-dependent ones, which fall on the same day each year (Ford 1972). These rituals are most frequent in late winter, when families whose harvests have been lean are most likely to be out of food. On some saints'

days, feasts are held and food and clothing may be thrown from the rooftops to the people below. Thus Pueblo groups have built a welfare system into their ritual celebrations.

Richard Ford (1972) suggests that this system depends on surplus and that in the face of real famine, the society would have to turn to other mechanisms that involve feedback from the environment. The best example of such a regulatory ritual system can be found among the Maring of highland New Guinea. Roy Rappaport (1967) has demonstrated that the ritual slaughter of pigs functions as a mechanism for redistributing surplus pigs, providing local populations with a supply of animal protein at critical times, and ultimately regulating the territorial distribution of Maring groups.

The Maring are inveterate fighters. Neighboring groups often fight sporadically for weeks until one group is driven from its ancestral territory. The victors then perform a ritual called "planting the *rumbim*." Every man places his hand on the ritual rumbim plant, and the ancestors are addressed as follows:

> "We thank you for helping us in the fight and permitting us to remain on our territory. We place our souls in the rumbim as we plant it on our ground. We ask you to care for this rumbim. We will kill pigs for you now, but they are few. In the future, when we have many pigs, we shall again give you pork and uproot the rumbim and stage a kaiko [pig festival]. But until there are sufficient pigs to repay you, the rumbim will remain in the ground" [Rappaport 1967:23–24].

This ceremony is accompanied by the ritual slaughter of some pigs. These animals are dedicated to the ancestors, and their meat is distributed among the group's allies in payment for military assistance. A period of truce follows. Until the kaiko is staged and the rumbim is uprooted, the group may not engage in hostilities. The Maring believe that until these rituals are completed, they have not fully paid their debts to their ancestors and allies and therefore will not be given further military aid. Rappaport maintains that by limiting warfare, this taboo on fighting ensures that the regional population level does not become dangerously low.

The dynamics of this system are evident at the local level. Before the rumbim can be uprooted, a tribe must raise a sufficient number of pigs. If a place is "good," the Maring say, this process requires only about five years. If a place is "bad," however, it sometimes takes ten to twenty years. A bad place is one in which frequent misfortunes require people to kill large numbers of pigs (ritual demands that whenever group members are injured or fall ill, they and their families must be given pork to eat—a practice that ensures the afflicted of high-quality protein at a time when they need it most). Even in a bad place, however, the number of pigs eventually increases. And as the herds become larger, they require more and more food, and Maring women are forced to expend more energy in caring for the pigs. When this situation becomes intolerable, and pigs are actually competing with humans for food, the community normally decides that it is time to hold a kaiko. The ceremony begins with the uprooting of the rumbim and generally lasts for most of the year, with many feasts, weddings, and tribal alliances. It concludes with a wholesale sacrifice of pigs and distribution of pork to tribes throughout the region. Once a group has completed this ritual cycle, it is free to begin fighting again and to start a new cycle of territorial shifts, population redistribution, and manipulation of food sources.

Religion as Validation: Sociopolitical Functions

Religious beliefs and rituals provide more than ways of dealing with resources. They also contribute to the validation of the status quo, to the integration of society, and to the maintenance of social stability. Under certain circumstances, they may also serve as catalysts for violent change, as we see in revolutionary movements and religiously-inspired warfare. One important and basic social function of religion is simply to bring people together periodically and thus to maintain lines of communication and cooperation. Most religious rituals involve groups of people. In the Mbuti Pygmy molimo, in the weekly meetings of Christian and Muslim congregations, even in the awesome ceremonies the Aztecs once performed to appease their gods, people come together. The express purpose of their meeting is to perform some ritual or reaffirm an ideology, but while they are together, a range of social and economic activities may also take place. The *haj*, or once-in-a-lifetime pilgrimage to Mecca required of all Muslims, brings more than a million believers to one holy place at the same time each year. This huge gathering has political and economic implications. Not only is commerce carried out in the process, but members of different national and political entities make contact, exchange ideas, and reinforce their social and political aspirations.

Our interest in the social functions of religion, however, goes well beyond the coming together of people. Following the lead of Émile Durkheim, A. R. Radcliffe-Brown (1952) argued that the main function of religion is to establish, codify, reaffirm, and enforce fundamental social values. Religion helps to promote social unity and stability in many ways. Here we will consider four aspects of religious belief and practice which have wider social implications: the provision of a set of shared values, response to external oppression or internal turmoil, provision of psychological support, and promotion of social control. Each of these functions has a negative as well as a positive side: many nations have crumbled in the face of religious strife, many millions have died for their beliefs, and in addition to offering hope and consolation, religious ideology can bring fear and anxiety to the believer.

Reinforcement of Shared Values

When disputes arise, religion can serve to structure points of disagreement and then provide a common ground that all the participants can accept as valid for the entire community, whatever subsequent course of action is chosen. Individuals and groups constantly rely on religious values to explain and justify often very different courses of action. Murray Leaf (1972) has described the case of two political factions in an Indian village. In political campaigns, court contests, and a variety of day-to-day events, the members of these factions justify the rightness of their own position and the fallacy of their opponents' by claiming that theirs is the only one consistent with the tenets of the Sikh religion, dominant in the area. In this case, some of the "true Sikh" are members of the Congress Party and others of the Communist Party.

Religious ideologies are sufficiently general and ambiguous to support many conflicting patterns of action. Any course of action that is chosen can be validated by appeal to commonly held beliefs, and such an appeal creates a sense of rightness in the community.

Reduction of Conflict

The potential for tension and strife in social roles and relationships—between kinfolk, spouses, men and women, and rulers and subjects, for example—is inherent in every society. Ritual is frequently used as a way of channeling and controlling conflicts that arise when a person is caught between incompatible social obligations or when the moral norms of the social order as a whole run counter to the interests of particular groups.

Rites of conflict, for example, publicly express both the bonds of social unity and the tensions inherent in these bonds. Among the Shilluk of Sudan, the coronation ritual is a rite of conflict that dramatizes the surface struggles between rival settlements of kin groups. At a deeper level, it also represents the conflict that arises because a single prince who comes from a particular kin group and settlement is supposed to represent Shilluk unity. Before the new king can take office, competing groups stage a mock battle. One army carries the effigy of Nyikang, the symbol of Shilluk unity; the other army includes the king-elect. The army of the effigy captures the king from his clansmen and takes him to the capital. Here he is placed on the throne and the spirit of Nyikang is said to enter his body. Physically and symbolically separated from his relatives and followers, the new king is placed above sectional loyalties. By confronting the sources of social tensions, such rituals help to promote cooperation and reduce conflict.

Validation of Change: Revitalization

Religious beliefs and rituals can be vehicles or catalysts for social change. At times strain and tension within a society become so great that conflict and instability can no longer be contained. Religious **revitalization movements**—conscious efforts to build an ideology that will be relevant to changing cultural needs—are often part of the social eruption that follows. As Anthony Wallace has explained: "Societies are not, after all, forever stable; political revolutions and civil wars tear them apart, culture changes turn them over, invasion and acculturation undermine them. Reformative religious movements often occur in disorganized societies; these new religions, far from being conservative, are often radically destructive of existing institutions" (1966:30). The primary if unstated goal of such revitalization movements is to resolve conflict and promote stability by reorganizing society. These movements often serve an important function in the adaptation of a society to external forces that threaten to overwhelm it.

Umbanda, a rapidly spreading Afro-Brazilian religion, incorporates aspects of Catholicism, European spiritualism, and Brazilian Indian shamanism with an African base. This *pajé*, or shaman, in Altamira is in a trance brought on by calling the spirits at the bottom of a well during a curing ceremony. New religions such as this one, which resembles Vodoun in some respects, are spreading rapidly in Brazil. Evangelical protestant churches are gaining adherents throughout Latin America as well. (JACQUES JANGOUX/PETER ARNOLD)

Because anthropologists have often been eyewitnesses to (and sometimes even agents of) the drastic impact of Western culture on other societies, there is a substantial anthropological literature on nativistic revitalization movements. In the late 1880s, for example, the Ghost Dance appeared among the Indians of the western United States. Promoted as a nonpolitical religious vision by an Indian named Wovoka, the Ghost Dance expressed the belief that dead Indian forebears were soon to return on trains to take possession of the technology of the whites, all of whom would be simultaneously exterminated in a great explosion. This vision soon became a rallying cry for many Indian tribes, as the return of their dead ancestors

would so increase their strength that they would certainly outnumber the whites. Sioux warriors, in particular, were encouraged to challenge the U.S. Army: they had only to perform the Ghost Dance and wear special shirts, they were assured, to become impervious to bullets. After several years of raids and counterraids, the last remnant of 200 Sioux was killed at Wounded Knee, South Dakota, on December 29, 1890 (Mooney 1978).

In Melanesia, adherents of periodic "cargo cults" believed that ships or airplanes were soon to arrive, bringing white technology and wealth to the area (we will discuss this phenomenon shortly). Some of these belief systems call for passive behavior; others call for rebellion. In all instances, however, an unstable and conflict-ridden society uses a combination of old and new symbols to define a new view of the world and its own place in it. This response can be the basis for successful political and cultural resistance to external threats and hostility.

Both Christianity and Islam have their origins in what amount to revitalization movements. Both arose in the context of cultural and social disruption and both developed an ideology that mobilized their followers to construct a utopian social order, to right the wrongs that afflicted the present. Christianity arose among a people defeated by an imperial power, Rome. The subsequent course of the movement was very similar to that of others before and since: a visionary leader, an emphasis on a return to fundamental virtues, the bypassing of the established religious structure, and triumph in the face of persecution. In fact, persecution and oppression are often essential to the ultimate success of revitalization movements, because they are seen to confirm the righteousness of the members.

Anthony Wallace (1966) analyzed the nature of such movements in North America in his study of the Handsome Lake movement among the Iroquois during the late eighteenth and early nineteenth centuries. In the decade preceding the appearance of this movement, the Iroquois had increasingly suffered from disease, poverty, death, and confinement to reservations as the result of policies pursued by the U.S. government. The prophet Handsome Lake claimed to have received word of a means of resolving these problems in a series of visions. His first visions emphasized the need to return to traditional Iroquois practices, and the symbols he used emphasized traditional religion. A second set of visions revealed proscriptions—against drinking and witchcraft, for example. A third set prescribed radical departures from traditional Iroquois practices. White farming patterns were to be employed, and men, not women, should do the labor. Couples should live in neolocal, not matrilocal extended households. The husband-wife relationship was held to take precedence over the mother-child bond. What had at the outset seemed like an extremely conservative movement ultimately embodied a program for radical societal change. It is precisely because of the richness and the ambiguity of religious symbols that old symbols can be manipulated and recombined to justify what is or what should be, even if the new program differs markedly from currently accepted social practices.

Peter Worsley (1968) has examined a similar but more recent instance of religious response to the political subjugation of one society by a technologically more advanced one. In Melanesia, the arrival of European colonial administrators, merchants, and missionaries had a dramatic impact on the traditional social order. Worsley shows that the spread of cults announcing the end of the world—cargo cults—was one means by which people adapted to their new circumstances. Members of the cults, such as the John Frumm Cult of the New Hebrides, built airstrips and bamboo towers from which they summoned planes with "microphones" fashioned from tin cans, constructed jetties to receive ships, and worked themselves up to a state of great anticipation. Much like the cults in the United States whose members gather to await the second coming of Christ or the end of the world, the failure of the prophecy does not usually discourage the believers. Failure is explained as the result of errors in the ritual performances or of treachery. In Melanesia the belief in the treachery of white administrators who diverted the awaited cargo became a rallying cry against colonial government. The John Frumm Cult, named after an American serviceman who apparently served in the Pacific during World War II, is just one of many; a Lyndon Johnson Cult arose in 1964 (Lawrence 1964). The cults all shared certain features: a set of beliefs spread, people began to organize in reference to them, and gradually the beliefs came to acquire an anti-European orientation. Finally they evolved into active forces for political opposition to foreign rule.

"Cargo" is Pidgin English for much-coveted trade goods. The cults of New Guinea and elsewhere start with the belief that when the present world ends, as it shortly will in a terrible cataclysm, all wrongs will be righted and ultimately the riches or cargo of the whites will accrue to the Melanesians. Although the followers are inevitably doomed to disappointment when the prophecy is not fulfilled, they usually persevere in their beliefs, anticipating the arrival of the cargo at any moment. The followers continue to await the millennium, which has been described as "something you go to but never arrive at." The cults help make sense of a changing social order. More pragmatically, they end up being the means by which scattered groups come together and gain the motivation to resist the outsiders. Once resistance is successful, much of the protest nature of the cults is forgotten; many of the independence movements and postindependence labor movements in Melanesia have their origins in cargo cults.

A more recent revitalization movement is the Islamic revolution that led to the overthrow of the Iranian monarchy in 1979 and the establishment of a state based on Islamic law, which would, its proponents assured the world, restore the moral order the Shah had abandoned. On January 16, 1979, His Imperial Majesty Muhammad Reza Pahlavi, Shah of Shahs, Light of the Ayrans, and not coincidentally a close ally of the United States, ignominiously fled his country, never to return. The Shah's ouster followed several years of increasingly violent confrontations between government police and troops and masses of people united in their opposition to what they saw as a foreign-dominated, corrupt, and immoral regime. Religious leaders provided both the organizational stimulus and, through a radical interpretation of Islamic ideology, the justification for a massive outpouring of people to the streets. The day before the Shah left, crowds estimated at 2 to 4 million filled the streets of Teheran to chant a principal slogan of the movement:

> Khomeini, you are the light of God, the cry of our hearts!
> Khomeini is our leader, Shari'ati [a theologian] our inspirer!
> Death to the Shah!
> Shah, we shall kill you because you killed our fathers!
> Death to the American dog!
> Shah held on a leash by the Americans!
> We will destroy Yankee power in Iran!
> Hang this American king!   [Munson 1988:63].

In the two decades before the revolution Iran had experienced very rapid economic and social change. Large numbers of formerly rural families had migrated to urban centers in search of a better life, many with little success. While the country had been transformed economically through urbanization, industrialization, and oil revenues invested in massive development projects, a large segment of the population was bypassed by these processes. Moreover, the Shah had systematically suppressed most secular forms of opposition in the country; thus the clergy alone was in a favorable position to express popular discontent.

From an economic perspective, the spreading discontent was fueled by a decline in oil revenues, rampant inflation, and a drop in employment. From a sociopolitical point of view,

Religion and Economics: The Production of Christians in Guatemala

In his classic study *The Protestant Ethic and the Spirit of Capitalism,* Max Weber postulated that the individualistic values of Protestantism encouraged the rise of modern European capitalism and entrepreneurship. Though most social scientists today consider Weber's generalizations too sweeping, Sheldon Annis (1988) finds in Guatemala something close to Weber's "Protestant ethic"—an emphasis on individual salvation which justifies self-interested economic activity, in contrast to the traditional focus on the community. In Guatemala, however, this emphasis is the result of economic change rather than the force that drives it. In recent years a tide of evangelical Protestantism has swept through Latin America, long a bastion of Catholicism. Annis found that by 1987 well over 20 percent of Guatemalans had been converted to Protestantism, and some enthusiasts were predicting that the country would be half Protestant by 1990.

During the 1960s and 1970s Guatemala was racked not only by natural disasters, most notably a catastrophic earthquake in 1976, but also by fierce guerrilla warfare. During the administration of General Romeo Lucas García, government-linked violence swept the country as the army struck out at guerrillas and at villagers who were suspected of supporting them. The government's claim to moral legitimacy rested largely on a vague ideology of "anticommunism" that had little meaning to people in the villages. The guerrillas, though not numerous enough to defeat the army, held the moral high ground among many villagers. Their legitimacy as potential liberators was reinforced by their connections to the progressive wing of the Catholic church, with its liberation theology.

In 1982, in the midst of this conflict, a military coup placed Efraín Ríos Montt, a member of an evangelical sect called the Church of the Complete Word, in the presidency. His legitimacy, he said, lay in the power of God. In a situation of endemic violence with a Prot-

estant zealot leading the government, membership in an evangelical church could safeguard a villager from government-linked repression. Further, Ríos Montt challenged the guerrillas' right to the moral high ground in the conflict by helping to "give voice and social identity to still-inchoate forces that had been jelling for years at the grassroots" (p. 7). What has caused Protestantism to flourish in an overwhelmingly Catholic country? And what are the underlying dynamics of the competition between Catholicism and Protestantism? Annis argues that the key to religious behavior is rooted in economic production.

Annis bases his argument on an analysis of the ideology of the traditional milpa economy—an ideology of egalitarianism and communalism that is central to Indian culture. What he describes as "*milpa* logic" evolved as an expression of the Indians' place in Guatemalan colonial society; they occupied a separate and unequal sphere in which economic subordination was offset by a limited cultural autonomy (p. 105). And "*milpa* logic is 'Catholic.'" As the milpa economy is gradually breaking down "undramatically, Protestantism makes its entry at the frayed edges, where stable systems of economic production, culture, and social relations are beginning to come apart" (p. 10).

A milpa is a plot of corn interplanted with beans and small quantities of secondary crops. Despite the low rate of return, almost all highland Indian families grow corn as their first crop. Planting a milpa in fact optimizes resources in a very particular way. First, corn is remarkably hardy and will survive misuse, neglect, and drought; and when eaten with beans and some fresh vegetables, it makes a nutritionally sound diet. Second, the milpa makes use of household resources that may be abundant but otherwise unusable—dawn weeding hours, after-school hours, waste water, and so forth. Third, it reinforces the family and household unit as the basis of social organization by optimizing the resources of the family—a grandmother's knowledge of herbs and her availability for weeding, for example. Fourth, because milpa horticulture is built upon the principle of optimizing inputs rather than maximizing outputs, it works against the accumulation of capital. The milpa's product is consumed by the family or traded within the village. Because of this system's fundamentally anti-entrepreneurial character, it reinforces the egalitarian nature of the village—a central characteristic of Indian society (pp. 37–38).

The cultural stability of the milpa system has been disrupted during this century by population pressure with its resultant increase in landlessness and environmental deterioration, by military repression, by new technology and development programs, and by expanding primary education. These pressures have led to a skewing of the distribution of wealth within the ostensibly egalitarian Indian community, and this development has undermined the cultural rationale of milpa production (p. 75).

In a sense, two different modes of production have developed, each centered on the way in which peasant families choose to handle surplus. Those whom Annis describes as "*milpa*-promoting" are willing to invest their surplus in symbolic acts that celebrate and reinforce communalism. By doing so they not only tie themselves to a stable and coherent cultural system but are restrained from purchasing significant power or prestige outside the community. The Catholic church has historically been very active in promoting pan-community activities and associations, all of which call upon the villagers to spend a good part of their family income above household needs. As Annis notes, people say that "it is expensive to be a Catholic." Even poor Catholic families spend as much as a quarter of their combined income on ceremonial events (pp. 93–94).

In the mode of production associated with Protestantism, families either have no surplus (they are "dispossessed" peasants) or choose to invest in expanding their economic opportunities. They turn their backs on communal values to reach for a different set of rewards that confer personal prestige, family well-being, or spiritual gratification (p. 75). By investing in consumer goods, trucks and buses, and cash crops, they explicitly reject the ideology of the milpa.

The Protestant message provides an ideological rationalization for personal gain. And in general, Annis found that Protestants were better prepared and far more motivated than Catholics to pursue lifestyles that would either lift them out of poverty or protect hard-won financial gain. Despite the fact that Catholics own 1.41 times as much land and rent twice as much, Protestants have higher disposable incomes from agriculture—money they can deploy for immediate personal benefit or to invest in future production. Protestants own better land (as a consequence of frequent buying and selling of plots), plant more intensively, and plant a higher proportion of cash crops than Catholics. The only crop the Catholics produce more intensively than the Protestants is corn—presumably because of their greater reliance on the milpa. A contrast between Catholic and Protestant can be seen also in the matter of textile weaving, a traditional Indian pursuit: for the Catholic women, handweaving is a "kind of celebration of the integrative power of the identity of Indianness . . . for Protestants, handweaving and textile entrepreneurship are a path leading away from Indianness" (p. 141). The very fact of their success, whether they started at the bottom or further up the economic scale, reinforces the spiritual choices of the Protestants with a material rationale.

The early Protestant missionaries viewed the Indians as being "spiritually, biologically, and economically enslaved" (p. 106). And they viewed the Catholic church, alcohol, and debt as the instruments of that enslavement. They attacked the culture of the Indians. In the late 1970s and early 1980s the rate of conversion increased as Protestants found fertile ground for conversions among people who had become marginalized economically by extreme poverty or socially by increased entrepreneurship. The disintegration of the milpa ideology has created an atmosphere in which Protestant fundamentalism can flourish.

The force of religion as a source for political legitimacy is nowhere better illustrated than in Iran, since 1979 ruled by Shi'ite Moslem clerics. Here mullahs leave for the front shortly before the end of the war with Iraq in 1988. This war, which was pursued by Iran as a religious cause, resulted in almost a million deaths until it came to an inconclusive halt. (MORADABADI/REFLEX PICTURE AGENCY)

important factors included the alienation of the traditional middle classes and old elites and the partial erosion of the clergy's power and economic base during the "white revolution," or land reform. The traditional merchant classes were losing their edge to an emerging technocratic and Western-trained class. The cities of Iran were swollen with rural settlers who found themselves cut off from the wealth they could see around them. However prosaic the causes, much of the discontent was expressed in moral terms: disgust with a highly visible foreign presence in the country (in 1979 there were more than 20,000 U.S. technicians, businessmen, and military personnel in Iran, and many Europeans besides) and the spread of such non-Islamic customs as the use of alcohol, public displays of ostentatious consumption, and the Western dress adopted by substantial numbers of urban women. The so-called modern aspects of society were seen as immoral and corrupt, and more and more people responded to the call for "purification." As opposition grew, each act of repression by the government fueled the movement. Every person arrested, injured, or killed became a martyr whose fate reinforced the legitimacy of the revolution.

When the revolution was finally successful, its leaders, like those of other successful revolutions, had to face the mundane job of reconstituting a social order and perpetuating their rule. Many of the clergy, formerly in the streets as revolutionary leaders, became parliamentarians, government officials, militia leaders, and administrators.

Religion and Individual Coping: Psychological Functions

"Religion," Malinowski observed, "is not born out of speculation and reflection, still less out of illusion or misapprehension, but rather out of the real tragedies of human life, out of the conflict between human plans and realities" (1931:99). Religions reduce anxiety by supplying some answers to the imponderables of human experience: Why do we suffer? Why do we die? Why are we subject to natural disasters? In addition to supplying a system of meaning, a way of thinking about human existence, religion prescribes clear-cut institutional ways of dealing with the often frightening uncertainties of life.The Trobriand Islanders, for example, despite their highly developed skills as navigators and fishermen, perform magico-religious rituals before embarking on a long ocean voyage. They do not bother with such rituals for everyday fishing expeditions, but a long voyage on the open sea in a fragile canoe is a dangerous undertaking, and the rituals help to allay their apprehensions.

A reduction in anxiety is not simply a more peaceful state of mind. A patient's attitude is as important as medical treatment to recovery from many diseases; a lessening of anxiety may strengthen a person's commitment to recovery and tip the balance toward a return to health. In the same way, a crew paralyzed by fear is less likely to complete a dangerous canoe voyage than one that is confident of the protection of providence. The same can be said for warriors, and despite the cynical observation that "God is on the side of the heaviest artillery," every military organization from the tribal to the very modern makes liberal use of adrenalin-arousing ideology and rituals to bolster the resolve to fight.

Socialization

Religious beliefs and rituals provide more than ways of dealing with anxiety and suffering and of regulating resources; they also contribute to the integration of society and the maintenance of social stability. They help to socialize individuals, express and reinforce social solidarity, offer a means of adjusting to events or conflicts that threaten to disrupt the social fabric, and help to perpetuate forms of social organization.

Religion is a means by which people are led to accept propositions about activities and events remote from any experience or sensation. No society would survive if people did not accept some things they cannot prove. It is not simply a matter of taking on faith what earlier generations have verified for themselves, but rather of accepting abstract principles about what is ultimately unknowable. This ability is important in a number of activities with an ideological base, from politics to aesthetics. Through religious symbols and their manipulation, people are taught not only how to accept certain beliefs but also how to demonstrate those beliefs in socially effective ways.

Promotion of Social Control: The Vodoun Church of Haiti

In the Vodoun religion of Haiti, with its associated secret societies, called *bizango*, we see one way in which religion can promote social control. The processes by which it does so reveal much more than a simple mechanism for maintaining social order. They lead one to see how the natural world merges with the supernatural, how religion merges with magic, how religion can be the basis for the practice of medicine, and how a proud people have maintained their identity through the beliefs of their forebears. Vodoun (often called voodoo) is poorly understood and often associated with very negative connotations, especially where zombies are concerned. The truth is far less lurid and rather more interesting.

Until 1791 Haiti was a rich colony of France. Its plantations, worked by slaves under conditions that must have been incredibly severe, produced prodigious quantities of sugar. The slaves, imported from West Africa, suffered such high mortality that they were continually replaced by new arrivals; in the last year of French rule more than 350,000 slaves were imported (Davis 1988:25). The slaves came from many societies and from many walks of life.

Among them were potters and other craftworkers, farmers, hereditary chiefs, warriors, herbalists, sorcerers, and priests. The Haitian revolution of 1791, which abruptly ended direct colonial rule, marked the first successful slave revolt in history and the birth of the world's first black republic. It also ended the plantation system and opened the hinterlands of the country for settlement by newly freed slaves—many only recently brought from their homelands. The Vodoun religion is one aspect of the African heritage that took root in the New World.

Vodoun believers preponderate among the rural population of Haiti and are found in significant numbers in the urban centers, where the Vodoun church exists in an uneasy relationship with the Catholic church. The beliefs and rituals have their origins in West Africa. The

A woman dances in a Vodoun ceremony in Port-au-Prince, Haiti. The purpose of such ceremonies is to summon *loa* spirits, which then possess one or more of the congregants. (ANTHONY SUAU/BLACK STAR)

core of the belief system is that the spirits, *loa*, are multiple expressions of God. It is not an animistic religion. True, the believers recognize Agwe, the sovereign of the sea; Ogoun, the spirit of fire and metallurgical elements; and numerous others; but they also recognize Erzulie, goddess of love; Ghede, the spirit of the dead; and Legba, the spirit of communication among all the spheres. "Vodounists, in fact," writes Wade Davis (1988:47), "honor hundreds of loa because they so sincerely recognize all life, all material objects and even abstract processes as the sacred expressions of God." God thus stands as the supreme force at the apex of a vast pantheon; but he is distant, and it is with the spirits that one interacts on a daily basis.

Vodoun not only embodies a set of spiritual beliefs but prescribes a way of life. It is a code of ethics, a philosophy, a view of human nature. "As surely as one can refer to a Christian or Buddhist society, one may speak of a Vodoun society, and within that world one finds completeness: art and music, education based on the oral transmission of songs and folklore, a complex system of medicine, and a system of justice based on indigenous principles of conduct and morality" (ibid.). It cannot be abstracted from the day-to-day lives of the people; the sacred and the profane are one.

The Vodounist defines health, both that of the individual and that of the community, as a coherent state of equilibrium between physical and spiritual components. "Health is wholeness, which in turn is conceived as something holy, and in this regard Vodounist perceptions are not far removed from beliefs once held by our own society" (ibid.:43). The words "health," "whole" and "holy" are all derived from the Old English *hal*.

Vodoun medicine works on two levels, as do efforts to maintain social order within the community. For minor physical ailments, the individual seeks symptomatic treatment, often from a specialist called a "leaf doctor" because he uses pharmacologically active plants. When more serious trouble arises, breaking the harmony of the individual's spiritual components, responsibility for treatment falls on the Vodoun priest (the *houngan*) or priestess (the *mambo*) (ibid.:43, 45). Each individual case is unique and gets special attention—part of the strength of the treatment from a psychological perspective.

The houngan urges a patient with an obviously physical ailment, such as a broken limb, to go to a public hospital; he treats only the existential aspects of the trouble himself. The existential question "Why?" is never lost to sight. The patient knows very well that danger lurks everywhere; the question asked and answered is "Why me? Of all people, why was I stricken?" If the ailment is caused by sorcery, as is often assumed, the supernatural malevolent forces can be treated only by the mambo or houngan.

Community equilibrium is likewise sought and maintained, and trouble and troublemakers are eschewed. Here again the houngan and the mambo are important. As spiritual leaders, the Vodoun priests and priestesses are called upon to interpret a complex set of spiritual concepts and to perform complex rituals. They may direct ceremonies to restore community health, to divine the future, and to protect society against evildoers and sorcerers. Sorcery and magic are very much part of the Vodoun belief system and practice. Individuals and communities must confront the evil intentions of enemies, and must themselves turn to the malevolent forces that threaten them. Witchcraft and sorcery must be used to confront witchcraft and sorcery, and to this end the community may condone and support the efforts of a professional sorcerer, the *bokor*.

In many ways the antithesis of the priest, the bokor commands an arsenal of spells, potent potions, powders, and supernatural entities. For every force that harms, there is one that heals, and vice versa. The roles of houngan and bokor merge as each needs the other; every religious ceremony requires magic, and magic itself is worthless without knowledge of the loa, or spirits, commanded by the houngan. Even the most powerful bokor cannot kill a man unless his death is sanctioned by Baron Samedi, the lord of the dead and guardian of the graveyard (Davis 1988:54). The bokor may be feared, even despised, but he is an essential member of the community.

It is in this ideological context that the belief in zombies, or the "living dead," has to be understood. The word itself is probably derived from the Congolese *nzambi,* or "spirit of a dead person." It is the interplay between life and death, the forces of good and evil, and their human expressions in priests and sorcerers that makes Vodoun and the fear of zombifacation such a powerful social force. The bokor, if sufficiently skilled, can do more than cast powerful spells and assume animal form; he is thought to be capable of creating two forms of zombies. One is a spirit of a person, sold to or captured by a bokor, who is doomed to wander the world endlessly. The second is the more familiar "living dead," raised from the grave by the sorcerer and led away as a slave. Zombies are recognizable by their docile natures, glassy, empty eyes, and evident lack of will and emotion. Zombies are not feared; they are viewed as pathetic relics of their former selves. What is feared is zombification (ibid.:57–60). This is why the concept has such force as a means of social control.

Wade Davis, a Harvard-trained ethnobiologist, has investigated numerous accounts of individuals who had been pronounced dead, whose burial had been witnessed, and who were later encountered displaying some semblance of life. He has worked closely with bokor sorcerers and has observed the preparation of both spells and poisons designed to induce zombification. The formulas and ingredients have been analyzed in the laboratory: some, such as parts of human cadavers, possess no active pharmacological properties; others contain potent toxins capable of killing or inducing paralysis.

Davis has also examined zombification as it is perceived by adherents of Vodoun. This is the most important aspect of the phenomenon, as it appears to be in cases of sorcery everywhere. Yet he did, he claims, find strong evidence to support the occasional occurrence of empirically verifiable zombification (ibid.:193–196). Davis found that the toxin used by the bokor is the same nerve-paralyzing chemical, tetrodotoxin, found in the Japanese fish *fugu.* The Japanese biomedical literature describes occasional victims who were thought to be dead but who subsequently revived. While more direct evidence is lacking and his hypotheses may well be contested by others, the evidence is congruent both with the way the bokor's poison is administered (directly into the blood through skin abrasions) and with folk belief. Most often the poison is administered in lethal doses, but on rare occasions, Davis suggests, it may lead to temporary but nearly complete paralysis followed by recovery, often with severe mental impairment. In either case, lethal or not, the bokor's work is remembered for its success— the immobilization of an intended victim.

This hypothesis still does not explain why the bokor, with his fearful powers, is tolerated in the community. In fact, Davis makes clear, he would not be tolerated if he were to use his presumed powers in an unacceptable fashion. In examining many cases of popularly attributed zombification, he found one common element. All victims were peripheral to the community and had incurred its displeasure. In addition, he posits, the bizango, or secret societies, play a role in mediating the occurrence of sorcery and determining its targets. The secret societies, each with its own territory, bring men and women of the community together for ritual dance, songs, and prayer—and recreation, it would seem. Each is an exclusive grouping with an elaborate hierarchy among its members. Outsiders are forbidden to participate in its meetings, and members carry symbols and insignia, including "passports." Bizango societies, working with bokors, may have the critical role in the creation of zombies. "A zombie is not an innocent victim, but an individual who has transgressed the established and acknowledged codes of his or her society. The act of zombification represents the ultimate social sanction" (Davis 1988:284).

Religion, as we see from this case, does more to promote social stability than simply defuse conflict through ritual. Every religion is a system of ethics that defines right and wrong ways to behave, and prescribes sanctions against wrongdoers. When moral standards of conduct are invested with supernatural authority, their values and prescriptions are made more compelling. The Bible, for instance, describes in graphic detail the severe punishment awaiting one who breaks the Lord's commandments. In other belief systems, misdeeds are thought to provoke the wrath of ancestral spirits. The ancestors may bring misfortune to the person who fails to carry out obligations to the spirits themselves, or to one who engages in antisocial behavior toward close kin (Gluckman 1965).

Obviously, the people who act as intermediaries between ancestors (or saints or gods) and mortals, such as the mambos, houngans, and bokors of the Vodoun church and the priests, rabbis, and mullahs of Christianity, Judaism, and Islam, may occupy positions of great power. And while they serve as instruments of social control, it also happens that their tremendous power is sometimes used for worldly rather than religious ends. In Haiti the overthrow of the Duvalier regime was marked by public rage directed at houngans who were tied to the regime through memberships in the semisecret, paramilitary Tonton Macoute, a bizango organization that had served the state. Elsewhere the mullahs of Iran have effectively run the country since the Shah's ouster in 1979. They employ their power much as would any secular administrator. But on occasion the religious nature of their rule comes into play. Not only have they presided over legislation designed to bring Iran's laws into strict conformity with Islamic teaching, but the late Ayatollah Khomeini, paramount leader, used the call of Islam to mobilize the country for war with Iraq, a war in which Iranians were urged to seek "martyrdom" for the faith. As many as half a million did just that.

Summary

There is no society in which religion does not play an important role. Religion and cosmology encode not only a model of the world but also a model for the world—a plan of what it should be like. Thus religion can, and often does, guide economic and political behavior. A functional definition of religion must encompass the wide variety of religious beliefs and practices that we find in human society, but in general we can say that all religions include a dimension of the supernatural and express an ideology. Some anthropologists have defined religion as any system of beliefs, symbols, and rituals that serve to make existence meaningful and intelligible.

The sociologist Émile Durkheim posited that religion is each community's way of expressing its moral values and collective beliefs. He suggested that each society distinguishes between the *sacred*, the world of supernatural forces, and the *profane*, the everyday, natural world. Religious beliefs, according to Durkheim, embody the sacred. Actually the distinction between the natural and the supernatural is not always clear. The natural world is central to some religions, and in others supernatural forces play an important role in secular life, as in the case of *divination, witchcraft,* and *spirit possession.*

As ideology, religion has a powerful emotional appeal, particularly in the use of symbols, and it provides a rationale for human existence. Lévi-Strauss has argued that myths are symbolic formulas for the resolution of conflicts of values and moral quandaries within a society.

A belief system is inherent in every religion. The nineteenth-century anthropologist E. B. Tylor thought that all religion was based on the idea of a soul, or a personal supernatural force that is distinct from the physical body. He called the belief in the soul *animism* and argued that early people assigned a soul to all living things. Tylor's contemporary R. R. Marett believed that a less sophisticated notion, which he called *animatism*, preceded animism historically; animatism is the belief in an impersonal supernatural force that bestows good and evil on animate and inanimate objects alike.

Some religions conceive of supernatural beings, either of human origin (as in the case of ghosts and spirits) or of extrahuman origin (as in the case of a god or gods). The latter pattern of belief is called *theism.* Religions characterized by *polytheism*, or the belief in many gods, often portray gods as having human emotions and preoccupations. *Monotheism* is a belief in one supreme god. In many monotheistic religions, however, lesser figures, both supernatural and human, are deified.

Guy Swanson, in his extensive study of the relationship between religion and social organization, has found that beliefs reflect the basic characteristics of the social order: as societies become more highly stratified, so do their religious concepts.

All peoples embody their basic religious beliefs in *rituals*—highly formalized and stereotyped behaviors that frequently involve the manipulation of symbols. Religious ritual performs two basic functions: it reinforces group soli-

darity and brings about change (as in the release of tensions in the course of a ritual). The two major categories of ritual identified by anthropologists are *rites of passage* and *rites of intensification.* By celebrating such events as birth, puberty, and marriage, rites of passage note an individual's transition from one social circumstance to another. Rites of intensification are practiced to bolster a life-giving natural process or to emphasize the society's commitment to a set of values or beliefs.

Religion is organized in different ways in different societies. Some use highly individualistic rites, in which the worshiper relies on himself or herself to draw on powers of the supernatural. Other societies organize their rituals communally, and assign special roles to people on a one-time basis. In most societies people seek help from individuals with special abilities to mediate between the community and the supernatural. In many nonindustrialized societies, a *shaman*, or medium of the supernatural, performs ritual services, usually for a fee. Shamans are found in every society, and the term includes curers, fortune-tellers, astrologists, and diviners. Politically centralized societies usually have a professional, bureaucratized clergy to perform religious functions on a calendrical basis for the entire community.

Religions serve society as means of explaining existential questions, validating social or political systems (or future ones), and helping the individual to cope with life crises.

Religion can serve to maintain a balance between people and their environment. The practice of many religious customs regulates the way a society views and uses its resources. Religious practices also adapt to changes in the environment. The relationship between ritual and ecology, anthropologists have discovered, is a dynamic one.

Religious beliefs and rituals tend to validate the status quo and maintain social stability. They express and reinforce social solidarity by providing a set of shared values, responding to external oppression and internal turmoil, providing psychological support, and promoting social control. Each of these functions has a negative as well as a positive side, as can be seen in the cases of the Vodoun church of Haiti and the Islamic revolution in Iran. Religious *revitalization movements*, which may arise in response to a disorganized social system, incorporate new goals and symbols to fill changing needs. The psychological functions of religion are to relieve personal anxiety and suffering by providing a system of meaning and a source of comfort and stability.

Key Terms

animatism	polytheism	rites of intensification	shaman
animism	profane	rites of passage	spirit possession
divination	revitalization	ritual	theism
monotheism	movements	sacred	witchcraft

Suggested Readings

CHARLESWORTH, M., H. MORPHY, D. BELL, AND K. MADDOCK (EDS.). 1984. *Religion in Aboriginal Australia: An Anthology.* St. Lucia, Queensland, Australia: University of Queensland Press. A systematic study of unity and diversity in Aboriginal religious life. Though Australian religions are distinguishable from other regional groupings, they differ quite radically among themselves. This anthology is directed at the general reader who is interested in the main features of Aboriginal religion.

DAVIS, W. 1988. *Passage of Darkness: The Ethnobiology of the Haitian Zombie.* Chapel Hill, N.C.: University of North Carolina Press. Anthropological investigation and ethnobotanical research are used in this study to taxonomically identify the plant and animal ingredients of a folk toxin that had long been rumored to play a part in the process of zombification. The ethnographic context of zombification is also examined.

HERDT, G. 1987. *The Sambia: Ritual and Gender in New Guinea.* New York: Holt, Rinehart and Winston. A detailed ethnographic report of long-term institutionalized homosexuality as ritualized preparation and training for warrior status, political participation, and warfare.

RAPPAPORT, R. 1979. *Ecology, Meaning and Religion.* Berkeley: North Atlantic Books. A collection of essays that relate religious consciousness to the naturalistic assumptions of ecological and evolutionary theory.

WORSLEY, P. 1968. *The Trumpet Shall Sound: A Study of "Cargo" Cults in Melanesia.* New York: Schocken. 2nd ed. This detailed and now classic account of the rise of large numbers of millenarian cults in Melanesia attempts to define the conditions under which "cargo" cults occur.

Chapter **17** Cultural Change and Development: Anthropology at Work

Studying the present can be a means of glimpsing the future. Every society is in a state of flux or change, and what will emerge in the future must have ties to the present. The urban anthropologist Roger Sanjek and the sociologist Robert Bach are carrying out research based on just that premise. They are studying two communities in Queens, New York, in order to predict some of the urban dynamics of American society in the year 2100 (*New York Times*, July 10, 1988, p. 22). In each of these communities, among the most ethnically diverse in the nation, the researchers investigate intergroup relations, the reception accorded new immigrant families, their means of adjustment, and the form taken by community leadership. The researchers have found that a few very active individuals emerge as community leaders. A few determined women have been instrumental in introducing newcomers to such unfamiliar customs as garbage pickup, day care, and baby-sitting pools. They have also been instrumental in demanding better service from the city, responding to vandalism and street crime in their communities, and improving the quality of the schools.

As the U.S. Census Bureau predicts that in the year 2100 the United States population will be 10 percent Asian, 17 percent black, 28 percent Hispanic, and 46 percent white, the Queens study offers a window into the future. American neighborhoods are likely to accommodate an ever-changing ethnic mix of peoples; the way they adapt to each other and the way immigrants respond to American ways of doing things will affect the nature of our society. The Ford Foundation and the National Science Foundation are financing the project, which is a model for similar studies in Miami, Chicago, Houston, Philadelphia, San Francisco, and Garden City, Kansas. The findings of these and similar studies will shape urban planning policy. The ways in which the people of Queens have coped with crime, refurbished homes and stores, and adapted to cultural diversity offer guidance to other places experiencing similar changes. Anthropology and anthropologists are very much part of this process. By trying to understand general processes of change, anthropologists pave the way for a better understanding of the way society can cope with its consequences.

People react to change in a variety of ways. First, they may not perceive their cultural traditions to be in a state of flux. Sometimes the rate of change is so slow that people are hardly aware that it is occurring. When women entered the U.S. work force in great numbers during World War II and later in the 1960s, few people observed, let alone anticipated, the social consequences. Only many years later did public policy come to recognize the changes taking place in the way we lived, married, and reared our children (see Susser 1986). Even today little or no attempt has been made to shift public policy in ways that would cushion the social costs of this transformation borne by women and children (Sidel 1986).

Anthropologists have found a marked tendency for human populations to maintain the status quo. "If it ain't broke, don't fix it" seems to be the cultural watchword; and if it is broke, make do. People do not usually seek and accept change easily, for change always has inherent risks. As we have seen, innovation is often instigated either by people who have little to lose or by those who have the resources with which to absorb the risk.

431

PERSPECTIVES ON CHANGE

There are as many ways to view cultural change as there are points of view within anthropology—and we noted in Chapters 1 and 2 the diversity of theoretical positions within the discipline. Anthropologists who draw on psychological theory tend to look for and explain change in terms of individual motivation, personality, and attitudes toward risk. Those interested in cognition may stress the role of religion, world view, or cosmology in people's adoption of new beliefs and new ways of behaving and in their ways of reconciling innovations with their traditional behavior.

A new mother rests on a "roasting bed" and warms her abdomen with a *tungku* stone. Malay villagers have been quick to adapt such traditional practices in the light of modern clinical services. (CAROL LADERMAN/FORDHAM UNIVERSITY)

When Carol Laderman (1983), a specialist in religion and ideology, studied traditional and modern medical beliefs and practices associated with childbirth and midwives in rural Malaysia, she found what others before her have noted: that the Malay country people follow what appears to be an ancient and seemingly rigid ideology incorporating food taboos following childbirth and medical beliefs based on a complex view of the body as comprising "humors" or balanced fluids—some "hot," some "cold." Disease is thought to be caused and cured by "hot" or "cold" foods and medicines. Spirits, too, play a big role in bringing disease to humans, and they must be treated with special rituals or potions. Despite the conclusions of earlier observers, however, Laderman found that actual Malay practice is flexible, quickly adjusts to prevailing food resources, and is able to incorporate modern clinical procedures

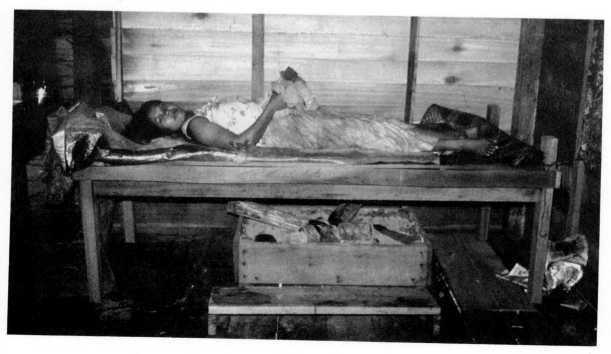

when they are needed and available. In actual practice, postpartum food restrictions do not negatively affect the mother's health and may have benefits; some of the ritual and dietary customs, for example, seem to be designed to ease the new mother through postpartum physiological stress and even postpartum depression.

Foods that are classified as "cold" are taboo: shellfish, eggplant, some fruits and vegetables, and certain fish. "Hot" foods are prescribed, including a common variety of fish, teas and other warm liquids made of special leaves, rice, and meat. The mother is considered to be in a special ritual state of transition for forty days after she has given birth. During this time she is paid almost constant attention; she is kept warm under blankets and a box of warm stones is placed beneath her bed to heat it. During this period she is encouraged to eat carefully and make the shift back to a normal diet gradually. In short, through experimentation, each woman is led back to her normal social status and natural health; the actual diet and ritual observances are adjusted to each case. The ritual period of transition, Laderman suggests, helps the new mother cope with both the physiological and psychological consequences of childbirth. The strongly voiced ideology does not stop people from adopting new practices and from adjusting their behavior as circumstances dictate. When necessary, the women incorporate modern drugs in their diet and visit medical doctors. Not only is the traditional system constantly changed to meet individual needs, but it is changing altogether as new ideas and technologies reach the Malaysians.

Despite the multiplicity of anthropological perspectives on change, most research has focused on the costs and benefits of change to the people involved. One researcher may try to determine which social grouping or class benefits from innovation and which pays the costs. Another, economics-oriented researcher may in-vestigate who within a social setting is likely to introduce new techniques of production or marketing. Still another may look at the environmental impact of a new agricultural technique. But common to all is some measure of costs and benefits, success and failure.

Innovation

In earlier chapters we discussed the need for all societies to achieve a balance between social rules and deviance. Deviance is essential in the area of innovation. When certain members of a society violate a social rule and their actions succeed in resolving some problem, they are called entrepreneurs or inventors rather than deviants. As a result, most innovations are as much a matter of serendipity as of cold, clear calculation.

Nevertheless, considerable attention has been given to the social and psychological characteristics of innovators. When Everett Rogers (1962, 1971) studied patterns of innovation in rural villages in Colombia, he found that innovators were more literate, listened to the radio and read newspapers more often, and made more trips to the city than noninnovators. They were also less fatalistic—less prone to believe that people have no control over their lives—and more empathetic—able to project themselves into new and different roles. Innovators, too, tended to be the larger landowners—perhaps because wealth permits experimentation and entails less risk in the event of failure, perhaps because experimentation leads to wealth.

Rogers was able to identify several personal characteristics that innovators had in common, but it was much more difficult for him to use these data to explain why change occurred. The success of innovation depends not simply on its occurrence but also on its acceptance, and acceptance is very much a matter of the surrounding situation. Our historic records show that many important innovations have been introduced simultaneously in different places (see Table 17-1). This finding prompts the conclusion that the introduction and acceptance of innovations are not random. Consequently, the current trend in studies of cultural innovations is to focus less on the psychological characteristics of innovators than on the conditions under which innovations are adopted and then

---

TABLE 17-1:   Some Simultaneous Discoveries and Inventions

Telescope: Jansen, Lippershey, Metius, 1608

Sunspots: Fabricius, Galileo, Harriott, Scheiner, 1611

Logarithms: Napier, 1614; Burgi, 1620

Calculus: Newton, 1671, publ. 1687; Leibnitz, 1676, publ. 1684

Nitrogen: Rutherford, 1772; Scheele, 1773

Oxygen: Priestley, Scheele, 1774

Water is H_2O: Cavendish, Watt, 1781; Lavoisier, 1783

Steamboat: Jouffroy, 1783; Rumsey, 1787; Fitch, 1788; Symington, 1788

Theory of planetary disturbances: Lagrange, Laplace, 1808

Telegraph: Henry, Morse, Steinheil, Wheatstone and Cooke, ca. 1837

Photography: Daguerre and Niepce, Talbot, 1839

Surgical anaesthesia by ether: Long, 1842, results disregarded; Jackson, Liston, Morton, Robinson, 1846

Sunspot variations correlated with disturbances on earth: Gauthier, Sabine, Wolfe, 1852

Natural selection: Darwin, Wallace, 1858

Telephone: Bell, Gray, 1876

Phonograph: Cros, Edison, 1877

Rediscovery of Mendel's laws: De Vries, Correns, Tschermak, 1900

Flight orientation of bats due to hearing reflections of uttered sounds: Griffin and Galambos, U.S.A., 1941–42; Dijkgraat, Holland, 1943—during total severance of communications in war years

---

Source: Abridged from *Anthropology,* by A. L. Kroeber, copyright 1923, 1948 by Harcourt Brace Jovanovich, Inc. and renewed 1976 by Theodora K. Quinn, reprinted by permission of the publisher.

become routine. All people innovate to some degree, and all populations include at least a handful of highly inventive individuals. Change occurs when these people and their ideas are accepted as legitimate and not rejected as deviant.

Frederick Barth's study (1963) of fishing villages in northern Norway reveals that conditions of ambiguity can prompt acceptance of innovation. Isolated geographically and culturally, the villagers (most of whom were Lapps) occupied a marginal position in Norwegian society. Many wanted the goods that industrialization promised but lacked the means to obtain them. Fishing for export and farming for home consumption made for a precarious existence. The villagers had neither the capital nor the financial know-how to make connections with the modern world.

Such conditions create a niche for the people that Barth identifies as **entrepreneurs**—individuals who are willing to take risks and break with traditional practices in order to make a profit (see Chapter 14). Barth suggests that in marginal communities the entrepreneur acts as an agent of change by playing the role of mediator between local communities and outside institutions. By making use of existing possibilities in ways neither local people nor state bureaucrats perceive or plan, the entrepreneur is able to bring together a relatively self-conscious group of people who see the utility of change. Under other conditions, entrepreneurs may be considered deviant or even criminal. Here they fill a need.

The acceptance of innovations depends to a great extent on the fact that customary ways of acting are always subject to variation. Individuals constantly make decisions in every society, and decision making gives rise to behavioral variation. There are enough conflicting versions of proper behavior in every society to create some ambiguity and thus allow for the introduction and acceptance of innovation.

Innovation and Adaptation

Whatever the internal processes that affect the acceptance of innovations, their long-term survival depends on their adaptiveness. Innovations may be accepted immediately and permanently because they help a group to cope with day-to-day changes in its social and natural environment. Or an innovation may remain relatively insignificant until major environmental changes make it an important part of a population's adaptive mechanisms.

Perhaps the best way to begin a discussion of adaptation within a social context is to examine a case in which very similar populations responded quite differently to contact with new groups. Consider the case of the Pimas and Papagos of southern Arizona (Hackenberg 1962). These two Native American groups are similar in language, in artifacts and tools, and in physical appearance, but they differ in critical ways. In the recent past the Pimas derived roughly 60 percent of their subsistence from agriculture and 40 percent from hunting and gathering. They lived in approximately a dozen permanent villages along the Gila River, where they practiced irrigation agriculture. The Papagos, on the other hand, had a semimigratory lifestyle. They lived in "field villages" adjacent to locations used for floodwater farming, but also in "well villages," hunting-and-gathering base camps located around permanent sources of water. The Pimas' headmen had much greater authority than the Papagos', their wealth was more unevenly distributed, and they had more formal mechanisms of intervillage interaction.

Both ethnohistoric and archaeological data suggest that the reasons that these two groups, with similar habitats, cultures, and languages, developed such significant differences in subsistence strategies, settlement patterns, and social organization lie about four hundred years in the past. Until then the area seems to have been inhabited by populations whose subsistence strategies ranged from almost total reliance on hunting and gathering to heavy reliance on irrigation agriculture supplemented by hunting and gathering. But instead of two easily distinguishable cultural traditions, the subsistence and settlement patterns ranged along a continuum, with populations varying their strategies in response to changing climatic conditions.

During the sixteenth century, the Spaniards and the Apaches came to Arizona, and both groups had an impact on the ways of life of native peoples. The Spaniards introduced winter wheat, which proved to be a successful crop in the irrigated fields of small villages along the river. Because winter was the traditional hunting-and-gathering season, dependence on hunting and gathering decreased in these villages. But winter wheat did not prove successful in the floodwater fields of the more migratory groups, so their reliance on hunting and gathering did not decline.

The Apaches, too, had a significant effect on the ways of life of the Pimas and Papagos. A predatory group, the Apaches frequently raided agricultural populations in the area. Consolidation and a stronger political organization centered on defense enabled local people in the more sedentary villages to protect themselves. Less sedentary groups became increasingly mobile in order to avoid the invaders. Thus the joint arrival of the Spaniards and Apaches seems to have resulted in two very distinct patterns of subsistence, settlement, and social organization—one we now call Papago, the other Pima.

Ecological factors seem to have played a central role in this outcome. Slight differences in subsistence strategies and economic behavior among the original populations proved to be critical in their responses to contact with the Spaniards and Apaches. The people in one set of ecological circumstances reacted by decreasing their mobility and centralizing their political organization, while those in another set of circumstances reacted by increasing their mo-

bility and flexibility and decreasing their dependence on agriculture.

Acculturation

The Pima and Papago case also illustrates the process of **acculturation**—cultural change that occurs in response to extended firsthand contacts between two or more previously autonomous groups. Studies of acculturation offer anthropologists insights into the range of factors that affect the outcome of contact between societies.

The Influence of Social Types and Circumstances

One basic factor involved in acculturation lies in the types of individuals who make contact and the kind of contact they have. Those individuals tend not to represent a broad cross-section of their societies. The native peoples of South America, for example, experienced their initial contact with Europeans when they encountered military expeditions, missionaries, and seamen—hardly a representative sample of European society. Once the indigenous states and chiefdoms were subdued, the principal aims of the newcomers were to convert the Indians to Christianity, to acquire their lands, and to make use of their labor in the newly opened mines and on the haciendas.

The first Europeans to make contact with the people of highland New Guinea—a rugged region that had deterred exploration by outsiders for centuries—were prospectors seeking gold or oil in the 1920s. Here the native peoples were seen largely as a cheap labor force; their land was not taken from them. In parts of Amazonia the first people to make sustained contact with such indigenous tribes as the Yąnomamö tended to be missionaries. Their motives may have been beneficent but their activities were not always beneficial to the people. Missionaries often believe that if they are to make Christians of native peoples, they must systematically discredit their traditional culture in order to separate them from their religious practices and beliefs.

Needless to say, the conquistadors and the later missionaries had quite different effects on the native society. Shortly after the Spaniards came to the New World, vast numbers of peoples perished. Nicaragua alone lost 92 percent of its native population in the first few generations of contact (Newson 1988). The great empires of the Aztecs and Incas were destroyed, the indigenous religions were suppressed by force, and thousands of distinct cultures all but disappeared. In New Guinea, which was colonized very recently, indigenous peoples retain their lands, their religions, and much of the cultural content of their precontact way of life. Today Papua New Guinea is an independent country, and to the extent that any people can determine their cultural future, they will do so. The Yąnomamö, as we shall see in more detail later, are in a more precarious position. They are racked by new diseases brought by the newcomers and their forest lands threatened by the lumbermen's chainsaws and the developers' bulldozers. Their cultural future is still in doubt.

The Adoption of New Behaviors

A second basic factor in acculturation is the specific behaviors that are modified as a result of contact. A society that gradually adopts the practices of another culture does not adopt *every* behavior or belief of that other culture. On the contrary, cultural influences meet with varying degrees of acceptance and resistance, so rates of culture change are highly variable. In Guatemalan towns, for example, native Indians and *ladinos* (people who speak Spanish and have a modern lifestyle) live side by side.

As a result of their contact, few Indians use traditional sweat baths any longer; most Indians speak Spanish as well as the Quiché language; and most wear modern Western-style clothing. But in other areas of behavior, Indians are not becoming ladinos at so fast a pace. Most still pursue the traditional agricultural life; few live in ladino-style houses or cook on modern stoves; and while most dress in Western clothes, only 13 percent of the men wear shoes rather than the traditional sandals (Woods and Graves 1973).

Societal Flexibility

A third factor influencing acculturation consists of the characteristics of the societies in contact, particularly the flexibility and openness of their boundaries and internal structures. When a society's boundaries are very rigid, marriage with members of another group may not be permitted. The interactions of the Spaniards and the British with Native American groups were quite different in this respect. The Spaniards intermarried, while the British did not. This is one of the reasons that the population of modern Mexico is substantially a blend of New World and Old World people, while in North America, the population is largely of European and African extraction with a distinct Native American minority. In general, the more permeable the boundaries of a given society and the more flexible its internal structure, the more open it is to acculturative change (Broom et al. 1954).

Political and Military Strength

A fourth factor influencing the effects of culture contact is the relative political and military strength of the two groups. A society of greater strength is often capable of forcing its cultural patterns on a weaker one. This is precisely what happened in the encounters between European

colonizers and native peoples. Existing political systems were destroyed and new ones imposed. Even new tribes were created and chiefs imposed by the outsiders; relations between men and women were transformed, often with a loss of political and social autonomy on the part of women (Etienne and Leacock 1988; Gailey 1987). It must be recognized, however, that strength is not simply a matter of numbers. Many numerically smaller groups have had a dominant influence over larger ones. Han Chinese military colonizers in imperial times, for example, were frequently outnumbered by so-called national minority peoples, but they did not lose their cultural identity. In fact, as a result of their influence, the numerically superior people often became more like the Han Chinese.

The Yąnomamö Enter the Twentieth Century

The Yąnomamö of Venezuela and Brazil are experiencing acculturation in much the same manner as are other Indian tribes of the Amazon rain forest. Their present predicament is very similar to that experienced by native populations throughout North and South America in the early days of colonization by Europeans. They have been abruptly brought into contact with a technologically advanced and alien cultural system. When Napoleon Chagnon arrived

(Top) Shavante men dancing during an initiation rite for young boys in 1958. (Bottom) Twenty-four years later, when anthropologists David and Pia Maybury-Lewis revisited the Shavante, they found that the style of dancing had become well known throughout Brazil. The running shorts testify to the passage of time between the two pictures. (TOP: DAVID & PIA MAYBURY-LEWIS/ANTHRO-PHOTO; BOTTOM: WILLIAM CRAWFORD)

in 1964, the villages closest to European settlements had seen only a handful of whites, and those of the interior none at all. Trade goods had been reaching them, passed on through intermediate groups, but no extended contact had occurred between the Yąnomamö and the outside world. Since the period of first contact, change as a result of acculturation has been occurring rapidly and often against a backdrop of misery and misfortune. Along with contact have come diseases to which the Yąnomamö had no immunity. They have been decimated repeatedly by epidemics; one disastrous influenza epidemic in 1973 killed a quarter of the population in the villages sampled (Chagnon and Melancon 1983:59). These scourges have had a severe impact on the traditional social organization; ritual specialists have died before passing on their knowledge and skills, kin groups have been broken up and forcibly resettled, and leaders have succumbed to these new diseases.

In 1974 the Perimetral Norte highway reached the Brazilian Yąnomamö, who until then had had only sporadic contact with outsiders, and brought with it a veritable flood of lumbermen (Saffirio and Hammer 1983). Here, too, epidemics took an almost instant toll: villages studied soon after the road was constructed had lost between 30 and 51 percent of their populations. Soon, however, the Indians nearest the road came to depend on it. They ranged themselves alongside the road to beg and barter for shorts, shirts, food—doubtless it seemed like an easier way to make a living than their traditional horticulture and hunting. Soon they built a village near the road and went to work on farms and sawmills; for twenty or thirty days' work they received a little money, not more than $2 or $3, and some cigarettes and used clothes. They came to try to emulate the ways of the Brazilians or *civilizados* and not to appear to be *indios bravos* (wild Indians).

The "roadside" Yąnomamö came to differ from the unacculturated villagers of the interior. They adopted Brazilian haircuts, took up smoking cigarettes, bought canned foods and candy, and added lots of salt to their food. In fact, their traditional diet was superior to that of the average Brazilian farmer, and with contact their diet declined in terms of calories earned per unit of labor expended. But because they wanted to appear like the Brazilians and to interact more with them, they adopted as many Brazilian practices as they could. Not only did they adopt such utilitarian items as aluminum pots and pans, steel axes, shotguns, and other things that facilitated subsistence activities, they also came to depend on large numbers of consumer items that tied them ever more closely to the Brazilian suppliers. As John Saffirio and Raymond Hammer write (1983), it is doubtful that they would have embraced this alien culture so wholeheartedly if they had understood that in so doing they were losing their political autonomy and entering Brazilian society at the very bottom of the social and economic hierarchy.

The Spectrum of Acculturation

Thus the conditions under which culture contact takes place have a large effect on the results. At one extreme we have instances in which one society is virtually taken over by another, its own cultural traditions being replaced by those of the dominant society. At the other extreme we find populations that respond to contact with other societies by attempting either to avoid or to expel the newly arrived group. The Papagos, for example, tried to avoid the Apaches by adopting a more migratory lifestyle. Similarly, revitalization movements (such as those described in Chapter 16) and armed rebellions are efforts to ward off or reverse the influence of intruding societies.

Somewhere between these two extremes are situations in which a society incorporates some new traits into its cultural practices but avoids a pervasive loss of traditional customs. Accul-

turation, to a greater or lesser degree, is a two-way street. Most groups are selective in their adoption of traits from other societies, and they modify what they borrow to blend with their own beliefs and practices. Catholicism in Latin America adapted and incorporated many pre-Columbian beliefs and practices as it made converts. In Haiti people combined elements of a variety of West African religions with selected Catholic myths and rituals into a new religious system, the Vodoun church. This faith, organized around its churches and priesthood, while much maligned and misunderstood, acted as a means for the Haitians to express themselves against their colonial masters in earlier days, and more recently as a system of social control (Davis 1988).

METHODS OF VIEWING CHANGE

Oral Histories

One obvious way to learn about change is to ask informants what life was like in the past, and how and why their world has changed. Some of the best accounts of traditional culture are based on long, intensive interviews, and anthropologists working with contemporary indigenous societies in Latin America, Asia, and Australia are eager to record oral histories related by people who still remember the tales and traditions that are fast being lost. Scott Cane (1987), for example, has spent many months over the past six years working with Gugadja informants, visiting old campsites and documenting the subsistence activities of a people who only recently gave up hunting and gathering as a way of life in the great Western Desert of Australia. He records firsthand information on the final phase of hunter-gatherer activity in arid Australia, and documents the seasonal round of harvesting and food preparation, traditional techniques of hunting and storage, the plants, insects, and animals that were used, and the myths and lore associated with this vanished nomadic way of life. Nevertheless, we have to recognize that these are recollections, not directly observed behavior.

Historical Documents

Anthropologists also use historical documents to study culture change. Of course, journalists, historians, and record keepers are selective storytellers. But by uncovering and comparing numerous sources, a researcher can sometimes arrive at a reasonably close approximation of the chronology of change in a population and the reasons for it. Burton Pasternak's study of family history and demography in Taiwan (1982), as we saw in Chapter 8, drew on detailed genealogical archival documents going back several generations.

A study by Sidney Mintz (1986), based on archival and historical documents of several countries, shows how Europeans transformed sugar from a rare luxury to a necessity of everyday life and how world history was altered in the process:

Some of the best accounts of traditional native American culture are based on long, intensive interviews. Here a Hopi woman demonstrates how to fire a pot. (K. ROSENTHAL/STOCK, BOSTON)

Sugar—or rather the great commodity market which arose demanding it—has been one of the massive demographic forces in world history. Because of it, literally millions of enslaved Africans reached the New World, particularly the American South, the Caribbean and its littoral, Guiana and Brazil. This migration was followed by those of East Indians, both Moslem and Hindu, Javanese, Chinese, Portuguese, and many other peoples in the nineteenth century. It was sugar that sent East Indians to Natal and the Orange Free State (now South Africa), sugar that carried them to Mauritius and Fiji. Sugar brought a dozen different ethnic groups in staggering succession to Hawaii, and sugar still moves people in the Caribbean   [Mintz 1986:91].

The documents that Mintz used include early botanical observations, accounts by explorers and travelers, ships' manifests, plantation records, and government records on slavery, trade, migration, and tax revenues. His long-term fieldwork in many countries of the Caribbean gave him a vivid understanding, too, of what life on a sugar plantation was like. The result is a unique insight into the way a commodity we all take for granted spread from obscurity in 1650 to become by 1900 part of the everyday diet of Europeans and now a staple almost everywhere in the world. This is cultural change writ large.

Restudies

Another, more particularistic way to investigate change is to visit the site of a field study conducted some years earlier. Margaret Mead went back to the South Pacific island of Manus twenty-five years after her original study of this isolated, nonliterate, kin-based society. In the interim, Americans had been using the island as a military base. Through regular contacts during the occupation, the people of Manus had adopted a whole new set of perceptions, desires, and norms (Mead 1956). Since Napoleon Chagnon first went to Venezuela to study the Yąnomamö in 1964, he has made more than fifteen return visits, some of them lengthy. As a result of his work, that of his graduate students and research associates, and even that of others who wished to challenge some of his theories, the Yąnomamö have become one of the best-studied tribal populations in the world. Thanks to these efforts, we have in-depth data on the demographic processes, warfare, health and nutrition, land use, and economy of a people whose way of life is rapidly disappearing. This information is of value to the Yąnomamö themselves as they face an uncertain future. The Venezuelan government's policy is to assimilate such populations as the Yąnomamö, and already the effects of this policy are evident.

Missionaries are encouraged; ranchers, miners, and lumber companies have encroached on their territories; travel companies bring tourists in power boats; outsiders have hunted and trapped many game species out of existence; and road and other projects threaten the Yąnomamö's physical and cultural survival. The anthropologists who have worked with the Yąnomamö of Venezuela and Brazil have been the principal defenders of their sovereignty and right to continue living in their own fashion on their own lands. Data collected by Marcus Colchester, an English anthropologist (1985), and by Napoleon Chagnon and Tom Melancon

(1983) and others document the ravages of introduced diseases and have helped marshal medical assistance. Their techniques are varied, but repeated trips to the same study sites are basic to their ability to document ongoing change and acculturation.

Impact Studies

Change may also be studied through the special surveys sometimes called "impact" studies. Most economic development projects, for example, are accompanied by social impact analyses prepared by social scientists. It is known that any major project, such as the building of a dam, a new highway, or even a rural road, will have social costs as well as benefits for the people affected. These studies, which take many forms—including before-and-after studies, as we have seen in the Yąnomamö case—use an initial study conducted before the project is undertaken as a basis for comparison.

Another common approach is to select a sample of communities directly affected by the project and compare them with communities of a similar sort elsewhere. In Kenya, where many thousands of miles of new rural roads have been built in recent years, studies have compared households or villages alongside new roads with those still at some distance from a motorable trail. Such impact studies identify a selection of newly built roads in various agricultural areas and attempt to see how the coming of the road has affected economic and social life. Households that suddenly have easier access to markets and towns are seen to adopt quickly such new technologies as metal tanks to store water and tin roofs. These people also go to town more frequently to avail themselves of entertainment, educational opportunities, and health care. The economic benefits are, of course, better access to marketing facilities and extension services; the possible costs associated with the new road (admittedly hard to measure) may include the drawing of men into urban employment, with attendant hardship for their spouses, and disruption of patterns of household and community self-sufficiency. Other social costs include increased expenditure on transport and increased exposure to deleterious consumer items such as alcohol and the venereal diseases that are prevalent in market towns. Studies of this kind can readily document such changes as the adoption of new technologies and consumer goods, altered modes of subsistence, and the introduction of new patterns of communication. What they cannot do reliably is predict the long-term consequences of these short-run changes. One way to see the long-term consequences of specific adaptations is to go back in time: archaeological data offer us an insight into the long-term processes of change.

Archaeological Research: Viking Settlements

One example of an accumulation of short-term adaptations that result in an ultimately dramatic long-term change illustrates most of the preceding points, including the importance of always keeping environmental consequences in mind in assessing change. Thomas McGovern and other archaeologists who specialize in Norse or Viking history have attempted to unravel the checkered history of Norse settlement in the North Atlantic (McGovern 1980; McGovern et al. 1988). Numerous islands were settled between A.D. 790 and 1000, including the Shetland and Faroe islands, Iceland, and Greenland, and very likely the east coast of North America as well. The colonies had rather different histories, and the westernmost ones, Iceland and Greenland, mark the outer limits of significant Viking settlement. The once thriving settlements of Greenland, which ultimately failed by 1500, and Iceland, which suffered a significant decline in population after several centuries, offer some insights into processes of long-term adaptation.

The Viking settlers brought with them an established food-procurement system: they raised cattle and sheep, fished, and, where it was feasible to do so, cultivated wheat or barley. They also came equipped with a social and political hierarchy that separated the free from the slaves and encompassed quite rigid distinctions among servants, tenants, landowners, and chiefs. By law every free landowning farmer or household had to be associated with a particular chief. Each tenant—a family that was contracted to run a farmstead for a specified period—was bound to a landowning householder. The entire colony was run by an elite comprising chiefs and, in the later periods, the Norwegian king's appointees and church dignitaries. The early colonial period was quite successful; most of the settlers were free, and they established independent holdings on which to raise sheep and cattle wherever they found sufficient pasturage. The settlers were quick to incorporate the rich marine life into their diets. The population of Greenland's settlements grew, as did that of Iceland, the two together reaching some 60,000.

With success, however, came the gradual transformation of the Viking colonies. In the beginning each settlement was relatively autonomous, and the predominant form of homestead was that of a free family working pastures and lands that they owned and on which they paid taxes. Though slaves were brought over initially, no more were imported, and such labor as nonfamily members performed was provided by servants and tenants. As time passed and settlements grew, churches were erected and homesteads spread to the outer limits of pasturage in this severe environment. Gradual social and political changes had profound effects. First, the number of tenant farmers increased in relation to freeholders as many freeholders had to sell their lands to pay the taxes levied. Thus land became much more subject to indirect management. The people who worked the land were under pressure to produce as much hay or to raise as many sheep and cattle as possible, with little thought to possible long-term effects. Evidence of overgrazing and soil erosion is abundant. Second, what were formerly petty chiefs became powerful leaders, controlling considerable land and often warring with rivals. By the mid-thirteenth century a few families had come to control most of the land. In short, land use became intensified; socially the society was more stratified; specialized priests, warriors, smiths, and urban craftworkers proliferated; and decision making became more centralized as power accrued to the chiefs and bishops.

In 1262–1264 Greenland and Iceland came under the direct control of the Norwegian state, and most land was now controlled by church and crown. The church sent bishops to rule and encouraged the building of monumental structures quite disproportionate to the size and resources of the colonies. Taxes and tithes were collected, administered, and forwarded to the state by foreign-born appointees. The colonies were closely integrated into a growing North European economic system. But economic integration did not bring prosperity to most of the people of the colonies, and ultimately it had dire consequences. Environmental degradation through soil erosion and depletion of marine resources caused hardship. Much of the pasturage became barren rock, and by 1500 the colony on Greenland had become extinct, unable to cope with the demands of its topheavy administration, a depleted resource base, and the harsh climate. Greenland was once more left to its North American inhabitants—the Eskimos, whose time-proven adaptation the Vikings chose to ignore or dismiss. By 1600, 94 percent of Iceland's people were reduced to tenant farming and the population declined sharply. This colony survived, but prosperity returned only in this century, when Iceland reorganized itself as an independent and locally self-sufficient society.

The Lessons of the Viking Settlements

Such dire consequences can, of course, be avoided. In numerous instances long-term growth in population and intensification of land use have endured for centuries in combination with political centralization, as in China and the Middle East. But the lessons taught by the failure of the Viking settlements should not be dismissed lightly. Highly integrated and centralized political systems entail special risks. Even technologically sophisticated systems are vulnerable to the negative effects of centralized planning.

The Soviet Union is today facing an ecological disaster of almost unparalleled magnitude. The Aral Sea, in 1960 the fourth largest lake in the world, is drying up so rapidly that by the end of the century it will be nothing more than vast briny swamp (Micklin 1988:1170–1173). Water that formerly fed the Aral has been diverted to complex and distant irrigation schemes, some more than 1,300 kilometers away. The water that does flow into the Aral from surrounding agricultural schemes is contaminated by chemical fertilizers and pesticides. Gone is the rich fishing industry, and communities once strung around the lake shore are being stranded as the shoreline recedes. The rapidly diminishing surface area of the lake is already resulting in hotter, drier summer temperatures and lower winter temperatures in the surrounding regions; the falling of the water table has disrupted oasis farming in the region and is causing more rapid desertification.

The main culprit in this case and in many others is an abstraction: a highly centralized system of planning and decision making with inadequate ability to anticipate long-term costs. Of course we know that abstractions have no influence over environmental events: the decisions are made and carried out by myriad individuals united in a bureaucratic hierarchy, each concerned with such mundane matters as career advancement, job security, and day-to-day survival. Keeping to "productivity" goals, limiting one's liability and responsibility for mistakes, demonstrating bureaucratic achievement in extending the scope of one's authority are critical to the success of individuals in bureaucracies. In this context, local information and early warning signs that might signal impending environmental or social problems are easily ignored.

Problems in the Study of Change

No approach to the study of change is without problems. Informants may have selective memories and may consciously or unconsciously slant their accounts. Historical documents and records tend to shape the facts to justify practices current at the time they were written. The problem with restudies is that they tend to create the impression that groups move steadily in one direction, ignoring the possibility of short-term fluctuations. And when different anthropologists conduct the initial and follow-up studies, the results may reflect differences in their orientations and methods rather than cultural changes. Even large-scale surveys, such as impact analyses, have their limitations, as a truly controlled comparison is difficult if not impossible to make. It is hard to prove that the social changes or innovations observed in the Kenyan road studies, for example, were actually caused by the roads. The roads, after all, were laid out along the best existing trails; thus they linked communities that already had better-than-average access to markets and also, not coincidentally, had leaders with the political connections to have the roads run to their communities.

New Frontiers of Research

Because none of the commonly used methods of studying change is independently reliable,

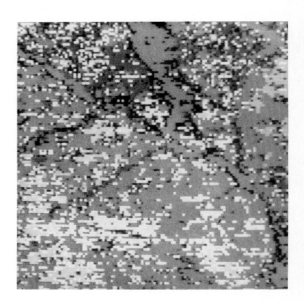

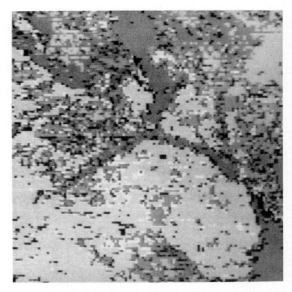

(Top) Pokot herders had abandoned the region shown in this Landsat imagery for five years. During this period, the region had become overrun by acacia thorn bushes, a tenacious weed. (Bottom) Farmed or grazed areas show up in the Landsat imagery quite differently, allowing the interpretation of land use and habitation. (TOP & BOTTOM: FRANCIS CONANT/HUNTER COLLEGE)

most research incorporates a variety of methods. Anthropologists are also trying more sophisticated ways of obtaining data on change. To perceive change as a periodic interruption of stability is no longer justifiable; we now know that change is continuous through time in every society. Rather than simply reconstruct patterns of culture change, anthropologists must try to find ways of conducting studies of change that stretch over many years, yielding precise records of change as it occurs over the long run.

One interesting development in this area is the information available from satellite scans. Earth satellites are currently gathering data about every part of our world, including data on such aspects of human culture as demographic settlement, and agricultural patterns. Francis Conant, in his work with the Pokot of Kenya (1982), has used such data to show how grazing patterns have been altered as a consequence of warfare, with the result that large areas of former pastures have reverted to acacia (thorn tree). In years to come, satellite records may prove invaluable to anthropologists even though the evidence they provide is on a very large scale.

THE PROCESS OF LONG-TERM CHANGE

Patterns of general evolution indicate some recurring long-term processes of systemic change. The number of regularities in the transformation of human societies over millennia is limited. These patterns of general evolution—the patterns of behavior or organization that can be observed in a group or population—are the products of short-term changes, and none is universal. With that caveat in mind, let us review some very general processes involved in long-term cultural change, many of them already illustrated:

Intensification. The trend toward intensification is the basis of Leslie White's theory of energy capture, discussed in Chapter 2. Agricultural **intensification**, as we saw in Chapter 8, refers simply to an increase in the product derived from a unit of land or labor. Over millennia, the general trend has been toward greater intensification of food production. As we saw earlier, most societies that rely on hunting and gathering obtain less food from a unit of land than societies that rely on intensive agriculture. In the latter societies, increasing numbers of people rely on a constant amount of land to produce increasing amounts of food. We have seen this dynamic at work in the Viking settlements and in other agricultural societies.

Specialization and differentiation. Another process involved in long-term change is **specialization,** the increasingly limited range of productive activities in which a single individual is likely to be engaged. As specialization increases, the average person is engaged in a smaller and smaller percentage of the entire set of activities carried out in a society. Industrial society (or postindustrial society) is simply the latest point reached in a process that is as old as human culture. As individuals have become increasingly specialized, societies have tended to be characterized by increasing **differentiation**; that is, organization in separate units for various activities and purposes.

Centralization. A third evolutionary process has been **centralization,** the concentration of political and economic decisions in the hands of a few individuals or institutions. As we saw in Chapter 15, this process has been related to the growth of political, economic, and social differentiation: a strong centralized power is useful in efforts to orchestrate diverse activities and interests, not to mention efforts to defend extant resources—and possibly to acquire those of neighboring populations.

Stratification. Another trend in the long-term evolution of cultures is **stratification**—the division of a society into groups that have varying degrees of access to resources and power. We saw in Chapter 13 that the long-term evolutionary trend has been from consensual to authoritative leadership. Band societies have no clearly defined, legally or militarily established elite leadership.

Settlement nucleation. In almost every part of the world, stratification and centralization have been associated with **nucleation,** the tendency of populations to cluster in settlements of increasing size and density. Cities are an exclusive characteristic of state-organized societies. Without question, the world's population is increasingly focused or dependent on cities.

Political conflict. As other changes have taken place in the organization of human cultures and behavior patterns, an additional long-term trend concerns the nature of **conflict**. While it is likely that the causes for war and violent political conflict have remained the same through human history, the consequences have themselves changed dramatically. As the generations now living know all too well, political violence can exact a truly unparalleled toll in human lives and misery. Most Soviet women now in their sixties have been widows since World War II. Millions have died in the war-related famine in Ethiopia; wars in Vietnam, Cambodia, Afghanistan, and the Middle East have contributed their millions. The increasing integration of the world's societies as well as changes in technology now make the consequences of political conflict even more widely felt.

These trends are not, of course, inevitable. New developments in technology, especially in areas related to communication and produc-

tion, may alter things dramatically. Nor are these general, long-term evolutionary trends independent in a causal sense. First, important systemic relationships link them. Second, changes in each may be responses to similar environmental changes. Intensification and specialization, for example, may both serve to extract more resources from a deteriorating environment through the reorganization of work. Centralization may accomplish the same end through increased efficiency in the flow of resources or information concerning their availability. Also, we have to make a clear distinction between trends or processes that can be seen in individual populations or social systems and those that appear to extend to societies around the globe. Any particular society may as easily be in the process of decentralizing or deintensifying land use as not. The Viking settlements are again a case in point: after several centuries of political and economic centralization, the trend was reversed—rather dramatically. Anthropologists prefer to view these trends as continua over which social organization varies rather than as linear processes in human development.

Though it is true that if we consider all societies over the course of human existence as a whole, cultural evolution has tended to proceed from the simple to the complex, it is a mistake to believe that all societies pass smoothly or uniformly in this direction. And it is also a mistake to equate increasing complexity with "progress" or with improved adaptation, as we have just seen in Greenland and the Aral Sea region.

APPLIED ANTHROPOLOGY

Anthropologists have become increasingly interested in analyzing the relationship between general trends and innovations on the one hand

and development on the other. In the process of assessing the impact of change on society, some of them become personally involved in efforts to bring about change. George Foster has described this process, or **applied anthropology,** as the activity of professional anthropologists "in programs that have as primary goals changes in human behavior believed to ameliorate contemporary social, economic, and technological problems" (1969:54).

Anthropologists work all over the globe on development projects as diverse as construction of rural roads in Kenya, irrigation schemes in Pakistan, conservation of rangeland in Tunisia, and amelioration of the social impact of AIDS in the United States. Others are increasingly practicing their profession in the world of government administration, social services, and business. Today such efforts are no longer on the fringe; they are part of mainstream anthropology. At least half of practicing American anthropologists are employed outside of academic institutions. A brief and incomplete list of specialties in applied anthropology includes health care and medicine, nutrition, care of the aging, forensic science and criminology, legal assistance, housing, civil rights advocacy, education, and public administration.

Social scientists in other disciplines are involved in similar activities, but the anthropologist's approach is distinguished by the holistic perspective discussed in Chapter 1. Anthropologists emphasize the cultural complexity of even the smallest and most piecemeal innovation—the values, attitudes, and social relations that are likely to affect its success or failure.

Impact Assessment and Evaluation

George Appell, who has worked on development projects in Indonesia, offers a set of principles that, in somewhat abridged form, aptly summarize the sorts of negative impacts that planned change occasions and that have to be weighed against possible benefits (Appell 1988:272):

Every act of development necessarily involves an act of destruction.

Any new activity introduced is likely to displace an indigenous activity.

Each act of change has the potential to cause physiological, nutritional, psychological, and/or behavioral impairment among some segment of the subject population.

Modernization can erode indigenous mechanisms for coping with social stress, such as regulating conflict and solving family problems.

To this list we might add one more caution:

The costs and benefits of any innovation or planned changed are not going to be distributed equally throughout the population; some people will benefit and some will lose. What has to be kept in mind is whether the distribution of costs and benefits is fair or desirable.

The ultimate cost-benefit outcome of any development project or effort to effect some form of desired social change can be influenced by many factors. Some of the most important are environmental and ecological factors, traditional values and beliefs, and social ties.

Environmental and Ecological Factors

A proposed innovation may have a profound effect on the ecological system, as we have just seen in the case of the Aral Sea in the Soviet Union. Large dams, for example, almost always have a legacy of large-scale environmental damage, such as downstream pollution, increased salinity of the soil as a result of a rise in the water table, increased risk of flooding and erosion, and even, many people argue, an increase in the risk of earthquakes (Goldsmith and Hildyard 1984). But innovations need not be so massive as a huge irrigation scheme or a giant dam to have significant effects on ecological systems.

The introduction of shotguns, for example, has dramatically reduced the numbers of many game species used by the Yąnomamö. A new strain of rice introduced in Nepal increased yields as much as 200 percent, but because the rice grew on short, tough stalks that produced little fodder for cattle and required threshing machinery that was not available locally, the innovation was not without serious costs (Foster 1969). The more intensive cultivation has led to loss of topsoil from erosion, and an increased dependence on firewood instead of straw for fuel has resulted in deforestation and increased risk of downstream flooding. Everywhere we see the effects of fertilizers, pesticides, and herbicides in contaminated water sources. Environmental costs must figure in any evaluation of the effectiveness of a proposed innovation.

Traditional Values and Beliefs

Innovations may also have dramatic effects on traditional beliefs and values. Though it is not easy to measure such costs, certainly the breakdown of traditional belief systems can bring psychological stress, disrupt families, and precipitate alcohol abuse. It was U.S. government policy until very recently to encourage many Indian tribes to send their children to boarding schools, which ostensibly would prepare them for careers in mainstream American society. These schools, in addition to the usual curriculum, imparted a further message: that American Indian culture was inferior to that of the whites. Students were forbidden to use an American Indian language, even outside the classroom; most references to Indian tradition and values were of a demeaning sort; and every effort was made to draw the students away from their traditional culture. This policy aroused great controversy within the affected communities. Such schooling was ostensibly the reason for a major division among the Hopi in 1906, when communities hostile to white education severed ties with the "progressives"; it is in these communities that the full Hopi ceremonial cycle is still practiced (Whiteley 1988). The causes underlying community factions are everywhere complex, but it is not unusual for innovations, forced or voluntary, to exacerbate them. It is hard, too, to estimate the impact of this policy of enforced assimilation or acculturation through education on the self-esteem of the students, but it must have been considerable, though many students undoubtedly acquired valuable skills. Happily, the beliefs and traditions of American Indians have proved to be remarkably resilient in the face of great pressures for assimilation. Many languages on the verge of extinction only a few years ago are again being taught to children, and traditional practices and beliefs are being adapted to current situations and so are being maintained.

Social Ties

Innovations may have unintended consequences for social relations as well. If these consequences are negative, they must be included among the costs of innovation and planned change. Attempts to introduce improved clothes-washing facilities, for instance, may cause women to lose the opportunity to meet and exchange information with their neighbors at a community washing place. Changes in cattle management, as with the Dinka of Sudan, may deprive elders of their special status as camp group leaders (Lako 1988). The building of modern highrise apartment houses to replace slum housing may have nega-

New York State's SOB Problem: Acceptable Risk

We accept the fact that modern life entails risks: any day a major industrial accident may devastate our area. We rely on technology that we do not understand and we have little say in its deployment and regulation. Consider just two frightening examples of the many that could be cited: In 1983 the entire town of Times Beach, Missouri, had to be bought by the federal government because toxic levels of dioxin were found in its soil. And in 1984 a chemical leak from a Union Carbide plant in Bhopal, India, killed more than 2,600 people.

These disasters had at least one thing in common: *organizations* played primary roles in both the genesis of the problems and the search for solutions. The victims had no control over either of these situations, and for protection, they had necessarily to rely on organizations—local, regional, national, international, and private agencies. Lee Clarke (1989) gives us the anatomy of one such disaster—not a major one by global standards, but one serious enough to have all the elements necessary to permit us to see how the organizations we must rely on handle their responsibilities.

The eighteen stories of the State Office Building in Binghamton, New York—the SOB, as it is locally known—make it the tallest building in town, and it incorporates most of the modern building technologies. One of its fire-protection systems automatically opens doors on the roof; another uses a solution of 65 percent polychlorinated biphenyls (PCBs) and 35 percent chlorinated benzenes to cool the SOB's electrical transformers, located in the basement. PCBs have now been banned because they cause cancer, liver ailments, and other problems; moreover, in combination with other elements they can produce the deadly toxin dioxin. Still PCBs remain in wide use in transformers and electrical capacitors built before the ban.

At 5:33 A.M. on February 5, 1981, a switch gear (which functions much as a fuse box or circuit breaker does) in the SOB's mechanical room failed, causing an electrical arc that lasted twenty to thirty minutes. The heat in the room rose to an estimated 2000 degrees Fahrenheit, causing a ceramic bushing on one of the two nearby transformers to crack. About 180 gallons of the transformer's PCB-containing coolant were released by the accident.   [Clarke 1989: 6]

The coolant was vaporized by the intense heat and the vaporized PCBs mixed with dense soot given off by burning electrical insulation. The automatic fire doors worked perfectly; unfortunately, as soon as they opened, the building turned instantly into an eighteen-story chimney: the draft sucked the PCB-contaminated soot upward, spread it throughout the building, and spewed it out to downtown Binghamton. (Had the building been privately owned, nothing of the sort would have happened; as a state building it was exempted from codes that prohibit air shafts from reaching directly into mechanical rooms.) Every room, every desk, file cabinet, and closet, the airways between walls and ceilings—all were coated with soot that contained significant quantities of deadly dioxin.

The morning after the fire, media personnel, politicians, and state and country officials convened on the scene. In view of the highly toxic substances involved, it was immediately apparent that the fire was potentially a major environmental, health, and political problem. In the absence of any single chain of command, federal, state, and local politicians, health workers, and department heads all offered separate and usually conflicting assessments of the problem and its solution. As the SOB was managed by the state's Office of General Services (OGS), this department was involved from the start; as PCBs are derived from oil, the state Department of Transportation (DOT) was called in; and appeals went out to the federal Small Business Administration (because of the multimillion-dollar losses suffered by local businesses), the Occupational Safety and Health Administration (because of hazards faced by workers), the National Institute of Occupational Safety and Health (because of long-term health threats), and the Environmental Protection Agency (because of environmental impacts). After some initial uncertainty, the DOT (the only agency that had had experience with PCBs) decided it lacked jurisdiction because the "oil spill" had occurred indoors rather than outdoors. Under high-level political pressure, the OGS then ordered an immediate clean-up and sent in teams of janitors and security guards. In some respects, the clean-up itself was a disaster. Many of the crew worked without face masks; some used toilets in the SOB, flushing toxins into the city's sewer system; some took home contaminated food, cigarettes, money, lottery tickets, and other items they found in offices; some left contaminated work clothes in neighboring buildings. As a result, more than five hundred people were directly or indirectly exposed to toxic soot.

Within a month after the fire, lawsuits for damages totaling over $1 billion had been filed against the state, many occasioned by the botched clean-up. One might, Clarke notes, attribute the OGS's decision to hire janitors (rather than people trained to deal with chemical spills) to a callous disregard for the health of its workers in its rush to respond to political pressure. Actually, OGS officials had acted in a manner that would have been appropriate in 99 percent of the circumstances they faced following a fire in a state building; unfortunately, this was an exceptional case. Organizations, by nature conservative, are rarely prepared to handle exceptional circumstances. No single person or office was sufficiently in charge to define the problem; in the absence of a well-defined objective, the OGS simply did what it had been organized to do: it "cleaned" the SOB.

Once the seriousness of the problem became apparent, the bureaucratic behavior changed. The officials who had rushed to the scene to issue plans and assessments now scurried in the other direction: one agency after another disclaimed responsibility, until no one was left to deal with the problem but the OGS and the Binghamton health authorities.

The clean-up was redone with greater inputs by specialized consultants from the chemical industry, with less publicity, and under the aegis of one agency. Today the State of New York declares that the level of contaminants remaining in the building is "acceptable." The question remains: What is an acceptable risk, and for whom?

Far from a rational, precise, scientific endeavor, risk assessment is a haphazard process, the result of the colliding and colluding of competing and complementary organizational interests. However precisely a risk may be expressed, it is the outcome of assumptions based on bad or missing data and of compromise among competing interests. And contrary to what one would expect, most risk assessments are made, like this one, after the disaster has occurred.

Lee Clarke sees two distinct phases in the sociology of risk management. Phase one he calls "the interorganizational garbage can": a multitude of competing lines of authority, no clear definition of the problem, and a lack of political accountability on the part of decision makers (p. 168). At the time when rational decision making is most crucial, it is virtually nonexistent. Decisions occur in a chaotic swirl of competing organizational interests. Phase two (which in Binghamton came nine months after the first) he terms "the action set": all but one or two governmental organizations pull out or are forced out of the problem area, groups of semi-independent nongovernmental organizations establish a division of labor representing victims (unions, health workers, merchants, environmental activists), and one organization takes official responsibility for directing operations and announcing formal risk assessments (here the OGS). Still, the degree of risk is assessed *after* all the key decisions have been made (p. 171).

tive social consequences by breaking down established social networks, patterns of social control, and even pride of residence. We saw such consequences in Los Peloteros, and they are now widely recognized to be among the social costs of almost all large-scale housing projects. Of course, an innovation may have an even more significant impact on traditional social ties, as when a traditionally subordinate group is placed in an economically competitive position with a traditional elite. This was the case in Syria, where the French during the mandate period before World War II recruited members of the small Aloui sect to the army and police forces. They now rule the country.

Managing Social Change

Any country faces problems when it sets out to manage social change and tries to anticipate the costs. Such problems are as pressing in the United States' efforts to house the homeless and treat drug addicts as in Sudan's efforts to manage agricultural projects. The anthropologist can help at the community level, where detailed knowledge can mean the difference between success and failure. Anthropologists' respect for indigenous solutions and ways of doing things can also make a difference. All too often planners work from the top down, with little interest in or respect for traditional, time-proven methods. Indigenous solutions in the areas of land use and food production are almost always critical to the long-term success of a new strategy.

Much of the present crisis in food production is attributable to the fact that the growth rates of the populations of many countries in the tropics have outstripped their ability to feed themselves. But most of the techniques that are being imported by such countries are based on farming methods first developed in temperate climates (see Hemming 1985, vol. 1; Posey et

al. 1984). In the Amazon region, large development schemes involving the clearing of forests, introduction of new food crops, and mechanization have had very poor economic results. Most cleared land in the Brazilian Amazon is used for cattle ranching; 85 percent of recently cleared land is now altogether unproductive because of soil degradation (Posey et al. 1984:95). Tropical soils are generally thin and subject to rapid erosion and breakdown of nutrients once the protective cover of the rain forest is removed. As a consequence, intensification of agriculture or other uses of once forested land often result in less rather than more food. Many people who have worked in tropical agricultural systems think the way out of this dilemma is to pay more attention to developing more productive farming on the basis of plants and techniques already locally well established.

Impact Statements

Since 1973 anthropologists have become increasingly involved in new areas of work. In that year Congress passed legislation mandating a variety of impact assessments to be carried out when federal funds are to be used in large-scale projects, both at home and abroad. Also, development projects are required to be directed toward benefiting the "poorest of the poor" and ensuring growth with equity (see Horowitz 1988:2). A variety of state and national environmental protection acts require evaluations of the impact of government-supported projects on biological, geological, social, historical, and cultural resources. An agency that proposes to undertake a potentially disruptive project must prepare an impact statement that identifies any adverse consequences, direct or indirect, that the project will have. These consequences must be taken into account at the earliest possible stage of planning. If the impacts are judged to be damaging, procedures must be designed to alleviate the problem. Anthropologists, like other social scientists, have been drawn into planning and development work that was formerly the almost exclusive domain of engineers and economists.

As a consequence, anthropologists have become involved in preparing statements describing, for example, the impact of resource exploitation on historic and prehistoric sites and modern peoples. They argue that without such actions, most historic and prehistoric remains in this society would be destroyed. The environmental protection laws also require assessment of the impact of government-funded projects on the life of existing communities, and cultural anthropologists have become involved in this area of research as well. In both instances, anthropologists are working to help resolve the conflicts between society's growth and development and the preservation of cultural heritage and current traditions.

Extensive fieldwork is a beginning point for such studies. In the case of highway projects, for example, planners identify several alternative "corridors" in which the highway might be built. Archaeologists then attempt to determine how many important sites would be destroyed by construction in the various corridors. Cultural anthropologists, as we saw earlier in regard to rural roads in Kenya, assess the impacts on existing communities. Recommendations concerning the desirability of particular alternatives or modifications that will alleviate problems are based on such studies.

Case Studies in Applied Anthropology

In many of the cases we have referred to, the role of the applied anthropologist has been to analyze a situation that has already occurred and draw lessons for future policies. In other cases, anthropologists are actively involved in planning and implementing (or preventing) development projects.

An Analysis of the Sahelian Drought

Between 1969 and 1973, a famine and drought ravaged the Sahel, a hot, dry belt of savannah stretching 4,000 miles across Africa, just south of the Sahara Desert. It is estimated that between 100,000 and 250,000 deaths occurred in a total nomadic population of 2.5 million. The immediate and most obvious cause of famine was the failure of the summer monsoons: vegetation dried up and animals and humans starved.

Yet drought is not a new problem in the Sahel. Such pastoral nomads as the Tuareg and the Fulani have successfully adapted to these conditions for millennia. Jeremy Swift (1974), who studied the catastrophic effects of this drought on several nomadic groups, argues that the disaster was caused by human, not environmental, changes. The severe consequences of scanty rainfall were exacerbated by overgrazing, overstocking, and efforts to extend intensive agriculture into ecologically fragile zones.

The economy of the Sahelians was well adapted to the dry environment and a nomadic pastoral mode of production. It depended on animals, mostly camels and goats, as the basic units of a nonmarket redistribution system that ensured each family of enough animals to support itself. Animals and animal products were also traded for grains, cloth, and other needs that could be supplied by local agricultural groups. Less benignly, the nomads also exacted tribute from sedentary groups or used slaves to work oasis fields. Still, the two modes of production were interdependent and the produce of a broad area was exchanged by one mechanism or another so as to sustain economically diversified groups.

Because the Sahel has almost always experienced large annual fluctuations in rainfall, the nomadic lifestyle incorporated strategies for adapting to yearly changes in resources. The population was sparse, owing to a combination of high male-to-female sex ratio, low birth rate, and high female sterility. The pastoral system had also developed built-in mechanisms for weathering drought years. During extended dry periods, both nomads and farmers moved south to greener lands. As the drought passed, they moved north again. Another drought strategy was diversification: nomadic groups responded to drought periods by using the land resources for hunting and gathering as well as for pasture.

The three strategies of population control, mobility, and intensification allowed Sahelians to maintain an ecological balance even in times of drought. But this equilibrium was disturbed when French colonizers and several generations of development planners introduced changes in the twentieth century. The French increased security, enabling more land to be used for pasture (herdsmen could spread out without fear of raids from neighboring tribes). Veterinary medicine and new wells provided by the French enabled herds to grow larger. Thus the Sahelians adapted to a more sedentary life and to a market economy by raising more and different animals: sheep and cows began to replace sturdier herds of camels and goats. In sum, earlier, flexible subsistence strategies were replaced by a more fixed and less weather-resistant lifestyle. The tragic collapse brought by the drought was, unfortunately, almost directly comparable to what has happened elsewhere in North and East Africa, and even in the arid zones of China and South America. Herds increased in areas where they could graze for extended periods. The newly dug wells encouraged herders to overgraze the pastures around them, so that plant cover was destroyed. The extension of intensive cultivation into the Sahel eliminated the traditional buffer zone into which people had moved in bad years. At the edge of the Sahel, soils made thin and fragile by tilling became denuded and transformed into desert. In the end, only the desert has won.

Spreading desertification continues to be a major threat to human use of the arid zone, and many planning efforts simply exacerbate rather than relieve the situation.

The Sahelian case illustrates a paradox that is central to applied anthropology: the difficulty of sorting out beneficial change from harmful change. Until the drought, the nomadic groups seemed to be reaping benefits from development. They were more secure; food and water were ample for the first time; and even a few luxuries, such as tea and sugar, were available. But though development brought short-term benefits, it destroyed the Sahelians' ability to cope with environmental change.

Unplanned (or misplanned) change occurs frequently in the modern world. Can such tragedies as the Sahelians' be avoided and can the Sahelians themselves be saved from future droughts? Finding answers to such questions and helping to plan policies that will minimize the dangers of change are important roles of applied anthropologists.

The Vicos Project

To plan and carry out positive change are also tasks of applied anthropologists. A classic case of this sort was the Cornell University project in Vicos, Peru, in the 1950s. Vicos was a farm, or hacienda, purchased by a charitable society. At the time of the Cornell project, a *patrón* could rent the hacienda for a period of five to ten years. Traditionally the patrón reserved the best land for his own use and sublet less profitable plots to Indian tenants. Each tenant family paid its rent by sending one adult to work the patrón's land for three days a week; the peasants also provided cooks, grooms, servants, watchmen, and the like. For the most part, the *vicosinos* were illiterate subsistence farmers who lacked modern skills, health care, social respect, and any hope of participating in decisions that affected their lives.

In a year when the potato crop failed, however, Vicos was put up for rent. In January 1952 Cornell University signed a five-year lease on Vicos. The goals of the Cornell anthropologists were to give the vicosinos the right to self-determination by gradual diffusion of power; to raise the standard of living by increasing productivity and sharing the wealth; to introduce modern agricultural techniques and medical care; to bring Indians into the modern world by schooling and other means; and to raise their status among their neighbors.

The Cornell anthropologists proceeded on the assumptions that innovations in areas where people felt most deprived would be most readily accepted, and that an integrated approach to the introduction of innovations would last longer and produce less conflict than would a piecemeal approach (Holmberg 1958). They began by paying the vicosinos back wages (a symbolic gesture, for the pay amounted to 3 cents a week) and hiring volunteers to perform services the Indians had long been forced to provide without pay. In the first year the new patrones introduced modern seeds, fertilizers, and agricultural techniques, and plowed the profits from their cash crop back into the hacienda. Between 1952 and 1957, productivity rose from $100 to $400–600 per acre. All residents shared in the profits from the bottomlands, and all learned modern techniques for farming their own land. They built a health clinic and school with a capacity of 400 students (the old school accommodated 10 to 15 students).

Initially the Cornell administrators did not attempt to alter the traditional hierarchy among overseers and workers. However, the weekly meetings at which previous patrones had distributed work assignments were now used to explain innovations, discuss goals and plans, draw vicosinos into the decision-making process, and give residents news of the outside world. By 1957 a council of ten elected delegates had taken over the management of the community's affairs. Younger men committed to improvement rather than to tradition had largely replaced the elders in positions of village authority.

In addition, Cornell sought to regularize relations with the local authorities and to create numerous occasions on which vicosinos could meet neighboring mestizos (people of mixed Spanish and Indian blood) on an equal footing. By 1957, mestizos were turning to the peones they had once regarded as unworthy of the slightest respect for advice on agricultural techniques.

Despite strong resistance from the local elite, the Indians were able to purchase Vicos—and their independence—in July 1962. Since then, the Peruvian government has initiated five similar programs on other haciendas, in some cases with vicosinos acting as advisers (Holmberg 1958). In almost all respects, then, the project was a success. Cornell took power (something anthropologists have rarely had the opportunity or inclination to do) in order to restore power to the Indians, with the deliberate intention of changing their way of life. Many of the innovations tested in this project have been adopted elsewhere, and no other project has ever been subjected to the scrutiny that this one has. Some people, however, have debated whether the Cornell approach was ethical.

THE ETHICS OF ANTHROPOLOGY

Ethical issues are a major concern in anthropological work, from the time anthropologists make their initial decisions as to where and how they will do fieldwork through their final evaluations of the effects of their projects. Taking a simple right-or-wrong position on the issues raised by a practical project is easy; a thoughtful and creative approach to ethical problems is more difficult. While ethical issues may be more sharply focused in such work, they are present in all kinds of anthropological research. Whenever people are the subjects of scientific investigation, ethical considerations inevitably arise.

The Means and Ends of Research

A major ethical problem is how anthropological research should be used; and for whose benefit. The debate here has centered on two basic issues: objectivity and relevance. Both of these issues, for example, are involved in anthropologists' response to the rising incidence of AIDS.

Objectivity

Some anthropologists argue that, as scientists, they have an obligation to strive for the objectivity that is generally associated with the physical sciences. This position is based on the belief that it is possible to suspend one's cultural and theoretical biases in the field and to observe and report what one sees with detached objectivity. Other anthropologists believe that this approach ignores one of the most basic tenets of anthropology: that every individual is a product of his or her culture. Total objectivity is thus impossible. A researcher's cultural background, academic training, and personality influence both what is perceived and what is reported. By pretending to objectivity, then—by leaving biases unstated instead of clearly identifying them—anthropologists may be deceiving themselves.

Perhaps what is called for is a matter less of objectivity than of rigor. By using the most rigorous methods possible to evaluate their conclusions, anthropologists guarantee, if not absolute objectivity, at least comparability in the evaluation of theories and ideas.

Relevance

Equally controversial are questions about the relevance of topics that anthropologists choose to study. Again we find many anthropologists who believe that the pursuit of knowledge is its own justification, and that researchers should address themselves to questions that will increase our understanding of human culture over the long run. Critics of this view argue that it is immoral to place the needs of the discipline ahead of human needs, and that anthropologists should address with equal vigor the pressing social problems of their day. They add that a discipline that focuses on only theoretical issues is destined to become involuted and obsolete.

Consider the Vicos project. It was one of the first opportunities for anthropologists to act as policy makers, not just as theorists or advisers and go-betweens (Manners 1956). Some anthropologists consider it unethical to interfere so directly in other people's lives. But others respond to this charge by asking if it is ethical for anthropologists not to put their expertise to practical use.

The Case of AIDS

The response of anthropology to the rising incidence of AIDS is a good indication of the discipline's way of responding to a global health crisis. (See the box in Chapter 10.) Somewhat surprisingly, the initial response was minimal, reflecting both the prejudices of society toward this sexually transmitted disease and the still strong feeling in the discipline that theoretical research is of primary concern (Herdt 1987:1–3). Complicating the issue was the initial reluctance of funding agencies to support research that was not medical. Given the fact that the impact of AIDS had been felt primarily by traditionally stigmatized and disadvantaged groups, together with the fact that cultural factors play an important role in the spread of the disease, anthropologists might have been expected to be in the forefront of AIDS research. And though they are handicapped by the funding problem, anthropologists have undertaken both theoretical research on AIDS and projects designed to deliver better health care to its victims. At the first appearance of the disease in the United States in 1981, some anthropologists responded with proposals for relevant research. Others moved into AIDS research as it became clear that the epidemic touched upon their areas of specialization, whether medical research, social behavior, or interests in regions hard hit by the virus. Somewhat belatedly, the American Anthropological Association officially declared such work to have the highest

priority and undertook to form a task force of experts. Today at least two hundred anthropologists are working full or part time on AIDS-related research or projects.

AIDS in Brazil

In Brazil, a country that documented its first case of AIDS in 1983 and that now has an estimated 300,000 to 500,000 carriers of the virus,

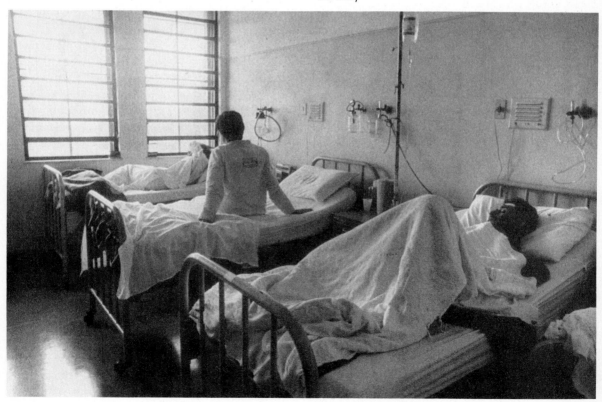

An AIDS ward in Sao Paulo, Brazil. AIDS, a global disease, has spread through different sectors of the population in various countries. Which populations are affected in a given country depend largely on behavioral and cultural factors. (CARLOS HUMBERTO/CONTACT PRESS IMAGES)

anthropologists who had formerly been working in unrelated areas have turned their attention to the epidemic. Nancy Flowers, who has worked among Amazonian populations, is concerned with two issues: the potential of the disease to spread from urban areas to rural ones, thus putting far more people at risk; and the effect AIDS will have on indigenous populations of the Amazon—such people as the Yąnomamö, who have already suffered much from introduced diseases (Flowers 1988). These complex questions have no simple answers. Some rural areas seem to be at considerable risk as members of the poorest segments of urban society migrate to the frontiers in search of work in mining, logging, cattle raising, and trucking. The cultural isolation and marital endogamy of the Amazonian Indians is thought to afford them some protection against sexually transmitted diseases, but should such a disease enter a small, relatively closed population, it would spread rapidly. Prostitutes have followed the young men to the frontiers. The AIDS virus may easily spread along the same route.

Richard Parker's primary interest was Rio de Janeiro's famous *carnaval*, but he found the sexual symbolism and activities associated with the festival shifting his attention to sexual practices and attitudes in urban Brazil. When the AIDS epidemic appeared, his understanding of Brazilian sexual culture led him to suggest that models and predictions based on the experience of the United States may not be relevant to Brazil (Parker 1987:164–166). Others have suggested the same for Africa, where AIDS is also a very serious health problem (Conant 1988). There the disease is spreading rapidly among heterosexuals. In Brazil the disease first appeared among urban, middle-class male homosexuals, as in the United States. But in Brazil it is much more likely to spread throughout the population, because bisexual behavior in men is condoned there, particularly if they maintain their masculine gender identity. Further, the Brazilians' emphasis on a bride's virginity en-

courages unmarried women to engage in anal sex in order to avoid vaginal penetration, and anal sex is known to be a major mode of transmission among both heterosexuals and homosexuals. Clearly Parker's work is sensitive and potentially controversial. Whatever the outcome of such studies, they are undertaken in the belief that anthropology has insights of immediate value to offer.

The Responsibilities of Anthropologists

Of particular importance in all anthropological research are two specific questions: What obligations do anthropologists have to the people they study? And what obligations do anthropologists have to their own government and to that of their hosts? Let us look first at some of the problems concerning anthropologists' responsibilities to the people they study.

Responsibilities to Informants

In the early 1960s Oscar Lewis published a life history of the Sánchez family (a pseudonym for a poor family in Mexico City) as part of his continuing investigation of the culture of poverty (see Rigdon 1988). Lewis allowed the members of the family to tell their own story, and he transcribed their accounts verbatim, without censoring obscene language, political opinions, or the seamier aspects of their lives. He called *The Children of Sánchez* (1961) an autobiography. In keeping with the belief that scholars in host countries should see and have an opportunity to criticize foreign researchers' observations, Lewis arranged for a Spanish translation, which was issued in Mexico in early 1965.

The reaction in the Mexican newspapers was totally unexpected. Lewis was accused of both fabricating data and obtaining information with hidden recording devices; of characterizing Mexicans in general "as the most degraded, miserable and vile people of the whole world"; by stating that Mexicans were incapable of self-government; and of serving as an undercover agent for the FBI—all false accusations. Some Mexican reporters defended Lewis. He had been entirely open about his sponsorship and research goals; he had obtained the Sánchez family's permission to publish their story and had taken every precaution to conceal their identity. Nevertheless, the Mexican Geographical and Statistical Society filed suit against him for obscenity and slander against the Mexican people. The attorney general ultimately rejected the suit. But suppose the case had gone to court. Would Lewis have been able to protect the identity of the Sánchez family, who had revealed embarrassing and potentially incriminating facts about themselves because he had guaranteed them anonymity?

A similar incident involving possible violation of the right to privacy occurred some years earlier in the United States. In this case, it was the informants themselves, rather than the press or the local scholars, who objected to public exposure. Arthur Vidich, one member of a team of researchers who had conducted a study of a small town in upstate New York, wrote and published an unofficial account of the study. Having given both the town and the individuals described fictitious names, Vidich believed he had fulfilled his obligation to the community. The townspeople thought otherwise. They knew who he was talking about when he referred to the mayor or the school principal (after all, it was a very small town). And they were incensed by what they considered to be a sensationalized representation of their private lives.

Anthropologists heatedly debate the extent of the researcher's responsibility to informants. Obtaining their consent and guaranteeing their anonymity may not be enough. The informants may not understand the full implications of having the details of their lives and their opinions examined and published, particularly if they have little education and experience of the outside world.

Indeed, anthropologists themselves may not anticipate the reactions to their findings. Once a study is published, it may be put to any use by anyone. Physicians, psychiatrists, lawyers, and priests have the legal right to withhold from a court of law information that is given to them in confidence. Anthropologists do not. They may be required to submit their records or to testify in court (or else go to jail, as some reporters have done). Thus living up to a felt responsibility toward the subjects of investigation may prove difficult or impossible. On the other hand, if a researcher explains these problems in full detail to informants, they may well choose not to cooperate. Unfortunately, such problems are exacerbated by the behavior of some anthropologists. None of us is above reproach. We make mistakes, sometimes serious ones. Some researchers consider sensitive materials essential to their research, and others seek to avoid such materials, focusing on what is public knowledge in the community they study. Some are concerned only with issues of interest to themselves, while others seek to identify topics that are of interest to the inhabitants of the communities they study. Some make an effort to disseminate their results in a form understandable to the study community and others feel no such obligation. The issue is, in short, complex.

Responsibilities to Government

Just as anthropologists are attempting to determine their responsibilities to individuals, so they are seeking to clarify their proper relationship with governments.

Today many countries restrict fieldwork, in particular the activities of ethnographers. Why? Some governments resent the fact that anthropologists are more interested in the "backward" segments of their countries than in the progress they have made. Some undoubtedly fear that researchers will expose the lack of grass-roots support for the government and their failure to control corruption at the local level. Some governments believe that anthropologists are covert agents of American neo-colonialism. Even within our own country, Native American groups have accused anthropologists of exploiting them for their own gain and of failing to defend their interests in the face of corporate and governmental pressure.

Two generations ago, anthropologists might have dismissed such accusations outright. At that time the common complaint among anthropologists was that the government neither funded their research nor listened to their advice. More recently, however, the U.S. government has become increasingly interested in the social sciences and has funded research through a variety of agencies. Some of these agencies are considered "neutral" and scientific by most (though not all) anthropologists; others, such as the Central Intelligence Agency and the Department of Defense, are considered suspect by most (but again not all) anthropologists.

A Code of Ethics

In 1968, in response to years of soul-searching discussion and often heated debate inflamed by the political controversies of the decade, the American Anthropological Association (AAA) appointed a committee on ethics. That committee proposed a code of ethics that was eventually approved by the AAA membership.

The Principles of Professional Responsibility, as the code was titled, describes anthropologists' responsibilities to the people studied and to both home and host governments. The document states that the researcher's paramount responsibility is to the people under study. A thorough and honest explanation of the investigation, the right to remain anonymous, and

fair compensation for all services are due to everyone involved. In addition, the researcher has a moral obligation to consider possible repercussions of the investigation and to communicate them to informants, making sure they understand.

The anthropologist's responsibilities to the public center on the commitment to disseminate results in a truthful and candid manner. No researcher should knowingly falsify or color any findings, or provide to sponsors, authorities, or others any information that has been withheld from the public.

As teachers, anthropologists are admonished to evaluate students solely on the basis of their intellectual abilities (not of their race, sex, or any other criterion); to alert students to ethical problems; to inform them realistically as to what will be expected of them in graduate school and what their career opportunities will be; to acknowledge all student assistance in print; and to encourage and assist students in their efforts to find secure positions and legitimate sources of research funds.

In their dealings with sponsors, anthropologists should be honest about their qualifications and research goals and should require that sponsors disclose the sources of funds and grant the researchers the right to make all ethical decisions.

Finally, the anthropologists' relationships with their own and host governments must be honest and candid. Under no circumstances should an anthropologist agree to secret research, reports, or debriefings of any kind.

Several distinct positions have emerged from the debates over the issues we have considered. A small but significant minority of anthropologists believe values and politics have no place in social science. As A. R. Radcliffe-Brown wrote some years ago, the anthropologist is not (that is, should not be) concerned, as an anthropologist, with whether such things as slavery and cannibalism or institutions of the

United States or Russia are or are not right, good, reasonable, or just (1952). According to this view, moral judgments and social or political activism are incompatible with solid scientific investigation.

Most anthropologists are concerned about the ethics of research and the problems of the peoples among whom they work, but they are wary of rendering judgments or interfering in other people's lives. This position is based on a deep commitment to cultural relativism—the belief that no custom is right or wrong in and of itself, but each must be viewed in its context.

However, as the impact of development is increasingly felt by the societies that have traditionally been of concern to anthropologists, more and more action-oriented anthropologists are questioning the notions that a detached, objective stance is possible and that silence on social issues equals neutrality. According to these anthropologists, failure to speak out and refusal to become involved is tantamount to support of the status quo. These anthropologists see the fieldworker's role as making resources available to the people being studied and helping them to understand possible alternatives and articulate their views. They support cultural relativism—so long as it does not become an excuse for inaction.

There are no simple solutions for today's social scientist. Our consciousness of ethical issues has been raised; the need for each anthropologist to determine the relative merits of each case is clear. Equally clear is the need to found our ethics, approaches, and interventions in change situations on solid theoretical principles.

Summary

Change is constant in all societies, despite a marked human tendency to maintain the status quo. Anthropologists focus on a variety of aspects of social change, but common to all approaches is some measure of costs and benefits, success and failure.

Considerable attention has been focused on the conditions that foster the acceptance of innovations. Conditions of ambiguity have been found to create a niche for *entrepreneurs*, individuals who are willing to take risks and break with tradition in order to make a profit. The acceptance of innovations depends to a great extent on the fact that customary behavior is always subject to variation. The long-term survival of an innovation depends on its adaptiveness.

The extent of *acculturation*, or cultural change that occurs in response to extended contacts between two or more previously autonomous groups, depends on various factors, including the types of individuals who make contact and the kind of contact they have, the specific behaviors that are modified, the flexibility of the societies in contact, and their relative political and military strength. Depending on the situation, the results of culture contact can be a drastic replacement of cultural traditions by those of the dominant society or incorporation of new traits without a pervasive loss of traditional customs.

Anthropologists collect data on change by obtaining accounts of the past from informants and from historical documents, by following up years later on a field study, by studying the impacts of development projects on local groups, and by studying archaeological evidence. Although all these methods add to our understanding of culture change, none is independently reliable. Consequently, most research on change incorporates a variety of methods. And new methods of collecting data, such as satellite scans, may prove invaluable in years to come.

Patterns of general evolution indicate that the following processes are involved in long-term cultural change: *intensification*, *specialization* and *differentiation*, *centralization*, *stratification*, *nucleation*, and political *conflict*. None of these processes is inevitable. Anthropologists prefer to see these trends as continua over which social organization varies rather than as linear patterns in human development.

The problems facing today's world—such as food shortages, rapid population growth, depletion of resources, pollution, and the difficulty of adapting to rapid and continuous change—are many and complex. The area of anthropology concerned with using the practical and theoretical aspects of the discipline in an effort to alleviate current social, economic, and technological problems is called *applied anthropology*. The ultimate outcome of any project can be influenced by many factors, among them environmental and ecological conditions, traditional values and beliefs, and social ties.

Applied anthropologists may work to analyze problems in order to draw lessons for future policy (as in the case of the Sahelian drought analysis) or they may get involved in actually implementing (or preventing) change (as in the Vicos project). Recently a new area of applied work has developed in our own society. The enactment of environmental protection laws has required an evaluation of the impact of any government-supported project on biological, geological, social, historical, and cultural resources. Anthropologists are becoming heavily involved in the task of impact assessment.

Ethical issues are a major consideration in all kinds of anthropological research. One ethical issue on which there is much debate is objectivity. Some anthropologists strive for total ob-jectivity, while others maintain that as every individual is a product of his or her culture, anthropologists who claim objectivity are deceiving themselves. Total objectivity may be unattainable, but anthropologists should strive to evaluate their research by the most rigorous methods possible.

Another controversial issue is the relevance of the topics that anthropologists choose to study. Some anthropologists feel that the pursuit of knowledge is its own justification; others urge that human needs be placed before those of the discipline. An evident compromise is to focus research on theoretically important topics that also address practical problems, such as the rising incidence of AIDS.

Anthropologists have responsibilities to their informants—to protect them from embarrassment and other repercussions. But sometimes it is difficult to draw the line between the need to know and the informants' right to privacy. It is also difficult for anthropologists to distinguish their obligations to the host country from those to their sponsors or home governments. The American Anthropological Association has drawn up a code of ethics outlining the anthropologist's responsibilities to the people studied, the public, the discipline, students, sponsors, and both home and host governments.

Several positions have emerged from the debates over ethics in research. Some anthropologists hold that moral judgments and social or political activism are incompatible with scientific investigation. Others are concerned about the ethics of research, but their commitment to cultural relativism makes them wary of rendering judgments or interfering in other people's lives. A growing number of action-oriented anthropologists see a refusal to become involved as tantamount to support of the status quo; they support cultural relativism only so long as it does not become an excuse for inaction.

Each anthropologist must determine the merits of each case. Anthropologists' ethics, approaches, and interventions need to be based on solid theoretical principles.

Key Terms

acculturation	**conflict**	**intensification**	**specialization**
applied anthropology	**differentiation**	**nucleation**	**stratification**
centralization	**entrepreneurs**		

Suggested Readings

BODLEY, J. H. 1985. *Anthropology and Contemporary Human Problems*. Palo Alto, Calif.: Mayfield. 2nd ed. An examination of resource depletion, hunger and starvation, and other problems of our industrialized world. The author re-examines tribal cultures and compares their solutions with those of our society.

CHAMBERS, E. 1985. *Applied Anthropology: A Practical Guide*. Englewood Cliffs, N.J.: Prentice-Hall. A synthesis of the field of applied anthropology that reviews the ways in which the profession has adapted to new career opportunities, the ethical concerns associated with applied work, and the training of applied anthropologists.

DAVIS, S. H. 1977. *Victims of the Miracle: Development and the Indians of Brazil*. New York: Cambridge University Press. This book documents the effects of Brazil's program of development on indigenous populations that have often suffered in the name of economic progress.

GRILLO, R. AND A. REW (EDS.) 1985. *Social Anthropology and Development Policy*. New York: Tavistock Publications. A collection of papers that examines the role of the anthropologist in different political contexts, the contribution to be made by anthropologists to policy, and what working in the applied field might mean for anthropologists and those who hire them.

KENNEDY, J. G. 1977. *Struggle for Change in a Nubian Community*. Palo Alto, Calif.: Mayfield. An account of the changes brought about in a remote Nubian village by the construction of the Aswan Dam. It focuses on one man in the community, who guided the important changes faced by his people when they were forced to resettle in a distant and alien region.

KOTTAK, C. P. 1983. *Assault on Paradise: Social Change in a Brazilian Village*. New York: Random House. A fascinating account of the transformations that have occurred in the Brazilian coastal community of Arembepe during the two decades that the author has been doing research there.

LOGAN, M., AND E. E. HUNT (EDS.). 1978. *Health and the Human Condition: Perspectives on Medical Anthropology*. North Scituate, Mass.: Duxbury Press. Applied anthropology is increasingly concerned with health, and medical anthropology has emerged as an important area of specialization. This collection of essays examines the ways in which societies have learned to cope with disease and discusses how health care might be improved.

MAIR, L. 1984. *Anthropology and Development*. London, Eng.: Macmillan. A survey of the types of development policy that require the cooperation of the grass-root levels of population for their success. This study examines ways in which misunderstandings can prevent development policies intended to raise living standards from working.

MINTZ S. W. 1986. *Sweetness and Power: The Place of Sugar in Modern History*. New York: Penguin Books. An absorbing account of how sugar has changed and continues to change global eating habits, work patterns, and international trade.

NEWSON, L. A. 1988. *Indian Survival in Colonial Nicaragua*. Norman, Okla.: University of Oklahoma Press. A detailed description of the colonial experiences of Indians in Nicaragua that focuses on the cultural and demographic factors that have resulted in different rates of survival for indigenous populations.

Glossary

acculturation cultural change that occurs in response to extended firsthand contacts between two or more previously autonomous groups

adaptation the process by which organisms or populations of organisms make biological or behavioral adjustments that facilitate their survival and reproductive success in their environment

administrative system a twentieth-century system of ownership in which land is owned and managed by the state; found in China, the Soviet Union, and some parts of Africa and Latin America

affinal kin persons related by marriage

age grade a group of people of the same sex and approximately the same age who share a set of duties and privileges

alienation the fragmentation of individuals' relations to their work, the things they produce, and the resources with which they produce them

allomorphs forms contained in morphemes that differ in sound but not in meaning

allophones sounds that belong to the same phoneme

ambilineal descent a descent ideology based on ties traced through either the paternal or the maternal line

ambilocality residence of a married couple with or near the kin of either husband or wife, as they choose

animal husbandry the breeding, care, and use of herd animals, such as sheep, goats, camels, cattle, and yaks

animatism belief in an impersonal supernatural force

animism belief in a soul, a spiritual essence that differs from the tangible, physical body

aphasia a language disorder resulting from brain damage

applied anthropology the activity of professional anthropologists in programs that have as primary goals changes in human behavior believed to ameliorate contemporary social, economic, and technological problems

archaeology the study of the relationship between material culture and behavior; investigations of the ways of life of earlier peoples and of the processes by which their ways of life changed; *historical archaeology* is concerned with patterns of everyday life in periods from which written documentation has survived

authority the ability to exert influence because of one's personal prestige or the status of one's office

avunculocal residence residence of a married couple with or near a brother of the husband's mother who is usually a senior member of his matrilineage

balanced reciprocity gift giving that clearly carries the obligation of an eventual and roughly equal return

band a loosely integrated population sharing a sense of common identity but few specialized institutions

bifurcation a basis of kin classification that distinguishes the mother's side of the family from the father's side

bilateral descent a descent ideology in which individuals define themselves as being at the center of a group of kin composed more or less equally of kin from both paternal and maternal lines

bilocal residence regular alternation of a married couple's residence between the household or vicinity of the wife's kin and of the husband's kin

biological imperatives the basic human drives for food, rest, sexual satisfaction, and social contact

biological species a group of interbreeding populations that is reproductively isolated from other such groups

bound morphemes morphemes that must be attached to other morphemes to convey meaning

bride price payment made by a man to the family from whom he takes a daughter in marriage

bride service service rendered by a man as payment to a family from whom he takes a daughter in marriage

bridewealth property given by the family of the groom to the family of the bride to compensate them for the loss of their daughter's services

call system   a repertoire of sounds, each of which is produced in response to a particular situation

carrying capacity   the point at or below which a population tends to stabilize

caste   a social category in which membership is fixed at birth and usually unchangeable

cattle complex   an East African socioeconomic system in which cattle represent social status as well as wealth

census   a comprehensive survey of a population designed to reveal its basic demographic characteristics

centralization   concentration of political and economic decisions in the hands of a few individuals or institutions

ceremonial fund   the portion of the peasant budget allocated to religious and social activities

chiefdom   a society distinguished by the presence of a permanent central political agency to coordinate the activities of multicommunity political units

clan   a group that claims but cannot trace precisely their descent from a common ancestor

closed corporate community   a community that strongly emphasizes community identity and discourages outsiders from settling there by restricting land use to village members and prohibiting the sale or lease of property to outsiders

code sheets   anthropologists' checklists of observed behaviors and inferred motivations for or attitudes toward them

cognates   words so similar from one language to the next as to suggest that both are variants of a single ancestral prototype

cognitive imperative   the human need to impose order on the world by mental processes

cognitive processes   ways of perceiving and ordering the world

collateral relatives   people to whom one is related through a connecting person

community identity   an effort by speakers to identify themselves with a specific locality and to distinguish themselves from outsiders

conflict   in its political manifestation, conflict exacts an ever-increasing toll in human lives and misery

conjugal relationship   the relationship between spouses

consanguineal kin   persons related by birth

controlled comparison   a method in which hypotheses are tested by comparing two or more populations that are similar or identical in most respects other than that which has been defined as the independent variable

conversion   the use of a sphere of exchange for a transaction with which it is not generally associated

corporate ownership   control of land and other productive resources by a group rather than by individuals

corporateness   the sharing of group members in specific rights

corvée   unpaid labor in lieu of taxation, usually on road construction and maintenance

creole   a pidgin language than has evolved into a fully developed language, with a complete array of grammatical distinctions and a large vocabulary

cross-cousins   mother's brothers' children and father's sisters' children

cross-cultural research   (holocultural research) a method that uses a global sample of societies in order to test hypotheses

cultural anthropology   the study of specific contemporary human cultures (*ethnography*) and of the underlying patterns of human culture in general (*ethnology*)

cultural ecology   an approach to the study of cultural diversity that requires the simultaneous investigation of technology, culture, and the physical environment

cultural materialism   the theory, espoused by Marvin Harris, that ideas, values, and religious beliefs are the means or products of adaptation to environmental conditions ("material constraints")

cultural relativism   the ability to view the beliefs and customs of other peoples within the context of their culture rather than one's own

culture   a system of shared beliefs, values, customs, behaviors, and artifacts that the members of a society use to cope with one another and with their world and that are transmitted from generation to generation through learning

culture area   a region in which several groups have similar culture complexes

culture of poverty   a self-perpetuating complex of escapism, impulse gratification, despair, and resignation; an adaptation and reaction of the poor to their marginal position in a class-stratified, highly individuated, capitalistic society

deep structure   an abstract two-part mental model consisting of a noun phrase and a verb phrase, with the optional addition of an adverb or adverbial phrase

demographic transition   a rapid increase in a society's population with the onset of industrialization, followed by a leveling off of the growth rate due to reduced fertility

descent group   a group of consanguineal kin united by presumed lineal descent from a common ancestor

descent ideology   the concept of kinship as a basis of unambiguous membership in a group and possibly of property rights and political obligations

descent relationship   the ties between mother and child and between father and child

diachronic studies   use descriptive data from one society or population that has been studied at many points in time

differentiation   organization in separate units for various activities and purposes

diffusion   the spread of an aspect of culture from the society in which it originated by migration or imitation

divination   a practice in which an element of nature acts as a sign to provide supernatural information to the diviner

domestic cycle   the changes in household organization that result from a series of demographic events

domestic mode of production   the organization of economic production and consumption primarily in the household

domestication   the process by which people try to control the reproductive rates of animals and plants by ordering the environment in such a way as to favor certain species

dowry   payment made by the bride's family to the groom or to the groom's family

early cultural evolutionists   early cultural anthropologists who held to the basic premise that cultures progress through a sequence of evolutionary stages

ecology   the study of the interplay between organisms (or the populations to which they belong) and their environment

economic class   a group that is defined by the economic position of its members in relation to the means of production in the society—the wealth and relative economic control they may command

economic system   the ideas and institutions that people draw upon and the behaviors in which they engage in order to secure resources to satisfy their needs and desires

ecosystem   the cycle of matter and energy that includes all living things and links them to the nonliving

empiricism   reliance on observable and quantifiable data

endogamy   marriage within a particular group with which one is identified

entrepreneurs   individuals who are willing to take risks and break with traditional practices in order to make a profit

entrepreneurship   economic innovation and risk taking

equilibrium   a balance among the components of an ecosystem

ethnicity   a basis for social categories that are rooted in socially perceived differences in national origin, language, and/or religion

ethnocentrism   the tendency to judge the customs of other societies by the standards of one's own

ethnographic present   describes the point in time at which a society or culture is frozen when ethnographic data collected in the field are published in a report

ethnography   the gathering of information on contemporary cultures through fieldwork, or firsthand study

ethnohistory   the study of the process of societal change by reconstruction of the recent histories of groups that have undergone rapid cultural change in recent years but have no written record of those changes

ethnology   the uncovering of general patterns and "rules" that govern social behavior

evolution   the process by which small but cumulative changes in a species can, over time, lead to its transformation; may be divided into two categories: *physical evolution* (adaptive changes in biological makeup) and *cultural evolution* (adaptive changes in thought and behavior)

evolutionary ecology   the study of living organisms within the context of their total environment, with the aim of discovering how they have adapted

exchange   the distribution of goods and services among members of a society

exogamy   marriage outside a particular group with which one is identified

extended family household   a multiple-family unit incorporating adults of two or more generations

family household   a household formed on the basis of kinship and marriage

fictive kin   persons such as godparents, *compadres,* "blood brothers," and old family friends whom children call "aunt" and "uncle"

field dependence   the tendency to see the field of vision as a single unit, with separate objects existing only as part of the whole

field independence   the tendency to see the objects in one's field of vision as discrete units, distinct from the field as a whole

fieldwork   the firsthand observation of human societies

floodwater farming   the practice of planting crops in areas that are flooded every year in the rainy season, the floodwaters thus providing natural irrigation

formal interview   an interview that consists of questions designed to elicit specific facts, attitudes, and opinions

formal organization   a group that restricts membership and makes use of officially designated positions and roles, formal rules and regulations, and a bureaucratic structure

formalism   a school of economic anthropology which argues that if the concepts of formal economic theory are broadened, they can serve as analytic tools for the study of any economic system

fossils   the naturally mineralized remains of earlier forms of plant and animal life

fraternal polyandry   marriage of one woman with a set of brothers

free morphemes   morphemes that are complete words when standing alone

freehold   private ownership of property

French structuralism   the theoretical school founded by Claude Lévi-Strauss that finds the key to cultural diversity in cognitive structures

functionalism   the theory that all elements of a culture are functional in that they serve to satisfy culturally defined needs of the people in that society or requirements of the society as a whole

gender   a cultural construct consisting of the set of distinguishable characteristics associated with each sex

generalized reciprocity   informal gift giving for which no accounts are kept and no immediate or specific return is expected

genetics   the science of the biological transmission of traits from parents to offspring

grammar   the formal structure of a language, comprising phonology, morphology, and syntax

grammatical structure   the rules for organizing elements of a language into meaningful utterances

great English vowel shift   a linguistic change during the Middle English period, when speakers of English began to alter the sounds of vowels, eventually changing all vowel sounds in the language

group   a number of individuals who interact on a regular basis and have a sense of collective identity

habitat   the specific area where a species lives

historical particularism   an anthropological approach characterized by the collection of detailed ethnographic data

holism   the philosophical view that no complex entity can be considered to be only the sum of its parts; as a principle of anthropology, the assumption that any given aspect of human life is to be studied with an eye to its relation to other aspects of human life

holocultural research   *see* cross-cultural comparison

Homo sapiens   the human species

horizontal migration   a nomadic pattern characterized by regular movement over a large area in search of grass; also called *plains migration*

horticulture   a simple form of agriculture based on the working of small plots of land without draft animals, plows, or irrigation; also called *extensive agriculture*

household   a domestic residential group whose members live together in intimate contact, rear children, share the proceeds of labor and other resources held in common, and in general cooperate on a day-to-day basis

Human Relations Area Files (HRAF)   a compilation of reports on 330 societies that are used for cross-cultural research

hunting and gathering   involves the systematic collection of vegetable foods, hunting of game, and fishing

hypothesis a statement that stipulates a relationship between a phenomenon for which the researcher seeks to account and one or more other phenomena

independent family household a single-family unit that resides by itself, apart from relatives or adults of other generations

industrialism a form of social organization in which the population's needs for food, manufactured products, transportation, and many services are met through the use of machines powered largely by fossil fuel

informal interview an unstructured question-and-answer session in which the informant is encouraged to follow his or her own train of thought, wherever it may lead

institutions a society's recurrent patterns of activity, such as religion, art, a kinship system, law, and family life

intensification an increase in the product derived from a unit of land or labor

intensive agriculture a form of agriculture that involves the use of draft animals or tractors, plows, and often some form of irrigation

inventory of resources a catalogue of the kinds of materials the people under investigation take from their environment in order to clothe, house, and feed themselves; the amount of time they spend procuring these materials; the quantity of food they collect or produce; and the distribution of the research population per unit of land

joint family household a complex family unit formed through polygyny or polyandry or through the decision of married siblings to live together in the absence of their parents

juncture the linkage or separation of syllables by pauses

kin terminology the terms that systematically designate distinctions between relatives of different categories

kindred a collection of bilateral kin

law a rule of social conduct enforced by sanctions administered by a particular source of legitimate power

legitimacy the right to rule on the basis of recognized principles

leveling mechanism a social or economic practice that serves to lessen differentials in wealth

levirate a social custom under which a man has both the right to marry his dead brother's widow and the obligation to provide for her

lineage a unilineal descent group composed of people who trace their genealogies through specified links to a common ancestor

lineal relatives direct ascendants and descendants

lingua franca any language used as a common tongue by people who do not speak one another's native language

linguistic anthropology a subdivision of anthropology that is concerned primarily with unwritten languages (both prehistoric and modern), with variation within languages, and with the social uses of language; traditionally divided into three branches: *descriptive linguistics*, the systematic study of the way language is constructed and used; *historical linguistics*, the study of the origin of language in general and of the evolution of the languages people speak today; and *sociolinguistics*, the study of the relationship between language and social relations

low energy budget an adaptive strategy by which a minimum of energy is used to extract sufficient resources from the environment for survival

mapping drawing a map showing the physical features of a community; usually an early step in a field project

market exchange the trading of goods and services through a common medium of value

Marxist anthropology the study of internal sources of social change, with a focus on a society's distinctive set of elements and contradictions

matriclan a group that claims but cannot trace their descent through the female line from a common female ancestor

matrifocal centered on the mother; said of a family situation common to the urban poor worldwide in which the woman and her relationships with her children and her female kin form the core of family life

matrifocal family household a family unit based solely on the bond between a mother and her children

matrilineage a lineage whose members trace

their genealogies through specified female links to a common female ancestor

matrilineal descent   descent traced through the female line

matrilineal descent group   a unilineal descent group in which membership is inherited through the maternal line

matrilocal residence   residence of a married couple with or near the wife's kin

mechanical solidarity   the unity of a society formed of social units that are comparable (Durkheim)

mechanization   the replacement of human and animal labor by mechanical devices

mercantile system   a system of ownership common in Europe and elsewhere after the eighteenth century in which land became the private property of individual owners

moiety   one of the two subdivisions of a society with a dual organizational structure

monogamy   an exclusive union of one man and one woman

monotheism   belief in one god

moral economy approach   views peasants as being less concerned with individual profit than with the security of knowing they will be protected in adversity

morphemes   the smallest units of speech that convey meaning

morphology   the system by which speech units are combined to form meaningful words

multilineal evolutionism   an anthropological approach that focuses on the development of individual cultures or populations without insisting that all follow the same evolutionary pattern

natural selection   the process whereby members of a species who have more surviving offspring than others pass their traits on to the next generation, whereas the less favored do not do so to the same degree

negative reciprocity   an exchange between enemies or strangers in which each side tries to get the better end of the bargain

neolocal residence   residence of a married couple in a new household established apart from both the husband's and the wife's kin

network   a web of social ties of various kinds

niche   the environmental requirements and tolerances of a species; sometimes seen as a species' "profession" or what it does to survive

nomadic pastoralism   the strategy of moving the herds that are one's livelihood from pasture to pasture as the seasons and circumstances require

nonunilineal descent group   a kin group in which descent may be traced through either parent or through both

nuclear family household   an independent family unit formed by a monogamous union

nucleation   the tendency of populations to cluster in settlements of increasing size and density

organic solidarity   the unity of a society formed of dissimilar, specialized groupings, each having a restricted function (Durkheim)

paleontologists   experts on animal life of the distant past

parallel cousins   mother's sisters' children and father's brothers' children

participant observation   actual participation in a culture by an investigator, who seeks to gain social acceptance in the society as a means to acquire understanding of her or his observations

pastoralism   a form of social organization based on herding

patriclan   a group that claims but cannot trace their descent through the male line from a common male ancestor

patrilineage   a lineage whose members trace their genealogies through specified male links to a common male ancestor

patrilineal descent   descent traced through the male line

patrilineal descent group   a unilineal descent group in which membership is inherited through the paternal line

patrilocal residence   residence of a married couple with or near the husband's kin

patrimonial system   a system of ownership, followed in northern and central Europe during the Middle Ages, in which land was controlled by feudal lords who held their domains by hereditary right

patron–client relationship   a mutually obligatory arrangement between an individual who has authority, social status, wealth, or some other personal resource (the *patron*) and another person who benefits from his or her support or influence (the *client*)

peasants   farmers who lack control over the means of their production—the land, the other resources, and the capital they need to grow their crops, and the labor they contribute to the process

phoneme   a class of sounds that differ slightly from one another but that may be substituted for one another without any change of meaning

phonology   the sound system of a language

phratry   a group that typically consists of several clans that extend the rights and obligations of kinship to one another but retain distinct identities

physical anthropology   the study of the human species, past and present, as a biological phenomenon

pidgin   a language based on a simplified grammar and lexicon taken from one or more fully developed languages

political economy approach   assumes that peasants rationally calculate the advantages their immediate families can expect to derive from a collective venture and decline to participate unless they see a benefit in doing so; also called *rational peasant approach*

politics   the process by which a community's decisions are made, rules for group behavior are established, competition for positions of leadership is regulated, and the disruptive effects of disputes are minimized

polyandry   marriage between one woman and two or more men simultaneously

polygamy   plural marriage

polygyny   marriage between one man and two or more women simultaneously

polytheism   belief in many gods

power   the ability to exert influence because one's directives are backed by negative sanctions of some sort

prebendal system   a system of ownership common in the centralized bureaucratic states that arose in China, Mogul India, Peru, and the Ottoman Empire, in which land was temporarily assigned to administrators or tax collectors by the ruler

primates   a grouping of mammals that includes humans, apes, and New and Old World monkeys

primatology   the study of living nonhuman primates

processors   hunter-gatherers who occupy one permanent settlement, from which they move to temporary camps to exploit seasonally available resources (a *foraging pattern*)

production   the conversion of natural resources to usable forms

productive life span   the period bounded by the culturally established ages at which a person ideally enters and retires from the work force

productivity   the amount of work a person accomplishes in a given period of time

profane   the sphere of the ordinary and routine; the everyday, natural world

psychological anthropology   the study of the relationship between culture and individual personality

random sample   a sample in which each individual in a population has the same chance of being selected as any other

ranked societies   societies in which access to valued positions of status is limited in some way

rational economic decisions   the weighing of available alternatives and calculation of which will provide the most benefit at the least cost

reciprocity   mutual giving and taking (such as sharing food and other goods) between people who are bound by social ties and obligations

redistribution   reallocation of a society's wealth by means of obligatory payments or services

regulation of access to resources   control over the use of land, water, and raw materials

rent fund   the portion of the peasant budget allocated to payment for the use of land and equipment

replacement fund   the portion of the peasant budget allocated to the repair or replacement of materials depleted by normal wear and tear

resilience   the ability of an ecosystem to undergo change while still maintaining its basic elements or relationships

revitalization movements   conscious efforts to build an ideology that will be relevant to changing cultural needs

rites of intensification   rituals intended either to bolster a natural process necessary to survival or to reaffirm the society's commitment to a particular set of values and beliefs

rites of passage   rituals that mark a person's transition from one set of socially identified circumstances to another

ritual   behavior that has become highly formalized and stereotyped

role   a set of behavioral expectations appropriate to an individual's social position

sacred   the sphere of extraordinary phenomena associated with awesome supernatural forces

sampling bias   the tendency of a sample to exclude some members of the sampling universe and overrepresent others

sampling universe   the largest entity to be described, of which the sample is a part

scarce resources   a central concept of Western economics which assumes that people have more wants than they have resources to satisfy them

scientific theory   a statement that postulates ordered relationships among natural phenomena

sedentary pastoralism   animal husbandry that does not involve mobility

sedentism   the practice of establishing a permanent, year-round settlement

segmentary lineage   a descent group in which minimal lineages are encompassed as segments of minor lineages, minor lineages as segments of major lineages, and so on

selective attention   unconscious focusing on and response to stimuli that are perceived to be important, to the exclusion of other stimuli

semantic domains   groups of related categories of meaning in a language

semantics   the study of the larger system of meaning created by words

serial monogamy   an exclusive union followed by divorce and remarriage, perhaps many times

shaman   a medium of the supernatural who acts as a person in possession of unique curing, divining, or witchcraft capabilities

sharecropping   working land owned by others for a share of the yield

slash-and-burn agriculture   a method of farming, also called *swidden agriculture,* by which fields are cleared, trees and brush are burned, and the soil, fertilized by the ash, is then planted

slavery   a practice that permits some people within a society to own other persons and to claim the right to their labor

social category   a category composed of all people who share certain culturally identified characteristics

social class   a category of people who have generally similar educational histories, job opportunities, and social standing and who are conscious of their membership in a social group that is ranked in relation to others and is replicated over generations

social control   a framework of rewards and sanctions that channel behavior

social division of labor   the process by which a society is formed by the integration of its smaller groups or subsets

social pressure   a means of social control in which people who venture over the boundaries of society's rules are brought back into line

socialization   the process by which a person acquires the technical skills of his or her society, the knowledge of the kinds of behavior that are understood and acceptable in that society, and the attitudes and values that make conformity with social rules personally meaningful, even gratifying; also termed *enculturation*

sociobiology   the application of Darwinian ideas of natural selection to human culture and social behavior

sociolinguistics   the study of the interrelationship of social variables and language

sororate   a social custom under which a widower has the right to marry one of his deceased wife's sisters, and her kin are obliged to provide him with a new wife

specialization   the limited range of activities in which a single individual is likely to be engaged

specialized pastoralism   the adaptive strategy of exclusive reliance on animal husbandry

speech community   a socially distinct group that develops a dialect; a variety of language that diverges from the national language in vocabulary, pronunciation, and grammar

spheres of exchange   the modes of exchange—reciprocity, redistribution, and market exchange—that apply to particular goods or in particular situations

spirit possession   the supposed control of a person's behavior by a supernatural spirit that has entered the body

stability   the ability of an ecosystem to return to equilibrium after disturbances

state   a complex of institutions that transcend kinship in the organization of power

statistical analysis the application of probability theory to quantified descriptive data

status a position in a pattern of reciprocal behavior

stratification the division of a society into groups that have varying degrees of access to resources and power

stratified sample a sample obtained by the process of dividing a population into categories representing distinctive characteristics and then selecting a random sample from each category

stratified society a society in which extensive subpopulations are accorded differential treatment

structural functionalism the theory that the central function of the various aspects of a society is to maintain the social structure—the society's pattern of social relations and institutions

substantivism a school of economic anthropology that seeks to understand economic processes as the maintenance of an entire cultural order

surface structure the particular arrangement of words that we hear or read

synchronic studies rely on research that does not make use of or control for the effects of the passage of time

syntax the arrangement of words into meaningful utterances

terms of address the terms people use when they address their kin directly

terms of reference the terms by which people refer to their kin when they speak about them in the third person

theism belief in one or more gods of extrahuman origin

totem a plant or animal whose name is adopted by a clan and that holds a special significance for its members, usually related to their mythical ancestry

transformational grammar Noam Chomsky's theory of linguistics, based on the fact that a single meaning may be expressed in different forms

transformational rules according to transformational grammar, the techniques by which deep structure is translated into surface structure

transhumance seasonal movement of livestock between upland and lowland pastures

travelers hunter-gatherers who follow a regular yearly round, occupying a series of campsites for brief periods when a valued resource is available in the vicinity of each site (a *logistical pattern*)

tribe a descent- and kinship-based group in which subgroups are clearly linked to one another, with the potential of uniting a large number of local groups for common defense or warfare

unilineal descent group a kin group in which membership is inherited only through either the paternal or the maternal line, as the society dictates

unilineal evolution a pattern of cultural progress through a sequence of evolutionary stages; the basic premise of the early cultural evolutionists

water table the level of water under the earth

witchcraft use of religious ritual to control, exploit, or injure unsuspecting, or at least uncooperating, other persons

workday the culturally established number of hours that a person ideally spends at work each day

Bibliography

Aberle, D. F., et al.
1963   The Incest Taboo and the Mating Patterns of Animals. *American Anthropologist* 65:253–265.

Abramson, A.
1987   "Beyond the Samoan Controversy in Anthropology: A History of Sexuality in the Eastern Interior of Fiji." In *The Cultural Construction of Sexuality*, ed. P. Caplan, pp. 193–216. New York: Tavistock.

Abruzzi, W.
1987   Ecological Stability and Community Diversity During Mormon Colonization of the Little Colorado River Basin. *Human Ecology* 15:317–338.

Abu Lughod, L.
1988   *Veiled Sentiments.* Berkeley: University of California Press.

Adams, J. W., and A. B. Kasakoff
1976   Factors Underlying Endogamous Group Size. In *Regional Analysis: Social Systems*, vol. 2, ed. C. Smith, pp. 149–172. New York: Academic Press.

Adams, R. M.
1966   *The Evolution of Urban Society: Early Mesopotamia and Prehispanic Mexico.* Chicago: Aldine.

Annis, S.
1988   *God and Production in a Guatemalan Town.* Austin: University of Texas Press.

Antoun, R. T.
1968   On the Significance of Names in an Arab Village. *Ethnology* 7:158–170.

Appell, G. N.
1988   Casting Social Change. In *The Real and Imagined Role of Culture in Development: Case Studies from Indonesia*, ed. M. R. Dove, pp. 271–284. Boulder, Colo.: Westview Press.

Armelagos, G.
1987   Biocultural Aspects of Food Choice. In *Food and Evolution: Towards a Theory of Human Food Habits*, ed. M. Harris and E. B. Ross, pp. 565–578. Philadelphia: Temple University Press.

Bailey, R. C., and N. R. Peacock
1990   Efe Pygmies of Northeast Zaire: Subsistence Strategies in the Ituri Forest. In *Uncertainty in the Food Supply*, ed. I. De Garine and G. A. Harrison. New York: Cambridge University Press.

Balikci, A.
1970   *The Netsilik Eskimo.* New York: Natural History Press.

Barnet, R. J., and R. E. Muller
1974   *Global Reach: The Power of the Multinational Corporations.* New York: Simon & Schuster.

Barry, H., III, I. L. Child, and M. K. Bacon
1959   Relation of Child Training to Subsistence Economy. *American Anthropologist* 61:51–63.

Barry, J. W.
1965   *A Study of Temne and Eskimo Visual Perception: Preliminary Report.* Psychology Laboratory Report no. 28. Edinburgh: University of Edinburgh.

Barth, F.
1961   *The Nomads of South Persia: The Basseri Tribe of the Kamseh Confederacy.* New York: Humanities Press.

———.
1963   *Role of the Entrepreneur in Social Change in Northern Norway.* Bergen: Norwegian Universities Press.

———.
1966   The Problem of Comparison. *Royal Anthropological Institute*, occasional paper no. 23, pp. 22–23.

———.
1969   *Ethnic Groups and Boundaries: The Social Organization of Cultural Difference.* Boston: Little, Brown.

———.
1981   *Process and Form in Social Life.* London: Routledge & Kegan Paul.

Bates, D. G.
1973   *Nomads and Farmers: The Yörük of Southeastern Turkey.* University of Michigan Museum of Anthropology Monograph, p. 52. Ann Arbor: University of Michigan.

———.
1974   Normative and Alternative Systems of Marriage Among the Yörük of Southeastern Turkey. *Anthropological Quarterly* 47:270–287.

Bates, D. G., and S. H. Lees.
1977   The Role of Exchange in Production Specialization. *American Anthropologist* 79:824–841.

———.
1979   The Myth of Population Regulation. In *Evolutionary Biology and Human Social Behavior: An Anthropological Perspective*, ed. N. A. Chagnon and W. Irons, pp. 273–289. North Scituate, Mass.: Duxbury Press.

Bates, D. G., and A. Rassam
1983   *Peoples and Cultures of the Middle East.* Englewood Cliffs, N.J.: Prentice-Hall.

Beals, A. R.
1962   *Gopalpur: A South Indian Village.* New York: Holt, Rinehart and Winston.

Beattie, J.
1964   *Other Cultures.* New York: The Free Press.
Beck, L.
1986   *The Qashqa'i of Iran.* New Haven, Conn.: Yale University Press.
Beckerman, S.
1983   Does the Swidden Ape the Forest? *Human Ecology* 11:1–12.
Benedict, R.
1959   *Patterns of Culture.* New York: New American Library. First published 1934.
Bentley, G.
1985   Hunter-Gatherer Energetics and Fertility: A Reassessment of !Kung San. *Human Ecology* 13:79–110.
Berleant-Schiller, R., and E. Shanklin (eds.)
1983   *The Keeping of Animals.* Totowa, N.J.: Allenheld, Osmun.
Bernard, H. R.
1988   *Research Methods in Cultural Anthropology.* Beverly Hills, Calif.: Sage.
Berreman, G. D.
1972   Race, Caste, and Other Invidious Distinctions in Social Stratification. In *Race* 13:500–536. London: Institute of Race Relations.
Bettinger, R. L.
1987   Archaeological Approaches to Hunter-Gatherers. *Annual Review of Anthropology* 16:121–142.
Binford, L. R.
1968   Post-Pleistocene Adaptations. In *New Perspectives in Archaeology,* ed. S. R. Binford and L. R. Binford. Chicago: Aldine.

——.
1983   *Working at Archaeology.* New York: Academic Press.

——.
1989   Ancestral Lifeways: The Faunal Record. In *Applying Anthropology: An Introductory Reader,* ed. A. Podolefski, and P. J. Brown. Mountain View, Calif.: Mayfield Press.
Blackwood, E.
1984   Sexuality and Gender in Certain Native American Tribes: The Case of Cross-Gender Females. *Signs* 10:27–42.
Bloomfield, L.
1965   *Language,* ed. H. Hoijer. New York: Holt, Rinehart and Winston.
Boas, F.
1940   *Race, Language and Culture.* New York: Macmillan.

——.
1966   *The Limitations of the Comparative Method of Anthropology.* New York: Free Press. First published 1896.
Bogen, J. E.
1969   The Other Side of the Brain: An Oppositional Mind. *Bulletin of the Los Angeles Neurological Societies* 34:135–162.

Bohannan, P.
1960   Africa's Land. *Centennial Review* 4:439–449.

——.
1965   The Tiv of Nigeria. In *Peoples of Africa,* ed. J. L. Gibbs, Jr. New York: Holt, Rinehart and Winston.
Bongarts, J.
1988   Modeling the Demographic Impact of AIDS in Africa. In *AIDS 1988: American Association for the Advancement of Science Symposia Papers,* ed. R. Kulstad, pp. 85–94. Washington, D.C.: AAAS.
Boserup, E.
1970   *Women's Role in Economic Development.* Chicago: Aldine.
Boster, J.
1983   A Comparison of the Diversity of Jivaroan Gardens with That of the Tropical Forest. *Human Ecology* 11:47–68.
Bott, E.
1957   *Family and Social Networks.* London: Tavistock.
Boulding, K.
1961   *Economic Analysis,* 4th ed. New York: Harper & Row.
Bourguignon, E., and L. Greenbaum
1973   *Diversity and Homogeneity.* New Haven, Conn.: HRAF Press.
Bowen, E. S.
1964   *Return to Laughter: An Anthropological Novel.* New York: Doubleday/American Museum of Natural History.
Bowlby, J.
1969   *Attachment.* Attachment and Loss Series, vol. 1. New York: Basic Books.
Boyd, R., and P. J. Richerson
1985   *Culture and the Evolutionary Process.* Chicago: University of Chicago Press.
Brace, C., M. L. Brace, and W. R. Leonard
1989   Reflections on the Face of Japan: A Multivariate Craniofacial and Odontometric Perspective. *American Journal of Physical Anthropology* 78:93–114.
Bradburd, D.
1980   Never Give a Shepherd an Even Break: Class and Labor Among the Komanchi of Kerman, Iran. *American Ethnologist* 7:604–620.

——.
1984   The Rules and the Game: The Practice of Komanchi Marriage. *American Ethnologist* 11:738–754.
Briggs, J. L.
1970   *Never in Anger: Portrait of an Eskimo Family.* Cambridge, Mass.: Harvard University Press.
Brooke, J.
1987   Informal Capitalism Grows in Cameroon. *New York Times,* November 30, p. 8.
Broom, L., et al.
1954   Acculturation: An Exploratory Formulation. *American Anthropologist* 56:973–1000.

Buchler, I., and Selby, H. A.
1968   *Kinship and Social Organization: An Intro-duction to Theory and Method.* New York: Macmillan.

Burling, R.
1970   *Man's Many Voices: Languages in Its Cultural Context.* New York: Holt, Rinehart and Winston.

———.
1974   *The Passage of Power.* New York: Academic Press.

Cane, S.
1987   Australian Aboriginal Subsistence in the Western Desert. *Human Ecology* 15:391–434.

Cann, R. L.
1988   DNA and Human Origins. *Annual Review of Anthropology,* vol. 17, pp. 127–143. Palo Alto, Calif.: Annual Reviews, Inc.

Caplan, P. (ed.)
1987   *The Cultural Construction of Sexuality.* New York: Tavistock.

Carneiro, R. L.
1981   The Chiefdom: Precursor to the State. In *The Transition to Statehood in the New World,* ed. G. D. Jones and R. R. Kautz, pp. 37–77. New York: Cambridge University Press.

Carrington, J. F.
1949   *Talking Drums of Africa.* London: Carey Kingsgate Press.

———.
1971   The Talking Drums of Africa, *Scientific American* 255:90–94.

Chagnon, N. A.
1967   Yąnomamö Social Organization and Warfare. In *War: The Anthropology of Armed Conflict and Aggression,* ed. M. Fried, M. Harris, and R. Murphy. New York: Natural History Press.

———.
1983   *Yąnomamö: The Fierce People.* 3rd ed. New York: Holt, Rinehart and Winston.

Chagnon, N. A., and R. Hames
1979   Protein Deficiency and Tribal Warfare in Amazonia: New Data. *Science* 203, 4383:10–15.

Chagnon, N., and W. Irons (eds.)
1979   *Evolutionary Biology and Human Social Behavior: An Anthropological Perspective.* North Scituate, Mass.: Duxbury Press.

Chagnon, N. A., and T. Melancon
1983   Epidemics in a Tribal Population. In *The Impact of Contact: Two Yąnomamö Cases,* pp. 53–75. Report no. 11. Cambridge, Mass.: Cultural Survival International.

Chibnik, M. (ed.)
1987   *Farm Work and Fieldwork: American Agriculture in Anthropological Perspective.* Ithaca, N.Y.: Cornell University Press.

Chomsky, N.
1972   *Language and Mind.* New York: Harcourt Brace Jovanovich.

Clark, K., and C. Uhl
1987   Farming, Fishing, and Fire in the History of the Upper Rio Negro Region of Venezuela. *Human Ecology* 15:1–26.

Clarke, L.
1989   *Acceptable Risk? Making Decisions in a Toxic Environment.* Berkeley: University of California Press.

Colchester, M.
1985   *The Health and Survival of the Venezuelan Yąnomamö,* IGWA document no. 53. Cambridge, Mass.: Cultural Survival International.

Collier, J., Jr.
1967   *Visual Anthropology: Photography as a Research Method.* New York: Holt, Rinehart and Winston.

Collins, W. T.
1974   An Analysis of the Memphis Garbage Strike of 1968. *Public Affairs Forum* (Memphis State University) 3:1–6.

Colson, E.
1954   Ancestral Spirits and Social Structure Among the Plateau Tonga. *International Archives of Ethnography* 1:21–68.

Conant, F. P.
1965   Korok: A Variable Unit of Physical and Social Space Among the Pokot of East Africa. *American Anthropologist* 67:429–434.

———.
1982   Thorns Paired Sharply Recurved: Cultural Controls and Rangeland Quality in East Africa. In *Anthropology and Desertification: Dryland Ecology in Social Perspective,* ed. B. Spooner and H. Mann, pp. 111–122. London: Academic Press.

———.
1984   Remote Sensing, Discovery, and Generalizations in Human Ecology. In *The Ecosystem Concept in Anthropology,* ed. E. Moran. Boulder, Westview Press.

———.
1988   Social Consequences of AIDS: Implications for East Africa and the Eastern United States. In *AIDS 1988: American Association for the Advancement of Science Symposia Papers,* ed. R. Kulstad, pp. 147–156. Washington, D.C.: AAAS.

Cook, S.
1966   The Obsolete "Anti-Market" Mentality: A Critique of the Substantive Approach to Economic Anthropology. *American Anthropologist* 68:323–345.

Coughenour, M. B., and J. E. Ellis, D. M. Swift, D. L. Coppock, K. Galvin, J. T. McCabe, and T. C. Hart
1985   Energy Extraction and Use in a Nomadic Pastoral Ecosystem. *Science* 230:619–625.

Coult, A. D., and R. W. Habenstein
1965   *Gross Tabulations of Murdock's World Ethnographic Sample.* Columbia: University of Missouri Press.

Curran, J. W., H. W. Jaffe, A. M. Hardy,
W. M. Morgan, R. M. Selik, and T. J. Dondero
1988   Epidemiology of AIDS and HIV Infection in the United States. In *AIDS 1988: American Association for the Advancement of Science Symposia Papers*, ed. R. Kulstad, pp. 19–34. Washington, D.C.: AAAS.

Cyriax, R. J.
1939   *Sir John Franklin's Last Arctic Expedition.* London: Methuen.

Dalton, G.
1962   Traditional Production in Primitive African Economies. *Quarterly Journal of Economics* 76:360–378.

———.
1972   Peasantries in Anthropology and History. *Current Anthropology* 13:385–415.

D'Andrade, R. G.
1973   Cultural Constructions of Reality. In *Cultural Illness and Health: Essays in Human Adaptation*, ed. L. Nader and T. W. Maretski. Washington, D. C.: American Anthropological Association.

D'Aquili, E.
1972   *The Biopsychological Determinants of Culture.* McCaleb Module in Anthropology. Reading, Mass.: Addison-Wesley.

Davis, W.
1988   *Passage of Darkness: The Ethnobiology of the Haitian Zombie.* Chapel Hill: University of North Carolina Press.

Dawson, J. L. M.
1967   Cultural and Psychological Influences upon Spatial Perceptual Processes in West Africa. *International Journal of Psychology* 2:115–128, 171–185.

Denevan, W., J. Treacy, J. Alcorn, C. Paddoch,
J. Denslow, and S. Paitan
1984   Indigenous Agroforestry in the Peruvian Amazon: Bora Indian Management of Swidden Fallows. *Interciencia* 9:346–357.

Dietz, T.
1987   *Pastoralists in Dire Straits.* Netherlands Geographical Studies, no. 49. Amsterdam: University of Amsterdam, Institute for Social Geography.

Divale, W., and M. Harris
1978   The Male Supremacist Complex: Discovery of a Cultural Invention. *American Anthropologist* 80:668–671.

Douglas, M.
1962   The Lele—Resistance to Change. In *Economic Anthropology: Readings in Theory and Analysis*, ed. E. E. LeClair, Jr., and H. K. Schneider. New York: Holt, Rinehart and Winston.

Dove, M. R.
1984   The Chayanov Slope in a Swidden Society: Household Demography and Extensive Agriculture in Western Kalimantan. In *Chayanov, Peasants, and Economic Anthropology*, ed. P. Durrenberger, pp. 97–132. New York: Academic Press.

———.
1988   Introduction. In *The Real and Imagined Role of Culture in Development: Case Studies from Indonesia*, ed. M. R. Dove, pp. 1–37. Honolulu: University of Hawaii Press.

Downs, J. F.
1965   The Social Consequences of a Dry Well. *American Anthropologist* 67:1387–1417.

Dozier, E. P.
1970   *The Pueblo Indians of North America.* New York: Holt, Rinehart and Winston.

Draper, P.
1976   Social and Economic Constraints on Child Life Among the !Kung. In *Kalahari Hunter-Gatherers*, ed. R. B. Lee and I. DeVore, pp. 199–217. Cambridge, Mass.: Harvard University Press.

Duben, A.
1986   The Significance of Family and Kinship in Urban Turkey. In *Sex Roles, Family and Community in Turkey*, ed. C. Kagitcibasi. Indiana University Turkish Studies no. 3. Bloomington: Indiana University Press.

Durkheim, E.
1961   *The Elementary Forms of the Religious Life.* New York: Collier. First published 1912.

———.
1964   *The Division of Labor in Society.* New York: Free Press.

Durrenberger, P. (ed.)
1984   *Chayanov, Peasants, and Economic Anthropology.* Orlando, Fla.: Academic.

Dyson-Hudson, N., and R. Dyson-Hudson
1982   The Structure of East African Herds and the Future of East African Herders. *Development and Change* 13:213–238.

Dyson-Hudson, R.
1988   Ecology of Nomadic Turkana Pastoralists: A Discussion. In *Arid Lands: Today and Tomorrow*, ed. E. Whitehead, C. Hutchinson, B. Timmerman, and R. Varady, pp. 701–703. Boulder, Colo.: Westview.

Dyson-Hudson, R., and M. A. Little (eds.)
1983   *Rethinking Human Adaptation: Cultural and Biological Models.* Boulder, Colo.: Westview.

Dyson-Hudson, R., and E. A. Smith
1978   Human Territoriality. *American Anthropologist* 80:21–42.

Eder, J. F.
1988   Batak Foraging Camps Today: A Window to the History of a Hunting-Gathering Economy. *Human Ecology* 16:35–57.

Edgerton, R. B.
1971   *The Individual in Cultural Adaptation: A Study of Four East African Peoples.* Berkeley and Los Angeles: University of California Press.

Ehrlich, P., and A. H. Ehrlich
1972   *Population, Resources, Environment: Issues in Human Ecology.* 2nd ed. San Francisco: Freeman.

Eicher, M.
1988   *Nonsexist Research Methods: A Practical Guide.* London: Allen & Unwin.

Eliade, M.
1975   *Myths, Rites, Symbols: A Mircea Eliade Reader,* vol. 2, ed. W. C. Beane and W. G. Doty. New York: Harper & Row.

Ember, C. R.
1978   Myths About Hunter-Gatherers. *Ethnology* 17, 4:439–448.

——.
1983   The Relative Decline in Woman's Contribution to Agriculture with Intensification. *American Anthropologist* 85:285–304.

Ember, C. R., M. Ember, and B. Pasternak
1974   On the Development of Unilineal Descent. *Journal of Anthropological Research* 30:69–94.

Ember, M., and C. R. Ember
1971   The Conditions Favoring Matrilocal versus Patrilocal Residence. *American Anthropologist* 73:571–594.

Engels, F.
1972   *The Origin of the Family, Private Property, and the State,* ed. E. B. Leacock. New York: International Publishers. First published 1884.

Estioko-Griffin, A., and P. B. Griffin
1981   Woman the Hunter: The Agta. In *Woman the Gatherer,* ed. F. Dahlberg, pp. 121–151. New Haven, Conn.: Yale University Press.

Etienne, M., and E. Leacock (eds.)
1988   *Women and Colonization: Anthropological Perspectives.* South Hadley, Mass.: Bergin & Garvey.

Evans-Pritchard, E. E.
1940   *The Nuer: A Description of the Modes of Livelihood and Political Institutions of a Nilotic People.* Oxford: Clarendon Press.

Fadlan, I.
922 A.D.   *Observations on the Manners and Customs of the Northmen Encamped on the Volga,* trans. R. Blake and R. Frye. Reprinted in and cited from *A Reader in General Anthropology,* C. Coon, ed. pp. 411–416. New York: Holt, 1948.

Farb, P.
1974   *Word Play: What Happens When People Talk.* New York: Knopf.

Fay, R. E., C. F. Turner, A. D. Klassen, and J. H. Gagnon
1989   Prevalence and Patterns of Same-Gender Sexual Contact Among Men. *Science* 243:338–348.

Feinberg, R.
1988   Margaret Mead and Samoa: *Coming of Age* in Fact and Fiction. *American Anthropologist* 90:656–663.

Feinmen, G., and J. Neitzel
1984   Too Many Types: An Overview of Sedentary Prestate Societies in the Americas. In *Advances in Archaeological Methods and Theory,* 7:39–102. Orlando, Fla.: Academic Press.

Feit, H. A.
1973   The Ethno-Ecology of the Waswanipi Cree; or How Hunters Can Manage Their Resources. In *Cultural Ecology: Readings on the Canadian Native Peoples,* ed. B. Cox. Toronto: McClelland & Stewart.

Ferguson, B. R. (ed.)
1984   *Warfare, Culture, and Environment.* New York: Academic Press.

Fischer, J. L.
1958   Social Influences on the Choice of a Linguistic Variant. *Word* 14:47–56.

Fisher, H. E.
1987   The Four-Year Itch: Do Divorce Patterns Reflect Our Evolutionary Heritage? *Natural History* 10:22–33.

Fisher, M.
1980   *Iran: From Religious Dispute to Revolution.* Cambridge, Mass.: Harvard University Press.

Fishman, C.
1988   *Anthropology Newsletter* 26.

Flinn, M.
1986   Correlates of Reproductive Success in a Caribbean Village. *Human Ecology* 14:225–245.

Flowers, N. M.
1988   The Spread of AIDS in Rural Brazil. In *AIDS 1988: American Association for the Advancement of Science Symposia Papers,* ed. R. Kulstad, pp. 159–168. Washington, D.C.: AAAS.

Flowers, N., D. Gross, M. Ritter, and D. Werner
1975   Protein Capture and Cultural Development in the Amazon. *American Anthropologist* 3:526–549.

——.
1982   Variation in Swidden Practices in Four Central Brazilian Indian Societies. *Human Ecology* 10:203–217.

Ford, R. I.
1972   An Ecological Perspective on the Eastern Pueblos. In *New Perspectives on the Pueblos,* ed. A. Ortiz. Albuquerque: University of New Mexico Press.

Foster, B.
1974   Ethnicity and Commerce. *American Ethnologist* 1:437–448.

Foster, B., and S. Seidman
1982   Urban Structures Derived from Collections of Overlapping Subsets. *Urban Anthropology* 11:171–182.

Foster, G. M.
1969   *Applied Anthropology.* Boston: Little, Brown.

Frank, A. G.
1969   *Capitalism and Underdevelopment in Latin America.* New York: Monthly Review Press.

Frayser, S.
1985   *Varieties of Sexual Experience.* New Haven, Conn.: HRAF Press.

Frazer, J.
1959   *The New Golden Bough.* Abr. ed. New York: Criterion. First published 1900.

Freeman, D.
1983   *Margaret Mead and Samoa: The Making and Unmaking of an Anthropological Myth.* Cambridge, Mass.: Harvard University Press.

Freeman, J. D.
1961   On the Concept of the Kindred. *Journal of the Royal Anthropological Institute* 91:192–220.

Freeman, M. M. R.
1971   A Social and Ecological Analysis of Systematic Female Infanticide Among the Netsilik Eskimo. *American Anthropologist* 73:1011–1019.

Freilich, M.
1971   *Meaning of Culture: A Reader in Cultural Anthropology.* Lexington, Mass.: Xerox College.

Fried, M.
1967   *The Evolution of Political Society: An Essay in Political Anthropology.* New York: Random House.

Fromkin, V., and R. Rodman
1988   *An Introduction to Linguistics,* 4th ed., New York: Holt, Rinehart and Winston.

Gailey, C. W.
1987   *Kinship to Kingship: Gender Hierarchy and State Formation in the Tongan Islands.* Austin: University of Texas Press.

Galvin, K. A.
1988   Nutritional Status as an Indicator of Impending Food Stress. *Disasters* 12:147–156.

Gardner, A., and B. Gardner
1969   Teaching Sign Language to a Chimpanzee. *Science* 165:664–672.

Geertz, C.
1966   Religion as a Cultural System. In *Anthropological Approaches to the Study of Religion,* ed. M. Banton. New York: Praeger.

———.
1969   Two Types of Ecosystems. In *Environment and Cultural Behavior,* ed. A. P. Vayda. New York: Natural History Press.

Gibbs, J. L., Jr.
1963   The Keplle Moot. *Africa* 33:1–10.

Gilmore, D. D.
1987   *Aggression and Community: Paradoxes of Andalusian Culture.* New Haven, Conn.: Yale University Press.

———.
1990   *Manhood in the Making: The Cultural Construction of Masculinity.* New Haven, Conn.: Yale University Press.

Gladwin, C., and J. Butler
1982   Gardening: A Survival Strategy for the Small, Part-Time Florida Farm. *Proceedings Florida State Horticultural Society* 95:264–268.

Gluckman, M.
1965   *Politics, Law, and Ritual in Tribal Society.* Chicago: Aldine.

Goldschmidt, W.
1947   *As You Saw.* New York: Harcourt, Brace.

———.
1971   *Exploring the Ways of Mankind.* New York: Holt, Rinehart and Winston.

Goldsmith, E., and N. Hildyard
1984   *The Social and Environmental Effects of Large Dams.* San Francisco: Sierra Club.

Goleman, D.
1988a   Sex Roles Reign Powerful as Ever in the Emotions. *New York Times,* August 23, pp. C1–C2.

———.
1988b   An Emerging Theory on Blacks' IQ Scores. *New York Times,* April 10, Education Supplement, pp. 22–24.

Goodall, J. Van L.
1971   *In the Shadow of Man.* Boston: Houghton Mifflin.

Goodenough, W. H.
1955   A Problem in Malayo-Polynesian Social Organization. *American Anthropologist* 57:71–83.

———.
1970   *Description and Comparison in Cultural Anthropology.* Chicago: Aldine.

Gorman, E. M.
1989   The AIDS Epidemic in San Francisco: Epidemiological and Anthropological Perspectives. In *Applying Anthropology,* ed. A. Podolefsky, and P. J. Brown, pp. 192–201. Mountain View, Calif.: Mayfield Press.

Gossen, G. H.
1972   Temporal and Spatial Equivalents in Chamula Ritual Symbolism. In *Reader in Comparative Religion: An Anthropological Approach,* ed. W. A. Lessa and E. S. Vogt. New York: Harper & Row.

Gough, E. K.
1959   The Nayars and the Definition of Marriage. *Journal of the Royal Anthropological Institute* 89:23–34.

———.
1971   Nuer Kinship: A Reexamination. In *The Translation of Culture,* ed. T. O. Beidelman, pp. 79–122. London: Tavistock.

Gould, J. L., and P. Marler
1987   Learning by Instinct. *Scientific American* 256:74–85.

Gould, S. J.
1986   Cardboard Darwinism: This View of Life. *Natural History* 95:14–21.

———.
1989   Tires to Sandals: This View of Life. *Natural History* 98:8–16.

Graves, T. D.
1970   The Personal Adjustment of Navajo Indian Migrants to Denver, Colorado. *American Anthropologist* 72:35–54.

Gregor, T.
1985   *The Sexual Lives of an Amazonian People.* Chicago: University of Chicago Press.

Grigg, D. B.
1974   *The Agricultural Systems of the World: An Evolutionary Approach.* Cambridge, Eng.: Cambridge University Press.

Gross, D. R.
1983   Village Movement in Relation to Resources in Amazonia. In *Adaptive Responses of Native Amazonians,* ed. R. B. Hames and W. T. Vickers, pp. 429–499. New York: Academic Press.

———.
1984   Time Allocation: A Tool for the Study of Cultural Behavior. *Annual Review of Anthropology* 13:519–558.

Gross, D. R., and B. A. Underwood
1971   Technological Change and Caloric Costs: Sisal Agriculture in Northeastern Brazil. *American Anthropologist* 73:725–740.

Hackenberg, R.
1962   Economic Alternatives in Arid Lands: A Case Study of the Pima and Papago Indians. *Ethnology* 1:186–195.

Hames, R.
1983   Monoculture, Polyculture, and Polyvariety in Tropical Forest Swidden Cultivation. *Human Ecology* 11:13–34.

Harris, M.
1966   The Cultural Ecology of India's Sacred Cattle. *Current Anthropology* 7:51–66.

———.
1974   *Patterns of Race in the Americas.* New York: Norton.

———.
1984   A Cultural Materialist Theory of Band and Village Warfare: The Yąnomamö Test. In *Warfare, Culture, and Environment,* ed. B. R. Ferguson, pp. 111–140. New York: Academic Press.

———.
1985   *Good to Eat: Riddles of Food and Culture.* New York: Simon & Schuster.

———.
1987   Comment on Vayda's Review of *Good To Eat: Riddles of Food and Culture. Human Ecology* 15:511–518.

———.
1988   *Culture, People, Nature: An Introduction to General Anthropology,* 5th ed. New York: Harper & Row.

Hart, T. D., and J. A. Hart
1986   The Ecological Basis of Hunter-Gatherer Subsistence in African Rain Forests: The Mbuti of Eastern Zaire. *Human Ecology* 14:29–57.

Hart, C. W., and A. R. Pilling
1960   *The Tiwi of North Australia.* New York: Holt, Rinehart and Winston.

Headland, T.
1987   The Wild Yam Question: How Well Could Independent Hunter-Gatherers Live in a Tropical Forest Ecosystem? *Human Ecology* 15:463–492.

Hemming, J. (ed.)
1985   *Change in the Amazon Basin,* vol. 2: *Man's Impact on Forests and Rivers.* Manchester: Manchester University Press.

Herdt, G.
1987   AIDS and Anthropology. *Anthropology Today* 3:1–3.

Herskovits, M.
1924   A Preliminary Consideration of the Cultural Areas of Africa. *American Anthropologist* 26:50–63.

Hertzberg, H. T. E.
1989   Engineering Anthropology: Past, Present, and Potential. In *Applying Anthropology: An Introductory Reader,* ed. A. Podolefsky and P. J. Brown. Mountain View, Calif.: Mayfield Press.

Hiatt, L. R.
1980   Polyandry in Sri Lanka: A Test Case for Parental Investment. *Man* 15:583–598.

Hill, K., K. Hawkes, M. Hurtado, and H. Kaplan
1984   Seasonal Variance in the Diet of the Ache Hunter-Gatherers in Eastern Paraguay. *Human Ecology* 12:101–136.

Hockett, C. F., and R. Ascher
1964   The Human Revolution. *Current Anthropology* 5:135–168.

Hoebel, E. A.
1954   *The Law of Primitive Man.* Cambridge, Mass.: Harvard University Press.

Hoijer, H.
1954   The Sapir-Whorf Hypothesis. In *Language in Culture,* no. 79, ed. H. Hoijer. Washington, D.C.: American Anthropological Association.

Holling, C. S.
1973   Resilience and Stability of Ecological Systems. *Annual Review of Ecology and Systematics* 4:1–23.

Holmberg, A.
1958   Research and Development Approach to the Study of Change. *Human Organization* 17:12–16.

Holmes, R.
1984   Non-Dietary Modifiers of Nutritional Status in Tropical Forest Populations of Venezuela. *Interciencia* 9:386–391.

———.
1985   Nutritional Status and Cultural Change in Venezuela's Amazon Territory. In *Change in the Amazon Basin,* vol. 2, *Man's Impact on Forests and Rivers,* ed. J. Hemming. Manchester, Eng.: Manchester University Press.

Hopkins, N.
1983   The Social Impact of Mechanization. In *Migration, Mechanization, and Agricultural Labor Markets in Egypt,* ed. A. Richards and

P. L. Martin, pp. 181–197. Boulder, Colo.:
Westview Press.

Horgan, J.
1988   The Violent Yanamomö: Science and Citizen.
Scientific American 255:17–18.

Horowitz, M.
1988   Anthropology and the New Development
Agenda. In *Bulletin of the Institute for Development Anthropology, Development Anthropology Network* 6:1–4.

Howell, N.
1976   *Normal Selection Rates of the Demographic
Patterns of the !Kung San.* Paper presented at
the 1976 meeting of the American Anthropological Association, Washington, D.C.

———.
1979   *Demography of the Dobe !Kung.* New York:
Academic Press.

Hughes, A. L.
1988   *Evolution and Human Kinship.* New York:
Oxford University Press.

Ingold, T.
1980   *Hunters, Pastoralists, and Ranchers.* Cambridge, Eng.: Cambridge University Press.

Irons, W.
1975   *The Yomut Turkman: A Study of Social Organization among a Central Asian Turkic-
Speaking Population.* Anthropological Papers,
no. 58. Ann Arbor: University of Michigan,
Museum of Anthropology.

Johnson, G. A.
1983   Decision-Making Organization and Pastoral
Nomad Camp Size. *Human Ecology* 11:175–
200.

Johnson, P. L.
1988   Women and Development: A Highland New
Guinea Example. *Human Ecology* 16:105–122.

Jorgenson, J.
1971   Indians and the Metropolis. In *The American
Indian in Urban Society*, ed. J. O. Waddell and
O. M. Watson. Boston: Little, Brown.

Katz, S. H., M. L. Hediger, and L. A. Valleroy.
1974   Traditional Maize Processing in the New
World. *Science* 17:765–773.

Keesing, R. M.
1975   *Kin Groups and Social Structure.* New York:
Holt, Rinehart and Winston.

Kelly, R.
1985   *The Nuer Conquest.* Ann Arbor: University of
Michigan Press.

Kemp, W. B.
1971   The Flow of Energy in a Hunting Society. *Scientific American* 225:104–115.

Khaldun, I.
1377 A.D.
        The Muqaddimah: An Introduction to History,

vol. 1, trans. Franz Rosenthal. London: Kegan
Paul, 1958.

Kimball, J. C.
1984   *The Arabs 1984/85: An Atlas and Almanac.*
Washington, D.C.: The American Educational
Trust.

Kirkby, A. V.
1973   *The Use of Land and Water Resources in the
Past and Present, Valley of Oaxaca, Mexico.*
Ann Arbor: Museum of Anthropology, University of Michigan.

Konner, M.
1983   *The Tangled Web.* New York: Harper & Row.

———.
1988   Body and Mind: The Aggressors. *New York
Times Magazine,* August 14, pp. 33–34.

Koop, C. E.
1988   Foreword: Current Issues in AIDS. In *AIDS
1988: American Association for the Advancement of Science Symposia Papers*, ed. R. Kulstad, pp. vii–viii. Washington, D.C.: AAAS.

Kopytoff, I.
1977   Matrilineality, Residence, and Residential
Zone, *American Ethnology*, 4:539–558.

Korte, C., and S. Milgram
1970   Acquaintance Networks Between Racial
Groups: Application of the Small World
Method. *Journal of Personality and Social Psychology* 15:101–108.

Kramer, M.
1987   *Three Farms: Making Milk, Meat, and Money
from the American Soil.* Cambridge, Mass.:
Harvard University Press.

Kroeber, A. L., and C. Kluckhohn
1952   *Culture: A Critical Review of Concepts and Definitions.* New York: Knopf.

Labov, W.
1964   Phonological Correlates of Social Stratifica-
tions. *American Anthropologist* 66, special issue, pt. 2, pp. 164–176.

Laderman, C.
1983   *Wives and Midwives: Childbirth and Nutrition in Rural Malaysia.* Berkeley: University
of California Press.

Lako, G. T.
1988   The Impact of the Jonglei Scheme on the Economy of the Dinka. In *Tribal Peoples and Development Issues: A Global Overview*, ed. J. H.
Bodley. Palo Alto, Calif.: Mayfield Press.

Lardy, N. R.
1985   State Intervention and Peasant Opportunities.
In *Chinese Rural Development: The Great
Transformation*, ed. W. L. Parish, pp. 33–56.
Armonk, N.Y.: M. E. Sharpe.

Laswell, H.
1936   *Politics: Who Gets What, When, and How.*
New York: McGraw-Hill.

Lawrence, P.
1964   *The Road Belong Cargo: A Study of the Cargo*

Movement in the Southern Madang District, New Guinea. Manchester: University of Manchester Press.

Leach, E. R.

1954   *Political Systems of Highland Burma.* New York: Humanities Press.

——.

1965   *Political Systems of Highland Burma.* Boston: Beacon Press.

——.

1982   *Social Anthropology.* Glasgow: Fontana Paperbacks.

Leaf, M. J.

1972   *Information and Behavior in a Sikh Village: Social Organization Reconsidered.* Berkeley and Los Angeles: University of California Press.

Leavitt, G. C.

1989   The Disappearance of the Incest Taboo. *American Anthropologist* 91:116–131.

Lee, R. B.

1968   What Hunters Do for a Living, or, How to Make Out on Scarce Resources. In *Man the Hunter,* ed. R. B. Lee and I. De Vore. Chicago: Aldine.

——.

1969   !Kung Bushmen Subsistence: An Input-Output Analysis. In *Environment and Cultural Behavior,* ed. A. P. Vayda. New York: Natural History Press.

——.

1979   *The !Kung San.* Cambridge, Eng.: Cambridge University Press.

Lee, R. B., and I. De Vore (eds.)

1968   *Man the Hunter.* Chicago: Aldine.

——.

1976   *Kalahari Hunter-Gatherers: Studies of the !Kung-San and Their Neighbors.* Cambridge, Mass.: Harvard University Press.

Lees, S. H.

1973   *Sociopolitical Aspects of Canal Irrigation in the Valley of Oaxaca.* Memoir no. 6. Ann Arbor: University of Michigan, Museum of Anthropology.

——.

1974a   Hydraulic Development as a Process of Response. *Human Ecology* 2:159–175.

——.

1974b   The State's Use of Irrigation in Changing Peasant Society. *Anthropological Papers of the University of Arizona,* no. 25.

Lennihan, L.

1988   Wages of Change: The Unseen Transformation in Northern Nigeria. *Human Organization.*

Leslie, P. W., and P. H. Fry

1989   Extreme Seasonality of Births Among Nomadic Turkana Pastoralists. *American Journal of Physical Anthropology.*

Leslie, P. W., P. H. Fry, K. Galvin, and J. T. McCabe

1988   Biological, Behavioral, and Ecological Influ-

ences on Fertility in Turkana Pastoralists. In *Arid Lands: Today and Tomorrow,* ed. E. Whitehead, C. Hutchinson, pp. 705–726. Boulder, Colo.: Westview.

Lessa, W. A. and E. Z. Vogt

1962   *Reader in Comparative Religion: An Anthropological Approach,* 2nd ed. New York: Harper & Row.

Lévi-Strauss, C.

1943   The Social Use of Kinship Terms Among Brazilian Indians. *American Anthropologist* 45:398–409.

——.

1955   The Structural Study of Myth. *Journal of American Folklore* 67:428–444.

——.

1969   *The Raw and the Cooked,* trans. J. and D. Weightman. New York: Harper Torch Book.

——.

1988   *The Jealous Potter,* trans. Benedicte Chorier. Chicago: University of Chicago Press.

Levine, N. E.

1988   *The Dynamics of Polyandry: Kinship, Domesticity, and Population on the Tibetan Border.* Chicago: University of Chicago Press.

Levine, R., and B. LeVine

1963   Culture and Personality Development in a Gushii Community. In *Child Rearing in Six Societies,* ed. B. B. Whiting. New York: Wiley.

Levinson, D., and M. J. Malone

1980   *Toward Explaining Human Culture.* New Haven, Conn.: HRAF Press.

Lewis, H. T., and T. A. Ferguson

1988   Yards, Corridors, and Mosaics: How to Burn a Boreal Forest. *Human Ecology* 16:57–78.

Lewis, O.

1959   *Five Families.* New York: Basic Books.

——.

1960   *Tepoztlán: A Village in Mexico.* New York: Holt, Rinehart and Winston.

——.

1961   *The Children of Sánchez.* New York: Random House.

——.

1966   *La Vida: Puerto Rican Family in the Culture of Poverty—San Juan and New York.* New York: Random House.

Lewis, R. L.

1987   *Black Coal Miners in America: Race, Class, and Community Conflict, 1790–1980.* Lexington: University Press of Kentucky.

Lieberman, P., and E. Crelin

1971   On the Speech of Neanderthal. *Linguistic Inquiry* 2:203–222.

Linton, R.

1937   One Hundred Percent American. *The American Mercury* 40:427–429. Reprinted in *The Nacerima,* ed. J. P. Spradley and M. A. Rynkiewich, pp. 405–406. Boston: Little Brown.

Little, M. A.
1988   Introduction to the Symposium: The Ecology of the Nomadic Turkana Pastoralists. In *Arid Lands Today and Tomorrow: Proceedings of an International Research and Development Conference,* ed. E. E. Whitehead, C. F. Hutchinson, B. N. Timmerman, and R. G. Vardy, pp. 696–734. Boulder, Colo.: Westview Press.

Little, M. A., K. Galvin, and P. W. Leslie
1988   Health and Energy Requirements of Nomadic Turkana Pastoralists. In *Coping with Uncertainty in Food Supply,* ed. I. de Garine and G. A. Harrison, pp. 288–315. Oxford, Eng.: Oxford University Press.

Livingstone, F. B.
1968   The Effects of Warfare on the Biology of the Human Species. In *War: The Anthropology of Armed Conflict and Aggression,* ed. M. Fried, M. Harris, and R. Murphy. New York: Natural History Press.

Lorenz, K.
1965   *Evolution and Modification of Behavior.* Chicago: University of Chicago Press.

Lowie, R. H.
1954   *Indians of the Plains.* New York: McGraw-Hill.

Mahdi, M.
1971   *Ibn Khaldun's Philosophy of History.* Chicago: University of Chicago Press.

Mair, L.
1965   *Introduction to Social Anthropology.* New York: Oxford University Press.

Malinowski, B.
1927   *Sex and Repression in Savage Society.* London: Routledge & Kegan Paul.

———.
1931   Culture. In *Encyclopedia of the Social Sciences,* vol. 4. New York: Macmillan.

———.
1954   *Magic, Science, and Religion and Other Essays.* Garden City, N.Y.: Anchor/Doubleday.

———.
1961   *Argonauts of the Western Pacific.* New York: Dutton. First published 1922.

Manners, R.
1956   Tabara: Subculture of a Tobacco and Mixed Crop Municipality. In *The People of Puerto Rico,* ed. J. Steward. Urbana: University of Illinois Press.

Marett, R. R.
1909   *The Threshold of Religion.* London: Methuen.

Marshall, L.
1960   !Kung Bushman Bands. *Africa* 30:325–354.

———.
1961   Sharing, Talking, and Giving: Relief of Social Tensions Among !Kung Bushmen. *Africa* 31:233–249.

———.
1965   The !Kung Bushman of the Kalahari Desert. In *Peoples of Africa,* ed. J. L. Gibbs, Jr. New York: Holt, Rinehart and Winston.

Mayer, A. C.
1968   The Indian Caste System. *International Encyclopedia of the Social Sciences,* 2:339–344.

Mayr, E.
1963   *Animal Species and Evolution.* Cambridge, Mass.: Harvard University Press.

McGovern, T., G. Bigelow, T. Amorosi, and D. Russell
1988   Northern Islands, Human Error, and Environmental Degradation. *Human Ecology* 18:225–270.

McGovern, T. H.
1980   Cows, Harp Seals, and Churchbells: Adaptation and Extinction on Norse Greenland. *Human Ecology* 8:245–276.

Mead, M.
1935   *Sex and Temperament in Three Primitive Societies.* New York: Morrow.

———.
1949   *Male and Female.* New York: William Morrow.

———.
1956   *New Lives for Old: Cultural Transformation—Manus, 1928–1953.* New York: Morrow.

———.
1971   *Coming of Age in Samoa.* New York: Morrow. First published 1928.

———.
1975   *Blackberry Winter.* New York: Random House.

Meggars, B. J.
1971   *Amazonia: Man and Culture in a Counterfeit Paradise.* Chicago: Aldine.

Meggitt, M. J.
1964   Male–Female Relationship in the Highlands of Australian New Guinea. *American Anthropologist* 66, special issue, pt. 2, pp. 204–224.

Micklin, P. P.
1988   Desiccation of the Aral Sea: A Water Management Disaster in the Soviet Union. *Science* 241:1,170–1,175.

Middleton, J.
1960   *Lugbara Religion: Ritual and Authority Among an East African People.* London: Oxford University Press.

Milan, F.
1970   The Demography of an Alaskan Eskimo Village. *Arctic Anthropology* 71:26–43.

Mills, C. W.
1959   *The Power Elite.* New York: Oxford University Press.

Milton, K.
1985   Ecological Foundations for Subsistence Strategies Among the Mbuti Pygmies. *Human Ecology* 13:71–78.

Mintz, S. W.
1986   *Sweetness and Power: The Place of Sugar in Modern History.* Harmondsworth: Penguin.

Mooney, K. A.
1978   The Effect of Rank and Wealth on Exchange Among the Coast Salish. *Ethnology* 17:391–406.

Moore, O. K.
1957   Divination—A New Perspective. *American Anthropologist* 59:69–74.

Moorehead, A.
1963   *Cooper's Creek.* New York: Harper & Row.

Morgan, L. H.
1963   *Ancient Society.* New York: World. First published 1877.

Morren, G. E. B., and D. C. Hyndam
1987   The Taro Monoculture of Central New Guinea. *Human Ecology* 15:301–315.

Mundy-Castle, A. C.
1966   Pictorial Depth Perception in Ghanaian Children. *International Journal of Psychology* 1:290–300.

Munson, H., Jr.
1988   *Islam and Revolution in the Middle East.* New Haven, Conn.: Yale University Press.

Murdock, G. P.
1949   *Social Structure.* New York: Macmillan.

———.
1967   *The Ethnographic Atlas.* Pittsburgh, Pa.: University of Pittsburgh Press.

Murphy, R. F.
1986   *Cultural and Social Anthropology: An Overture.* 2nd ed. Englewood Cliffs, N.J.: Prentice-Hall.

Nadel, S. F.
1935   Nupe State and Community. *Africa* 8:257–303.

Nader, L. (ed.)
1965   The Ethnology of Law. *American Anthropologist* 67, special issue, pt. 2.

Nash, M.
1966   *Primitive and Peasant Economic Systems.* San Francisco: Chandler.

Navarro, M.
1989   The Personal Is Political: Las Madres de la Plaza de Mayo. In *Protest and Resistance: Latin American Experience,* ed. S. Eckstein. Berkeley: University of California Press.

Newson, L. A.
1988   *Indian Survival in Colonial Nicaragua.* Norman: University of Oklahoma Press.

Nimkoff, M. F., and R. Middleton
1960   Types of Family and Types of Economy. *American Journal of Sociology* 66:215–225.

Noble, D.
1984   *The Forces of Production.* New York: Knopf.

Obbo, Christine
1988   Is AIDS Just Another Disease? In *AIDS 1988: American Association for the Advancement of Science Symposia Papers,* ed. R. Kulstad, pp. 191–198. Washington, D.C.: AAAS.

O'Brien, D.
1984   Women Never Hunt: The Portrayal of Women in Melanesian Ethnography. In *Rethinking Women's Roles: Perspectives from the Pacific,* ed. D. O'Brien and S. Tiffany. Berkeley: University of California Press.

Odum, H. T.
1971   *Environment, Power, and Society.* New York: Wiley-Interscience.

Oliver, D. L.
1955   *A Solomon Island Society: Kinship and Leadership Among the Siuai of Bougainville.* Cambridge, Mass.: Harvard University Press.

Otterbein, K. F.
1970   *The Evolution of War: A Cross-Cultural Study.* New Haven, Conn.: HRAF Press.

Parish, W. L.
1985   Introduction: Historical Background and Current Issues. In *Chinese Rural Development: The Great Transformation,* ed. W. L. Parish, pp. 3–32. Armonk, N.Y.: M. E. Sharpe.

Parker, R. G.
1987   Acquired Immunodeficiency Syndrome in Urban Brazil. *Medical Anthropology Quarterly* 1:155–175.

———.
1988   Sexual Culture and AIDS Education in Urban Brazil. In *AIDS 1988: American Association for the Advancement of Science Symposia Papers,* ed. R. Kulstad, pp. 169–174. Washington, D.C.: AAAS.

Parker, S.
1976   The Precultural Basis of the Incest Taboo: Toward a Biosocial Theory. *American Anthropologist* 78:285–301.

Pasternak, B.
1972   *Kinship and Community in Two Chinese Villages.* Stanford, Calif.: Stanford University Press.

———.
1976   *Introduction to Kinship and Social Organization.* Englewood Cliffs, N.J.: Prentice-Hall.

———.
1978   Seasons of Birth and Marriage in Two Chinese Localities. *Human Ecology* 6:299–324.

———.
1983   *Guests in the Dragon: Social Demography of a Chinese District, 1895–1946.* New York: Columbia University Press.

———.
1985   On the Causes and Consequences of Uxorilocal Marriage in China. In *Family and Population in East Asian History,* ed. S. Hanley and A. Wolf, pp. 310–335. Stanford, Calif.: Stanford University Press.

Pasternak, B., and Wang Ching
1985   Breastfeeding Decline in Urban China: An Exploratory Study. *Human Ecology* 13:433–465.

Peacock, N.
1984   The Mbuti of Northeast Zaire: Women and Subsistence Exchange. *Cultural Survival Quarterly* 8:15–17.

Pehrson, R.
1957   *The Bilateral Network of Social Relations in Kön Kämä Lapp District.* Bloomington: Indiana University Press.

Perlmutter, D.
1986   No Nearer to the Soul. *Natural Language and Linguistic Theory* 4:515–523.

Piaget, J.
1954   *The Construction of Reality in the Child.* New York: Basic Books.

Pianka, E. R.
1974   *Evolutionary Biology.* New York: Harper & Row.

Popkin, S.
1979   *The Rational Peasant.* Berkeley: University of California Press.

Posey, D.
1983   Indigenous Ecological Knowledge and Development. In *The Dilemma of Amazonian Development*, ed. E. Moran, pp. 225–257. Boulder, Colo.: Westview Press.

———.
1984   Ethnoecology as Applied Anthropology in Amazonian Development. *Human Organization* 43:95–107.

Posey, D., J. Frecchone, J. Eddins, and L. F. DaSilva
1984   Ethnoecology as Applied Anthropology in Amazonian Development. *Human Organization* 43:95–107.

Pospisil, L. J.
1963   *The Kapauku Papuans of West New Guinea.* New York: Holt, Rinehart and Winston.

Powdermaker, H.
1966   *Stranger and Friend: The Way of an Anthropologist.* New York: Norton.

Price, D.
1981   Complexity in Non-Complex Societies. In *Archaeological Approaches to the Study of Complex Society*, ed. S. E. van der Leeuw, pp. 57–97. Amsterdam: University of Amsterdam's Albert van Giffen Institute for Prehistory.

Putterman, L.
1981   Is a Democratic Collective Agriculture Possible? *Journal of Development Economics* 9:375–403.

Radcliffe-Brown, A. R.
1952   *Structure and Functions in Primitive Society.* New York: Free Press.

Rapoport, A.
1981   "Realism" and "Relevance" in Gaming Simulations. *Human Ecology* 9:137–150.

Rappaport, R. A.
1967   Ritual Regulation of Environmental Relations Among a New Guinea People. *Ethnology* 6:17–30.

———.
1968   *Pigs for the Ancestors: Ritual in the Ecology of a New Guinea People.* New Haven, Conn.: Yale University Press.

———.
1979   *Ecology, Meaning, and Religion.* Berkeley, Calif.: North Atlantic Books.

Rasmussen, K.
1929   *Report of the Fifth Thule Expedition, 1921–1924*, vol. 7, no. 1: *Intellectual Culture of the Iglulik Eskimos.* Copenhagen: Glydendalske Boghandel.

Redman, C. L.
1978   *The Rise of Civilization: From Early Farmers to Urban Society in the Ancient Middle East.* San Francisco: Freeman.

Rensberger, B.
1989   Racial Odyssey. In *Applying Anthropology: An Introductory Reader*, ed. A. Podelefski and P. J. Brown. Mountain View, Calif.: Mayfield Press.

Riegelhaupt, J.
1967   Saloio Women: An Analysis of Informal and Formal Political and Economic Roles of Portuguese Peasant Women. *Anthropology Quarterly* 40:109–126.

Rigdon, S. M.
1988   *The Culture Facade: Art, Science, and Politics in the Work of Oscar Lewis.* Urbana and Chicago: University of Illinois Press.

Rindos, D.
1980   Symbiosis, Instability, and the Origins and Spread of Agriculture. *Current Anthropology* 21: 751–765.

Rogers, E. M.
1962   *Diffusion of Innovations.* New York: Free Press.

Rogers, E. M., and F. F. Shoemaker
1971   *Communication of Innovations: A Cross-Cultural Approach.* New York: Free Press.

Roosevelt, A.
1987   The Evolution of Human Subsistence. In *Food and Evolution: Towards a Theory of Human Food Habits*, ed. M. Harris and E. B. Ross, pp. 565–578. Philadelphia: Temple University Press.

Rubin, J., N. Flowers, and D. R. Gross
1986   The Adaptive Dimensions of Leisure Time. *American Anthropologist* 13:524–536.

Safa, H. I.
1974   *The Urban Poor of Puerto Rico: A Study in Development and Inequality.* New York: Holt, Rinehart and Winston.

Saffirio, J., and R. Hammer
1983   The Forest and the Highway. In *The Impact of Contact: Two Yanomamö Case Studies*, report no. 11, pp. 3–48. Cambridge, Mass.: Cultural Survival, Inc.

Sahlins, M. D.

1961   The Segmentary Lineage: An Organization of Predatory Expansion. *American Anthropologist* 63:332–345.

————.

1963   Poor Man, Rich Man, Big Man, Chief: Political Types in Melanesia and Polynesia. *Comparative Studies in Society and History* 5:285–303.

————.

1965   On the Sociology of Primitive Exchange. In *The Relevance of Models for Social Anthropology*. Association of Social Anthropologist, monograph no. 1. New York: Praeger.

————.

1968   *Tribesmen*. Englewood Cliffs, N.J.: Prentice-Hall.

————.

1972   *Stone Age Economics*. Chicago: Aldine.

Salzman, P. C.

1971   Movement and Resource Extraction Among Pastoral Nomads: The Case of the Shah Nawazi Baluch. *Anthropological Quarterly* 44:185–197.

————.

1980   *When Nomads Settle: Processes of Adaptation and Response*. New York: Praeger.

Sanjek, R.

1977   Cognitive Maps of the Ethnic Domain in Urban Ghana: Reflections on Variability and Change. *American Ethnologist* 4:603–622.

Sankoff, G.

1972   A Quantitative Paradigm for the Study of Communicative Competence. Paper prepared for the Conference on the Ethnography of Speaking, Austin, Texas, April 20–23.

Sapir, E.

1921   *Language: An Introduction to the Study of Speech*. New York: Harcourt Brace and World.

————.

1929   The Status of Linguistics as a Science. *Language* 5:207–214.

Saunders, L., and S. Mehenna

1986   Village Entrepreneurs: An Egyptian Case. *Ethnology* 25:75–88.

Schama, S.

1987   *An Embarrassment of Riches*. New York: Knopf.

Scheper-Hughes, N.

1979   The Margaret Mead Controversy: Culture, Biology, and Anthropological Inquiry. *Human Organization* 43:443–454.

Schneider, B. E.

1988   Gender and AIDS. In *AIDS 1988: American Association for the Advancement of Science Symposia Papers*, ed. R. Kulstad, pp. 97–106; Washington, D.C.: AAAS.

Schneider, D. M., and K. Gough (eds.)

1961   *Matrilineal Kinship*. Berkeley: University of California Press.

Schneider, H. K.

1970   *The Wahi Wanyaturu: Economics in an African Society*, Viking Fund Publications in Anthropology, no. 48. Chicago: Aldine.

————.

1974   *Economic Man: The Anthropology of Economics*. New York: Free Press.

Schoepf, B. G., R. wa Nkera, P. Ntsomo, W. Engundu, and C. Schoepf

1988   AIDS, Women, and Society in Central Africa. In *AIDS 1988: American Association for the Advancement of Science Symposia Papers*, ed. R. Kulstad, pp. 175–182. Washington, D.C.: AAAS.

Schrire, C.

1984   Wild Surmises in Savage Thoughts. In *Past and Present in Hunter-Gatherer Societies*, ed. C. Schrire. Orlando, Fla.: Academic Press.

Scott, J. C.

1976   *The Moral Economy of the Peasant*. New Haven, Conn.: Yale University Press.

Service, E. R.

1971   *Primitive Social Organization: An Evolutionary Perspective*. 2nd ed. New York: Random House.

Sheets, P.

1989   Dawn of a New Stone Age. In *Applying Anthropology: An Introductory Reader*, ed. A. Podolefsky and P. J. Brown. Mountain View, Calif.: Mayfield Press.

Shepher, J.

1983   *Incest: A Biosocial View*. New York: Academic Press.

Sheridan, T. E.

1988   *Where the Dove Calls: The Political Ecology of a Peasant Corporate Community in Northwestern Mexico*. Tucson: University of Arizona Press.

Sidel, R.

1986   *Women and Children Lost*. New York: Viking-Penguin.

Simon, H. A.

1966   *Models of Man: Social and Rational; Mathematical Essays on Rational Human Behavior in a Social Setting*. New York: Wiley.

Slobodkin, L. B.

1968   Toward a Predictive Theory of Evolution. In *Population Biology and Evolution*, ed. R. C. Lewontin. Syracuse, N.Y.: Syracuse University Press.

Smil, V.

1984   *The Bad Earth*. Armonk, N.Y.: M. E. Sharpe.

Smith, R.

1984   Social Class. In *Annual Review of Anthropology*, pp. 467–494. Palo Alto, Calif.: Annual Reviews.

Sorensen, C. W.

1988   *Over the Mountains Are Mountains: Korean Peasant Households and Their Adaptation to*

Rapid Industrialization. Seattle: University of Washington Press.

Southwold, M.
1965   The Ganda of Uganda. In *Peoples of Africa*, ed. J. L. Gibbs, Jr. New York: Holt, Rinehart and Winston.

Spence, J.
1988   *The Question of Hu*. New York: Knopf.

Speth, J. D.
1988   Seasonality, Resource Stress, and Food Sharing in Egalitarian Foraging Societies. Paper presented at the symposium Coping with Seasonal Constraints, 86th Annual Meeting of the American Anthropological Association, Chicago, 1987.

Spiro, M. E.
1952   Ghosts, Ifaluk, and Teleological Functionalism. *American Anthropologist* 54:495–503.

Stephan, C. W., and W. C. Stephan
1985   *Two Social Psychologies*. Homewood, Ill.: Dorsey Press.

Steward, J.
1953   Evolution and Process. In *Anthropology Today*, ed. A. L. Kroeber. Chicago: University of Chicago Press.

———.
1972   *Theory of Culture Change: The Methodology of Multilinear Evolution*. Urbana: University of Illinois Press.

Sturtevant, W. C., and D. Damas (eds.)
1984   *Handbook of North American Indians*, vol. 5: *Arctic*. Washington, D.C.: Smithsonian Institution.

Susser, I.
1986   Work and Reproduction: Sociologic Context. *Occupational Medicine: State of the Art Reviews* 1:517–530.

Swanson, G. E.
1960   *The Birth of the Gods: The Origin of Primitive Beliefs*. Ann Arbor: University of Michigan Press.

Sweet, L. E.
1965   Camel Pastoralism in North Arabia and the Minimal Camping Unit. In *Man, Culture, and Animals: The Role of Animals in Human Ecological Adjustment*, publication no. 78, ed. A. Leeds and A. P. Vayda. Washington, D.C.: American Association for the Advancement of Science.

Swift, J.
1974   The Future of Tuareg Pastoral Nomadism in the Malian Sahel. Paper presented at the SSRC Symposium on the Future of Traditional Societies, December.

Tapper, R.
1979   *Pasture and Politics*. London: Academic Press.

Thomas, D. H.
1986   *Refiguring Anthropology*. Prospect Heights, Ill.: Waveland Press.

Thompson, L.
1950   *Culture in Crisis: A Study of the Hopi Indians*. New York: Harper & Row.

Thompson, L., and A. Joseph
1947   *The Hopi Way*. Chicago: University of Chicago Press.

Tierney, J., L. Wright, and K. Springen
1988   The Search for Adam and Eve. *Newsweek* January 11.

Trevathan, W. R.
1987   *Human Birth: An Evolutionary Perspective*. Hawthorne, N.Y.: Aldine.

Tsiang, H.
1884   *Buddhist Records of the Western World*, vol. 1, trans. S. Bell. London: Trubner. Reprinted in and cited from *A Reader in General Anthropology*, ed. C. Coon. New York: Holt, 1948, pp. 452–463.

Turnbull, C.
1961   *The Forest People*. New York: Simon & Schuster.

———.
1965   The Mbuti Pygmies of the Congo. In *Peoples of Africa*, ed. J. L. Gibbs, Jr. New York: Holt, Rinehart and Winston.

Turner, V. W.
1967   *The Forest of Symbols: Aspects of Ndembu Ritual*. Ithaca, N.Y.: Cornell University Press.

Tylor, E. B.
1871   *Primitive Culture: Researches into the Development of Mythology, Philosophy, Religion, Language, Art, and Custom*, 2 vols. 2nd ed. London: John Murray.

USAID
1982   *Sudan: The Rahad Irrigation Project*. Impact Evaluation Report no. 31. Washington, D.C.

U.S. Public Health Service
1986   The Coolfont Report. *Public Health Report* 101.

Van Gennep, A.
1960   *The Rites of Passage*. Chicago: University of Chicago Press.

Vayda, A. P.
1974   Warfare in an Ecological Perspective. *Annual Review of Ecology and Systematics* 5:183–193.

———.
1976   *Warfare in Ecological Perspective*. New York: Plenum.

———.
1987   Explaining What People Eat: A Review Article. *Human Ecology* 15:493–510.

Vondal, P. J.
1987   Intensification Through Diversified Resource Use: The Human Ecology of a Successful Agricultural Industry in Indonesian Borneo. *Human Ecology* 15:27–52.

Wallace, A. F. C.
1966   *Religion: An Anthropological View.* New York: Random House.

———.
1970   *The Death and Rebirth of the Seneca.* New York: Knopf.

Washabaugh, W.
1986   *Five Fingers for Survival.* Ann Arbor, Mich.: Karoma.

Weisman, S.
1988   Where Births Are Kept Down and Women Aren't. *New York Times,* January 29, p. 4.

Wells, M.
1987   Sharecropping in the United States: A Political Economy Perspective. In *Farm Work and Fieldwork: American Agriculture in Anthropological Perspective,* ed. M. Chibnik, pp. 211–243. Ithaca, N.Y.: Cornell University Press.

Werner, D., N. Flowers, M. Ritter, and D. Gross
1979   Subsistence Productivity and Hunting Effort in Native South America. *Human Ecology* 7:303–315.

Westermarck, E. A.
1922   *The History of Human Marriage,* 3 vols. New York: Allerton. First published 1889.

White, L.
1949   *The Science of Culture.* New York: Farrar, Straus & Cudahy.

Whiteley, P. M.
1985   Unpacking Hopi Clans: Another Vintage Model out of Africa. *Journal of Anthropological Research* 41:359–374.

———.
1988   *Deliberate Acts: Changing Hopi Culture Through the Oraibi Split.* Tucson: University of Arizona Press.

Whiting, B. B. (ed.)
1963   *Six Cultures: Studies of Child Bearing.* New York: Wiley.

Whiting, J. W., and I. L. Child
1953   *Child Training and Personality: A Cross-Cultural Study.* New Haven, Conn.: Yale University Press.

Whiting, B. B., and J. W. Whiting
1973   Methods for Observing and Recording Behavior. In *A Handbook of Method in Cultural An-*
thropology, ed. R. Naroll and R. Cohen. New York: Columbia University Press.

———.
1974   *Children of Six Cultures: A Psycho-Cultural Analysis.* Cambridge, Mass.: Harvard University Press.

Whorf, B. L.
1956   The Relation of Habitual Thought and Behavior to Language. In *Language, Thought, and Reality: Selected Writings of Benjamin Lee Whorf.* Cambridge, Mass.: MIT Press.

Wilcox, S., and S. Wilbers
1987   The Case for Academic Acceptance of American Sign Language. *Chronicle of Higher Education* 33:1.

Williams, T. R.
1967   *Field Methods in the Study of Culture.* New York: Holt, Rinehart and Winston.

Williams, W. L.
1986   *The Spirit and the Flesh: Sexual Diversity in American Indian Culture.* Boston: Beacon.

Wilson, A., H. Ochman, and M. E. Prager
1987   Molecular Time Scale for Evolution. *Trends in Genetics* 3:241–247.

Wolf, E. R.
1966   *Peasants.* Englewood Cliffs, N.J.: Prentice-Hall.

———.
1982   *Europe and the People Without History.* Berkeley: University of California Press.

Woods, C. M., and T. D. Graves
1973   *The Process of Medical Change in a Highland Guatemalan Town.* Los Angeles: Latin American Center, University of California.

Worsley, P.
1968   *The Trumpet Shall Sound: A Study of Cargo Cults in Melanesia.* New York: Schocken.

Wright, H. T., and G. A. Johnson
1975   Population, Exchange, and Early State Formation in Southwestern Iran. *American Anthropologist* 77:267–289.

Yellen, J. E., and R. B. Lee
1976   The Dobe-/Du/da Environment: Background to a Hunting and Gathering Way of Life. In *Kalahari Hunter-Gatherers,* ed. R. B. Lee, Cambridge, Mass.: Harvard University Press.

Index